W9-BKM-304

Published by Simon and Schuster
A Division of Gulf & Western Corporation
Simon & Schuster Building
Rockefeller Center
1230 Avenue of the Americas
New York, New York 10020
ISBN 0-671-21548-5
Library of Congress Catalog Card Number 73-9361
Manufactured in the United States of America

8 9 10 11

THE COMPLETE BOOK OF

BREADS

by Bernard Clayton, Jr.

SIMON AND SCHUSTER · NEW YORK

To my wife, who lets me use her kitchen

Contents

Farming
Germany, 1470

Acknowledgments

Recognition of help in writing this book must span oceans and generations if proper acknowledgment is to be given to all those whose creativity and imagination before an open hearth or a bake stove have touched this book in so many ways. They are a multitude; even though I cannot name them, my gratitude is deep.

Fortunately, I do know the names of many of the people and organizations who gave me immeasurable help in compiling material, and whose enthusiasm and kindness gave me strength to complete the long task.

To each of these I direct heartfelt thanks.

The Bobbs-Merrill Co., for permission to quote from *The Joy of Cooking* by Irma S. Rombauer and Marion Rombauer Becker.

Bovril, Ltd., Middlesex, England, for permission to use its Bovril and Cheese recipe.

Brian Bristow, Balcombe Bakery, Sussex, England, for permission to use his recipe for Lardy Loaf.

The Junior League of Charleston, South Carolina, for permission to quote from its *Charleston Receipts*.

Betty Crocker of General Mills, for permission to use the recipe for C. D. Q. White Bread.

Elizabeth David, of Elizabeth David, Ltd., London, for permission to quote from *The Baking of an English Loaf*, written by her and published in 1969.

E. P. Dutton & Co., for permission to reprint the recipe for James Beard's Cuban bread.

Hindostan (Indiana) Women's Booster Club, for permission to quote from its *Community Favorite Cookbook*.

Hobart Manufacturing Company, for permission to use its recipe for 30-Minute White Bread.

International Multifoods Corporation, for permission to use CoolRise recipes from its *Let's Bake* recipe book.

Ladies Aid Society of the First Presbyterian Church, Polson, Montana, for permission to quote from its 1912 cookbook.

Jack Mabee, for permission to quote from *Sourdough Jack's Cookery*.

F. Marian McNeill, Edinburgh, Scotland, for permission to quote from *The Scots Kitchen*.

The Pillsbury Company, for permission to use recipes for Easy Mixer White Bread and Toasting White Bread.

Charles Scribner's Sons, for permission to quote from *Cross Creek Cookery* by Marjorie Kinnan Rawlings.

George and Cecilia Scurfield, London, for permission to quote from *Home Baked*.

Standard Brands, for permission to quote from Fleischmann's *New Treasury of Yeast Baking*.

Sunset magazine for permission to quote from its *Cook Book of Breads* and the August 1971 issue relative to building an outdoor adobe oven.

Shambala Publications, Inc., Berkeley, California, for permission to quote from *The Tassajara Bread Book* by Edward Espe Brown.

The Misses Ola and Minnie Turnipseed, for permission to adapt their recipe for white bread made with a hops starter.

United Methodist Women's Society, Delphi, Indiana, for permission to quote from *A Cook Book of Tested Recipes*, 1907.

Universal Foods Corporation, for permission to use its recipes for Instant Blend White Bread and Old Milwaukee Rye Bread.

My thanks also to: Agricultural Research Service, U.S. Department of Agriculture; Mrs. Jerry Di Vecchio; Mrs. Dorothy Eggert; Ruth M. Emerson, American Institute of Baking; André Gaulier, Bayeux, Normandy, France; Paul Jensen; Bernadine Landsberg; Yves Montfort, Benodet, Brittany, France; Pierre Poilane, Paris; Ministère du Tourisme, Gouvernement de Quebec; Mrs. Diane Shadley, Carnation Company; the late Mrs. Maude Smith, Delphi, Indiana; Standard Milling Company, Kansas City; Wheat Flour Institute; Don and Marie Whitehead.

Foreword

Farmer's Calendar
Germany, 1493

A very exaggerated idea of the difficulty of breadmaking prevails amongst persons who are entirely ignorant of the process.

—*Eliza Acton,* The English Bread Book, *1857*

It happened on holiday in Ireland.

We had stopped at an inn in the small fishing village of Dungarvin to warm after a miserably cold, wet day behind a horse pulling a rented gypsy wagon over miles of narrow, crooked Irish roads.

At dinner, the bread came in slices of varying thicknesses served from a wicker basket covered with a starched linen cloth. Our waitress, Bridget, a pretty girl with black hair and sparkling white teeth, held a menu in one hand and the bread basket in the other. In the basket were three breads—currant-filled Tea Brack, a brown whole wheat or wholemeal loaf and soda bread. I took a bite of each. Then, I took a second, and a third. It seemed to me, as I sat there slowly warming myself in the moist heat of the dining room, that I had never tasted anything so good. I knew, too, that I wouldn't be passing through Dungarvin again very soon, and the only way I could be assured of ever having that bread again was to bake it myself. When Bridget brought another tiny crock of sweet butter for my second order of bread, I asked her who had baked it.

"Sir, it is Mr. Kelly's mother, it is," she said (making the "sir" sound like "sar"). "Baked in the kitchen, there," and she pointed toward the dark oak door behind me. Mr. Kelly owned the Devonshire Arms, as had his father and grandfather before him, and his mother had been baking those same delicious loaves every day of the week for more than five decades.

"Our compliments to Mr. Kelly's mother, and ask her if she would part with the recipes, especially the one for the Tea Brack," I said. Bridget returned in a few moments and said the old lady would be delighted to share them. (Mr. Kelly's mother's Tea Brack is on page 535. Bridget's father, one of six bakers in Dungarvin, gave me the white soda bread on page 56.)

As she gave me the recipes Mr. Kelly's mother pointed out that an Irish baker would ask for five things to create the perfect loaf—smooth baking powder, freshly churned buttermilk, freshly milled flour, a covered iron pot and, under it, a glowing red turf fire. Some of the fire and ash, she continued, would be heaped on top of the lid to seal in the heat.

While I had doubts that those exact conditions could be duplicated in my kitchen, I felt reasonably certain I could do as well with no loss in looks, texture and downright good taste with the ingredients I could find in the United States.

I thanked her. We hitched up the horse and left. I did not know then where the newborn interest in baking would take me; therefore, I uttered no unforgettable words to mark the beginning of my pleasurable affair with bread.

The history of bread stretches back to when man turned from a nomadic hunting life to a more settled existence that allowed the cultivation of small grains. The first bread was an unleavened wafer-thin cake made from a mixture of grain meal and water and baked on hot stones. Bread-baking did not become a skilled craft until the Egyptians and the Mesopotamians made it one about 5,000 years ago. Their bread was leavened with yeast-rich foam scooped from the top of fermenting wines. A variety of breads was found in the tombs of the Pharaohs—some flavored with poppy and sesame seeds and even camphor.

Later, the Greeks developed a wide variety of breads, using such ingredients as oil, cheese, and "milk from grass feeding cows." However, it was the Romans who supported commercial baking on a grand scale and made it an art. According to early records, in 79 A.D., a mill-bakery in Pompeii *daily* processed 1,000 bushels of flour to bake between 100,000 and 150,000 loaves. In Rome, as in Pompeii, there was a mill-bakery for about every 1,500 Roman citizens.

However, the quality of a loaf of Roman bread should not be romanticized. It was generally coarse and heavy, although the best grade could conceivably be served to a dinner guest today—one with courage and strong teeth. The bread available to the family of a Roman scribe, for instance, was so heavy it sank in water like a rock.

Throughout history, bread has been such an important part of man's diet that bakers have been controlled by law. In Caesar's era, strict measures were taken governing the kind of flour, from white to coarse dark, to be sold to each class of people. In the Middle Ages, German bakers were required by law to provide full measure; they often added an extra bun to each dozen rather than risk punishment in the stocks for short-changing customers; hence, the phrase *baker's dozen*. During that same period, English law called for the baker's head if he cheated on the weight of his product. He, too, added an extra bun to every dozen.

Clearly, the European or Middle Eastern baker was an important tradesman in his town or village. The housewife either bought his bread or carried the prepared dough to him for baking, a pattern that has changed little in many parts of the world.

In America something very different happened. The art of baking developed in the home because the sparse settlements in the New World could not support a baker. The home baker learned to use materials at hand, largely corn in the beginning, and later, as the pioneers pushed into the West, they began using wheat.

Baking in many pioneer homes was done on the hearth before an open fire or in a heavy iron pot buried deep in the hot coals. In other homes, baking was done in a clay or brick oven, the fire being built directly on the chamber floor. When the chamber was sufficiently hot the coals were shoveled out and the loaves were placed directly on the floor. Such an oven was similar to the early Roman oven and the adobe oven of the Pueblo Indians.

There were yet other refinements to come. Some readers may remember the wood-burning ranges their grandmothers used, shoving in a stick of oak to get the temperature just so. It was an unexcelled baking machine, or so it seemed to a small boy who sampled the product. The step from the range, invented in the 1820's, to today's stove with its lights, bells, timers, sensors, and chrome was a relatively easy one.

Home baking today is the distillation of all of the lore, love, magic, common sense, skill, nonsense, art, technique, understanding, and luck that has come down through countless generations of bread bakers, women and men, in both the home and the shop. This book is a further distillation of that knowledge.

Once upon a time almost everyone agreed that bread was good to eat and good for you. It was the staff of life. But, people wanted more white bread rather than whole grain loaves. At first, flour was bleached naturally by storing and aerating it—a process that also strengthened the gluten and made it better for baking. Since the natural process took from eight to twelve weeks, millers began to bleach flour chemically to speed it through the mills. Chemical bleaching was generally erratic at best, and strange bleaching agents were used, even chalk dust. Finally, the Food and Drug Administration stepped in to set standards for harmless bleach compounds and for chemicals that aged the flour and strengthened the gluten. Then, when it was enriched with B vitamins and iron, flour regained most of its old properties. Most of today's flour is unexcelled. Some commercial bread products are poor but this is usually the fault of the baker, not of the flour.

Wheat products are rich in carbohydrates, proteins, vitamins and minerals. Also, they are relatively low in calories. The average slice of bread, made with enriched white flour, contains 63 calories—a cup of whole milk, 155.

Indeed, bread can be an important element in common-sense weight reduction and control, as demonstrated at the University of Nebraska where a group of students lost an average of 19.2 pounds in 8 weeks on a calorie-controlled diet containing large amounts of bread.

Dr. Jean Mayer, the Paris-born professor of nutrition at Harvard University and a food consultant for the White House, recommends serving more fruit, more vegetables and *more bread* to lower the fat intake in the American diet. He is careful to point out that he means more *good* bread. Calling store-bought bread nothing more than an "edible napkin," Dr. Mayer says that if we make better bread, we will use fewer spreads, jams, and other sandwich fillings.

The rise in interest in natural foods is reflected in the use of all sorts of organic ingredients in bread-making. As you use the recipes in this book, you will see the many opportunities to use such ingredients as stone-ground flours, wild yeast, raw sugar, organic honey, and wheat-germ. The recipe for Sprouted Wheat Bread is an example of a remarkable bread made with natural ingredients.

Introduction

Farmer's Calendar
Germany, 1493

This is a working cookbook.

Its aim is to encourage anyone to bake a good-tasting loaf of any of the dozens of breads the Western world offers. Every recipe has been tested in the author's kitchen. Hundreds of loaves have been baked with a regular Tappan electric stove whose double ovens, finally, when the book was about done, refused to turn off. The thermostats were worn out. For days, between loaves, the ovens kept at a steady 180 degrees.

My search for recipes led me to several old cookbooks and family recipe files. In earlier days, it was not uncommon to be admonished to sift the flour to remove such foreign objects as twigs, insects, chaff and the like. Today the art of milling and packaging is so sophisticated that there is no need for such a warning. Also, it is clear in the old volumes, that the authors were struggling with a crude yeast that often had to be soaked overnight to start its growth. They had to allow many hours for the first step in preparation of a loaf. (Compare this to today's instant dry yeast that goes to work within moments after warm liquid is added.) I have, therefore, updated some of these old recipes.

A number of them have been left untouched, however, and are responsible for some of the best bread in the book. The Salt-rising Bread by the women of Montana's Flathead Valley, page 307, is from a recipe dating back to the turn of the century. The scalding hot milk is poured over the cornmeal and left overnight just as it was done by those Western women in 1900. The Butter Bran Bread is another old one. The only change is the name; it was too delectable to be called "Bran Cornmeal."

With one or two small exceptions, all recipes stand alone without reference to another recipe. (When one is deep in the preparation of a bread, hands covered with flour, there is nothing more vexing than to be told: "now turn to page 7 and follow instructions for the basic dough but add . . .") When the reader is referred elsewhere, it is either to a chart on dough volume to help determine which pans to select for how many loaves, or to the chapter on making starters and wild yeasts for sour dough loaves.

The instructions in the recipes are divided into timed steps so that the home baker can determine if there is time for a phone call or a trip to the school between *Rising* and *Shaping*. There usually is. This helps you to know whether a loaf started in the evening can be finished before bedtime, or whether it should be stopped after kneading and placed overnight in the refrigerator.

Once the dough has had a healthy start and the yeast is at work reproducing itself, the whole baking process should be a relaxed one. If necessary, the preparation can be stopped at almost any stage by refrigerating the dough. If you wish to stretch it only a few minutes or for as long as an hour or two, punch the dough down and let it rise again. Remember, the texture will get progressively finer each time it rises. Even dough rising in pans can be knocked down, kneaded and shaped again, if for some reason it cannot be put in the oven on schedule.

A relaxed baker means relaxed dough and that is one of the secrets of baking good bread.

Ingredients, Techniques, and Equipment

Gardening Tools
Venice, 1593

About the Ingredients

Flour

Every flour milled from a basic grain—barley, buckwheat, corn, oat, rye, white, whole wheat—has its own collection of recipes in this book. There is one exception—rice—and it is in only one recipe.

While each flour is described in the introduction to its chapter, there are certain things common to working with them all.

Unless the recipe specifies otherwise, flour is *not* sifted.

The amount of flour for dough that is to be kneaded is *approximate* because flour varies greatly in its power to absorb moisture. For instance, bread flour absorbs more moisture than all-purpose flour. Flour stored during the humid summer months will absorb less of the mixing liquid than the same flour that has been kept in a dry house in wintertime.

In those recipes that specify an exact amount of flour, principally those for batter breads, this is done only for convenience, not precision. The batter is stirred or beaten, not kneaded by hand, and a little more time in the oven will compensate for the slight difference in the moisture content of the batter because of different flours.

Self-rising flour may be used interchangeably with all-purpose flour by omitting the baking powder and salt in the recipe.

Leavening

Air, steam, and carbon dioxide are all involved in varying degrees in the leavening action of all baked goods. Even with minimum mixing, it is impossible to combine ingredients without incorporating some air. The gas—carbon dioxide—is produced either by the fermentation of the yeast, by baking powder activated by heat and moisture, or by baking soda reacting with an acid such as buttermilk or orange juice. A loaf would be solid as a brick were it not for the action of one of these leavening agents.

Yeast

There are about 130 billion living cells in one package of active dry yeast and these will double in number in a warm dough mixture in about 2 hours. Feasting on the sugars in the flour, the yeast will send out carbon dioxide gas to make the bread rise.

When yeast is called for in this book, it is active dry yeast. Compressed yeast is not mentioned simply because the packets of dry yeast are so readily available, are easy to use, and they keep for months without refrigeration. The compressed cakes may be substituted, of course. (One yeast cake is equivalent to one packet dry yeast.)

The term "to proof" originally meant to test the yeast to prove that it was alive and ready to work. Since World War II there have been remarkable improvements in yeasts and there is little reason to question the reliability of a package of yeast used within the time period stamped on the envelope.

Both Fleischmann's and Red Star active dry yeast are of this new breed—finely ground yeast granules that tolerate much higher temperatures (120°–130°) than the old. They can be added directly to the dry ingredients without first being dissolved. When recipes in this book call for the yeast to be dissolved beforehand, this is because doing so makes it easier to follow the recipe's original sequence.

Brewer's yeast, on the other hand, is not a leavening agent. Known also as nutritional or primary yeast, it is an excellent source of biologically complete and digestible protein and is sometimes used as an added ingredient in bread-making but *never as a substitute for regular yeast.*

Salt inhibits and can regulate the growth of yeast. Sugar is food for it. Too much heat will kill it (140°), while too little warmth (below 80°) will delay its growth and limit its leavening power.

Baking Soda and Baking Powder

Baking soda, which was the first chemical leavener, reacts with acids such as sour cream or buttermilk to produce carbon dioxide. The reaction is almost instantaneous, requiring fast assembly of ingredients and immediate baking.

Double-acting baking powder, on the other hand, has a multiple action which releases a small amount of gas while the ingredients are put together. The main thrust comes from the heat of the oven.

Self-rising flour and cornmeal contain a leavener and salt added at the mill.

Starters

See the chapters on Starters and Sour Dough Breads, pages 281 and 287.

Milk

A loaf made with milk has a velvety grain, a browner crust and a creamy white crumb. It is softer and stays that way longer than bread made without milk.

The majority of the recipes in the book specify non-fat dry milk, which is much easier to use in bread-making than liquid milk. The milk granules are usually added to the mixture along with the other dry ingredients. Liquid milk always presents the danger of scorching while being heated.

Shortening

Shortening makes bread rich, tender, and flaky. Not only does it improve the texture, it also contributes to the flavor, especially if the shortening is butter or lard. Shortening can be animal (butter or lard) or vegetable (cottonseed, peanut, soybean or coconut oil, cocoa butter, etcetera). The choice is dictated primarily by flavor, cost, availability, and personal preference.

Salad and cooking oils may be substituted in recipes when melted shortening is specified.

An Explanation of Techniques

Mixing and Kneading

In the normal preparation of bread dough, liquid and yeast are added to the flour, which swells and forms a rough mass. When this mass is mixed and kneaded, the gluten in the flour is developed and forms an elastic mesh throughout the dough. Gluten, a plant protein found in wheat flour, has great elasticity which allows the dough to rise as carbon dioxide is produced by the yeast.

In yeast-leavened breads, the gluten must be developed to give volume to the loaf. In other breads—those leavened by baking powder, baking soda or other means—the concern is to *prevent* the gluten from developing and making them tough. Biscuit dough, for example, is mixed very little to avoid developing the gluten. In batters, the gluten is dispersed, so they can be mixed thoroughly without concern for making the product tough.

Gluten is found only in wheat flour. Since there is no gluten in cornmeal, corn bread batter may be beaten until smooth without danger of toughening it. This is true of several of the other flours, such as rye, barley, and buckwheat, but these are usually combined with wheat flour in bread and cake recipes to achieve sufficient volume.

How to Knead

The ideal place for kneading is a counter top or table at a height that will allow the arms to be fully extended, with the hands resting palms down on the work surface. (When the table is too high, there is a considerable loss of power in pushing against the dough; when it is too low, you are likely to wind up with a tired back.)

The kneading process may be started in the bowl as the dough is worked with the fingers and thumbs until it has absorbed most of its quota of flour, forming a ragged, shaggy mass.

Turn the shaggy mass onto the floured work surface. Fold the dough roughly in half, pushing down with both hands. As you draw back, give the dough a turn on the board. Fold the dough and repeat the sequence—push-turn-fold. Do this over and over again. The outside surface of the dough will be less sticky than the inside, and frequently some of the moist dough from inside will break through to the surface. Sprinkle it with flour and fold it in.

This rhythmic pattern of push-turn-fold should be broken occasionally by lifting the dough head-high and crashing it down against the work surface. Don't be gentle with the dough in this first stage—pummel it and punch it.

In a French bakery in Bayeux, I watched fascinated as an electrically driven trip-hammer beat a fast bang-bang-bang on a big lump of dough turning beneath it. It would become a solid, fine-textured specialty bread called "*brie*."

Suddenly you discover the dough is no longer an unresponsive blob in your hands but something soft and smooth. It is warm, springy, and alive, and small air bubbles may push their way up to the surface of the dough.

Rising

After bread dough has been kneaded to a smooth, elastic consistency, it is placed in a large bowl, covered with plastic wrap, and put in a warm place (80°–85°). The yeast continues to grow, giving off carbon dioxide, which stretches the gluten. The cell walls become thin (and the mass becomes "light") as the expanding ball of dough rises to about twice its original size.

The Wheat Flour Institute suggests using a warm place between 79° and 90°, but I like 80° to 85° because the lower temperatures produce a more flavorful bread. The high temperatures will, of course, increase the rate of fermentation and reduce the time of rising. All of the recipes in this book call for the lower range, although it is not a critical factor.

To test the dough, press it with two fingers near the edge of the bowl. If the indentations remain, the dough has risen enough.

A yeast batter cannot be tested by denting. When it has doubled, it will appear bubbly rather than smooth.

There is no rising for breads made with chemical leaveners, although a few will be allowed to rest for a short period of time to condition the ingredients before going into the oven.

Punching, Shaping, and Panning

After it has risen to twice its size, yeast dough is punched down by jabbing it with the fingers and fist and pulling the sides into the middle—actually turning the dough inside out. To achieve a uniform grain, the bubbles are worked out of the dough by kneading for about 30 seconds. If a particularly fine texture is desired, the dough may be left in the bowl for a second rising. Otherwise the dough is shaped and placed in pans or, for hearth loaves, on baking sheets or in cloth-lined baskets. Dough will double in volume the second time in about two-thirds of the time necessary for the first rising.

Batter breads are baked in a variety of pans to give them different personalities and characteristics.

Dough Volume Chart

Fitting dough into a loaf pan of the right size is an important part of the art of bread-making. While it will not alter the taste, too little or too much in a pan can spoil the visual effect of something that should be attractive.

Determine the total volume (in number of cups) or the total weight of the dough. (I use a 5-pound postal scale for this.) Then check the dough volume chart. The choice is yours as to how many loaves of what size you wish to bake.

PAN SIZE		VOLUME	WEIGHT
Large	9 x 5	3 cups	2 pounds
Medium	8½ x 4½	2½ cups	1½ pounds
Small	7½ x 3½	1½ cups	1 pound
Miniature	5½ x 3	¾ cup	½ pound
Sub-mini	4½ x 2½	½ cup	5 to 6 ounces

Refrigerating the Dough

Placing dough in the refrigerator substantially slows down the yeast action. If you double the amount of yeast specified in a recipe, you can refrigerate almost all yeast doughs and batters.

If the dough is shaped and placed in pans *before* it is refrigerated, it can go into the oven 10 minutes after it comes out of the cold. If the unshaped ball of dough has been refrigerated, it must wait two to three hours at room temperature before it can be shaped and put in pans.

Baking

One of the minor miracles of baking is "oven-spring"—the quick rising of the dough during the first 10 to 15 minutes in a hot oven. The hot gases literally spring the dough into shape, with the crust lifting above the edge of the pan and exposing the "shred" along one side.

Too hot an oven will form a crust too quickly and set the gluten before the loaf is fully developed. Not enough heat will create a thin crust and a loaf of poor quality. Doughs made with sugar or milk brown more rapidly than the leaner doughs and are baked at somewhat lower temperatures.

A reminder to home bakers who live in the Rocky Mountains and other high places: baking times or temperatures must be increased. For the statistical minded this means 2° for each 1,000 feet above sea level.

Oven Temperatures

TEMPERATURE	DESCRIPTION
250° to 275°	Very slow
300° to 325°	Slow
350° to 375°	Moderate
400° to 425°	Hot
450° to 475°	Very hot

When Is It Done?

A hearth loaf on a baking sheet in the oven is the easiest of all breads to test for doneness. Pull the oven shelf out a bit, and with a potholder in each hand turn the loaf on its side. Tap the bottom crust with an index finger. If the loaf has a hard, hollow sound, it is done. If it is soft and unresponsive, return the bread to the oven for an additional five or ten minutes. Test again.

A yeast loaf may be slipped from its baking pan and tested in the same manner. Also at this point if the crust is not brown enough to please, it can be left out of the pan and returned to the oven to produce a richer color.

A classic way to test many baked products is to insert a wooden toothpick, a slender metal probe, or even a broom straw into the heart of the loaf. If moist particles cling to the probe, return the loaf to the oven.

Quick breads, which are soft and fragile even when done, should be tested *only* with a probe. A metal one costs a dime at a variety store.

When Bread Is Not Done

When bread is not done, return it to the pan or the baking sheet, and if a slice has been cut off, simply replace it. Slip the pan into the oven for an additional 15 minutes at the recommended oven heat. Test it again. If it needs more oven time, send it back once more.

Freezing

The freshness of a baked loaf can best be preserved by freezing. Bread should first be cooled to room temperature, slipped into a bag or wrapped in plastic, and then sealed. It will freeze more quickly, too, if it is placed directly against the sides or back of the freezer.

Thaw bread at room temperature and then reheat, if you wish, for 15 minutes in a 350° oven. A solidly frozen loaf can be thawed by placing it in a 300° oven for 25 to 40 minutes.

Staling

Staling is the baker's no-nonsense word to describe what begins to happen to any loaf the moment it comes from the oven. When bread stales, there is a subtle change in flavor and aroma. While the inside of the bread begins to dry out, the crust absorbs the moisture and becomes soft and leathery.

But stale bread is not lost bread. Reheating greatly freshens it, and so does toasting.

In several studies by the flour companies, the most surprising finding was that bread stored in the refrigerator *stales faster* than bread at room temperature.

Ideally, bread should be stored in a clean, dry place at room temperature. There is nothing better than the traditional bread box or bread drawer. Bread in a plastic bag will be equally fresh but moist. Bread stored in the box (without a wrapping) will better retain its crispness. Nevertheless, a loaf to be held for a long period should go into the refrigerator to prevent mold from forming.

Basic Equipment

Of utmost importance to the home baker is his oven. If he bakes frequently, he should have the utility company check it at least every 18 months to be certain that the oven is heating as it should and according to the dial settings. The temperature gauges and thermostats on the best ovens go astray occasionally and need to be adjusted by an expert.

Next in importance is a bowl or earthenware crock. (My favorite for a two-loaf recipe is an old brown crock, rimmed in white—9½ inches in diameter and 5 inches deep. It has been in our family for years.) Then come measuring spoons and measuring cups; a long-handled wooden spatula or spoon for stirring; a work surface on which to knead the dough; finally, pans in which to place the dough.

Here are more details, and other desirable items.

Large Baking Sheet

I use it for hearth loaves, some festive breads, biscuits, yeast rolls, and for toasting crumbs and seeds. A Teflon-coated sheet is probably the best because it does not have to be oiled and can be wiped clean afterwards with a paper towel.

Rolling Pin

The best is the French rolling pin which has no handles but is simply a long, graceful piece of wood, tapered from the ends to the center. Great for beating beaten biscuit dough.

Pastry Scraper

A rectangular piece of steel with a wooden handle that is used in the kitchen for lifting and turning sticky doughs, and scraping the work surface after kneading is finished. A putty knife with a four-inch blade does equally well.

Atomizer

The plastic atomizer from a window-cleaner bottle placed in a glass or bottle of water to spray a fine mist over loaves about to go into the oven, or to spray *into* the oven to create steam during the baking period.

Peel

A flat board with a long handle to move baked goods in and out of a large oven. The French call it *la pelle.* I use one in my outdoor oven.

Baskets

French bakers have used these for generations to form hearth loaves. They call them *bannetons*. Any small woven basket lined with a folded cloth and sprinkled liberally with flour will do. The ball of dough rises in the basket and then is placed on the sheet for baking.

Bowls and Crocks

I prefer a heavy crock which will retain the heat as evenly as possible while the dough rises. Although I use the stainless steel bowl under the dough hook of the electric mixer, I often transfer the dough to a warm crock before letting it rise.

Loaf Pans

Bread will not brown as well in a bright metal pan (such as aluminum) as it will in a dark metal one, which holds the heat sufficiently to produce a deep brown, thick crust overall. (If your loaf is not brown enough, you can, however, remove it from the pan and bake 5 minutes or so more.) Glass (pyrex) also holds the heat exceptionally well and makes a beautiful golden crust. A Teflon-coated pan eliminates sticking and is easy to clean. It also produces a nice dark crust. Pyrex containers are by all odds my favorites.

I keep a selection of empty tin cans for special projects such as Russian Kulich and Boston Brown Bread. Those with printing on them absorb the heat much better than bright ones. For easy removal of the loaf, it is helpful to put a disk of wax paper on the bottom of the can (greasing well before and after). However, if the loaf refuses to budge, the easiest way is to cut the bottom of the can with an opener and simply push the bread out.

Pans for French bread are described in the section on French bread.

Electric Mixer

Heavy batters and doughs are a strain on the tiny electric motors of even the best home electric mixers. (Even my Kitchen Aid, one of the best, gets uncomfortably hot during the 5 or 6 minutes it takes to knead a batch of dough with the hook.) So, I beat almost all bread mixtures by hand rather than use a portable or hand-held electric mixer. The chance of damage to a small mixer is too great.

The larger mixers, on stationary mounts, can be used for batters and yeast doughs in the early stages of preparation. A dough hook, however, is necessary when more flour is added and the dough becomes firm.

Thermometer

Until you are familiar with every nook and cranny of the oven, use either a columnar or dial-type thermometer to gauge the uniformity of the heat. You may find the oven thermometer does not always agree with a good thermometer like a Taylor, so adjust the heat accordingly. And, move the loaves once or twice during the baking period to expose them to the various heats in the oven.

Bread Knife

A fine loaf of bread deserves to be sliced with a razor-sharp knife. Invest in a good one; there is none better than a 14-inch knife with a serrated blade made by a Swiss firm and sold in the U.S. by R. H. Forschner Co. It is the Victorinox #460-9 and sells for about $5. Reserve it for *bread only* and it will stay sharp for several years.

Toaster

Home-baked breads adapt more easily to the old-fashioned toaster, with sides that fold out to accommodate a variety of slice sizes and textures, than to the more modern ones. While you must watch the toast in the old model, it does a custom job that an automatic machine cannot equal. I use a Canadian toaster manufactured by the Toastess Corporation, Model 202.

Standard Weights and Measures

Herbman
Strasbourg, 1529

Make certain all measurements are level.

Dash	= 8 drops
1 tablespoon	= 3 teaspoons
4 tablespoons	= ¼ cup
5⅓ tablespoons	= ⅓ cup
8 tablespoons	= ½ cup
16 tablespoons	= 1 cup (dry)
1 fluid ounce	= 2 tablespoons
1 cup (liquid)	= ½ pint
2 cups (16 ounces)	= 1 pint
2 pints (4 cups)	= 1 quart
4 quarts	= 1 gallon
8 quarts	= 1 peck (dry)
4 pecks	= 1 bushel
16 ounces (dry measure)	= 1 pound

U.S.	EUROPEAN
1 teaspoon	= 1 coffee spoon
1 tablespoon	= 1 soup spoon
2 tablespoons	= 1 English tablespoon
2 teaspoons	= 1 English teaspoon
20 fluid ounces	= 1 English pint
10 ounces (dry measure)	= 1 English cup

ONE

A Beginning

Caraway
Lyons, 1579

Wheat and Flours

The tiny wheat kernel, no more than a quarter of an inch long, is one of the most important seeds on earth. It feeds about half of the globe's peoples and it is rapidly overtaking rice as the number-one grain.

When the whole wheat kernel is ground, it becomes whole wheat or graham flour. When it is very finely ground, wheat meal can be separated into three elements—white flour, bran, and the germ. The bran and germ are then sifted out and used for other purposes.

Millers struggled for centuries to perfect a way to grind wheat so that white flour could be sifted out. The Egyptians sifted or "bolted" the crushed grain through papyrus strands. George Washington was especially proud of the high quality of "bolted" flour produced by his Mount Vernon mill and shipped it as far away as the West Indies. Today, white flour must pass through a sieve having at least 4,225 openings per square inch.

An experienced home baker knows and uses several kinds of white flour. Most often he will use bread flour which is milled from hard wheat grown in the prairie states and Canada, soft wheat flour from U.S. regions with less severe winters, and all-purpose flour, a combination of hard and soft.

Bread flour, because of its higher protein content, will produce a stronger and better network of gluten to hold the carbon dioxide and produce loaves of greater volume. However, it is difficult to find in supermarkets and neighborhood stores. A flour mill or bakery will have it although they might not wish to bother with an order for less than 25 pounds.

Dough made with bread flour must be kneaded longer than that made from all-purpose flour to develop the greater amount of gluten. (Many electric mixers have a dough-hook attachment which is very useful for kneading this kind of dough. Of course, you can also do it by hand.) When bread flour is used in recipes, additional liquid is often necessary.

Soft wheat flour, low in gluten, will make a tender product, and is used chiefly in cake flours and cake mixes. Commercially, it finds its way into crackers, pretzels, cakes, cookies, and pastries.

All-purpose flour, a blend of the two, is perhaps the most versatile flour in the kitchen. It has been blended at the mill to produce enough gluten for yeast breads, yet not too much for use in quick breads and certain kinds of cakes.

There are about a half-dozen or so other kinds of white flour available, including: "self-rising," which has leavening agents and salt added; phosphated and bromated flours, with additives to improve baking quality; gluten flour, for dietetic breads; and "instant" flour, a granular product that is free-pouring like salt and disperses instantly in cold water. Because "instant" flour is more expensive than regular flours and is not especially useful in bread-making, I have not specified it in any of the recipes. There is a special white flour available in health food stores which contains finely ground wheat-germ, but generally speaking the germ is not used in white flours.

First Five Lessons

The first five lessons for the new home baker—and an equally rewarding exercise for the experienced one—could well be five new methods of making bread with white flour and the new superfine instant dry yeast. There could be no better first sally into the baking field than to bake each of the five before moving on to the rest of the book. These five also hold great promise to those who have been baking for a long time.

The five methods, developed by the home economists of milling and yeast companies working in their kitchen laboratories, have simplified bread-baking while retaining all of the good old-fashioned taste. Such names as "Can-Do-Quick" and "Easy Mixer" may suggest ease of preparation obtained by sacrifice of quality, but this is not so. These breads are *good*.

These five are important, too, because variations of these recipes will appear again and again in the book. (Perhaps it would be possible to adapt *all* recipes to the new methods, but then the fun and excitement of finding new and different recipes done in new and different ways would be gone.)

CAN-DO-QUICK WHITE BREAD

[ONE TALL LOAF OR TWO SMALLER ONES]

The home economists in the Betty Crocker Kitchens call this new baking development their "Can-Do-Quick" method. C.D.Q. shortens bread-making time by about half with results that compete nicely with breads made the conventional way. The combination of yeast and baking powder —and buttermilk—gives a flavor that is reminiscent of bread baked on Western cattle ranches.

INGREDIENTS	2 packages dry yeast ¾ cup warm water (105°–115°) 1¼ cups buttermilk at room temperature 5 cups (approximately) all-purpose or bread flour 2 tablespoons sugar 2 teaspoons baking powder 1 tablespoon salt ¼ cup shortening at room temperature 2 tablespoons melted butter Melted butter for brushing (optional)
BAKING PANS	One large (9 x 5) loaf pan, or one medium (8½ x 4½) and one small (7½ x 3½) loaf pan, greased or Teflon. If glass pans are used, reduce oven heat 25°.
PREPARATION 15 mins.	In a large mixing bowl dissolve the yeast in warm water. Stir with a fork or metal whip to hasten the action and put aside for 3 minutes. Add buttermilk, 2½ cups flour, sugar, baking powder, salt, and shortening. (Use lard for a real back-country flavor.) With electric mixer on low, blend for 30 seconds, scraping down the sides of the bowl. Turn the mixer to medium and beat for 2 minutes. Stir in the remaining flour gradually. (Do this by hand unless your mixer is heavy duty or has a dough hook. Don't overburden a small hand-held mixer.) When thoroughly blended, the dough will be soft and slightly sticky. Add more flour if it seems too moist or slack.
KNEADING 6 mins.	Turn the dough out on a floured board or counter top, and knead for about 6 minutes until the dough is smooth and elastic. (You may have to dust additional flour on the board if the dough sticks.)

SHAPING
5 mins.

With rolling pin, roll into a rectangle slightly longer than the loaf pan (or pans). Lift one of the long sides and lay it over the other. Pinch to seal the seam, and turn loaf so that seam is at the bottom. Pat dough into final shape and place gently in the loaf pan. Brush loaf lightly with melted butter.

RISING
1 hour

Cover the pan with wax paper held above the pan at least 3 inches by a couple of cans or glasses and put in a warm place (80°–85°) until the dough is doubled. It will push about 2 inches above the pan in about 1 hour. Preheat oven to 425°.

BAKING
425°
10 mins.
375°
35 mins.

Bake in the hot oven for 10 minutes, turn temperature down to 375°, and continue baking for about 35 minutes, or until a loaf tests done when thumped on the bottom crust (sounds hollow). Smaller loaves, however, should be taken out 10 minutes sooner.

FINAL STEP

Remove from oven and place loaves on a wire rack to cool. If a soft crust is desired brush loaves with melted butter. An even softer crust can be obtained by placing a tea towel over the hot bread after brushing.

COOLRISE© WHITE BREAD

[TWO MEDIUM LOAVES]

This is a white loaf to prepare one day and bake the next. The remarkable thing about this recipe is placing the panned loaves in the refrigerator rather than in the oven. During the time the dough cools, it also rises so that 2 (or 20) hours later it is well above the edge of the pan, and ready to be baked. Nevertheless, it takes some mental readjustment to slip a cold, moist pan and loaf into a hot oven. The results: good to excellent.

The method was developed in the Consumer Kitchens, Robin Hood Flour.

INGREDIENTS

6–7 cups all-purpose or bread flour
2 tablespoons sugar
1 tablespoon salt
2 packages dry yeast
¼ cup shortening, at room temperature
2¼ cups very hot tap water (120°–130°)

Cooking oil for brushing
Melted butter for brushing (optional)

BAKING PANS — Two medium (8½ x 4½) loaf pans, greased or Teflon. If glass pans are used, reduce oven temperature 25°.

PREPARATION
15 mins. — Thoroughly blend 2 cups flour, sugar, salt, and undissolved yeast in mixing bowl. Add shortening. Add water to the dry ingredients. Beat 2 minutes at medium speed, scraping bowl occasionally. Add 1 cup of flour, which will make a thick batter. Beat at high speed for 1 minute.

Stop the beater if it is a lightweight portable, and use a large wooden spoon. Work in additional cups of flour to make a soft dough.

KNEADING
10 mins. — Turn dough out onto a lightly floured board or counter top. Knead 8 to 10 minutes until it is smooth and elastic. Small bubbles will have formed under the skin of the dough. Form into a ball.

RESTING
20 mins. — Place the ball of dough on the board or counter top, cover it with a piece of plastic wrap, and let it rest 20 minutes.

SHAPING
5 mins. — Punch down the dough. Divide in half with a knife, shape into loaves. (The loaves can be formed either by patting and molding them by hand into shape, or by making rectangles with a rolling pin and folding them in half along the length—like Parker House rolls—and placing them seam down in the baking pans.) Brush with cooking oil. Cover loosely with plastic wrap to allow for an expansion of 1 or 2 inches above the edge of the pan. (The pressure of the rising dough may split the wrap if it is put on tightly.)

REFRIGERATION
2–24 hours — Refrigerate 2 to 24 hours. Loaves may be removed and baked whenever it is convenient during that time span.

RESTING
10 mins. — Set the oven at 400° and remove loaves from the refrigerator. Carefully peel back the plastic wrap. Let stand, uncovered, for 10 minutes while the oven heats. If bubbles have formed on the surface of the dough, prick them with a toothpick or metal skewer.

BAKING
400°
40 mins. — Bake 40 minutes, or until the loaves are golden brown and sound hollow when thumped on the bottom crust.

FINAL STEP

Remove loaves from pans immediately and place on wire rack to cool. For a soft crust, brush with butter. Leave untouched and uncovered for a firm crust.

EASY MIXER WHITE BREAD

[A CHOICE OF LOAVES]

Another good bread for the beginner is this easy-to-make loaf, which has good texture and pleasant taste, and which makes excellent toast. It also freezes well. This recipe uses the electric mixer for much of the blending. And kneading time is short—1 minute.

The method was developed in the Pillsbury Kitchens.

INGREDIENTS

2½ cups warm water (105°–115°)
2 packages dry yeast
½ cup instant non-fat dry milk
2 tablespoons sugar
1 tablespoon salt
⅓ cup vegetable oil
7 cups all-purpose or bread flour, approximately

BAKING PANS

One large (9 x 5) and one small (7½ x 3½) loaf pan, greased or Teflon, or two medium (8½ x 4½) pans. If glass, reduce oven heat 25°.

PREPARATION
15 mins.

Place warm water in a large mixing bowl and sprinkle yeast over the top. Add dry milk, sugar, salt, oil, and about 3 cups of the flour. Blend well at low speed of mixer, scraping the sides of the bowl clean with a rubber scraper. Increase speed to medium and beat for 3 minutes.

Remove bowl from mixer and stir in remaining flour, first with a wooden spoon and then with your hand. The dough will be stiff.

RESTING
15 mins.

Turn the dough out on a lightly floured board or counter top, cover with a towel or wax paper and let rest 15 minutes.

KNEADING AND RESTING
5 mins.

Knead only until smooth—about 1 minute. Divide the dough into two pieces with a sharp knife. Shape into balls and let rest under a towel for 4 minutes.

SHAPING 6 mins.	Form a loaf by pressing a ball of dough into a flat oval, roughly the length of the baking pan. Fold the oval in half lengthwise, pinch the seam tightly to seal, tuck under the ends, and place seam down in the pan. Repeat for the other loaf.
RISING 1 hour	Place the pans in a warm place (80°–85°), cover with wax paper, and leave until the center of the dough has risen 1 inch above the level of the edge—about 1 hour.
BAKING 400° 10 mins. 350° 35 mins.	Preheat oven to 400°. Bake in a hot oven for 10 minutes, reduce heat to 350° and continue for another 35 minutes. Halfway through the baking period turn pans. Turn again 10 minutes before done. Turn loaves out and test for doneness. When fully baked they sound hollow when thumped on the bottom crusts.
FINAL STEP	Turn from pans onto wire racks to cool.

INSTANT BLEND WHITE BREAD

[ONE LARGE OR TWO MEDIUM LOAVES]

In this recipe, the active dry yeast is scattered directly on top of a third of the flour, then blended and boosted into almost immediate action by the very high temperature of the liquids. A second time-saver consists of reducing the usual hour-long first rising of the dough to a "rest" of 20 minutes. The bread is light, even-textured, and crusty brown.

This recipe was developed by Red Star Yeast's Home Service Department.

INGREDIENTS	4¾ to 5 cups all-purpose or bread flour, approximately 2 packages dry yeast 1 cup milk ¾ cup water 2 tablespoons shortening 2 tablespoons sugar 1 tablespoon salt
BAKING PANS	One large (9 x 5) or two medium (8½ x 4½) loaf pans, greased or Teflon. For other pan combinations, see dough volume chart (p. 23). If glass pans are used, reduce oven heat 25°.

PREPARATION
15 mins.

Measure 1¾ cups of flour into a large mixing bowl. Add the dry yeast and blend either with a wooden spoon or electric mixer.

In a saucepan, stir together milk, water, shortening, sugar, and salt. Heat until it is warm (about 125°), being careful not to scorch. Combine with the flour-yeast mixture and beat at a low speed for one-half minute. Scrape the bowl. Beat at high speed for 3 more minutes. Add 1 additional cup flour. Beat another minute. If the mixer is a lightweight portable, switch to a wooden spoon and continue beating. Gradually add remaining flour until the ball of dough is soft but not sticky.

KNEADING
8 mins.

Turn out the dough onto a lightly floured board or counter top and knead for 7 or 8 minutes. The dough will be smooth and elastic.

RESTING
20 mins.

(This is called a "resting" rather than a "rising.") Cover the dough with the inverted mixing bowl and let it rest in place on the counter top for 20 minutes.

SHAPING
10 mins.

Knead the dough briefly—30 seconds. For one large loaf, roll the dough into an 8 x 16-inch rectangle. Roll from the narrow end into a tight roll. Pinch the ends to seal and turn under. For two medium loaves, divide the ball and pat or roll the dough into 2 7 x 14-inch rectangles. Roll from narrow end. Pinch the seam and ends to seal. Place seam down in baking pans.

RISING
45 mins.

Cover pans with wax paper or foil and place in a warm spot (80°–85°) until dough has doubled in volume—about 45 minutes. The center of large loaf will be about 2 inches above pan edge; center of medium loaves, 1 inch above pan edge.

BAKING
400°
10 mins.
350°
40 mins.

Preheat oven to 400°. Bake for 10 minutes; then reduce heat to 350° and continue baking for about 40 additional minutes, or until the loaves test done when thumped on the bottom crust (hollow sound).

FINAL STEP

Turn loaves out onto wire racks to cool.

RAPIDMIX WHITE BREAD

[TWO MEDIUM OR THREE SMALL LOAVES]

Blend the dry yeast with the other dry ingredients—some of the flour, all of the sugar, salt, and non-fat dry milk—pour in the warm liquids, and a new bread-making process begins. This recipe, developed in the Fleischmann's Yeast Test Kitchens, calls for use of the electric mixer through the third cup of flour, and then hand blending (unless you have a heavy duty mixer like the Kitchen Aid with dough hook). This bread makes delicious toast.

Variations of this basic Rapidmix recipe are elsewhere in this volume, including 100% Whole Wheat Bread, Kulich, Buttermilk Bread, Low Cholesterol and Raisin Casserole.

INGREDIENTS

5 to 6 cups all-purpose or bread flour, approximately
3 tablespoons sugar
2 teaspoons salt
1 package dry yeast
¼ cup non-fat dry milk
2 cups hot tap water (120°–130°)
3 tablespoons shortening

BAKING PANS

Two medium (8½ x 4½) or three small (7½ x 3½) loaf pans, greased or Teflon. If glass pans are used, reduce oven heat 25°. Refer to the dough volume chart (p. 23) for other pan combinations.

PREPARATION
15 mins.

In a large bowl, mix 2 cups of flour, sugar, salt, yeast and non-fat milk. In a small bowl or saucepan, pour the hot tap water over shortening to soften. Add to dry ingredients and beat with electric mixer for 2 minutes at medium speed, scraping bowl occasionally. Add 1 cup flour and beat at high speed for 3 minutes. Stop the beater and continue with a wooden spoon (unless it is a heavy duty mixer). Add about 2 cups more flour and blend well with the spoon, then by hand as it gets less sticky. When the dough is no longer sticky, turn it out onto floured board or counter top.

KNEADING
8 mins.

Knead 8 minutes by hand (5 minutes if using a dough hook). The dough will be smooth and quite elastic.

FIRST RISING
1 hour

Place the dough in a lightly greased bowl. Cover with plastic wrap and set in a warm place (80°–85°) until the dough has doubled in bulk—about 1 hour.

SHAPING
10 mins.

Turn back the plastic wrap and punch down the dough. Turn it onto the floured work surface and knead for 1 minute to force out bubbles. Divide the dough into two (or three) pieces with a sharp knife. Shape into balls, and let rest under a towel for 3 minutes. Form a loaf by pressing a ball of dough into a flat oval roughly the length of the baking pan. Fold the oval in half, pinch the seam tightly to seal, tuck under the ends, and place seam down in the pan. Repeat for second (and third) loaf.

SECOND RISING
45 mins.

Place the pans in the warm place (80°–85°), cover with wax paper and leave until the dough has doubled in volume—about 45 minutes.

BAKING
400°
10 mins.
350°
25–30 mins.

Preheat oven to 400°. Place the loaves in the hot oven for 10 minutes, then lower the heat to 350° for an additional 25 to 30 minutes. When the loaves are a golden brown and sound hollow when thumped on the bottom crust, they are done.

FINAL STEP

Turn out onto wire racks to cool. Brush the hot loaves with melted butter or margarine if you want a soft tender crust.

TWO

White Breads

Corn Poppy
Lyons, 1579

In spite of the current interest in whole grain and dark breads—which I share—white flour is the dominant flour in bread-baking. White breads have a variety of tastes and textures that add delight to meals and snacks. In this chapter there are forty-nine recipes for predominantly white loaves, the largest chapter in the book.

This varied collection offers such delicious loaves as a true Hungarian loaf, Irish Soda Bread, Frisian Sugar Loaf, Scottish Buttermilk Bread, and many others. As will be seen in later chapters, white flour is also an important ingredient in many dark breads which would not rise sufficiently without the gluten contributed by the white flour.

COTTAGE BREAD

[TWO CASSEROLE LOAVES]

Cottage Bread is moist and flaky. It has, however, a somewhat coarser texture than other white loaves. Baked in a casserole, it is easy to prepare and can go in the oven in about an hour. When it comes out of the oven an hour later, brush with melted butter, sprinkle with salt and serve. It is a surprisingly tasty loaf for such little work.

INGREDIENTS

2¾ cups warm water (105°–115°)
2 packages dry yeast
3 tablespoons sugar
1 tablespoon salt
2 tablespoons vegetable shortening
6½ cups all-purpose flour
Vegetable oil
Melted butter, salt

BAKING PANS

Two 1½ quart casseroles, greased or Teflon. If glass, reduce oven heat 25°.

PREPARATION
10 mins.

Place the warm water in a mixing bowl and sprinkle with yeast. Stir briskly to dissolve. Blend in sugar, salt, shortening, and 3 cups of flour. Beat with an electric mixer for 2 minutes at medium speed, or for an equal time with a wooden spoon.

Gradually add remaining flour, a half-cup at a time, and beat until smooth and somewhat stiff.

FIRST RISING
40 mins.

Cover the bowl with plastic wrap and put in a warm place (80°–85°) until the batter has doubled in volume, about 40 minutes.

FORMING
5 mins.

Stir down the batter and beat for 30 seconds with a wooden spoon. Turn half the batter into one casserole and the balance into the other. With moist fingers, pat the tops smooth.

SECOND RISING
30 mins.

Cover casseroles with wax paper and return them to the warm place until the dough is level with the edge of the casserole, about 30 minutes. In the meantime, heat the oven to 375°.

BAKING
375°
40–50 mins.

Brush the loaves with oil and place them in the moderately hot oven until they are light brown and test done when a metal testing pin or skewer inserted in the center of the loaf comes out clean and dry, about 40 to 50 minutes. (If moist particles cling to the probe, return loaves to the oven for an additional 10 minutes.)

FINAL STEP

Remove the loaves from the casseroles and place on wire rack to cool. Brush tops with melted butter and sprinkle with a little salt.

TOASTING WHITE BREAD

[TWO LOAVES]

This white bread is good just as it is but it also makes an absolutely first-rate piece of toast. The dough can either be baked right away or the pans can be slipped into plastic bags and refrigerated for several hours or overnight.

INGREDIENTS
2½ cups warm water (105°–115°)
2 packages dry yeast
½ cup instant non-fat dry milk
2 tablespoons sugar
1 tablespoon salt
¼ cup cooking oil or shortening
7 to 7½ cups all-purpose flour, approximately
Melted butter for brushing

BAKING PANS
Two medium (8½ x 4½) loaf pans, greased or Teflon. If glass, reduce oven heat 25°.

PREPARATION
10 mins.
Place the warm water in a large mixing bowl. Sprinkle the yeast over and stir briefly. Add dry milk, sugar, salt, oil, and 3 cups flour to make a thick batter. Blend at low speed in electric mixer for 30 seconds. Increase speed to medium-high and beat for 3 minutes. Turn off mixer and, by hand, gradually add remaining flour to form a stiff dough that pulls away from the sides of the bowl.

KNEADING
4 mins.
Turn the dough onto a lightly floured work surface—counter top or bread board—and knead with a strong push-turn-fold motion until no longer sticky, about 4 minutes.

SHAPING
5 mins.
Divide the dough in half, shape into balls and let rest under a towel for 3 minutes. Form the loaf by pressing each ball of dough into a flat oval roughly the length of the baking pan. Fold the oval in half, pinch the seam tightly to seal, tuck under the ends, and place in the pan, seam down. Repeat for the second ball.

RISING
If you want to bake them right away, cover the pans with wax paper and let rise in a warm place (80°–85°) until dough has doubled in size, about 1 hour.

REFRIGERATING — If you choose, the pans can now be slipped into large plastic bags—allowing enough room for the bread to rise—and refrigerated for several hours or overnight. Then skip Rising and bake as directed. (Before baking, prick any air bubbles on the surface.)

BAKING
375°
35–40 mins. — Preheat oven to 375°. Bake for 35 to 40 minutes, or until the loaves test done. Turn one loaf out of its pan and tap with a forefinger. If it sounds hollow and hard, the bread is done. If not, return the loaf (without the pan, if you wish a deep brown crust) for an additional 10 minutes and test again.

FINAL STEP — Remove from the pans immediately and brush with melted butter for a soft shiny crust. Cool on wire racks.

CHUREK

[EIGHT TO TEN PIECES]

Churek, an Armenian bread, is a flat, crisp bread sprinkled with sesame seeds and traditionally baked on a griddle or stone. I bake mine in an oven. They are rather irregular circles, rolled very thin and baked until they are puffed and crisp.

Churek is a traditional bread of the Russian Caucasus found in almost all Armenian and Georgian homes and restaurants. It will keep for several days at room temperature if wrapped securely in plastic wrap or foil.

INGREDIENTS
- 4 cups all-purpose flour, approximately
- 1 tablespoon sugar
- 1 package dry yeast
- 2 teaspoons salt
- 4 tablespoons butter, melted
- 1 cup hot tap water (120°–130°)
- ¼ cup sesame seeds, approximately

BAKING SHEET — One baking sheet, greased or Teflon.

PREPARATION
15 mins. — No kneading is required, only vigorous beating with mixer and spoon.

Measure 2½ cups flour into a large mixing bowl and stir in the sugar, yeast, salt, melted butter, and hot tap water. Beat with electric mixer at medium-high speed for 3 minutes.

Stop mixer. With a large spoon, beat in the balance of the flour, continuing to beat for 8 to 10 minutes, or until a soft, spongy dough is formed. (If the dough sticks to the bowl or spoon add additional flour. It may be helpful to use a pastry scraper or wide putty knife to turn and work the soft dough.)

RISING
50 mins.

Form the soft dough into a ball in the bowl and cover tightly with plastic wrap. Place the bowl in a warm place (80°–85°) until dough doubles in volume, about 50 minutes. Preheat oven to 400°.

SHAPING
12 mins.

Punch down the dough and knead for 30 seconds to press out the bubbles. Divide the dough into 8 or 10 equal parts. Roll each into a 6″ to 8″ circle as thin as possible, and place 2 or 3 on the prepared baking sheet. Brush lightly with water and sprinkle with sesame seeds.

BAKING
400°
20 mins.

Set the baking sheet on the lowest rack of the oven and bake 20 minutes or until the bread is a pale golden brown. Transfer the breads to a wire rack and repeat with the remaining rounds.

INSTANT BLEND BUTTERMILK BREAD

[TWO 1-POUND LOAVES]

This is a good buttermilk bread and easy to make. Three minutes under the beaters, 8 minutes of hand kneading (or 6 minutes by dough hook), and a short rest of 20 minutes before rolling the two pieces into long tapered loaves. For variety, I sprinkle one with sesame and the other with poppy seeds.

INGREDIENTS

4½ cups of all-purpose flour, approximately
2 packages dry yeast
1 cup buttermilk
¾ cup water
2 tablespoons *each* shortening and sugar
1 tablespoon salt
A sprinkle of poppy and sesame seeds (optional) and warm water for brushing

BAKING SHEET

One baking sheet, greased or Teflon.

PREPARATION
20 mins.

Stir together in a large mixing bowl 2 cups flour and the yeast.

In a saucepan combine buttermilk, water, shortening, sugar and salt. Place over low heat until warm (120°–130°). If the buttermilk curdles, no matter. Add to dry ingredients and beat ½ minute at low speed. Scrape the sides of the bowl. At high speed, beat for 3 minutes.

Stop the mixer. Using first a wooden spoon, then your hands, gradually add remaining flour, a half-cup at a time, stirring and mixing until a soft dough is formed.

KNEADING
8 mins.

Turn the dough onto a heavily floured work surface and knead 8 minutes (6 minutes with a dough hook). The dough will be smooth and elastic.

RESTING
20 mins.

Form into a ball, cover with a tent of wax paper or towel and let it rest for 20 minutes.

SHAPING
15 mins.

Punch down the dough and knead 30 seconds to press out the bubbles. Divide into two pieces; set one aside while shaping the first. With a rolling pin or by hand, shape one piece into a 6 x 12-inch rectangle. Roll up tightly, starting at the wide side. Pinch the seam and ends together securely, and roll back and forth between your palms to taper the loaf. Repeat with second piece. Place on baking sheet.

RISING
45 mins.

Place a length of wax paper over the loaves and put them in a warm spot (80°–85°) to rise until doubled in size, about 45 minutes. After the dough has risen for 25 minutes, slash the tops of the loaves with 3 or 4 diagonal cuts with a sharp razor or knife. Brush with warm water and leave for remaining 20 minutes.

BAKING
400°
45 mins.

Preheat the oven to 400°. Brush loaves again with the warm water and sprinkle with sesame and/or poppy seeds. Bake in the hot oven for about 30 minutes. Then shift loaves around for even baking and bake for another 15 minutes, or until the loaves are golden brown. Test one loaf by tapping the bottom crust with a forefinger. A hard hollow sound means the bread is baked. If not, return to the oven for 10 additional minutes.

FINAL STEP

Remove the loaves from the oven and brush with water immediately. Place on a wire rack to cool.

THIRTY-MINUTE WHITE BREAD

[TWO LOAVES]

This is an excellent, light and airy loaf. The panned dough is placed in a *cold* oven, the heat turned on for 60 seconds, turned off and then the dough is allowed to rise for exactly *30 minutes* (hence, the name) before the oven is turned up for baking.

The recipe for this dough was created by the Kitchen Aid home economists to respond particularly well to the dough hook attachment for their mixer. It can be done by hand, of course.

INGREDIENTS

2 packages dry yeast
3 tablespoons warm water (105°–115°)
1 cup milk, scalding hot
2 tablespoons shortening
3 teaspoons salt
1 cup cold water
2 tablespoons sugar
6 to 7 cups all-purpose or bread flour, approximately

BAKING PANS

Two medium (8½ x 4½) loaf pans, greased or Teflon. If glass, reduce oven heat 25°.

PREPARATION
20 mins.

In a small bowl, dissolve the yeast in warm water (105°–115°). Beat briskly with a metal whisk or fork to hasten the action. Set aside.

Bring the milk to the boiling point in a saucepan, and add shortening and salt. Remove from the heat and add cold water.

In a large mixing bowl combine the cooled milk (not above 130°), the yeast mixture and sugar. Stir in 2 cups flour and beat 3 minutes at medium speed in the electric mixer—or 150 strong strokes with a wooden spoon. Gradually add 2 more cups flour, and continue beating for 3 minutes—or 150 strokes.

Turn off mixer and add about 2 cups of flour. Work it in with the spoon, and, when it becomes stiff, with your hands. When the dough has a rough form and is cleaning the sides of the bowl, turn it out briefly on the floured surface to make certain it is ready for kneading.

KNEADING
8 mins.

Knead for about 8 minutes, or replace dough in bowl and put under dough hook for 5 minutes.

SHAPING
10 mins.

Divide the dough in half, and shape into balls. Let rest under a towel for 3 minutes. Form the loaves by pressing each ball (with your palms or a rolling pin) into a flat oval, roughly the length of the baking pan. Fold the oval in half, pinch the seam tightly to seal, tuck under the ends, and place seam down in pan. Brush the tops with melted butter or shortening.

RISING
30 mins.

Place the pans in a cold oven and turn the heat to 400° for *1 minute*. Turn it off!

BAKING
400°
50 mins.

Thirty minutes later turn on the oven to 400° and bake for about 50 minutes or until the loaves are brown. When done, they will sound hollow when tapped on the bottom crust with a forefinger. If the crust is soft, return to the oven without the pans for 10 minutes.

FINAL STEP

Place loaves on a metal rack to cool. The bread makes fine sandwiches and toast. It also freezes very well.

AIR BREAD

[TWO LOAVES AND A HALF DOZEN MUFFINS]

James Beard discovered that this slightly sweet batter for muffins was even better as bread, but only when toasted. The batter is so thick you can scarcely stir it, and it rises grandly. Don't let it touch the wax paper or foil because it sticks tenaciously. One batch of dough—poured to the halfway mark in the tins—will produce one medium loaf, one small loaf and a half-dozen muffins made in brioche pans.

INGREDIENTS

2 packages dry yeast
2¼ cups warm water (105°–115°)
5 cups all-purpose flour
¾ cup instant non-fat dry milk
½ cup (1 stick) butter, at room temperature
½ cup sugar
1 tablespoon salt
2 lightly beaten eggs, at room temperature

BAKING PANS

One medium (8½ x 4½) and one small (7½ x 3½) loaf pan and a muffin pan or brioche cups (about a half-dozen), all greased or Teflon. If glass, reduce oven heat 25°.

PREPARATION 20 mins.	In a large bowl, dissolve yeast in water and stir briskly with a fork or metal whisk to speed the action. Let stand for 3 to 5 minutes until it begins to foam. Stir into the yeast mixture 2 cups flour, dry milk, butter, sugar, and salt. Stir in the eggs, and gradually add the remaining flour, a half-cup at a time, beating vigorously to form a thick stringy batter.
FIRST RISING 1 hour	Cover dough with plastic wrap and let rise until double in volume in a warm (80°–85°), draft-free place, about an hour.
FORMING 15 mins.	Stir down the dough and divide among the loaf and muffin or brioche tins. Wet the tips of the fingers to press the soft dough into place.
SECOND RISING 45 mins.	Cover loosely with wax paper (resting it on water tumblers above the pans) until the dough has risen to twice the bulk, about 45 minutes.
BAKING 375° 45/20 mins.	Preheat oven to 375°. Bake the bread for about 45 minutes. The muffins will take approximately 20 minutes.
FINAL STEP	Turn out on a metal rack to cool before serving or freezing.

ARAB BREAD

[SIXTEEN SMALL PUFF LOAVES]

A Middle Eastern bread (also known as "Armenian"), these small loaves puff into hollow balls that can be filled with sandwich spread or butter and honey. The traditional way, however, is to tear the warm loaf open and wrap it around bits of lamb pulled from a shish kebab skewer.

It is easy to make, but instructions must be followed explicitly. One side left too thick or rolled too thin will produce a lopsided loaf. (Delicious, nevertheless.)

INGREDIENTS	6 cups all-purpose flour, approximately 2 packages dry yeast 1½ teaspoons salt 2½ cups hot tap water (120°–130°) 3 tablespoons olive or salad oil

BAKING EQUIPMENT

Sixteen seven-inch squares of aluminum foil.

PREPARATION
15 mins.

Place 3 cups flour, yeast, and salt in a large mixing bowl. Pour in hot tap water and oil. Beat with electric mixer at low speed until the ingredients are moist, then turn to high for 3 minutes. (This can also be mixed by hand with a large wooden spoon—150 strokes.) Stop the mixer and with the wooden spoon blend in the remaining flour, one cup at a time, until the dough holds together and cleans the sides of the bowl.

KNEADING
10 mins.

Turn out on a floured surface and knead for about 10 minutes or until the dough is smooth and satiny. If it is sticky in the early stages of kneading, add a bit more flour—a quarter-cup at a time—until it no longer sticks to the counter surface or the fingers.

FIRST RISING
1½ hours

Return dough to the bowl and grease the ball lightly so a crust will not form as it rises. Cover the bowl with plastic wrap and put in a warm place (80°–85°) until dough has doubled in bulk, about 1½ hours.

SHAPING
20 mins.

Punch down and turn out on a lightly floured surface. Knead for a minute or two to work out the bubbles. Form into a round ball and divide into sixteen equal pieces. (I use a postal scale to assure equality.)

Now comes the moment of truth. Form each piece into a round ball, and then, with a rolling pin, roll each one into a circle 6½ inches in diameter and about $\frac{3}{16}$ inch thick. It is more important to work for *uniform* thickness—whatever the measurement—so when it puffs with steam it will rise uniformly and not be lopsided. Don't worry about the shape of the circle. Irregularity adds charm.

SECOND RISING
1 hour

Place each circle of dough on a piece of aluminum foil and let stand uncovered—repeat, *uncovered*—at room temperature for 1 hour. (Do not place in a warm spot to hurry the rising.)

BAKING
500°
5 mins.

Preheat oven to 500° and place oven rack at the lowest possible position. Place 3 or 4 breads at a time—on foil—directly on the oven rack. Bake for about 5 minutes, or until they are puffed and start to brown.

FINAL STEP

Remove from oven and either serve at once or keep them warm and moist by slipping them into plastic bags until serving. Or, let cool and freeze. Thaw before using. To reheat, stack several in a pile, wrap with foil and place in a 375° oven for 10 to 15 minutes.

MOTHER'S SALLY LUNN

[ONE LOAF]

Sally Lunn is made both as a quick bread and as a yeast bread. This quick bread recipe is an adaptation of one from a famous Charleston cookbook. It's simple and quick.

INGREDIENTS

2 eggs at room temperature, separated
½ cup sugar
1½ cups all-purpose flour
3 teaspoons baking powder
½ teaspoon salt
¾ cup milk
2 tablespoons butter, melted

BAKING PAN

One 8- or 9-inch square loaf pan, greased or Teflon. If a glass pan, reduce oven heat 25°.

PREPARATION
15 mins.

Preheat oven to 350°. Separate the eggs. In a large mixing bowl combine the yolks and sugar. Stir in the dry ingredients—flour, baking powder, and salt—alternately with the milk. Add butter. Stir well. Beat the egg whites until stiff and fold into the batter.

FORMING
3 mins.

Pour into the prepared pan. Push into the corners and smooth with a spatula or spoon. (Dampened fingertips also work well.)

BAKING
350°
40 mins.

Bake for 40 minutes or until it tests done (a wooden toothpick inserted in the bread comes out clean and dry).

FINAL STEP

Let cool in the pan for 10 minutes and then turn onto a wire rack to finish cooling. Cut into squares and serve.

BUTTERMILK BREAD

[TWO LOAVES]

The name "buttermilk bread" has a country-kitchen lilt, and this loaf has a country-kitchen taste. It is light, of good texture, has a golden-brown crust and creamy white insides. It keeps for a long period deep-frozen and makes delicious toast.

INGREDIENTS

5½ to 6½ cups all-purpose or bread flour
3 tablespoons sugar
2½ teaspoons salt
¼ teaspoon baking soda
1 package dry yeast
1 cup water
⅓ cup shortening
1 cup buttermilk

BAKING PANS

Two medium loaf pans (8½ x 4½), greased or Teflon. If glass pans are used, reduce oven heat 25°.

PREPARATION
20 mins.

In a large mixing bowl, stir together 2½ cups flour, sugar, salt, baking soda and dry yeast. Combine water, shortening, and buttermilk in a saucepan and place over low heat until warm. (The shortening does not need to melt. And, because of the buttermilk, the mixture may appear curdled, but this does not matter.) Gradually add the liquid to the dry ingredients and beat for 2 minutes at medium speed. Scrape bowl once or twice during the process.

Add about 1 cup flour to make a thick batter, and beat at high speed for another 2 minutes. From this point forward, use a wooden spoon and fingers to work in additional flour. When the mass of dough is soft and not sticky, turn out on a lightly floured board or counter top. Or return the dough to the mixing bowl if you have a dough hook.

KNEADING
8 mins.

Knead until the ball of dough is smooth and elastic—about 8 minutes. (It will take about 5 minutes with the dough hook.) If the dough is too slack or soft and has a tendency to stick, add a small amount of flour—but only in the early stages of kneading.

FIRST RISING
1 hour

Place in a greased bowl, turning to make certain the entire mass has a light film of grease to keep a crust from forming while it rises. I sometimes rub shortening on my hands and pat the top of the dough when I put it in the bowl.

Cover tightly with plastic wrap and put in a warm place (80°–85°) until the dough has doubled in bulk, about 1 hour. If the dough has risen enough, you will be able to tell by poking a finger into it—the dent will remain.

SHAPING
5 mins.

Punch down dough and cut into two pieces with a large knife. For each piece, turn the cut side under and gently press and pat it into an oblong shape that will barely touch the ends of the pan. Place in pans.

SECOND RISING
45 mins.

Cover with wax paper and return to the warm place for about 45 minutes or until the dough has risen about 1 inch above the pan.

BAKING
375°
40 mins.

Preheat oven to 375°. Bake for about 40 minutes, or until the crust is golden brown and a loaf sounds hollow when thumped on the bottom. If the bottom is soft and does not resound, return the loaf to the oven (without the pan) for another 5 to 10 minutes, and test again. (You can test for doneness also by inserting a metal skewer or toothpick in the center; it will come out dry and clean.)

FINAL STEP

Remove from pans immediately and cool on wire racks.

CUBAN BREAD

[TWO PLUMP LOAVES]

A large dose of yeast—twice the usual yeast-flour ratio—gives a fast rise to this unusually crusty white loaf comprised of only water, flour, yeast, salt and sugar. The crust is cut with a sharp knife or razor blade before it goes into the oven and it opens in the heat like a giant blossom.

A number of food authors have lauded this bread, first popularized by James Beard in his cooking classes, because it is so quick and easy, even for beginners. (You don't even need to preheat the oven.)

INGREDIENTS

5 to 6 cups all-purpose or bread flour, approximately
4 packages dry yeast
1 tablespoon salt
2 tablespoons sugar
2 cups warm water (105°–115°)
½ cup flour for the board
Sesame seeds (optional)

BAKING SHEET

One baking sheet, greased or Teflon.

PREPARATION
15 mins.

Place 4 cups of flour in a large mixing bowl and add yeast, salt and sugar. Stir these dry ingredients until they are well blended. Pour in water and beat with 100 strong strokes. Gradually work in remaining flour (using fingers if necessary), a half cup at a time, until the dough takes shape and is no longer sticky.

KNEADING
6 mins.

Sprinkle work surface—counter top or bread board—liberally with flour. Work in the flour as you knead, keeping a layer of it between the dough and the work surface. Knead for about 6 minutes or until smooth, elastic and feels alive under the hands.

RISING
15 mins.

Place dough in a greased bowl, cover with plastic wrap and put it in a warm place (80°–85°) until doubled in bulk, about 15 minutes. You can test if it is light or risen by poking a finger in it; the dent will remain.

SHAPING
10 mins.

Punch down the dough, turn it out on the work surface and cut into two pieces. Knead each piece 30 seconds to squeeze out the bubbles and form into round, plump loaves. Place on baking sheet. With a sharp knife or razor, slash an "X" on each of the loaves, brush with water, and, if desired, sprinkle with sesame seeds.

BAKING
400°
50 mins.

Place baking sheet on middle shelf of a *cold* oven. Set the temperature at 400°, place a large pan of hot water on the shelf below and turn on the heat. The bread, of course, will continue to rise while the oven is heating. Bake for about 50 minutes or until the loaves are a deep golden brown. Thump on the bottom crust to test for doneness. If they sound hollow and hard, they are done.

FINAL STEP

Place on metal racks and cool. Since this bread has no shortening it will not keep beyond a day or so. It does, however, freeze as well as other loaves. Serve warm, but not hot.

FORK BREAD

[ONE LOAF]

This bread is rich and tender—a deep, dark brown crust surrounding a lovely yellow interior. The contrast between the two is striking. The eggs give it a surprising sheen that makes it one of the most handsome loaves to grace the table. It is a yeast-raised batter bread requiring no kneading.

To serve, do not cut with a knife, no matter how sharp, but gently pull it apart with forks.

INGREDIENTS

2 packages dry yeast
¼ cup warm water (105°–115°)
3 tablespoons sugar
3 eggs, at room temperature
½ cup (1 stick) butter, at room temperature
½ teaspoon salt
2 cups all-purpose or bread flour

BAKING PAN

One medium (8½ x 4½) loaf pan or 9-inch tube pan, greased or Teflon. If a glass pan is used, reduce oven heat 25°.

PREPARATION
15 mins.

Dissolve yeast in water and stir briskly with a fork or whisk. Set aside.

In a large bowl beat together the sugar, eggs, butter, salt, and 1 cup flour. Beat 150 strokes or 3 minutes at high speed with an electric mixer. Stir in remaining flour with wooden spoon.

FORMING
3 mins.

Pour the batter into pan, and spread it evenly with the spoon.

RISING
2–2½ hours

Cover pan with plastic wrap and put in a warm place until the batter has doubled in volume. This is usually a lengthy process—from 2 to 2½ hours.

BAKING
450°
20 mins.

Preheat the oven to 450°. Bake for 20 minutes or until the loaf is a deep, rich brown. It will test done when a skewer or toothpick inserted in the loaf comes out dry and clean.

FINAL STEP

Turn onto a wire rack to cool. Serve on a platter with two forks. Let each guest break off his own serving.

IRISH SODA BREAD

[TWO ROUND LOAVES]

This is a white soda bread with a sweet, crusty smell. It can be enlivened, if you wish, with 1 to 2 cups of raisins or currants. The Irish put a lid over the pan when it goes into the oven. Try one with the lid on and one without, and see which you like best.

INGREDIENTS

4 cups all-purpose or bread flour
1 teaspoon salt
3 teaspoons baking powder
1 teaspoon baking soda
¼ cup sugar
⅛ teaspoon (a pinch) of cardamom or coriander, or 1 to 2 cups raisins or currants
¼ cup (½ stick) butter or margarine
1 egg, at room temperature
1¾ cups buttermilk, at room temperature

BAKING PANS

Two 8-inch cake or pie pans, greased or Teflon. Lids, if desired. If glass pans are used, reduce heat 25°.

PREPARATION
10 mins.

In a large bowl, combine flour, salt, baking powder, baking soda, sugar, and spice. (If you plan to add currants or raisins—later—don't use the spice.) Add butter or margarine, and cut in with two knives or a pastry blender, or work it in with the fingers.

In another bowl, beat the egg and mix with buttermilk. (It is important for these to be at room temperature, for either cold milk or cold eggs can be a shock to the batter and slow the baking process.) Pour the buttermilk mixture into the dry ingredients and stir until well blended. At this point add the fruit, if desired.

KNEADING
3 mins.

Turn out on a floured surface and knead gently for three minutes, or until the dough is smooth.

SHAPING
10 mins.

Divide dough into two pieces, shape each into a round loaf, and place each loaf in a pan. Press down until the dough fills the pan. With a sharp knife or razor blade, cut a cross about ½-inch deep on top of each loaf. Cover the pans with lids, Irish style, or leave uncovered.

BAKING
375°
40 mins.

Preheat oven to 375°. Bake for about 40 minutes. Thump the bottom of one to test for doneness. If it sounds hollow, it's done.

FINAL STEP

Turn out on a wire rack to cool. Do not cut for about 4 hours. Then, cut in wedges to serve.

SALLY LUNN

[ONE LARGE ROUND LOAF]

A sweet bread rich in eggs and butter, this one is said to have gotten its name on the Continent many years ago from *soleil et lune,* French for "sun and moon." At that time, the dough was shaped into buns and, to many, the golden top crust and the white bottom evoked an image of the two heavenly bodies.

It is a yeast batter bread *not* to be kneaded—beaten only. (Carelessly, I once kneaded the dough. It then tripled in volume in the oven and almost rose out of the angel food cake pan.) Here it is prepared by the rapid-mix method—sprinkling the yeast onto the flour.

INGREDIENTS

3½ to 4 cups all-purpose flour
⅓ cup sugar
1 teaspoon salt
1 package dry yeast
½ cup *each* milk and water
½ cup (1 stick) butter
3 eggs, at room temperature

BAKING PAN

One 9-inch tube pan, greased or Teflon. If a glass container, reduce oven heat 25°.

PREPARATION
20 mins.

In a large bowl, mix 1½ cups flour, sugar, salt, and yeast.

In a saucepan, combine the milk, water and butter. Place over low heat until the liquid is warm and the butter soft (the butter need not melt).

Gradually pour the liquid into dry ingredients and beat for about 3 to 4 minutes with a wooden spoon or 2 minutes with an electric mixer at medium speed. Add eggs and 1 cup flour—or enough flour to make a thick batter. Continue to beat for 2 minutes with the spoon or at high speed with the electric mixer. Stop beating and stir in enough additional flour to make a stiff batter.

FIRST RISING
1 hour

Cover bowl with plastic wrap and put in a warm place (80°–85°), free from draft, until the dough has doubled in bulk, about 1 hour.

FORMING
5 mins.

Stir the batter down and beat well for about 30 seconds. Pour into the pan.

SECOND RISING
1 hour

Cover pan with wax paper and let rise in the warm place until dough has doubled in volume, about 1 hour.

BAKING
325°
50 mins.

Preheat oven to 325°. Bake for 50 minutes, or until the loaf tests done. (A wooden toothpick or metal skewer inserted in the loaf will come out clean and dry.)

FINAL STEP

Carefully remove the loaf from the pan. (It will be quite heavy and somewhat fragile while it is hot.) It is best served while still warm. To cool, place on a wire rack.

DIET BREAD

[TWO LOAVES]

This diet loaf is salt-free, sugar-free, and has no shortening; water is used instead of milk. Made only with yeast and flour, it is a lovely light brown loaf that toasts well, and has a surprisingly good flavor despite its lack of salt. (Actually, if salt is added, it becomes French Peasant Bread.)

While it will freeze and keep nicely for months, it will not remain soft and fresh for more than a day or two because it contains no fat.

INGREDIENTS

1 package dry yeast
¼ cup warm water (105°–115°)
2 cups warm water (105°–115°)
6 to 6½ cups all-purpose or bread flour, approximately

BAKING PANS

Two medium (8½ x 4½) loaf pans, greased or Teflon. If glass, reduce oven heat 25°.

PREPARATION
20 mins.

In a large bowl sprinkle yeast over the ¼ cup warm water, stir briskly with a metal whisk or fork, and leave for about 10 minutes until it begins to bubble and foam.

Add the 2 cups of warm water, and flour a cup at a time. With a wooden spoon, stir in each cup until the batter is smooth. When it can no longer be worked in with the spoon, use your fingers. Fold and work the dough between the fingers and press roughly against the sides of the bowl. When it forms a mass and cleans the sides of the bowl (it will be a moist, sticky dough) turn it out on a floured work surface—counter top or bread board.

KNEADING
7 mins.

Because it is sticky, it will be easier to turn it with a metal spatula or scraper (I use a broad putty knife). Keep the dough dusted with flour during the kneading or it will stick to your hands and work surface. Be rough with the dough. Slam it against the counter top a dozen or so times. Each time, turn and lift it with the spatula and bang it down again. Soon it will become elastic and lose most of its stickiness. Knead for about 7 minutes, including the slamming, etc.

FIRST RISING
1 hour

Place dough in bowl, cover, and leave in a warm place (80°–85°) for about 1 hour or until it has doubled in bulk. (It will be stark white, in contrast to white bread doughs somewhat tinted by milk and/or shortening.)

SHAPING
5 mins.

Turn out onto a lightly floured surface and knead for a moment or two to press out bubbles. Divide in two and shape into loaves. Place in pans, pressing it into the corners.

SECOND RISING
45 mins.

Place pans in the warm place, cover with wax paper and leave until the center of the dough has risen to the edge of the pan, about 45 minutes. Meanwhile, preheat oven to 375°.

BAKING
375°
30 mins.

Bake for 30 minutes or until it is light brown. (Because it contains no salt, it will not become golden brown.) Turn one loaf out and test for doneness by thumping the bottom crust with a forefinger. If it sounds hard and hollow, it is done.

FINAL STEP

Turn out on a metal rack to cool. This toasts well, but don't expect the deep brown color that comes with a richer dough. It is good, nevertheless, and a sprinkle of salt will make it right for the non-dieter.

SCOTTISH BUTTERMILK BREAD

[ONE LOAF]

The traditional Scottish Buttermilk Bread is closely akin to Irish Soda Bread. I discovered this bread in Pitlochry, a small town in the Highlands, and was delighted to find that in my Indiana kitchen it blossomed into the same lovely brown loaf, flaky and rough textured, that I had eaten there. There is no baking powder in this recipe; it relies entirely on the buttermilk and baking soda for the leavening. I mark the round loaf in quarters or "farls" and break them off, rather than slice the bread. It takes less than an hour to mix, bake and serve.

INGREDIENTS	2 cups all-purpose flour, approximately ½ teaspoon *each* baking soda and cream of tartar ¼ teaspoon salt 1 teaspoon sugar 1 tablespoon butter, at room temperature ¾ cup buttermilk, at room temperature
BAKING SHEET	One baking sheet, greased or Teflon.
PREPARATION 10 mins.	Measure flour into a medium-size bowl, and add baking soda, cream of tartar, salt, and sugar. Work in the butter and add buttermilk. If it is too moist to handle without sticking, dust with additional flour.
SHAPING 3 mins.	Pat into a round loaf about 8 inches across and flatten slightly. With a razor, cut an "X" about ¼-inch deep in the top. Sprinkle flour on the bottom of the pan and add the loaf.
BAKING 375° 35–40 mins.	Preheat oven to 375°. Bake for 35 to 40 minutes or until the loaf has blossomed open and is a lovely golden brown. Turn out the loaf and tap the bottom crust with a forefinger. If it has a hard, hollow sound it is done.
FINAL STEP	Place the loaf on a metal rack to cool before serving. This freezes well.

EGG BRAID

[ONE LARGE OR TWO SMALL LOAVES]

This is an instant-blend recipe. A rest period of 20 minutes substitutes for one of the two rising periods, saving you a half-hour's work.

Sprinkled with poppy seeds, these braids are big and handsome, and have an excellent flavor.

INGREDIENTS	4 to 4½ cups all-purpose flour, approximately 2 packages dry yeast ½ cup milk, room temperature ½ cup warm water (105°–115°) 2 tablespoons shortening 2 tablespoons sugar 2 teaspoons salt 3 eggs, at room temperature For the glaze: 1 egg, slightly beaten, and a sprinkle of poppy seeds
BAKING SHEET	One baking sheet, greased or Teflon.
PREPARATION 15 mins.	Measure 2 cups flour into a large mixing bowl. Add yeast and stir together. Add milk, water, shortening, sugar, and salt, and beat to blend. Break in the eggs. Beat with an electric mixer at low speed for 30 seconds. Beat 3 more minutes at high speed, scraping the bowl once or twice. Stop mixer and gradually add remaining flour to form a soft mass that pulls away from the bowl.
KNEADING 8 mins.	Turn out onto a floured work surface and knead with a strong push-turn-fold motion until the dough is smooth and elastic, about 8 minutes (6 minutes with a dough hook).
RESTING 20 mins.	Cover dough with inverted mixing bowl and let rest 20 minutes. Knock down the dough and knead for 30 seconds to squeeze out the bubbles.
BRAIDING 25 mins.	For one large loaf, divide the dough into three equal parts. Let rest for 3 minutes before continuing. Roll each, under your palms, into a 15-inch-long roll. Place side by side and braid loosely, beginning in the center and braiding first to one end and then to the other.

Seal ends by pinching and tucking under the braid. Place on the baking sheet.

For the two smaller loaves, divide the dough in half and form each half as described above.

RISING
45 mins.

Cover loaves with wax paper and let rise until doubled, about 45 minutes.

BAKING
400°
25–30 mins.

Preheat the oven to 400°. Brush braids with beaten egg and sprinkle with poppy seeds. Bake in the hot oven for 25 to 30 minutes or until brown. A thump on the bottom crust with the forefinger will sound hard and hollow if the loaf is done.

FINAL STEP

Remove to wire racks and cool before serving or freezing.

LOW CHOLESTEROL BREAD

[TWO LARGE LOAVES]

To anyone with a special concern about cholesterol, this loaf can be a pleasant diet aid. It is a good bread, with only 1 tablespoon of low cholesterol margarine in the dough, and it can be served without comment or apology to any guest at the table, diet problem or not. A solid loaf, it freezes and keeps well.

INGREDIENTS

7 to 8 cups all-purpose flour, approximately
2 tablespoons sugar
2 teaspoons salt
1 package dry yeast
1 tablespoon margarine (low cholesterol, if available) at room temperature
2½ cups hot tap water (120°–130°)

BAKING PANS

Two large (9 x 5) baking pans, greased or Teflon. If glass, reduce oven heat 25° For other pan sizes, see dough volume chart, page 23.

PREPARATION
15 mins.

In a large bowl, stir together 2 cups flour, the sugar, salt and yeast. Add the margarine. Add the hot tap water and beat for 2 minutes at medium speed in an electric mixer, or for the same time with a wooden spoon. Add 1 cup flour and beat for 2 more minutes either at high speed or with the spoon.

Stop the mixer and stir in the remaining flour a

half-cup at a time, first with the spoon and then using your hands. The dough will be a rough, shaggy mass that will clean the sides of the bowl. If the dough is slack and moisture comes through, add small sprinkles of flour.

KNEADING
8 mins.

Turn the dough onto a lightly floured work surface—counter top or bread board—and knead with a push-turn-fold motion. The dough will become smooth and elastic, and bubbles will form under the surface. Sprinkle more flour on if it sticks to your hands or work surface. Occasionally, pick up the dough and bang it down hard against the surface. Knead for about 8 minutes altogether or 6 minutes with the dough hook.

FIRST RISING
1 hour

Drop the dough back into the mixing bowl and pat with margarine or oil to keep the surface from crusting. Cover the bowl tightly with plastic wrap and put in a warm place (80°–85°) until the dough has risen to about twice its original height, about 1 hour.

SHAPING
10 mins.

Punch down dough and knead for 30 seconds to press out the bubbles. Cut ball into two pieces with a sharp knife. Shape into balls and let rest under a towel for 3 to 4 minutes. Form each loaf by pressing a ball into a flat oval, roughly the length of the baking pan. Fold the oval in half lengthwise, pinch the seam to seal, tuck under the ends, and place seam down in the pan.

SECOND RISING
45 mins.

Place the pans in a warm place (80°–85°), cover with wax paper, and leave until the center of the dough has risen ½–1 inch above the pan, or has about doubled. This will take about 45 minutes. Meanwhile, preheat oven to 400°.

BAKING
400°
40–45 mins.

Bake loaves in the hot oven for about 40 to 45 minutes. Midway in the bake period and again near the end of it, shift the loaves so they are exposed equally to temperature variations in the oven. Bake until they have a lovely golden crust and test done. (Turn out one loaf and tap the bottom crust with a forefinger. If it gives a hollow, hard sound, the bread is done. If it is soft, return to the oven for an additional 10 minutes.) If the loaves are browning too quickly, cover with a piece of foil or brown sack paper.

FINAL STEP

Remove from pans and cool on metal racks.

ENGLISH MUFFIN BREAD

[TWO LOAVES]

English Muffin Bread is for the English Muffin buff. It will win few awards for its beauty, delicate crumb or golden crust, but, sliced and toasted, it is delicious. (Imagine an English Muffin pulled apart and laid open to reveal its interesting foundation of irregular air pockets.) It came originally from a bakery on the Oregon coast, where it was developed as a batter bread—leavened with yeast but reinforced with baking soda late in the production stage.

Try it under Eggs Benedict.

INGREDIENTS

1 package dry yeast
Pinch of sugar
½ cup warm water (105°–115°)
1½ cups of warm milk (100°)
1 tablespoon salt
3 cups all-purpose flour
¼ teaspoon baking soda dissolved in one tablespoon warm water (100°)

BAKING PANS

Two medium (8½ x 4½) loaf pans, greased or Teflon. If glass, reduce oven heat 25°.

PREPARATION
15 mins.

An unusual step in the preparation of this recipe consists of proofing the dough before all of the ingredients are added.

Sprinkle yeast and sugar over the warm water. Stir briskly with a fork and set aside until it has started to foam and bubble, about 5 minutes.

In a large bowl, combine yeast mixture and milk. With a large wooden spoon stir in salt and flour a cup at a time. Stir until smooth and well blended, about 30 strokes.

FIRST RISING
1 hour

Cover the bowl with plastic wrap and put in a warm (80°–85°) draft-free place for about 1 hour. The dough will double in bulk and be quite bubbly.

Stir down the batter-like dough and add the dissolved baking soda. (It is the chemical action of the soda that gives the bread its network of peculiarly large cells.) Stir well.

SHAPING
5 mins.

Pour or spoon into the pans, pushing the dough into the corners with a spatula. (The pans will be about a quarter-filled.)

SECOND RISING
1 hour

Cover pans with plastic wrap and return to the warm place for about 1 hour. The dough will rise about half-way up the pan.

BAKING
375°
1 hour

Preheat oven to 375°. Bake the loaves for about 1 hour. The loaves will be well browned and pull away from the sides of the pans when done. You may have to add another 10 minutes. Unless thoroughly baked, they can collapse.

FINAL STEP

Turn out from pans and cool on wire racks. You may wish to try it sliced as it comes from the oven, but it is best toasted. It freezes fine and keeps for months.

KHOUBZ ARABY BREAD

[SIX 8-INCH ROUND LOAVES]

Almost as soon as these thin flat disks of Arab bread are in the hot oven, they begin to solemnly puff into round balls. While some will make only a half-hearted attempt to fully blossom and will puff only slightly, all will be equally delicious served at a meal where pieces of bread can be wrapped around bits of meat. The plainness of the bread, while exotic in form, allows the diner to appreciate fully the other flavors of the meal. It is the perfect accompaniment to barbecued and grilled meats.

INGREDIENTS

4 cups bread or all-purpose flour, approximately
1 package dry yeast
2 teaspoons salt
2 tablespoons olive oil
1 cup hot tap water (120°–130°)
For the glaze (optional): 1 egg white
1 tablespoon water
1 tablespoon sesame seeds

FOR BAKING

One baking sheet, floured or Teflon. Aluminum foil in which to wrap loaves when they come from the oven.

PREPARATION
15 mins.

Measure 2 cups flour into a large mixing bowl and stir in the yeast, salt, olive oil, and hot tap water. Blend at low speed of electric mixer for 30 seconds, increase to high for 3 minutes, or beat vigorously with a wooden spoon for an equal length of time.

Stop mixer. Stir in the balance of flour, a half-cup at a time, first with the spoon and then with your hands. The dough will be a rough, shaggy mass that will clean the sides of the bowl. If the dough is moist and sticky, add a small amount of additional flour.

KNEADING
8 mins.

Turn the dough onto a lightly floured work surface—counter top or bread board—and knead with the rhythmic 1-2-3 motion of push-turn-fold. Break the kneading rhythm occasionally by throwing the dough down hard against the counter top. Knead for about 8 minutes total, or 6 minutes with a dough hook.

RESTING
25 mins.

Divide the dough into 6 pieces. Roll into balls, cover with a towel, and let rest for 25 minutes.

SHAPING AND GLAZING
25 mins.

The secret of success in Arab bread is the thinness of the rolled-out rounds or disks. They must be no more than one-eighth-inch thick. Their thinness is more important than making them exactly round.

With a rolling pin, flatten each ball into a disk about 8 inches in diameter and one-eighth-inch thick. Place as many as will fit on baking sheet. If desired, brush with a mixture of egg white and water and sprinkle liberally with sesame seeds.

RESTING
25 mins.

Cover all with wax paper and let rest for 25 minutes. Meanwhile, arrange the oven shelves so that the loaves can be placed first on the lowest shelf and then moved 3 or 4 inches up to a higher shelf.

BAKING
500°
10 mins.

Preheat oven to 500°. Place the baking sheet on the lowest shelf for 5 minutes and then transfer to the higher shelf for an additional 5 minutes, or until the loaves are puffed and lightly browned.

Remove the breads and wrap together in foil. Set aside for 15 minutes. Place the remaining unbaked rounds on the baking sheet and repeat baking procedure.

FINAL STEP

Unwrap the loaves. The tops will have fallen and there will be a pocket in the center. Serve warm or at room temperature.

PANE ITALIANO

[TWO ROUND OR LONG LOAVES]

Pane Italiano comes in many sizes and shapes. Like the classic French loaf, Italian bread is simple—flour, salt, yeast, and water. French, on occasion, may have shortening and a little sugar, but not so Italian.

Long kneading is the key to good Italian bread. Knead 15 to 20 minutes, or 10 minutes under the dough hook. The dough must be stiff yet elastic.

This is a fine dough for small individual loaves and hard rolls.

INGREDIENTS

6 to 7 cups bread or all-purpose flour, approximately
1 package dry yeast
1 tablespoon salt
2 cups hot tap water (120°–130°)
For the glaze: 1 egg white
1 tablespoon water

BAKING SHEET AND PAN

One baking sheet, greased or Teflon. Also, a shallow pan partially filled with water and placed on the lowest rack in the oven during baking gives the loaves thick, crisp crusts.

PREPARATION
15 mins.

The formation of gluten is important to the success of this loaf, so it needs hard mixing and long kneading.

Measure 3 cups flour into a mixing bowl and stir in the yeast, salt, and hot tap water. Blend at low speed in the electric mixer for 30 seconds; increase to high for 4 minutes.

Stop the machine. Stir in the balance of the flour, a half-cup at a time, first with a spoon and then using your hands. The dough will be a rough, shaggy mass that will clean the sides of the bowl. If the dough is slack and the moisture breaks through, add small quantities of flour, a teaspoon at a time.

KNEADING
15–20 mins.

Turn the dough onto a lightly floured work surface—counter top or bread board—and knead with the rhythmic 1-2-3 motion of push-turn-fold. The dough will become smooth and elastic, and bubbles will rise under the surface of the dough. If the dough continues to be sticky, sprinkle additional flour. Break the kneading rhythm by occasionally throwing the dough down hard against the counter top. Knead this particular dough 15 to 20 minutes (10 minutes under the dough hook).

FIRST RISING
1½ hours

Place the dough in the mixing bowl and pat with buttered or greased fingertips to keep the surface from crusting. Cover the bowl tightly with plastic wrap and move to a warm place (80°–85°) until the dough has risen to about twice its original size, about 1½ hours.

SECOND RISING
1 hour

Turn back the plastic wrap, and punch down the dough with your fingers, pulling the edges into the center. Turn the dough over, and replace the plastic. Let double in volume, about 1 hour. If you are uncertain, press a fingertip an inch deep into the dough. If the dent remains, it is ready to shape.

RESTING
10 mins.

Divide the ball of dough into two pieces, cover and let rest for 10 minutes.

SHAPING
15–20 mins.

There are a number of shapes in which Italian bread can be formed.

Long Loaves: Roll each piece of dough into a rectangle, 12 by 15 inches, and about ¼ of an inch thick. Roll up tightly, beginning with the *long* side, and at each turn press the surface of the roll into the remaining flat dough. (Do this with the fingertips which are in position to do so during the rolling process.) This will prevent the loaf from unrolling when it begins to expand. Taper ends under your palms. Place loaf, seam side down, on the baking sheet.

Plump Loaves: Roll each piece of dough into an 8 x 15-inch rectangle, about ½ inch thick. Roll up tightly, beginning with the short side, and seal with the fingertips (as done above) as you roll. Taper ends under your palms until the loaf is about a foot long and plump.

Round Loaves: Shape each piece of dough into an evenly rounded loaf, and place on the baking sheet.

THIRD RISING
1 hour

Cover with wax paper and return to the warm place for 1 hour, or until the loaves have doubled in volume.

BAKING
425°
15 mins.
350°
30 mins.

Place the shallow pan of water on lowest rack and preheat the oven to 425°. *Long Loaves:* Cut diagonal slashes with a razor blade on the top and brush with egg white and water mixture. *Plump Loaves:* Cut a lengthwise slice down the center and brush with egg white and water mixture. *Round Loaves:* Make 4 shallow cuts across the top, then 4 crosswise cuts. Brush with egg white and water mixture.

Place in the hot oven for 15 minutes then reduce heat to 350° for an additional 30 minutes. Midway in the baking period—after the loaves have started to brown—brush again with the egg white and water solution. Shift the loaves during the baking period so they are exposed equally to temperature variations in the oven.

When done, the loaves will be golden brown and crusty. To test, turn one loaf over and tap the bottom with a forefinger. If it gives a hollow, hard sound, the bread is done. If not, return to the oven for an additional 10 minutes. If the loaves appear to be browning too quickly, cover with a piece of foil or brown sack paper.

FINAL STEP — Place loaves on wire rack to cool. Italian bread should be eaten within 24 hours. It has no fat in it and it simply dries out. But, it does freeze well to be reheated later, if you wish.

SWEDISH CARAWAY BREAD

[ONE SMALL LOAF]

The zest of an orange, a little brown sugar, a dollop of butter and a sprinkle of caraway seeds are boiled in water for 3 minutes to begin a Swedish caraway bread made with white flour only. Caraway seeds in a Swedish loaf usually call for one of the dark grains, but not in this fine loaf. It is excellent toasted. The inside is speckled with orange flecks and is somewhat shaded because of the brown sugar.

INGREDIENTS
- 2 tablespoons brown sugar
- ¾ cup water
- Zest (peel) of 1 orange, grated
- 1 tablespoon butter
- 1 teaspoon caraway seeds
- 1 teaspoon salt
- 1 package dry yeast
- 2 cups all-purpose flour, approximately

BAKING PAN — One small (7½ x 3½) baking pan, greased or Teflon. If glass, reduce oven heat 25°.

PREPARATION
15 mins.

Boil the brown sugar, the water, the orange zest, the butter, and caraway seeds in a small saucepan for 3 minutes. Pour into a large mixing bowl to cool to lukewarm (105°–115°). When cooled, add salt, yeast and 1 cup flour. Stir together well. Beat 2 minutes with an electric mixer at medium-high speed, or for an equal length of time with a wooden spoon.

FIRST RISING
1½ hours

More flour will be added later. For now, scrape down sides of the bowl, cover with plastic wrap, and put in a warm place (80°–85°) for 1½ hours.

KNEADING
8 mins.

Stir down the dough with a wooden spoon. Add the balance of the flour a half-cup at a time, first with the spoon and then using your hands. The dough will be a rough, shaggy mass that will clean the sides of the bowl. If the dough is sticky, sprinkle with additional flour.

Turn the dough onto a lightly floured work surface—counter top or bread board—and knead with the rhythmic 1-2-3 motion of push-turn-fold. The dough will become smooth and elastic, and bubbles will rise under the surface of the dough. Occasionally, break the kneading rhythm by throwing dough down hard against the counter top. Knead about 8 minutes altogether.

SHAPING
10 mins.

Shape the dough into a ball and let rest under a towel for 3 to 4 minutes. Form the loaf by pressing the ball into a flat oval, roughly the length of the baking pan. Fold the oval in half, pinch the seam tightly to seal, tuck under the ends, and place in the pan, seam down.

SECOND RISING
45 mins.

Cover the pan with wax paper and put in the warm place for about 45 minutes or until the dough has doubled.

BAKING
350°
1 hour

Preheat oven to 350°. Bake for 1 hour, or until the loaf is brown and crusty. Midway in the bake period turn the pan around so the loaf will be exposed to temperature variations in the oven. Turn the loaf out of its pan and tap the bottom crust with a forefinger. If it sounds hollow and hard, the bread is done. If not, return to the oven for an additional 10 minutes. If the top of the loaf appears to be browning too quickly, cover with a piece of brown sack paper or foil.

FINAL STEP

Remove from the pan and place on a metal rack to cool before slicing.

SALT-FREE WHITE BREAD

[ONE LARGE LOAF]

This is an unusual loaf, for without the control which salt has over yeast, the leavening action is dramatic. Don't let it rise above the level of the pan, however, or it may collapse just as grandly as it rose. It has a flat taste that I enjoy as do many people. Those not on a restricted diet can sprinkle on a little salt if they wish.

INGREDIENTS

1 package dry yeast
1 tablespoon sugar
3 to 3½ cups all-purpose flour, approximately
1 cup hot tap water (120°–130°)
2 tablespoons cooking oil

BAKING PAN

One large (9 x 5) baking pan, greased or Teflon. If glass, reduce oven heat 25°.

PREPARATION
15 mins.

In a large mixing bowl, stir the yeast and sugar into 1 cup flour. Pour in the hot tap water and the oil. Beat 2 minutes at medium speed with an electric mixer, or for equal time with a wooden spoon. Add a half-cup flour. Beat for 2 minutes at high speed or with the spoon.

Stop mixer and stir in the balance of the flour, a half-cup at a time, first with the spoon and then using your hands. The dough will be a rough, shaggy mass that will clean the sides of the bowl. If the dough is moist and sticky, add small sprinkles of flour.

KNEADING
10 mins.

Turn the dough onto a slightly floured work surface—counter top or bread board—and knead with the rhythmic 1-2-3 motion of push-turn-fold. The dough will become smooth and elastic, and bubbles will form under the surface of the dough. Occasionally change the kneading rhythm by raising the dough above the table and banging it down hard against the table top. Knead for about 10 minutes altogether, or 8 minutes with the dough hook.

FIRST RISING
1 hour

Drop the dough back into the mixing bowl and pat with buttered fingers to keep the surface from crusting. Cover the bowl tightly with plastic wrap and move to a warm place (80°–85°) until the dough has risen to about twice its original size (judged by how it creeps up the sides of the bowl), about 1 hour.

SHAPING
10 mins.

Punch down dough and knead for 30 seconds to press out the bubbles. Shape into a ball and let rest under a towel for 3 to 4 minutes to relax the dough. Form the loaf by pressing the ball into a flat oval roughly the length of the baking pan. Fold the oval in half, pinch the seam to seal, tuck under the ends, and place in the pan, seam down.

SECOND RISING
45 mins.

Place the pan in a warm place (80°–85°), cover with wax paper and leave until the center of the dough has risen above the edge of the pan, or has about doubled. This will take about 45 minutes.

BAKING
400°
30 mins.

Preheat the oven to 400°. Bake the loaf in the hot oven about 30 minutes, or until it has a lovely light brown crust. Midway in the bake period and again near the end of it, shift the loaf so that it is exposed equally to temperature variations in the oven. To test for doneness, turn out and tap the bottom crust with a forefinger. If it gives a hollow, hard sound, the bread is done. If not, return to the oven (without the pan) for an additional 10 minutes.

FINAL STEP

Remove from pan and cool on a metal rack.

PITA (*ISRAELI FLAT BREAD*)

[SIX SMALL ROUND LOAVES]

These small packets come out of the oven ready to receive a sandwich filling. Light brown and puffed in the center, Israeli flat breads will be crusty and hard when they are put on the rack to cool but will soon soften. Simply tear open and spread with butter and/or sandwich material.

It is a simple creation—water, flour, salt, and yeast.

INGREDIENTS

1 package dry yeast
1¼ cups warm water (105°–115°)
3 to 4 cups all-purpose or bread flour, approximately
2 teaspoons salt

BAKING SHEET

One baking sheet, greased or Teflon.

PREPARATION
10 mins.

In a mixing bowl, dissolve yeast in the warm water. Stir in 2 cups of flour and the salt. Beat with 50 vigorous strokes. Add additional flour, a half-cup at a time, first with the spoon and then using your hands, until a rough, shaggy mass is formed.

KNEADING
8 mins.

Turn onto a lightly floured work surface—counter top or bread board—and knead with a rhythmic 1-2-3 motion until the dough is soft, satiny and feels alive under the hands. Knead for 8 minutes altogether or 6 minutes with the dough hook.

SHAPING
12 mins.

Divide the dough into six pieces and form each into a round ball. Flatten with a rolling pin. Each should be about 4 to 5 inches in diameter and ¼ inch thick.

RISING
45 mins.

Cluster the loaves on the work surface and cover with a towel or wax paper. Leave them for 45 minutes, or until slightly puffed.

BAKING
500°
15–18 mins.

Preheat oven to 500°. Turn the rounds over (upside down) onto the baking sheet and place in the oven for 15 to 18 minutes, or until they are light brown and puffed in the center.

FINAL STEP

Place on wire rack to cool. The breads will be hard when they are removed from the oven but the crusts will soften and flatten as they cool. These should be served within a day or so since they soon lose their freshness. They freeze well, however.

CRACKED WHEAT BREAD

[TWO LOAVES]

The first time I made this loaf I didn't cook the cracked wheat, simply because the recipe didn't mention that important step. Uncooked it is like biting down on buckshot. So, cook the cracked wheat twenty minutes, drain and mix with the dough. (There are breads for which uncooked grain is soaked for three days as part of a sponge and becomes quite tender.)

It is an intriguing loaf with bits of the cracked wheat sticking out of the crusts. It is excellent toasted.

INGREDIENTS

½ cup uncooked cracked wheat
5 to 6 cups all-purpose flour
2 packages dry yeast
3 tablespoons sugar
4 teaspoons salt
⅓ cup non-fat dry milk
2 cups hot tap water (120°–130°)
3 tablespoons shortening, at room temperature

BAKING PANS

Two medium (8½ x 4½) baking pans, greased or Teflon. If glass, reduce oven heat 25°.

PREPARATION
30 mins.

Cook the cracked wheat in water to cover for thirty minutes. It will expand to about double. Drain and set aside.

20 mins.

In a large mixing bowl stir 2 cups flour, yeast, sugar, salt, and non-fat dry milk. In a saucepan, pour the hot tap water over the shortening, and stir.

Gradually add the liquid to the dry ingredients. With an electric mixer, beat first at low speed to blend and then at medium speed for 2 minutes. Scrape bowl occasionally. Add cracked wheat and beat at high speed for 2 minutes. Stop the mixer and beat in enough additional flour to make a soft dough that drops away from the sides of the bowl.

KNEADING
5 mins.

Turn out onto a floured work surface, counter top or bread board, and knead for 5 minutes until the dough is smooth and elastic. If the dough is damp or slack and sticks to the hands, sprinkle with a small amount of additional flour.

RESTING
15 mins.

Cover the dough on the counter top with the inverted bowl and let it rest for 15 minutes.

SHAPING
5 mins.

Divide the dough into two pieces. Shape each into a ball, flatten with the palms, fold in half, pinch the seam tightly and shape into a loaf. Drop in the prepared pan, seam down.

RISING
50 mins.

Cover with wax paper and put in a warm place (80°–85°), free from draft, until the loaves are twice the size, approximately 50 minutes.

BAKING
400°
30–40 mins.

Preheat oven to 400°. Bake for about 40 minutes. Test for doneness by inserting a wooden pick in the center of one of the loaves—if it comes out clean and dry, the loaf is done.

FINAL STEP

Remove from pans and cool on wire racks before serving or freezing.

BARM BRACK

[TWO LOAVES]

Barm Brack (literally "yeast bread") is one of the few examples of yeast being used in traditional Irish cooking. It is a light, fruit-filled loaf that is best eaten spread thickly with butter. On All Hallow's Eve, October 31, this festive tea bread is baked with a wedding ring, wrapped in paper, in the dough. This recipe follows the new no-dissolve method of using dry yeast mixed in the flour.

INGREDIENTS

4½ to 5½ cups all-purpose flour, approximately
½ cup sugar
1½ teaspoons salt
1 teaspoon grated lemon peel
3 packages dry yeast
¼ cup (½ stick) shortening (butter or margarine)
¾ cup water
½ cup milk
2 eggs, room temperature
1¼ cups golden seedless raisins
⅓ cup chopped mixed candied fruits
Glaze: 1 teaspoon sugar dissolved in 1 tablespoon water

BAKING PANS

Two medium (8½ x 4½) loaf pans, greased or Teflon. If glass, reduce oven heat 25°.

PREPARATION
15 mins.

In a large mixing bowl measure 1½ cups of flour, sugar, salt, lemon peel, and undissolved yeast. In a saucepan combine shortening, water and milk and heat over low heat until the liquid is warm. Add to dry ingredients and beat in electric beater at medium speed for two minutes, scraping the bowl occasionally. Add eggs and ¾ cup of flour, or enough to make a thick batter. Beat at high speed for two minutes.

KNEADING
6–8 mins.

Unless your mixer has a dough hook, it now becomes a hand job. Add enough flour to make a soft dough. Turn it onto a lightly floured work surface and knead until smooth and elastic, about 6 or 8 minutes. (If you use a dough hook, reduce kneading time by half.)

FIRST RISING
45 mins.

Put the dough back in the mixing bowl and pat with buttered or greased fingers to keep the surface from crusting. Cover the bowl tightly with plastic wrap and move to a warm place (80°–85°) until the dough has risen to about twice its original size (judged as it expands up the sides of the bowl). You can test if the dough has risen sufficiently by poking a finger in it; the dent will remain.

SHAPING
20 mins.

Punch dough down, and turn out again onto the lightly floured work surface. Work in the raisins and candied fruit. If this is done at an earlier stage the fruit begins to break apart and color the dough. Divide the dough into two pieces with a sharp knife. Shape the pieces into balls, and let them rest under a towel for 3 or 4 minutes. Form the loaf by pressing each ball, under the palms or with a rolling pin, into a flat oval, roughly the length of the baking pan. Fold the oval in half, pinch the seam tightly to seal, tuck under the ends, and place in the loaf pan, seam down. Repeat with the second piece.

SECOND RISING
1 hour

Cover loosely with wax paper and let rise in the warm place until it has doubled in bulk, about one hour—or until the top of the dough is a ½ inch above the edge of the loaf pan.

BAKING
375°
35–40 mins.

Preheat oven to 375°. Bake in the moderately hot oven until the loaves test done. Turn one loaf out of its pan and tap the bottom crust with a forefinger. A hard hollow sound means the bread is done. If not, return to the oven—without the pan, if you wish a deep brown overall crust—for an additional 10 minutes. However, if the loaves appear to be browning too quickly, cover with a piece of foil or brown sack paper.

Finally, brush the crusts with a thin syrup made from 1 tablespoon water and 1 teaspoon sugar. Return to the oven for 2 or 3 minutes or until shiny.

FINAL STEP

Remove bread from the oven. While the loaf is still warm, cut in thick slices and serve with ample butter. This bread will keep for several days wrapped tightly in plastic or foil. It also freezes nicely.

AN ENGLISH LOAF

[ONE LOAF]

Angered over the quality of bread from commercial bake shops in her country, a fine English home baker and food editor, Elizabeth David, developed this recipe and technique, and set down these words:

This is basic guidance to those who have already reached the conclusion that it is pretty ludicrous to spend three days planning menus to include shrimp-filled avocados, fillet of beef in puff pastry and no end of palaver over the grinding and percolation of the coffee, if they cannot offer their guests a decent piece of bread.

In those households where home-made bread and well-made bread is on offer, nobody needs worry about all that prestige-type food. What will impress your friends and arouse the maximum envy in your rivals is the sight and taste of fresh, authentic, un-cranky bread, with its slightly rough and open texture, plain unvarnished crust, and perceptibly salty bite.

Her final words:

This is the kind of bread which should be cut in good thick chunky slices straight from the loaf left on the table for all to see and enjoy.

—from the booklet
The Baking of an English Loaf, 1969.

I believe her for I have baked her loaf many times.

INGREDIENTS

1 package dry yeast
¼ cup warm water (105°–115°)
3 to 4 cups bread or all-purpose flour, approximately
2 heaping teaspoons coarse rock or sea salt
½ pint (1 cup) warm water (105°–115°)
(Yeast and flour in England differ somewhat from those same ingredients in the U.S. With her permission I have made small adjustments.)

BAKING PAN

One medium (8½ x 4½) loaf pan, greased or Teflon, metal or glass. If the latter, reduce oven temperature 25°.

PREPARATION
20 mins.

In a teacup or small bowl "proof" the yeast by dissolving it in ¼ cup warm water. If it begins to foam in about five minutes, as it should, this is "proof" that the yeast is alive and ready to work.

In a big wide bowl place 3½ cups of flour. Fashion a well in the center of the flour and pour in the yeast mixture. Stir the flour into the mixture with a large wooden spoon. In the small bowl dissolve salt in the 1 cup of lukewarm water and pour it over the flour.

Mix the dough first with the spoon and then with the fingers. The mixture should clean the sides of the bowl. If the dough is too soft or wet, sprinkle on more flour, a tablespoon at a time.

FIRST KNEADING
2 mins.

If the bowl is large enough this small amount of dough can be kneaded right in the bowl. If not, turn the dough out onto a lightly floured work surface and knead for 2 minutes. *Two* minutes only.

FIRST RISING
45 mins.

Round the dough into a ball, butter it lightly, and place in the bowl. Cover tightly with plastic wrap and put in a warm place (80°–85°) until it has doubled in bulk. You can test if it has risen sufficiently by poking a finger in it; the dent will remain.

SECOND KNEADING
5 mins.

This unusual second kneading is more important than the first and the harder you treat the dough—throw it down hard against the counter—the better it will be. This checks the action of the yeast and forces bubbles out of the dough so the process can start anew.

SHAPING
15 mins.

Flatten the dough into a rough circle with your hands—fold in half—pinch the seam tightly closed. Turn the loaf upright, seam down, and pat into shape before placing it in the greased loaf pan. Sprinkle the top with a little flour which gives it a fresh-from-the-oven look.

SECOND RISING
45 mins.

Cover the tin with wax paper and return to the warm place until the edge of the dough has risen to the edge of the tin.

BAKING
450°
15 mins.
400°
30 mins.

Preheat oven to 450°. Place the bread in the center of the oven and bake in the very hot oven for 15 minutes. Reduce heat (to hot) and leave the bread in the oven for another 30 minutes until it is a rich deep brown. If it should brown too swiftly cover the loaf with a piece of brown wrapping paper. Halfway through the baking period turn the pan so that the loaf is exposed to the various heats in the oven.

The loaf will shrink slightly in the tin when it is fully baked and will sound hollow when tapped on the bottom crust with a knuckle or forefinger. If it feels soft, it is undercooked. Return it to the oven for another 10 minutes.

FINAL STEP

Remove bread from the oven. Cool the loaf on a wire rack so that air can circulate around it. When the loaf is cool, put it in a plastic bag and store. To keep the loaf crusty, Elizabeth David wraps her loaf, when it has cooled, in a clean cloth or puts it in a bread box or bread drawer.

FEATHER BREAD

[TWO LONG LOAVES]

Feather light precisely describes feather bread. My 16-inch-long loaf, with an ample girth of 12 inches, weighs only one or two ounces more than 1 pound. I use bread flour which gives it even greater volume than the usual all-purpose flour.

It has the looks and texture of a French loaf but it is a little richer and sweeter. The bread has a golden crisp crust, brushed beforehand with nothing but slightly beaten egg white. It is best eaten fresh although it can be frozen as soon as it is cool and put away in the deep freeze for a party occasion months hence with admirable results.

INGREDIENTS

6 cups bread or all-purpose flour, approximately
2 packages dry yeast
2 cups hot tap water (120°–130°)
⅓ cup butter, room temperature
1 tablespoon *each* sugar and salt
Glaze: 1 egg white, slightly beaten

BAKING SHEET

One baking sheet, greased or Teflon.

PREPARATION
20 mins.

In a large mixing bowl measure 3 cups of flour and yeast.

In another bowl combine 2 cups water, butter, sugar, and salt. Pour this slowly into the dry ingredients and blend at low speed in the electric mixer for 30 seconds, or with a wooden spoon. Add additional 1 cup of flour and beat at high speed for 3 minutes. Stop the mixer and add flour, a ½ cup at a time, until a soft mass is formed.

KNEADING
8 mins.

Turn out the dough on a lightly floured work surface and knead until the dough is smooth and elastic (5 minutes with a dough hook). The dough will be warm and alive under your hands.

RESTING
15 mins.

Invert the bowl over the dough and let it rest.

SHAPING
15 mins.

Knead for 30 seconds to flatten the dough and press out the air bubbles. Divide into two pieces. Roll each in a 12 x 15-inch rectangle. From the short side, roll into a tight loaf—pinching the seam and ends. Place on the baking sheet.

RISING
1¼ hours

Cover the loaves with wax paper and put in a warm place (80°–85°) until light and doubled in volume.

BAKING
425°
35 mins.

Preheat oven to 425°. Brush loaves with egg white and bake until they are light and shiny brown. Turn a loaf over and tap the bottom crust with a forefinger. A hard hollow sound means the bread is baked.

FINAL STEP

Remove from the oven and place on a metal rack to cool. Because of the ⅓ cup of butter in the dough, this bread, unlike a French or Italian, will keep for several days wrapped in foil or plastic. This is a great barbecue bread.

UNBLEACHED WHITE BREAD

[ONE OR TWO SMALL LOAVES]

Unbleached flour, which has been allowed to age naturally to bleach out the yellowness of newly milled or "green" flour, and to oxidize the proteins, makes an ordinary appearing loaf that does produce a wonderful slice of toast. The creamy white interior is dense and heavily textured.

INGREDIENTS

3½ cups unbleached flour, approximately
1 package dry yeast
2 teaspoons salt
1¼ cups hot tap water (120°–130°)
Glaze: 1 egg white and 1 tablespoon water

BAKING PANS

One large (9 x 5) baking pan, greased or Teflon, or two small (7½ x 3½) pans, glass or metal. If glass, reduce oven heat 25°.

PREPARATION
10 mins.

In a mixing bowl measure 2 cups of the unbleached flour, yeast, and salt. Pour in water and blend thoroughly. Add additional flour until the dough is soft and pulls free of the bowl.

KNEADING
8 mins.

Turn out on a floured work surface and knead until the dough is no longer sticky. It is not an alive dough, however, and will not be as elastic nor as responsive as dough made with other white flours.

FIRST RISING
2–2½ hours

Place the dough back in the bowl, pat with buttered fingers and cover the bowl tightly with plastic wrap. Put in a warm place (80°–85°) to rise until doubled in volume. This is a lengthy process of more than 2 hours.

SHAPING
5 mins.

Punch down, form 1 large or 2 small loaves and place in the prepared baking pans.

SECOND RISING
1 hour

Cover with wax paper and return to the warm place until the dough has doubled in bulk—about 1 hour.

BAKING
400°
40–45 mins.

Preheat the oven to 400°. Brush with egg white blended with water. Bake in the oven until loaves are loose in their pans. A hard hollow sound when tapped on the bottom crust means the bread is baked. For a crustier loaf, remove from pan or pans the last 10 minutes and place on the oven rack.

FINAL STEP

Remove from the oven and place on a metal rack to cool before serving.

SUNSET WHITE BREAD

[TWO LOAVES]

While there seems to be a limitless supply of recipes for "the perfect loaf" of white bread, now and then a particular recipe does produce better than ordinary results. One such is this loaf from the kitchens of *Sunset* magazine, the chief arbiter of life-styles for people in the Pacific Coast states.

Sunset calls it its basic loaf, with almost two dozen variations ranging from Herb to Oatmeal. Tomato Caraway, for example, can be made by simply adding two cups of warm tomato juice (in place of milk) and 1 tablespoon of caraway seed to the basic loaf.

Milk and butter help keep the loaf moist for days if wrapped in foil or plastic. It is delicious toasted, and freezes well.

INGREDIENTS

1 package dry yeast
¼ cup warm water (105°–115°)
2 cups warm milk (105°–115°)
3 tablespoons butter or margarine (melted) or vegetable oil
1 tablespoon salt
2 tablespoons sugar
6 cups all-purpose or bread flour, approximately

BAKING PANS

Two medium (8½ x 4½) loaf pans, greased or Teflon. If glass, reduce oven heat 25°.

PREPARATION
20 mins.

In a large mixing bowl dissolve yeast in water. Let stand for 5 minutes.

Stir in warm milk and add melted butter, salt and sugar—blend well.

Stir in 3 cups of flour, 1 cup at a time. Beat 50 strokes. Add 4th cup and beat until smooth. Put aside the spoon and work in the 5th cup with the fingers. The dough should be a rough mass, cleaning the sides of the bowl.

KNEADING
10 mins.

Turn out the dough on a liberally floured work surface —counter top or bread board. If the dough is slack or wet, add more flour and keep a coating of flour on the ball as you work it. With a strong push-pull-fold action, knead for about 10 minutes. Keep flour on the hands. You will soon notice bumps and bubbles under the skin of the dough. This is as it should be. The kneading is finished when the dough is soft and satiny —and no longer sticky.

FIRST RISING
1½ hours

Place the ball of dough in the bowl, butter it lightly and cover tightly with plastic wrap. Put it in a warm place (80°–85°) to rise for about 1½ hours—or until doubled in size. You can test if it has risen sufficiently by poking a finger in it; the dent will remain.

SHAPING
8 mins.

Punch down dough and work out the bubbles by kneading for 1 or 2 minutes. Divide the dough with a sharp knife or pull it apart. Form each loaf by pressing the dough into a rough oval the length of the pan, folding and pinching the seam tightly closed.

SECOND RISING
45 mins.

Place shaped loaves in pans—seams down. Cover with wax paper or foil and return to the warm place until doubled in bulk.

BAKING
375°
45 mins.

Preheat oven to 375°. Slide the pans into the moderately hot oven until the loaves are browned. They will pull away from the pan sides, and a wooden toothpick inserted in the center of a loaf will come out dry and clean. Also, when thumping on the bottom crust yields a hard and hollow sound, they are done. If the bottom crust is soft return to the oven for an additional 10 minutes, and test again.

FINAL STEP

Remove bread from the oven, turn from the pans, and place on wire cooling racks. You may wish to brush the hot loaves with melted butter (or the paper wrapping off a stick of butter) to get a soft crust.

SOUTHERN LOAF BREAD

[TWO MEDIUM LOAVES]

This is an exceptionally good loaf of white bread, lightly speckled with wheat germ. It is allowed to rise twice before it is shaped, and once following—a total of three times before it goes into a moderately hot oven. It is close kin to the loaf bread in the famous Southern cookbook written by the Charleston Junior League. The small difference is that the League's recipe calls for whole milk; this one, non-fat dry milk.

INGREDIENTS

1 package dry yeast
6 cups all-purpose or bread flour, approximately
⅓ cup non-fat dry milk
2 tablespoons sugar
2 teaspoons salt
4 tablespoons wheat germ
2½ cups hot tap water (120°–130°)
1 tablespoon butter or margarine, room temperature

BAKING PANS

Two medium loaf pans (8½ x 4½), greased or Teflon, glass or metal. If glass, lower temperature in oven 25°.

PREPARATION
15 mins.

In a large mixing bowl stir yeast, 3 cups flour, milk, sugar, salt, and wheat germ. Pour in the tap water and add butter or margarine. Beat at medium speed for about 4 minutes, or 150 strong strokes with a wooden spoon. The gluten will begin to form and the dough will be stringy from the sides of the bowl.

Add 3 additional cups of flour (perhaps a little

more if all-purpose flour), working it in with the spoon and fingers until the mass has absorbed the flour, and is soft but no longer sticky.

KNEADING
9 mins.

Knead the dough until it is smooth and satiny.

FIRST RISING
1 hour

Place in a lightly greased bowl—and turn to coat the ball of dough on all sides—and cover tightly with plastic wrap. Put in a warm place (80°–85°) until it has doubled in bulk.

SECOND RISING
45 mins.

With the fist and fingers, punch the dough down and turn the ball over. Let it stand for a second time.

SHAPING AND RESTING
10 mins.

Turn out on the bread board or counter top and cut the ball of dough into two equal pieces. Shape each piece into a ball, and rest briefly on floured surface.

Press each into a flat oval, the length of the baking pan. Fold the oval in half, pinch the seam tightly to seal, tuck under the ends, and place in the pans, seam down. Repeat with the second piece.

THIRD RISING
45 mins.

Cover lightly with wax paper and return to the warm place until doubled in bulk.

BAKING
400°
45 mins.

Preheat oven to 400° about 15 minutes before baking. Place the tins in the oven until the crusts are deep brown. A wooden toothpick or metal skewer inserted in the center will come out dry and clean. Tap the bottom of one loaf with a forefinger. A hard hollow sound means the bread is baked.

FINAL STEP

Remove bread from the oven and turn out immediately onto a metal rack to cool. For a soft crust, brush the tops with melted butter and lay a cloth over them while they cool.

SISTER VIRGINIA'S DAILY LOAF

[FOUR LOAVES]

The Shakers, a peaceful and industrious people who founded one of their religious colonies in central Kentucky in 1805, today are remembered chiefly for the simple, fine lines of their furniture. Unexcelled cooks and bakers, they could and did set a tidy and tasty table. The "daily loaf" of fine white bread was ever present.

The creator of this loaf, Sister Virginia was one of the Kentucky community's 500 members, all of whom were gone by the mid-1920's. Sister Virginia earned for herself a certain immortality for the recipe for four 1-pound "daily loaves."

The 12 cups of flour make a big ball of dough that is a large handful to work and knead. You may wish to halve the recipe for everything except the package of yeast. It is best made with lard.

INGREDIENTS

1 package dry yeast
¼ cup warm water (105°–115°)
2 cups milk, scalded
¼ cup sugar
4 teaspoons salt
8 tablespoons lard or vegetable shortening
2 cups water
12 cups all-purpose or bread flour, approximately
1 tablespoon melted butter

BAKING PANS

Four medium (8½ x 4½) loaf pans, greased, metal or glass. If glass, reduce baking temperature 25°. Teflon pans are excellent, too, and will give a rich brown crust to the sides and bottom.

PREPARATION
20 mins.

In a small bowl or cup dissolve yeast in warm water. Whip it briefly with a spoon or whisk to hasten the action. Set aside for 5 minutes.

Scald milk in a large saucepan, and add sugar, salt and lard. When the shortening has melted add water and allow the mixture to cool to lukewarm. Pour in the yeast mixture and stir well with a large wooden spoon. Mix in 3 cups of flour and beat 100 strong strokes until the batter is smooth. Continue adding flour, working the dough, first with the spoon and then with the fingers, until it cleans the sides and bottom of the bowl. The dough will form a rough ball.

KNEADING
8 mins.

Turn the dough onto a well floured work surface, counter top or bread board, and begin the kneading process—push and turn, push and turn. If the moist dough breaks through the skin of the ball, sprinkle liberally with flour and continue kneading. Keep flour on the board and on the fingers in the early phase of kneading. The dough will gradually become smooth and elastic.

FIRST RISING
1 hour

Return the dough to the bowl and cover tightly with plastic wrap which will prevent air from forming a crust on the surface of the dough. Place it in a warm spot (80°–85°), with constant heat, no drafts, and leave until it has almost doubled in bulk. You can test if it has risen by poking a finger in it; the dent will remain.

SHAPING
25 mins.

Turn out the dough, knead briefly to push out the bubbles and divide it into four equal pieces. Round each into a ball and put aside on the work surface, cover with the piece of plastic wrap and let them rest for about 15 minutes.

With the hands and a rolling pin, flatten out the first piece into a rough rectangle, and fold lengthwise. Stretch the dough and fold into thirds, the ends overlapping. Flatten out and roll up like a jelly roll. It should be about the length of the pan. Place it in the pan, seam down. Repeat with each piece. Brush with melted butter.

SECOND RISING
45 mins.

Cover the pans with wax paper and return them to the warm place until the dough has doubled in bulk—the center slightly above the edge of the pan.

BAKING
350°
35 mins.

Preheat oven to 350°. Bake the loaves until the crusts are golden brown and the loaves are loose in their pans. Thump the bottom crust with the forefinger. A hard hollow sound means the bread is baked.

FINAL STEP

Remove bread from the oven. Turn out the loaves onto a metal cooling rack. This bread makes excellent toast and will keep nicely wrapped in plastic for 8 or 10 days. It also freezes very well.

RICH WHITE BREAD

[TWO PLUMP LOAVES]

This loaf is deserving of its name. Ingredients include milk, lard or butter, sugar and two eggs. The loaf is big and plump. The slice is white and nicely textured. Toasts beautifully. Great sandwich bread, as well.

INGREDIENTS

1½ cups hot tap water (120°–130°)
½ cup non-fat dry milk
2 tablespoons sugar

2 teaspoons salt
2 packages dry yeast
5½ to 6 cups bread or all-purpose flour, approximately
2 tablespoons lard or butter, room temperature
2 eggs, room temperature

BAKING PANS
Two large (9 x 5) loaf pans, greased or Teflon. If glass, reduce oven heat 25°.

PREPARATION
15 mins.

Pour water in a mixer bowl and stir in milk, sugar, salt, yeast, and 3 cups of all-purpose flour. Add the lard and eggs. Beat with a spoon until the batter is smooth and sheets off the spoon, or at medium speed of the electric mixer for 2 minutes. Scrape the bowl occasionally.

Stir in the balance of the all-purpose flour, a half cup at a time, first with the spoon and then by hand. The dough will be a rough, shaggy mass that will clean the sides of the bowl. Scrape down the sides of the bowl with fingertips or the edge of a large metal spoon or spatula.

KNEADING
8 mins.

Turn the dough onto a lightly floured work surface—counter top or bread board—and knead with the rhythmic 1-2-3 motion of push-turn-fold. The dough will become smooth and elastic, and bubbles will form under the surface of the dough. Sprinkle more flour on the ball of dough if it continues slack or moist and sticks to the hands or work surface. Break the kneading rhythm occasionally by throwing the dough down hard against the counter top.

FIRST RISING
1½ hours

Place the dough back in the bowl and pat with greased or buttered fingertips to keep the surface from crusting. Cover the bowl tightly with plastic wrap and move to a warm place (80°–85°) until the dough has risen to about twice its original size as judged by how it creeps up the sides of the bowl.

SECOND RISING
30 mins.

Turn back plastic wrap and punch down the dough. Fold toward the center and turn over. Re-cover and let rise until almost doubled.

SHAPING
10 mins.

Punch down and knead for 30 seconds to press out the bubbles. Divide the dough into two pieces with a sharp knife. Shape into balls, and let rest under a towel for 3 to 4 minutes. Form the loaf by pressing each ball into a flat oval, roughly the length of the baking pan. Fold the oval in half, pinch the seam tightly to seal, tuck under the ends, and place in the pan, seam down. Repeat for the second loaf.

THIRD RISING
50 mins.

Cover the loaves with wax paper and leave in the warm place until the center of the dough has risen to an inch above the edge of the pan, about 50 minutes.

BAKING
400°
30–40 mins.

Preheat oven to 400°. Bake the loaves until they are a golden brown and test done. Turn one loaf out of its pan and tap the bottom crust with a forefinger. A hard hollow sound means the bread is done. If not, return to the oven for an additional 10 minutes. If the loaves appear to be browning too quickly, cover with foil or a piece of brown paper sack. Midway in the bake period, and again near the end of it, shift the pans so the loaves are exposed equally to the temperature variations of the oven.

FINAL STEP

Remove bread from the oven. Turn from pans and cool on metal racks before serving. For a soft crust brush with melted butter and cover with a towel.

TURNIPSEED SISTERS WHITE LOAF

[TWO LOAVES]

Two elderly spinster sisters, Ola and Minnie Turnipseed, legends as cooks in northern Indiana (RFD, Monticello), have been cooking and serving dinners for guests in their kerosene-lit farm home for more than thirty years. This is an adaptation of the big loaf of white bread they bake in a wood and corn-cob burning range stove in which they do upwards of 800 loaves each year.

The Turnipseed loaf is leavened with a fresh starter made with hops. The hops "start" used by the sisters has been alive and working since 1940.

INGREDIENTS

Sponge:
- 1 cup hops starter (see page 285)
- 2 cups warm water (105°–115°)
- 3 cups bread or all-purpose flour
- 2 teaspoons sugar

Dough:
- All of the sponge
- ½ cup lard or other shortening, room temperature

1 tablespoon salt
3½ to 4 cups bread or all-purpose flour, approximately
1 teaspoon butter, melted to brush crusts

BAKING PANS

Two medium (8½ x 4½) baking pans, greased or Teflon. If glass, reduce oven heat 25°.

PREPARATION
The Sponge
8 hours

In a large bowl stir together the hops starter, water, flour and sugar.

Cover with plastic wrap and put in a warm place (80°–85°) for 8 hours or overnight until the sponge has bubbled and is light and frothy. It will about double in volume during this time.

The Dough
15 mins.

Remove the plastic wrap, stir down the sponge, add lard or other shortening, salt and 2 cups of the bread or all-purpose flour. Stir vigorously for 3 minutes or in an electric mixer at medium-high speed for the same length of time. Stop the mixer. Stir in the balance of the flour, a half cup at a time, first with the spoon and then by hand. The dough will be a rough, shaggy mass that will clean the sides of the bowl. If the dough continues moist and is sticky, add a few sprinkles of flour.

KNEADING
8 mins.

Turn the dough onto a lightly floured work surface—counter top or bread board—and knead with the rhythmic 1-2-3 motion of push-turn-fold. The dough will become smooth and elastic, and bubbles will rise under the surface of the dough. If the dough should continue moist and sticky, sprinkle on additional flour. Break the kneading rhythm by occasionally throwing the dough hard against the counter top. Knead for 8 minutes (6 minutes under dough hook).

FIRST RISING
2 hours

Place the dough back in the bowl and pat with buttered or greased fingertips to keep the surface from crusting. Cover the bowl tightly with plastic wrap and move to a warm place (80°–85°) until the dough has risen to about twice its original size. This is a somewhat longer process than with yeast-raised dough so allow 2 hours.

SHAPING
10 mins.

Punch down the dough and knead for 30 seconds to press out the bubbles. Divide the dough into two pieces with a sharp knife. Shape into balls. Let them rest under a towel for 3 to 4 minutes. Form a loaf by pressing the ball of dough into a flat oval, roughly the length of the baking pan. Fold the oval in half, pinch the seam tightly to seal, tuck under the ends, and place in the pan, seam down. Repeat for the second loaf.

SECOND RISING
1 hour

Place the pans in the warm place, cover with wax paper and leave until the center of the dough has risen 1 inch above the level of the edge of the pan, or about 1 hour.

BAKING
425°
15 mins.
350°
30 mins.

Preheat oven to 425°. Bake the loaves in the hot oven for 15 minutes, reduce heat to 350° and continue baking for an additional 30 minutes, or until the loaves are a light gold. Turn one loaf out of its pan to test for doneness. Tap the bottom crust with a forefinger. A hard hollow sound means the bread is done. If not, return to the oven for an additional 10 minutes. If the loaves seem slow to brown (because of the chemical makeup of hop-raised dough), brush the loaves with milk halfway through the bake period. At the same time, shift the pans in the oven so the loaves are exposed equally to temperature variations in the oven.

FINAL STEP

Remove bread from the oven. Turn from pans and place on a metal rack to cool. Brush crusts with melted butter.

PORTUGUESE SWEET BREAD

[TWO BRAIDED OR ROUND LOAVES]

A delicious example of Iberian baking, Portuguese Sweet Bread is a rich yeast loaf, with a close, fine texture. The dough can be fashioned in several ways. One is to simply press out a flattened round loaf to bake in a pie plate. Another is to braid the dough, brush with beaten egg and sprinkle with coarsely granulated decorating sugar. Or, work half the dough into a long rope, about 30 inches in length and about 1½ inches in diameter, and coil it inside a pie pan. Brush it with egg, and sprinkle with a dozen or so raisins. My own preference is the coil.

INGREDIENTS

2 packages dry yeast
¼ cup warm water (105°–115°)
1 cup sugar
5 to 6 cups all-purpose flour, approximately
1 teaspoon salt
1 cup milk, room temperature

3 eggs, room temperature
¼ pound (1 stick) butter, small bits
¼ cup dried currants (for braid)
Optional for glaze: 1 egg, beaten
¼ cup raisins
1 tablespoon coarse granulated sugar

BAKING SHEET OR PAN

Baking sheet (for braid), greased or Teflon, or 9-inch pie pan (for round loaf or coil). If glass pie pan, reduce oven heat 25°.

PREPARATION
20 mins.

In a small bowl or cup dissolve the yeast in warm water.

In a large mixing bowl combine sugar, 4 cups of flour and salt. Make a well in the center of the flour, pour in the yeast and milk. Break eggs into the mixture, and gently stir with a large wooden spoon until all ingredients are combined. Beat in butter, then add more flour, ¼ cup at a time, until the dough can be gathered into a rough, soft ball. When the dough becomes difficult to stir, work in the flour with your fingers.

KNEADING
10 mins.

Turn out the dough onto a floured work surface—counter top or bread board—and knead it with the heel of the hand until it is smooth and elastic.

FIRST RISING
1 hour

Return the dough to the bowl, pat it with greased fingers, cover the bowl with plastic wrap and put it in a warm place (80°–85°) until dough has doubled in bulk. You can test if it has risen by poking a finger in it; the dent will remain.

SHAPING
20 mins.

Punch down the dough, divide into half, and put aside to rest for 10 minutes. Each piece can be shaped in one of the following ways—

—Pat the dough into a flattened round, about 8 inches across, and place in a greased 9-inch pie pan.

—The Portuguese call the coiled loaf *caracois*. Roll the piece into a long 30-inch rope and coil it in the 9-inch pie pan.

—The braid is called *tranca a tricana*. First, work ¼ cup of dried currants into the dough. Cover it with a towel or piece of wax paper and let it rest for 30 minutes. Divide the dough into 3 equal parts, roll each into a 14-inch-long rope. Lay them side by side and weave them into a thick braid.

Pinch the ends together and turn under slightly. Place on baking sheet.

SECOND RISING
40 mins.

Cover the different loaves with wax paper and move them to the warm place until they have doubled in volume.

BAKING
350°
1 hour

Preheat the oven to 350°. Prepare the tops of the loaves before baking. Brush the flat loaf with beaten egg. Brush the coil with the beaten egg and dot it with a dozen or so raisins. Brush the braid with the egg—and sprinkle with sugar or coarsely granulated decorating sugar.

These loaves will be done when a wooden toothpick or skewer inserted in the loaf comes out clean and dry.

FINAL STEP

Remove bread from the oven. Handle the hot loaves with special care when removing them from the baking sheet or pie pan to the wire rack to cool. A spatula will help in lifting the coil and braid.

POPPY SEED BUBBLE LOAF

[ONE LARGE TUBE LOAF]

This handsome and spectacular loaf is made with yeast dough from which small 1-inch balls are pinched, dipped into melted butter and poppy seeds. They rise in a tube pan to triple their original depth and resemble a tall, seed-studded crown. Serve warm to guests and let them pick their own irregularly-shaped piece, each with its own crown of poppy seeds. It can also be sliced.

INGREDIENTS

1 package dry yeast
¼ cup warm water (105°–115°)
2 cups hot tap water (120°–130°)
⅔ cup non-fat dry milk
2 tablespoons shortening
2 teaspoons salt
2 tablespoons sugar
6 to 6½ cups all-purpose or bread flour, approximately
Dip: 4 tablespoons melted butter and ¼ cup poppy seeds

BAKING PAN

Lightly greased 10-inch tube pan. Mine is Teflon and does beautifully.

PREPARATION
20 mins.

In a small bowl or cup dissolve yeast in warm water. Stir with a fork or whisk to hasten the action.

In a large mixing bowl pour in tap water and add milk, shortening, salt, sugar, and 3 cups of flour. Stir briskly with a wooden spoon about 150 strokes or 2 minutes with the electric mixer. Pour in the yeast and blend it into the dough. Add 3 cups of flour, a cup at a time, and work it into the moist dough with a heavy wooden spoon. When the dough is soft and has lost most of its stickiness, turn it out onto a lightly floured counter top or bread board.

KNEADING
8 mins.

Dust the dough with a sprinkle of flour and begin to knead with a push-turn-fold, push-turn-fold movement. If the moisture breaks through the skin and the dough begins to stick, sprinkle on ¼ cup of flour. Soon it will become elastic and loose its stickiness. Knead for a total of 8 minutes by hand (5 minutes with a dough hook).

FIRST RISING
1 hour

Put the dough in a greased bowl, cover tightly with plastic wrap and put in a warm place (80°–85°), free of drafts, until the dough has doubled in bulk. You can test if the dough is ready to shape by poking a finger in it; the dent will remain.

SHAPING
20 mins.

Melt 4 tablespoons of butter in a small saucepan, and pour poppy seeds in a shallow saucer.

Punch down the dough and force out the bubbles with the palms of your hands. Pinch off pieces of dough that will make tiny balls about 1 inch in diameter. The size need not be exact since they will all rise in different shapes, but some uniformity is important. Pinch off a dozen or so—dip them, one at a time, first in the butter and then in the poppy seeds. Place them on the bottom of the pan, seed side up. Continue on, one batch after another, placing them close together. When the bottom is filled, begin a second row by stacking on top of the first. The balls usually fill two rows comfortably.

SECOND RISING
45 mins.

Cover the pan with wax paper and return it to the warm place until the balls have risen two-thirds the way up the sides of the pan.

BAKING
375°
1 hour

Preheat oven to 375°. Bake until the loaf tests done. A slender metal skewer inserted in the loaf will come out dry and clean. Also, after it has been turned out of the pan, tap it on the bottom with a forefinger. A hard hollow sound means the bread is baked.

FINAL STEP

Remove bread from the oven. This handsome loaf can come apart if handled roughly while still hot. Be careful. Place it on the metal cooling rack and then set it on a plate or dish before it is moved to the table. Let your guests have the fun of pulling out their own piece of warm bread. After it has cooled, the loaf can be sliced and served—and also toasted.

WEISSBROT MIT KÜMMEL
(German White Bread with Caraway Seeds)

[ONE LARGE ROUND LOAF]

This fine white bread, with a hint of caraway, is made with wheat flour and is called *Weissbrot mit Kümmel.* More than 500 years ago, a portrait painter put a Nuremberg baker on canvas, surrounded by big round loaves of white bread and smaller loaves of dark ones. This loaf is a descendant of the white.

Brushed or sprayed with water several times during the bake period, this bread will produce a deep golden crust with a satisfying crackle.

INGREDIENTS

3 packages dry yeast
¼ cup warm water (105°–115°)
4 cups of all-purpose or bread flour, approximately
2 teaspoons sugar
½ cup warm milk (105°–115°)
2 eggs, room temperaturc
¼ pound (1 stick) butter, room temperature
1 tablespoon salt
1 tablespoon caraway seeds

BAKING SHEET

One baking sheet, greased or Teflon.

PREPARATION
20 mins.

In a small bowl or cup sprinkle yeast over lukewarm water and stir briskly with a fork or whisk to dissolve. Set aside for 5 minutes or until yeast begins to foam and bubble.

In a large mixing bowl combine flour and sugar, and form a well in the center. Pour in the yeast mixture and the lukewarm milk (without refrigerator chill). With a large wooden spoon pull the flour into the liquid to form a thin batter. Beat in eggs, one at a time, and the butter. Continue to pull in the flour until it makes a rough mass that can be worked with the hands. Form into a rough ball and rest it on the bottom of the bowl.

WATER RISING
15 mins.

Fill the bowl with cold water (65°–70°) to cover the dough by 2 inches. The dough will rise above the water.

Remove the dough from the water and pat dry with paper toweling. Place on a floured work surface, punch down and knead out the air bubbles. Work in the salt and caraway seeds. Keep the dough sprinkled with flour to control the stickiness.

KNEADING
10 mins.

Knead the dough until it is smooth and elastic.

SHAPING
5 mins.

Pat the dough into a round loaf, slightly mounded in the center, about 8 inches in diameter. Place on a baking sheet.

SECOND RISING
35 mins.

Cover the dough with a tent of foil, shaped so that it does not touch the ball. It will double in bulk and be ready for the oven.

BAKING
375°
1 hour

Preheat the oven to 375°. Place the loaf on the middle shelf of the oven. Brush or spray with water twice during the bake period. The crust will be golden brown but if it appears to be browning too quickly, cover with a piece of foil or brown sack paper the last 10 or 15 minutes. Turn over the loaf and tap the bottom crust with a forefinger. A hard hollow sound means the bread is baked. If not, return to the oven for an additional 10 minutes. Midway in the baking period turn the loaf on the baking sheet so that it is exposed equally to the vagaries of the oven.

FINAL STEP

Remove bread from the oven. Turn out on a metal rack and allow to cool before slicing.

ARMENIAN PEDA BREAD

[TWO LARGE OR A DOZEN SMALL LOAVES]

The olive oil in this recipe sets this loaf apart from most other flat Armenian-type breads. The ball of dough for each loaf must be pressed down to a thickness of 1 inch or it will rise into an un-peda hump. This peda has a thick, crisp crust that is marvelous with barbecue meats, steaks, hamburgers, and, especially, lamb.

A small peda or roll can be made by dividing the dough into a dozen pieces and flattening each into a peda about 6 inches across.

INGREDIENTS
2 packages dry yeast
1 teaspoon sugar
2 cups warm water (105°–115°)
5 to 6 cups all-purpose or bread flour, approximately
2 teaspoons salt
2 tablespoons sugar
2 tablespoons olive oil (or salad oil)
Glaze: 1 beaten egg, sprinkle of sesame seeds

BAKING SHEET OR PANS
One baking sheet, greased or Teflon, or two 8-inch cake layer pans.

PREPARATION
15 mins.
In a small bowl sprinkle yeast and sugar over the surface of water. Stir with a fork or whisk until dissolved. Let stand for 3 to 5 minutes or until it begins to bubble and foam. Add 3 cups of flour to the liquid and measure in the salt and sugar. Beat until smooth—about 75 strong strokes with a wooden spoon. Stir in the olive oil. Gradually work in flour until a soft mass has formed and it can be worked with the fingers without sticking.

KNEADING
8 mins.
Turn dough onto a lightly floured work surface—counter top or bread board. Keep a sprinkling of flour on the dough, fingers and counter top. If the moisture begins to work through the skin of the dough and it clings to the fingers, add a little flour. Within 3 or 4 minutes the dough will begin to feel elastic and push back against the hands. Knead for about 8 minutes (6 minutes under the dough hook).

FIRST RISING
1 hour

Drop the ball of dough back into the mixing bowl, pat it with greased or buttered fingers and cover the bowl with plastic wrap. Put it in a warm place (80°–85°) until it has expanded to about double its size.

SHAPING
20 mins.

Punch down the dough, knead briefly to force out the bubbles, and let the dough rest for 5 minutes. Divide the ball in half for two large loaves, or into a dozen pieces for the small individual loaves. Round each into a ball and place on the baking sheet. The large pieces can also be baked in the round layer pans. Flatten under the palms to a thickness of 1 inch.

With a sharp razor, cut tops to form a diamond pattern. Brush with the beaten egg (or milk). Sprinkle liberally with sesame seeds.

SECOND RISING
30 mins.

Cover lightly with wax paper and let rise in the warm place until they have almost doubled in volume.

BAKING
425°
20–30 mins.

Preheat oven to 425°. Bake in a hot oven until brown and crusty. The small loaves will be done in about 20 minutes while the larger loaves will take about 30 minutes. When tapping the bottom crust yields a hard and hollow sound, the loaves are done.

FINAL STEP

Remove from the oven and place on a metal rack to cool. These may be frozen.

OLD ORDER AMISH BREAD

[THREE LOAVES]

Among the Old Order Amish families on farms in northern Indiana this is a prized loaf. The women bake it only with a premium bread flour milled from hard spring wheat, which is seldom found in stores since it is sold primarily in bulk to commercial bakers. This is the recipe of a farm wife who bakes six loaves a week for her family and buys the flour in 100 pound bags from a trucker who has a route among farm families, delivering from door to door.

This loaf can be made with all-purpose flour, of course, but to bake it as these farm women do, use bread flour made with spring or winter wheat.

INGREDIENTS

1 package dry yeast
¼ cup lukewarm water (105°–115°)
2 cups hot tap water (120°–130°)
½ cup sugar
2 teaspoons salt
½ cup vegetable oil
7 to 8 cups *bread* flour, approximately

BAKING PANS

Three medium (8½ x 4½) baking tins, greased or Teflon—or any desired combination of pans, according to dough volume chart page 23. If glass, reduce oven heat 25°.

PREPARATION
20 mins.

In a small bowl or cup dissolve yeast in lukewarm water, stirring briskly with a whisk or fork to hasten the action. Set aside for a moment.

In a large mixing bowl measure hot tap water, sugar, salt, vegetable oil and 2 cups flour. Stir with a wooden spoon or beat with an electric mixer until it is well blended, and add the yeast. Add 2 more cups of flour and beat 125 strokes or 2 minutes at medium speed with the electric machine. Gradually add more flour, working it together first with the spoon and then with the hands, until a rough mass has formed and the dough has cleaned the sides of the bowl. The dough will be elastic but not sticky. If moisture does break through the surface, dust with flour.

KNEADING
8 mins.

Turn the dough out on a generously floured work surface—counter top or bread board—and knead with a strong push-turn motion (6 minutes with a dough hook but be careful with this much dough that it doesn't climb over the protective collar into the lock mechanism). If the dough seems slack and doesn't hold its shape, add ½ cup additional flour and work it into the mass.

FIRST RISING
1 hour

Return the ball of dough to the large bowl (which has been washed and greased) and cover tightly with a length of plastic wrap. Put the bowl in a warm (80°–85°), draft-free place until dough has doubled in bulk.

SECOND RISING
50 mins.

Turn back the plastic wrap and punch down the dough. Replace the wrap and leave dough until it has risen again.

SHAPING
10 mins.

Turn out dough on the work surface, punch down and knead for about 1 minute to work out the air bubbles. Divide into three pieces and form into loaves. Place in the pans.

THIRD RISING
45 mins.

Cover the loaves with wax paper and return to the warm place until the dough has risen about 1 inch above the edge of the pans.

BAKING
400°
10 mins.
350°
30 mins.

Preheat oven to 400°. Put the loaves in a hot oven for 10 minutes, reduce heat and bake for an additional 30 minutes until the loaves are a golden brown. They will be done when a toothpick inserted in the center of the loaf comes out dry and clean. Also, when tapping the bottom crust yields a hard hollow sound, the loaves are done.

FINAL STEP

Remove bread from oven, turn out from pans immediately, and leave on metal rack to cool. This bread makes delicious toast and keeps well in the freezer for 6 or 8 months.

STARTER WHITE BREAD

[TWO LARGE LOAVES]

The life and movement in dough is a constant wonder. This loaf, leavened only with a starter, begins as a heavy blob of dough about the size of an orange on the bottom of the bowl. Warm water is poured over it, and eight hours later the sponge is foamy and light on the surface of the water.

INGREDIENTS

Sponge: 1 cup starter (see page 285)
1½ cups all-purpose flour, approximately
¼ cup sugar
½ teaspoon ginger
2 cups water

Dough: All of the sponge
1 cup non-fat dry milk
6 cups all-purpose flour, approximately
½ teaspoon *each* baking soda and cream of tartar
1 tablespoon salt
½ cup lard, room temperature, or other shortening

BAKING PANS

Two large (9 x 5) loaf pans, greased or Teflon. If glass, reduce oven heat 25°.

PREPARATION
Overnight

The night before, stir the starter and about 1½ cups of flour together in a bowl—to form a soft ball. Use a wooden spoon rather than fingers because it will be moist and sticky. Let stand for about 2 hours uncovered.

Meanwhile, in a small bowl or measuring cup, combine sugar, ginger and water.

Pour the liquid over the dough, cover the bowl tightly with plastic wrap and set in a warm place (80°–85°).

20 mins.

Next day, turn back the plastic cover and thoroughly blend the floating sponge into the water. Add milk, 1 cup of flour, baking soda, cream of tartar, and salt. Beat 50 strokes. (Lard makes a softer, richer texture and that's why I use it here.) Add the lard or other shortening and 2 cups flour and beat into a smooth batter. Work in the balance of the flour—about 2 cups or so—first with the spoon and then by hand. The dough will be a rough, shaggy mass that will clean the bowl. If the dough is slack, however, and moisture breaks through, add small amounts of additional flour as you work the dough.

KNEADING
8 mins.

Turn dough onto a lightly floured work surface—counter top or bread board—and knead with the rhythmic 1-2-3 motion of push-turn-fold. The dough will become smooth and elastic, and bubbles will rise under the surface of the dough. Sprinkle more flour on the dough if it sticks to the hands or the work surface. Break the kneading rhythm occasionally by throwing the dough down hard against the counter top. Knead for about 8 minutes (or 5 with a dough hook).

RESTING
20 mins.

Let the dough rest on the counter top, covered with a towel or length of wax paper, for 20 minutes.

SHAPING
15 mins.

Try a twin roll. Divide each loaf portion into halves, and make each into a roll the length of the pan. Place each side by side in the pan and brush generously with shortening so the division will remain during baking.

Brush tops with lard or butter.

RISING
2 hours

Place the pans in the warm place, cover with wax paper and leave until the dough has risen to double its original size. Starter is not a fast leavening agent (as compared to yeast) so it will take much longer to rise.

BAKING
375°
1 hour

Preheat oven to 375°. Bake the loaves in the oven. When the loaves are a golden brown and tapping the bottom crust yields a hard hollow sound, they are done. If not, return to the oven—without the pan, if you wish a deep brown overall crust—for an additional 10 minutes. Midway in the bake period and again near the end of it, shift the pans so the loaves are exposed equally to temperature variations in the oven.

FINAL STEP

Remove bread from the oven and turn the loaves onto a metal rack to cool before serving or freezing. This loaf will keep several months in the deep freeze. Excellent toasted, too.

METHODIST WHITE BREAD

[TWO LARGE LOAVES]

A two-day-old fermented potato starter—improbably called Witch Yeast by the Ladies of the Trinity M. E. Church of Delphi, Indiana—is the leavening in this creamy white and fully textured loaf from a 1907 church cookbook. Dry yeast can be substituted for the Witch Yeast with good results. The taste and aroma of this bread will carry one back to Hoosier wood-fired bake stoves of a century ago. Lovely toasted.

Witch Yeast (see page 282), according to the old cookbook, is made like this: "One quart mashed potatoes, 1 cup sugar, 2 tablespoonsful salt, 1 quart warm water. Let stand two days until it ferments, then use as other yeast—Mrs. Levi Rothenberger."

INGREDIENTS

5 medium potatoes to make 2 cups, mashed
1½ tablespoons salt
¼ cup sugar
2 cups water (from the boiled potatoes)
7 cups all-purpose or bread flour, approximately
1 cup Witch Yeast or 1 package dry yeast

BAKING PANS

Two large (9 x 5) loaf pans, greased or Teflon. If glass, reduce oven heat 25°.

PREPARATION 30 mins.	Six or more hours before— In a saucepan cover 5 medium potatoes with about 3 cups water, boil, covered, until well done—about 25 minutes. Pour off the water, reserve but keep hot. Mash potatoes until they are fine.
6 hours	In a large bowl mix mashed potatoes, salt, sugar, hot potato water, and 1 cup flour. Stir until thoroughly blended and the mixture is lukewarm to the touch. Sprinkle in the yeast (or mix in 1 cup Witch Yeast). Stir. Cover with plastic wrap and set in a warm place. Stir once or twice during the period.
	To continue—
20 mins.	Remove the plastic wrap, stir again and add 2 cups flour. Beat about 50 times, and then add 4 additional cups flour, one at a time, until the mixture is too thick to beat with a spoon. The use of Witch Yeast will require about 1 additional cup of flour to offset the added moisture. Work and blend by hand (or dough hook). When the dough cleans the sides of the bowl and is no longer sticky, turn the ball out on a floured board or counter top.
KNEADING 8 mins.	Knead until smooth and elastic.
FIRST RISING 1 hour	Place the dough back in the large bowl (which has been washed and greased) and place in a warm spot to double in volume. Cover with plastic wrap.
SHAPING 10 mins.	Punch down the dough and knead for 30 seconds to press out the bubbles. Divide the dough into two pieces with a sharp knife. Shape into balls, and let rest under a towel for 3 to 4 minutes. Form a loaf by pressing a ball of dough into a flat oval, roughly the length of the baking pan. Fold the oval in half, pinch the seam tightly to seal, tuck under the ends, and place in the pan, seam down. Repeat for the second loaf.
SECOND RISING 50 mins.	Cover the pans with wax paper and return to the warm spot until dough has doubled in bulk—about 2 inches above the edge of the pan.
BAKING 400° 10 mins.	Preheat oven to 400°. Bake the loaves in a hot oven for 10 minutes then reduce heat to moderately hot for an additional 40 minutes. When the loaves are a golden

350°
40 mins.

brown and tapping the bottom crust yields a hard hollow sound, they are done. If the finger strikes a soft, dull thud, return the loaves to their pans and put them back in the oven for an additional 10 or more minutes. Test again. A metal skewer will come out clean when inserted in the center of the loaf.

FINAL STEP

Remove the bread from the oven and turn the loaves out on wire cooling racks. Specially good when served warm from the oven, or toasted.

PEDA BREAD

[TWO ROUND LOAVES]

Looking peculiarly like a crown brioche in low profile or a brown tam-o-shanter sprinkled with sesame seeds, this two-part loaf with its center insert is a specialty of Armenian bake shops in the western United States. This one from California's San Joaquin Valley can be served sliced in wedges or used whole as a giant bun for a big hamburger patty or for barbecue meat slipped from 6 or 8 small skewers. The shaped loaves are held in the refrigerator 2 to 24 hours before baking which makes it an easy matter to time the arrival of the hot bread with the arrival of the meat.

INGREDIENTS

2 packages dry yeast
2 cups warm water (105°–115°)
½ cup non-fat dry milk
2 tablespoons sugar
1 teaspoon salt
3 tablespoons olive oil
6 cups all-purpose flour, approximately
Olive oil to brush tops
Glaze: 1 egg yolk and 1 teaspoon water; 4 tablespoons sesame seeds

BAKING SHEETS

Two baking sheets, greased or Teflon. It is unlikely a home oven will hold both loaves at once but since they can be taken one at a time from the refrigerator this is no problem.

PREPARATION
20 mins.

In a large mixing bowl stir the yeast into the warm water, and put it aside for about 5 minutes. With the electric mixer stir in milk, sugar, salt and olive oil.

Add 3 cups of the flour, and beat at medium speed for about 5 minutes. Remove the beaters and with a heavy wooden spoon work in 2 more cups of flour. If the spoon becomes difficult, use the fingers to work in the flour.

KNEADING
5 mins.

Turn the soft dough onto a bread board or counter top that has been floured with the remaining 1 cup of flour. Knead until the ball is smooth and elastic.

RESTING
20 mins.

Leave the dough on the counter top to rest. Cover it with plastic wrap, however. When you return to it, knead it lightly again to work out any air bubbles.

SHAPING
15 mins.

To begin, pinch off two small pieces of dough—about ½-cup size, and divide the large piece of dough in half. Shape each portion into a smooth ball.

On a baking sheet flatten the large piece into a flat round cake. Poke a hole in the center and, working with your fingers pulling in opposition, enlarge the hole to about 4 inches. Flatten the dough until it reaches a 10-inch diameter. Place one of the small balls of dough in the 4-inch center and flatten gently to fill the hole. Lightly brush with olive oil. Repeat with the second loaf.

REFRIGERATION
2–24 hours

Cover each with plastic wrap and place in the refrigerator. When ready to bake, remove loaf or loaves, uncover and let stand at room temperature for 10 minutes while the oven heats to 350°. Brush with beaten egg and sprinkle with sesame seed.

BAKING
350°
40 mins.

Bake in oven until the crust is a deep golden color and tapping the bottom crust yields a hard hollow sound. They are done when a wooden toothpick inserted in the center comes out clean.

FINAL STEP

Remove bread from oven and cool on a wire rack slightly before cutting. If for a giant sandwich, split the warm peda loaf in half horizontally, making the bottom section less than 1-inch thick. Slosh cooked marinade over the bottom, top it with tomato and meat and cover with the top of the loaf. Three pounds of lean ground beef in 8 large wedge-shaped patties makes a fine filling when covered with thin slices of cheese, onion, lettuce, and dill pickle.

PUSSTABROT

[TWO LARGE OR FOUR MEDIUM LOAVES]

This is a magnificent loaf of Hungarian white bread—a golden flaky crust sprinkled liberally with fennel seed, and a white slice with a tender, moist crumb. The sponge is started an hour or so beforehand by pouring the yeast mixture into a deep well in the center of 7 cups of flour—and allowing a thin batter to bubble up and over the reserve flour. This makes two big round loaves or four medium loaves. Whichever, the bread is fine with any meal, and, sliced, it makes noteworthy sandwiches.

INGREDIENTS

3 packages dry yeast
¾ cup warm water (105°–115°)
2 teaspoons sugar
¼ teaspoon fennel seed
8 cups all-purpose or bread flour, approximately
3 cups warm water (100°)
3 tablespoons sugar
1 tablespoon salt
3 tablespoons vegetable oil
Glaze: 1 beaten egg white
2 tablespoons water
½ teaspoon salt

BAKING SHEET

One large baking sheet, greased or Teflon.

PREPARATION
15 mins.

In a small bowl combine yeast, water, sugar and fennel seed. Beat it briskly for a moment or two to get the yeast action started. Set aside while you prepare the flour.

Use your largest bowl. Place in it 7 cups of flour and with a wooden spoon form a well in the center. Pour in warm water, sugar, and yeast mixture. With the spoon carefully draw in enough flour from the sides of the well to form a thin batter.

SPONGE
1 hour

Cover the bowl with plastic wrap and set in a warm place (80°–85°) until the sponge in the center has risen up and over the unmixed flour along the sides of the bowl.

With the spoon, and then the hands, work the flour into the sponge, pulling it from the sides with the spoon. Add salt and vegetable oil. Mix with the hands until the dough is firm but elastic. Add another cup of flour, in small portions, if necessary.

KNEADING
8 mins.

Sprinkle the work surface—counter top or bread board—with ½ cup of flour and turn the dough onto it. Knead under the heel of the hand until the dough is light, elastic, soft and alive.

FIRST RISING
1 hour

Return the dough to the large bowl and pat it lightly with a little vegetable oil spread over the hands. Cover the bowl tightly with plastic wrap so the top of the dough will not dry out and prematurely form a crust. Let the dough double in bulk.

SHAPING
10 mins.

Turn the dough back onto the work surface and knead with 10 strong strokes to work out the bubbles. With a sharp knife cut the dough into two or four pieces—depending on the number of loaves you wish to make. Form each into a ball, and place on baking sheet.

SECOND RISING
50 mins.

Cover the loaves with a length of wax paper and put in the warm place.

Meanwhile, preheat the oven to 350° and place a shallow pan of hot water on the lower shelf. The oven broiling pan is good for this.

BAKING
350°
50 mins.

Cut a ½-inch slash down the center of each loaf, brush with the egg white, water and salt solution and sprinkle with a little fennel seed. Put the loaves on the middle rack in the oven. Midway in the bake period shift the loaves and again near the end of the bake. When the loaves are golden brown and tapping the bottom crust yields a hollow sound, they are done. If not, return to the oven for 10 minutes.

FINAL STEP

Remove from oven and place the loaves on a metal rack to cool before serving or packaging to freeze.

HUNGARIAN WHITE BREAD

[TWO ROUND LOAVES]

Crushed anise and fennel seeds flavor these two fat golden brown loaves of white bread. I use bread flour but all-purpose flour is a perfectly acceptable substitute. These loaves are particularly attractive with a diamond pattern slashed on the tops and sprinkled with one of several seeds or coarse salt. It rises twice in the bowl and once on the baking sheet. A thoroughly satisfying loaf to make and to eat.

INGREDIENTS

2 cups warm water (105°–115°)
2 packages dry yeast
6 to 7 cups bread or all-purpose flour, approximately
3 tablespoons sugar
1 tablespoon salt
2 tablespoons cooking oil
¼ teaspoon anise seeds, crushed
½ teaspoon fennel seeds, crushed
Glaze: Egg yolk, 2 teaspoons of milk, and choice of poppy, fennel or sesame seeds or coarse salt

BAKING SHEET

One large baking sheet, greased or Teflon, or two small sheets.

PREPARATION
20 mins.

Pour warm water into a large bowl and sprinkle yeast over it. Stir to dissolve and let stand for 5 minutes or until the yeast begins to foam and bubble.

Blend in 4 cups of flour with sugar, salt, oil, and crushed seeds. Beat briskly until the mixture is smooth—about 100 strokes with a wooden spoon. Add more flour, ½ cup at a time, first with the spoon and then with the hand, until the dough is a rough mass and cleans the sides of the bowl.

KNEADING
8 mins.

Turn onto a lightly floured work surface—counter top or bread board—and knead with the 1-2-3 motion of push-turn-fold, push-turn-fold, etcetera. The dough will become smooth and elastic, and small bubbles can be seen just under the surface of the dough. Sprinkle more flour if the dough is slack (moist) and sticks to the hands or work surface. Occasionally raise the dough 2 or 3 feet above the table and bang it down hard against the counter. This is a relief from kneading and is equally effective in forming the gluten network.

FIRST RISING
1 hour

Put the dough back in the mixing bowl and pat all over with greased or buttered fingers to keep the surface moist. Cover with plastic wrap and move to a warm place (80°–85°) until the dough has risen to about twice its original size (as judged as it creeps up the sides of the bowl). You can test if it has risen by poking a finger in it; the dent will remain.

SECOND RISING
15 mins.

Turn back the plastic wrap and punch down the dough with the fist and fingers. Fold the edges of the dough into the center. Turn the ball of dough over, and reseal the plastic wrap. It will rise only partially in 15 minutes but that is sufficient.

SHAPING
5 mins.

Again, punch down the dough. Place it on the work surface, knead for 30 seconds to press out the bubbles and cut into two pieces with a sharp knife. Form each into a ball. Place on the opposite corners of the baking sheet (or use two smaller sheets if more convenient with your particular oven.)

THIRD RISING
40–50 mins.

Place the baking sheet in the warm place and cover carefully with a length of wax paper. If the paper tends to stick to the dough, rest it above on water glasses. The loaves will about double in size. You can test if dough is ready for oven by poking a finger in it; the dent will remain.

BAKING
425°
15 mins.
375°
25 mins.

Preheat the oven to 425°. With a sharp knife or razor blade slash tops of loaves to form a diamond pattern. Brush with the egg yolk and milk mixture. Sprinkle with choice of poppy, fennel, or sesame seeds, or coarse salt.

Bake in the hot oven for 15 minutes, reduce heat to moderately hot and bake an additional 25 minutes. When the loaves are a deep golden brown and tapping the bottom crust yields a hard hollow sound, they are done. If not, return to the oven for an additional 10 minutes. If the loaves brown too quickly, cover them with a piece of foil or brown sack paper.

FINAL STEP

Remove bread from the oven and lift the loaves to a wire rack to cool before serving or freezing. Allow the frozen loaf to thaw overnight in the refrigerator. Reheat in a 350° oven for 15 minutes.

SWISS BRAIDED BREAD

[TWO LOAVES]

This is a handsome, decorative loaf in fat braids brushed with heavy cream and beaten egg and sprinkled with poppy or sesame seeds. The dough is faintly yellow, and reminiscent of challah, the delicious Jewish loaf.

INGREDIENTS

1 package dry yeast
1¼ cups warm water (105°–115°)
1 stick (½ cup) butter, room temperature
2 tablespoons sugar
2 eggs, room temperature and slightly beaten
2 teaspoons salt
⅓ cup non-fat dry milk
5 cups all-purpose or bread flour, approximately
Glaze: 1 beaten egg, 2 tablespoons heavy cream or milk and sesame and/or poppy seeds

BAKING SHEET

One baking sheet, greased or Teflon.

PREPARATION
15 mins.

In a large mixing bowl sprinkle yeast over warm water. Stir to dissolve and set aside for 3 or 4 minutes.

Stir in the soft butter, sugar, eggs, salt and dry milk.

Gradually add flour, ½ cup at a time, first with a wooden spoon and, when it becomes a firm dough, by hand. Work the flour into moist ball until it cleans the sides of the bowl and has lost much of its stickiness. The dough will be a rough, shaggy mass.

KNEADING
8 mins.

Turn out the dough onto a floured work surface and knead with a strong push-turn-fold motion until it becomes smooth, elastic and alive under the hands. If it is moist and sticky, sprinkle a bit more flour on the work surface and dust the hands. Bang it down hard against the work surface several times during the kneading process to help form the gluten.

FIRST RISING
1½ hours

Return the dough to the bowl (which has been brushed and scraped clean), pat it over with buttered or greased fingers and stretch a length of plastic wrap over the top of the bowl. Place the bowl in a warm spot (80°–85°) until dough has risen to double its volume.

SHAPING
25 mins.

Divide the dough into 6 equal pieces and shape each into a round ball. Cover and let rest on the counter top for 15 minutes to relax the dough. Roll and shape each into a strip 1 inch wide by 18 inches long. Lay 3 strips side by side and braid from the middle to the ends. Pinch the ends securely together, tuck under and place on the baking sheet. Repeat with second piece.

SECOND RISING
50 mins.

Cover the braids with wax paper and return them to the warm place until they have risen to double their size.

BAKING
375°
35–40 mins.

Preheat oven to 375°. Brush the loaves with a mixture of 1 beaten egg and 2 tablespoons cream or milk. I often sprinkle the braids with poppy seeds or sesame seeds—or one of each.

Bake in the hot oven until the braids are a deep brown. They will test done if a wooden toothpick inserted in the center of a loaf comes out dry with no dough clinging to it.

FINAL STEP

Remove bread from the oven and carefully lift the braids with a spatula and place them on a wire rack to cool before serving.

HOME ROMAN MEAL BREAD

[TWO LOAVES]

One cup of Roman Meal cereal plus a half cup of wheat germ produces a solid, rough-textured loaf that many think is superior to one of the good commercial breads on the market, Roman Meal Bread. The cereal, a blend of whole wheat, whole rye, bran and defatted flaxseed meal, was fed to the Roman Legions, according to the box top. The slice is moist and chewy. It toasts beautifully and freezes and holds well for several months.

INGREDIENTS

5½ to 6 cups all-purpose flour, approximately
1 package dry yeast
1 cup Roman Meal cereal
¼ cup non-fat dry milk
½ cup wheat germ
2 teaspoons salt
¼ cup vegetable oil
2½ cups hot tap water (120°–130°)

BAKING PANS

Two medium (8½ x 4½) loaf pans, greased or Teflon. If glass, reduce oven heat 25°.

PREPARATION
15 mins.

In a large mixing bowl measure 3 cups flour and stir in yeast, Roman Meal cereal, milk, wheat germ, salt, oil and water. Beat in electric mixer for 1 minute at medium speed, then turn to high for 2 minutes, or for an equal length of time with a wooden spoon.

Stop the mixer. Stir in the balance of the flour, a half cup at a time, first with the spoon and then by hand. The dough will be a rough, shaggy mass that will clean the sides of the bowl. If the dough continues slack and sticky, add small sprinkles of flour.

KNEADING
8 mins.

Turn the dough onto a lightly floured work surface—counter top or bread board—and knead with a rhythmic 1-2-3 motion of push-turn-fold. The dough will become smooth and elastic, and feel alive under the hands. Break the kneading rhythm occasionally by throwing the dough down hard against the work surface.

FIRST RISING
50 mins.

Place the dough back in the mixing bowl and pat with buttered or greased fingers. Cover the bowl tightly with plastic wrap and move to a warm place (80°–85°) until the dough has risen to twice its original size. You can test if it has risen by poking a finger in it; the dent will remain.

SHAPING
12 mins.

Punch down dough and knead for 30 seconds to press out the bubbles. Divide the dough into two pieces with a sharp knife. Shape into balls, and let rest under a towel for 3 minutes. Form the loaf by pressing a ball into a flat oval, roughly the length of the baking pan. Fold the oval in half, pinch the seam tightly to seal, tuck under the ends, and place in the pan, seam down. Repeat with second loaf.

SECOND RISING
45 mins.

Place the pans in the warm place, cover with wax paper and leave until the center of the dough has risen about one inch above the level of the pan.

BAKING
350°
45 mins.

Preheat oven to 350°. Bake loaves in the oven. When the loaves are golden brown and tapping the bottom crust yields a hard and hollow sound, they are done. If not, return to the oven for an additional 10 minutes. Midway in the bake period and again near the end, shift the pans so the loaves are exposed equally to the temperature variations in the oven.

FINAL STEP

Remove bread from oven and turn out onto the metal rack to cool before slicing.

FRISIAN SUGAR LOAF

[TWO LOAVES]

A yeast bread from Friesland, a province bordering the North Sea in the Netherlands, this sugar loaf is a delight and a surprise when it is cut for breakfast, brunch or tea. Sugar cubes—heavily dusted with cinnamon—will have created pockets of sweet, sticky goodness, flavored with spice which also gives the loaf a tint of brown. While it is baking and then cooling on the rack, it sends a delightful aroma through the house.

INGREDIENTS

1 package dry yeast
2 cups warm water (105°–115°)
1 pinch sugar
1 cup sugar cubes, roughly broken
1 tablespoon cinnamon
6 cups all-purpose or bread flour, approximately
⅓ cup non-fat dry milk
2½ tablespoons shortening
2 tablespoons sugar
2 teaspoons salt

BAKING PANS

Two medium (8½ x 4½) loaf pans, greased or Teflon. If glass, reduce oven temperature 25°. See the dough volume chart on page 23 for other combinations of loaf sizes.

PREPARATION
30 mins.

In a mixing bowl sprinkle yeast over the surface of water. Add a pinch of sugar. Stir briskly with a fork or metal whisk to hasten the yeast action. Set aside while preparing the sugar cubes.

With the handle of the kitchen shears, an ice cracker, or a tack hammer, crack a cup of sugar cubes. Don't crush them. Try to break them into halves or quarters. Place them in a small bowl and sprinkle with a tablespoon of cinnamon. Turn with a spoon until all of the broken pieces are well coated.

Measure 3 cups of flour, a cup at a time, into the yeast mixture, and add milk, shortening, sugar and salt. With a wooden spoon beat 100 strong strokes—or 4 minutes in the electric mixer at medium speed. Stop the mixer. Stir in additional flour, about 3 more cups, first with the spoon and then with the hands. The dough will be a rough, shaggy mass but it will clean the sides of the bowl.

KNEADING
8 mins.

The sugar cubes are added gradually during the kneading process. Turn the dough onto a lightly floured work surface—counter top or bread board—and knead for 2 minutes with the rhythmic 1-2-3 motion of push-turn-fold. Flatten the dough and sprinkle with approximately ¼ cup of the sugar cube mixture. Knead it into the dough for 1 minute, and add another portion of sugar cubes. Again work it into the dough with a kneading motion. Repeat with the balance of the sugar cubes.

Meanwhile, the dough will have taken on some of the color of the cinnamon but this is desirable. If some of the sugar bits work their way out of the dough during the kneading, press them in again.

FIRST RISING
1 hour

Place the dough in the mixing bowl and pat with buttered or greased fingers to keep the surface from crusting. Cover the bowl with plastic wrap and move to a warm place (80°–85°) until the dough has risen to about twice its original size (judged as it expands up the sides of the bowl). You can test if it has risen by poking a finger in it; the dent will remain.

SHAPING
15 mins.

Turn the dough onto the work surface, knead for a moment to press out the bubbles and divide with a sharp knife. When the dough is cut, moist pockets of sugar will be exposed. Carefully close the cut edge, pinch the seam tightly. Shape the pieces into balls, and let them rest under a towel for 3 or 4 minutes. Form a loaf by pressing or rolling each into an oval—roughly the length of a baking tin. Fold the oval in half, pinch the seam to seal, tuck under the ends and place in the loaf pan, seam down.

SECOND RISING
45 mins.

Place the pans in the warm place, cover with wax paper and leave until the center of the dough has risen ½ to 1 inch above the edge of the pan.

BAKING
400°
15 mins.
350°
40 mins.

Preheat oven to 400° about 15 minutes before baking. Place the loaves in a hot oven for 15 minutes, reduce heat to 350° and bake for an additional 40 minutes. When tapping the bottom crust yields a hard hollow sound, they are done. If not, return to the oven (without the pan, if you wish a deep brown crust) for an additional 10 minutes. Midway in the bake period shift the position of the loaves so they are exposed equally to temperature variations in the oven.

FINAL STEP

Carefully remove the loaves from the tins making certain the sugar syrup has not stuck to the sides. Allow the loaves to cool before serving. It makes fine toast but it must be carefully watched so the sugar does not burn.

ADOBE OVEN BREAD

[TWO TO EIGHT LOAVES]

If you happen to have a wood-fired earthen oven—an adobe one from the U.S. Southwest or one made of baked mud and straw used by French-Canadians on the Gaspé Peninsula in Quebec—this recipe is designed especially for you.

California's *Sunset* magazine, which does highly imaginative things with food and food preparation, developed this recipe as well as a build-it- yourself Pueblo mud-and-cement oven to bake it in (page 552).

This is good bread wherever it is baked so if you are not equipped with a primitive outdoor oven do it in the kitchen. While it is best served warm from the oven or eaten the first day, the bread keeps surprisingly well. It will begin to harden but it is excellent sliced thin under cheese or paté, or simply toasted. It is quite chewy.

This is a large recipe calling for 12 cups of all-purpose flour and it is too much for all home mixers. It will mean hand mixing and kneading.

INGREDIENTS

1 package dry yeast
4 teaspoons sugar
4 cups warm water (105°–115°)
2 tablespoons salt
11 to 12 cups all-purpose flour, approximately
Glaze: 1 egg
4 tablespoons water

BAKING SHEET

One baking sheet, greased or Teflon. If you are baking in an adobe oven, you will need a peel to thrust the loaves into the oven and slip them onto the floor. You will also need an atomizer (see Basic Equipment, page 26) and water.

PREPARATION
12 mins.

Stir yeast and sugar into a large bowl and pour in the water. Stir briskly. Let stand for 5 minutes until it begins to foam. Add salt.

With a heavy wooden spoon stir in the flour, a half cup at a time, until a rough mass has formed and it cleans the bowl. If the dough continues moist and sticky, sprinkle on additional flour.

KNEADING
10 mins.

Turn the dough onto a lightly floured work surface—counter top or bread board—and knead with the rhythmic 1-2-3 motion of push-turn-fold. The dough will become smooth and elastic and feel alive under the hands. Bubbles will rise under the surface of the dough. Break the kneading rhythm occasionally by throwing the dough hard against the counter top.

FIRST RISING
1 hour

Place the dough in the mixing bowl and pat with buttered or greased fingers to keep the surface from crusting. Cover the bowl tightly with plastic wrap and move to a warm place (80°–85°) until the dough has risen to about twice its original size. You can test if it has risen by poking a finger in it; the dent will remain.

SHAPING
10 mins.

Punch down the dough and knead for 30 seconds to press out bubbles. Cut into however many pieces you wish loaves of bread—two or four or even eight small loaves. Form each into a ball. Place on the baking sheet or in small baskets lined with a cloth liberally sprinkled with flour.

SECOND RISING
45 mins.

Place the loaves in a warm place, cover with wax paper and leave until they have doubled in volume.

BAKING
425°
15 mins.
375°
35 mins.

Preheat oven to 425°. If the loaves have risen in baskets, simply tip the raised loaf into your hand and quickly turn the loaf right side up onto the baking sheet.

Brush the loaves with the egg and water mixture. With a razor blade slash each loaf three times across the top, about ¼ inch deep. Place in the oven.

Bake in the hot oven for 15 minutes, reduce heat to 375° and bake for an additional 35 minutes. Ten minutes after placing the loaves in the oven, spray with water (use an atomizer—see Basic Equipment, page 26). Spray again ten minutes later.

When loaves are golden brown and tapping the bottom crust yields a hard hollow sound, the bread is done. Midway in the bake period shift the loaves so they are exposed equally to the temperature variations of the oven.

FINAL STEP — Remove bread from the oven and place on a metal rack to cool before serving.

WHITE BREAD WITH CHOCOLATE

[FOUR SMALL LOAVES]

A delicious white bread, with a sponge starter, adapted to satisfy the need for an American counterpart to the small white loaves baked around a chocolate core that French children carry for a snack at school. The loaves are small so they may be torn apart with forks or by hand rather than cut (which smears the chocolate). Without the chocolate, this is a fine bread for toasting. Perhaps bake two loaves with chocolate for the chocolate buffs in the family, and two loaves without for superior toast.

INGREDIENTS

1½ cups warm water (105°–115°)
2 tablespoons sugar
2 packages dry yeast
½ teaspoon ginger
2 cups all-purpose or bread flour
1 cup hot tap water (120°–130°)
⅓ cup non-fat dry milk
2 tablespoons sugar
1 tablespoon salt
3 tablespoons lard or other shortening, room temperature
5½ to 6 cups all-purpose or bread flour, approximately
8 one-ounce sweet or semi-sweet chocolate squares

BAKING PANS — Four small (7½ x 3½) loaf pans, greased or Teflon. If glass, reduce oven heat 25°.

PREPARATION
Overnight — The night before, prepare the sponge; in a medium bowl, measure the water, sugar, yeast and ginger. Stir well. Blend in 2 cups of flour with a wooden spoon. It will be a thin batter. Cover with plastic wrap and set aside in a warm place (80°–85°) overnight.

15 mins. — In the morning, turn back the plastic wrap and stir down the sponge which will have risen and fallen several times during the night. Add the water, milk, sugar, salt, and lard. Stir in the balance of the flour, a half cup at a time, first with the spoon and then by hand. The dough will be a rough, shaggy mass that will clean the

sides of the bowl. If the dough is slack and moisture breaks through, add small amounts of additional flour.

KNEADING
8 mins.

Turn the dough onto a lightly floured work surface—counter top or bread board—and knead with the rhythmic 1-2-3 motion of push-turn-fold. The dough will become smooth and elastic, and bubbles will rise under the surface of the dough. Sprinkle with more flour if the dough is moist or continues to stick to the hands or work surface. Occasionally, change the kneading rhythm by throwing the dough down hard against the work surface. Knead for about 8 minutes (or 5 minutes with the dough hook).

FIRST RISING
1 hour

Place the dough in the bowl and pat with buttered or greased fingers to keep the surface from crusting. Cover the bowl tightly with plastic wrap and move to the warm place until the dough has risen to about twice its original size (judged as it creeps up the sides of the bowl). You can test if it has risen by poking a finger in it; the dent will remain.

SHAPING
20 mins.

Now the chocolate is added. First, punch down the dough and knead for 1 minute to press out the bubbles. With a sharp knife, divide the dough into four pieces. Shape into balls, and let rest under a towel for 3 to 4 minutes. Form each loaf by pressing a ball—under the palms or with a rolling pin—into a flat oval, roughly the length of the baking pan. Break the 1-ounce squares of chocolate in halves and lay the pieces down the center of the oval. Fold the oval in half, pinch the seam tightly to seal, tuck under the ends, and place in the pan, seam down. Repeat with other pieces.

Brush the loaves with melted shortening.

SECOND RISING
40 mins.

Place the pans in the warm place, cover with wax paper and leave until the center of the dough has risen ½ to 1 inch above the edge. Meanwhile, preheat oven to 375°.

BAKING
375°
35 mins.

Bake the loaves. When the loaves are golden brown and tapping the bottom yields a hard hollow sound, they are done. If not, return to the oven for an additional 10 minutes. Midway in the bake period and again near the end of it, shift the loaves so they are exposed equally to the temperature variations of the oven.

FINAL STEP

Remove bread from the oven. Turn the loaves onto wire racks to cool. This bread is absolutely delicious served warm, but expect to smear the chocolate if you cut the slices with a knife.

ZEPPELIN

[THREE LONG FAT LOAVES]

Count von Zeppelin would be proud of this Viennese baton that resembles one of his lighter-than-air machines. It is a white bread recipe with only a small amount of shortening, but there are several touches in the preparation of the loaves that lift it out of the ordinary. A sponge, sprinkled with a layer of flour, is set aside for 3 hours before the actual making begins. To give an authentic baked-on-the-hearth flavor to the bread, a can of ashes—from the fireplace or the barbecue pit—is placed in the back of the hot oven.

INGREDIENTS

2 packages dry yeast
1 cup warm water (105°–115°)
1 pinch sugar
2 cups all-purpose or bread flour
1 tablespoon *each* non-fat dry milk and salt
2 cups water
5 cups all-purpose or bread flour, approximately
2 tablespoons vegetable oil
Glaze: 2 tablespoons salt
½ cup water

BAKING SHEET

Large baking sheet, greased or Teflon.
One cup ashes from fireplace or barbecue, in can.

PREPARATION

In a large bowl sprinkle yeast over water. Add sugar and, with a fork or whisk, beat the mixture until the yeast is dissolved.

Sponge
3 hours

Add 2 cups of flour and stir with a wooden spoon until it becomes a heavy batter or sponge. Sprinkle the surface with a thin layer of flour, cover the bowl with plastic wrap and let the dough rise in a warm place (80°–85°) for 3 hours. Holes will appear in the top and the sponge may drop or sink in the center. All the better.

Dough
15 mins.

In a small bowl stir milk and salt into 2 cups water. Pour this mixture over the sponge. Work it into a dough, gradually adding flour. Add vegetable oil and blend into the dough.

When the dough has cleaned the sides of the bowl and is a rough mass, not too sticky, it is ready to knead.

KNEADING
8 mins.

Turn the dough out onto a lightly floured work surface, counter top or bread board, and knead under the palm of the hand. The dough will be dry (not sticky), elastic and silky. It will feel alive under your hands.

FIRST RISING
1 hour

Pat the ball of dough lightly with vegetable oil spread on the fingers, and drop it into the large mixing bowl. Cover tightly with plastic wrap and place in a warm spot (80°–85°) until the dough doubles in bulk.

SECOND RISING
20 mins.

Punch down the dough and knead it for 3 minutes. Return it to the bowl, cover it, and let it rise again.

SHAPING
15 mins.

Turn the dough out onto the work surface and cut into three pieces. To give the loaves the zeppelin shape, roll the ends under the palms while leaving the center section fairly fat. Then pat it into a shape roughly the shape of a football. Point the ends. Place on the baking sheet.

THIRD RISING
20 mins.

Cover the loaves with wax paper and let them rise. Place a cupful of ashes in a small can and set in the back of the oven.

BAKING
400°
45 mins.

Preheat oven to 400°. Just before placing the loaves in the oven, with a sharp knife or razor blade cut three diagonal slashes across the top of each. Brush the loaves either with plain cold water or a mixture of salt and water. During the baking period, brush the loaves every 10 minutes with the salt-water solution. When tapping the bottom crust yields a hard hollow sound, they are done.

FINAL STEP

Remove bread from the oven, lift the loaves off the baking sheet and place them on a metal rack to cool.

THREE

Bran Breads

Hazel
Lyons, 1579

Bran, the brown, flaky outer covering of the wheat kernel, has a nutlike flavor and is often mistaken for one of several breakfast cereals with almost the same name. They are bran, too, but of different texture and form. Satisfactory results, however, can come with substituting these products, if the original is not readily available.

HILO BRAN BREAD

[A CHOICE OF LOAVES AND MUFFINS]

Hardly as exotic in flavor or appearance as its place of origin—Hilo, on the Big Island of Hawaii—this bread, from a recipe by a member of the Hilo Women's Club, is a good straightforward bran loaf. When I lived in Hawaii, the Big Island was noted for the good food prepared in the kitchens of the big sugar plantation homes along the Hamakua Coast.

Molasses for the bread came from a nearby sugar refinery; the bran by ship from flour mills more than 2,000 miles away.

This recipe will make 3 small loaves (¾ pound each) and a half-dozen muffins or 2 medium loaves. The mixture is easy to work, and is light and fluffy when it is spooned or poured into the pans.

INGREDIENTS 3 cups all-purpose or bread flour
3 cups bran

½ cup sugar
4 teaspoons baking powder
1 teaspoon *each* salt and baking soda
2½ cups milk (or 2¼ cups hot tap water and ⅔ cup non-fat dry milk)
6 tablespoons molasses

BAKING PANS

Pan sizes are suggested above. To facilitate turning out the loaf after it has baked, butter or grease the pan, line the long sides and bottom with a length of wax paper, and butter again. Leave tabs of paper sticking out about ½ inch so the loaf can be pulled from the pan.

PREPARATION
20 mins.

Before preparing the batter, set the oven at 350°. If glass pans are used, reduce oven heat 25°.

In a large mixing bowl measure the white flour, bran, sugar, baking powder, salt, and baking soda. In a small bowl pour the milk and molasses. Stir well. Pour this into the dry ingredients and mix thoroughly. Let the mixture rest for 10 minutes while preparing the baking pans.

FORMING
3 mins.

Pour the batter into the prepared pans.

BAKING
350°
1 hour

Place the pans in the oven until one tests done when a wooden toothpick inserted in the loaf comes out clean and dry.

FINAL STEP

Remove bread from the oven. Hot quick bread is fragile when taken from the pan, so do this with care. It is delicious served warm with butter.

BRAN AND MOLASSES BREAD

[ONE LOAF]

There is an unusual wheaty flavor about this bran bread that is underscored by the dark unsulphured molasses that I use in this recipe. Its good flavor relies also on whole wheat flour and raisins. Buttermilk can be substituted for sour milk with equally good results. It is a fine loaf to serve thinly sliced at a brunch, buffet, or breakfast.

INGREDIENTS
2 cups bran
2 cups whole wheat flour
2 teaspoons baking powder
1 teaspoon *each* salt and baking soda
1 egg, room temperature
1¾ cups sour milk or buttermilk
½ cup blackstrap molasses (or ¾ cup brown sugar)
1 cup raisins

BAKING PAN
One medium (8½ x 4½) metal (or glass) loaf pan, greased or Teflon. If glass, reduce oven heat 25°. To facilitate turning the loaf out after it has baked, butter or grease the pan, line the long sides and bottom with a length of wax paper—and butter again. Leave ends of the paper sticking out about ½ inch so the loaf can be pulled from the pan.

PREPARATION
10 mins.
In a medium bowl combine bran, whole wheat flour, baking powder, salt, and baking soda. In another bowl beat the egg, and add sour milk and molasses. Blend in the dry ingredients and add the raisins. Blend but don't overbeat.

FORMING
3 mins.
Spoon or pour the batter into the loaf pan. Push the mixture into the corners of the pan with the spoon or spatula. Form it slightly higher along the sides than in the middle—to compensate for the rising crown when it bakes.

RESTING
1 hour
Allow the batter to rest while the oven is preheated to 375°. Cover the pan with a piece of wax paper during the period.

BAKING
375°
1 hour
Bake in oven until the loaf tests done when pierced in the center with a metal skewer or wooden toothpick. If it comes out clean and dry, the loaf is done. If moist particles cling to the pin, return the loaf to the oven for an additional 10 minutes. Test again.

FINAL STEP
Remove bread from the oven and turn the loaf out of the pan onto a metal rack to cool. It will have an unusually crisp crust. If a soft crust is more to your taste, brush with melted butter and cover with a tea towel while it cools.

BRAN NUT BREAD

[ONE LOAF]

Nuts give this rough textured loaf a special richness that will come as a surprise since it is not as dark as some of the other bran loaves. The reason is that I make it with white flour mixed with bran rather than whole wheat. A crusty loaf with a broken ridge down the center that complements coarseness of the crumb, it is delicious sliced thinly and served with a soft cheese.

INGREDIENTS

2 cups all-purpose or bread flour
3 teaspoons baking powder
1 teaspoon salt
2 cups bran
1⅓ cups milk
1 egg, room temperature
2 tablespoons shortening, melted
2 tablespoons molasses
1 cup chopped walnuts

BAKING PAN

One medium (8½ x 4½) loaf pan, greased or Teflon, or glass. If the latter, reduce oven heat 25°.

PREPARATION
10 mins.

In a medium bowl sift the flour and sprinkle in the baking powder and salt. Blend well with a wooden spoon or resift. Add the bran. In another bowl combine the milk and egg. Stir this into the flour, and add shortening, molasses and nuts. Mix to blend—but don't beat.

FORMING
15 mins.

Pour into a baking pan and allow it to stand for 15 minutes before putting it into the oven.

BAKING
375°
1 hour

Preheat oven to 375°. Place the batter in the oven until the loaf tests done. It is baked when a wooden toothpick or metal skewer inserted in the center of loaf comes out dry and clean.

FINAL STEP

Remove bread from the oven. Turn the loaf from the pan with care and place on a metal cooling rack. It will be a crusty loaf unless it is brushed with butter and covered with a towel. Most like it crisp. Regardless, it is better if it is allowed to age overnight before slicing.

BRAN ROLLS

[TWO DOZEN]

It is disquieting at times to follow a recipe in which the author does not make it clear whether he intends to use *bran*, the unadorned by-product that comes from milling the wheat kernel, or one of several breakfast foods which are made mostly with bran, including 40% Bran Flakes, 100% Bran, All-Bran, and Bran Buds. Usually any will do but some do better than others.

This recipe is made with Kellogg's All-Bran, "the original laxative cereal." The rolls are yeast-raised and the product is light and tender.

INGREDIENTS	1 package dry yeast ½ cup warm water (105°–115°) ½ cup boiling water ⅓ cup shortening, room temperature ½ cup sugar 1½ cups Kellogg's All-Bran 1 teaspoon salt 1 egg, room temperature 1½ cups all-purpose flour
MUFFIN TINS	Muffin tins, with cups for two dozen, greased or Teflon.
PREPARATION 15 mins.	In a small bowl or cup dissolve yeast in water. Stir briskly to speed the action. In a mixing bowl pour boiling hot water over shortening. Stir in sugar, Kellogg's All-Bran, salt, and let stand until lukewarm (105°–115°). Beat egg and stir into the bran mixture. Add the yeast, and blend well. Mix in the flour, a half cup at a time. Beat with 50 strong strokes.
FIRST RISING 2 hours	Cover the bowl with plastic wrap and let dough rise in a warm place (80°–85°) until almost doubled.
FORMING 3 mins.	Stir down and drop dough by the spoonful into prepared muffin pans, filling no more than half full.
SECOND RISING 1 hour	Cover the pans with wax paper and return to the warm place until the dough reaches to the level of the edge of the tins.
BAKING 375° 15–18 mins.	Preheat oven to 375°. Bake in the hot oven until the bran rolls are raised and a deep brown.

FINAL STEP

Remove rolls from the oven and serve while warm. These are equally good served later at room temperature, and can be frozen and kept for months.

BUTTER BRAN BREAD

[ONE SQUARE OR TWO OBLONG LOAVES]

This is such a delicious loaf from an old cook book that I changed its name from prosaic "Bran Cornmeal Bread" to one that would in some measure capture the richness of its dark, crisp crust and coarse textured slice. It tastes like bran, which it is, but it also has a large helping of butter, eggs, cornmeal, raisins and nuts. The first word I wrote about this loaf is still on the corner of the recipe card—"tremendous."

INGREDIENTS

½ cup *each* butter and sugar
2 eggs, room temperature
2 cups bran
⅔ cup all-purpose or bread flour
1⅓ teaspoons baking powder
½ teaspoon salt
5½ tablespoons yellow cornmeal
1 cup milk
1 cup raisins, nut meats or dates or 1 cup of a mixture

BAKING PANS

One square (9 x 9) pan, or two small (7½ x 3½) pans, greased or Teflon, glass or metal. If glass, reduce oven heat 25°. To facilitate turning out the loaf after it has baked, line the long sides and bottom with a length of wax paper, and butter again. Leave paper tabs projecting about ½ inch so the loaf can be pulled from the pan. It also makes cleaning the pan much easier.

PREPARATION
15 mins.

In a large bowl beat the butter until soft and gradually add the sugar. Blend the mixture until it is light and creamy. Beat in the eggs, one at a time, and add the bran.

On a length of wax paper sift the all-purpose or bread flour—and resift with the baking powder and salt. Add the yellow cornmeal. Alternately, beat into the bran mixture the dry ingredients and the milk. Add the raisins and/or dates and nuts. Mix thoroughly into the batter.

FORMING
5 mins.

Spread the batter in the pan or pans which have been lined with buttered wax paper. Push a slight depression down the center of the batter to compensate for the expansion in the oven.

BAKING
375°
45 mins.

Preheat oven to 375°. Bake the bread in the oven; the loaves will be done when a wooden toothpick or metal skewer inserted in the center of a loaf comes out dry and clean.

FINAL STEP

Remove the tins from the oven. Turn on their sides and gently slip the loaves out by pulling the wax paper. Place on wire rack to cool. This loaf keeps for several days wrapped in foil, and can be kept frozen for several months.

FOUR

Whole Wheat Breads

Wheat
Lyons, 1579

The delicate and delicious aroma rising from a toasted slice of whole wheat bread has been likened to the faint but fragrant odor coming off a haying field on a hot afternoon in late summer.

Whole wheat, one of the most versatile of the dark flours the home baker can use, is also called wholemeal (by the English and Irish) and graham flour, after Dr. Sylvester Graham who in 1837 advocated flour from the whole grain.

Whole wheat is relatively easy to work and knead because it does have a full quota of gluten. Unfortunately, the sharp edges of the bran particles are believed to cut the gluten strands which reduces the size of the loaf compared to a loaf of white made with the same volume of flour.

Stone ground whole wheat flour which *is* ground between stones, the top one weighing more than one ton and revolving all the while, is coarser than whole wheat from a modern mill where the wheat is ground between pairs of steel rollers. Many like the rough texture it gives the slice.

BATTER WHOLE WHEAT BREAD

[TWO LOAVES]

This loaf made with all whole wheat flour is a batter bread, not to be kneaded. It produces a wheaty, chewy slice that is unusual in texture and taste. The second bite and second slice will be better than the first bite and first slice. It comes on slowly but with authority. Slice and serve with the soft cheeses, topped with a wisp of ham.

INGREDIENTS
6 cups of whole wheat flour
¾ cup sugar
1 tablespoon salt
2 packages dry yeast
3½ cups hot tap water (120°–130°)

BAKING PANS
Two medium (8½ x 4½) loaf pans, greased or Teflon. If glass, reduce oven heat 25°.

PREPARATION
10 mins.
In a large mixing bowl measure the whole wheat flour and stir in sugar, salt and yeast. Pour in water and stir 50 strong strokes to blend. It will be a soft batter. It is not to be kneaded.

FORMING
5 mins.
With a spoon, fill pans half to two-thirds full. Wet the fingertips to push the batter into the corners, and to smooth.

RISING
30 mins.
Cover with wax paper and put into a warm place (80°–85°) until the batter has doubled in volume—but no more.

BAKING
400°
15 mins.
350°
45 mins.
Preheat oven to 400°. Bake in a hot oven for about 15 minutes then reduce heat to 350° for an additional 45 minutes, or until the loaves test done. A metal skewer inserted in the center of the loaf will come out clean and dry if the loaf is done. If moist particles cling to the probe, return to the oven for an additional 10 minutes.

FINAL STEP
Remove bread from the oven, turn from the pans and place on a metal rack to cool before serving.

BANNOCK

[ONE ROUND LOAF]

Less splendid than the Royal Hibernian loaf, page 134, with its eggs and much butter, but nonetheless delicious, the recipe for this brown soda bread is woven into an Irish linen cloth hanging in my kitchen. Above the recipe, a young girl is preparing the loaf before the soft heat from the glowing turf fire. It is a wheaty, rough-textured compact loaf that is the right vehicle for a thin slice of ham or cheese.

INGREDIENTS

3 cups whole wheat (wholemeal) flour
2 cups all-purpose or bread flour
1 teaspoon salt
1¼ teaspoons soda
2 tablespoons butter, room temperature
1¼ cups buttermilk, room temperature

BAKING PAN

One 7- or 8-inch cake pan, greased or Teflon, with 2-inch sides. Select a lid to cover.

PREPARATION
12 mins.

In a bowl mix together the dry ingredients—both flours, salt and soda. Work in the butter with fingers or cut with two knives until the mixture resembles moist bread crumbs. Add sufficient buttermilk to make the dough moist and sticky to the hand. Don't rush the process—allow the flour to absorb the buttermilk.

KNEADING
3 mins.

Knead lightly until the dough is well mixed and loses its stickiness. If it is too moist and sticks excessively to the fingers, add a little flour.

FORMING
3 mins.

Turn it into the cake pan. Push the dough to the edges of the pan, and cover with a lid.

BAKING
425°
30 mins.
325°
15 mins.

Preheat oven to 425°. Bake for 30 minutes in the hot oven; reduce heat to 325° and continue baking for an additional 15 minutes. Pierce with a wooden toothpick or a metal skewer in the center of the loaf. If it comes out clean and dry, the loaf is done. If moist particles cling to the probe, return the loaf to the oven for an additional 10 minutes. Test again.

FINAL STEP

Remove bread from the oven and carefully turn out onto a wire rack to cool. The bread should not be sliced until it has set for at least 6 hours. It will keep well for two or three days in a plastic bag.

SOAKED-WHEAT BREAD

[TWO SMALL ROUND LOAVES]

Without benefit of leavening, this loaf is dense, heavy as an uncured brick—and wholly satisfying. Soaked-Wheat Bread is crisp and crusty on the outside, and moist and chewy on the in. It demands good teeth, of course. Because it is almost all wheat, with only a trace of salt and a little oil, it has a remarkable nut-like flavor. Eat plain and spread with butter or thin-sliced cheese. Viva natural foods!

INGREDIENTS

2 cups water
2 cups whole or cracked wheat grains
¼ cup corn or vegetable oil
1¼ cups water
1 tablespoon salt
4 cups whole wheat flour, approximately

BAKING SHEET

One baking sheet, greased or Teflon.

PREPARATION
24 hours

In a medium bowl pour 2 cups water over whole or cracked wheat grains. Cover tightly with plastic wrap and set aside for 24 hours.

15 mins.

At the same time measure the corn oil, water, salt, and flour into a mixing bowl and blend together. Work the dough with the hands for this will be a heavy ball. If the dough is slack or wet, sprinkle in ¼ cup flour. Turn the dough out onto a floured surface.

KNEADING
5 mins.

The dough will be tacky but not sticky. It will not, however, become elastic or smooth because it is unleavened. Knead. Return dough to bowl. Cover tightly with plastic wrap and put in a warm place (80°–85°) for 24 hours.

FIRST RESTING
24 hours

This period of rest is 24 hours, and during this time the dough will age and mature but not rise as there is no leavening in it.

SHAPING
15 mins.

Next day, drain the wheat grains; chop them coarsely in the blender. Uncover the dough and knead in the chopped kernels. Divide the ball into two pieces. Shape each into a round loaf, and flatten slightly. Place on baking sheet.

SECOND RESTING
20 mins.

Cover the loaves with wax paper and let rest.

BAKING
325°
1½ hours

Preheat oven to 325°. Bake loaves in the oven. When tapping the bottom crust yields a hard hollow sound, they are done.

FINAL STEP

Remove bread from the oven. The grains will be very much in evidence when the loaves are sliced. Eat warm with butter and/or cheese.

BUTTERMILK WHOLE WHEAT BREAD

[ONE LARGE OR TWO MEDIUM LOAVES]

The time-saving steps in this whole wheat loaf are less important than the even texture of the bread. There is only one rising of the dough, and that is in the pans. The liquid is warm buttermilk, and the leavening agents—there are two of them, yeast and baking powder—interact to give the loaf a different flavor.

INGREDIENTS

2 packages dry yeast
¾ cup warm water (105°–115°)
1¼ cups buttermilk, room temperature
1½ cups all-purpose flour, approximately
3 cups whole wheat flour
¼ cup shortening, room temperature
2 tablespoons brown sugar or molasses
2 teaspoons baking powder
2 teaspoons salt

BAKING PANS

One large (9 x 5) or two medium (8½ x 4½) loaf pans, greased or Teflon, metal or glass. If the latter, reduce oven heat 25°.

PREPARATION
15 mins.

In a large mixing bowl sprinkle the yeast over water and stir briefly and briskly to speed the action of the yeast granules. Let stand for 3 minutes while warming the buttermilk (if brought chilled from the refrigerator).

When warm, pour the buttermilk, flour, 1 cup whole wheat, shortening, brown sugar or molasses, baking powder and salt into the yeast mixture. Blend at low speed until the flour and dry ingredients are absorbed. Scrape down the bowl. Increase speed to medium fast for 2 minutes. Stop mixer. With a wooden spoon stir in the remaining whole wheat flour, ½ cup at a time, and, when it becomes thick, work with the fingers.

Allow the whole wheat time to fully absorb the liquid before adding more flour or deciding there is enough. This should take about 4 minutes.

The dough will be slightly sticky and soft. You may add an additional ¼ cup of white flour to help control the stickiness.

KNEADING
8 mins.

Sprinkle flour on the work surface—counter top or bread board—and turn out the soft dough. In the early stages of kneading a metal spatula or a wide knife blade will help keep the counter scraped clean. Dust with flour each time.

Knead with a strong push-turn-fold action, occasionally lifting the dough above the board and banging it down hard. Knead for about 8 minutes (or 5 minutes under the dough hook).

SHAPING
10 mins.

Divide the dough, if for two loaves, and allow the pieces to rest 5 minutes before rolling into a rectangle (the short side as wide as the pan). Roll the rectangle, jelly-roll-like, and seal the seam and ends. Place in the prepared pan and brush lightly with butter.

RISING
50 mins.

Cover with wax paper and put in a warm place (80°–85°) until the dough has risen 1 to 2 inches above the edge of the pan.

BAKING
425°
30–35 mins.

Preheat oven to 425°. Bake the loaf or loaves in the oven until they are golden brown and loose in the pans. Cover with foil or brown paper if the crusts brown too rapidly. When thumping the bottom crust yields a hard hollow sound, they are done.

FINAL STEP

Remove bread from the oven. Place on wire racks to cool before serving.

MAPLE SYRUP GRAHAM BREAD

[TWO LOAVES]

Maple syrup—the golden liquid boiled down from the clear sap of the maple tree—gives this loaf a golden color, taste and fragrance. More than a cup of maple syrup is blended with buttermilk and sour cream, and mixed with two flours, white and whole wheat or graham. It is uncommonly good simply sliced and served with sweet butter.

INGREDIENTS

2 cups all-purpose flour
2 teaspoons *each* baking powder and baking soda
1 teaspoon salt
2 cups whole wheat or graham flour
2 eggs, room temperature

1½ cups of buttermilk, room temperature
½ cup sour cream, room temperature
1⅓ cups maple syrup

BAKING PANS — Two medium (8½ x 4½) loaf pans, greased or Teflon, glass or metal. If glass, reduce oven heat 25°. Because the maple syrup caramelizes and sticks to the sides of the pans, they should first be greased, lined with wax paper and greased again.

PREPARATION
15 mins. — In a large mixing bowl blend together flour, baking powder, baking soda, and salt. Measure and stir in whole wheat or graham flour.

In a small bowl beat eggs thoroughly and blend in the buttermilk, sour cream and maple syrup. Pour this mixture into the dry ingredients and stir well.

FORMING
5 mins. — Pour the batter, which will be quite thin, into the prepared loaf pans.

BAKING
325°
1 hour — Preheat oven to 325°. Place the pans in the oven and bake until the loaves test done. A wooden toothpick or metal skewer inserted into the center of a loaf will come out dry and clean if the loaf is done.

FINAL STEP — Remove bread from the oven. Allow the loaves to cool on a metal rack before slicing.

WHOLE WHEAT BANANA BREAD

[TWO LOAVES]

This light, cake-like loaf has a pronounced banana-nut flavor that dominates the more subtle whole wheat I use to enrich the bread. It bakes for more than one hour in a moderately slow oven with delicious results.

INGREDIENTS
½ cup butter or margarine
1 cup sugar
2 eggs, room temperature and slightly beaten
3 medium bananas (1 cup mashed)
1 cup all-purpose flour
½ teaspoon salt
1 teaspoon baking soda
1 cup whole wheat flour
½ cup chopped walnuts

BAKING PANS — One large (9 x 5) loaf pan and two small (7½ x 3½) pans, greased or Teflon. If glass pans are used, reduce heat 25°.

PREPARATION
20 mins. — In a saucepan, melt butter and blend in sugar. Remove from heat and mix in eggs and banana, blending until smooth. Stir in the white flour, salt, baking soda, and whole wheat flour. Stir in the nuts.

SHAPING
10 mins. — Prepare the pans by oiling lightly, lining the bottom and the long sides with a length of wax paper which is oiled again after it is in place. (This is an almost foolproof way to get quick bread out of a pan.)

Pour the batter into the pans.

BAKING
325°
75 mins. — Preheat oven to 325°. Place the pans in a moderately slow oven until the loaves test done when pierced with a wooden toothpick or metal skewer. If it comes out clean and dry the bread is done.

FINAL STEP — Remove bread from oven. Turn the pans on their sides and gently pull the wax paper to bring the loaves onto the cooling rack.

Cool to serve. It is best when it has aged for a half a day or so. It can be frozen, and keeps well tightly wrapped in foil or plastic.

ROYAL HIBERNIAN BROWN LOAF

[TWO ROUND LOAVES]

An uncommonly rich version of the Irish national loaf—brown soda bread. The Royal Hibernian Hotel in Dublin, from whence this recipe came, serves the bread warm and thin-sliced. Its richness comes from generous portions of butter and eggs. It is a striking loaf when it comes from the oven—unfolded like a giant blossom along cuts across the top.

INGREDIENTS
- 5 cups whole wheat flour
- 2½ cups all-purpose or bread flour, approximately
- ⅓ cup sugar
- 2 teaspoons baking soda
- 1 teaspoon salt
- 1 cup butter (warmed a bit)
- 2 eggs, room temperature, lightly beaten
- 2¼ cups buttermilk or sour milk

BAKING SHEETS

Two baking sheets, greased or Teflon.

PREPARATION
15 mins.

In a large bowl mix together all of the dry ingredients—the two flours, sugar, baking soda and salt. With fingers work in the butter until it is absorbed by the flour, and the mixture resembles tiny, soft bread crumbs. Make a well in the center of the mixture. In a separate bowl lightly beat the eggs and stir in the milk. Gradually pour the egg-milk mixture into the well, mixing first with a spoon and then by hand until it forms a stiff dough. If the dough should crumble, however, add one or more tablespoons buttermilk.

KNEADING
3 mins.

Turn the dough out on a floured surface (a Formica counter is excellent), dust the hands in flour and knead the dough lightly. The butter in the dough will make it easy to work without sticking to the counter or the hands. Sprinkle with a bit more flour if it does stick.

SHAPING
3 mins.

With a knife cut the dough into two pieces and shape into plump round balls. Pat down the tops slightly, and with a knife or razor blade cut a ½-inch-deep cross on the tops.

BAKING
400°
40–50 mins.

Preheat oven to 400° (hot). Place the loaves on two baking sheets, and bake until they have browned and have opened dramatically along the cuts. Turn one over and tap the bottom crust. A hard hollow sound means the bread is baked.

FINAL STEP

Remove bread from the oven and place onto wire racks to cool. Serve thinly sliced. It can be frozen and reheated later, of course.

WHOLE WHEAT SPICE BREAD

[ONE LOAF]

Three spices—cinnamon, nutmeg, and allspice—blend to give a delicate aroma and taste to this part-white and part-whole-wheat loaf. An unusually good quick bread, it is solid, moist—and a dark brown color because of the whole wheat and spices. Chopped walnuts are mixed throughout the bread. It is a versatile loaf that can be served warm (especially aromatic) for breakfast, or as a luncheon or buffet bread.

INGREDIENTS

1 cup all-purpose flour
2 teaspoons baking soda
¼ teaspoon *each* salt, nutmeg, and allspice
½ teaspoon cinnamon
½ cup whole wheat flour
¼ cup (½ stick) butter or other shortening
¾ cup sugar
2 eggs, room temperature
⅔ cup milk
½ teaspoon vanilla
½ cup chopped walnuts

BAKING PAN

One medium (8½ x 4½) loaf pan, greased or Teflon, metal or glass. If the latter, reduce oven heat 25°. This loaf has a tendency to stick in the pan. Line the bottom (and the sides, if you wish) with a piece of wax paper which is coated lightly with oil or butter.

PREPARATION
15 mins.

In a bowl sift or stir together the flour, baking soda, salt, nutmeg, allspice, and cinnamon. Measure in the whole wheat. In a separate bowl cream the butter and sugar. Break in one egg at a time, beating each well.

Alternately, pour and stir the milk and the dry ingredients into the bowl with the egg mixture. Add vanilla. Beat until the mixture is smooth, and add walnuts.

FORMING
3 mins.

Pour batter into pan. Push the batter into the corners and leave a slight depression down the center to offset oven expansion. Set aside for 5 minutes while the oven preheats to 350°.

BAKING
350°
1 hour

Place pan in oven and bake until the crust is a deep brown. Test with a wooden toothpick inserted into the center of the loaf. If it comes out clean and dry the bread is baked. If batter clings to the pick, return the loaf to the oven for an additional 10 minutes. Test again.

FINAL STEP

Remove bread from the oven. (This loaf is fragile when first taken from the oven.) Leave in the pan for 5 or 10 minutes, then turn the pan on its side and gently pull out the loaf by tugging on the wax paper or coaxing it with a metal spatula.

WHOLE WHEAT ORANGE BREAD

[ONE LARGE OR TWO SMALL LOAVES]

To begin, the zest of 3 oranges is boiled till soft, mixed with a cup of honey and cooked to a syrup. The bread is *all* whole wheat, with ½ cup of nuts to enhance the wheaty flavor. The loaf, however, belongs to the orange rind which gives it both a unique flavor and color.

INGREDIENTS

The zest (peel) of 3 medium oranges, sliced in strips
1½ cups water
1 cup honey
2¾ cups whole wheat flour
4 teaspoons baking powder
1 teaspoon salt
1 cup cold milk
The orange-honey syrup
½ cup chopped nuts, dredged in flour

BAKING PANS

One medium (8½ x 4½) loaf pan or two small (7½ x 3½) loaf pans, greased or Teflon, metal or glass. If the latter, reduce oven heat 25°. Line the pans with wax paper to keep the loaves from sticking. Be sure to butter over the paper.

PREPARATION
45 mins.

Strip the zest (the peel minus the white inner skin) from 3 medium oranges with a French *zesteur* or an ordinary potato peeler. Cut the pieces into long strips and place them in a small saucepan with water. Bring to a boil and cook slowly over low heat until the peel is tender, about 30 minutes. Pour off all but ¼ cup of the remaining liquid. Add honey to the orange liquid and peel, and boil over low heat until the syrup is thick. Set aside.

20 mins.

In a mixing bowl sift or blend together with a spoon the whole wheat flour, baking powder and salt. Pour milk into the saucepan with the orange syrup, and mix. Add the liquid gradually to the dry ingredients, and beat well. Dredge the nuts with 1 tablespoon of flour, and stir this into the batter. Set aside for 10 minutes while the oven heats to 325°.

FORMING
3 mins.

Pour the batter into the prepared pans, and spread with a wooden spoon or spatula.

BAKING
325°
1 hour

Bake bread in the oven until the loaves test done when pierced in the center with a metal skewer or wooden toothpick. If it comes out clean and dry, the loaf is done.

FINAL STEP

Remove bread from the oven and turn out on a metal rack to cool before serving. The bread gets better with age. Any time during the first week it is delicious unheated, served thinly sliced.

WHEAT NUT BREAD

[TWO MEDIUM OR THREE INDIVIDUAL-SIZE LOAVES]

Honey, whole wheat, raisins and walnuts make this dark loaf equally good plain, with butter, or toasted. It is not quite as solid a loaf as 100% whole wheat, nor as dark, but the good wheat flavor is there nevertheless. It has a slightly sweet taste because of the honey.

INGREDIENTS

3 cups whole wheat or graham flour
2 cups warm water (105°–115°)
2 packages dry yeast
1 pinch of sugar
¼ cup honey
1 tablespoon salt
2½ to 3 cups all-purpose flour
¼ cup non-fat dry milk
3 tablespoons soft shortening
½ cup walnuts, broken
½ cup seedless raisins
Glaze: A brush of soft shortening for a tender crust

BAKING PANS

Two medium (8½ x 4½) or 3 small (7½ x 3½) bread pans, lightly greased or Teflon. If glass pans are used, reduce oven heat 25°.

PREPARATION
20 mins.

In a large bowl measure the whole wheat flour and make a well in the center. Pour water in the well, and sprinkle yeast on top. Stir yeast into the water with a metal whisk or fork to quicken the action. Add sugar. Let stand for 3 minutes.

With a large wooden spoon pull the flour into the yeast mixture—and stir until all of the flour is wet. Add the honey, salt, 1 cup all-purpose flour, and non-fat dry milk. Stir in the shortening, nuts, and raisins. Beat until blended and smooth—about 100 strokes. Add all-purpose flour, a little at a time, until the dough is stiff and cleans the sides of the bowl. It is now ready for kneading.

KNEADING
5 mins.

Turn the dough out on a lightly floured board or counter top, and knead—about 75 push-turn-fold strokes. The dough will be stiff, bouncy but not as elastic as white dough. It may be slightly tacky but not sticky. Keep flour on the fingers.

FIRST RISING
1 hour

Place the ball of dough in the large bowl (which has been washed and greased), cover tightly with plastic wrap, and put in a warm place (80°–85°) until double in bulk. You can test if it has risen by poking a finger in it; the dent will remain.

SHAPING
5 mins.

Punch down the dough and knead for 30 seconds to press out the bubbles. With a sharp knife, divide the dough. Form each into a ball and let rest under a towel for 3 to 4 minutes. Shape by pressing the ball of dough into a flat oval, roughly the length of the baking pan. Fold the oval in half, pinch the seam tightly to seal, tuck under the ends, and place in the pan, seam down. Repeat with the others.

SECOND RISING
45 mins.

Place the pans in the warm place, cover with wax paper and leave until the center of the dough has risen ½ inch above the level of the edge of the pan. This will be about 45 minutes.

BAKING
375°
40 mins.

Preheat oven to 375°. Bake in the oven. When the loaves are dark brown and tapping the bottom crust yields a hard and hollow sound, they are done. Midway in the bake period and again near the end of it, shift the pans so the loaves are exposed equally to temperature variations in the oven.

FINAL STEP

Remove bread from the oven and place the loaves on the wire cooling rack. Brush the tops with butter or margarine for tender crust. This loaf is good toasted, and keeps well in the deep freeze.

WHOLE WHEAT HERB BREAD

[TWO LOAVES]

The flavor and aroma of sage and nutmeg blend with that of crushed caraway seeds to give personality to this lightly textured loaf made with whole wheat and white flours. It can be made with butter or margarine but I use vegetable oil which seems to further enhance the honest wheaty flavor. It is an excellent sandwich bread, and toasts beautifully.

INGREDIENTS

2 cups whole wheat flour
2 packages dry yeast
⅓ cup non-fat dry milk
3 tablespoons sugar
2 teaspoons salt
2 teaspoons caraway seed, crushed
½ teaspoon *each* nutmeg and sage
1½ cups hot water (120°–130°)
2 tablespoons vegetable oil, or other shortening, room temperature
1 egg, room temperature
2 to 2½ cups all-purpose or bread flour, approximately

BAKING PANS

Two medium (8½ x 4½) loaf pans, greased or Teflon, glass or metal. If glass, reduce baking temperature 25°.

PREPARATION
20 mins.

In a large mixing bowl blend with the electric mixer—the whole wheat flour, yeast, milk, sugar, salt, caraway seed, nutmeg and sage. Pour in the hot water and beat at medium speed for 1 minute (or 50 strong strokes with a large wooden spoon). Add oil and egg. Beat for another 1½ minutes (or about 75 spoon strokes).

Stir in the all-purpose flour, a half cup at a time, first with the spoon and then by hand. The dough will be a rough, shaggy mass that will clean the sides of the bowl. If the dough is slack and the moisture breaks through, add a small amount of additional flour.

KNEADING
6 mins.

Turn out the ball of dough onto a floured surface—a bread board or counter top. Knead it, adding a little more flour to control the stickiness, if needed, until the dough is smooth. Small bubbles can be seen under the skin of the dough. (If you use the dough hook attachment on a heavy mixer such as a Kitchen Aid it will take about 4 minutes.)

FIRST RISING
1 hour

Place the dough in the mixing bowl and pat with buttered or greased fingers to keep the surface from crusting. Cover the bowl tightly with plastic wrap and move to a warm place (80°–85°) until the dough has risen to about twice its original size (judged as it expands up the sides of the bowl). You can test if it has risen by poking a finger in it; the dent will remain.

SHAPING
10 mins.

Turn out again on the floured surface and cut the dough in two pieces with a large sharp knife. Each piece can be formed into loaves either by simply pressing and rolling by hand into a shape that fits into the loaf pan, or rolling (with a rolling pin) a rectangle of dough which is folded, the seam pinched shut, the ends tucked in and placed in the pan. Either will produce a handsome loaf.

SECOND RISING
40 mins.

Cover the pans loosely with wax paper and return to the warm place until the loaves have doubled in bulk—or until the center of the dough is level with the top of the pan.

BAKING
375°
45 mins.

Preheat oven to 375°. Bake the loaves in the oven until they test done. Tap the bottom crust with a forefinger. A hard hollow sound means the bread is baked. If not, return to the oven for 10 minutes, and without pans if you wish a deep brown overall crust. Midway in the bake period shift the pans so the loaves are exposed equally to temperature variations in the oven.

FINAL STEP

Remove bread from the oven and immediately turn out the loaves onto wire racks to cool completely before slicing. These loaves freeze well.

SPROUTED WHEAT BREAD

[TWO BIG LOAVES]

A little gardening effort is called for to first produce a cup of whole wheat sprouts in a period of 3 or 4 days. When a sprout has grown the length of the seed, proceed with the bread baking. The liquid called for in the recipe is the water drained from the sprouting wheat.

It is a delicious deep-crusted loaf that has the rich wheaty flavor to be found only in an all-wheat loaf.

INGREDIENTS

¼ cup wheat seeds or berries
2 cups warm water (80°–90°)
2 packages dry yeast
2 cups liquid from wheat soaking, warm (100°)
¼ cup *each* brewer's yeast and honey
3 tablespoons oil
5 cups whole wheat flour, approximately
1 tablespoon salt

BAKING PANS

Two large loaf pans (9 x 5), greased or Teflon, glass or metal. If glass, reduce oven heat 25°.

PREPARATION
Sprouting
3–4 days

Three or four days beforehand, place ¼ cup of whole wheat seeds or berries in a quart jar. Cover mouth with cheesecloth and fasten securely with a rubber band or string. Don't remove during the growing period—about 3 or 4 days. Soak in water.

Turn the jar on its side. Keep the berries moist, warm and dark in a kitchen closet. Twice a day rinse the berries in tepid water (80°–85°) poured through the cheesecloth; drain and reserve the water for a total of 2 cups needed in the recipe.

When the sprouts are as long as the seed, continue with the bread making.

(The first time I made this bread I inadvertently used *beef* stock as the liquid ingredient rather than the water saved from soaking the wheat berries. The result was an exceptional loaf of bread. I heartily recommend it.)

15 mins.

On bake day, sprinkle the yeast over ½ cup of the reserved stock poured into a large mixing bowl. Stir briskly with a fork or whisk. Put aside for 3 or 4 minutes until the yeast begins to work and bubble.

Stir in the balance of the stock, brewer's yeast, honey and oil. Blend well. Measure in 3 cups of whole wheat flour and the salt. Beat vigorously for 3 minutes until the batter is smooth.

FIRST RISING
1 hour

Cover with plastic wrap and put in a warm place (80°–85°) to rise.

KNEADING
8 mins.

Stir down. Add the sprouts and about 1 cup of whole wheat flour. Turn onto the work surface and surround the dough with about 1 cup of whole wheat flour. As you work the dough, brush a bit of the flour onto the ball of dough and over the hands to help control the stickiness. Use the side of a spatula or a wide putty knife to scrape the film off the work surface as it accumulates. Use the spatula or putty knife to turn over the dough as you knead, thus lessening the opportunity it has to stick to the hands. Soon, however, it will become elastic and smooth, and not stick.

SECOND RISING
50 mins.

Return the dough to the bowl, pat with greased fingers and cover the bowl tightly with plastic wrap. Put in the warm place until the dough has doubled in size.

SHAPING
12 mins.

Punch down the dough and knead for 30 seconds to press out the bubbles. Divide the dough evenly into two pieces. Shape into balls and let rest on the counter top for 3 or 4 minutes. Form the loaf by pressing each ball of dough into a flat oval, roughly the length of the baking pan. Fold the oval in half, pinch the seam tightly to seal, tuck under the ends, and place in the pan, seam down. Repeat with the second loaf.

THIRD RISING
45 mins.

Place the pans in the warm place, cover with wax paper and leave until the center of the dough has risen slightly above the level of the edge of the pan.

BAKING
375°
25 mins.
300°
35 mins.

Preheat oven to 375°. Bake in the moderately hot oven for 25 minutes, reduce heat to 300° and continue baking for an additional 35 minutes. When the loaves are golden brown and tapping the bottom crust yields a hard and hollow sound, the bread is done. If not, return to the oven for an additional 10 minutes. Midway in the bake period and again near the end of it, shift the pans so the loaves are exposed equally to temperature variations in the oven.

FINAL STEP

Remove bread from the oven, turn loaves from pans and place on a metal rack to cool before serving. This bread makes delicious toast. The loaf freezes well, and will keep thus for several months.

MALT BREAD

[TWO SMALL LOAVES]

A tidy brown whole wheat loaf, with raisins, this bread is flavored with 2 tablespoons each of malt and molasses which gives it a rich dark taste that makes a delicious slice. I adapted this from a recipe by the English home bakers George and Cecilia Scurfield. Toasts beautifully.

INGREDIENTS

1 cup all-purpose flour, approximately
4 cups whole wheat flour
2 teaspoons salt
1 package dry yeast
2 tablespoons butter, room temperature
2 tablespoons molasses
2 tablespoons malt syrup
1½ cups hot tap water (120°–130°)
½ cup raisins
Glaze: 1 tablespoon of milk to brush

BAKING PANS

Two small (7½ x 3½) baking pans, greased or Teflon. If glass, reduce oven heat 25°.

PREPARATION
18 mins.

In a large mixing bowl measure ½ cup all-purpose flour, 2 cups of whole wheat, salt, yeast, butter, molasses, malt, and water. Stir well to blend.

Beat for 2 minutes in the electric mixer at medium-high speed, or for an equal length of time with a large wooden spoon.

Stop the mixer. Add the remainder of the whole wheat flour and, finally, the all-purpose flour, a half cup at a time, first with the spoon and then by hand. The dough will be a rough, shaggy mass that will clean the sides of the bowl. If the dough continues slack, add a small measure of additional white flour.

KNEADING
8 mins.

Turn the dough onto a lightly floured work surface—counter top or bread board—and knead with the rhythmic 1-2-3 motion of push-turn-fold. The dough will become smooth and elastic, and bubbles will rise under the surface of the dough. Sprinkle more flour on the dough if stickiness persists. Break the kneading rhythm occasionally by throwing the dough down hard against the counter top.

FIRST RISING
1 hour

Place the dough in the clean mixing bowl and pat with buttered or greased fingers to keep the surface from crusting. Cover the bowl tightly with plastic wrap and move to a warm place (80°–85°) until the dough has risen to about twice its original size. You can test if it has risen by poking a finger in it; the dent will remain.

SHAPING
10 mins.

Punch down the dough and knead for 30 seconds to press out the bubbles. Divide the dough into two pieces with a sharp knife. Shape into balls, and let rest under a towel for 3 or 4 minutes. Form a loaf by pressing a ball of dough into a flat oval, roughly the length of the baking pan. Fold the oval in half, pinch the seam tightly to seal, tuck under the ends, and place in the pan, seam down. Repeat with the second loaf.

SECOND RISING
45 mins.

Place the pans in the warm place, cover with wax paper and leave until the center of the dough has risen about 1 inch above the level of the edge of the pan.

BAKING
350°
45 mins.

Preheat oven to 350°. Bake loaves in the oven. When the loaves are a lovely brown and tapping the bottom crust yields a hard and hollow sound, they are done. If not, return to the oven for an additional 10 minutes. If the loaves seem to be browning too quickly, cover with a length of foil or a piece of brown sack paper. Midway in the bake period and again near the end shift the pans so the loaves are exposed equally to temperature variations in the oven.

FINAL STEP

Remove bread from the oven and turn the loaves from the pans onto wire rack to cool. Brush them with water. Malt bread keeps very well and will improve in flavor after aging 2 or 3 days.

MOLASSES WHEAT BREAD

[TWO LOAVES]

A velvety soft dough to knead, this bread gets its dark color from molasses. I use blackstrap unsulphured molasses which has more bite to it but either the light or dark Brer Rabbit product gives a nice flavor to the bread. It is a delicious whole wheat loaf, especially toasted. Before dropping it into the loaf pan, twist the dough 2 or 3 times. Some home bakers believe that twisting makes bread more tender. For certain, it gives the loaf an unusual shape.

INGREDIENTS

2 cups hot tap water (120°–130°)
¼ cup molasses
½ cup non-fat dry milk
1 tablespoon salt
2½ cups whole wheat flour
2½ cups all-purpose flour, approximately
2 packages dry yeast
3 tablespoons shortening, room temperature

BAKING PANS

Two medium (8½ x 4½) loaf pans, greased or Teflon. If glass, reduce oven heat 25°.

PREPARATION
15 mins.

In a mixing bowl pour water, molasses, milk, salt and 1 cup *each* whole wheat flour and all-purpose flour. Stir to moisten thoroughly. Sprinkle on the yeast and add shortening.

With an electric mixer beat for 1 minute at medium speed or 75 strokes with a wooden spoon. Add the balance of the whole wheat flour (1½ cups). Beat at high speed for 3 minutes or 150 strong strokes with the spoon. Stop the mixer. Gradually work in the all-purpose flour, first with a spoon and then by hand, until a rough and somewhat shaggy mass is formed.

KNEADING
6 mins.

Turn the dough onto a liberally floured work surface—counter top or bread board—and knead with a strong push-turn-fold motion. If the dough sticks to the work surface or to the fingers, dust lightly with more flour. Knead in this fashion for 6 minutes (or 4 minutes with a dough hook).

FIRST RISING
1 hour

Shape the dough into a ball and return it to the bowl. Pat the dough with greased or buttered fingers to keep it from drying out, and cover the bowl tightly with plastic wrap. Put it in the warm place (80°–85°) until dough has expanded to about twice its original size. (Judge by how it creeps up the sides of the bowl.) You can test if it has risen by poking a finger in it; the dent will remain.

SHAPING
18 mins.

Punch down the dough with the fingers and knead for 30 seconds to press out the bubbles that formed during the rising. Divide into two pieces. Roll out under the palms so that each piece is about half again as long as the pan. Let the rolls rest for about 3 minutes (or they will resist twisting!). Twist each piece 2 or 3 times and place in the pan.

SECOND RISING
45 mins.

Place the pans in the warm place, cover with wax paper and leave until the center of the dough has risen ½ to 1 inch above the edge of the pans. Meanwhile, preheat the oven to 375°.

BAKING
375°
35–45 mins.

Place pans in the oven. When the loaves are dark brown and tapping the bottom crust yields a hard hollow sound, they are done. If the crust is soft and gives off a dull thud, return the bread to the oven—without the pans—for an additional 10 minutes.

FINAL STEP

Remove bread from the oven and turn the hot bread onto a wire rack to cool before slicing.

INSTANT BLEND WHOLE WHEAT BREAD

[TWO LOAVES]

An easy loaf to make, this bread begins by scattering the yeast over half the flour before the hot tap water is measured in. The yeast comes alive fast to develop a plump, open-textured loaf of bread. It is sweetened with honey which helps make it good for toasting.

INGREDIENTS

3 cups all-purpose or bread flour, approximately
2 packages dry yeast
⅓ cup non-fat dry milk
1½ cups hot tap water (120°–130°)
2 tablespoons shortening, room temperature
2 tablespoons honey
2 teaspoons salt
1 egg, room temperature
1½ cups whole wheat flour

BAKING PANS

Two medium (8½ x 4½) loaf pans, greased or Teflon. If glass, reduce oven heat 25°.

PREPARATION
15 mins.

Measure 2 cups of all-purpose or bread flour into a large mixer bowl. Sprinkle yeast and milk over flour; stir to blend. Pour in the water. Stir briefly and add shortening, honey, salt, and egg.

Beat at low speed in electric mixer for 30 seconds, scraping the bowl constantly. Beat 3 minutes at high speed. Stop the mixer and stir in the whole wheat flour. Add the balance of the all-purpose or bread flour, a half cup at a time, first with a spoon and then by hand. The dough will be a rough, shaggy mass, somewhat sticky because of the whole wheat flour. Sprinkle on additional all-purpose flour to control the stickiness.

KNEADING
10 mins.

Turn the dough onto a lightly floured work surface—counter top or bread board—and knead with the rhythmic 1-2-3 motion of push-turn-fold. Sprinkle more flour on the dough and work surface if the dough persists in sticking. Scrape from the work surface with a metal spatula, and dust again. The dough will become smooth and elastic. Occasionally break the kneading rhythm by throwing the dough down hard against the counter top.

RESTING
20 mins.

Cover the dough with a cloth or wax paper and let rest.

SHAPING
10 mins.

Punch down the dough and knead for 30 seconds to press out the bubbles. With a sharp knife, divide the dough into two pieces. Shape into balls, and let rest under the cloth for 3 to 4 minutes to relax the dough. Form the loaf by pressing each ball into a flat oval, roughly the length of the baking pan. Fold the oval in half, pinch the seam tightly to seal, tuck under the ends, and place in the pan, seam down. Repeat with the second loaf.

RISING
30–45 mins.

Place pans in a warm place (80°–85°), cover with wax paper and leave until the center of the dough is about level with the edge of the pan, or doubled in size. Meanwhile preheat the oven to 375°.

BAKING
375°
35–45 mins.

Bake loaves in the oven. When the loaves are dark brown and tapping the bottom crust yields a hard and hollow sound, they are done. If not, return to the oven for an additional 10 minutes. Midway in the bake period and again near the end, shift the pans so the loaves are exposed equally to temperature variations in the oven.

FINAL STEP

Remove bread from the oven, turn the loaves from the pans and place on a metal rack to cool. Brush with butter for soft crusts.

WHEAT-GERM BREAD

[TWO LOAVES]

A dark brown loaf, moist and, in taste, honest to its whole wheat and wheat-germ antecedents. Molasses and butter enhance the good flavor. It makes beautiful toast, and will keep for a long time in the freezer tightly wrapped in foil or plastic.

INGREDIENTS

2 packages dry yeast
¼ cup warm water (105°–115°)
1½ cups hot tap water (120°–130°)
3 teaspoons sugar
2½ teaspoons salt
⅓ cup butter or margarine, room temperature
⅓ cup molasses
1 cup wheat germ
¾ cup milk, heated
4 cups whole wheat flour
1 to 2 cups all-purpose or bread flour, approximately

BAKING PANS

Two medium (8½ x 4½) baking tins, greased or Teflon. If glass, reduce oven heat 25°.

PREPARATION
20 mins.

In a large bowl dissolve the yeast in the warm water. Stir briefly and let stand for about 3 minutes.

In a saucepan mix the hot water, sugar, salt, butter and molasses. The water should be sufficient to warm the mixture and melt the butter. If not, place it over low heat until the butter is softened. Allow the mixture to cool to lukewarm. Meanwhile, measure wheat germ into a small bowl and pour milk over it. Let it stand until the liquid has been absorbed by the wheat germ, and is only warm to the touch.

Stir molasses mixture and wheat-germ mixture together in the large bowl that contains the yeast. Stir mixture well and add 2 cups of whole wheat flour and 1 cup all-purpose flour; stir together with a wooden spoon for 150 strong strokes. Stir in the remaining whole wheat flour and sufficient all-purpose flour to form a rough ball of dough. If the ball is sticky, add ½ cup or more all-purpose flour.

KNEADING
6 mins.

Turn the dough out on a floured work surface—counter top or bread board—and with a strong push-turn motion knead the dough until it is smooth and elastic.

FIRST RISING
1½ hours

Place dough in a greased bowl, cover tightly with plastic wrap and move to a warm place (80°–85°) until the dough has doubled in bulk. You can test if it has risen by poking a finger in it; the dent will remain.

SHAPING
10 mins.

Punch down the dough, work it briefly under your hands and divide into two equal portions. Shape these into loaves and place in the pans.

SECOND RISING
1¼ hours

Cover the pans with wax paper and return to the warm place until the dough has risen to 1 inch above the edge of the pan or doubled in bulk.

BAKING
400°
50 mins.

Preheat oven to 400°. Place the loaves in the oven. When tapping the bottom crust yields a hard and hollow sound, they are done.

FINAL STEP

Remove bread from the oven and turn the loaves out on metal racks to cool.

HONEY WHEAT-GERM BREAD

[TWO LOAVES]

While this qualifies fully as a natural food loaf—unbleached flour, wheat germ, honey, and whole wheat—this also is for the baker seeking the most nourishment in a loaf, and for the diner who wants a slice of good dark bread. This loaf does all of these things. It is fine served warm from the oven, toasted or reheated after a long period in the deep freeze.

INGREDIENTS

1½ to 2 cups unbleached flour, approximately
½ cup non-fat dry milk
3 tablespoons wheat germ
2 teaspoons salt
2 packages dry yeast
2 cups hot tap water (120°–130°)
¼ cup vegetable oil
¼ cup honey
3 cups whole wheat flour

BAKING PANS

Two medium (8½ x 4½) loaf pans, greased or Teflon. If glass, reduce oven heat 25°.

PREPARATION
15 mins.

In a large mixer bowl measure 1 cup unbleached flour and stir in milk, wheat germ, salt, yeast and water. Add vegetable oil, honey and 2 cups whole wheat flour.

Beat in the electric mixer at medium-high speed for 3 minutes.

Stop the mixer. Stir in the additional 1 cup of whole wheat flour and the unbleached flour; ½ cup at a time, first with a spoon and then by hand. The dough will be rather heavy because of the dark flour but it will clean the sides of the bowl nevertheless.

KNEADING
8 mins.

Turn the dough onto a lightly floured work surface—counter top or bread board—and knead with the rhythmic 1-2-3 motion of push-turn-fold. The dough will become smooth and elastic in about 4 or 5 minutes. If the dough continues sticky, sprinkle on more flour. Break the kneading rhythm occasionally by throwing the dough down hard against the counter top.

FIRST RISING
1 hour

Place the dough back in the mixing bowl and pat with buttered or greased fingertips to keep the surface from crusting. Cover the bowl tightly with plastic wrap and move to a warm place (80°–85°) until the dough has risen to about double its original size. You can test if it has risen by poking a finger in it; the dent will remain.

SHAPING
15 mins.

Punch down dough and knead for 30 seconds to press out the bubbles. With a sharp knife divide the dough into two equal pieces. Shape into balls, and let them rest under a towel for 3 to 4 minutes. Form a loaf by pressing a ball into a flat oval, roughly the length of the baking pan. Fold the oval in half, pinch the seam tightly to seal, tuck under the ends, and place in the pan, seam down. Repeat with the second loaf.

SECOND RISING
50 mins.

Place the pans in the warm place, cover with wax paper and leave until the center of the dough has risen level with the edge of the pan. Meanwhile, preheat the oven to 350°.

BAKING
350°
50–60 mins.

Brush the tops with oil and place in the oven. When tapping the bottom crust yields a hard and hollow sound, they are done. If not, return to the oven. If you wish a deep over-all crust, remove both loaves from the pans the final 10 minutes of baking. Midway in the bake period shift the pans so the loaves are exposed equally to temperature variations in the oven.

FINAL STEP

Remove bread from the oven. Place the loaves on a metal rack to cool before serving. This loaf freezes well and can be kept for months in the freezer.

HONEY LEMON WHOLE WHEAT BREAD

[TWO LOAVES]

This is a delicious refrigerated loaf of whole wheat, rising in the refrigerator from 2 to 24 hours before it is baked. A dough taken out of the cold and slipped into the oven carries with it a moist coating that gives a different color and texture to the finished crust. This loaf, for example, has a freckled appearance quite apart from the brown flecks of whole wheat against the white flour.

The recipe calls for a tablespoon of grated lemon peel which, with the honey, imparts a wonderful aroma and taste. However, rather than grate the lemon, I sometimes dice the peel into tiny bits to make a more interesting bite.

INGREDIENTS

3 cups of all-purpose flour
2 packages dry yeast
1 tablespoon salt
¼ cup honey
3 tablespoons shortening, room temperature
1 tablespoon grated or diced lemon peel
2¼ cups hot tap water (120°–130°)
2 to 3 cups whole wheat flour, approximately

BAKING PANS

Two large (9 x 5) baking tins, greased or Teflon. If glass, reduce oven heat 25°.

PREPARATION
15 mins.

In a large mixer bowl combine all-purpose flour, yeast and salt. Stir. Add honey, shortening and lemon peel. Pour in the water.

Beat with an electric mixer at medium speed for 2 minutes. Scrape bowl occasionally. Add 1 cup of whole wheat flour. Beat at high speed for 1 minute. The batter will be thick and elastic, and will pull away from the bowl in strands.

Stop the mixer. Stir in 1 or 2 cups of whole wheat flour, depending on the moistness of the developing dough. Allow to stand for 2 minutes to be fully absorbed. The dough should be elastic, soft, and, at this stage, not overly sticky. If the dough continues slack and moist, add small amounts of additional all-purpose flour.

KNEADING
8 mins.

Turn the dough onto a lightly floured work surface—counter top or bread board—and knead with the rhythmic 1-2-3 motion of push-turn-fold. The dough slowly will become smooth and elastic. Occasionally change the kneading rhythm by throwing the dough down hard against the counter top.

RESTING
20 mins.

Cover the dough with a towel or piece of wax paper and allow it to rest.

SHAPING
10 mins.

Knead the dough for 30 seconds to press out the bubbles. Divide into two pieces with a sharp knife. Shape into balls, and let rest under a towel for 3 to 4 minutes. Form the loaf by pressing each ball under the palms or with a rolling pin into a flat oval, roughly the length of the baking pan. Fold the oval in half, pinch the seam tightly to seal, tuck under the ends, and place in the pan, seam down. Repeat with the second loaf. Place in pans. Brush the surface of the dough with oil. Cover the pans loosely with wax paper, and then with plastic wrap.

REFRIGERATION
2–24 hours

Place in the refrigerator 2 to 24 hours. Some home bakers have found that dough refrigerated from 2 to 8 hours has the best volume.

BAKING
400°
30–40 mins.

Remove from the refrigerator when ready to bake. Uncover and let stand 10 minutes while the oven heats to 400°. Prick any surface bubbles with an oiled toothpick just before slipping the loaves into the oven.

Bake on lower oven rack. When the loaves are a golden brown and tapping the bottom crust yields a hard and hollow sound, they are done. If not, return to the oven for an additional 10 minutes. If you wish a deep brown over-all crust, remove loaves from pans the last 10 minutes of the bake period.

FINAL STEP

Remove bread from the oven, turn from pans immediately and place on metal rack. For a soft crust brush with melted margarine.

100% WHOLE WHEAT BREAD

[THREE LOAVES]

A lovely brown-flecked and plump loaf, this 100% whole wheat bread rises well above the pan level to demonstrate that this grain has almost the same gluten power as white flour. It is sweetened with honey. There is a quarter of a stick of butter in each loaf, and melted butter is brushed on the hot crust to give it a subdued glaze.

INGREDIENTS

9 to 10 cups whole wheat flour, approximately
4 teaspoons salt
2 packages dry yeast
1½ cups milk } or 3 cups hot tap water, 1 cup non-fat
1½ cups water } dry milk
½ cup honey
6 tablespoons (¾ stick) butter or margarine

BAKING PANS

Three medium (8½ x 4½) loaf pans, greased or Teflon, glass or metal. If glass, reduce oven heat 25°.

PREPARATION
15 mins.

In a large mixing bowl, thoroughly blend 3 cups of whole wheat flour, salt and yeast.

In a saucepan, over low heat, combine milk, water, honey and butter or margarine. When the liquid is warm, gradually add to dry ingredients in the bowl, and beat at medium speed in electric mixer for 2 minutes, scraping bowl once or twice. Add 1 cup of flour, or enough to make a thick batter. Beat at high speed 3 minutes. Stop the mixer and add additional flour, stirring with a spoon, and then by hand, until a soft mass is formed.

RESTING
10 mins.

Turn the soft dough onto a lightly floured work surface, cover with the inverted bowl and let rest.

KNEADING
8 mins.

Knead the dough until it is smooth and elastic, adding ¼ cup or more additional flour if the dough is moist or slack. Knead for about 8 minutes (5 minutes if using a dough hook).

FIRST RISING
50 mins.

Drop the dough into a greased bowl, cover the top tightly with plastic wrap and move to a warm (80°–85°), draft-free place until the dough has doubled in bulk.

SHAPING
10 mins.

Turn back the plastic wrap, punch down the dough and turn it out on the work surface. Divide into thirds and shape each into a loaf. This can be done by simply flattening each piece into an oval, folding in half, pinching tight the seam and placing with seam down in the baking pan.

SECOND RISING
50 mins.

Cover the pans with wax paper and let the loaves rise in the warm place until they have doubled in bulk and the centers have risen about 1 inch above the level of the edge of the pans.

BAKING
375°
40 mins.

Preheat oven to 375°. Place the pans in the oven. When the loaves are a deep brown and tapping the bottom crust yields a hard and hollow sound, they are done. If it has a dull thud, it is underdone, so return to the oven without the pan for an additional 10 minutes.

FINAL STEP

Remove bread from the oven, turn from the pans and place on a wire rack to cool. Brush with butter.

GRANARY BREAD

[TWO ROUND HEARTH LOAVES]

With a large pinwheel design cut in the top crust, this is a picture loaf. It is equally good—wheaty, moist and with a faint trace of the special sweetness of honey. It is a CoolRise© loaf—2 to 24 hours in the refrigerator which means this can be scheduled to be served warm from the oven with most of the work done the day or night before.

INGREDIENTS

3½ to 4 cups all-purpose flour, approximately
2 packages dry yeast
1 tablespoon salt
⅓ cup honey
3 tablespoons margarine or shortening, room temperature
2½ cups hot tap water (120°–130°)
2½ cups whole wheat flour
1 teaspoon oil to brush loaves

BAKING SHEET OR PANS

One baking sheet or two 9-inch round cake pans, greased or Teflon, with 1½ or 2 inch sides.

PREPARATION
15 mins.

In a large mixer bowl, measure 2½ cups all-purpose flour and stir in yeast, salt, honey and margarine. Pour in the water. Beat with electric mixer at medium speed for 2 minutes. Scrape the bowl occasionally. Add 1 cup whole wheat flour and beat at high speed for 2 minutes.

Stop mixer. Stir in the remaining whole wheat flour and 1 cup of all-purpose flour, a half cup at a time, mixing first with the spoon and then by hand. The dough will be a rough, shaggy mass that will clean the sides of the bowl. It may be sticky. If so, add small amounts of flour.

KNEADING
8 mins.

Turn the dough onto a lightly floured work surface—counter top or bread board—and knead with the rhythmic 1-2-3 motion of push-turn-fold. The dough will become smooth and elastic. Sprinkle more flour on the dough and the work surface if the dough continues slack or moist, or if it sticks to the hands. Occasionally, change the kneading rhythm by raising the dough above the table and banging it down hard against the surface. (Knead 6 minutes under the dough hook.)

RESTING
20 mins.

Cover the dough with a towel or piece of plastic wrap and let it rest on the counter top.

SHAPING
8 mins.

Punch down and knead for 30 seconds to press out the bubbles. Divide the dough in half. Shape each into a round loaf, about 8 inches in diameter. Flatten slightly.

While I think this loaf does better on a baking sheet it may be a problem to find space for it in the refrigerator. If so, use two 9-inch pans that are easier to place.

Brush dough lightly with oil.

REFRIGERATION
2–24 hours

Cover baking sheet or pans lightly with plastic wrap, allowing room for the dough to expand. Place in the refrigerator 2 to 24 hours. I find the dough does best with no more than 8 to 10 hours in the cold.

BAKING
400°
30–40 mins.

Remove the loaves from the refrigerator and set aside, uncovered, while the oven heats to 400°. About 10 minutes.

With a sharp knife or razor blade cut six graceful curves radiating from the center. Make slashes no more than ¼-inch deep. Place in the oven. When the loaves are a dark brown and tapping the bottom crust yields a hard and hollow sound, they are done. If the loaves are browning too quickly, cover with a piece of foil or brown paper. Midway in the bake period, and again near the end of it, shift the loaves so they are equally exposed to temperature variations in the oven.

FINAL STEP

Remove bread from the oven and place on a metal rack to cool.

WALNUT WHEAT BREAD

[TWO LOAVES]

The English walnuts complement and enhance the flavor of this bread made with no flour other than whole wheat. It is a large brown loaf, with nuts peeking through the crusts—top, bottom and sides. Inside, it is moist, open textured and rich with nuts. It keeps well for at least a fortnight wrapped in plastic.

The bread is fine for any meal or occasion but specially good for breakfast or brunch—sliced thinly and served with sweet butter.

INGREDIENTS

1 package dry yeast
¼ cup warm water (105°–115°)
2 cups hot tap water (120°–130°)
½ cup non-fat dry milk
2 tablespoons *each* butter (melted) and sugar
2 teaspoons salt
6 cups whole wheat or graham flour, approximately
1 cup whole walnuts

BAKING PANS

Two medium (8½ x 4½) baking tins, greased or Teflon, metal or glass. If glass, reduce the heat in the oven 25°.

PREPARATION
20 mins.

In a large mixing bowl, dissolve yeast in warm water. Stir briskly with fork or whisk to speed the action.

Stir in hot tap water, milk, butter, sugar and salt. Blend well and add 4 cups of whole wheat or graham flour. To beat in the flour, use either an electric mixer at high speed for 3 minutes—or wooden spoon for about 150 strong strokes.

Stop the machine, add 1 more cup of flour and work it into the mass by spoon and hand.

At this point let the dough rest for 3 minutes while the whole wheat flour absorbs the moisture. It is important to know before the kneading begins whether additional flour is needed or if the balance of flour to moisture is just right. If, after the rest period, the dough is wet and sticky, add ¼ cup or more flour.

KNEADING
8 mins.

Sprinkle the work surface lightly with flour and turn the dough onto it. The dough should be soft, not stiff. (Knead 6 minutes with the dough hook.) The dough will be light and satiny, and feel as alive as a good white dough.

FIRST RISING
1 hour

Place the dough in the bowl, cover tightly with plastic wrap and put in a warm place until it has doubled in bulk. You can test if it has risen by poking a finger in it; the dent will remain.

SHAPING
15 mins.

Turn back the plastic wrap, punch down the dough and transfer it to the work surface. Flatten the dough into a large oval and place the walnuts in the center. Fold the dough over the nuts and slowly work them into the dough. This will take about 5 minutes. Divide the dough. Press each piece into an oval, fold in half, pinch seam closed, and drop into pan, seam under.

SECOND RISING
45 mins.

Put the pans in the warm place, cover with wax paper and let rise until approximately doubled in volume.

BAKING
375°
45 mins.

Preheat oven to 375°. Bake the loaves in a moderately hot oven for 45 minutes. The loaves will be deep brown and will pull away from the sides of the pan when done. They can also be tested with a wooden toothpick inserted in the center of the loaf. If it comes out dry and clean, the bread is done.

FINAL STEP

Remove bread from the oven and turn the loaves onto a wire rack to cool before serving.

CHOPPED WHEAT BREAD

[TWO LOAVES]

It is two or three days before the chopped wheat loaf is finished, a period climaxed by grinding soaked wheat kernels—but worth every minute of it. I think it is one of the finest tasting wheat breads to be produced in the kitchen. It is so good that I felt it deserved a better name than the soggy one it had—"soaked wheat bread."

The ingredients, ranging from wheat kernels (the whole unmilled grain) to soy flour and brewer's yeast are all highly nutritional, and all enjoy high ratings as "natural foods."

INGREDIENTS

2 cups wheat kernels
Potato water to cover (or tap water, if preferred)
1½ cups hot tap water (120°–130°)
2 packages dry yeast
¼ cup oil (corn, peanut, safflower, etc.)
¼ cup molasses, dark
1 tablespoon salt
¼ cup brewer's yeast
2 tablespoons soy flour
3 cups whole wheat flour

BAKING PANS

Two medium (8½ x 4½) loaf pans, greased or Teflon. If glass, reduce oven heat 25°.

PREPARATION
Beforehand

Two or three days beforehand soak wheat kernels in potato water to cover.

Bake Day
30 mins.

On bake day, drain the kernels and grind in a food chopper, using the finest blade. Place in a large mixing bowl. Stir in the hot tap water, dry yeast, oil, molasses, salt, brewer's yeast, soy flour, and whole wheat flour. Add the flour gradually, a half cup at a time, stirring it into the mixture thoroughly after each addition.

KNEADING
10 mins.

This is a heavy, dense dough and it will require the hands—and much patience. Pour a ½ cup of oil in a small bowl and dip the fingers into this during the kneading process. Also pour small portions of oil on the work surface and spread it out with the hands before proceeding with the kneading. It will also be helpful to have a spatula or wide putty knife to flip the dough over during the kneading. It will never have the live and elastic feel of white dough.

FIRST RISING
1½ hours

Return the dough to the mixing bowl, cover with plastic wrap and put in a warm place (80°–85°) until dough has doubled in bulk.

SHAPING
10 mins.

Punch down the dough and knead for 30 seconds to press out bubbles. Divide the dough into two pieces with a sharp knife. Shape each into a ball. Form the loaf by pressing the ball into a flat oval, roughly the length of the baking pan. Fold the oval in half, pinch to seal and place in the pan, seam down. Repeat with the second loaf.

SECOND RISING
1 hour

Cover lightly with wax paper and return to the warm place until the loaves have risen to the level of the edge of the pans.

BAKING
325°
1¼ hours

Preheat oven to 325°. Place in the oven. When the loaves are a crusty deep brown and tapping the bottom crust yields a hard and hollow sound, they are done. If not, return to the oven for an additional 10 minutes. If you wish a deep brown over-all crust, remove the loaves from their pans about 10 minutes before the end of the bake period. Midway during the baking, and again near the end, shift the loaves so they are exposed equally to temperature variations in the oven.

FINAL STEP

Remove bread from the oven, turn from the pans and cool on the metal rack before serving. This keeps well for two weeks or more if wrapped in foil. It also freezes well.

HONEY WHOLE WHEAT

[TWO LOAVES]

Light in color and light in flavor, this loaf is sweetened with only a small amount of honey. It is understated and does not cloy. The recipe will make 2 medium 1½-pound loaves, or it can be doubled for 3 large 2-pound loaves.

INGREDIENTS

1 package dry yeast
¼ cup warm water (105°–115°)
2 cups hot tap water (120°–130°)
3 tablespoons lard or other shortening
3 tablespoons honey
2 cups whole wheat flour
½ cup instant potato
½ cup non-fat dry milk
1½ tablespoons salt
3–4 cups all-purpose white flour, approximately

BAKING PANS

Two medium (8½ x 4½) loaf pans, greased or Teflon, metal or glass. If glass, reduce oven heat 25°.

PREPARATION
15 mins.

In a small bowl dissolve yeast in warm water. Stir and set aside.

In a large mixing bowl measure hot tap water, lard and honey. Stir to blend. Add the whole wheat flour, instant potato, milk and salt. Pour in the yeast mixture and blend well.

With a wooden spoon stir in the all-purpose flour, ½ cup at a time, to make a rough ball of dough that leaves the sides of the bowl. Use the fingers when the dough gets too thick and stiff to be stirred by the spoon.

KNEADING
8 mins.

Sprinkle flour on a work surface—counter top or bread board—and turn the rough mass of dough onto it. Begin to knead with a strong push-turn-fold motion—adding a sprinkle of flour if the dough is slack or moist and sticks to the hands and work surface. The dough will knead to a smooth elastic ball in approximately 8 minutes (5 minutes with a dough hook).

FIRST RISING
1¼ hours

Return the dough to the bowl. Pat with greased fingers so a crust will not form, and cover the bowl tightly with plastic wrap. Move to a warm place (80°–85°) until doubled in bulk. You can test if it has risen by poking a finger in it; the dent will remain.

SHAPING
10 mins.

Punch down the dough, turn it out on the counter and cut into the number of pieces for however many loaves you have decided to make (see dough volume chart, page 23). Shape each into a ball and let stand 5 minutes to relax the dough. Flatten the ball into an oval roughly the width of the long side of the pan. Fold in half, pinch the seam together tightly, and plump into a loaf with the seam under. Place in the pan.

SECOND RISING
50 mins.

Cover the pans with wax paper and put in the warm place until the dough has doubled in volume or reached an inch or so above the edge of the pan.

BAKING
400°
45–50 mins.

Preheat oven to 400°. Place the pans in the oven. When the loaves are a light brown and tapping the bottom crust yields a hard and hollow sound, they are done.

FINAL STEP Remove bread from the oven and turn the loaves onto wire racks to cool before serving.

FRUIT-NUT GRAHAM BREAD

[TWO LOAVES]

The dough for this bread has a rough unkempt appearance. Nuts and fruit protrude on every surface and they pop out when the dough is being kneaded. Nevertheless, it makes a most delicious whole wheat bread, with slightly firm pieces of glacéed fruits adding a pleasant bite. It is the kind of loaf that disappears during the course of one meal.

INGREDIENTS

3 cups all-purpose flour, approximately
3 cups graham or whole wheat flour
1 package dry yeast
¾ cup non-fat dry milk
1 tablespoon salt
2 tablespoons brown sugar, packed into spoon
2 cups hot tap water (120°–130°)
2 tablespoons shortening, room temperature
1 cup glacéed fruit
1 cup chopped nuts
Topping: ½ cup confectioners' sugar, 2 teaspoons milk, ⅛ teaspoon vanilla

BAKING PANS Two medium (8½ x 4½) baking pans, greased or Teflon, metal or glass. If the latter, reduce oven heat 25°.

PREPARATION
20 mins.

In a large mixing bowl measure 1½ cups *each* white and graham (or whole wheat) flours, and stir in the yeast, milk, salt and brown sugar. Pour in the hot tap water and stir at medium speed in the electric mixer for 1 minute or until fully absorbed. Add the balance of the graham flour, and the shortening—beat at medium-high speed for 3 minutes. (The fruit and nuts will be worked into the dough *after* the first rising.)

Turn off the machine and add white flour, ¼ cup at a time, starting first with a wooden spoon and then mixing by hand. The dough will be a shaggy soft mass that will have pulled away from the sides of the bowl.

KNEADING
8 mins.

Sprinkle the work surface (counter top or bread board) liberally with flour and turn the ball of dough onto it.

If the dough is slack, or moist and sticky, work 1/4 cup additional flour into it. Soon it will become elastic and springy, and will no longer stick to the fingers or the work surface. Knead with a strong push-turn-fold motion for about 8 minutes (5 minutes with a dough hook, although this is a larger ball of dough than the hook can effectively handle).

FIRST RISING
1 1/4 hours

Return the dough to the mixing bowl, pat all over with greased fingertips and cover the bowl with plastic wrap to keep in the moisture. Put in a warm place (80°–85° is ideal) until doubled in bulk. You can test if it has risen by poking a finger in it; the dent will remain.

SHAPING
15 mins.

Dredge the sticky fruit and the nuts in a tablespoon of flour and spread on the work surface. Punch down the dough, and begin to work in the fruit and nuts. It will take about 4 minutes to do so. With a sharp knife cut the dough into two pieces. Form each into a round ball, flatten into an oval the length of the pan, fold in half —seal the seam by pinching with the fingers. Pat into shape and place the loaf, seam down, in the pan.

SECOND RISING
45 mins.

Cover the pans with wax paper and return to the warm place until the center of the dough has risen about 1 inch above the level of the edge of the pan.

BAKING
375°
45 mins.

Preheat oven to 375°. Slip the pans into the oven and bake until the crusts are a dark brown and the loaves have pulled away from the sides. If the crusts brown too quickly place a piece of foil or brown paper over them. When tapping the bottom crust yields a hard and hollow sound, they are done.

FINAL STEP

Remove bread from the oven and place on a wire rack to cool. While the loaves are still warm you may wish to drizzle the tops with confectioners' icing and sprinkle with a tablespoon of chopped walnuts. Confectioners' icing: 1/2 cup confectioners' sugar, 2 teaspoons milk, and 1/8 teaspoon vanilla.

VOLLKORNBROT

[TWO LOAVES]

This Viennese bread is a compact loaf with full wheaty flavor. Because it is all whole wheat or graham flour, the dough will not have the same elasticity as all white or blended doughs and it will be tacky even after the full kneading period. Because of the shortening, however, it will pull away from the work surface and the fingers. A scraper will help keep the film off the counter top. The addition of a little flour or shortening on the fingers will also help control the stickiness.

It is not as easy to work as other dough, but the result is worthwhile —a delicious heavy slice, fairly dense in texture that is clearly of peasant origin.

INGREDIENTS

2 cakes dry yeast
2 cups warm water (105°–115°)
1 pinch sugar
½ cup non-fat dry milk
1 tablespoon salt
¼ cup dark molasses
2 tablespoons butter, room temperature
6½ cups whole wheat flour, approximately
Glaze: 1 egg white
¼ cup water
½ teaspoon salt

BAKING PANS

Two medium (8½ x 4½) loaf tins, greased or Teflon, metal or glass. If the latter, reduce oven heat 25°.

PREPARATION
20 mins.

In a large mixing bowl dissolve yeast in warm water, and add a pinch of sugar. Let it stand for 5 minutes.

Add the milk, salt, molasses and butter. Stir well with a wooden spoon. Add the whole wheat flour, one cup at a time, until the dough is a soft mass.

It is easy to add too much whole wheat flour to the mixture so add the 5th and 6th cups with care. Let it stand for 5 minutes at this stage so you can be certain the flour has absorbed all of the liquid it will, and not suddenly become dry and solid.

KNEADING
8 mins.

Turn the dough out on a work surface sprinkled with white flour. Knead under the heel of the hand. Add a little more flour to the board and hands if the dough continues to be tacky. It calls for more patience than a white dough or a blend.

FIRST RISING
1½ hours

Shape the dough into a ball, put it in a warm greased bowl, turning it to film all sides, and cover the bowl tightly with plastic wrap. Place in a warm (80°–85°), draft-free spot.

SHAPING
10 mins.

Punch down with the fingers and turn from the bowl onto the floured work surface. Cut the dough in two pieces and shape into loaves. Place them in the tins.

SECOND RISING
1 hour

Cover tins with wax paper and return to the warm place until the dough expands to a height level with the edge of the pan.

BAKING
375°
45 mins.

Preheat oven to 375°. Uncover the tins and brush the tops of the loaves with a mixture of the egg white, water and salt. Place in the oven until they test done. The loaves will pull away from the sides of the tin, and tapping the bottom crust will yield a hard and hollow sound.

FINAL STEP

Remove bread from the oven and turn out on a metal rack to cool. These loaves freeze well.

FIVE

Rye Breads

Rye
Lyons, 1579

Rye is the glamour flour of the dark grains. It can be used alone in a loaf (Dutch Roggebrood), blended with white (Heidelberg), or joined by cornmeal, potato, and whole wheat (Pumpernickel). It can be made sweet (Raisin Rye) or traditionally sour (Old Milwaukee).

Rye, which is one of the most important European cereal grains, is hardier than wheat, resistant to cold, and is the only grain other than wheat from which leavened bread can be made. The all-rye loaf, however, has little capacity for developing a gluten network to entrap the fermenting gases, hence it is quite dense and heavy. More times than not rye is mixed with white flour.

There are four kinds of rye flour—white rye, medium rye, dark rye, and rye meal or pumpernickel. Medium is straight rye flour, the one commonly used in rye bread-making. Dark rye and pumpernickel have bran particles in them that will cut the gluten strands and thereby limit the size of the loaf. White rye, which is used to make a light rye bread, is seldom called for in home baking.

MODEST RYE BREAD

[THREE LOAVES]

Modest Rye is modestly rye. Unlike other rye loaves that are sometimes made with more than half rye flour, this bread has only 1 cup of rye blended into 5 cups of all-purpose flour. A modest proportion. Molasses gives it a dark look that belies its mild rye flavor. For an almost white loaf use sugar instead of molasses.

I sprinkle caraway seeds on the tops of the loaves before they go into the oven but in this recipe none are added to the dough.

For a more developed rye flavor with the same amount of rye flour, use one of the rye sour dough starters, page 287.

INGREDIENTS

5 cups all-purpose flour, approximately
1 package dry yeast
¾ cup non-fat dry milk
3 tablespoons shortening, room temperature
2 teaspoons salt
2 tablespoons molasses (or sugar)
2¼ cups hot tap water (120°–130°)
1 cup rye flour
Glaze: 1 egg white
1 tablespoon water
2 teaspoons caraway seeds

BAKING SHEET AND BAKING PANS

One baking sheet, greased or Teflon. You may wish to bake half of the dough in a large (9 x 5) baking pan, greased or Teflon. The large pan size is desirable because this loaf will have greater volume than most other dark breads. If a glass pan is used, reduce oven heat 25°.

PREPARATION
15 mins.

In a large mixer bowl measure 2 cups of all-purpose flour, the yeast, milk, shortening, salt, molasses and tap water. Blend at low speed of electric mixer for 30 seconds. Add the rye flour, blend at low speed and then increase speed to medium for 3 minutes.

Stop the mixer and stir in the balance of the flour, a half cup at a time, first with the spoon and then by hand. The dough will be a rough, shaggy mass that will clean the sides of the bowl. If the dough continues slack or moist, add sprinkles of flour. Scrape down the film or coating on the sides of the bowl with fingertips or the edge of a large metal spoon or spatula.

KNEADING
8 mins.

Turn the dough onto a lightly floured surface—counter top or bread board—and knead with the rhythmic 1-2-3 motion of push-turn-fold. The dough will become smooth and elastic, and bubbles will rise under the surface of the dough. Sprinkle more flour on the dough if it sticks to the hands or to the work surface. Break the kneading rhythm occasionally by throwing the dough down hard against the counter top. Knead 8 minutes (6 minutes with a dough hook).

FIRST RISING
1 hour

Place the dough in the bowl and pat with buttered or greased fingertips to prevent the surface from crusting. Cover the bowl tightly with plastic wrap and set in a warm place (80°–85°) until the dough has risen to about twice its original size as judged by how it creeps up the sides of the bowl. You can test if it has risen by poking a finger in it; the dent will remain.

SHAPING
10 mins.

Punch down and knead the dough for 30 seconds to press out the bubbles. Divide dough into thirds.

For a hearth loaf, pat one piece into a round ball. I drop it in a cloth-lined basket to rise. It can also be placed directly on the baking sheet. For a pan loaf, press the ball into a flat oval, roughly the length of the baking pan. Fold the oval in half, pinch the seam tightly to seal, tuck under the ends, and place in the pan, seam down.

SECOND RISING
45 mins.

Place the loaves in the warm place, cover with wax paper and leave until they have doubled in bulk.

BAKING
375°
45 mins.

Preheat the oven to 375°. For the hearth loaf in the basket, tilt the raised loaf onto the baking sheet—right side up. Brush loaves with a mixture of egg white and water. Sprinkle with caraway seeds. With a razor blade, slash the tops either in a tic-tac-toe design for the round hearth loaf, or diagonal or lengthwise cuts for the pan loaf. Place pans in oven.

When the loaves are a deep brown, crusty and tapping the bottom crust yields a hard and hollow sound, they are done. Midway in the bake period and again near the end of it, shift the loaves so they are exposed equally to temperature variations in the oven.

FINAL STEP

Remove bread from the oven and place the loaves on the metal rack to cool before slicing.

CARAWAY RYE BREAD

[TWO LOAVES]

Light in color yet surprisingly rye in flavor, this loaf is especially fine for sandwiches. I make this in loaf pans rather than forming hearth loaves on baking sheets, which is usually done. The bread is excellent for rye toast which few people try.

INGREDIENTS

2 packages dry yeast
2 cups warm water (105°–115°)
2 cups rye flour
3 tablespoons sugar
1 tablespoon salt
2 tablespoons caraway seeds
4 to 4½ cups all-purpose flour, approximately
2 tablespoons shortening, room temperature

BAKING PANS

Two medium (8½ x 4½) loaf pans, greased or Teflon, metal or glass. If the latter, reduce oven heat 25°.

PREPARATION
15 mins.

In a large bowl, add the yeast to water, stir briskly for a moment and put aside for 3 minutes.

Measure the rye flour into the bowl and add sugar, salt, caraway seeds, 1 cup flour, and shortening. Beat until smooth—about 100 strokes. Stir in the balance of the flour, a half cup at a time, first with the spoon and then by hand. The dough will be a rough, shaggy mass that cleans the sides of the bowl.

KNEADING
6 mins.

Turn dough onto lightly floured work surface—counter top or bread board—and knead until smooth, about 100 push-turn-fold motions. Sprinkle additional flour to control the stickiness.

FIRST RISING
1 hour

Return dough to the mixing bowl and pat with buttered or greased fingertips to keep the surface from crusting. Cover the bowl tightly with plastic wrap and move to a warm place (80°–85°) until the dough has risen to about twice its original size. You can test if it has risen by poking a finger in it; the dent will remain.

RESTING
15 mins.

Turn back the plastic wrap and punch down dough with the fingers. Fold the dough into the center and turn it over in the bowl. Replace the plastic wrap and let it rest for 15 additional minutes.

SHAPING
15 mins.

Punch down the dough, knead for 30 seconds to press out the bubbles, and divide into two pieces with a sharp knife. Shape into balls and let rest under a towel for 3 or 4 minutes. Form the loaves by pressing each ball into a flat oval, roughly the length of the baking pan. Fold the oval in half, pinch the seam tightly to seal.

Tuck under the ends and place in the pan, seam down. Repeat with the second piece.

SECOND RISING
45 mins.

Place the pans in the warm place, cover with wax paper and leave until the center of the dough has reached level with the top of the pan.

BAKING
400°
40–50 mins.

Preheat oven to 400°. Bake loaves in the oven. When tapping the bottom crust yields a hard and hollow sound, they are done. If not, return to the oven for an additional 10 minutes. Midway in the bake period shift the pans so the loaves are exposed equally to temperature variations in the oven.

FINAL STEP

Remove bread from the oven. Turn the loaves out of the pans and place on a metal rack to cool before serving.

COOLRISE© PUMPERNICKEL BREAD

[THREE ROUND OR OBLONG LOAVES]

Pumpernickel rye is a coarsely ground rye grain. The edges of the particles will actually cut through the gluten network that holds in the expanding gases—thereby limiting the size of the loaf. No problem, however, for it will be a smaller and more compact loaf. A delicious bread for spreads at a buffet or for sandwiches. Dark, dense, and flavorful.

It has equal parts pumpernickel and white flour, plus a cup of potato to give it extra firmness and taste. It goes into the refrigerator to rise for at least 2 hours, preferably overnight.

INGREDIENTS

4 to 5 cups all-purpose flour
2 packages dry yeast
4 teaspoons salt
⅓ cup molasses
2 tablespoons margarine or shortening, room temperature
2¼ cups hot tap water (120°–130°)
1 cup mashed potato, fresh or instant
4 cups pumpernickel rye flour
1 teaspoon cooking oil (to brush loaves)

BAKING PANS

Three 8-inch pie pans, greased or Teflon, for the round loaves, or 3 medium (8½ x 4½) loaf pans, greased or

Teflon, for oblong loaves. Metal or glass. If the latter, reduce oven heat 25°.

PREPARATION
20 mins.

Measure into a large mixing bowl 2 cups white flour, the undissolved yeast and salt. Stir to blend. Add molasses and margarine. Pour in water, and beat at medium speed for 2 minutes—or for an equal length of time with a wooden spoon. Scrape bowl occasionally.

Add the potato, and 2 cups additional white flour. Beat at high speed for 1 minute or until thick and elastic. Stop the mixer, and with a wooden spoon stir in the 4 cups of rye flour. If more flour is necessary to form a soft dough, add small amounts of white flour.

KNEADING
8 mins.

Turn out the dough onto a liberally floured work surface—counter top or bread board—and knead for 7 to 8 minutes. The dough will become smooth and elastic.

RESTING
20 mins.

Cover dough loosely with plastic wrap. Let it rest for 20 minutes.

SHAPING
8 mins.

Punch down the dough. Divide the dough into thirds. Shape each into a round loaf, flatten slightly before placing in the pie pans. The dough may also be fashioned into loaves for baking tins. Flatten each ball—fold in half, pinch the seam to seal and drop in the pan, seam down. Brush lightly with vegetable oil.

REFRIGERATION
2–24 hours

Cover pans loosely with plastic wrap. Place in the refrigerator for at least 2 hours—up to 24 hours.

BAKING
400°
35–45 mins.

Remove the loaves from the refrigerator, uncover and let stand for 10 minutes while the oven heats to 400°. Prepare to bake on the lower oven shelf for the best results. Place in the oven. If the crust browns too quickly cover with foil the last 10 minutes. When tapping the bottom crust yields a hard and hollow sound, they are done.

FINAL STEP

Remove from oven and turn onto wire racks to cool. For a nice soft finish to the crust, brush with butter.

DILL RYE BREAD

[TWO LOAVES]

Dill seeds *and* dill weed are mixed into the dough of this unusual rye loaf. Caraway seeds, too. The combination is noteworthy. An easy loaf to make, the dry yeast particles are stirred into the flour before the hot tap water is added. Since it is a hearth bread, I let my loaves rise in cloth-lined baskets until they are high and round, and then turn them directly onto the baking sheet.

INGREDIENTS

3 to 3½ cups all-purpose flour, approximately
2 packages dry yeast
½ cup non-fat dry milk
1¾ cups hot tap water (120°–130°)
2 tablespoons *each* shortening and sugar
2 teaspoons salt
1 teaspoon *each* caraway seeds, dill seeds and powdered dill weed
1½ cups rye flour

BAKING SHEET

One baking sheet, greased or Teflon.

PREPARATION
15 mins.

Measure 2 cups all-purpose flour into a mixer bowl. Stir in the yeast and milk. Pour in water, and add shortening, sugar, salt, caraway seeds, dill seeds, and dill weed.

Beat in the electric mixer at medium speed for 3 minutes. Stop the mixer. Add the rye flour and beat it into the batter with 25 vigorous strokes. Stir in the balance of the all-purpose flour, a half cup at a time, first with the spoon and then by hand. The dough will be a rough, shaggy mass. The rye will make it considerably more sticky than an all-white dough. Sprinkle on additional all-purpose flour to control the stickiness. Scrape off the film coating the bowl with the fingertips or the edge of a metal spoon or spatula.

KNEADING
8 mins.

Turn the dough onto a lightly floured work surface—counter top or bread board—and knead with the rhythmic 1-2-3 motion of push-turn-fold. If a film clings to the work surface, scrape it off with a spatula (I use a wide putty knife), and dust with flour. Crash dough down on the counter top occasionally to break the kneading rhythm.

RESTING 20 mins.	Round the dough into a ball, cover with a piece of foil or paper and let rest.
SHAPING 6 mins.	Knead the dough for 30 seconds to press out the bubbles. Divide in two equal pieces and shape into balls. Place at opposite corners of the baking sheet or in small baskets, loosely lined with cloths sprinkled with flour.
RISING 45 mins.	Cover the loaves with wax paper and put in a warm place (80°–85°) until they have risen to double their size.
BAKING 375° 35–45 mins.	Preheat the oven to 375°. If the loaves have risen in baskets, tip the raised loaf into your hand and quickly set it right side up on the baking sheet. With a razor blade, slash the top of each four times to form a tic-tac-toe design. Bake in the oven until crisp and brown. When tapping the bottom crust yields a hard and hollow sound, they are done. If not, return to the oven for an additional 10 minutes.
FINAL STEP	Remove bread from the oven and place on a metal rack to cool. For a chewy crust brush with water.

HEIDELBERG RYE BREAD

[TWO LOAVES]

A baker will often add cocoa to give his rye loaf a darker and richer look. It is done so in this recipe—and succeeds well. This handsome loaf rises slowly in the refrigerator, usually overnight, although it can be done in as little as 2 hours. After the bread is baked, the chocolate's contribution to taste is so slight as to go unnoticed. The dough is soft and velvety, a pleasure to knead.

INGREDIENTS

- 3 cups all-purpose or bread flour, approximately
- 3 cups rye flour
- 2 packages dry yeast
- ¼ cup cocoa
- 1 tablespoon *each* sugar and salt
- 1 tablespoon caraway seeds
- 2 cups hot tap water (120°–130°)
- ⅓ cup molasses
- 2 tablespoons shortening, room temperature

BAKING SHEET One baking sheet, greased or Teflon.

PREPARATION
20 mins.

In a large bowl measure 1½ cups of the all-purpose flour, 1½ cups of rye, yeast, cocoa, sugar, salt, and caraway seeds. Beat in electric mixer to blend the ingredients. Pour in the water, molasses and soft shortening. Beat slowly for 30 seconds until the flour is absorbed, and at high speed for 3 minutes. This can be done by hand with a large wooden spoon for approximately the same length of time. The dough will be thick, elastic and pull in ribbons from the sides of the bowl.

Stop the mixer and gradually add flour, ½ cup at a time of both white and rye, alternately, until the dough is a soft mass and is no longer wet and sticky.

KNEADING
5 mins.

Turn out on a well-floured work surface and knead. The dough may continue to be sticky because of the high rye content. Scrape it off the counter top with a spatula or scraper. Add a bit more flour and keep the fingers dusted. Finally it will become a soft velvety dough, a delight to work.

RESTING
20 mins.

Cover the dough with a towel, piece of wax paper or the inverted bowl and let rest on the work surface.

SHAPING
10 mins.

Punch down and divide the dough in half. Shape each into a round ball, flatten slightly. For a long loaf, roll the piece into an 8 x 15-inch rectangle. Roll up tightly, seal the seam and ends. Taper by rolling under the palms. Place on the bake sheet.

REFRIGERATION
2–24 hours

Brush the loaves with vegetable or salad oil, cover loosely (to allow for expansion) with plastic wrap and place the baking sheet in the refrigerator. Leave 2 or more hours but no longer than 24.

BAKING
400°
30–40 mins.

Allow the loaves to stand at room temperature for 10 minutes while the oven heats to 400°. With a sharp knife or razor blade cut a cross (X) on round loaves or cut diagonal slashes 3 inches apart in the long loaves just before baking. Place in the oven. When tapping the bottom crust yields a hard and hollow sound, they are done. A dull thud: return to the oven for an additional 10 minutes.

FINAL STEP Remove bread from the oven. Remove from baking sheet and place on metal rack to cool. You may wish to brush with soft butter to give a soft crust.

LIMPA RYE BREAD

[THREE ROUND, PLUMP LOAVES]

How a recipe travels up and down a region, across the country or around the block is often as intriguing as the product is good. This recipe for orange-flavored limpa was one of several exchanged by two fine home bakers meeting for the first time at a horse show in northern California, but not baked until several years later in an Indiana kitchen.

It does not have the pronounced cummin/fennel taste of many limpa loaves but relies instead on four kinds of flour and the orange rind for its unusually good flavor. This is a large recipe for a large family with large appetites—or for gifts.

INGREDIENTS

1 cup whole wheat flour
1 cup medium rye flour
1 cup oatmeal
Grated rind of 2 oranges
1 cup brown sugar, packed
1 tablespoon salt
4 cups milk, heated (120°–130°)
2 packages dry yeast
4 tablespoons vegetable shortening, room temperature
6 cups all-purpose or bread flour, approximately

BAKING SHEET

One large baking sheet, greased or Teflon.

PREPARATION
15 mins.

In a large bowl blend with a wooden spoon the whole wheat and rye flours, oatmeal, orange rind, brown sugar, salt and milk, heated but not scalded. (Four cups hot tap water and 1 cup milk powder may be substituted.) Stir until the mixture is well blended—about 30 strokes. When the mixture has cooled to lukewarm, sprinkle in the yeast. Stir.

FIRST RISING
1½ hours

The dough is not completed but now it is put to rest in a warm place. Cover the bowl tightly with plastic wrap. The batter-like mixture will bubble pleasantly and begin to ferment.

KNEADING
15 mins.

Remove the plastic wrap and mix 4 tablespoons shortening into the dough. Add the white flour, a cup at a time, until the dough has lost its stickiness. Work it with your hands. When the dough has absorbed about 6 cups of white flour, it will be soft and elastic.

SHAPING
5 mins.

Divide the dough into three pieces—about 1¼ pounds each. Shape by hand into round, plump loaves and place on the baking sheet. Space them apart.

SECOND RISING
50 mins.

Cover the loaves with wax paper and place in a warm spot (80°–85°) until the loaves have doubled in bulk.

BAKING
380°
10 mins.
350°
40 mins.

Preheat oven to 380°. Bake for 10 minutes at 380°, turn oven down to 350° for an additional 40 minutes. After 25 minutes change position of loaves to assure uniform browning. Ten minutes before the loaves are done move them again.

FINAL STEP

Remove bread from the oven and shift to wire racks to cool. This makes delicious toast.

OLD MILWAUKEE RYE BREAD

[TWO TO FOUR LOAVES]

This is a two or three day affair that produces a fine rye loaf. It can be made into 2 large round loaves—good for husky family sandwiches—or 3 or 4 long, slender loaves, best for the buffet.

Under the taut plastic wrap covering the bowl, the sponge will rise and fall as it bubbles to its maximum goodness in approximately 3 days, give or take a few hours. After a day or so, a whiff of the fermented sponge will make manifest the historic connection between the baker and the brewer.

I have made several hundred loaves of this wonderful bread, probably more than any other, and each time I have a warm thought for Bernadine Landsberg of Milwaukee, who sent me the recipe a long time ago.

INGREDIENTS

The sponge: 1 package dry yeast
1½ cups warm water (105°–115°)
2 cups medium rye flour
1 tablespoon caraway seed

All of the sponge
1 package dry yeast
1 cup warm water (105°–115°)
¼ cup molasses
1 tablespoon caraway seed
1 egg, room temperature
1 tablespoon salt

1 cup rye flour
5 to 5½ cups all-purpose flour, approximately
3 tablespoons vegetable shortening
Glaze: 1 egg
1 tablespoon milk
1 tablespoon caraway seed

BAKING SHEET

Baking sheet, greased or Teflon.

PREPARATION
1–3 days

Set the sponge in a large bowl by dissolving yeast in the water. Stir in rye flour. Add caraway seeds. Cover the bowl snugly with plastic wrap so that the sour loses none of its moisture which condenses on the plastic and drops back into the mixture. The dark brown paste will rise and fall as it develops flavor and a delicious aroma. The sponge, which will resemble a wet mash that's too thick to pour and too thin to knead, may be used anytime after 6 hours although the longer the better—up to three days when it will have ceased fermenting.

20 mins.

On bake day, uncover the sponge bowl, sprinkle on the new yeast and add water. Blend well with 25 strokes of a wooden spoon. Add molasses, caraway, egg, salt, rye flour, and about 2 cups of the white flour. Beat till smooth—about 100 strokes. Add shortening. Stir in the balance of the flour, a half cup at a time, first with the spoon and then by hand. The dough should clean the sides of the bowl but it will be sticky due to the rye flour.

KNEADING
5 mins.

Turn the dough out on a floured surface—counter top or bread board. Knead until the dough is smooth. It may help to grease fingers to keep the dough from sticking.

FIRST RISING
1 hour
10 mins.

Return the dough to the large bowl, pat the surface well with butter or shortening and place plastic wrap tightly over the top of the bowl. Put in a warm place (80°–85°) for about 1 hour, or until the dough has doubled in bulk. Punch down and let rise 10 additional minutes.

SHAPING
20 mins.

Divide the dough with a sharp knife. For two round loaves, mold each into a smooth ball and place on the baking sheet. For the long slender loaves, roll out a long rectangle of dough with a rolling pin. Starting at one long edge, roll tightly and pinch together firmly at the seam. Place these side by side on a baking sheet.

SECOND RISING
40 mins.

Cover the loaves with wax paper supported on glass tumblers so that paper will not touch the dough. Return to the warm place until loaves have doubled in bulk.

BAKING
375°
40 mins.

Preheat oven to 375°. With a sharp razor carefully slash 3 or 4 diagonal cuts on the top of each loaf. Brush the tops with water (for an unglazed crust) or a whole egg mixed with 1 tablespoon of milk for a shiny crust. Sprinkle the moist glaze with caraway seeds.

Bake the loaves in the oven. When tapping the bottom crust yields a hard and hollow sound, they are done. If the loaves appear to be browning too quickly, cover with a piece of foil or brown sack paper.

FINAL STEP

Remove from the oven and allow to cool on metal racks. This bread keeps for at least a week or more and freezes well.

OVERNIGHT RYE BREAD

[TWO LOAVES]

A sponge works overnight for this rye batter bread that is a mixture of rye and whole wheat flours in almost equal parts. Baked in loaf pans, the bread comes from the oven light in color but rough-textured like a pumpernickel or an all-wheat bread. A good loaf of bread.

INGREDIENTS

2 cups rye flour, approximately
2 cups whole wheat or graham flour
¼ cup brown sugar
2 teaspoons salt
2 tablespoons lard or other shortening, room temperature
4 teaspoons caraway seeds
2 packages dry yeast
2½ cups hot tap water (120°–130°)
1 tablespoon butter, melted, or milk for crust during baking

BAKING PANS — Two medium (8½ x 4½) baking pans, greased or Teflon, metal or glass. If the latter, reduce oven heat 25°.

PREPARATION
20 mins. — The night before:
In a large bowl mix 1 cup of rye flour, all of the wheat, brown sugar, salt, lard, caraway seeds, and yeast. Pour in water and beat 150 strokes until well mixed. Add additional rye flour to make a thick batter that nevertheless can be stirred.

FIRST RISING
8 plus hours — Cover the bowl tightly with plastic wrap and put in a warm place (80°–85°) overnight (or for at least 8 hours) where batter will bubble, rise and fall and develop a rich fermented fragrance.

FORMING
5 mins. — On bake day turn back the plastic covering and stir down the dough. Pour it into the pans.

SECOND RISING
1 hour — Cover pans with wax paper and return to the warm place until the batter has risen to the edge of the pans.

BAKING
350°
1½ hours — Preheat the oven to 350°. The bread will bake in the oven for about 1½ hours but at the end of 1 hour remove the bread from the oven, slip from the pans, brush with melted butter or milk, and return at once to the oven (without the pans). If loaves seem to brown too rapidly cover with foil or brown paper.

FINAL STEP — Carefully lift the loaves out of the oven and turn out on a metal rack to cool before slicing. This is a fine brunch, buffet, and picnic bread. Keeps well frozen.

DUTCH ROGGEBROOD

[TWO LOAVES]

This version of the famous Dutch Roggebrood is a solid brick of unleavened rye, and solidly good to eat.

A Dutch woman vacationing in a small English inn in East Anglia, where I was bicycling, gave me this recipe after I had described vividly a delicious bread I had eaten in Amsterdam a number of years before. Roggebrood is sliced wafer thin (⅛ inch) and served buttered with a very thin slice of ham and cheese on it. Roggebrood, one of three kinds of bread usually served at a Dutch breakfast, will keep almost indefinitely wrapped in plastic.

INGREDIENTS

2 cups potato water (from boiling 3 or 4 diced-up potatoes)
½ cup molasses
7 cups rye flour
1 tablespoon salt
½ cup brewer's yeast (for taste only; not for leavening)
2 tablespoons caraway seeds, ground

BAKING PANS

Two medium (8½ x 4½) loaf pans, greased. Also a larger pan in which to place these two pans while the bread is steamed.

PREPARATION
20 mins.

Beforehand, boil 3 or 4 diced-up potatoes to get 2 cups of potato water. The potatoes may be used in other dishes as only the water is used in this recipe.

15 mins.

Pour boiling potato water into a large mixing bowl and add molasses, rye flour, salt, brewer's yeast, and caraway seeds.

Be forewarned—this will be a sticky, clinging mess that won't get better no matter how long it is worked because there is little of the magic gluten in rye flour.

When the dough has cooled, use a spoon (and the hands, sparingly) to blend all the ingredients together.

FORMING
10 mins.

Spoon the dough into pans. Dampen the fingers and push the dough into the corners, and smooth the surface.

Cover the two pans tightly with foil. Place them in a large pan and fill with hot water an inch or so around the dough-filled tins. Cover the large pan with a lid or improvise a cover from aluminum foil to keep the steam from escaping.

BAKING
250°
5 hours

Preheat oven. Carefully lift the covered pan into the oven and turn the heat to 250° for a very slow oven. Steam, covered, for 3 hours. Remove foil and lift out bread pans. Uncover the pans but be careful of steam when you do. Remove the large water-filled pan and empty. Remove the foil from the bread pans and return to the oven for an additional hour, still at 250°.

Turn off the heat. Remove the bread from the pans but return to the oven to dry out on the oven shelf for one hour, or a total of 5 hours.

FINAL STEP — Place on metal racks to cool before slicing thinly (1/8 inch) to serve.

FINNISH SUOMALAISLEIPÄÄ

[TWO FLAT, ROUND LOAVES]

This loaf gets its rich brown color and good taste from brown sugar and rye, one of the principal grains that flourishes in the cool weather of Scandinavia. While it can be served sliced, the Finnish people cut it in wedges, split each wedge and serve warm with butter.

INGREDIENTS

- 2 packages dry yeast
- 2½ cups warm water (105°–115°)
- 3 cups medium rye flour
- 6 tablespoons dark brown sugar
- 2 tablespoons butter, melted
- 3 teaspoons salt
- 4 cups all-purpose or bread flour, approximately

BAKING SHEET — One baking sheet, greased or Teflon.

PREPARATION
20 mins.

In a large mixing bowl sprinkle yeast over the water. Stir briskly with a fork or whisk and set aside for 5 minutes.

Stir the rye flour, a cup at a time, into the yeast mixture and add the brown sugar, butter and salt. When this is blended, add 1 cup white flour and beat 100 strong strokes with a wooden spoon—or 3 minutes medium fast with the electric mixer. At this point the dough will be like batter, stringy from the sides of the bowl. Add the balance of the white flour, a portion at a time, first with the spoon and then by hand until the dough has pulled away from the sides of the bowl. The ball will be soft but not sticky.

KNEADING
8 mins.

Turn the dough out onto a floured work surface. Add small portions of additional flour if the dough seems slack (or moist beneath the skin). Knead with a rhythmic motion of push-turn-fold until the dough is elastic and smooth. It should be kneaded by hand about 8 minutes—or half that time with a bread hook.

RISING
50 mins.

Gather the ball of dough and drop it into a lightly buttered bowl. Turn the dough and pat it with your buttery hands so that the dough is coated all over. Stretch plastic wrap over the bowl and move it to a warm (80°–85°), draft-free place until dough has doubled in bulk.

SHAPING
10 mins.

Punch the dough down with your fist and fingers, work out the air bubbles and cut into two pieces with a sharp knife. Shape each into a round, flat loaf—about 9 inches in diameter and 1½ inches high. Place the round loaves on the baking sheet.

BAKING
375°
1 hour

Preheat oven to 375°. Place in the oven until the bread has a dark brown crust. Midway in the baking process move the loaves to different positions on the baking sheet so they are equally exposed to different heats in the oven. The bread is done when a wooden toothpick inserted in the center comes out dry and clean. Also, when turned over and tapped, the loaf will sound hard and hollow.

FINAL STEP

Remove bread from the oven. Place on wire racks to cool but the loaves are best served while still warm (or rewarmed). Cut in wedges, split and serve with country butter.

POPPY SEED RYE

[TWO ROUND HEARTH LOAVES]

Poppy and caraway seeds are blended into a dough that was begun four or five days before with a flour-yeast-water starter, and got a strong boost on bake day with more yeast. The dough is only mildly rye since there is less rye flour than white but it does form husky, handsome loaves that are great for parties, barbecues and picnics.

It can be made into an onion rye simply by adding a small portion of chopped raw onion to the dough and sprinkling some on top of the loaves before they go into the oven.

These are hearth loaves and are usually placed directly on a baking sheet to rise. However, I put the dough in cloth-lined baskets and then tip them onto the bake sheet when they are light and ready. This means the loaves won't spread or slump during the rise but will expand upward.

INGREDIENTS

Sponge: 1 cup Sour Rye Starter (see page 283)
2 cups rye flour
1 cup warm water (105°–115°)

Dough: All of the sponge
1 package dry yeast
2 teaspoons salt
1 tablespoon *each* caraway seeds and poppy seeds
2 tablespoons butter, room temperature
3 tablespoons sugar
4 cups all-purpose flour, approximately
½ cup chopped raw onion (optional)
Glaze: 1 egg, room temperature
1 tablespoon water

BAKING SHEET

One baking sheet, greased or Teflon.

PREPARATION

While there are several starters that can be used, the recipe calls for a simple one, prepared 4 or 5 days ahead.

Sponge:
Overnight

The sponge is made the night before bake day by pouring 1 cup of starter in a large bowl. Add the rye flour and water. Stir. Cover tightly with plastic wrap so there can be no loss of moisture, and put in a warm place (80°–85°) overnight.

Dough:
15 mins.

On bake day, remove the plastic wrap, sprinkle yeast over the surface of the sponge and stir down. Add salt, caraway seeds, poppy seeds, butter, sugar and 2 cups all-purpose flour. Beat 150 strong strokes with a wooden spoon, or 3 minutes at medium speed of an electric mixer.

(For an onion rye loaf stir the chopped onion into the batter. Reserve 1 tablespoon to sprinkle on the loaves before they go into the oven.)

Add balance of the flour, a half cup at a time, first with the spoon and then by hand. The dough will be a rough, shaggy mass that will clean the sides of the bowl. If it continues sticky, add small amounts of flour.

KNEADING
8 mins.

Turn dough onto lightly floured work surface. Knead with 1-2-3 motion of push-turn-fold. Add sprinkles of flour to control stickiness.

FIRST RISING
1½ hours

Return the dough to the mixing bowl and pat with buttered or greased fingertips. Cover the bowl tightly with plastic wrap and move to the warm place until the dough has risen to about twice its original size. This can be judged by how high it creeps up the sides of the bowl. You can test if it has risen by poking a finger in it; the dent will remain.

SHAPING
5 mins.

Remove the cover, punch down the dough. Turn it onto the work surface, knead for 30 seconds to press out the bubbles, and cut into two pieces with a sharp knife. Form each into a ball. Place on opposite corners of the baking sheet or in small baskets, lined loosely with a cloth lightly sprinkled with flour.

SECOND RISING
45 mins.

Place the baking sheet and/or the baskets in the warm place and cover carefully with a length of wax paper. If the paper clings to the dough, rest it on water glasses. Leave to rise.

BAKING
375°
35–45 mins.

Preheat the oven to 375°. If the loaves have raised in the baskets, tip the raised loaf into the hand and quickly turn the loaf right side up onto the baking sheet. Brush with egg and cold water mixture. Sprinkle on the onion bits if this is an onion loaf. With a razor blade or sharp knife, slash a tic-tac-toe design on the top of each loaf.

Bake in the oven. When the loaves are a light brown and tapping the bottom crust yields a hard and hollow sound, they are done. If not, return to the oven for an additional 10 minutes. If the loaves appear to be browning too quickly, cover with a piece of foil or brown sack paper. Midway in the bake period and again near the end, shift the loaves on the baking sheet so they are exposed equally to temperature variations in the oven.

FINAL STEP

Remove bread from the oven and place on a wire rack to cool. Cover the loaves with a towel for softer crusts.

RAISIN RYE BREAD

[TWO ROUND LOAVES]

A combination of light and dark raisins, plumped beforehand in warm water, gives this golden round loaf of rye a rich appearance and a fine taste. It does not have the sour flavor of most rye breads (because of the shorter sponge time) but tastes somewhat wheaty. It develops a rough, jagged crust in the rising that makes it unnecessary to slash with a sharp knife. The breaks expand naturally as the bread rises.

INGREDIENTS

1 package dry yeast
2 cups rye flour
1½ cups hot tap water (120°–130°)
½ cup *each* light and dark raisins, plumped
1 tablespoon molasses
1 tablespoon cooking oil
2 teaspoons salt
½ cup warm water (105°–115°)
1½ cups rye flour
1½ cups all-purpose flour, approximately
Glaze: 1 egg, beaten

BAKING SHEET

One baking sheet, greased or Teflon.

PREPARATION
2 hours–
3 days

In a large bowl combine yeast, 2 cups of rye flour and water. Blend well, cover the bowl with plastic wrap and put in a warm place (80°–85°) until the sponge is light and bubbly—approximately 1½ to 2 hours. It can be left longer (up to two or three days) to improve and strengthen the rye flavor.

30 mins.

In the meanwhile, plump the raisins in warm water for about 20 minutes. Drain and set aside. In a small bowl combine molasses, cooking oil, salt and warm water and pour into the sponge. Drop in the raisins.

Alternately add about 1½ cups *each* of rye and all-purpose flour to the sponge—first with a wooden spoon and then by hand. If the dough is slack and sticky, add ¼ cup or more white flour.

KNEADING
6 mins.

Sprinkle the work surface liberally with flour and turn the dough onto it. Knead until the dough is smooth and elastic. This will be a heavier than normal dough because of the high rye content.

FIRST RISING
1 hour

Put dough back in the bowl, pat the surface with greased fingertips and stretch a piece of plastic wrap tightly across the bowl. Carry the bowl to a warm place (80°–85°) and leave until dough doubles in size.

SHAPING
10 mins.

Punch down the dough, turn out on the work surface, divide into two pieces. Let rest 5 minutes to relax the dough before shaping either into round loaves, slightly flattened, or into oblong loaves. Place them on a baking sheet.

SECOND RISING
45 mins.

Cover loaves with wax paper and return to the warm place to double in size.

BAKING
350°
1 hour

Preheat the oven to 350°. Brush loaves with beaten egg just before sliding them into the oven. When the loaves are well browned and crusty and tapping the bottom crust yields a hard and hollow sound, they are done.

FINAL STEP

Remove the loaves from the oven and place on wire racks to cool before serving, or freezing.

PUMPERNICKEL RYE BREAD

[TWO ROUND LOAVES]

This dark brown, almost black loaf of rye, with its soft chewy crust, is considered to be one of my finest by my father-in-law who has considerable baking expertise himself. For many years he owned a widely patronized bakery on the courthouse square in a small town in northern Indiana. The loaf has a lot of yeast in it (3 packages) to give it a fast, vigorous start, and dark molasses for flavor and color. Use pumpernickel rye flour if possible because it gives the bread a pleasant roughness. The loaf is docked (stabbed) a dozen or so times with an ice pick or skewer to keep the crust from lifting off during baking.

INGREDIENTS

3 packages dry yeast
1½ cups warm water (105°–115°)
½ cup dark molasses
1 tablespoon caraway seeds
1 tablespoon salt
2 tablespoons vegetable oil
3 cups pumpernickel rye flour
3 to 4 cups all-purpose or bread flour, approximately

BAKING SHEET

One baking sheet, greased and flour-dusted, or one Teflon sheet.

PREPARATION
15 mins.

In a large bowl add yeast to the water. Stir briskly with a whisk or fork to dissolve. Stir in molasses, caraway, salt, oil and the rye flour. Beat about 100 strong strokes with a wooden spoon. Add all-purpose flour, a half cup at a time, until the dough is stiff and cleans the sides of the bowl.

KNEADING 6 mins.	Turn dough onto a lightly floured work surface, counter top or bread board, and knead until the dough is smooth and pliable. Because of the rye flour it will never become as responsive as white dough.
FIRST RISING 1½–2 hours	Place the dough in a greased bowl, turning once to film the entire ball of dough. Cover with plastic wrap and let rise in a warm place (80°–85°). You can test if it has risen by poking a finger in it; the dent will remain.
SHAPING 15 mins.	Turn back the plastic wrap and punch down the dough. Turn it out on the work surface. Divide into two pieces, cover and let rest for 10 minutes. Round each piece into a smooth ball. Place on opposite corners of the baking sheet.
SECOND RISING 45 mins.	Cover with a sheet of wax paper and return to the warm place.
BAKING 375° 40–50 mins.	Preheat oven to 375°. Before placing the loaves in the oven stab each 10 or 12 times with a metal skewer, ice pick or trussing needle. Bake in the oven until well browned. For a chewy crust, brush tops of loaves with warm water several times during the last half of the baking period. Also, move the loaves once or twice during the bake period so they are exposed equally to different temperatures in the oven.
FINAL STEP	Remove bread from the oven and place the loaves on a metal rack to cool. This bread will keep well for a week or ten days.

DARK PUMPERNICKEL

[THREE LOAVES]

Cornmeal, mashed potato, and rye and whole wheat flours are the body of this fine-tasting pumpernickel loaf. Moist as pumpernickel should be, it is more open-textured than others because of its leavening with two packages of active dry yeast. While no white flour is used in the recipe, I liberally sprinkle it on while kneading the dough and forming the loaves. The dough is less sticky when worked with white flour, and it adds only a tiny portion of white to the overall volume of the dark grains.

INGREDIENTS

1½ cups cold water
¾ cup cornmeal, white or yellow
1½ cups boiling water
1 tablespoon salt
2 tablespoons *each* sugar and shortening
1 tablespoon caraway seeds
2 packages dry yeast
2 cups potato, mashed
4 cups rye flour
4 cups whole wheat flour, approximately

BAKING PANS

Three medium (8½ x 4½) loaf pans, greased or Teflon. If glass, reduce oven heat 25°.

PREPARATION
30 mins.

In a saucepan, stir cold water into the cornmeal, add the boiling water, and cook. Stir constantly, until thick and smooth. Add salt, sugar, shortening, and caraway seeds. Let stand until the mixture is warm (105°–115°) to the touch.

Sprinkle yeast into the warm mixture, and blend it in. Add the mashed potato (or ½ cup instant potato and 1½ cups warm water). Stir in rye flour and follow with 1½ cups of the whole wheat flour.

This will be a heavy, dense dough to work with the spoon and hands. Add sufficient whole wheat flour to form a ball. It will be sticky at the beginning. Let it stand 5 minutes until the flours have fully absorbed the moisture.

KNEADING
10 mins.

Turn out on a work surface—counter top or bread board—that is liberally floured with white flour (see opening paragraph). It will be helpful to use a spatula or wide putty knife to turn the dough and, at the same time, to keep the work surface scraped clean. The dough will become somewhat elastic and smooth. It will never achieve the elasticity of white dough. Knead. (It will be too heavy to work with a dough hook.)

FIRST RISING
1 hour

Place the dough in a bowl and pat with buttered or greased fingers to keep the surface from crusting. Cover the bowl tightly with plastic wrap and move to a warm place (80°–85°) until the dough has risen to about twice its original size (as judged by how it creeps up the bowl).

SHAPING
15 mins.

Punch down dough and knead for 30 seconds to press out the bubbles. Divide the dough into three pieces with a sharp knife. Shape into balls. Let them rest under a towel for 3 minutes. Form a loaf by pressing a ball of dough under the palms or with a rolling pin into a flat oval, roughly the length of the baking pan. Fold the oval in half, pinch the seam tightly to seal, tuck under the ends, and place in the pan, seam down. Repeat with the other two loaves.

SECOND RISING
45 mins.

Place the pans in the warm place, cover with wax paper and leave until the center of the dough has risen to the level of the edge of the pan.

BAKING
375°
1 hour

Preheat oven to 375°. Bake the loaves in the oven. When tapping the bottom crust yields a hard and hollow sound, they are done. If not, return to the oven for an additional 10 minutes. Test again. If you wish a darker over-all crust, remove the loaves from the pans during the final 10 minutes of the bake period. Midway in the baking, and again near the end, shift the loaves so they are exposed equally to temperature variations in the oven.

FINAL STEP

Remove bread from the oven, turn from pans and cool the loaves on a metal rack. This loaf will keep for two weeks or longer and for several months in the freezer. Slice thinly.

PEASANT BLACK BREAD

[TWO HEARTH LOAVES]

These long and almost black loaves look and taste like a choice European peasant rye bread. The crusts are quite thick and hard when the bread comes from the oven but the loaves are kept for a day or two in a plastic bag until the crusts soften. It has the unsweet but full flavor of parched grain.

The bread gets its fine dark coloring from Postum (the granules for the cereal beverage) and finely ground bread crumbs toasted until they are very dark. Be careful, however, not to burn them. Keep the crusts and ends from new loaves to make crumbs for successively darker ones in the future.

INGREDIENTS

2 cups fine bread crumbs, toasted until dark
3 teaspoons Postum
2 cups hot tap water (120°–130°)
¼ cup dark molasses
3 packages dry yeast
½ cup warm water (105°–115°)
¼ teaspoon ground ginger
3 cups rye flour
4 tablespoons butter, melted
2 teaspoons salt
2 cups all-purpose or bread flour, approximately
Glaze: 1 teaspoon Postum
2 teaspoons water

BAKING SHEET

One baking sheet, greased or Teflon.

PREPARATION
30 mins.

Beforehand, toast 2 cups of bread crumbs until they are dark but not burned. The best crumbs for this recipe are made with rye crusts from other loaves. To make even successive loaves darker, save the ends and crusts from this new bread. Store in the freezer for the next baking of black bread.

In a large bowl dissolve the Postum in tap water. Stir in the molasses and bread crumbs. Allow to stand until the crumbs are soaked and soft, and the mixture is only warm to the touch.

In a separate cup or small bowl dissolve yeast in warm water and stir in the ginger. Let it stand 10 minutes and then stir it into the bread crumb mixture.

Add the rye flour, and stir thoroughly. Mix in the butter and salt. Spread the 2 cups of flour on the work surface, counter top or bread board, and turn the mixture out onto it. It will be quite solid and seem dry. Invert the bowl over the dough and let it rest for 15 minutes.

KNEADING
10 mins.

Work the flour into the damp mixture. Knead until a smooth but stiff dough is formed. Early in the kneading process it will be sticky but gradually it will become elastic.

FIRST RISING
1½ hours

Place the ball of dough in the mixing bowl and pat with greased fingers to keep the surface from crusting. Cover the bowl tightly with plastic wrap and move to a warm place (80°–85°) until the dough has risen to twice its original size.

SHAPING
15 mins.

Turn the dough onto the work surface, knead out the bubbles and cut into two pieces with a sharp knife. Form each into a round ball. Let rest for 3 minutes. Press each ball into a long flat oval under the palms or with a rolling pin. Double over and pound several times down the middle of the long piece with the edge of the hand. Fold over, seal, and roll back and forth under the palms to fashion a long (18″) loaf. Repeat with the second piece. Place on the baking sheet.

SECOND RISING
30 mins.

Cover lightly with wax paper and return to the warm place.

BAKING
400°
45 mins.

Preheat oven to 400°. Just before baking mix 1 teaspoon of Postum in 2 teaspoons of water. Brush the loaves.

Bake in the hot oven. When tapping the bottom crust yields a hard and hollow sound, they are done.

FINAL STEP

Remove bread from the oven. After the loaves have cooled on a metal rack, place them in long plastic bags for a day or two to soften the crusts. This loaf keeps for a fortnight or more wrapped in plastic. Will keep for months frozen.

SWEDISH LIMPA RYE

[TWO LARGE ROUND LOAVES]

This is one of the author's favorite loaves from among a dozen limpa recipes in his files. It has the chili-like flavor of crushed cummin seed, the unmistakable fragrance of fennel, and the pleasant goodness of orange. Studded with raisins, the loaf rises up to become a handsome brown ball. It sends forth a good aroma when toasted and buttered.

INGREDIENTS

2 packages dry yeast
2 cups warm water (105°–115°)
2½ cups medium rye flour
¼ cup *each* sugar and molasses
1 teaspoon *each* cummin and fennel, crushed or ground
Grated rind of 2 oranges
1 cup raisins, light or dark
4 cups all-purpose or bread flour, approximately
3 tablespoons shortening
1 tablespoon salt

BAKING SHEET — One baking sheet, greased or Teflon.

PREPARATION
20 mins.

In a large bowl or cup dissolve yeast in water. Stir briskly with a fork or whip. Let it stand 5 minutes to begin its fermentation.

With a large wooden spoon stir all of the rye flour, sugar, molasses, cummin, fennel, orange rind, raisins, and about 1½ cups of white flour into the bowl. Beat until smooth—about 100 strokes.

Add 1 cup flour, stir, and beat in the shortening and salt. By hand add more flour, a little at a time, until the dough cleans the sides of the bowl and is stiff. If a raisin works its way out, push it back into the dough. The slight discoloration that sometimes comes with working fruit into white dough will not be noticed in this dark loaf.

KNEADING
10 mins.

Turn dough out onto a lightly floured board or counter top. Since this will be a slightly sticky dough, it may help to grease the fingers before beginning. Knead until the dough is smooth and no longer sticky.

FIRST RISING
50 mins.

Put the dough into the large bowl (which has been washed and greased), cover tightly with plastic wrap and leave in a warm place (80°–85°) until it doubles in bulk. You can test if it has risen by poking a finger in it; the dent will remain.

SHAPING
15 mins.

Punch down dough with quick jabs of the fist and fingers. Turn it over; let rest for 10 minutes. Turn the dough onto the board, knead briefly to press out the air. With a sharp knife, cut into two pieces. Pat and roll the dough into round balls. Place on opposite corners of the baking sheet. Flatten slightly.

SECOND RISING
45 mins.

Cover the dough with wax paper or foil and return to the warm place until doubled in volume. You can test if it has risen by poking a finger in it; the dent will remain.

BAKING
375°
45 mins.

Preheat the oven to 375°. With a razor blade or sharp knife, slash a cross on the top of each loaf. Bake in the oven. When the loaves are crusty and tapping the bottom crust yields a hard and hollow sound, they are done. If not, return to oven for an additional 10 minutes. If the loaves appear to be browning too quickly, cover with a piece of foil or brown sack paper.

FINAL STEP — Remove from oven and place the loaves on a wire cooling rack. This limpa makes exceptionally good toast. The loaf freezes well.

PUMPERNICKEL SPONGE RYE

[TWO LOAVES]

The sponge in this recipe stands from 4 to 72 hours—the longer the better for a true sour rye (vs. sweet rye) flavor. The sponge will bubble in the bowl under the plastic wrap (which catches and returns all of the moisture), giving off a heady, fermented aroma. This recipe has almost equal parts of rye and white flours.

This is one of my long-time favorite rye loaves, unexcelled for buffets, picnics, or sandwiches anytime. I make it both in the long and round loaves, depending on the occasion.

Keeps for ten days or two weeks tightly wrapped in plastic or foil. Will hold in the freezer for months.

INGREDIENTS
- 2 packages dry yeast
- 1½ cups warm water (105°–115°)
- 2½ cups medium or pumpernickel rye flour
- 1 tablespoon salt
- 1 to 3 tablespoons caraway seeds
- 2 tablespoons vegetable shortening, room temperature
- ⅓ cup molasses
- 3 cups all-purpose flour, approximately

BAKING SHEET — One baking sheet, greased or Teflon.

PREPARATION
1–3 days — One to three days beforehand prepare the sponge by sprinkling yeast over water in a medium-size bowl, and adding the rye flour. Mix into a smooth paste. Cover tightly with plastic wrap and put in a warm place (80°–85°) for at least overnight—three days preferably.

15 mins. — On bake day, add and stir in the salt, caraway seeds, shortening, molasses and 1 cup all-purpose flour. Beat 100 strokes until it is smooth. Stir in additional flour, a little at a time, first with a wooden spoon and then with the hands, until a soft mass is formed and the sides of the bowl are dry and cleaned.

KNEADING
6 mins. — Turn the dough onto a lightly floured work surface—counter top or bread board. This is a sticky dough be-

cause of the rye so keep the work surface and fingers dusted with flour. Oil or butter on the fingers will also help overcome the stickiness. Knead until smooth and the stickiness is gone.

FIRST RISING
1 hour

Place the dough in the mixing bowl, pat with greased fingertips and cover the bowl with plastic wrap. Put in a warm place (80°–85°) until the dough has doubled in bulk. You can test if it has risen by poking a finger in it; the dent will remain.

SHAPING
8 mins.

Turn back the plastic wrap and punch down the dough. Place it on the floured work surface and cut it in two with a sharp knife. For a round loaf, shape into a ball and place on the baking sheet. For a long loaf, roll into a rectangle, roll up tightly and place on the sheet.

SECOND RISING
45 mins.

Cover with wax paper and return to the warm place.

BAKING
375°
40–45 mins.

Preheat oven to 375°. With a sharp knife or razor blade, make 3 slashes across the tops of the round loaves, and 6 diagonal cuts down the long loaves. Brush with warm water, sprinkle with caraway seeds and bake in the oven until well browned. When tapping the bottom crust yields a hard and hollow sound, they are done. If not, return to the oven for an additional 10 minutes. If the loaves appear to be browning too quickly, cover with a piece of foil or brown sack paper.

FINAL STEP

Remove from the oven to the metal racks to cool.

RUSSIAN BLACK BREAD

[TWO LARGE LOAVES]

A chewy dark, almost black bread that looks to onion powder, crushed fennel seed, instant coffee granules, molasses and vinegar for some of its good taste. I use coarse pumpernickel rye flour, rather than the usual medium rye, to give it a rough texture usually associated with European peasant breads. It is fine for buffets, especially when it is shaped long and slender. A fat round loaf, it is good for sandwich slices.

INGREDIENTS

2 packages dry yeast
3½ cups all-purpose flour, approximately
4 cups medium or pumpernickel rye flour

1 teaspoon sugar
1 tablespoon salt
2 cups whole bran cereal
2 tablespoons caraway seed, crushed
2 teaspoons *each* instant coffee and onion powder
½ teaspoon fennel seed, crushed
2½ cups water
¼ cup *each* vinegar and dark molasses
1 square (1 oz.) unsweetened chocolate
¼ cup shortening
Glaze: 1 teaspoon cornstarch mixed into ½ cup cold water

BAKING PANS OR BAKE SHEET

Two 8-inch cake pans, greased, or, if the loaves are fairly stiff and will hold their shapes, place them on a baking sheet, greased or Teflon.

PREPARATION

Here is a choice of two ways to begin—mixer or by hand.

If you do this with a small electric mixer, change to hand beating and mixing at the first hint that the mixer is laboring or slowing down—or if it begins to heat up. It is advisable to use a small portable mixer only in thin and medium batters before the dough begins to take on body.

20 mins.

In a large bowl mix the yeast, 1 cup white and 1 cup rye flours, sugar, salt, bran cereal, caraway seed, instant coffee, onion powder, and fennel seed. In a saucepan combine water, vinegar, molasses, chocolate and shortening. Place over low heat. When the liquid is warm (the chocolate and shortening need to soften) add to the dry ingredients. Beat at medium speed for 2 minutes, scraping the bowl occasionally. Add 1 cup white and 1 cup rye flours. This may be the time to start beating by hand if you have been using the electric mixer. Nevertheless, beat for 2 minutes, or about 100 strong strokes. Stir in 2 cups rye and enough white flour (about 1 cup) to make a soft dough.

20 mins.

By hand—(the order of ingredients varies here).
In a small bowl dissolve yeast in ½ cup warm water (105°–115°). In a saucepan place 2 cups water, chocolate, and shortening, and heat until the liquid is warm, and the chocolate has dissolved.

In a large mixing bowl place the bran cereal, rye

flour, sugar, salt, caraway seed, instant coffee, onion powder, fennel seed, and the chocolate mixture. Add vinegar and molasses and the yeast mixture. With a wooden spoon beat 100 times, and then gradually add the white flour until it is a soft but slightly sticky dough.

Both—

Work flour into the dough first with the wooden spoon and then with the fingers and hands. When it has body and is no longer a sticky blob, turn out on a floured work surface—counter top or bread board.

RESTING 15 mins.	Cover the dough with the bowl and let it rest for 15 minutes.
KNEADING 8 mins.	Knead until the dough is smooth and elastic. If the dough is sticky, dust it and your hands with a bit of flour. Scrape away any sticky film that forms on the work surface, and dust it afresh.
FIRST RISING 1 hour	Place in a greased bowl, turning to cover all of the dough with a light film of oil. Cover the bowl tightly with plastic wrap and put the bowl in a warm place (80°–85°) until the dough has doubled in bulk.
SHAPING 10 mins.	Punch down with the fingers and turn out onto the lightly floured work surface. With a sharp knife, cut the dough into two pieces. Let the pieces rest for 5 minutes. Shape each into a ball and place either in a cake pan or on a baking sheet.
SECOND RISING 45 mins.	Cover with a sheet of wax paper and place in the warm spot until the loaves have doubled in bulk.
BAKING 350° 1 hour	Preheat oven to 350°. Bake in the oven until a wooden toothpick or metal skewer inserted in the center of a loaf comes out dry and clean. When tapping the bottom crust yields a hard and hollow sound, they are done. Meanwhile, prepare the glaze. In a small saucepan mix the cornstarch and cold water. Cook over medium heat, stirring constantly, until the mixture boils. Hold the boil for 1 minute, stirring all the while. When the bread is baked, remove from the oven and brush the loaves with the cornstarch mixture. Place the loaves back in the oven for about 3 minutes, or until the glaze has set.

FINAL STEP — Remove bread from the oven, turn from baking sheet or pan and place on metal racks to cool.

SOUR CREAM RYE BREAD

[TWO LOAVES]

This crusty loaf is dark and heavy with full rye taste and texture. I adapted this in my kitchen from a recipe in the fine Tassajara Bread Book from the Zen Center in San Francisco. My loaves are hearth baked —round and stabbed with a metal skewer so the top crust can expand some but not lift up too dramatically. The original recipe called for nothing but rye flour but the addition of a small portion of white makes a better loaf.

INGREDIENTS

1 cup all-purpose flour, approximately
5 cups rye flour
2 packages dry yeast
1 cup sour cream, room temperature
¼ cup molasses
1 tablespoon salt
¼ cup cooking oil
1½ tablespoons caraway seeds
1 cup hot tap water (120°–130°)

BAKING SHEET — One baking sheet, greased or Teflon.

PREPARATION — The 5 cups of rye flour and only 1 of white makes this a heavy and sticky dough to work. A metal spatula or broad putty knife to turn the dough during kneading will help. Also a tablespoon of shortening nearby in which fingertips can be greased occasionally will control some of the stickiness.

Measure ½ cup all-purpose flour, 2 cups rye flour, yeast, sour cream, molasses, salt, oil and 1 tablespoon caraway seeds into a large mixing bowl. Pour in the water and blend ingredients thoroughly with a wooden spoon.

Beat in the electric mixer at medium speed for 3 minutes, or for an equal length of time with the wooden spoon.

Stop the mixer. Add the balance of the rye flour and, finally, the remaining ½ cup of all-purpose flour.

Stir in these flours, a half cup at a time, first with the spoon and then by hand. The dough will be a rough, shaggy mass that will clean the sides of the bowl. If the dough continues slack and moist, and is sticky, sprinkle on small amounts of all-purpose flour.

KNEADING
8 mins.

Turn the dough out onto floured surface. The dough will be a sticky mass to start. Keep turning it with the spatula and the fingers. Gradually it will become more workable. It will never become as elastic and alive as white dough, however. Knead.

FIRST RISING
1 hour

Place dough in the clean mixing bowl and pat with buttered or greased fingers to keep the surface from crusting. Cover the bowl tightly with plastic wrap and move to a warm place (80°–85°) until the dough has risen to twice its original size.

SHAPING
5 mins.

Punch down the dough and knead for 30 seconds to press out the bubbles. With a sharp knife divide into two pieces. Form each into a ball. Place on opposite corners of the baking sheet or in small baskets, lined loosely with cloths sprinkled with flour.

SECOND RISING
45 mins.

Cover with wax paper and return to the warm place until the loaves have doubled in size. If the paper clings to the dough, elevate it on glass tumblers.

If the loaves have raised in baskets, tip the raised loaf into your hand and quickly turn it right side up and onto the baking sheet.

BAKING
350°
50–60 mins.

Preheat oven to 350°. With a razor blade cut a tic-tac-toe design on the top of the loaves.

Brush with water and sprinkle with caraway seeds. Bake in the oven. When the loaves are dark brown and crusty and tapping the bottom crust yields a hard and hollow sound, they are done. If the loaves appear to be browning too quickly, cover with a piece of foil or brown sack paper. Midway in the bake period and again near the end of it shift the loaves so they are exposed equally to temperature variations in the oven.

FINAL STEP

Remove bread from the oven and lift to the metal rack to cool before serving. This loaf keeps well for two or three weeks if it is wrapped tightly in foil or plastic. Freezes equally well, too.

HAM IN RYE

[ONE LOAF]

This is an ideal picnic loaf—the rye bread surrounds the ham ready to be sliced. The bread itself is one of my favorite recipes that takes 3 days to prepare but the sour rye flavor and the ham make an unbeatable combination for an out-of-doors feast. On occasion I have used a small Canadian bacon piece but I think ham is best.

The rye does not cling to the ham so expect the loaf to have raised away from the meat. The meat slice will be loose in the bread but the guests will like it nevertheless.

INGREDIENTS	Rye dough, see Old Milwaukee Rye, page 176 1 three-pound piece cooked ham, room temperature Glaze: 1 egg white 1 tablespoon water
BAKING PAN	One 10-inch cake pan, greased or Teflon, with 1½-inch sides.
PREPARATION	Prepare the dough. When it has risen and has been punched down, turn it out on the floured work surface.
SHAPING 15 mins.	Let the dough relax 5 minutes. Roll the dough into a rectangle large enough to completely surround the ham. Place the ham in the center of the dough and draw it up over the meat. Pinch the folds together, and form a neat topknot. A long piece of Canadian bacon can be rolled into the rectangle, making certain the thick overlap is on the top when the loaf is placed in the pan.
RISING 45 mins.	Cover the loaf with plastic and let rise in a warm place (80°–85°).
BAKING 425° 10 mins. 375° 50 mins.	Preheat oven to 425°. Brush the loaf with the egg white and water mixture. Bake in the hot oven for 10 minutes, reduce heat to 375° and bake for an additional 50 minutes.
FINAL STEP	Remove bread from the oven and turn out of pan. Serve hot, or cool on rack and serve later at room temperature.

SPICY RYE BREAD

[TWO ROUND OR OBLONG LOAVES]

The first aromatic hint of the spiciness of this recipe will come when the cloves, allspice and caraway are mixed in hot water with the molasses and brown sugar. This is a dark brown rye loaf that carries 4 slashes across the crust to prevent the loaves from breaking on the sides. It also identifies the loaf as something special.

Like all recipes with rye flour this one will be sticky until, suddenly, there comes that moment in kneading when stickiness ceases and all is well. Remember: keep a light sprinkle of flour powdered on the dough and on the work surface. If the dough seems unusually tenacious in its stickiness, rub the fingertips with vegetable shortening.

INGREDIENTS

2 packages dry yeast
¾ cup warm water (105°–115°)
2 teaspoons salt
½ teaspoon *each* ground cloves and allspice
1 teaspoon caraway seeds
2 tablespoons brown sugar, packed
3 tablespoons molasses
1 cup hot tap water
2 tablespoons shortening
2½ cups rye flour
3 to 3½ cups all-purpose white flour, approximately

BAKING SHEET

One baking sheet, greased or Teflon.

PREPARATION
15 mins.

In a small bowl or cup sprinkle the yeast over lukewarm water. Stir briskly with a fork or whisk to dissolve the yeast granules. Set aside.

In a large mixing bowl measure the salt, cloves, allspice, caraway seeds, sugar, molasses and hot water. Add shortening. Blend well. Add yeast mixture, rye flour and 1 cup of white flour to the bowl. Beat until smooth with a wooden spoon—about 100 strokes—or 2 minutes at medium speed with an electric mixer.

Put aside the electric mixer and add more flour, first with the spoon and then with the fingers. The dough, which will clean the sides of the bowl, will be a rough mass, a bit sticky but firm.

KNEADING
8 mins.

Turn the dough out onto a lightly floured work surface —counter top or bread board—and knead firmly with a push-turn-fold motion until the dough is smooth and elastic under the hand.

FIRST RISING
1 hour

Place dough in a greased bowl, turning once to film all sides. Cover with plastic wrap and let rise in a warm place (80°–85°) until doubled. You can test if it has risen by poking a finger in it; the dent will remain.

SHAPING
10 mins.

Divide dough into two parts. Round up each into a smooth ball or oblong shape and place on the opposite corners of the baking sheet.

SECOND RISING
45 mins.

Cover with a sheet of aluminum foil, and shape it so that it does not touch the dough. Put in a warm place until double in size. You can test if it has risen by poking a finger in it; the dent will remain.

BAKING
375°
45 mins.

Preheat oven to 375°. With a sharp knife or razor slash the top of the loaves into a pattern. I make four slashes in the form of a square that identifies this type of loaf in my bread box and freezer. Bake loaves until they are brown and test done when pierced with a toothpick. If the pick comes out clean and dry the loaf is done. Also, when tapping the bottom crust yields a hard and hollow sound, they are done. Should the crust begin to darken too fast, cover with brown paper the last 15 minutes of the bake period.

FINAL STEP

Remove bread from the oven and shift from the baking sheet to the metal rack to cool. For slightly glazed crust, brush with water.

VORTLIMPA

[THREE LONG SLENDER LOAVES]

From the moment you pour the three cups of dark stout into the saucepan you know you are on to something special. Because of the stout and the molasses-water glaze, it is dark (almost black) and shiny and it confounds the tongue with a sweet dark taste. It was once voted the best loaf to ever come from my kitchen by a young woman who had studied for several years in Norway and had fallen under the spell of their dark breads. Others have found it too assertive. Try it with goat cheese or feta.

INGREDIENTS

4 packages dry yeast
Pinch of sugar
¼ cup warm water (105°–115°)
3 cups stout or dark beer
1 teaspoon salt
¼ cup or ½ stick butter, room temperature
1 cup dark molasses
6 cups medium rye flour
4 cups all-purpose flour, approximately
Peel of 2 oranges, finely chopped
2 tablespoons fennel, ground or pounded
Glaze: 1 tablespoon molasses
2 tablespoons water

BAKING SHEET

Baking sheet, greased or Teflon.

PREPARATION
20 mins.

Sprinkle yeast and sugar on the warm water in a small bowl. Stir it briskly and set aside. In a medium-sized saucepan heat the stout, salt, and butter. When the butter has melted remove from heat, add molasses, stir and let it cool to lukewarm.

This is a large batch (anything over 6 cups of flour is large) and requires a large bowl. With a wooden spoon, work 3 cups of rye flour and 1 cup of white flour into stout mixture. Beat well—about 100 strokes—until batter is creamy and smooth. Add yeast mixture, orange peel, fennel seed and remaining 3 cups of rye flour. Stir —and when new flour has been absorbed, add 2 cups or more of white flour. Stir with the spoon until it leaves the sides of the bowl, and then continue to mix by hand.

KNEADING
10 mins.

Turn out on a floured board or counter top. In the beginning it will be sticky. Rye dough always is. Handle the new dough gingerly, dusting well with flour, until you have struck a workable balance. This could mean the addition of a cup or more of white flour in the early part of the kneading process. Gradually it will take on an even texture and no longer stick to your hands or to the work surface. Knead for at least 5 minutes after the dough has reached this point.

FIRST RISING
1½ hours

Place the dough in a greased bowl, cover tightly with plastic wrap and let rise in a warm place (80°–85°) until double.

SHAPING
15 mins.

Turn out on the floured counter top and cut into three equal pieces. Flatten a piece with the palm of the hand, and with a rolling pin form a long rectangle. Roll it into a tight loaf. Seal the seam by pinching it shut along its length. You can also experiment by shaping the piece by hand, rolling it under the palms until the loaf is about 12 to 14 inches long. Repeat with the other pieces.

Place loaves on baking sheet. Be certain they are far enough apart that they won't touch when they rise. If they threaten, fold two kitchen towels, dust well with flour, and lay between the loaves.

SECOND RISING
45 mins.

Cover with wax paper and return to the warm place until they have doubled in volume.

BAKING
400°
30 mins.
325°
45 mins.

Preheat oven to 400°. Prick, or dock, the top of each loaf with a wooden toothpick, an inch or more deep in a dozen places, so steam can escape without lifting off the top.

Bake in the hot oven for 30 minutes; turn heat down to 325°. Continue baking for 45 minutes more. When tapping the bottom crust yields a hard and hollow sound, they are done.

Halfway through the baking, turn the loaves and brush with the molasses-water glaze. A few minutes before the loaves are done, brush them again with the glaze and return to the oven until the glaze has set (about 4 minutes).

FINAL STEP

Remove bread from the oven and place on a wire rack to cool. Wrap in foil or plastic wrap to keep crusts soft.

SPICED RYE BREAD

[FOUR MEDIUM LOAVES AND A DOZEN ROLLS]

This is a big recipe. There are about 10 cups of flour which yield approximately 7 pounds of dough when all is assembled. You may wish to reduce ingredients by half.

Dough can be a demanding mistress. Fight back! Since this is made with a starter only, no yeast, the periods of rising, or proofing, are longer than usual. On occasion, I have punched it down and put it in the refrigerator rather than wait past my bedtime for it to double in bulk.

In the morning I have set it in a warm room for an hour or so, and gone on from there to finish the bread. Dough, once it has come alive and is growing, can take a lot of abuse, so punch it down if it crests at an inopportune time.

This loaf has a delightful spicy taste.

INGREDIENTS

Cooked Potato Starter (see page 284)

Sponge:
- 1½ cups of starter, room temperature
- 2 cups warm water (105°–115°)
- 3 tablespoons molasses
- 3 cups rye flour
- 1 cup oatmeal

Dough:
- 2 cups warm water (105°–115°)
- 1 cup non-fat dry milk
- ½ teaspoon ginger
- 2 tablespoons salt
- 6 tablespoons shortening, room temperature
- 3 tablespoons molasses
- 3 tablespoons *each* crushed allspice and grated orange peel
- 8 cups all-purpose flour, approximately

Glaze:
- 1 tablespoon milk
- 1 teaspoon sugar
- ½ teaspoon cinnamon, optional

BAKING PANS AND BAKE SHEET

Four medium (8½ x 4½) loaf pans, greased or Teflon, and baking sheet for the rolls. If glass pans are used, reduce oven heat 25°.

PREPARATION
Overnight
8–12 hours

The night before, in a large bowl, make a sponge of 1½ cups of prepared potato starter, warm water, molasses, rye flour and oatmeal. Beat together, cover with plastic wrap and put in a warm place (80°–85°).

Bake Day
15 mins.

On bake day, turn back the plastic wrap, stir down the sponge and add 2 cups warm water, milk, ginger, salt, shortening, molasses, allspice, orange rind and 5 cups of all-purpose flour. Beat thoroughly—at least 200 strong strokes with a large wooden spoon. Add more flour, ½ cup at a time, to make a soft mass that pulls away from the sides of the bowl.

KNEADING
20 mins.

Spread flour over the work surface and turn the rough ball of dough onto it. Work with the fingers, kneading until it absorbs more flour and becomes smooth and elastic—approximately 10 minutes. Let it rest 5 minutes, and knead again for 5 additional minutes.

FIRST RISING
1½ hours

Return the dough to the bowl, pat all over with shortening, cover the bowl with plastic wrap and put in a warm place (80°–85°) until dough is light and doubled in bulk.

SHAPING
15 mins.

Punch down the dough, turn it out onto the floured work surface and divide and shape into loaves or rolls as desired. (See dough volume chart, page 23.) Brush with shortening.

SECOND RISING
1 hour

Cover with wax paper and return to the warm place until the dough has doubled in bulk. You can test if it has risen by poking a finger in it; the dent will remain.

BAKING
350°
30 mins.
1 hour

Preheat oven to 350°. Bake in the oven—rolls for 30 minutes, and the loaves for 1 hour or until a dark crusty brown. When tapping the bottom crust yields a hard and hollow sound, they are done.

FINAL STEP

Remove bread from the oven and turn loaves onto wire racks to cool before slicing. Brush tops with milk. For an added taste delight, mix sugar and cinnamon with the milk to be brushed on the loaves.

DARK RYE BREAD

[FOUR LOAVES]

There is a nut-like quality in a bite of this dark rye loaf that is a batter bread, no kneading. This does not mean that it is easy to make because it is not. It is hard work. The heavy, sticky glob of rye and white flour is difficult to beat especially in the large quantities of this recipe. I suggest cutting the recipe in half for the first endeavor.

The finished loaves—dark, moist, nutty and waxy—make it worth the effort, however. If the different kinds of rye flours (or meal) are not available, use the rye at hand.

INGREDIENTS

4 cups warm water (105°–115°)
1 cup dark molasses
2 packages dry yeast
½ cup cooking oil
2 tablespoons salt
4 egg yolks, room temperature
1 cup warm water (105°–115°)
½ cup instant mashed potato granules
2 cups non-fat dry milk
2 cups medium rye flour (or rye meal)
7 cups dark or pumpernickel rye flour
3 cups all-purpose flour

CASSEROLES OR PANS

Four 2-quart casseroles, greased or Teflon, or 4 large (9 x 5) loaf pans, or combination. If glass, reduce oven heat 25°.

PREPARATION
20 mins.

Pour the water into a large bowl and add the molasses and yeast. Stir and let stand while continuing with the recipe.

In a separate bowl beat together the oil, salt, egg yolks, 1 cup warm water, potato granules, and milk. Add this to the yeast mixture.

Stir in the medium rye flour and the dark or pumpernickel rye flour. Beat 100 strong strokes. Add the all-purpose flour, a half cup at a time, to make a stiff dough that pulls from the spoon after it has been beaten. About 100 strong strokes. The dough will be soft but not fluid.

FIRST RISING
1½ hours

Cover the bowl tightly with plastic wrap and move to a warm place (80°–85°) until the dough has risen to about twice its original volume.

SECOND RISING
50 mins.

Turn back the plastic wrap, stir down the dough. Replace the cover and allow to rise again.

SHAPING
6 mins.

Divide the dough into equal parts with a spoon and place in the prepared casseroles or baking pans. Wet the spoon or a spatula and mound the dough slightly.

THIRD RISING
45 mins.

Cover the pans with a length of wax paper but don't let it touch the moist dough. Place above on glass tumblers if necessary. Leave the loaves until doubled in bulk.

BAKING
400°
15 mins.

Preheat the oven to 400°. Carefully brush the tops with vegetable oil. Bake in the hot oven for 15 minutes, reduce heat to 350° and bake for an additional 40 min-

350°
40 mins.

utes, or until the loaves are a deep brown. When tapping the bottom crust yields a hard and hollow sound, they are done. If not, return to the oven for an additional 10 minutes.

FINAL STEP

Remove bread from the oven. Let the loaves cool in the casseroles or pans for 10 minutes before turning onto metal racks.

PUMPERNICKEL BREAD

[ONE LARGE ROUND LOAF]

Baked with all dark grains, this pumpernickel bread, as delicious as it is, should not be undertaken by an amateur who could be discouraged by the difficult job of kneading a batch of sticky dough. This has no white flour, only rye (with no gluten) and whole wheat. It is a loaf for an advanced amateur, a baker who will tolerate the tedium of stickiness until, finally, the gluten forms and the dough kneads easily under the palms.

The loaves cut into dark brown, almost black slices of moist wheaty bread. Ideal for buffets, and sandwiches. Or served with sliced cheese—and a cold beer on the side. It is too heavy to toast, of course, but it freezes well.

INGREDIENTS

1½ cups water
½ cup cornmeal
¾ cup molasses
1 tablespoon *each:* butter and salt
2 teaspoons sugar
1½ teaspoons caraway seed, pounded slightly
½ square unsweetened chocolate
1 package yeast
¼ cup warm water (105°–115°)
1 cup mashed potato (prepared from instant)
3 cups rye flour
1 cup whole wheat flour, approximately
Glaze: 1 egg white mixed with 1 tablespoon cold water

BAKING SHEET

One baking sheet, greased or Teflon.

PREPARATION
25 mins.

Combine water and cornmeal in a medium saucepan and cook the mixture, stirring with a wooden spoon, until it is thickened. Remove from the heat and add molasses, butter, salt, sugar, caraway seed and chocolate. Stir until it is well blended, pour into a large mixing bowl and set aside until it has cooled to warm (105°–115°).

Meanwhile, dissolve yeast in water. Add the yeast and potato to the mixture in the bowl. Blend well and stir in the rye flour and 1 cup whole wheat. The dough will be stiff and sticky.

KNEADING
10–12 mins.

Turn the dough onto a work surface liberally sprinkled with whole wheat flour. Put a little vegetable shortening or oil on your fingers and hands before you start to knead. Keep the surface of the dough powdered with flour. Also have a scraper handy to remove the gummy film of dough that accumulates on the work surface.

(I find this heavy dough almost impossible to knead with a dough hook on an electric mixer. The dough just sets in the bowl while the rotating hook carves a big hole in the center.)

Be patient and presently the dough will respond and begin to clear the work surface, and your fingers. Knead until it is elastic, though stiff.

FIRST RISING
1 hour

Place the dough in a greased bowl, cover with plastic wrap and put in a warm place (80°–85°). The dough will seem so heavy you may wonder how it could possibly rise. But it will and it will double in bulk.

SHAPING
5 mins.

Punch down the dough, knead out the air bubbles for 30 seconds and form the dough into a round, smooth ball. It may be divided into half and formed into two smaller loaves if you wish. Place on the baking sheet dusted with cornmeal.

SECOND RISING
50 mins.

Cover the loaves with wax paper and return to the warm draft-free place until they have doubled in bulk.

BAKING
375°
50 mins.

Preheat oven to 375°. Brush the loaves with egg white blended with water, and place in the oven. When tapping the bottom crust yields a hard and hollow sound, they are done. If not, return to the oven for an additional 10 minutes. If the loaves appear to be browning too quickly, cover with a piece of foil or brown sack paper.

FINAL STEP

Remove bread from the oven and place on a metal rack to cool. The bread will keep for several weeks, wrapped in foil or plastic.

SIX

Barley Breads

Barley
Lyons, 1579

Barley is one of the most ancient of the cultivated cereal grains. Grown by the Swiss lake dwellers in the Stone Age, barley mixed with water was one of the medicines prescribed by Hippocrates. The English and Dutch brought the grain to the early settlements in America while the Spanish introduced it into California.

Barley flour bakes into a dark loaf, and is the principal ingredient of several of the European black breads.

Barley flour, milled by Cellu of La Grange, Ill., is available at most health food stores. Rye flour, however, can be substituted for barley with good results.

BARLEY BANANA BREAD

[ONE LARGE LOAF]

A mild flour, barley allows the full flavor of the bananas and the nuts to dominate this loaf of smooth textured bread. While there is no wheat in this loaf, there is 1 cup of rice flour which is quite bland but it combines well with the barley to make a good-tasting and moist loaf.

INGREDIENTS
1 cup sugar
½ cup shortening, room temperature
2 eggs, room temperature and beaten
1⅓ cups mashed banana
1½ cups barley flour
1 cup rice flour
2 teaspoons baking powder
½ teaspoon salt
¾ cup walnuts

BAKING PAN
One large (9 x 5) baking pan, greased or Teflon. If glass, reduce oven heat 25°. To aid in turning out the loaf after it has baked, butter or grease the pan, line the long sides and bottom with a length of wax paper, and butter again. Leave tabs of paper sticking out a ½ inch so the loaf can be pulled from the pan.

PREPARATION
15 mins.
Preheat oven to 350°. In a mixing bowl, cream the sugar and shortening. Break in the eggs and stir in the mashed banana.

In another bowl, combine the barley flour, rice flour, baking powder and salt. Stir the dry ingredients into the egg-banana mixture. When this is well blended, add the walnuts.

FORMING
5 mins.
Pour the batter into the baking pan. With a rubber spatula or spoon, push the batter slightly higher around the edges of the pan than in the center to compensate for the rising crown in the oven.

BAKING
350°
1 hour
Place the pan in the oven and bake until it tests done when a wooden toothpick, inserted in the loaf, comes out clean and dry.

FINAL STEP
Remove bread from the oven. Carefully remove the loaf from the pan and allow to cool on a metal rack.

BARLEY ORANGE BREAD

[ONE LARGE OR TWO SMALL LOAVES]

The orange rind is rather elaborately prepared in this recipe but it subdues an otherwise dominant flavor that could overpower the subtleness of the gentle barley. If you like a strong orange flavor forego the boiling process and let the orange come through.

This loaf is light brown in color, with a shiny golden crust. There is something velvety soft about barley flour and it gives this loaf some of the same quality.

INGREDIENTS

Skin of two oranges
½ cup *each* sugar and water
2 cups barley flour, sifted
½ cup sugar
½ teaspoon salt
3 teaspoons baking powder
2 eggs, room temperature and beaten
½ cup orange juice (fresh or frozen)
3 tablespoons melted shortening

BAKING PAN

One medium (8½ x 4½) loaf pan, greased, glass or metal, or two small (7¼ x 3½) tins. If glass, reduce oven temperature 25°. The loaf will come out of the pan much easier if you line the long sides and bottom of the pan with a length of wax paper after having greased the pan. Be certain to grease the paper as well.

PREPARATION
1½ hours

First, the orange peels. Barely cover the rind from 2 oranges with water and boil for 10 minutes. Pour off the water; add more water and boil 10 minutes longer, or until tender. Pour off the water, and hold for a moment or so under cold running water. Chop the peels or grind them in a food chopper. Add ½ cup each sugar and water and cook until thick—about 25 minutes.

Later, when the orange mixture has cooled, sift flour, sugar, salt and baking powder into a large bowl. Add the eggs, the orange juice, shortening and the orange mixture. Combine—but don't overmix—and pour into either the large or two small loaf pans.

BAKING
350°
1 hour

Preheat oven to 350°. Bake in the oven. To test, insert a metal skewer into the center of the loaf. If it comes out clean and dry, the loaf is done. If moist particles cling to the skewer, the loaf is not baked. Return it to the oven for an additional 10 minutes. Test again. A wooden toothpick is a satisfactory probe for small loaves.

FINAL STEP

Remove bread from the oven. Let the bread cool for 10 minutes before turning it out of the pan. Warm quick bread is more fragile than a yeast loaf so handle it with care. Usually the loaf can be pulled from the pan (turned on its side) by the ends of wax paper lining sticking out. Peel off the paper and let the loaf cool on a metal rack before slicing. It will develop a richer flavor if allowed to mature at least a day at room temperature wrapped in plastic or foil.

RIESKA

[ONE 14-INCH FLAT LOAF OR TWO 8-INCH LOAVES]

Rieska, a velvety textured flat bread made with barley flour, is a traditional loaf from Lapland and northern Finland. There is no wheat flour in this bread but the barley alone produces a delightfully light and tasteful loaf. It is cut in pie-shaped wedges, spread with plenty of butter and served immediately.

INGREDIENTS

2 cups barley flour (or rye)
¾ teaspoon salt
2 teaspoons sugar
2 teaspoons baking powder
1 cup undiluted evaporated milk or light cream
2 tablespoons butter, melted

BAKING SHEET

Baking sheet, greased or Teflon.

PREPARATION
15 mins.

In a medium-size bowl combine the flour, salt, sugar and baking powder. Stir in the milk or cream and the butter until a soft dough forms. Preheat oven to 450°.

SHAPING
5 mins.

Spoon the dough onto the baking sheet. It will be soft and sticky so dust your hands lightly with flour before patting the mass into a circle about 14 inches in diameter, and about ½-inch thick. The dough may be divided in half to form two smaller 8-inch flat loaves. With the point of a knife lightly score the top to indicate the 8 or 10 servings, but do not cut. Prick all over with the tines of a fork.

BAKING
450°
10 mins.

Place in the oven until lightly browned.

FINAL STEP

Remove bread from the oven. Cut into pie-shaped pieces after it has cooled for 5 minutes, and serve immediately, spread with butter.

SEVEN

Corn Breads

Turkish Corn
Basle, 1542

Three truths keep bubbling to the surface in a search for a good piece of corn bread.

Southerners like their corn bread thin—about one inch deep in the pan. They want it made with white cornmeal. White looks pure.

The North likes a thick corn bread—sometimes three to four inches deep in the pan—and made with yellow cornmeal. Yellow looks rich.

Few Europeans care for corn in any form. They consider it a "gross food."

Corn was first seen by Columbus in Cuba on November 5, 1492. In 1616, a European author wrote of corn bread—

> There is as yet no certain experience of the naturall vertues of this corne. The bread that is made thereof is drye and hard, having very small fatness or moysture, wherefore men may easily judge, that it nourisheth but little, and is evill of digestion, nothing comparable to the bread made of wheat, as some have falsy affirmed.

To the colonists, in a cold land unfriendly to the growing of wheat, corn was manna. Indians taught them how to grow and prepare it. Pioneer women improved on the cooking techniques, invented dozens of kinds of corn bread, and put together hundreds of variations that became regional specialties.

To the new bread bakers without regional preferences, I confess that I find no difference in taste as between white and yellow. I will choose one over the other, on occasion, because of the color.

Here are a dozen and a half of the best corn bread recipes.

BACON SPOON BREAD

[ONE SOUFFLÉ DISH]

The Cheddar cheese, the hint of garlic, and the bits of bacon combine to make an unusually good spoon bread. It rises impressively in the oven and is served puffed and creamy. Carry it to the table in the casserole and spoon into individual dishes.

INGREDIENTS

½ pound fried bacon, in bits
2 cups sharp Cheddar cheese, shredded
¾ cup cornmeal, yellow preferred
1½ cups cold water
¼ cup butter or shortening, room temperature
2 garlic cloves, crushed
½ teaspoon salt
1 cup milk
4 egg yolks
4 egg whites, stiff-beaten

BAKING DISH

One 2-quart casserole or soufflé dish, greased.

PREPARATION
20 mins.

Beforehand, fry the bacon. Cut or chop into small bits. Shred the cheese.

Preheat oven to 325°.

20 mins.

Stir cornmeal into the cold water in the saucepan and place over medium heat. Bring to a bubbling boil, stirring constantly. When it is thick—perhaps 60 seconds —remove from heat. Stir in cheese, butter, garlic and salt. When cheese is melted pour in the milk. Stir in egg yolks and add bacon bits.

Beat egg whites stiff, and fold them into the batter.

FORMING
3 mins.

Pour into the casserole or soufflé dish. Level the batter with the rubber scraper or spatula.

BAKING
325°
1 hour

Bake in the oven. The bread will be nicely browned, high and puffy. Slip a knife blade into the center of the casserole. If the blade comes out clean and dry, the spoon bread is done. If not, return to the oven for an additional 10 minutes.

FINAL STEP

Remove bread from the oven. Serve while hot.

JOHNNYCAKE

[FOUR TO SIX SERVINGS]

In early America it was called journey cake—fine to pack for a long horseback trip. This recipe is a particularly good one—eggs, butter, milk, white flour and cornmeal. It is eggy, of course, thanks to 2 beaten eggs. Best served warm from the oven.

INGREDIENTS	2 eggs, room temperature and beaten ½ teaspoon salt 2 tablespoons *each* sugar and butter, melted 1 cup *each* cornmeal and all-purpose flour 2 teaspoons baking powder 1 cup milk, room temperature
BAKING PAN	One 8-inch square pan, greased or Teflon.
PREPARATION 15 mins.	Preheat oven to 425°. Into a large bowl break the eggs and add the salt. Whip until the eggs are light in color. Beat in sugar and butter. On a length of wax paper sift the cornmeal, flour and baking powder. Alternately, add this and the cup of milk to the bowl. Blend well.
FORMING 3 mins.	Pour the batter into the buttered square pan, and work it into the corners with a spatula or spoon.
BAKING 425° 20 mins.	Bake in the oven. Pierce the center of the loaf with a wooden pick. If it comes out clean and dry the bread is done.
FINAL STEP	Remove bread from the oven. Serve while warm or on a journey.

VIRGINIA SPOON BREAD

[SIX SERVINGS]

It is one home baker's opinion that this is one of the South's best food exports. It is simply made—a base of cornmeal, the yolks of three eggs, and the beaten whites of four folded in. The delicious result: a puffed and brown-crusted dish to be spooned into individual side dishes.

INGREDIENTS	1 cup cornmeal, white 2 cups boiling water ¼ cup (½ stick) butter, melted 1 teaspoon salt 1½ cups milk 3 egg yolks 4 egg whites, stiffly beaten
BAKING DISH	One 1-quart baking dish, greased or buttered.
PREPARATION 15 mins.	Preheat oven to 350°. Stir cornmeal gradually into the rapidly boiling water. When the mixture is smooth, add butter, salt and stir in the milk. Remove from heat and stir in the egg yolks. Allow the mixture to cool to warm (90°–100°). Meanwhile, beat the egg whites to hold a peak. Fold into the mixture.
FORMING 3 mins.	Pour batter into the baking dish. It should come to no more than three quarters of the way up the sides. Level with rubber scraper or spatula.
BAKING 350° 30 mins.	Bake in the oven until it is puffed and nicely browned. A knife blade slipped into the bread will come out clean and dry when it is done.
FINAL STEP	Remove bread from the oven. Serve immediately, and with a spoon.

PLYMOUTH BREAD

[TWO LOAVES]

Pioneer America handed down this fat brown loaf that relies in large measure on cornmeal and molasses for its good taste and unusual texture. An important first step in the preparation of the dough is to sprinkle the cornmeal slowly into the saucepan of boiling water to keep the mixture smooth and free of troublesome and unattractive little balls of congealed meal.

INGREDIENTS	1 package dry yeast ½ cup warm water (105°–115°) 2 cups boiling water ½ cup yellow cornmeal 2 tablespoons shortening

½ cup molasses (light is preferred)
2 teaspoons salt
4½ cups all-purpose or bread flour

BAKING PANS

Two medium (8½ x 4½) baking pans, greased or Teflon, metal or glass. If the latter, reduce oven heat 25°.

PREPARATION
25 mins.

Sprinkle the yeast over the warm water in a small bowl or cup. Stir briskly and set aside.

Bring water to a boil in a saucepan and *very slowly* pour the cornmeal into it—stirring all the while. Boil for 5 minutes. Set it off the burner, add shortening, molasses and salt. Pour into a mixer bowl and set aside to cool to warm (105°). When cool, add the yeast mixture and blend in the electric mixer for 60 seconds —or with a wooden spoon.

Gradually add 2 cups of flour and beat at medium speed for 3 minutes—or 150 strokes with the wooden spoon. Stop machine and stir in additional flour with the spoon, and then by hand, until a rough mass is formed. If slack or sticky, add ¼ cup more flour and work it into the dough.

KNEADING
8 mins.

Turn out on a floured surface and knead. (The dough can be returned to the mixer for kneading if the machine has a dough hook—about 5 minutes.) The dough will be smooth, elastic and feel alive.

RISING
1 hour

Place the ball of dough in a lightly greased bowl, cover tightly with plastic wrap and put in a warm place (80°–85°) until dough has doubled in volume.

SHAPING
10 mins.

Punch down the dough. Knead briefly to push out the air bubbles, and divide in two pieces. Press each into a flattened oval—fold in half, pinch seam, plump into shape and place in pans.

BAKING
350°
1 hour

Preheat oven to 350°. Bake in the oven until the loaves are nicely brown and tapping the bottom crust yields a hard and hollow sound. If the bottom is soft, the bread is underdone. Return to the oven, out of their pans, for an additional 10 minutes.

FINAL STEP

Remove bread from the oven. Turn out on wire racks to cool. A brush of milk across the crust will give it a nice soft glaze. This bread makes delicious toast. It freezes well for months.

SOUTHERN CORN BREAD

[NINE SERVINGS]

There is no wheat flour in this corn bread, only white cornmeal. Nor is there shortening. It is essentially corn, and that is what good corn bread is all about. It is a thin slab which is the way a Southerner likes it. This batter is also excellent for corn sticks, enough for about 12 to 14.

INGREDIENTS	2 eggs, room temperature 2 cups buttermilk, room temperature 1 teaspoon baking soda 2 cups white cornmeal 1½ teaspoons salt
BAKING PAN	One 9 x 9 x 2 pan, greased or Teflon.
PREPARATION 15 mins.	Heat oven to 450°. Generously grease the pan; heat it in the oven while mixing the batter. In a small bowl beat the eggs and add the buttermilk. In a mixer bowl stir together baking soda, cornmeal and salt. Pour in the egg-buttermilk mixture and beat in an electric mixer or with rotary beater until the batter is smooth.
FORMING 3 mins.	Carefully pour batter into heated pan.
BAKING 450° 20–25 mins.	Return immediately to the oven and bake until it sets. Insert a knife blade in the center of the bread, if it comes out clean and dry the corn bread is done.
FINAL STEP	Remove bread from the oven. Serve hot, cut in squares, with lots of butter.

SOUR MILK CORN BREAD

[APPROXIMATELY EIGHT SERVINGS]

This is a thin corn bread, of yellow cornmeal, made with eggs, sour milk and butter. The result is a fine open texture, not dense like many other corn breads, and a pleasant eggy flavor. Try breaking serving pieces off the yellow square rather than cutting it. It seems to taste better that way.

INGREDIENTS

1 cup *each* all-purpose flour and yellow cornmeal
1 teaspoon salt
1 teaspoon baking soda
1 cup sour milk or buttermilk, room temperature
2 eggs, room temperature
2 tablespoons butter or other shortening, melted

BAKING PAN

One 9 x 9 baking tin, greased or Teflon. This mixture can also be baked in muffin tins or corn stick molds.

PREPARATION
15 mins.

Preheat oven to 450°.

In a large bowl, blend together the flour, yellow cornmeal and salt. In a smaller bowl or cup, stir the soda into the sour milk or buttermilk. Pour this into the bowl of dry ingredients, and add 2 eggs, well beaten. Stir in the melted butter. While the mixing should be done quickly, the batter should not be overbeaten.

FORMING
3 mins.

Pour the batter into the baking tin which has been coated with either bacon drippings or melted shortening.

BAKING
450°
30 mins.

Bake in the oven until it is well browned, and tests done when pierced with a wooden toothpick. If it comes out clean and dry, the loaf is done. If moist particles cling to the probe, return to the oven for 5 minutes.

FINAL STEP

Remove bread from the oven. This bread is best served hot and broken into pieces, rather than cut.

ANADAMA BREAD

[TWO LOAVES]

There are a number of stories about the name of this plump, light bread. One: "Anna, damnit, this is the way I want it," shouted the New England farmer as he mixed yeast and white flour into the despised porridge of corn meal and molasses prepared by his wife each morning of their long married life. He did the right thing, certainly, because it produced a fine textured bread, yellow in color, with a taste of molasses. I use blackstrap unsulphured molasses that is dark in color and tangy in flavor. If you want a more subtle flavor, try Brer Rabbit's light New Orleans molasses.

INGREDIENTS

5 to 6 cups all-purpose or bread flour, approximately
2½ teaspoons salt
1 cup yellow cornmeal
2 packages dry yeast
¼ cup (½ stick) margarine or butter, room temperature
2 cups hot tap water (120°–130°)
⅓ cup molasses

BAKING PANS

Two medium (8½ x 4½) loaf pans, greased or Teflon, glass or metal. If glass pans are used, reduce oven heat 25°.

PREPARATION
15 mins.

In a large mixing bowl stir together 2½ cups of flour, salt, cornmeal and yeast. Add margarine or butter.

In a saucepan or bowl combine water and molasses, and stir. Gradually pour molasses mixture into dry ingredients, and beat 2 minutes at medium speed of an electric mixer. Add enough flour to make a thick batter —about ½ cup—and beat at high speed for 2 minutes, scraping the sides of the bowl clean once or twice during the process.

Put aside the mixer and stir in balance of the flour with a large wooden spoon, and as it stiffens, begin to work it with the fingers. When the dough is soft but no longer sticky, turn it out on a lightly floured bread board or counter top.

KNEADING
8 mins.

Knead until the dough is smooth and elastic. (Five minutes is sufficient with a dough hook.) The dough will show small bubbles under its skin.

FIRST RISING
50 mins.

Place the dough in a greased bowl—turning to film it all over—and cover tightly with plastic wrap. Place in a warm spot (80°–85°), free of drafts, until it doubles in bulk.

SHAPING
6 mins.

Punch down the dough and cut into two pieces with a sharp knife. With the hands, form each into a neat oblong ball, the seam under. It should just touch the ends of the pan when dropped in. See the dough volume chart on page 23 for other combinations of pan sizes.

SECOND RISING
45 mins.

Cover the pans with wax paper and return to the warm place until the dough doubles in bulk—or has risen in the center to about 1 inch above the edge of the pan.

BAKING
375°
45 mins.

Preheat oven to 375°. Bake in the oven. Midway through the bake period, turn the pans so they are evenly exposed to the temperature variations in the oven. When the loaves have a golden crust and tapping the bottom crust yields a hard and hollow sound, they are done.

FINAL STEP

Remove bread from the oven and turn out on metal cooling racks. Brush with melted butter. It is delicious toasted.

YANKEE CORN BREAD

[PAN OF NINE SERVINGS]

Unlike Southerners who prefer little or no sugar in their corn bread and like it baked thin in the pan, Northerners bake a sweeter, thicker bread. This is made with yellow cornmeal which is also preferred in the North, except in some of the New England states.

A surprising discovery for someone cutting into this pan of corn bread will be bits of bacon scattered throughout the batter.

INGREDIENTS

1 cup all-purpose flour
¼ cup sugar
4 teaspoons baking powder
¾ teaspoon salt
1 cup yellow cornmeal
2 eggs, room temperature
1 cup milk
¼ cup (½ stick) margarine, room temperature
⅓ cup chopped crisp bacon

BAKING PAN

One 9 x 9 x 2 pan, greased. If Teflon, there is no need to oil it. Reduce oven heat 25° if bake pan is glass.

PREPARATION
20 mins.

In a medium bowl sift together the flour, sugar, baking powder and salt. Stir in the cornmeal.

In a small bowl beat eggs with a fork, and add milk and shortening. Stir all, including bacon, into the cornmeal mixture with a wooden spoon or fork only enough to moisten the flour. Add the bacon bits. Don't overstir even if the batter is lumpy.

FORMING
15 mins.

Pour into the pan and level with the spoon or rubber spatula. Let rest 10 minutes.

BAKING
425°
25 mins.

Preheat oven to 425°. Bake in the oven. Test with a wooden toothpick or metal skewer for doneness. Don't, however, overbake, or it will be dry.

FINAL STEP

Remove bread from the oven. Cut in squares and serve immediately from the pan—with ample butter.

BATTER CORN BREAD

[TWO LOAVES]

A golden loaf from the oven, Batter Corn Bread has the rough texture of quick corn breads. It is a batter bread, however, that relies on yeast for leavening. Although there is no kneading the soft mixture, it is turned into pans and allowed to rise for about 1 hour before baking. It has a good corn flavor and aroma, and can be frozen and reheated.

INGREDIENTS

2 packages dry yeast
3½ cups all-purpose flour
1¾ cups yellow cornmeal
⅓ cup non-fat dry milk
1½ cups hot tap water (120°–130°)
1 stick (½ cup) margarine or other shortening, room temperature
6 tablespoons sugar
2 teaspoons salt
2 eggs, room temperature and lightly beaten
To brush: 1 tablespoon milk, 1 tablespoon cornmeal

BAKING PANS

Two medium (8½ x 4½) loaf pans, greased or Teflon. If glass, reduce oven heat 25°.

PREPARATION
20 mins.

In a large bowl stir together yeast, flour, cornmeal and milk. In another bowl pour water over the margarine, sugar, salt and eggs. Combine. Beat until well blended —about 50 strokes. The batter will be stiff.

FORMING
5 mins.

Turn the batter into the loaf pans and push into the corners with a rubber scraper.

RISING
1 hour

Cover the tins with wax paper and move to a warm place (80°–85°) until batter has doubled in bulk.

BAKING
375°
35 mins.

Preheat oven to 375°. Before putting the loaves in the oven, carefully brush the tops with milk and sprinkle lightly with cornmeal.

Bake in the oven. When tapping the bottom crust yields a hard and hollow sound and a wooden toothpick inserted in the center comes out dry and clean, they are done.

FINAL STEP

Remove bread from the oven and turn the loaves out onto cooling racks. This bread is especially good warm. Freezes well.

CORN BUBBLE BREAD

[ONE LARGE ROUND LOAF]

Cornmeal gives this essentially white flour loaf a nice coarse texture but it is stacking small balls of dough in a tube pan that gives it its bubbles. When the balls are stacked two-deep in the large pan they will appear almost lost but they soon expand in rising to make an intriguing solid loaf 3 to 4 inches deep.

The loaf can be sliced or each bubble can be pulled off and served.

While this recipe calls for putting the prepared dough in the refrigerator 2 to 24 hours before baking, it can be done straightaway with the usual 1-hour rising in a warm place.

INGREDIENTS

5 to 6 cups of all-purpose flour, approximately
2 tablespoons sugar
1 tablespoon salt
1 cup yellow cornmeal
2 packages dry yeast
1¾ cups milk
½ cup water
3 tablespoons shortening
2 teaspoons melted margarine, to brush

BAKING PAN

One 10-inch tube pan, greased or Teflon.

PREPARATION
20 mins.

In a large mixer bowl blend 2 cups of flour, sugar, salt, cornmeal and yeast.

In a saucepan, over low heat, combine milk, water and shortening. When the liquid mixture is warm to the touch, pour it into the dry ingredients—and beat 2 minutes at medium speed of the electric mixer. Add about ½ cup of flour to make the batter thick. Beat at high speed for 2 minutes. Scrape down sides of the bowl twice during the beating.

The beating can also be done by hand. With a wooden spoon, beat for approximately the same length of time or until the batter pulls away from the sides of the bowl in strands.

Turn off mixer and stir in additional flour to make a rough mass that can be worked with the hands.

KNEADING
8 mins.

Turn the dough onto a lightly floured work surface and knead with a strong push-turn-fold action. The dough will be smooth and elastic, and feel alive under the hands. (Five minutes with a dough hook.)

RESTING
20 mins.

Cover the ball of dough with the inverted bowl. Leave on the counter to rest.

SHAPING
20 mins.

Uncover the dough, punch it down and knead briefly to collapse the air pockets.

Divide the dough into 32 small pieces. The quickest and most accurate way is to divide the dough, with a knife, successively into 2–4–8–16–32 pieces.

Roll into balls between the palms. Arrange half of them in the first layer in the tube pan. They will not necessarily touch. Place the remaining 16 balls in a layer on top. Any irregularity of form will be lost when the loaf rises. Brush with margarine.

REFRIGERATION
2–24 hours

Cover tightly with plastic wrap and place in the refrigerator from 2 to 24 hours.

BAKING
375°
55–60 mins.

Preheat oven to 375°. Bring the pan out of the refrigerator and allow it to stand uncovered for 10 minutes. With a greased toothpick puncture any gas bubbles that have pushed out from the surface of the loaf.

Bake in the oven. When the loaf is a deep brown and tapping on the bottom crust yields a hard and hollow sound, it is done. If it is soft, return to the oven (without the pan) for an additional 10 minutes.

FINAL STEP

Remove bread from the oven and place the loaf on a metal rack to cool. Brush with melted butter.

CUSTARDY CORN BREAD

[FOUR TO SIX SERVINGS]

A thin batter is sandwiched between a dollop of melted butter on the bottom of the pan and milk poured over the top to produce a custard-like loaf—soft, moist, slightly sweet and very good. It is served on the dinner plate. The surprising thing about this bread is that it tastes different cold than when warm, but equally good both ways.

INGREDIENTS
¾ cup white cornmeal
¼ cup all-purpose flour
1 to 2 tablespoons sugar
½ teaspoon salt
1 tablespoon baking powder
1½ cups, plus 2 tablespoons milk
1 egg, room temperature and beaten
2 tablespoons butter

BAKING PAN
One square 8-inch pan, buttered. In this recipe a Teflon pan must be buttered according to instructions.

PREPARATION
20 mins.
Preheat oven to 400°.
In a large bowl, measure the cornmeal, all-purpose flour, sugar, salt and baking powder—blend thoroughly with a spoon. Stir in 1 cup plus 2 tablespoons of milk and the egg. Mix this only enough to dampen the dry ingredients—don't overbeat.

FORMING
5 mins.
Drop the butter in a square baking pan, place over low heat or in the preheated oven until it melts. Remove from heat. Spread the butter over the bottom of the pan and pour in the mixture. Pour the remaining ½ cup of milk over the batter—do not stir.

BAKING
400°
30 mins.
Carefully place pan in the oven and bake.

FINAL STEP
Remove bread from the oven. The bread is cut in the pan and served on the dinner plate.

JALAPEÑO CORN BREAD

[TWO PANS]

Among my recipes this ranks as one of the best corn breads. While it is of direct Mexican descent, even those who have reservations about South-of-the-border food should like this one. Chopped Jalapeño peppers (the very hot kind) are in the bread but they lose their fierceness when baked. They give the loaves a provocative and spicy flavor that happily embraces the sharp Cheddar cheese, the creamed corn and cornmeal. It is a handsome pan of bread—the yellow corn and the deeper yellow streaks of cheese, highlighted with bits of green pepper. It is delicious any time. Served with or without butter, it is almost a meal in itself. It is good with Mexican food, of course, also barbecue meats, grilled steaks, and hot dogs. It is an equally good companion to soup, a glass of red wine or a bottle of cold beer.

INGREDIENTS

2½ cups yellow cornmeal
1 cup all-purpose flour
2 tablespoons sugar
1 tablespoon salt
4 teaspoons baking powder
½ cup non-fat dry milk
3 eggs, room temperature
1½ cups warm water (110°)
½ cup cooking oil
1 one-pound can cream-style corn
6 to 8 Jalapeño chili peppers, chopped
2 cups sharp Cheddar cheese, grated
1 large onion, grated

BAKING PANS

Two 9 x 11 or 9 x 9 pans, greased or Teflon.

PREPARATION
15 mins.

Preheat oven to 425°. Because they are so hot, Jalapeño peppers should be treated with respect. I cut them up on a plate rather than the regular chopping board because they leave behind a hot afterglow that I might not want on the next food to be chopped. I am aware, too, that a bit of juice rubbed into an eye will bring a rush of tears and stop all preparations for a few moments. But nevertheless, even that is worth it for a bite of the product.

In a large bowl stir together the cornmeal, flour, sugar, salt, baking powder and milk. In a smaller bowl lightly beat the eggs and stir in the water and oil. Pour the liquid mixture into the cornmeal mix and stir in the corn, the chopped peppers, cheese and grated onion.

FORMING
3 mins.

Pour the batter into the baking pans and spread evenly with a rubber scraper or the wooden spoon.

BAKING
425°
30 mins.

Bake in the oven until the bread tests done—a wooden toothpick or metal skewer inserted in the center comes out clean.

FINAL STEP — Remove bread from the oven. Let the pans cool somewhat on metal racks before cutting into serving pieces.

REBECCA'S CORN BREAD

[NINE SERVINGS]

This recipe from a fine home baker in Hawaii is a far cry from a basic corn bread, what with ¾ cup sugar, ¾ cup of butter, and 3 eggs but there will be few who won't enjoy its delicious overstatement.

INGREDIENTS

¾ cup yellow cornmeal
2¼ cups all-purpose flour
¾ cup sugar
3 teaspoons baking powder
½ teaspoon salt
1 cup milk
¾ cup (1½ sticks) butter, melted
3 eggs, beaten

BAKING PAN — One 9 x 9 x 2 baking pan, greased or Teflon.

PREPARATION
12 mins.

Preheat oven to 400°.

In a large bowl measure cornmeal, flour, sugar, baking powder and salt. Blend well. Add milk and butter slowly. Pour in eggs. Stir only enough to blend the mixture thoroughly.

FORMING
3 mins.

Pour into the pan and level with a spoon or spatula.

BAKING
400°
20 mins.

Bake in the oven until the bread tests done when pierced with a metal skewer, wooden toothpick or the blade of a knife. If it comes out clean and dry, the corn bread is done.

FINAL STEP — Remove bread from the oven. Cut into nine servings.

BROA—PORTUGUESE CORN BREAD

[ONE ROUND LOAF]

The yellow cornmeal in this yeast-raised Portuguese corn bread is spun in the blender until it is finely pulverized. It is not coarse and solid like many corn breads but lightly textured, thanks to the yeast leavening. It is served warm or cold, and it is particularly good with soups. It can be frozen for several months and reheated in a 250° oven.

INGREDIENTS	1 package dry yeast 1 sprinkle of sugar ¼ cup warm water (105°–115°) 1½ cups yellow cornmeal (blendered) 1½ teaspoons of salt 1 cup boiling water 1 tablespoon olive oil 1¾ to 2 cups all-purpose flour, approximately
BAKING SHEET	Baking sheet, greased or Teflon.
PREPARATION 30 mins.	In a small bowl dissolve yeast and sugar in warm water. Beat with a whisk or fork to speed the process. Set aside while preparing the cornmeal. Pulverize the cornmeal in a blender, ¼ cup at a time, until it is fine and powdery. The bread can be made without this step but the texture will not be as smooth. In a large mixing bowl combine 1 cup of cornmeal, salt and boiling water. Stir until smooth. Stir in 1 tablespoon olive oil and cool the mixture until it is lukewarm. Add the yeast. Gradually add the rest of the cornmeal and 1 cup of flour, stirring constantly. Work the dough into a ball, adding ¼ cup or more flour if necessary to overcome the stickiness, and place a length of plastic wrap over the bowl.
FIRST RISING 30 mins.	Place the bowl in a warm spot (80°–85°), free from drafts, until dough has doubled in volume.
KNEADING 5 mins.	Turn the dough out onto a floured work surface, and knead it with a strong push-turn-fold motion. Meanwhile add up to 1 cup additional flour to make a firm but not stiff dough.
SHAPING 3 mins.	Shape into a round ball and flatten slightly. Place on the baking sheet.
SECOND RISING 30 mins.	Cover the ball with wax paper and return to the warm place until it doubles in bulk again.
BAKING 350° 40 mins.	Preheat oven to 350°. Bake in the middle of the oven. When the crust is golden and tapping the bottom crust yields a hard and hollow sound, it is done. If it doesn't,

return to the oven for an additional 10 minutes. Test again.

FINAL STEP

Remove bread from the oven and place on a metal rack to cool before serving. In Portugal the bread is served with a famous dish of peas and eggs, and a potato-sausage soup.

CORN AND RICE BREAD

[FOUR TO SIX SERVINGS]

A different kind of corn bread, this one has yellow crusts, top and bottom, thanks to eggs and butter, and a layer of custard-like batter of cooked rice and cornmeal in between. It is a moist but not wet loaf that can be eaten either with a fork or the fingers. The batter is quite thin but bakes into a solid loaf in half an hour in a hot oven. It is very good—hot or cold.

INGREDIENTS

2 cups white cornmeal
1 tablespoon baking powder
1 teaspoon salt
1½ cups milk
3 eggs, room temperature and well beaten
1 cup cold cooked rice
2 tablespoons melted butter

BAKING PAN

One 8 x 8 square baking tin, greased or Teflon.

PREPARATION
15 mins.

While preparing the bread, preheat oven to 400°.

In a large bowl blend the white cornmeal, baking powder and salt. Stir or sift together thoroughly. In a small bowl, combine the milk, eggs, cooked rice and butter. Add to the dry ingredients. Stir the mixture together but do not overbeat.

FORMING
3 mins.

Pour the batter into the baking pan and level it with a spatula or spoon.

BAKING
400°
30 mins.

Bake bread in the oven. Pierce with a wooden toothpick or metal skewer. If it comes out dry and clean, the bread is done.

FINAL STEP

Remove bread from the oven. This delightful bread is best served warm but it is almost as good cold later on.

RICH CORN BREAD

[SIX SERVINGS]

This recipe is a produce man's dream. As its name implies, it is an unusually rich corn bread using cream, milk, butter and eggs. Since some judge their corn bread as much by its thickness as by its flavor—the batter is only ½ inch deep in the pan and rises to about 1½ inches. Nevertheless, absolutely delicious hot from the oven.

INGREDIENTS

1½ cups yellow cornmeal
½ cup all-purpose flour
1 teaspoon *each* salt and sugar
3 tablespoons baking powder
1 cup milk
3 eggs, room temperature
¼ cup heavy cream, room temperature
⅓ cup butter, melted

BAKING PAN

One shallow baking pan, 16 by 12 inch greased or Teflon, or a combination of smaller pans with the equivalent volume. For example, two 9 by 9 inch pans are about right.

PREPARATION
10 mins.

Preheat oven to 400°.

In a mixing bowl measure cornmeal, flour, salt, sugar and baking powder. In a small bowl or measuring cup lightly beat the milk into the eggs and pour this into the bowl of dry ingredients. Beat until thoroughly blended. Pour in cream and butter. Blend the mixture.

FORMING
2 mins.

Pour the batter into the baking pans to the depth of about ½ inch.

BAKING
400°
20–25 mins.

Bake in the oven until it is nicely brown and tests done when a wooden toothpick inserted in the bread comes out clean and dry.

FINAL STEP

Remove bread from the oven. Serve hot cut in rectangles.

STEAMED CORN BREAD

[THREE SMALL LOAVES]

Steamed corn bread has the color and texture of Boston Brown Bread and is steamed in the same way. The loaf, however, is less demanding in its ingredients. There is no blend of several flours. Cornmeal and all-purpose only. Molasses, as in the brown bread, gives the loaf its sweetness and some of its taste. Its brown rounds are great for sandwiches served with coffee, tea or milk.

INGREDIENTS

2 eggs
2½ cups buttermilk
½ cup molasses
1 cup all-purpose flour
2 cups cornmeal, white or yellow
2 teaspoons *each* salt and baking soda

BAKING CANS AND KETTLE

Three #2 cans or 1-pound coffee cans, greased. Tight fitting lids or aluminum foil held in place with string, rubber band, or masking tape. Fit rounds of buttered wax paper in the bottoms of the cans to facilitate removing the loaves.

Large kettle with a lid to hold the cans during the steaming.

PREPARATION
12 mins.

Beat eggs, buttermilk and molasses in a large mixing bowl with electric beater or large wooden spoon until blended. Sift flour, cornmeal, salt and baking soda into the liquid mixture, and stir until smooth.

FORMING
5 mins.

Pour the batter into the prepared cans—about two-thirds full. Cover tightly. Steam leaking into the cans can ruin the bread.

STEAMING
3 hours

Place the cans on a rack in the large kettle of boiling water. Water should come about halfway up the sides of the containers. Cover the kettle. (If no lid is available, fashion one out of aluminum foil and tie with a cord.)

Steam in continuously boiling water (over a low heat). If necessary, add boiling water during the steaming.

FINAL STEP

Remove the cans from the water and take off their lids. Place them in a 400° oven for 10 minutes to partially dry. Let the loaves rest on a metal rack 15 minutes before turning them out. It may be necessary to loosen the loaves with a knife run around the inside edge of the can—done gently.

Slice into rounds and serve.

TOASTED CORNMEAL BREAD

[THREE LOAVES AND A DOZEN ROLLS]

This delightful bread, far more sophisticated than the quick corn breads, is leavened first with a potato starter and then with yeast. Toasted cornmeal, found in some specialty food stores, is called for but I toast the necessary 3 cups in a 350° oven for about 30 minutes. The quantities in the recipe are substantial and produce 3 medium loaves and a dozen large crusty rolls.

It is a loaf with a nice open texture, light brown in color, and with a good nut-like taste. It toasts beautifully, and freezes well for an indefinite period.

INGREDIENTS

2 cups raw potato starter (see page 284)
1½ cups all-purpose flour
1½ cups cold water
3 cups toasted cornmeal
1 package dry yeast
1 teaspoon sugar
½ teaspoon ginger
½ cup warm water (105°–115°)
2 cups warm water (105°–115°)
1 cup non-fat dry milk
4 tablespoons maple or maple-flavored syrup
5½ cups all-purpose flour, approximately
3 teaspoons salt
4 tablespoons butter or margarine, room temperature

BAKING PANS

Three medium (8½ x 4½) baking pans, greased or Teflon. One muffin pan, greased or Teflon, with cups 2½ inches in diameter. If glass pans are used, reduce oven heat 25°.

PREPARATION
Overnight

The day before baking, empty the raw potato starter into a mixing bowl and stir in 1½ cups *each* white flour and cold water. Cover tightly with plastic wrap and set in a warm place overnight. Scald the starter jar and set aside.

Toast the cornmeal unless you have the prepared product.

On bake day, stir the starter and return 2 cups to the starter jar. Cover and place in the refrigerator for later use. Reserve the remaining 2 cups of starter.

20 mins.

In a small bowl or cup dissolve yeast, sugar and ginger in ½ cup lukewarm water. Stir briskly with a fork or whisk to hasten the action.

In a large mixing bowl pour the 2 cups of reserved starter, add 2 cups warm water, milk, syrup, toasted cornmeal and 3 cups all-purpose flour. Mix thoroughly. Add yeast mixture, salt, butter and 1½ cups additional flour. Stir 125 strokes or until the dough has formed a rough mass and has cleaned the sides of the bowl.

KNEADING
8 mins.

Spread 1 cup of flour on the work surface—counter top or bread board—and turn the dough onto it. Knead with a strong push-turn-fold motion, using only as much of the flour as necessary to make a smooth, elastic dough that is not sticky.

FIRST RISING
1 hour

Return the dough to the bowl, pat with buttered fingers, cover tightly with plastic wrap and set in a warm place (80°–85°) until light and doubled in size.

SHAPING
20 mins.

Turn out the dough, divide in 4 equal pieces and knead briefly to expel the bubbles. For the bread, shape 3 pieces into loaves. Place in the pans. For the rolls, roll an 8 x 10 inch rectangle, brush with butter, roll up from the long side and cut into as many slices as there are cups in the muffin pan—9 or 12, usually. Drop one in each cup, cut side up.

SECOND RISING
50 mins.

Cover loaves and rolls with wax paper and return to the warm place until light and doubled in volume.

BAKING
375°
25 mins.
45 mins.

Preheat oven to 375°. Place pans in the oven. The rolls will bake in about 25 minutes so plan to remove them earlier than the loaves which will bake in about 45 minutes. When they are golden brown and loose in their pans, and tapping the bottom crust yields a hard and hollow sound, they are done.

FINAL STEP

Remove bread from the oven and turn out from pans onto a wire rack to cool.

EIGHT

Buckwheat Breads

Buckwheat
Lyons, 1579

Buckwheat is more legend than reality in most kitchens. When praise of it is sung, infrequently at best, it is usually for a stack of buckwheat pancakes. It is sorely underrated as a flour for bread; it deserves better.

Buckwheat was discovered in the cool mountain regions of China about 1000 A.D. It was brought to this country from Europe by the Dutch and grown along the Hudson River before 1625. The name derives from two old words—boc (beech) and whoet (wheat). It is not a true grain, however, since it is not a grass but an herb.

SPECIAL BUCKWHEAT BREAD

[CHOICE OF LOAVES]

At first bite it is overwhelmingly buckwheat but then it shades into another flavor—prune or raisin. There is no flour other than buckwheat in it so it is dark chocolate in color. You must like buckwheat to enjoy this loaf.

INGREDIENTS
½ cup coarsely chopped prunes or raisins
1¾ cups of buttermilk
½ cup brown sugar

2 cups buckwheat flour
1½ teaspoons salt
½ teaspoon baking powder

BAKING PANS

One medium (8½ x 4½) loaf pan, or 1 small (7½ x 3½) and 3 miniature (4½ x 2½) loaf tins, greased or Teflon. If glass is used, reduce oven heat 25°.

PREPARATION
10 mins.

Beforehand, coarsely chop ½ cup of prunes. Grease and line the pans with wax paper.

In a bowl pour buttermilk and stir in sugar, flour, salt, baking powder and prunes (or raisins).

FORMING
3 mins.

Pour batter into prepared pan or pans and work it into the corners with a spatula. Level off the tops. Let the pans stand for 10 minutes while the oven heats to 325°.

BAKING
325°
30–45 mins.

Place pans in the oven for about 45 minutes (30 minutes for the miniature loaves) or until the loaves test done when a wooden toothpick inserted in the center of one comes out clean and dry.

FINAL STEP

Remove bread from the oven. Turn the pans on their sides and gently pull the wax paper to slip the loaves onto the metal rack to cool. The loaf is good warm from the oven but even more so the next day.

BUCKWHEAT BREAD

[FOUR SMALL LOAVES]

The ratio of white flour to buckwheat is 2 to 1, but the latter comes on strong, especially when it is toasted. It will bring back memories of buckwheat cakes on a cold winter's day, and it seems to go best with bacon or sausage and eggs. Also, it can be fried in a batter and be as good as any buckwheat griddle cake ever served. (See Pain Perdu, page 528.)

The recipe calls for 2 cups from an established potato starter (page 284) but when I don't have an active starter in the refrigerator, I make an overnight sponge.

INGREDIENTS

Overnight Sponge: 2 cups hot tap water (120°–130°)
2 cups all-purpose flour
1 tablespoon *each* salt and sugar
1 package dry yeast

Dough: 1 package dry yeast
½ cup warm water (105°–115°)
1 teaspoon sugar
½ teaspoon ginger
2 cups potato starter (page 284) or overnight sponge (above)
1 cup warm water (105°–115°)
⅓ cup non-fat dry milk
4 tablespoons brown sugar or sorghum molasses
2 cups buckwheat flour
4 tablespoons butter or margarine, room temperature
2 teaspoons salt
4 cups all-purpose flour, approximately

Glaze: 2 tablespoons cream or canned milk, to brush

BAKING PANS AND TINS

The dough weighs about 4 pounds so I usually plan to make four loaves. It is nice to bake part of the dough in 1-pound coffee tins which make nice cylindrical loaves for sandwich slices or French toast. Oil the tins well. I place a round of buttered wax paper in the bottom of the coffee cans because I want the loaves to drop out when I turn the tins over.

For regular 1-pound loaves, I use small (7½ x 3½) loaf pans, greased or Teflon. If glass, reduce oven heat 25°.

PREPARATION
Overnight

If preparing overnight sponge, mix together in a bowl the water, all-purpose flour, salt, sugar and yeast. Cover with plastic wrap and set in a warm place (80°–85°) overnight. There will be enough sponge remaining to use as a starter for other recipes.

20 mins.

In a small bowl or cup, dissolve yeast in warm water, and add sugar and ginger. Beat for a moment with a fork or whisk to hasten the fermentation action.

In a large mixing bowl, pour 2 cups of the starter or sponge and reserve the rest for other breads. Add 1 cup warm water, milk, the brown sugar or sorghum, and buckwheat flour. Add the yeast mixture and beat 25 strokes. Add butter or margarine, salt and stir about 150 strong strokes until the batter strings from the sides of the bowl. Add 3 cups white flour, a cup at a time, working first with a wooden spoon and then with the fingers. The dough will be moist and rough but it will clean the sides of the bowl.

KNEADING
8 mins.

Turn the dough out onto a working surface—a counter top or a bread board. Spread the remaining flour around the edge of the ball of dough and gradually work the additional flour into the dough as you knead. Don't force the dough to accept more flour than it will take. The dough will be elastic, smooth and not sticky. Knead.

FIRST RISING
1 hour

Return the dough to the bowl, grease the top and sides lightly with oil or butter, cover with plastic wrap and place in a warm (80°–85°) draft-free spot until the dough has doubled in bulk.

SHAPING
15 mins.

Turn the dough out, knead briefly and lightly, and shape as desired.

SECOND RISING
45 mins.

Brush tops with butter, cover with wax paper and return to the warm place.

BAKING
375°
45 mins.

Preheat oven to 375°. Bake small loaves in a moderately hot oven for 45 minutes; the larger loaves about 10 minutes longer. Five minutes before the end of the baking, brush the tops of the loaves with cream or canned milk to give the crust a rich, russet color.

Turn out one loaf from its pan and thump the bottom crust with a forefinger. A hard hollow sound means the bread is baked. If not, return to the oven (without pan, if you wish) for an additional 10 minutes. If the loaves appear to be browning too quickly, cover with a piece of foil or brown sack paper.

FINAL STEP

Remove bread from the oven and turn onto a metal rack to cool before slicing.

BAUERNBROT

[TWO ROUND LOAVES]

While this Austrian peasant loaf has the subtle, not-too-strong flavor of buckwheat, it is a moist bread that is excellent served at a buffet or at tea. It is heavy, and ideal for a continental breakfast—to be eaten with cheese and slices of thin ham. The loaf has a salty light tan crust but a slice reveals a dark brown interior.

This loaf begins with *Sauerteig* (starter).

INGREDIENTS	*Sauerteig* (Witch Yeast or Sour Rye), page 282 4 cups buckwheat flour 2 cups all-purpose flour 1 package dry yeast 1½ cups warm water (105°–115°) ½ cup starter 1½ teaspoons salt 1 tablespoon caraway seeds ¼ cup dark molasses Glaze: 1 tablespoon salt dissolved in ¼ cup water
BAKING SHEET	One large baking sheet, greased or Teflon.
PREPARATION Overnight	The starter can be one of those suggested above, or, a quick overnight starter or sponge can be made by combining ¼ cup each of white and buckwheat flours, 1 package yeast, a pinch of sugar and enough water to form a thick but wet batter. Cover with plastic wrap and let it work overnight. It will be light and frothy the following morning and ready to use in this recipe.
Bake Day 1¾ hours	In a large bowl blend together buckwheat and white flour, and set aside. In a large mixing bowl dissolve yeast in warm water, and add 2 cups of combined flour mixture. Beat with a wooden spoon until smooth. It will have the consistency of a batter-like porridge. Cover the bowl with plastic wrap and let it stand in a warm place for 1½ hours.
15 mins.	Stir down with the spoon—and add ½ cup of the starter or *Sauerteig,* salt, caraway seeds and molasses. Add remaining flour a cup at a time until the ball of dough is roughly formed and has pulled away from the sides of the bowl. Don't force the dough to accept more of the flour than it needs to make a firm, but not stiff or hard ball.
KNEADING 6 mins.	Turn the dough onto a lightly floured work surface and knead with a strong push-turn-fold action. The dough

should be firm enough to hold its shape in a round ball. Add more buckwheat-white flour mixture if needed.

SHAPING
5 mins.

Divide the dough into equal parts and shape into round balls. Brush immediately with water and place them on the baking sheet.

RISING
30 mins.

Cover the loaves with a length of wax paper and leave in a warm place.

BAKING
350°
40 mins.

Preheat oven to 350°. Bake the loaves in the oven for 10 minutes. Open the oven door and quickly brush them with the salt water. Bake for 30 minutes longer, brushing them with the salt water every 10 minutes. Test the loaves for doneness by inserting a wooden toothpick in the center of a loaf. If it comes out dry and clean the loaf is done.

FINAL STEP

Remove bread from the oven and place on a metal rack to cool.

NINE

Oat Breads

Oats
Venice, 1560

Oats have had a plebeian upbringing, mentioned as a weed by the classical writers of Rome, and used infrequently in medicines. In the early Christian era they gained some stature as a foodstuff, yet despite their ability to add flavor and good texture to bread, oats have come down through the centuries principally as a food for livestock, especially horses.

All of the recipes here are made with rolled oats or oatmeal (one and the same) except one which calls for Scotch oatmeal, the cracked and unflattened whole grain. The oat groat is the edible part of the oat kernel, and whole groats become rolled oats.

The flour has no gluten strength and is seldom used in bread except in hypoallergenic diets.

BUTTERMILK OATEN BREAD

[FOUR "FARLS," OR QUARTERS]

This County Cork recipe was originally in pints and gills but here it is in cups and fractions thereof. The results, thankfully, are the same—golden triangles, or "farls," medium brown and crisp on the outside, and moist on the in.

INGREDIENTS
2 cups oatmeal, instant or old-fashioned
1¼ cups buttermilk or sour milk
2½ cups all-purpose or bread flour
1 teaspoon salt
1 teaspoon baking soda

BAKING SHEET
One baking sheet, greased or Teflon. Cornmeal alone on the baking sheet may be used to facilitate removing the baked loaf.

PREPARATION
Overnight
Night before: in a bowl mix the oatmeal and buttermilk, cover tightly with plastic wrap and let stand until you are ready to proceed the next day.

10 mins.
The next day: preheat the oven to 350°.

In a separate bowl mix the flour, salt and soda together and mix it gradually into the oatmeal. Use wooden spoon or fingers. If the mixture is difficult to work, add a little more milk. Keep the mixture soft.

KNEADING
4 mins.
Knead in the bowl until the dough is smooth.

SHAPING
5 mins.
Pat the dough into a round loaf about 2-inches thick. With a sharp knife or scissors cut the dough into quarters, or farls, and place the sections side by side on the baking sheet.

BAKING
350°
40 mins.
Bake in the oven until the quarters are a medium to deep brown. To test for doneness, turn one farl over and tap. A hollow sound means it is baked.

FINAL STEP
Remove bread from the oven. Place the farls on a wire rack to cool. When they have cooled, break them open with fingers rather than cut them.

ENGLISH OATMEAL BREAD

[TWO LOAVES]

This nice dark loaf of oatmeal, whole wheat and white flours has a solid, pleasing bite. The oatmeal, which is not to be seen once it becomes a part of the dark dough, is quite evident, however, in the moist texture of the slice. The oatmeal is soaked in milk for two hours beforehand.

The fine English home bakers George and Cecilia Scurfield suggest that buns as well as bread be made with this dough.

INGREDIENTS

2 cups oatmeal
1½ cups milk
1 package dry yeast
¼ cup warm water (105°–115°)
2 tablespoons butter, room temperature
1 tablespoon salt
1 cup whole wheat flour
1½ cups all-purpose flour, approximately

BAKING PANS

Two small (7½ x 3½) baking pans, greased or Teflon. If glass, reduce oven heat 25°.

PREPARATION
2 hours

Two hours or more beforehand, soak the oatmeal in milk in a large bowl.

In a cup or small bowl, dissolve the yeast in water. Beat briskly with a fork or whisk to hasten the action. Set aside for 5 minutes.

15 mins.

Stir the yeast into the oatmeal mixture, add butter, salt and whole wheat flour. Beat in an electric mixer at medium speed for 1 minute. Add ½ cup of the all-purpose flour and continue beating for an additional 2 minutes, or the same length of time stirring vigorously with a large wooden spoon.

Stop mixer. Stir in the balance of the all-purpose flour, ½ cup at a time, first with the spoon and then by hand. The dough will be a rough, shaggy mass that will clean the sides of the bowl. If the dough continues moist and slack, and sticks to the fingers or work surface, sprinkle on additional flour.

KNEADING
8 mins.

Turn the dough onto a lightly floured work surface—counter top or bread board—and knead with the rhythmic 1-2-3 motion of push-turn-fold. The dough will become smooth and elastic. Occasionally change the kneading rhythm by raising the dough above the table and crashing it down hard against the surface. Knead for about 8 minutes. (Six minutes with the dough hook.)

FIRST RISING
1½ hours

Place the dough back in the mixing bowl and pat with buttered or greased fingers to keep the surface from crusting. Cover the bowl tightly with plastic wrap and move to a warm place (80°–85°) until the dough has risen to about twice its original size—as judged by how it creeps up the sides of the bowl. You can test if it has risen by poking a finger in it; the dent will remain.

SHAPING
6 mins.

Punch down dough, turn it onto work surface again, and knead for 30 seconds to press out the bubbles. Divide the dough into two pieces with a sharp knife. Shape into balls, and let them rest under a towel for 3 to 4 minutes. Form a loaf by pressing a ball, under the palms, into a flat oval, roughly the length of the baking pan. Fold the oval in half, pinch the seam tightly to seal, tuck under the ends, and place in the pan, seam down. Repeat with the second loaf.

SECOND RISING
45 mins.

Place the pans in the warm place, cover with wax paper and leave until the dough has risen to double the volume, or until the center of the dough has risen 1 inch above the level of the edge of the pan. Meanwhile, preheat the oven to 400°.

BAKING
400°
30 mins.
350°
20–30 mins.

Bake the loaves in the hot oven for 30 minutes, reduce heat to 350° and continue baking for another 20 to 30 minutes, or until the loaves are a golden brown and test done. Turn one loaf out of its pan and tap the bottom crust with a forefinger. A hard hollow sound means the bread is baked. If the tops of the loaves appear to be browning too quickly, cover with a piece of foil or brown paper. Midway in the bake period, and again near the end of it, shift the pans so the loaves are exposed equally to temperature variations in the oven.

FINAL STEP

Remove bread from the oven and place the loaves on a metal rack to cool before slicing. This loaf will keep nicely wrapped in plastic wrap or foil.

GRANDMA'S OATMEAL BREAD

[TWO LOAVES]

There is instant identity to this light brown loaf that has oats sprinkled generously on the top crust and stuck in abundance on the sides and bottom. The dough has 2 cups of quick-cooking oats that are plumped almost instantly when boiling hot water is poured over them. Grandma's original recipe called for ½ cup of molasses but it seemed too strong so I have reduced it by half.

INGREDIENTS

5 to 5½ cups all-purpose flour, approximately
2 packages dry yeast
1 tablespoon salt
1¾ cups boiling water
2 cups quick-cooking oatmeal
¼ cup molasses
⅓ cup lard or other shortening
2 eggs, room temperature
2 tablespoons rolled oats
Topping: 1 egg white mixed with 1 tablespoon water
Rolled oats to sprinkle

BAKING PANS

Two medium (8½ x 4½) baking tins, greased or Teflon, metal or glass. If the latter, reduce oven heat 25°.

PREPARATION
20 mins.

In a large mixing bowl, measure 2 cups of flour and over it sprinkle yeast and salt. Stir this with a spoon, or an electric mixer, at low speed.

In a saucepan, pour water over the oatmeal and add molasses and lard. Add this mixture to the flour and beat with an electric mixer at slow speed for 30 seconds or until blended. Increase speed to medium-fast for 3 minutes, or beat with a wooden spoon for equal length of time. Stop the mixer and add the eggs and 2 additional cups of flour. If this is too stiff for the beaters, beat with a wooden spoon. Add additional flour, ¼ cup at a time, until the dough is soft and is no longer clinging to the sides of the bowl.

KNEADING
16 mins.

Turn the dough out onto a lightly floured surface; cover with a length of wax paper and let it rest for 10 minutes. With a strong push-turn-fold motion, knead until the dough is smooth and elastic.

FIRST RISING
1½ hours

Place the dough in a mixing bowl, pat it with buttered fingers and cover the bowl tightly with plastic wrap. Place the bowl in a warm spot (80°–85°) until the dough has doubled in volume.

SHAPING
12 mins.

First, grease the baking pans heavily and coat with 2 tablespoons rolled oats tumbled slowly in the pans.

Turn the dough out onto a floured work surface and divide in half. Shape each into a loaf by pressing flat, folding in half, sealing the seam, and placing it seam down in the pan.

SECOND RISING
50 mins.

Cover the pans with wax paper, return to the warm place and let dough rise until double.

BAKING
375°
40 mins.

Preheat oven to 375°. Before putting the loaves into the oven, brush with the egg white and water mixture—sprinkle lightly with rolled oats. Bake in the oven. When the loaves are golden brown and tapping the bottom crust yields a hard and hollow sound, they are done.

Watch the loaves during the last half of the baking period and if the tops are getting too brown, cover them with a piece of foil or brown paper.

FINAL STEP

Remove bread from the oven and turn the loaves out on metal racks to cool.

OATMEAL SESAME BREAD

[THREE SMALL ROUND LOAVES]

Each of the three loaves of this delightful bread is about the size of a large orange, and each is marked into six wedges to be broken apart by guests. It is fine eating—moist and flavored with 1½ cups of oatmeal. The bread is brushed with egg white, dipped into a bowl of sesame seeds before it goes into the oven. It makes a handsome, though small loaf.

INGREDIENTS

1½ cups of rolled oats
2½ to 3 cups all-purpose flour, approximately
1 package dry yeast
2 tablespoons sugar
1 tablespoon salt
2 tablespoons butter, room temperature
1½ cups hot tap water (120°–130°)
Topping: 1 egg white
1 tablespoon water
3 tablespoons sesame seeds

BAKING SHEET

One baking sheet, greased or Teflon.

PREPARATION
15 mins.

In a large mixing bowl, measure the rolled oats and 1 cup all-purpose flour and stir in yeast, sugar, salt, butter and water. Beat in the electric mixer at medium speed for two minutes, or for an equal length of time with a wooden spoon.

Stop the mixer. Stir in balance of the flour, a half cup at a time, first with the spoon and then by hand. The dough will be a rough, shaggy mass that will clean the sides of the bowl.

KNEADING
8 mins.

Turn the dough onto a lightly floured work surface—counter top or bread board—and knead with the rhythmic 1-2-3 motion of push-turn-fold. The dough will become smooth and elastic. Sprinkle more flour on the dough and the work surface if the dough continues slack and sticky. Break the kneading rhythm occasionally by throwing the dough down hard against the counter top. Knead for 8 minutes (6 minutes under a dough hook).

FIRST RISING
1 hour

Place the dough in the bowl and pat with buttered or greased fingers to keep the surface from crusting. Cover the bowl tightly with plastic wrap and move to a warm place (80°–85°) until the dough has doubled in size. You can test if it has risen by poking a finger in it; the dent will remain.

SHAPING
20 mins.

Turn back the plastic wrap and punch down the dough. Knead for 30 seconds to press out the bubbles. Divide the dough into 3 equal pieces. Let rest 5 minutes.

Beat the egg white and 1 tablespoon of water together in a cup until frothy. Sprinkle the sesame seeds onto a plate or into a bowl.

Shape each part of dough into a round ball, slightly flattened on top. Hold loaf in the fingers, brush top and sides with the egg white mixture. Invert the loaf in the sesame seeds, pressing down lightly to cover with seeds. Carefully place the loaf on the baking sheet, seed side up. Repeat with the other 2 pieces.

With a sharp knife, mark 6 equal wedges on each loaf with 3 deep grooves across the top. Cut lightly, about ½ inch deep.

SECOND RISING
45 mins.

Place the baking sheet in the warm place and cover carefully with a length of wax paper. The loaves will double in size.

BAKING
400°
20–25 mins.

Preheat oven to 400°. Bake the loaves in the oven until they are golden brown and test done. Turn one loaf over and tap the bottom crust with a forefinger. A hard hollow sound means the bread is baked. Don't over-bake these small loaves. Midway in the bake period and again near the end of it, shift the loaves so they are exposed equally to the temperature variations in the oven.

FINAL STEP Remove bread from the oven and place the loaves on a metal rack to cool. These keep for several days wrapped securely in foil or plastic, and freeze well for several months.

ORANGE OATMEAL BREAD

[ONE LARGE OR FOUR MINIATURE LOAVES]

The orange fruit and skin flavor this loaf while the oatmeal gives it a rough texture that is good to chew. The crust is waxy and the slice is moist and speckled with bits of the peel. I make miniature loaves and serve one to each breakfast or brunch guest. Delicious warm and spread with sweet butter.

INGREDIENTS
1 orange (for its peel and fruit)
2 tablespoons sugar
1½ cups all-purpose flour
¾ cup sugar
4½ teaspoons baking powder
½ teaspoon salt
¼ teaspoon baking soda
1 cup rolled oats
2 eggs, room temperature
2 tablespoons butter, melted
⅔ cup water

BAKING PANS One large (9 x 5) baking pan, or 4 miniature (4½ x 2½) pans, greased or Teflon, metal or glass, but if the latter reduce oven heat 25°. Line the pan with wax paper to keep the loaves from sticking. Be certain to butter again after lining.

PREPARATION
25 mins.
Beforehand, grate the rind of 1 orange and reserve it in a small bowl. Peel off the outer white membrane, and, with a sharp knife, cut the meat out of each section, leaving the sectional membranes intact. Discard the

membranes and seeds. Cut the flesh into small pieces and add to the rind; sprinkle with 2 tablespoons sugar and mix well. Set aside. Preheat oven to 350°.

In a large bowl, measure the flour, sugar, baking powder, salt and baking soda. Stir in the rolled oats. In a separate bowl, lightly beat the eggs and mix with the melted butter, reserved orange mixture and water. Blend the liquid into the dry ingredients.

FORMING
15 mins.

Pour the batter into the prepared loaf pan or pans. Let rest for 10 minutes.

BAKING
350°
1 hour
(45 mins. for miniature loaves)

Bake the loaf in the oven until the loaf tests done when a wooden toothpick inserted in the center of the loaf comes out clean and dry.

FINAL STEP

Remove bread from the oven. Carefully remove the bread from the pan and allow it to cool on a metal rack before serving.

RAISIN OATMEAL BREAD

[ONE LARGE OR TWO SMALL LOAVES]

A dark, chocolate-colored loaf, this bread has a molasses flavor that comes on much stronger than do the three flours, the buttermilk or the raisins and nuts. Nevertheless, combined in a moist compact loaf, they make an unusual and delicious bread. The knife, slicing the loaf, will cut through the rolled oats to leave an intriguing pattern of light streaks against the almost-black bread.

INGREDIENTS

1 cup *each* all-purpose flour, rye flour and oatmeal
1 teaspoon *each* salt, baking soda and baking powder
¼ cup sugar
½ cup molasses
1¼ cups buttermilk
1 cup raisins
½ cup chopped walnuts

BAKING PANS — One large (9 x 5) baking tin, or 2 small (7½ x 3½) pans, greased or Teflon, glass or metal. If glass, reduce oven temperature 25°. To facilitate turning out the loaf after it has baked, butter or grease the pan, line the long sides and bottom with a length of wax paper and butter again. Leave tab ends of the paper projecting out about ½ inch so the loaf can be pulled from the pan.

PREPARATION
15 mins. — Preheat oven to 350°.

Combine in a large bowl the all-purpose flour, rye flour, oatmeal, salt, baking soda, baking powder and sugar. In a small bowl, mix the molasses and buttermilk, and pour into the dry ingredients. Blend but don't beat. Add the raisins and walnuts. Stir together thoroughly.

FORMING
5 mins. — Pour the batter into the pan, or pans, and level with a spoon or rubber spatula.

BAKING
350°
1 hour — Place the pans in a moderate oven and bake for 1 hour. Smaller loaves will require only 45 minutes. Test for doneness with a wooden toothpick.

FINAL STEP — Remove bread from the oven. Allow the bread to cool for 15 minutes in the pan; then turn out onto a metal rack to finish cooling.

SCOTCH OATMEAL BREAD

[FIVE MEDIUM LOAVES]

There is no yeast in these loaves yet they are as fat and pregnant as any made with two or three packages of yeast. Cooked Potato Starter (page 284) is the leavening force.

This is a large recipe—five medium loaves, or 3 medium loaves, 1 large loaf and a dozen rolls. Scotch oatmeal is cracked whole-grain oats which is mixed with the starter the night before, and, on bake day, blended with maple syrup, ginger, butter, and bread flour. Cinnamon and grated maple sugar are sprinkled on rectangles of dough, rolled tightly and baked. The result is a colorful brown swirl through the loaves.

INGREDIENTS

2 cups boiling water
2 cups Scotch oatmeal (cracked whole-grain oats)
2 cups all-purpose or bread flour
3 tablespoons brown sugar
1½ cups Cooked Potato Starter (page 284)
2 cups warm water (105°–115°)
1 cup non-fat dry milk
½ teaspoon ginger
5 teaspoons salt
6 tablespoons *each* soft butter and maple or maple-flavored syrup
8 to 10 cups all-purpose or bread flour, approximately
2 tablespoons cinnamon
½ cup grated block maple sugar or loose brown sugar
Softened butter to brush crusts

BAKING PANS

Baking pans, greased or Teflon, according to the number of loaves desired. See the dough volume chart on page 23 for suggestions. If glass, reduce oven temperature 25°.

PREPARATION
Overnight

The night before baking, pour boiling water over Scotch oatmeal in a medium mixing bowl. Stir, and when cooled to lukewarm (100°), add flour, brown sugar and starter. Cover tightly with plastic wrap and put in a warm place until morning.

20 mins.

Turn back the plastic covering, stir, and add warm water, milk, ginger and salt. Blend in the butter, syrup and five cups of flour. Stir 150 strong strokes with a wooden spoon until the ingredients are mixed and the batter strings from the sides of the bowl. Gradually add more flour, ½ cup at a time—first with the spoon and then by hand—until the dough forms a soft mass.

KNEADING
10 mins.

Turn the dough out onto a work surface spread with flour. Keep flour on the dough and on the hands until it is no longer sticky. Knead until the dough is smooth and elastic, and feels alive under the hands.

FIRST RISING
1 hour

Return dough to the bowl, pat with buttered fingers, and cover tightly with plastic wrap. Transfer to a warm place (80°–85°) free from drafts, until the dough is light and doubled in bulk.

SHAPING
20 mins.

Punch down the dough, turn it out on the floured work surface and divide into as many pieces as you want loaves of bread. For the loaves, roll each piece into a rectangle, sprinkle with the cinnamon and grated maple sugar or brown sugar. (A few raisins can be sprinkled on the dough.) Roll the rectangle tightly, pinching the seam together and tucking under the ends. Brush the tops with butter. Drop into pans. For rolls, divide one portion of dough into desired number, roll into shape under the palms and place them on a baking sheet. Brush the tops with melted butter.

SECOND RISING
50 mins.

Cover the loaves with wax paper and place them in a warm place until they have risen to at least double in volume.

BAKING
350°
½–1 hour

Preheat oven to 350°. Place the loaves and rolls in the oven. Bake the loaves for about 1 hour, while the rolls will take no more than 30 minutes. Test for doneness with a wooden toothpick inserted in the loaf; it will come out dry and clean if properly baked.

FINAL STEP

Remove bread from the oven and turn from the pans. Place on the metal rack to cool before serving.

TEN

Blended Grain Breads

Millet
Lyons, 1579

The breads made with the blended grains are coarser, denser, and darker than most other loaves. They taste of no one grain but the meld of them all. In the seven recipes there is a total of seven different flours and cereals. Sennebec Hill has six and War Bread four.

Surprisingly, perhaps, Boston Brown Bread is in this chapter. While it is a steamed bread—a process almost but not quite unusual enough to deserve a place of its own—Boston Brown is made with cornmeal and rye and whole wheat flours. The baked version has these three plus all-purpose white.

THREE FLOURS BREAD

[TWO LARGE OR FOUR SMALL LOAVES]

A blend of three flours—whole wheat, soy and white—produces an unusual flavor in this crusty brown yeast loaf. The dough will weigh about 4 pounds so I usually divide it into quarters and bake four 1-pound loaves in small tins. These light and wheat-textured loaves are fine to send off with a departing house guest or to leave with a host or hostess.

INGREDIENTS

2 packages dry yeast
½ cup warm water (105°–115°)
2¼ cups hot tap water (120°–130°)
½ cup brown sugar, firmly packed

1 tablespoon salt
½ cup shortening, room temperature
4 cups whole wheat flour
1 cup all-purpose flour, approximately
1½ cups soy flour

BAKING PANS

Two large (9 x 5) or 4 small (7½ x 3½) loaf pans, greased, metal or glass. If glass, reduce oven heat 25° or the crust may scorch.

PREPARATION
20 mins.

In a small bowl or cup stir yeast into water with a metal whisk or fork This will hasten the yeast action. Set aside.

In a large mixing bowl, pour tap water over brown sugar, salt and shortening. Gradually beat in 3 cups of whole wheat flour and 1 cup of white flour. Pour in the yeast mixture and beat with an electric mixer at medium speed for about 5 minutes—or 100 strong strokes with a large wooden spoon. Mix in the soy and the remaining 1 cup of whole wheat. It will now be too stiff to mix with a beater (unless it has a dough hook) so turn it out on a floured surface—a bread board or counter top.

KNEADING
6 mins.

If the dough is sticky in the hands as kneading begins, add a small amount of white flour. Depending on the flour, the dough may absorb up to a cup additional white flour before it begins to feel light and springy. Knead.

FIRST RISING
1 hour

Return to the bowl (washed and greased), cover tightly with plastic wrap and place in a warm spot (80°–85°) until doubled in bulk.

SHAPING
5 mins.

Remove the plastic wrap and turn the dough out on a floured surface to knead lightly for about 45 seconds. Divide the dough in half or quarters and shape to fit the prepared loaf tins.

SECOND RISING
45 mins.

Cover with wax paper and return to the warm place until the center of the dough has risen about 1 inch above the level of the edge of the pans.

BAKING
375°
45 mins.
(35 mins. for small loaves)

Preheat oven to 375°. Bake in the oven until well browned. The loaves are done when a wood toothpick or testing skewer inserted in the center comes out clean. However, if the bread has been baked in shiny tins, the loaves may not be brown enough on the sides and bottoms to please you. Turn them out of the tins and return them to the oven for an additional 5 minutes.

FINAL STEP

Remove bread from the oven. Allow the loaves to cool completely on metal racks before slicing.

WAR BREAD

[TWO LARGE LOAVES]

While the name of this loaf may be provocative to some, the bread is not. It has many admirable qualities, including a 150-year-old history as a farmhouse loaf in the New England states. When white flour was scarce, often in wartime, this blend of rolled oats, cornmeal, and whole wheat was added to the flour to make it go farther. It makes a delicious loaf that tastes equally good in less troubled times.

A young friend who likes it has suggested the name be changed to peace-meal bread.

INGREDIENTS

1 cup rolled oats
1 cup cornmeal
1 cup whole wheat flour
1 tablespoon lard or other shortening
⅓ cup molasses
1 tablespoon salt
3 cups boiling water
1 package dry yeast
5 to 6 cups all-purpose flour, approximately

BAKING PANS

Two large (9 x 5) baking pans, greased or Teflon. If glass, reduce oven heat 25°.

PREPARATION
25 mins.

In a large bowl, mix together rolled oats, cornmeal, whole wheat, lard, molasses and salt. Pour in the boiling water, stirring constantly, until the mixture is smooth. Set aside to cool to lukewarm (105°–115°). Sprinkle yeast on the batter, and blend.

Stir in the all-purpose flour, a half cup at a time, first with the spoon and then by hand. The dough will be somewhat heavy and dense and will not have the full elasticity of white dough. Nevertheless, the dough will form a shaggy mass that cleans the sides of the bowl. Sprinkle on flour to control the stickiness, if needed.

KNEADING
8 mins.

Turn the dough onto a lightly floured work surface—counter top or bread board—and knead with the rhythmic 1-2-3 motion of push-turn-fold. The dough will become smooth. Sprinkle on more flour if the dough continues to stick to the work surface or the fingertips. Shortening on the fingertips will help with the stickiness. Knead. This recipe is almost too large to put under the dough hook of the two smaller Kitchen Aid models. It can be done but the dough must be held below the protective shield with a rubber scraper.

FIRST RISING
1 hour

Place the dough back in the clean mixing bowl and pat with buttered or greased fingers to keep the surface from crusting. Cover the bowl tightly with plastic wrap and move to a warm place (80°–85°) until the dough has risen to twice its original size—judged by how it creeps up the sides of the bowl. You can test if it has risen by poking a finger in it; the dent will remain.

SHAPING
10 mins.

Punch down the dough and knead for 30 seconds to press out the bubbles. With a sharp knife, divide the dough into two pieces. Shape into balls, and let them rest under a towel for 3 to 4 minutes. With the hands form a loaf by pressing a ball into a flat oval, roughly the length of the baking pan. Fold the oval in half, pinch the seam tightly to seal, tuck under the ends, and place in the pan, seam down. Repeat with the second loaf.

SECOND RISING
50 mins.

Place the pans in the warm place, cover with wax paper and leave until the center of the dough has risen to an inch above the edge of the pan.

BAKING
350°
1 hour

Preheat oven to 350°. Bake the loaves in the oven until they are nicely browned and test done. Turn one loaf out of its pan and tap the bottom crust with a forefinger. A hard hollow sound means the bread is baked. If not, return to the oven for an additional 10 minutes. If the loaves brown too quickly, cover them with brown sack paper or foil. Midway in the bake period, and again near the end, shift the pans so the loaves are exposed equally to temperature variations in the oven.

FINAL STEP

Remove bread from the oven and turn from the pans. Place on a metal rack until cool.

SENNEBEC HILL BREAD

[TWO LARGE OR FOUR SMALL LOAVES]

There are six cereals and flours in this fine and flavorsome dark loaf—cornmeal, wheat germ and rolled oats, and rye, whole wheat and white flours. While it is a stiff dough to work, it raises well, and has a rough texture and a nutlike flavor. The 4 egg yolks give it richness and add to the color of this blend of dark grains. Makes a fine toast.

INGREDIENTS

2 packages dry yeast
2 cups warm water (105°–115°)
¼ cup molasses
4 egg yolks, room temperature
2½ teaspoons salt
⅓ cup cooking oil
1 cup non-fat dry milk
½ cup *each* rolled oats, yellow cornmeal, and wheat germ
1 cup rye flour
2 cups whole wheat flour
3 cups all-purpose or bread flour, approximately

BAKING PANS

Four small (7½ x 3½) pans or two large (9 x 5) pans, greased or Teflon. If glass, reduce oven heat 25°.

PREPARATION
20 mins.

In a large mixing bowl, sprinkle yeast over water. Add molasses, which will hasten the fermentation as well as give the bread flavor. Stir with a fork or whisk and let stand for 2 or 3 minutes.

Add egg yolks, salt, oil, milk, oats, cornmeal and wheat germ. Beat on low speed of electric mixer or with a wooden spoon until well mixed. It will be a heavy batter; so with the spoon and by hand, add the rye flour, whole wheat and 1 or 2 cups of all-purpose white flour to make a firm dough.

KNEADING
6 mins.

Turn the dough out on a floured work surface and knead. If the dough is sticky (or slack) add ¼ cup of all-purpose flour and work it into the dough.

FIRST RISING
50 mins.

Grease the bowl lightly, drop the ball of dough into it, turning it so that all surfaces are lightly filmed with oil. Cover the bowl tightly with plastic wrap, place in a warm spot (80°–85°) and let rise until nearly doubled. For a somewhat finer texture the dough may be punched down at the end of this time and allowed to rise again. However this is not necessary.

SHAPING
10 mins.

Turn the dough out on a floured surface; knead to press out the bubbles and divide the dough into two or four pieces, whichever number you choose to make. (See the dough volume chart on page 23.) Shape into balls, and let rest under a towel 3 or 4 minutes. Form a loaf by pressing a ball of dough into a flat oval, roughly the length of the baking pan. Fold the oval in half, pinch the seam tightly to seal, tuck under the ends, and place in pan, seam down. Repeat with the other loaves.

SECOND RISING
45 mins.

Cover the pans with wax paper, return to the warm place, and let the dough rise until it is doubled in volume.

BAKING
375°
25 mins.
350°
20 mins.

Preheat oven to 375°. Bake in a moderately hot oven for 25 minutes; then reduce heat to 350° and bake for an additional 20 minutes. Turn one loaf out of the pan and tap the bottom crust with a forefinger. A hard hollow sound means the bread is baked. If not, return to the oven for an additional 10 minutes.

FINAL STEP

Remove bread from the oven. Turn the loaves out on a metal rack to cool.

BOSTON BROWN BREAD

[TWO 1-POUND LOAVES]

One of the prime ingredients of this version of New England's legendary steamed bread is rye, a grain that the Puritans found would grow well in their cool climate. The rye is mixed with two other flours, whole wheat and cornmeal, and steamed on top of the stove for about 2 hours to produce a moist brown cylinder that is spongy to the touch when done.

Raisins are optional and they must be dusted with flour to keep them from sinking in the batter-like dough. Serve this bread warm with a pot of molasses-flavored beans or a boiled dinner.

Two 1-pound coffee cans are my molds. A coffee can with printing and art work on the side will brown the bread faster than will a plain shiny can.

INGREDIENTS

1 cup cornmeal
1 cup rye flour
1½ teaspoons baking soda
1 teaspoon salt
1 cup whole wheat or graham flour, unsifted
¾ cup molasses
2 cups sour milk or buttermilk, room temperature
1 cup raisins, well dusted with flour

BAKING CANS

Two 1-quart cylindrical molds, No. 2 cans or 1-pound coffee cans, greased.

PREPARATION
15 mins.

In a large bowl sift together cornmeal and rye flour, baking soda and salt. Add whole wheat or graham flour.

In a small bowl stir the molasses into the buttermilk or sour milk. When it is thoroughly blended, add it to the dry ingredients, a little at a time and stir just enough to blend. Don't overstir. Add the raisins.

SHAPING
15 mins.

Butter the coffee cans or molds and, to make certain the bread will slip out, cut rounds of buttered wax paper to place in the bottom of each.

Divide the batter between the two cans. The mix will come to slightly more than half the height of the coffee can. Double a piece of foil and press it tightly across the top of each can. Tie each foil top securely in place with a length of cord. Don't puncture the foil.

STEAMING
2 hours

On the bottom of a large kettle (with cover) place a rack on which the two cans rest. Pour in hot water to half the height of the cans or molds—and bring the water to a slow boil. Steam until the bread is springy to the touch and no longer sticky. It may be necessary to add more hot water to the kettle during the 2-hour period.

FINAL STEP

Remove bread from the kettle and allow the tins to cool for 5 to 10 minutes before turning them on their sides and slipping the bread out. Work with care because the hot loaves are fragile. Place them on a cooling rack and, ideally, serve them warm. These freeze nicely.

DARK GRAINS BREAD

[TWO MEDIUM LOAVES]

Dark Grains Bread has the consistency of a fine pumpernickel (which is chiefly rye) but a far-ranging flavor—buckwheat, whole wheat, wheat germ, white, and only a modest portion of rye. It is sticky and stiff to work but it rises surprisingly well, more than 1 inch above the edge of the pan in less than 1 hour. It is too heavy for the dough hook. Good dark color and a faint taste of molasses.

INGREDIENTS

2 packages dry yeast
2½ cups warm water (105°–115°)
⅓ cup non-fat dry milk
¼ cup molasses
1 tablespoon salt
½ cup *each* wheat germ and buckwheat flour
2 tablespoons shortening, room temperature
1 cup rye flour
3 cups whole wheat flour
1 to 1½ cups all-purpose or bread flour, approximately

BAKING PANS

Two medium (8½ x 4½) baking pans, greased or Teflon, metal or ovenproof glass. If the latter, reduce oven heat 25°.

PREPARATION
20 mins.

In a large bowl, dissolve yeast in water and stir briskly to hasten the action. Set aside for 3 minutes.

Measure and stir in milk, molasses, salt, wheat germ and buckwheat flour. Stir 50 strokes to blend well. Add the shortening and stir into the mixture. Add, gradually, ½ cup at a time, the rye flour and whole wheat. It will be thick but stir 150 times until it pulls away in strands from the sides of the bowl. Add the all-purpose or bread flour, ½ cup at a time, first with the spoon and then by hand. It will create a rough mass that will not adhere to the sides of the bowl. If it is wet, add a little more all-purpose flour. It may continue to stick to the hands until after it has been kneaded for several minutes.

KNEADING
8 mins.

Spread flour on the work surface—counter top or bread board—and turn the dough onto it. Keep flour dusted on the dough, the work surface and the hands while you knead. Shortly the dough will lose its stickiness. It will, however, remain firm and dense throughout the kneading process. At no point will it be as elastic or as responsive as white dough. Because it is so sticky, use a dough scraper or metal spatula to keep the work surface scraped clean during the kneading.

FIRST RISING
1 hour

Place the dough in the mixing bowl, pat it well with buttered fingers, cover the bowl tightly with plastic wrap and place in a warm spot (80°–85°) until dough has doubled in bulk.

SHAPING
6 mins.

Knock down the dough, divide in two equal pieces, flatten each into an oval, and fold in half. Pinch the seams together and plump into a loaf, seam down. Place in pans.

SECOND RISING
50 mins.

Cover pans with wax paper and return to the warm place until the center of the dough has reached level with the tops of the pans.

BAKING
375°
50 mins.

Preheat the oven to 375°. Place in the oven. Test for doneness by turning one loaf out of its pan and thumping it on the bottom crust with a forefinger. A hard hollow sound means the bread is baked.

FINAL STEP

Remove bread from the oven. Place the hot loaves on a metal rack to cool. This is a delicious rough-textured bread that is excellent for sandwiches and buffets.

WHEAT AND OAT BREAD

[TWO LOAVES]

Boiling water plumps both the raisins and the oatmeal in this loaf that is made with three wheat products—bran, whole wheat and white flour. Its good looks and equally good taste deserved something better than a name it once had—Health Bread—which to many connotes blandness and even strangeness. This light brown loaf is neither. It is a bit on the sweet side, however, because of the ¾ cup of molasses, a rather heavy portion that can be reduced.

INGREDIENTS

2 packages dry yeast
½ cup warm water (105°–115°)
1 cup oatmeal
2 teaspoons salt

2 tablespoons shortening, room temperature
1 cup raisins
1 cup bran
2¾ cups boiling water
¾ cup molasses
1 cup whole wheat flour
6 cups all-purpose flour, approximately

BAKING PANS

Two medium (8½ x 4½) loaf tins, greased or Teflon, metal or glass. If glass, reduce heat in the oven 25°.

PREPARATION
40 mins.

In a small bowl dissolve yeast in ½ cup warm water. Stir to dissolve and set aside.

In a large bowl combine oatmeal, salt, shortening, raisins, bran—and pour over this the boiling water. Stir and set aside to cool to lukewarm. This may take a half hour or so unless the bowl is placed in cold water to cool. Test the mixture with a thermometer (or finger) to determine that it is not above 120°. Add the yeast mixture and molasses.

Stir in whole wheat flour and 2 cups of all-purpose flour. Gradually add additional flour, a half cup at a time, to make a rough mass that cleans the sides of the bowl. If it is slack and inclined to be sticky, add ¼ cup more flour.

KNEADING
8 mins.

Lightly flour the work surface—bread board or counter top—and turn the dough into the center of it. Knead until smooth and elastic.

FIRST RISING
1 hour

Place in a greased bowl. Turn the dough once to cover the entire ball with a film of oil. Cover the bowl with plastic wrap, and put in a warm place (80°–85°) until the dough has doubled in bulk.

SHAPING
20 mins.

Punch down the dough, divide and cover the two pieces with a towel or wax paper. Let the dough rest on the counter for 10 minutes. Press each piece flat, fold in half, seal the seam by pinching tightly, and place each into a pan.

SECOND RISING
45 mins.

Cover with wax paper, return to the warm place and let the dough rise until it has doubled in volume.

BAKING
350°
1 hour

Preheat oven to 350°. Place the pans in the oven and bake until the crusts are nicely browned. Turn one loaf out of its pan and tap the bottom crust with a forefinger. A hard hollow sound means the bread is baked. If not, return to the oven for an additional 10 minutes.

FINAL STEP — Remove bread from the oven and place the loaves on wire rack until cooled. Freezes well.

BAKED BROWN BREAD

[ONE LARGE LOAF]

Baked brown bread or Dutch-oven bread is very much like Boston brown bread but with one major difference. Boston brown bread is steamed whereas this is put into a cold oven, the heat turned on and baked at a moderate setting for less than 90 minutes. This is about half the time required for a steamed bread. Baked brown bread is a hearty, wholesome dark loaf, filled with raisins and walnuts. It does not, however, have the softness nor fine texture of a steamed bread.

INGREDIENTS
- ½ cup white or yellow cornmeal
- 1½ cups all-purpose or bread flour
- 1 cup *each* rye flour and whole wheat flour
- ½ cup *each* brown sugar, packed tightly, and molasses
- 2 teaspoons *each* baking soda and salt
- 2 cups buttermilk or sour milk
- 1 cup broken walnuts

BAKING CONTAINER — Dutch-oven (9-inch diameter) or equivalent covered casserole or other pan, greased.

PREPARATION 15 mins. — In a large bowl, measure the cornmeal, all-purpose or bread flour, rye flour, whole wheat flour, brown sugar, molasses, baking soda and salt. Pour in the buttermilk or sour milk and mix well. Stir in the walnuts.

FORMING 3 mins. — Pour the mixture into the Dutch oven, or casserole.

BAKING 350° 1 hour — Do *not* preheat oven. Place the bread in the cold oven. Turn the heat to moderate and bake the bread. It is done when a wooden toothpick inserted in the bread comes out clean and dry. If moist particles cling to the probe, return the loaf to the oven for an additional 10 minutes. Test again.

FINAL STEP — Remove bread from the oven. This is a rather large loaf. Use care in removing from the Dutch oven, to place on the wire rack to cool.

ELEVEN

French Breads

Sesame
Lyons, 1579

In France, bread is seldom baked in the home because the *boulangerie* is just around the corner producing its bounty of golden loaves, long ones and round ones, six days of the week. The considerable aim of this chapter is to have the home baker do as well.

It is somewhat exacting to produce a loaf of fine French bread, but it is not difficult.

The dough for the bread is the least complicated of all to make. Flour, water, salt and yeast. The baking procedure is not elaborate but there are several steps that must be done correctly and in sequence to produce the classic crusty loaf.

The French make their bread with flour milled from western European wheat. It is a soft wheat, with a low gluten content, and somewhat akin to the mix of hard and soft wheat in all-purpose flour. While the large French bakeries use some U.S. and Canadian hard wheat flour to enable the dough to withstand rough machine mixing and shaping, the small *boulanger* produces his loaf of bread without it. By using all-purpose flour the reader can do almost as well.

To give the dough time to develop its large open patternwork of cells, it must be allowed to rise in the bowl until it has at least fully doubled in volume. The shaped loaves, in their turn, must fully develop before they are placed in the oven. Less than full proof means smaller loaves, and a more dense slice.

To achieve the legendary crispness that sends golden chips flying across the room when the loaf is broken or cut, the bread must be baked in an oven that is first *moist* and then *dry*.

In U.S. bakeries and French *boulangeries,* steam under pressure is shot into the oven moments before the loaves are put in, and again at intervals while the bread expands under the heat. The steam prevents the crust from forming too quickly and allows full oven-spring enabling the loaf to swell to maximum size. Approximately 15 minutes of the allotted bake time is required. The steam is turned off, the oven heat becomes dry and gives color to the thin, late-forming crust.

The home baker can reach almost the same results by placing a broiler pan partially filled with water in the hot oven several minutes before putting the bread in to bake. Expect steam to puff harmlessly from cracks around the oven door. With no more than 1 or 1½ cups of water in the pan, it will completely evaporate during the first 15 minutes, which is as it should be.

Before the loaves go into the oven they are brushed with water or sprayed with an atomizer. Two or three times during the first half of the bake period, brush or spray the loaves. The steam from the pan will also keep the loaves moist. When the loaves are fully formed and color comes faintly to the crust, use no more water. If there is water in the pan, remove it. The oven heat will dry and bake the loaves to a lovely crackly brown.

In France the basic dough takes many shapes. There is the long, slender *baguette,* the *bâtard* and the *ficelle.* The round plump loaves—the *miche* and the *boule.* The husky long and ample *pain boulot.* For the family, *pain de ménage.* In the country, the peasant loaf—*pain de campagne.*

I spent a pre-dawn morning in Bayeux, in Normandy, watching a young twenty-five-year-old *boulanger,* Monsieur André Gaulier, put his own touch to large round loaves by jabbing his outstretched fingers deep into the raised dough just before it went into the oven. Everyone in Bayeux knew the dimpled loaf was made by M. Gaulier and no one else.

In a small one-man bakery in the resort town of Bénodet, in Brittany, I helped Monsieur Yves Montfort load lengths of soft dough into long black-metal baguette pans, open-ended and trough-shaped. These we stacked in a large wooden cabinet to rise. The three-foot loaves could not be turned out of the pans to go into the oven for they would have been unmanageable. The pans with their raised loaves were pushed into the ovens.

From the moment I walked into his bakery at three o'clock in the morning until I left at eight o'clock, M. Montfort scarcely looked up from his work. When the last hot loaves were resting on end in wire baskets, and the sound of hard crust crackling in the cool air was the only noise in the bakery, he looked across the table, waved at the bread, and smiled wearily—

"*Trop, trop!*" Too much indeed for one man.

His recipe for French bread is on page 266.

But in Paris the most famous loaf is baked by Monsieur Pierre Poilane in his two bakeries where a staff of thirty-eight turn out more than fifteen hundred loaves each day for a clientele that ranges from Elysée Palace to the bistros in the neighborhood.

M. Poilane's genuine love of his profession and the pride he has in his position as the city's premier *boulanger* is evident at the very entrance to his shop at 8 rue du Cherche-Midi. The door pulls are of hand wrought brass fashioned into sheaves of wheat. On the walls of the shop are dozens of paintings and sketches of the celebrated proprietor, his famous black beret and the plump peasant loaves that have brought him fame. On shelves above the bins of bread are a dozen ceramic replicas of the Poilane loaf. Each is a tureen.

The peasant loaf which weighs 2 kilograms (4½ pounds) is made with unbleached flour milled to his own specifications and is somewhat darker than most French bread. He takes particular pride in pointing out that the ovens are hand-fired with apple wood.

The Poilane loaf is described in verse on his business card—

> If you have a friend
> for whom you wish well
> recommend to him your baker
> for his bread is baked with wood,
> on tile, made with *levain** and wheat
> flour, with germ, ground by millstones.

M. Poilane has a gourmet's palate and a reputation to match, and he is welcomed into every restaurant in Paris even though he appears before the maître d' in his gray shopkeeper's smock and beret, with a loaf of Poilane bread under his arm.

When I dined with him at a favorite restaurant, Le Borghèse, we ate his country bread, rough and delicious, with a choice pâté, accompanied by a superb wine. M. Poilane laughingly explained that his country loaf sells for 90¢ which the Borghèse management claims is too costly for their tables as *pain ordinaire*. Nevertheless, the owners and waiters eat the Poilane loaf in the staff dining room.

M. Poilane was philosophical when he picked up another baker's bread from the basket on the table.

"Today more and more bread in France is being made by those who spend their time watching clocks and gauges. The proper way to make bread is by hand, in wood-burning ovens, and to feel the life of the dough."

The French peasant bread on page 269 was inspired by this great *bou-*

* *A starter of dough from the previous batch.*

langer. While it is not possible in the U.S. to bake with the kind of flour M. Poilane has grown and ground especially for him, the starter of whole wheat flour gives it the flavor and texture of the Poilane loaf.

Sour Dough French Bread is an American creation, specifically from the San Francisco Bay Area. Two recipes for French-type bread are included in the chapter on sour dough breads, page 287, and should not be overlooked, for they are different and delicious.

MONSIEUR MONTFORT'S FRENCH BREAD

[TWO MEDIUM ROUND OR FOUR LONG LOAVES]

Two things were quickly apparent during my visit to Monsieur Montfort's *boulangerie* in Bénodet (page 264), and each contributed importantly to the making of his excellent French loaf.

Despite a gas-fired oven going full blast in the room, the air in the bakery was relatively cool—70°. In baskets, pans, and large mixing bowls, the dough was slowly rising in a relaxed way to develop the full wheaty flavor characteristic of French bread. It took almost twice as long to rise as it would in a room 10° to 15° warmer.

I pinched off a small ball of dough from a batch resting in a large mixing bowl and discovered to my surprise that it was softer than anything to which I was accustomed. I could *force* it to stick to my fingers but handled gingerly it would not. It was just one step beyond the sticky stage, and I would have been inclined to firm it up with more flour. Not M. Montfort. He sprinkled flour liberally over the work surface but this didn't affect the consistency of the dough.

This recipe takes both of these factors into consideration—temperature of the room and the consistency of the dough. Because of the extended period allowed for resting the dough at lower temperatures, five to six hours are needed to prepare, raise, shape and bake the bread. But worth every minute of it.

INGREDIENTS	7 cups all-purpose flour (a little more if excessively sticky) 2 packages dry yeast 4 teaspoons salt 3 cups hot tap water (105°–115°)
BAKING SHEETS OR PANS	One baking sheet for hearth loaves, greased or Teflon, or if available, four 18-inch French bread pans, greased (see suppliers, page 545).

PREPARATION
10 mins.

Place a pastry scraper or putty knife to one side before you begin.

In a large bowl measure the flour and stir in yeast and salt. Form a well in the bottom of the bowl and pour in the water. With a wooden spoon slowly pull the flour into the liquid until it is fully absorbed. Work it into a ball with the fingers and place on lightly floured work surface or bread board.

KNEADING
10 mins.

The dough should be tacky but not hopelessly sticky. Begin turning and folding the dough with the pastry scraper or putty knife. Sprinkle small amounts of flour on the work surface and hands if you must but do so sparingly. Continue to lift, fold and turn for 10 minutes. Throw the dough down against the work surface to break the lift-fold-turn rhythm. The dough will become elastic but will continue to stick to moist fingers unless powdered with flour.

FIRST RISING
2–3 hours

Wash the large bowl, grease and place the dough in it. Cover tightly with plastic wrap. Find a constant 70° place for the bowl. Allow the dough to expand fully to double its volume.

PUNCH DOWN
2 mins.

Turn back the plastic, punch down the dough, re-cover the bowl and return it to its 70° place.

SECOND RISING
1–2 hours

Allow the dough to double in volume.

SHAPING
15 mins.

Turn the dough onto the floured work surface, punch down and knead briefly to press out the bubbles. Divide the dough, which will weigh about 3¾ pounds, into as many loaves as you wish to make.

One fourth of the recipe (about 1 cupful or ¾ pound of dough) will make one long, slender loaf—18 by 2 inches. Half the recipe will make two husky long loaves (14 by 4 inches) or two round hearth loaves.

Form the divided dough into balls, and let them rest for 5 minutes.

For a long loaf, flatten the ball into an oval. Fold over, flatten with the side of the open hand, fold again and roll with the palms. If the dough resists, let it rest for another 3 or 4 minutes while preparing the other pieces. Return to the partially formed length and continue to roll under the palms until it is shaped. The seam will disappear.

The long pieces of dough can be placed directly on the baking sheet to rise although they will slump somewhat because the dough lacks stiffness. They can be placed in a long basket lined with a cloth and liberally sprinkled with flour. The baskets will direct the dough upwards during the rise period.

By placing the shaped dough on a length of canvas (or pastry cloth) and pulling the cloth up between the loaves to separate them, the home baker can do as M. Montfort does with large loaves. Sprinkle liberally with flour beforehand. The dough expands upwards and puts pressure on the loaf or loaves adjoining to do the same. This can be done on the work surface if the room temperature is the desired 70°.

A third and perhaps the best way is to place the long loaves in half-cylindrical, French-type metal pans.

Round loaves can be placed on the corners of the baking sheet to rise but because of the softness of this particular dough it is better to use the round cloth-lined baskets.

THIRD RISING
1 hour

Place the shaped dough in the 70° location and rest wax paper above on water glasses. Leave until the loaves are fully doubled. More proof rather than less is desirable. The longer it is allowed to rise the larger the cell structure will be in the baked loaf. Approximately 20 minutes before putting the dough in the oven preheat to 425°.

BAKING
425°
25–30 mins.

Prepare the oven by placing the broiler pan or a similar vessel on the lowest shelf. Five minutes before baking, pour 1½ cups of hot tap water in the pan.

If the loaf was raised in a basket, tip onto the hand and lower gently onto the baking sheet. The dough raised on canvas is gently rolled onto a flat cardboard or cookie sheet held in one hand and transferred to the baking sheet.

With a razor blade, slash the top of the round loaves in a tic-tac-toe design. Hold the blade at a 45 degree angle as you make the cut. For the long loaves, cut a series of diagonal cuts.

Brush or spray loaves with water as you place them in the hot oven.

At 3-minute intervals, during the first 15 minutes,

spray the loaves. Do it from the oven door. Don't pull out loaves or the moist hot air will be lost.

The loaves will be fully ovenproof (expanded) in about 18 minutes, at which time color will begin to tinge the crusts. If water remains in the pan, empty it.

Bake in the oven until the loaves are a golden brown. Turn over one loaf and tap the bottom crust with a forefinger. A hard hollow sound means the bread is baked. If not, return to the oven for an additional 5 minutes. If the loaves appear to be browning too quickly, cover with a piece of foil or brown sack paper.

Midway in the bake period and again near the end of it, shift the loaves to expose them equally to the temperature variations in the oven.

FINAL STEP

Remove bread from the oven. Place the loaves on a wire rack to cool. The French baker stands his loaves on end so that cool air freely circulates around them. For a bright shiny crust brush lightly with water, slightly salted.

Bon Appétit!

FRENCH PEASANT BREAD

[TWO LOAVES]

This fine bread came out of my kitchen after a summer in France watching M. Poilane in Paris and the village bakers in the provinces begin new dough that had all of the goodness of the traditional French loaf by adding a portion of sponge from the previous batch.

To give it the color and taste of the peasant loaf, I add one cupful of sour dough whole wheat sponge to the recipe for the basic white loaf. There is a special and unique flavor that develops in the fermentation of whole wheat flour that is lost in a dough made entirely of white flour. Whatever bacteria is responsible, it transplants easily from whole wheat to white, with delightful results.

Since it is a peasant-type bread, put the dough to rise in small cloth-lined baskets; later, turn the raised loaves right onto the baking sheet, and slice with a razor blade.

There is water steaming in the oven broiler pan and this evaporates away, as it should, about the time the loaves begin to brown.

INGREDIENTS

Starter: Peasant Bread starter (page 286)
Sponge: All of the starter
2 cups warm water (105°–115°)
3 cups all-purpose flour
Dough: All of the sponge
1 tablespoon salt
3 cups all-purpose flour, approximately

BAKING SHEET

One baking sheet, greased or Teflon.

PREPARATION

Give the starter and the sponge each at least one day to fully develop. Plan to bake on the third day.

1 day

Prepare the Peasant Bread starter.

1 day

Into a large bowl pour the starter and stir in water and 3 cups flour. Mix it well. Replace the plastic wrap and return to the warm place for another day. It will be a wet mix like the starter.

On bake day, remove the plastic and stir down the sponge. Add salt. Stir in flour, a half cup at a time, first with a wooden spoon and then by hand, until it is firm and no longer sticky. Small sprinkles of flour will control the stickiness if the moisture should break through the dough.

KNEADING
10 mins.

This dough works particularly well under a dough hook. Turn it onto a lightly floured work surface—counter top or bread board—and knead with the rhythmic 1-2-3 motion of push-turn-fold. The dough will become smooth and elastic, and bubbles will form under the surface of the dough. Sprinkle with more flour if the dough is slack or moist, or if it sticks to the hands or work surface. Occasionally change the kneading rhythm by raising the dough above the counter and smashing it down hard against the top. (This is a large batch for the dough hook and it may try to climb over the shield above the hook. Hold it down with a rubber spatula as the hook turns.)

FIRST RISING
1 hour

Put the dough back in the mixing bowl and pat with buttered or greased fingers to keep the surface moist. Cover the bowl tightly with plastic wrap and move to a warm place (80°–85°) until the dough has risen to twice its original size (as judged by how it creeps up the sides of the bowl).

SHAPING
10 mins.

My kitchen has an assortment of small baskets—the kind used to serve bread at dinner—and I chose two to help shape this peasant loaf. Fold and lay a tea towel in the basket, letting the cloth drape over the sides. Dust liberally with flour, some of which will stick to the loaf to give it an attractive finish. My round baskets are about 8 inches in diameter. The long basket, about 14 inches long and 3 inches wide.

Divide the dough. Shape each piece to fit the shape of the basket you have chosen—long or round. Simply drop the dough in the basket.

SECOND RISING
50 mins.

Cover with wax paper and leave in the warm place (80°–85°) for about 50 minutes, or until it has raised to about double its volume.

In the meanwhile, preheat the oven to 425° with water in a pan on the bottom shelf. One cup of water poured in a broiler pan 15 minutes before putting in the bread is usually sufficient to steam the oven during the important first 20 minutes of the bake period.

BAKING
425°
35–40 mins.

(See paragraph above.) Carefully tip the raised dough out of each basket and onto the baking sheet. With a razor blade, cut diagonal slashes in a long loaf and criss-crosses on a round one. Place in the oven.

Bake the loaves in the oven until they are golden brown and test done. Turn over one loaf and tap the bottom crust with a forefinger. A hard hollow sound means the bread is baked. Midway in the bake period, and again near the end of it, shift the loaves so they are exposed equally to the eccentricities of the oven.

FINAL STEP

Remove bread from the oven and place on metal racks to cool. Try a slice of this toasted served with cheese. Absolutely great.

FRENCH BREAD—THE ENGLISH WAY

[THREE LARGE LOAVES]

This French bread comes from England, only a Channel's width away. It is a delicious and handsome hard-crusted loaf that has the creamy interior so much sought after by French bread devotees. A big loaf, it is light when held in the hand—hardly more than a pound for all of its 16-inch length and 12-inch girth.

Because it has no shortening—only flour, yeast, salt and water—it will not keep much beyond 24 hours. Bake it the day you intend to serve it, or freeze for another day.

When I have unbleached flour at hand, I set the sponge with all-purpose flour but use unbleached for the dough. It is not essential but somehow the loaves always seem more golden and more crusty when I do.

INGREDIENTS

Sponge: 2 packages dry yeast
2 cups warm water (105°–115°)
3 cups all-purpose flour

Dough: All of the sponge
1 tablespoon of salt
1½ cups warm water (105°–115°)
5 cups unbleached or all-purpose flour, approximately

BAKING SHEET AND PAN

One baking sheet, greased or Teflon. A shallow roasting pan to contain hot water in the oven during the early part of the bake period.

PREPARATION

While this is a process that takes 6 hours or more before a loaf is baked it has a time span that can be broken into several easy segments, some today and some tomorrow.

Sponge
10 mins.
2–24 hours

Sprinkle yeast over the water in a large bowl. Stir with a fork or metal whisk to dissolve.

Stir in flour to make a batter. If the batter is too thick, thin it down with a tablespoon or two of water. It must be liquid to allow the bubbles to work their way up during the period of fermentation.

Cover the bowl with plastic wrap and put aside in a warm place (80°–85°) for at least 2 hours, or better, overnight. The longer it is left during a 24-hour period the better flavor it will have. The sponge will spread out in the bowl, creep up the sides and fall back. Under its cover, it will be giving off the strong odor of fermentation.

Dough
12 mins.

Uncover the sponge bowl. Dissolve the salt in water and pour it over the sponge. Mix together. Add flour, a half cup at a time, first with the spoon and then by hand. Keep plenty of flour in the bowl so the hands are always working with flour at the edge of the dough. The dough will be a rough, shaggy mass that will clean the bowl. If it continues moist and is sticky, sprinkle on additional flour.

KNEADING
10 mins.

French bread is the product of unrestrained and uncurbed kneading. Turn the dough onto a lightly floured work surface—counter top or bread board—and knead with the rhythmic 1-2-3 motion of push-turn-fold. The dough will become smooth and elastic, and bubbles will rise under the surface of the dough. Change the kneading rhythm by throwing the dough down hard against the work surface. The dough will feel warm and alive in your hands.

FIRST RISING
1½ hours

Return the dough to the bowl and pat with buttered or greased fingers to keep the surface from crusting. Cover the bowl tightly with plastic wrap to retain the moisture. Move to a warm place (80°–85°) until the dough has risen to more than double its original size. You can test if it has risen by poking a finger in it; the dent will remain.

SHAPING
15 mins.

Turn back the plastic cover and punch down the dough. Place it on the lightly floured work surface and knead for 30 seconds to press out the bubbles. With a sharp knife divide the dough into three equal pieces. Place them under a towel and let them rest for 5 minutes.

Form each piece into a ball. For a round loaf, place the ball on the corner of the baking sheet or put it in a small basket, lined loosely with a cloth and sprinkled with flour. (The basket will direct the dough upwards rather than allowing it to spread out on the baking sheet.)

For a long loaf, roll the ball into a rectangle, 10 x 16 inches. Roll up the dough, beginning with the short side, and stopping after each full turn to press the edge of the roll firmly into the flat sheet of dough to seal. Press with fingertips. The long loaf can be placed directly on the baking sheet or in a long cloth-lined basket to be placed on the baking sheet later.

SECOND RISING
50 mins.

Place the baking sheet and/or the baskets in the warm place and cover carefully with a length of wax paper. If the paper clings to the dough rest it on water glasses. The loaves will double in bulk.

Prepare the oven by placing the large shallow roasting pan, partially filled with hot water, on the bottom shelf. Fill only one-third full as, ideally, the water should boil away midway in the bake period when the loaves will have started to brown (and steam is no longer necessary). Preheat the oven to 400°.

At 400° the water will boil gently and steam will begin to puff harmlessly from around the door.

BAKING
400°
45 mins.

If the loaves have raised in baskets, tip the raised loaf into the hand and quickly turn it right side up onto the baking sheet. Brush with cold water. With a razor blade or a sharp knife, slash the round loaves with a tic-tac-toe design; the long loaves with diagonal cuts.

Bake the loaves in the oven until the crusts are a golden brown. Turn over one loaf and tap the bottom crust with a forefinger. A hard hollow sound means the bread is baked. If not, return to the oven for an additional 10 minutes. Midway in the bake period and again near the end of it, shift the loaves on the baking sheet so they are exposed equally to the temperature variations of the oven. Each time the loaves are shifted brush them with water or spray with an atomizer.

FINAL STEP

Remove bread from the oven and place on a wire rack where they will crackle and pop as they cool.

BLUE RIBBON FRENCH BREAD

[TWO LOAVES]

The crustiness and salty good taste of this French bread made with all-purpose flour (rather than bread flour) won for me a Blue Ribbon at the Indiana State Fair. A shallow pan of steaming water on the bottom of a hot (400°) oven keeps the loaves in a cloud of moist air during the early stages of oven-spring. It is an easy loaf to make.

INGREDIENTS

1 package dry yeast
¼ cup warm water (105°–115°)
1¾ cups hot tap water (120°–130°)
2 tablespoons non-fat dry milk
1 tablespoon sugar
1 tablespoon butter, room temperature
1 tablespoon salt

5½ to 6 cups all-purpose flour, approximately
Topping: 1 tablespoon cold water
1 tablespoon coarse salt

BAKING SHEET AND PAN

One baking sheet, greased or Teflon. A shallow roasting pan for hot water in the oven during baking.

PREPARATION
15 mins.

Dissolve yeast in lukewarm water. Stir with a fork or metal whisk and set aside for 3 minutes.

In a large mixing bowl, pour the hot tap water and stir in milk, sugar, butter and salt. Add the yeast mixture.

Stir in 2 cups of all-purpose flour and beat in the electric mixer at medium-high speed for 3 minutes.

Stop mixer. Stir in the balance of the flour, a half cup at a time, first with the spoon and then by hand. The dough will be a rough shaggy mass that will clean the sides of the bowl. If it continues moist and sticky, sprinkle on additional flour.

KNEADING
20 mins.

Turn the dough onto a lightly floured work surface and let the dough rest for 10 minutes. Knead with the rhythmic 1-2-3 motion of push-turn-fold. The dough will become smooth and elastic, and bubbles will rise under the surface of the dough. Break the kneading rhythm by throwing the dough down hard against the counter top. Knead for 10 minutes (or 8 under a dough hook).

FIRST RISING
1¼ hours

Return the dough to the mixing bowl and pat with buttered or greased fingertips. Cover the bowl tightly with plastic wrap to retain the moisture. Move to a warm place (80°–85°) until the dough has risen to twice its original volume. This can be judged by how high up the sides of the bowl it creeps. You can test if it has risen by poking a finger in it; the dent will remain.

SHAPING
15 mins.

Punch down the dough and turn it onto the lightly floured work surface again. Knead for 30 seconds to press out the bubbles, and cut into two pieces with a sharp knife. Form each piece into a ball.

For a round loaf, place on a corner of the baking sheet or in a small basket, lined loosely with a cloth and sprinkled with flour. For a long loaf, roll the ball into a rectangle, 10 x 16 inches. Roll up the dough, beginning with the short side, and stopping after each full turn to press the edge of the roll firmly into the flat sheet of dough to seal. Press with the fingertips. The long loaf can be placed directly on the baking sheet or in a long cloth-lined basket to be placed on the baking sheet later.

SECOND RISING
50 mins.

Place the baking sheet and/or the baskets in a warm place and cover the loaves carefully with a length of wax paper. If the paper clings or sticks to the dough, rest it on water glasses. Leave until the loaves have doubled in volume.

Prepare the oven by placing a large, shallow roasting pan, partially filled with hot water, on the bottom shelf. Fill only one-third full since, ideally, the water should boil away midway in the bake period when the loaves will have started to brown (and steam is unnecessary).

BAKING
400°
45 mins.

Preheat the oven to 400°. If the loaves have raised in baskets, simply tip the raised loaf into your hand and quickly turn the loaf right side up onto the baking sheet. Brush with cold water and sprinkle with the coarse salt. With a razor blade or a sharp knife, slash the round loaves with a tic-tac-toe design; the long loaves with diagonal cuts.

Bake the loaves in the oven until they are a golden brown. Turn over one loaf and tap the bottom crust with a forefinger. A hard hollow sound means the bread is baked. If not, return to the oven for an additional 10 minutes. Midway in the bake period and again near the end of it, shift the loaves on the baking sheet so they are exposed equally to the temperature variations of the oven.

FINAL STEP

Remove bread from the oven and place on wire racks to cool. Scrub the water out of the roasting pan since it may have picked up some mineral deposits from the boiling water.

This bread is delicious reheated. Place uncovered in a 350° oven for 20 minutes. It also keeps well frozen.

FRENCH BREAD WITH UNBLEACHED FLOUR

[TWO LOAVES]

While unbleached flour is often difficult to find (and often expensive), it is the flour used by the French *boulanger* to make bread. Unbleached flour, he feels, is important to help form the crisp crust. Unbleached flour is also closer to the natural product, with fewer things changed in the milling process.

My favorite is Ceresota, milled in Kansas City. Ceresota flour, which dates back to 1891, achieves its whiteness through a natural aging process while stored at the mill. The exact number of weeks is a company secret.

INGREDIENTS

5½ to 6 cups unbleached flour, approximately
1 package dry yeast
2 teaspoons sugar
1 tablespoon salt
½ cup non-fat dry milk
2 cups hot tap water (120°–130°)
To brush: ½ cup water
½ teaspoon salt

BAKING SHEET AND PAN

One baking sheet, greased or Teflon. Also shallow roasting pan on the bottom shelf of the oven for hot water.

PREPARATION
15 mins.

In a large mixing bowl measure 2½ cups flour and add yeast, sugar, salt, milk and tap water. Beat in an electric mixer 30 seconds at slow speed to blend, and increase speed to medium-fast for 3 minutes, or an equal length of time beating with a wooden spoon.

Stop mixer. Stir in the balance of the flour, a half cup at a time, first with the spoon and then by hand. The dough will be a rough, shaggy mass that will clean the sides of the bowl. If the dough continues slack and sticky, add several sprinkles of flour.

KNEADING
10 mins.

Turn dough onto a lightly floured work surface—counter top or bread board—and knead with the rhythmic 1-2-3 motion of push-turn-fold. The dough will become smooth and elastic. However, if the stickiness persists, sprinkle on additional flour. Break the kneading rhythm by throwing the dough down against the counter top. Knead for about 10 minutes (6 minutes under the dough hook).

FIRST RISING
1 hour

Return the dough to the bowl and pat with buttered or greased fingertips. Cover the bowl tightly with plastic wrap to retain the moisture. Move the bowl to a warm place (80°–85°) until the dough has risen to double its original size. You can test if it has risen by poking a finger in it; the dent will remain.

SHAPING
15 mins.

Punch down the dough. Place it on the work surface, knead for 30 seconds to press out the bubbles and cut into two equal pieces with a sharp knife. Form each into a ball. For a round loaf, place on a corner of the prepared baking sheet or in a small basket, lined loosely with a cloth sprinkled with flour. For a long loaf, roll the ball into a rectangle, 10 x 16 inches.

Roll up the dough, beginning with the short side, and stopping after each full turn to press the edge of the roll into the flat dough to seal. Press with the fingertips. The long loaf can be placed directly on the baking sheet or in a long cloth-lined basket to be placed on the baking sheet later.

SECOND RISING
45 mins.

Place the baking sheet and/or the baskets of dough in the warm place and cover carefully with a length of wax paper. Leave until the loaves have doubled in volume.

Prepare oven by placing a large, shallow roasting pan partially filled with hot water on the bottom shelf. Fill only about one-third as ideally the water should boil away midway in the bake period, after the loaves have started to brown.

BAKING
400°
15 mins.
350°
20 mins.

Preheat to 400°. If the loaf has raised in a basket, simply tip the loaf into your hand and quickly turn the loaf right side up onto the baking sheet. Brush the loaves with the salt water solution. With a razor blade cut diagonal slashes (about ¼ inch deep) in the long loaf, and a tic-tac-toe design on the round one.

Bake the loaves in the hot oven for 15 minutes, reduce heat to 350° and continue baking for 20 minutes. Halfway through the baking, brush the loaves with the salt water solution and at the same time shift the loaves on the baking sheet so they are exposed equally to the temperature variations of the oven.

Turn over one loaf and tap the bottom crust with a forefinger. A hollow, hard sound means the bread is baked. If not, return to the oven for an additional 10 minutes.

FINAL STEP — Remove bread from the oven and place the loaves on a metal rack to cool before serving.

COOLRISE© FRENCH BREAD

[TWO LOAVES]

One of the nice things about this loaf of good French bread is that it can be mixed, kneaded and shaped ahead of time—up to 24 hours—and slipped into the refrigerator to be kept until it is time to bake. It has a beautiful deep brown crust but not as crispy and crackly as some of the other French loaves. Nevertheless, the texture of the slice is open, not fine grained, and it has a delightfully salty taste.

INGREDIENTS

- 5 to 6 cups all-purpose or bread flour
- 2 packages dry yeast
- 1 tablespoon sugar
- 1 tablespoon salt
- 2 tablespoons vegetable shortening, room temperature
- 2¼ cups hot tap water (120°–130°)
- 1 tablespoon cooking oil
- 1 tablespoon cold water

BAKING SHEET — One baking sheet, greased or Teflon.

PREPARATION
15 mins. — Combine 2 cups of all-purpose or bread flour, undissolved yeast, sugar and salt in a large mixing bowl. Stir to blend. Add shortening. Pour in tap water. Beat in an electric mixer at medium speed for 2 minutes, or for an equal length of time with a large wooden spoon. Add 1 cup flour and increase speed to high for 1 minute, or beat with a spoon. Scrape bowl occasionally.

Stop mixer. Stir in the balance of the flour, a half cup at a time. The dough will leave the sides of the bowl. If the dough continues moist and sticky, add a few sprinkles of flour.

KNEADING
10 mins. — Turn the dough onto a lightly floured work surface—counter top or bread board—and knead with the rhythmic 1-2-3 motion of push-turn-fold. The dough will become smooth and elastic, and bubbles will rise under

the surface of the dough. If the dough is sticky, sprinkle flour on the work surface and the hands. Knead for 8–10 minutes (6 minutes under the dough hook).

RESTING
20 mins.

Cover the dough with plastic wrap and let rest for 20 minutes.

SHAPING
15 mins.

Punch down the dough. Divide into two equal pieces. Roll each into a rectangle 10 x 16 inches. Roll up the dough, beginning with the short side, and stopping after each full turn to press the edge of the roll into the flat dough to seal. Press with the fingertips.

Place on the baking sheet. Brush the loaves with oil and cover loosely with a length of plastic wrap.

REFRIGERATION
2–24 hours

Place the loaves in the refrigerator (moderately cold). The best volume is obtained with not more than 8 hours in the refrigerator, however.

BAKING
400°
40–55 mins.

Remove the bread from the refrigerator, peel back the plastic wrap and leave uncovered for 10 minutes while the oven heats to 400°. Brush with cold water, and with a razor blade, slash tops of loaves with curving diagonal strokes.

If you wish, ten minutes after the bread is in the oven, spray with water from an atomizer, or brush it on. Ten minutes later repeat. Midway in the bake period and again near the end of it, shift the loaves on the baking sheet so that they are exposed equally to the temperature variations of the oven.

Bake in the oven until they are golden brown. Test by turning over one loaf and tapping the bottom crust with a forefinger. A hollow, hard sound means the bread is baked. If not, return to the oven for an additional 10 minutes.

FINAL STEP

Remove bread from the oven and place on a metal rack to cool.

TWELVE

Starters

Hop Plant
Antwerp, 1574

The creation of a bubbling and aromatic pot of starter—beloved by pioneer housewives and frontiersmen without wives—is the first and most important step in making breads of the sour dough family. It is a mixture of flour and a liquid into which bacteria, wild or otherwise, is introduced. Normally it is made and stored in small quantities, usually about two cups.

The next step is adding more flour and liquid to make a sponge which is essentially a larger bowl of starter. Now about half of the flour and liquid is fermenting, and the yeast cells are multiplying by the millions.

The final step—the sponge becomes the dough.

The starter was in use for a long time before yeast moved from the brewery and bakery to appear in its little silver envelope on the grocer's shelf. On the American frontier and in Alaska, starters substituted for yeast as the leavener for breads, biscuits, and flapjacks, and became famous. While it was developing its own peculiar flavor, it was also gathering around it a following of fierce defenders who gave it a mystique of its own.

No longer was the question one of getting the dough to rise—packaged yeast could do that—it was the unique tart flavor and aroma that was sought and prized.

A true starter, be forewarned, can be whimsical and maddening in its formative days. Once established it is a joy to have in the refrigerator.

Some starters have yeast boosters, but the amount is small and its presence will be lost in the long fermentation period that follows. No yeast should be used to help along salt-rising bread because it overpowers the delicate aroma and flavor of the sour.

A starter can be passed down in a family for generations or it can be only a few days old. The Turnipseed Sisters (page 88) have a hops starter that they have kept alive for more than 30 years, yet bread I bake with a new hops starter is equally flavorful. Starters available in specialty food stores or by mail order are satisfactory but no more so than any of the starters described here.

There are two easy ways to replenish starters.

The first is to replace the cupful taken out of the jar with ¾ cup of flour and ¾ cup of liquid (water, potato water, or milk). Stir, then allow it to ferment at room temperature for a day or so before returning, covered, to the refrigerator.

The other is to pour all of the starter into a bowl and add 1 cup of flour and 1 cup of liquid. This is an opportunity to wash and scald the jar in which the starter has been stored. Stir the mixture well and take out however much starter is required by the recipe. Return the balance to the freshly washed jar. Allow it to ferment at room temperature for a day and then return, covered, to the refrigerator.

A starter should be used at least once a week. If not, stir down after 3 or 4 weeks, spoon out and discard half of it and replenish the balance.

Some starters can be frozen successfully, but if it doesn't bounce back to life after thawing it may need to be helped with a sprinkling of dry yeast. Stir in the yeast and allow it to bubble before using.

Here are the starters—wild as well as yeast-fortified—that are used in recipes in the book. Not all breads made with starters or sponges can be properly termed "sour dough," hence, they are not a part of this sour dough section. Those are the sour rye breads, salt-rising breads, the white loaf by the Turnipseed Sisters (a hops starter), and others. There is a fine starter—*Sauerteig*—used in making a delicious Austrian buckwheat loaf, Bauernbrot (page 237), that should not be overlooked. The rye and hops starters are described here since in a venturesome spirit you may wish to substitute these for other kinds.

Not listed among the starters are several exotic ones, including those made with beer, soft drinks, and leaves of trees.

Witch Yeast

This is from the cookbook published by the Methodist Church women of Delphi, Indiana, more than a half century ago.

1 cup mashed potato
¼ cup sugar
2 teaspoons salt
1 cup warm water (105°–115°)

Stir together in a quart glass jar, cover with a cloth and leave in a warm place (80°–85°) for two days or until it ferments, bubbles up, and smells pleasantly sour. Use, or seal and refrigerate.

Can be used in the Methodist White Bread, page 101, or in other sour dough recipes if you choose.

Sour Rye Starter

2 cups rye flour
1½ cups warm water (105°–115°)
1 package dry yeast
1 slice onion

Mix the flour, water, yeast, and onion together in a wide-mouth quart jar. Cover with a cloth and put in a warm place (80°–85°) for 3 or 4 days or until it is well fermented, frothy, and smells pleasantly sour. Remove the onion. Either use, or seal and refrigerate.

Can be used as part of the sponge in all sour rye breads.

San Francisco Starter

While this is not the true San Francisco bacterial strain, it does give the bread a respectable sour fragrance, open texture, dark crust, and a chewy bite.

1 cup milk
1 cup unbleached or all-purpose flour

Pour the milk in a glass jar or bowl and leave uncovered at room temperature for a day. Measure in the flour, stir and leave uncovered in a warm place (80°–85°) for two to five days, depending on how soon the bacteria begin the fermentation process. If the mixture should dry out, stir in a little warm milk. When the starter is bubbly, frothy, and gives off a pleasantly sour aroma, it is ready. Either use at that time, or cover tightly and store in the refrigerator.

A variation of this is to mix the milk and flour *together* in a 1-quart glass jar, and seal immediately with a rubber sealing ring and a substantial wire clamp. Allow the mixture to ferment for 5 days. Stir down each day (thereby letting the accumulated gas escape), and replace the lid.

This starter obviously relies on the bacteria in the milk.

Cooked Potato Starter

This is made in two steps, several days apart.

4 tablespoons cornmeal
2 tablespoons sugar
1½ teaspoons salt
1 cup milk

Stir the cornmeal, sugar, salt, and milk together in a saucepan and bring to the scalding point. Stir constantly. Pour this into a small bowl or glass container, cover tightly with plastic wrap and leave in a warm place (80°–85°) for 2 to 4 days or until it ferments and becomes light and frothy. Stir each day. When the mixture is spongy prepare:

3 medium potatoes
1 quart water
3 tablespoons sugar
2 teaspoons salt

Cook the potatoes in the water until tender. Reserve the water, and add more, if necessary, to make 3 cups of liquid. Mash the potatoes and put through a sieve or food mill. Stir in the reserved liquid, sugar, and salt. When cool, stir in the fermented cornmeal. Cover and let stand in a warm place (80°–85°). Stir down each time it becomes bubbly. Next day put it into a two-quart jar, cover and place in the refrigerator to age before using in about 3 days. Stir each time before using, and replenish when the starter has been reduced to 1 or 1½ cups. Prepare a new mixture of potato, potato water, sugar, and salt and proceed as before.

Raw Potato Starter

1 cup warm water (105°–115°)
1¼ cups all-purpose flour
1 teaspoon *each* salt and sugar
1 medium potato, grated

Mix together the water, flour, salt, and sugar in a 2-cup measure. Add grated potato sufficient to make a full 2 cups.

Pour the mixture into a wide-mouth glass jar or small bowl that will hold about 1 quart (to allow for expansion during fermentation).

Place a piece of cheesecloth over the container and allow it to rest in a warm place (80°–85°) for 24 hours. Stir and cover tightly with plastic wrap which will retain the moisture. The mixture will become light and foamy in 2 or 3 days. Stir down each day.

Pour the fermented starter into a glass jar, fitted with a tight lid, and place in the refrigerator. In 3 or 4 days, when a clear liquid collects on top of the mixture, it will have ripened sufficiently to use.

Honey Starter

This is a yeast-boosted starter.

1 package dry yeast
2½ cups warm water (105°–115°)
2 tablespoons honey (or sugar)
2½ cups unbleached or all-purpose flour

Combine the yeast, water, honey (or sugar), and flour in a quart jar which has a tight fitting cover. Seal the jar and let the mixture ferment for 5 days, stirring daily.

Replenish the starter with water and flour in equal portions.

Sheepherder's Starter

1¾ cups bread or all-purpose flour
1 tablespoon *each* salt and sugar
1 package dry yeast
2½ cups warm water (105°–115°)

In a large bowl, mix together the flour, salt, sugar, yeast, and water. Cover the bowl tightly with plastic wrap to retain the moisture and put in a warm place (80°–85°) for 4 days. Each day stir and re-cover. When it has fermented and smells pleasantly sour, it may be used or refrigerated.

This starter is used in the Sheepherder's Bread, page 300.

Hops Starter

3 cups water
1 quart fresh hops or ¼ cup packaged dry hops
½ cup cornmeal, white or yellow
2 cups mashed potato
3 tablespoons sugar
2 teaspoons salt

In a saucepan bring water to a boil and steep hops for 20 minutes. Drain and reserve the liquid; discard the hops. If necessary add water to make 3 full cups of liquid.

Pour 1 cup of the hops liquid in a saucepan and stir in the cornmeal. Bring to a boil over medium heat, stirring constantly. When it thickens slightly, remove from heat.

In a large mixing bowl combine cornmeal mixture, mashed potato, sugar, salt, and the remaining 2 cups of hops liquid. Cover the bowl with a length of cheesecloth and set in a warm place (80°–85°) for 24 to 48 hours or until well fermented and bubbly. Stir every 8 hours or so during this period.

When the starter is frothy and smells pleasantly fermented, pour it into a two-quart glass jar with a tight fitting lid. Store in the refrigerator until clear liquid has risen to the top of the mixture in about 2 days. Stir down—and it is ready to use.

To replenish when only 1 cup remains: add water, cornmeal, mashed potatoes, sugar, and salt (as to begin). Set in a warm place. It will ferment and become active in about 8 hours. Store in the refrigerator.

Peasant Bread Starter

The recipe for French Peasant Bread (page 269) uses all of the starter prepared below. If you want starter left for later, double these ingredients except the yeast. Use only 1 yeast.

1 package dry yeast
1 cup warm water (105°–115°)
1 tablespoon non-fat dry milk
1 cup whole wheat flour

In a medium-size bowl dissolve yeast in water. Add milk and whole wheat flour. Mix thoroughly. It should be a soft, pablum-like mixture that will bubble and work for 24 hours. Cover tightly with plastic wrap and put in a warm place (80°–85°) for a day.

THIRTEEN

Sour Dough Breads

Maize
Seville, 1535

SOUR DOUGH LOAF

[TWO LARGE LOAVES]

There is no uncertainty about this sour dough loaf since it is made with store yeast, and its fermentation over a period of several days as well as how high and well it rises can be anticipated beforehand. Not so always with wild yeast spores which are the foundation of the true sour dough starters and sponges.

Nevertheless, this is a fine bread—creamy white on the inside, golden brown on the out, and the pleasant sharpness that comes with a long fermentation.

The sponge can be heard bubbling across a quiet kitchen during the first 2 days of active fermentation, and then it becomes passive and quiet.

INGREDIENTS

Sponge:
- 1 package dry yeast
- 1¾ cups bread or all-purpose flour
- 1 tablespoon salt
- 1 tablespoon sugar
- 2½ cups hot tap water (120°–130°)

Dough:
- 5 to 6 cups bread or all-purpose flour, approximately
- 3 tablespoons sugar
- 1 teaspoon salt
- 1 package dry yeast

⅓ cup non-fat dry milk
1 cup hot tap water (120°–130°)
2 tablespoons margarine or other shortening
1½ cups sponge
(Refrigerate the balance of the sponge for later uses. To replenish fully, add 1½ cups warm water [105°–115°], ¾ cup flour and 1½ teaspoons sugar.)

BAKING PANS

Two large (9 x 5) baking pans, greased or Teflon. If glass pans are used reduce oven heat 25°.

PREPARATION
Sponge
4 or 5 days

Blend yeast, bread or all-purpose flour, salt and sugar in a medium bowl and pour in the water. Stir for 30 seconds. Cover with plastic wrap to retain the moisture, and place in a warm spot (80°–85°). Stir down each day.

Bake Day
Dough
15 mins.

In a large bowl measure 1 cup of bread or all-purpose flour and stir in sugar, salt, yeast, milk and 1 cup hot tap water. Add the margarine or other shortening and 1½ cups of the sponge.

Beat for 3 minutes at medium-high speed in the electric mixer, or for an equal length of time with a wooden spoon.

Stop the mixer. Stir in the balance of the flour, a half cup at a time, first with the spoon and then by hand. The dough will be a rough, shaggy mass that will clean the sides of the bowl. If the dough continues moist and sticky, sprinkle with flour.

KNEADING
8 mins.

Turn the dough onto a lightly floured work surface—counter top or bread board—and knead with the rhythmic 1-2-3 motion of push-turn-fold. The dough will become smooth and elastic, and feel alive under the hands. Bubbles will rise under the surface of the dough. If the dough should be sticky, sprinkle on small additions of flour. Occasionally break the kneading rhythm by raising the dough above the work surface and throwing it down hard against the table. Knead for 8 minutes (6 minutes under the dough hook).

FIRST RISING
1 hour

Return the dough to the bowl and pat with buttered or greased fingers to keep the surface from crusting. Cover the bowl tightly with plastic wrap. Move to a warm place (80°–85°) until the dough has risen to about twice its original volume. It can be judged by how high it creeps up the sides of the bowl. You can test if it has risen by poking a finger in it; the dent will remain.

SHAPING
10 mins.

Punch down the dough with the fingertips and knead for 30 seconds to press out the bubbles. Put the dough on the lightly floured work surface and cut into two equal pieces with a sharp knife. Shape each into a ball, and let rest under a towel for 5 minutes. Form a loaf by pressing a ball of dough into a flat oval, roughly the length of the baking pan. Fold the oval in half, pinch the seam tightly to seal, tuck under the ends, and place in the pan, seam down. Repeat for the second loaf.

SECOND RISING
50 mins.

Return the pans to the warm place, cover with a length of wax paper and leave until loaves have doubled in size. Ideally, the top of the dough should have risen about 1 inch above the level of the edge of the pans.

BAKING
400°
30–40 mins.

Preheat the oven to 400°. Bake the loaves in the oven until they are golden brown and test done. Turn one loaf out of its pan and tap the bottom crust with a forefinger. A hard hollow sound means the bread is baked. If not, return to the oven for an additional 10 minutes. If you wish a darker over-all crust, remove the loaves from the pans during the final 10 minutes of the bake period. Midway in the bake period and again near the end of it, shift the loaves so they are exposed equally to the temperature variations of the oven.

FINAL STEP

Remove bread from the oven. Turn from pans and cool on wire rack. Brush with melted margarine for a softer crust.

CALIFORNIA SOUR DOUGH WHOLE WHEAT BREAD

[TWO LOAVES]

The development of this unusual loaf of sour dough bread was one of my first baking achievements. In the 60's I went professional when California's *Sunset* magazine, at home in the Bay Area where devotees of sour dough French bread are legion (and vocal), bought and published the recipe.

During the three days when the sponge is fermenting in the bowl, a whiff under the plastic wrap will be strongly alcoholic. I use a cup of wheat grains, whole or cracked, in the sponge to give the bread the texture of a provincial loaf. The bread makes exceptionally good toast.

INGREDIENTS

Sponge: 2 cups warm water (105°–115°)
2 packages dry yeast
⅓ cup non-fat dry milk
3 cups whole wheat flour
1 cup whole or cracked wheat grains (optional)

Dough: All of the sponge
¼ cup dark molasses
1 tablespoon salt
3 tablespoons vegetable shortening
2½ to 3 cups all-purpose flour, approximately

BAKING PANS

Two medium loaf pans (8½ x 4½), greased or Teflon, glass or metal. If glass, reduce baking temperature 25°.

PREPARATION
Sponge
3 days

Begin the sponge 3 days before bake day by blending, in a large bowl, the warm water, yeast, milk, whole wheat flour and the wheat grains. Stir well. Cover the bowl tightly with plastic wrap so moisture will not evaporate. Put in a warm place—80° to 85°. Once each day stir the mixture briefly and replace the plastic wrap.

Bake Day
Dough
15 mins.

Remove the plastic wrap and lay aside. Stir in the molasses, salt and shortening. Stir in the all-purpose flour, a half cup at a time, first with the spoon and then by hand. The dough will be heavy and moist but when it cleans the sides of the bowl it is ready for kneading.

KNEADING
8 mins.

Turn the dough onto a floured work surface, counter top or bread board, and knead with the rhythmic 1-2-3 motion of push-turn-fold. It is a heavier dough than an all-white but presently the gluten will begin to form and the dough will become soft and pliable. Continue kneading. (The dough hook does not work well in this dough.) Add small portion of flour (a teaspoon or so) to control the stickiness, if necessary.

FIRST RISING
2 hours

Place the dough back in the mixing bowl and pat with buttered or greased fingers to keep the surface from crusting. Cover the bowl again with the piece of plastic wrap and move to a warm place (80°–85°) until the dough has risen to about twice its original size (judge how high it creeps up the sides of the bowl). Because this is leavened with only the 3-day-old sponge, it will not rise as fast as if it had been made with a fresh charge of yeast.

SHAPING
15 mins.

Punch down dough. Knead for 30 seconds to press out the bubbles. With a sharp knife divide the dough into two pieces. Shape into balls, and let rest under a towel for 5 minutes. Shape by pressing each ball—under the palms or with a rolling pin—into a flat oval, roughly the length of the baking pan. Fold the oval in half, pinch the seam tightly to seal, tuck under the ends, and place in the pan, seam down. Repeat with the second loaf.

SECOND RISING
1¼ hours

Place the pans in the warm place, cover with wax paper and leave until the center of the dough has risen even with the edge of the pan.

BAKING
375°
40–50 mins.

Preheat the oven to 375°. With a sharp razor, slash each down the center just before placing the loaves in the oven. This allows the bread to expand without raising up the crust as well as to give this loaf an identification of its own. Bake in the oven until they are deep brown and crusty. Turn one loaf out of its pan and tap the bottom crust with a forefinger. A hard hollow sound means the bread is baked. If not, return to the oven—without the pan—for an additional 10 minutes. If the tops of the loaves appear to be browning too quickly, cover with a piece of foil or brown paper sack. Midway in the bake period shift the pans to different parts of the oven or simply exchange positions.

FINAL STEP

Remove bread from the oven. Turn the loaves onto a metal rack to cool before serving. This bread will keep for at least two weeks, tightly wrapped, and can be frozen for 6 months or more. Toasting brings out the special flavor and aroma of this delicious bread.

SOUR DOUGH FRENCH BREAD

[TWO LOAVES]

Allow a full day—24 hours—to make this good-tasting and crusty version of San Francisco's sour dough French bread. Since it is leavened with only a starter (no commercial yeast), it needs more time for the sourness and bubbly yeast action to develop. The starter is simply one cup of milk and one cup of flour mixed together and allowed to ferment for several days (page 283).

Unlike the traditional French loaf made with a soft wheat flour, San Francisco sour dough is made with bread flour milled from hard wheat to enable it to withstand the rigors of a long fermentation.

This recipe was developed several years ago by home economists in the heart of California's sour dough country.

INGREDIENTS

Sponge: 1 cup starter
1½ cups warm water (105°–115°)
4 cups bread or all-purpose flour
2 teaspoons *each* sugar and salt

Dough: All of the sponge
½ teaspoon baking soda
2 cups bread or all-purpose flour, approximately

Wash: ½ cup water
1 teaspoon salt

BAKING SHEET

One baking sheet, greased or Teflon.

PREPARATION

Four or five days beforehand prepare a starter, if one is not available.

Starter
4 or 5 days
Sponge
18 hours

In a large bowl or crock, one day prior, combine the starter, water, flour, sugar and salt. Mix thoroughly, cover the bowl with plastic wrap and leave at room temperature (70°) until sponge has doubled in volume.

Bake Day
Dough
12 mins.

Stir down the sponge, sprinkle on the soda. Stir in all-purpose flour, a half cup at a time, first with the spoon and then by hand. The resulting dough should be stiff but if it should continue slack and sticky, add a tablespoon of flour.

KNEADING
8 mins.

Turn the dough onto a lightly floured work surface—counter top or bread board—and knead with a rhythmic 1-2-3 motion of push-turn-fold. The dough will become smooth and elastic, and bubbles will form under the surface of the dough. Work in a quarter cup more flour if the dough will accept it. Break the kneading rhythm occasionally by throwing the dough down hard against the counter top. Knead 8 minutes (6 under the dough hook).

SHAPING
10 mins.

Cut the ball of dough into two pieces. Let them rest under a towel for 5 minutes. Form each into a ball.

For a round loaf, place on a corner of the prepared bake sheet or in a small basket, lined loosely with a cloth and sprinkled with flour. For a long loaf, roll the ball into a 10 x 16 inch rectangle. Roll up the dough, beginning with the short side, and stopping after each turn to press the edge of the roll into the flat dough to make a firm seal. Press with the fingertips. The long loaf can be placed directly on the baking sheet or in a long cloth-lined basket to be placed on the bake sheet later.

RISING
3–4 hours

Place the baking sheet and/or the baskets in a warm place (80°–85°) until the loaves are nearly doubled in bulk. This is a natural leavening and the dough will not expand as vigorously as with commercial yeast.

Place a shallow pan of hot water on the lower shelf of the oven and preheat to 400°—near the end of the rise period.

BAKING
400°
45 mins.

If the loaves have been raised in baskets, tip the raised loaf into the hand and quickly turn the loaf right side up onto the baking sheet. Brush with water and with a razor blade slash a tic-tac-toe design on the round loaves, and diagonal cuts on the long ones.

However, for a more tender crust, brush loaves with cooking oil or melted butter instead of water and don't place the hot water on the lower shelf.

Bake in the oven until the loaves are medium dark and test done. Turn one loaf over and tap the bottom crust with a forefinger. A hard hollow sound means the bread is baked. If not, return to the oven for an additional 10 minutes. Midway in the bake period and again near the end of it, shift the loaves on the baking sheet so they are exposed equally to temperature variations.

FINAL STEP

Remove bread from the oven and place on metal rack to cool somewhat but serve warm.

SOUR DOUGH OATMEAL BREAD

[THREE LARGE OR FOUR MEDIUM LOAVES]

A thick crusty loaf, mildly sour or tart, its creamy insides are flecked with oats. It is a big bubbly recipe that produces about 6 pounds of dough, or enough for 3 or 4 medium loaves. Use a large bowl for mixing.

This is one of the first sour dough recipes I collected and it came via another cookbook author, Jack Mabee, of San Francisco. His small sour dough cookbook has sold literally tens of thousands of copies.

INGREDIENTS

Sponge: 1 cup starter (see page 283)
2 cups warm water (105°–115°)
2½ cups bread or all-purpose flour

Dough: All of the sponge
2 cups hot tap water (120°–130°)
¾ cup non-fat dry milk
¼ cup honey
1 package dry yeast
2 cups quick cooking oatmeal
2 tablespoons sugar
2 teaspoons *each* salt and baking soda
4 to 5 cups bread or all-purpose flour, approximately

BAKING PANS

Three large (9 x 5) or four medium (8½ x 4½) baking pans, greased or Teflon. For other combinations of pan sizes, see dough volume chart, page 23. If glass, reduce oven temperature 25°.

PREPARATION
Sponge
8–10 hours

Begin the night before by mixing the starter, warm water and flour in a large bowl. Cover with plastic wrap and put in a warm place (80°–85°) for 8 to 10 hours, or overnight. It will bubble and foam to about double its original size.

Bake Day
Dough
15 mins.

Turn back the plastic wrap, stir down the sponge and measure in water, milk and honey. Sprinkle on the yeast. Stir in oatmeal, sugar, salt and baking soda.

Measure in the flour, a half cup at a time, first with a wooden spoon and then by hand. The dough will be a rough shaggy mass that will clean the sides of the bowl. If the dough continues moist, add a tablespoon or more additional flour.

KNEADING
5 mins.

Turn the dough onto a lightly floured work surface—counter top or bread board—and knead about 100 times with the rhythmic 1-2-3 motion of push-turn-fold. Knead until the dough feels smooth and satiny under the hands. (This is too large a batch to knead with the dough hook on most home mixers.)

RESTING
10 mins.

Let the bread rest under a towel.

SHAPING
10 mins.

Knead the dough for 30 seconds to press out the bubbles. With a sharp knife, divide it into three (or four) pieces. Shape into balls, and let rest for 3 to 4 minutes under the towel. Form a loaf by pressing a ball of dough into a flat oval, roughly the length of the baking pan. Fold the oval in half, pinch the seam tightly to seal, tuck under the ends, and place in the pan, seam down. Repeat with the second loaf, and so on.

RISING
1¼ hours

Place the pans in a warm spot (80°–85°), cover with wax paper and leave until the center of the dough has risen 1 inch above the level of the edge of the pan.

BAKING
400°
20 mins.
350°
25 mins.

Preheat oven to 400°. I identify sour dough loaves with a slash lengthwise down the center of the crust. You may wish to do the same. It also allows the bread to expand along the slash and not pull the top crust away from the sides.

Bake the loaves in the hot oven for 20 minutes, reduce heat to 350° and continue baking for an additional 25 minutes, or until the loaves test done. Turn one loaf out of its pan and tap the bottom crust with a forefinger. A hard hollow sound means the bread is baked. If not, return to the oven for an additional 10 minutes. Midway in the bake period and again near the end of it, shift the pans so the loaves are exposed equally to the oven's temperature variations.

FINAL STEP

Remove bread from the oven and place on a metal rack to cool. Brush with melted butter if you want a soft crust. This makes delicious toast, and freezes well in the deep freeze for 2 or 3 months.

SOUR DOUGH ANADAMA BREAD

[TWO BIG LOAVES]

Anadama is corn—a flavor enriched appreciably by the sourness of the bread. The leavening is a sour dough starter, strengthened midway in the process with a packet of yeast. The crust is dark, thick and crisp.

INGREDIENTS

Sponge: 1 cup starter (see page 283)
2 cups warm water (105°–115°)
2½ cups all-purpose or bread flour

Dough: 1½ cups boiling water
1 cup cornmeal, white or yellow
1 tablespoon cooking oil
½ cup molasses, light
2 tablespoons salt
4 cups sponge
1 package dry yeast
4 to 5 cups all-purpose or bread flour, approximately

BAKING PANS

Two large (9 x 5) baking pans, greased or Teflon. If glass, reduce oven heat 25°.

PREPARATION
Sponge
10–12 hours

In a medium-size bowl, measure a cup of starter. Stir in water and all-purpose or bread flour. Beat 30 seconds until smooth. Cover tightly with plastic wrap so there will be no evaporation. Put in a warm place (80°–85°) until the sponge has fermented and bubbles to double its volume. It will be light and spongy, and smell of fermentation.

Bake Day
Dough
15 mins.

In a large bowl, pour water over cornmeal, stirring constantly. Add oil, molasses and salt. When the mixture has cooled to warm (heat will kill the sponge), stir in the 4 cups of sponge. Sprinkle yeast over the surface, and mix thoroughly—30 seconds of strong beating with a wooden spoon.

Stir in 2 cups of flour. Beat at medium-high speed in electric mixer for 3 minutes.

Stop beater. Stir in the balance of the flour, a half cup at a time, first with the spoon and then by hand. The dough will be a rough, shaggy mass that will clean the bowl. If the dough continues moist and sticky, sprinkle the dough with flour.

KNEADING
8 mins.

Turn the dough onto a lightly floured work surface—counter top or bread board—and knead with the rhythmic 1-2-3 motion of push-turn-fold. The dough will become smooth and elastic, and bubbles will rise under the surface of the dough. Occasionally change the kneading rhythm by raising the dough above the work surface and banging it down hard. Knead for 8 minutes (6 under the dough hook).

FIRST RISING
1¼ hours

Place the dough back in the mixing bowl and pat with buttered or greased fingers. Cover the bowl tightly with plastic wrap to retain the moisture. Move to a warm place (80°–85°) until the dough has risen to about twice its original size, as judged by how high it creeps up the sides of the bowl. You can test if it has risen by poking a finger in it; the dent will remain.

SHAPING
12 mins.

Punch down the dough and knead for 30 seconds to press out the bubbles. With a sharp knife, divide into two pieces. Shape into balls, and let rest under a towel for 5 minutes. Form a loaf by pressing a ball of dough into a flat oval, roughly the length of the baking pan. Fold the oval in half, pinch the seam tightly to seal, tuck under the ends, and place in the pan, seam down. Repeat with the second loaf.

SECOND RISING
50 mins.

Place the pans in the warm place, cover with wax paper and leave until the center of the dough has risen 1 inch above the level of the edge of the pan. Meanwhile, preheat oven to 400°.

BAKING
400°
15 mins.
350°
30 mins.

Bake in the hot oven for 15 minutes, reduce heat to 350° and continue baking for an additional 30 minutes, or until the loaves are a deep brown and test done. Turn one loaf out of its pan and tap the bottom crust with a forefinger. A hard hollow sound means the bread is baked. If not, return to the oven for an additional 10 minutes. Midway in the bake period and again near the end of it, shift the pans so the loaves are exposed equally to the temperature variations in the oven.

FINAL STEP

Remove bread from the oven and place on a wire rack to cool. If a soft crust is desired, brush with melted butter.

SOUR DOUGH POTATO BREAD

[FOUR MEDIUM LOAVES]

There is no yeast in this loaf of potato bread—only potato starter—yet the loaves rise large and majestic, and have a wonderful taste and texture that potato alone can produce. Instant mashed potato is used in the sponge so there is no fuss about peeling and boiling potatoes.

This is a large recipe—enough for 4 medium loaves, or 2 loaves and several dozen rolls or buns.

INGREDIENTS	Sponge: 1 cup potato starter, raw or cooked (see page 284) 1½ cups all-purpose flour ½ cup sugar ½ teaspoon ginger 2 cups water ⅔ cup instant mashed potato Dough: All of the sponge 1 cup warm water (105°–115°) 1 cup non-fat dry milk 7 cups all-purpose flour, approximately ½ teaspoon *each* baking soda and cream of tartar ½ cup vegetable shortening, room temperature 1½ teaspoons salt
BAKING PANS	Four medium (8½ x 4½) loaf pans, greased or Teflon, or a selection of pans and baking sheets according to dough volume chart, page 23. If glass, reduce oven heat 25°.
PREPARATION Starter	Several days beforehand you will have made the potato starter (raw or cooked), page 284.
Sponge 2 hours Overnight	In a stoneware or glass bowl (not metal or plastic) stir together 1 cup starter and 1½ cups all-purpose flour. A soft ball will form. Let it rest uncovered for 2 hours. In a separate bowl stir together the sugar and ginger in 2 cups water. Pour over the starter. Sprinkle potato over the surface of the water. Cover tightly with a length of plastic wrap and set in a warm place (80°–85°) overnight.
Bake Day Dough 15 mins.	Eight or ten hours later the sponge will be foamy and expanding up the sides of the bowl. Stir down. Add warm water, milk, 3 cups of flour, baking soda and cream of tartar. Beat 100 strokes. Measure in the shortening and salt. Stir in the balance of the flour, ½ cup at a time, first with a spoon and then by hand. The dough will be a rough, shaggy mass that will clean the sides of the bowl. If the dough continues sticky, add sprinkles of flour.

KNEADING
8 mins.

Turn the loaf onto a lightly floured work surface—counter top or bread board—and knead with the rhythmic 1-2-3 motion of push-turn-fold. The dough will be smooth and elastic, and bubbles will rise under the surface of the dough. Sprinkle more flour on the dough if it is slack or moist, and continues to stick to the hands or work surface. Occasionally change the kneading rhythm by raising the dough above the table and crashing it down hard against the counter top. Knead for 8 minutes (6 minutes with the dough hook).

RESTING
20 mins.

Form into a ball, put to one side on the counter or bread board, and cover with a cloth to rest.

SHAPING
15 mins.

Punch down the dough and knead for 1 minute to press out the bubbles. Divide the dough into as many pieces as you want loaves—see dough volume chart, page 23. Shape the pieces into balls, and let them rest for 3 or 4 minutes. Form the loaf by pressing the ball under the palms or with a rolling pin into a flat oval, roughly the length of the bake pan. Fold the oval in half, pinch the seam tightly to seal, tuck under the ends, and place in the pan, seam down. Repeat with the others.

To fashion rolls or buns see pages 519–520.

RISING
45 mins.

Brush the tops with butter, cover loosely with wax paper and put in a warm place (80°–85°) until the dough has doubled in size. The center of the top will be about ½ inch or so above the edge of the pan.

BAKING
375°
45 mins.

Preheat oven to 375°. Bake the loaves in the oven until they are a lovely golden brown and test done. Turn one loaf out of its pan and tap the bottom crust with a forefinger. A hard hollow sound means the bread is baked. If not, return to the oven for an additional 10 minutes. If you wish a deep brown, over-all crust remove the loaves from the pans during the last 10 minutes of the bake period. Midway in the bake period shift the pans so the loaves are exposed equally to temperature variations in the oven.

Five minutes before the end of the bake period brush the loaves with a swish of cream or soft butter for a rich-looking crust.

FINAL STEP

Remove bread from the oven and turn from the loaf pans. Place loaves on a metal rack to cool before serving. This bread toasts beautifully, keeps well wrapped in plastic for a week or more, and will freeze for an indefinite period. A very admirable loaf.

SHEEPHERDER'S BREAD

[TWO ROUND LOAVES]

From the Idaho mountain ranges comes this loaf of sour dough bread traditionally baked in a Dutch oven tucked in the hot coals of a sheepherder's campfire. The bread baked by a Basque sheepherder might not be as elegant as this loaf for his probably would be made only with starter, flour, salt and water. The bread can be baked in the oven, or out-of-doors in a Dutch oven with wonderful results. Allow four days for the starter to ferment to be ready for baking.

INGREDIENTS
1½ cups Sheepherder's Starter (see page 285)
5 to 6 cups bread or all-purpose flour, approximately
3 tablespoons sugar
2 teaspoons salt
1 package dry yeast
½ cup non-fat dry milk
1 cup hot tap water (120°–130°)
2 tablespoons margarine, room temperature

BAKING SHEET
One baking sheet, greased or Teflon.

PREPARATION
Starter
4 days
Four days beforehand prepare the starter.

Bake Day
Dough
25 mins.
Measure out 1½ cups of the starter, and refrigerate the remainder in a glass jar for future use.

In a large mixing bowl stir together 1 cup flour, sugar, salt, yeast and milk. Pour in the water and stir to moisten the dry ingredients. Add margarine and the starter. Beat in the electric mixer at medium speed for 2 minutes, or 150 strokes with a spoon. Add 2 cups of flour, ½ cup at a time, beat 2 minutes at high speed or 175 strong strokes with a spoon.

Stop the mixer.

Stir in the additional flour, ½ cup at a time, to make a soft elastic dough. At this point it will be shaggy and rough. If it persists in sticking, sprinkle a little more flour—about ¼ cup.

KNEADING
8 mins.

Sprinkle the work surface—counter top or bread board—with flour and place the dough on it. Knead with the 1-2-3 motion of push-turn-fold until the dough has lost its roughness and stickiness, and has become elastic, smooth and alive under the hands. If it sticks, sprinkle on a little flour.

FIRST RISING
1¼ hours

In the large bowl place the dough and pat with greased or buttered fingers. Cover tightly with plastic wrap and put in the warm place (80°–85°) until the dough has expanded to at least twice its original size. You can test if it has risen by poking a finger in it; the dent will remain.

RESTING
15 mins.

Knead the dough for 30 seconds to press out the bubbles. Cover with a piece of wax paper and a towel and let it rest.

SHAPING
6 mins.

Punch down the dough and knead for 30 seconds to press out the bubbles. Place on the floured work surface and cut into two pieces with a sharp knife. Form each into a ball. Place on the opposite corners of the baking sheet or in small baskets, lined with loose cloth or tea towel liberally sprinkled with flour. (The two loaves may be combined and made into a large loaf to place in a Dutch oven.)

SECOND RISING
50 mins.

Place the baking sheet in the warm place and cover carefully with a length of wax paper. Leave until loaves have doubled in size.

BAKING
400°
35–40 mins.

Preheat the oven to 400°. If the loaves have raised in baskets, simply tip the raised loaf into your hand and quickly turn the loaf right side up onto the baking sheet. Brush the loaves with water. With a razor, slash four times in a tic-tac-toe design.

Bake in the oven until bread is a golden brown and tests done. Turn one of the loaves over and tap the bottom crust with a forefinger. A hard hollow sound means the bread is baked. Midway in the bake period and again near the end of it, shift the loaves on the baking sheet so they are exposed equally to the temperature variations in the oven.

FINAL STEP

Remove bread from the oven. Place on a metal rack to cool. This bread freezes well, and is delicious toasted.

HOMECOMING SOUR DOUGH FRENCH BREAD

[TWO LOAVES]

This loaf came out of my oven the first time to feed guests coming from afar for an Indiana University Homecoming football game. The I. U. team lost but the bread, said one guest, made it all worthwhile.

The sponge, which begins with a sour dough starter, can be left to ferment for one or two days—depending on the degree of sourness desired. The egg white wash just before the loaf goes into the oven and again at the end of it gives a glossy shine over a fine crackly crust. It is a delicious bread that is best when it is served warm or rewarmed.

INGREDIENTS

Sponge: 1 cup starter (see page 287)
1½ cups warm water (105°–115°)
2½ cups bread or all-purpose flour
2 teaspoons *each* sugar and salt

Dough: 1 package dry yeast
¼ cup warm water (105°–115°)
All of the sponge
½ teaspoon baking soda
3 to 4 cups bread or all-purpose flour, approximately

Glaze: 1 egg white
1 tablespoon water

BAKING SHEET AND PAN

One baking sheet, greased or Teflon. Also shallow roasting pan for hot water on the bottom shelf of the oven.

PREPARATION
Sponge
1 or 2 days

In a large mixing bowl combine starter, water, flour, sugar and salt. Stir well and cover bowl with plastic wrap. Put in a warm place (80°–85°). Stir each day.

Bake Day
Dough
12 mins.

On bake day dissolve yeast in water in a small bowl. Stir briskly for a moment or two to help dissolve the yeast granules and pour into the sponge. Add baking soda. Blend thoroughly. Stir in additional flour, a half cup at a time, first with the spoon and then by hand. The dough will be a rough, shaggy mass that will clean the sides of the bowl. If the dough continues moist and sticky, add several sprinkles of flour.

KNEADING
8 mins.

Turn the dough onto a lightly floured work surface—counter top or bread board—and knead with the rhythmic 1-2-3 motion of push-turn-fold. The dough will become smooth and elastic and feel alive under the hands.

Break the kneading rhythm occasionally by throwing the dough down hard against the work surface. Knead 8 minutes (6 under the dough hook).

SHAPING
20 mins.

This dough does not rise *before* shaping, as with most yeast breads. When kneading is completed put dough under a towel to rest for 10 minutes.

Punch down the dough and, with a sharp knife, cut into two pieces. Form each into a ball. For a round loaf, place on a corner of the bake sheet, or in a small basket, lined loosely with a cloth and sprinkled with flour. For a long loaf, roll the ball into a rectangle, 10 by 16 inches. Roll up the dough, beginning with the short side, and stopping after each full turn to press the edge of the roll into the flat dough to seal. Press with the fingertips. The long loaf, like the round one, can either be placed on the bake sheet or in a long cloth-lined basket to be placed on the baking sheet later.

RISING
1½ hours

Place the baking sheet or the baskets in a warm place (80°–85°) and cover carefully with a length of wax paper. Support the wax paper on glass tumblers if the paper sticks to the dough. Leave until loaves have doubled in volume.

Prepare oven by placing a large, shallow roasting pan, partially filled with hot water, on the bottom shelf. Fill only about one-third full as ideally the water should boil away midway in the bake period when the loaves have started to brown.

BAKING
400°
45 mins.

Preheat oven to 400°. If the loaf has raised in a basket, tip it into your hand and quickly turn the loaf—right side up—onto the bake sheet. Brush the loaves with the mixture of egg white and water. With a razor blade, cut diagonal slashes in a long loaf, and a tic-tac-toe design on a round one. (Make the cuts no more than ¼ inch deep.)

Place in the oven. Midway in the bake period and again near the end of it, shift the loaves on the baking sheet so they are exposed equally to the temperature variations of the oven. Ten minutes before the bread is done, brush again with the egg water.

Bake until the loaves are a glossy brown. Turn over one loaf and tap the bottom crust with a forefinger. A hard hollow sound means the bread is baked. If not, return to the oven for an additional 10 minutes.

FINAL STEP — Remove bread from the oven. It makes a delightful crackling sound on the rack as it cools. Serve warm or rewarmed.

SOUR DOUGH WHOLE WHEAT

[FOUR LOAVES]

A sponge of whole wheat flour, water and a cup of sour dough starter bubbles and foams for 24 hours before it takes command of this delicious loaf of almost all whole wheat. It is a satisfying dough to work, soft and pliable, but it makes a large mix, almost 6 pounds. This is too much dough for a bread hook or an inexperienced or not-too-strong kneader. You may reduce all the ingredients by half, except the starter portion, the yeast and all-purpose bread flour.

INGREDIENTS

Sponge: 1 cup starter (see page 287)
3 cups warm water (105°–115°)
4 cups whole wheat flour

Dough: All of the sponge
1 package dry yeast
1 tablespoon salt
5 cups whole wheat flour
1 to 2 cups all-purpose or bread flour

BAKING PANS — Four medium (8½ x 4½) loaf pans, greased or Teflon. If glass, reduce oven heat 25°.

PREPARATION
Sponge
8–10 hours

The night before, mix the starter, water and flour in a bowl. Cover with a length of plastic wrap and put in a warm place (80°–85°) for 8 to 10 hours, or overnight. It will bubble and foam and rise to double its original volume.

Bake Day
Dough
20 mins.

Turn back the plastic wrap, stir down sponge and sprinkle yeast over the surface of the mixture. Add salt. Measure in whole wheat flour, a half cup at a time, mixing first with a spoon and then by hand. When all of the flour has been mixed in, let the dough rest for 8 to 10 minutes while the flour completely absorbs the moisture.

Stir in the all-purpose or bread flour, a half cup at a time, to make a soft dough that can be formed into a ball. It will be somewhat sticky because of the considerable amount of whole wheat flour.

KNEADING
8 mins.

Instead of using only the hands to knead—as with white flour doughs—hold a spatula, putty knife, or scraper in one hand. Scrape and turn the dough with the implement—pressing and pushing with the palm of the other hand. Slowly the dough will become responsive and less sticky. Lay down the scraping device and knead with the hands until the dough is elastic. If it persists in sticking, sprinkle on additional small portions of white flour. This dough will be softer than normal yeasted breads.

RESTING
15 mins.

Cover the dough with plastic wrap or a towel and let rest on the work surface.

SHAPING
10 mins.

Push down and knead for 30 seconds to press out the bubbles. With a sharp knife, divide the dough into four pieces. Shape into balls, and let rest for 3 to 4 minutes under a towel. Form a loaf by pressing a ball of dough into a flat oval, roughly the length of the baking pan. Fold the oval in half, pinch the seam tightly to seal, tuck under the ends, and place in the pan, seam down. Repeat with the second loaf, third and fourth.

RISING
2 hours

Place the pans in the warm place, cover with wax paper and leave until the center of the dough has risen to the level of or slightly above the edge of the pan. Preheat oven to 425° about 15 minutes before the bread is ready to be transferred.

BAKING
425°
20 mins.
350°
35 mins.

Slit the top of each loaf with one stroke of a razor blade lengthwise. Brush with water, and bake in the hot oven for 20 minutes. Brush the loaves again with water, reduce heat to 350° and continue baking for an additional 35 minutes or until the loaves are browned and test done. Turn one loaf out of its pan and tap the bottom crust with a forefinger. A hard hollow sound means the bread is baked. If not, return to the oven for an additional 10 minutes. Midway in the bake period and again near the end of it, shift the pans in the oven so they are exposed equally to its temperature variations.

FINAL STEP

Remove bread from the oven. Place on a metal rack to cool.

FOURTEEN

Salt-rising Breads

Sugar Cane
London, 1633

The phrase *salt-rising* refers to the old kitchen practice of keeping the bowl of starter nested overnight in a bed of warm salt, which retains heat nicely. It does not refer to the bread's peculiar taste.

The starter to begin salt-rising bread is a true starter. No yeast is used. It is, however, temperamental. If it doesn't bubble up during the night to produce its oddly sweet odor, have no patience. It is only a sacrifice of cornmeal and milk. Begin again, but put it together in another way. Use a different milk, or another kind of cornmeal. There is no easy explanation of why one combination will work and another will not.

Salt-rising bread loves warmth. Warm everything it touches—the bowl, the cups, and the spoons. Don't let it chill. With an ordinary household thermometer search out a place where the temperature is consistent over a 24-hour period. The ideal temperature for the starter is between 90° and 95°, and in my house that is on a shelf near the hot water heater in the utility room. An alternative place is a pan of water over a pilot light on the stove.

The sponge and dough demand less heat and attention as the bacterial strain grows and strengthens.

Use pasteurized whole milk. I have used non-fat dry milk but not always with success.

SALT-RISING BREAD

[TWO LOAVES]

This is an uncomplicated way to make a loaf of good salt-rising bread. The recipe is one published in 1912 by the Ladies Aid Society of the First Presbyterian Church in Polson, Montana—in the heart of the Flathead Indian country. The women of Flathead Valley were fine cooks and bakers, and salt-rising bread was a specialty.

It begins the day before with only 2 tablespoons of cornmeal in a small bowl over which scalding hot milk is poured. It will ferment and be light and foamy by morning. The active mixture is added to a batter in a large bowl to begin the fermentation process over again but on a larger scale. It will have a strong smell not unlike a soft ripe cheese, and it is here the lovers of salt-rising bread are usually sorted out from among those who are not. To the former, it is a glorious aroma; to the latter, an unpleasant smell.

INGREDIENTS

¼ cup milk, scalding hot
2 tablespoons of cornmeal
1 teaspoon sugar
2 cups boiling water
1 teaspoon *each* sugar, salt, baking soda
7 to 8 cups bread flour, approximately
⅓ cup shortening (lard)

BAKING PANS

Two medium (8½ x 4½) loaf pans, greased or Teflon, metal or glass. If the latter, reduce baking heat 25°.

PREPARATION
15 mins.

The evening before—
In a small bowl pour scalding (but not boiling) milk over the cornmeal and teaspoon of sugar. Stir together and cover tightly with plastic wrap. Place in a warm spot (90°–95°) where it will remain 8 to 10 hours. A bubbly foam will be over the surface of the cornmeal and it will smell sweet and fermented.

Overnight

Bake Day
Dough
20 mins.

In a large mixing bowl, pour water over sugar, salt and baking soda. Stir this briefly with a large wooden spoon. Gradually add 2½ cups of flour to make a batter. Stir this until it is smooth—about 50 strokes. The batter should be lukewarm (100°) to the touch. It must not be hot. Stir in the fermented cornmeal mixture.

FIRST RISING
2 hours

Cover the bowl tightly with plastic wrap, return to the warm place until the batter has bubbled and foamed to more than double its volume. When you turn back the plastic wrap the smell will be quite strong.

10 mins.

With the wooden spoon mix in the lard (or other shortening). Gradually add the additional flour, ½ cup at a time, first with the spoon and then by hand. Work it well between the fingers, adding more flour (if necessary) until the dough has lost its wetness and a rough mass is formed.

KNEADING
10 mins.

Turn the dough onto a floured work surface—counter top or bread board—and begin the kneading process. This is a particularly alive dough under the hands—elastic and soft. Knead for about 10 minutes. (Eight minutes with a dough hook.) Let it rest on the board under a cloth or towel for 10 minutes.

SHAPING
10 mins.

Divide the dough. Roll each piece into a rectangle, fold in half, pinch the seam closed and shape the dough into a loaf. Place in the pan, seam to the bottom. Brush the tops lightly with oil or melted lard.

SECOND RISING
50 mins.

Cover with wax paper and return to the warm place until the dough has doubled. The dough usually fills only a third of the pan when I set it aside and it is sufficiently risen when it reaches two-thirds up the side of the pan.

BAKING
375°
45 mins.

Preheat the oven to 375°. Place the pans in the oven. When the loaves are nicely browned and tapping the bottom crust yields a hard and hollow sound, they are done.

FINAL STEP

Remove bread from the oven. Turn out immediately onto a metal cooling rack. Salt-rising bread toasts very well, and can be kept frozen for several months.

SISTER ABIGAIL'S SALT-RISING BREAD

[TWO LOAVES]

Sister Abigail, of one of Ohio's Shaker communities, began her salt-rising bread recipe quite simply: "Take scalded milk and pour over cornmeal." It became more complicated as she heated more milk, added this ingredient and that, and then put everything in a saucepan set in a bowl filled with hot water.

This is to caution the home baker that this Shaker recipe, while it produces a good loaf of salt-rising bread, is a painstaking one, calling for a warm kitchen, and a work schedule that will accommodate the rather unpredictable risings of the starter and dough. The feeling of accomplishment when taking a well-raised loaf from the oven, however, can be considerable.

While Sister Abigail used both bread and all-purpose flours, the home baker can use all of the latter with good results.

INGREDIENTS

1 cup scalded fresh pasteurized milk
½ cup cornmeal
3 cups fresh pasteurized milk
¾ teaspoon salt
1 tablespoon sugar
5 tablespoons lard or shortening
3 cups bread flour (or all-purpose)
2½ cups all-purpose flour, approximately

BAKING PANS

Two medium (8½ x 4½) baking pans, greased or Teflon. If glass, reduce oven heat 25°.

PREPARATION
Starter
2–6 hours

Scald milk and pour it over cornmeal in a small bowl. Stir to mix. Do not cover. Leave open to the air, and move to a warm place—90° to 95°. This is a higher temperature than dough requires so I have a place on the top of my water heater where I put only this starter. Leave until the mixture bubbles. This must be an active fermentation—not just one or two solitary bubbles making their way through the cornmeal. The action must expand the mixture and make it light and fluffy. If it doesn't, start a new starter. You are at the mercy of bacteria!

In a large saucepan, heat the milk to lukewarm (105°–115°) and stir in salt, sugar and lard or shortening. Add the starter.

1–2 hours

Fill a large bowl with hot water and carefully set the saucepan in it to provide a constant flow of warmth while this bigger batch ferments and begins to bubble. Change the hot water 2 or 3 times during the period.

Dough
20 mins.

Empty the warm bowl, wipe it dry and use it to combine the milk mixture and the flour. Stir in the flour—first the bread flour and then the all-purpose flour. Do so a half cup at a time, first with the spoon and then by hand. The dough will be a rough, shaggy mass that will clean the sides of the bowl. However, if the dough continues slack and moist, and sticks to the fingers and bowl, add additional sprinkles of all-purpose flour.

KNEADING
8 mins.

Turn the dough onto a lightly floured work surface—counter top or bread board—and knead with the rhythmic 1-2-3 motion of push-turn-fold. Expect the dough to have a slightly different consistency than the usual all-white dough. It will not feel as alive nor will it be as elastic. Knead for about 8 minutes. (Six minutes under the dough hook.) If the dough sticks to the counter top or fingers, sprinkle on additional flour.

SHAPING
5 mins.

The dough goes directly into the pans.

With a sharp knife, divide it into two pieces. Shape each into a flat oval, roughly the length of the baking pan. Fold the oval in half, pinch the seam tightly to seal, tuck under the ends, and place in the pan, seam down. Repeat with the second loaf.

RISING
2–3 hours

Place the pans in a warm place (90°), cover with wax paper and leave until the dough has doubled in volume. It may be 2 or 3 hours depending on how warm the loaves are kept during this period. A temperature of about 90° is ideal.

BAKING
350°

Preheat oven to 350°. Bake in a moderate oven for 15 minutes, advance heat to 425° and bake for an additional 45 minutes, a total of 1 hour, or until a light brown.

When tapping the bottom crust yields a hard and hollow sound, the bread is done. If not, return to the oven for an additional 10 minutes. Midway in the bake period, and again near the end of it, shift the pans so the loaves are exposed equally to temperature variations in the oven.

FINAL STEP

Remove bread from the oven. Turn from the pans and place on the metal rack to cool before slicing.

Expect salt-rising bread to be a heavy, solid loaf. It will not have the lightness or the buoyancy that a yeast-leavened loaf will have. But expect it to be fine tasting.

SALT-RISING WHOLE WHEAT

[TWO LOAVES]

The salt-rising method is a natural way to make bread. There is no yeast. Cornmeal and milk, fermented in a warm place overnight, is the leavening agent. In this recipe, an adaptation of the one developed by the Flathead Valley women (page 307), several cups of whole wheat flour are mixed with white to make a blend of dark and light. The odor of salt-rising bread hot out of the oven or toasted is one of baking's most distinctive odors. The taste and texture are equally so.

INGREDIENTS

½ cup milk, scalding hot
2 tablespoons cornmeal, white or yellow
1 teaspoon sugar
2 cups boiling water
1 teaspoon *each* sugar, salt and baking soda
3 cups all-purpose or bread flour, approximately
3½ cups whole wheat flour
⅓ cup shortening (lard, if you have it)
1 teaspoon lard, melted (to brush crusts)

BAKING PANS

Two medium (8½ x 4½) baking pans, greased or Teflon, metal or glass. If glass, reduce oven heat 25°.

PREPARATION
Starter
Overnight

Start the small bowl of starter by pouring the milk over the cornmeal and sugar. Stir briefly and cover with plastic wrap. The single most important factor in success in making salt-rising bread is to have the starter not too hot nor too cool—90° to 95° is near-perfect for this recipe. I find that I can hold this temperature constant throughout the night by placing the bowl near the hot water heater in the utility room.

In the morning, the surface of the mixture will be light and foamy—and have its distinctive sweet, fermented odor.

Bake Day
Sponge
10 mins.

In a large bowl pour hot water over the sugar, salt and baking soda. Stir well with a wooden spoon. Combine in the bowl 1 cup of white flour and 1½ cups of whole wheat. Stir until it is well blended—100 strong strokes. When this batter has cooled to lukewarm, pour in the cornmeal starter and stir it into the mixture. The shortening comes later, during kneading.

FIRST RISING
2 hours

Cover the bowl tightly with plastic wrap and return it to the same warm place. The sponge will more than double in volume.

Dough
10 mins.

Stir down the sponge, and add the lard or other shortening. Work in the balance of the flour, a half cup at a time, first with the spoon and then by hand. The dough will be a rough, shaggy mass that will pull away from the sides of the bowl.

KNEADING
10 mins.

Turn the dough onto a lightly floured work surface—counter top or bread board—and knead with the rhythmic 1-2-3 motion of push-turn-fold. The dough will become smooth and elastic, and bubbles will rise under the surface of the dough. Sprinkle more flour on the dough if it is slack or moist, and continues to stick to the hands or work surface. Salt-rising dough, however, is a lovely dough to work—alive, springy and smooth under the hands.

Put it under a towel to rest for 10 minutes.

SHAPING
5 mins.

Punch dough down and knead for 1 minute to press out the bubbles. With a sharp knife, divide the dough. Shape the pieces into balls, and let them rest under a towel for 3 or 4 minutes to relax. Form the loaf by pressing each ball under the palms or with a rolling pin into a flat oval—roughly the length of the baking tin. Fold the oval in half, pinch the seam tightly to seal, tuck under the ends and place in the loaf pan, seam down. Brush the tops with melted lard.

SECOND RISING
1 hour

Cover with foil or wax paper and put in the warm place until the dough has doubled in volume. It will rise to fill about two-thirds of the pan.

BAKING
375°
45 mins.

Preheat the oven to 375°. Place loaves in the oven. When they are nicely brown and tapping the bottom crust yields a hard and hollow sound, the bread is done. If not, return to the oven (without the pan, if you wish a browner crust) for an additional 10 minutes.

FINAL STEP

Remove bread from the oven. Turn the loaves out of the pans onto a wire rack to cool. It is delicious toasted and will keep for many days tightly wrapped.

FIFTEEN

Festive Breads

Anise
Lyons, 1579

There is no surer sign of the approaching holidays than the appearance on the grocer's shelves in mid-October of that colorful and priceless ingredient for the festive breads—candied fruit in all its wonderful variety. In summer they would have melted in the heat and their sweetness would have drawn the ants. But now, as the days grow short and the nights cool, it is safe to bring them home and begin preparation for a joyous time of baking from early November through Thanksgiving, Christmas, New Year's, and on into the Easter celebration.

Of course, not all festive breads are baked for the holidays, or made with candied fruit. A child's birthday, any time of year, deserves a festive creation. Challah, the delicious Jewish loaf, is a Sabbath bread. Panettone is for weddings and christenings as well as the holidays.

MOTHER'S CHRISTMAS BREAD

[TWO LARGE LOAVES]

Dates, nuts, candied fruit and butter make this one of the best tasting and most colorful of the festive loaves. I traced the recipe back to the Indiana kitchen of Mrs. Maude Smith, whose father's mother first baked this loaf in her Norwegian kitchen in 1870. It is delicious toasted.

INGREDIENTS

2 cups all-purpose flour
2 cups warm milk (105°–115°)
2 packages dry yeast
1 egg, room temperature
½ cup sugar
1 teaspoon salt
1 cup (2 sticks) butter, room temperature
5 cups all-purpose flour, approximately
1 cup glacé cherries, halved
1 cup mixed candied fruit, diced fine
1 cup dates, bits or crystals
1 cup English walnuts or pecans, coarsely broken

BAKING PANS

Two large (9 x 5) loaf pans, greased or Teflon. If glass pans are used, reduce oven heat 25°. See dough volume chart (page 23) for other combinations.

PREPARATION
2 hours

In a large bowl combine 2 cups of flour, milk and yeast. If more convenient, substitute for the milk 2 cups warm water (105°–115°) and ½ cup non-fat dry milk. Mix, cover the bowl with plastic wrap and let stand for 2 hours.

15 mins.

Lightly beat the egg and add to the mixture. Add sugar, salt and butter. Beat well—about 50 strokes. Continue beating and add flour, 1 cup at a time, until the dough is soft and no longer sticky.

KNEADING
10 mins.

Turn the dough out on a floured board or counter top, and knead until the dough is smooth and elastic. Add a small amount of flour (1 or 2 tablespoons) if the dough sticks to the board. However, it is a rich mixture and will pull free from the fingers and the board. Mix together the glacé cherries, candied fruit, dates, and nuts.

10 mins.

Press the dough flat and sprinkle on about half of the fruit-nut mixture. Work it into the dough. Repeat with the balance of the fruit-nuts. Knead until the mixture is well distributed through the dough.

FIRST RISING
1 hour

Return dough to the large bowl, cover with plastic wrap and put in a warm place (80°–85°) until doubled in volume.

SHAPING
10 mins.

Punch down the dough and knead for 30 seconds to press out the bubbles. With a sharp knife, divide the dough into two pieces. Shape into balls, and let rest under a towel for 3 to 4 minutes. Form a loaf by pressing a ball of dough into a flat oval, roughly the length of the baking pan. Fold the oval in half, pinch the seam tightly to seal, tuck under the ends, and place in the pan, seam down. Repeat with the second loaf.

SECOND RISING
45 mins.

Cover the pan with wax paper and return to a warm place until the dough has doubled in bulk.

BAKING
350°
50 mins.

Preheat oven to 350°. Bake the loaves in the oven until they are golden brown. When tapping the bottom crust yields a hard and hollow sound, they are done. If not, return to the oven for an additional 10 minutes. If the tops of the loaves appear to be browning too quickly, cover with a piece of foil or brown sack paper. Midway in the bake period and again near the end of it, shift the pans so the loaves are exposed equally to temperature variations in the oven.

FINAL STEP

Remove bread from the oven. Slip the hot loaves carefully from the tins and leave on wire racks until they are cool.

SUGARPLUM BREAD

[ONE LARGE AND SIX BABY LOAVES]

The name "sugarplum" calls forth memories of holidays past and stirs an eagerness about holidays to come. Sugarplum Bread, made with a rich dough, flavored with nutmeg, candied mixed fruit, peel and raisins, is part of that scene.

In this recipe the dough is made into one large round loaf and six small ones. The latter is fine for holiday callers, young carolers, especially.

INGREDIENTS

5 to 5½ cups of all-purpose flour, approximately
½ cup sugar
1½ teaspoons salt
2 packages dry yeast
⅓ cup non-fat dry milk
1⅓ cups hot tap water (120°–130°)
¼ cup shortening
2 eggs, beaten
½ teaspoon vanilla
¼ teaspoon nutmeg
½ cup candied mixed fruit and peel
1 cup seedless raisins
Icing: 1 cup confectioners' sugar
1 tablespoon lemon juice, fresh

BAKING SHEET AND MUFFIN TINS

For the round loaf, one baking sheet, greased or Teflon. For the small ones, a large muffin pan with 6 cups, greased or Teflon.

PREPARATION
15 mins.

In a large bowl measure 2 cups of flour and stir in sugar, salt, yeast, milk, and water. Blend thoroughly and add the shortening, eggs, vanilla, nutmeg, chopped mixed fruit and peel and the seedless raisins. Stir for 2 minutes with a wooden spoon, or with an electric mixer at medium speed for an equal length of time.

Stop the mixer. Stir in the balance of the flour, a half cup at a time, first with the spoon and then by hand. The dough will be a rough, shaggy mass that will clean the sides of the bowl. If the dough continues moist and sticky, add several sprinkles of flour.

KNEADING
8 mins.

Turn the dough onto a lightly floured work surface—counter top or bread board—and knead with the rhythmic 1-2-3 motion of push-turn-fold. The dough will become smooth and elastic, and bubbles will rise under the surface of the dough. If the dough is sticky, sprinkle on a small amount of flour. Occasionally break the kneading rhythm by throwing the dough hard against the work surface. Knead about 8 minutes (6 minutes under the dough hook).

FIRST RISING
2 hours

Place the dough back in the mixing bowl and pat with buttered or greased fingers. Cover the bowl tightly with plastic wrap and move to a warm place (80°–85°) until the dough has risen to about twice its original size.

SHAPING
15 mins.

Divide the dough in half. Knead each piece for 30 seconds to press out the bubbles. Shape one piece into a ball, flatten slightly on top and place on the baking sheet. Divide the second portion into 6 pieces. Shape each into a ball. Place in muffin pans, and press down. They will be almost level with the top of the cups.

SECOND RISING
1 hour

Cover the loaf and pans with wax paper and put in the warm place until dough has nearly doubled in volume.

BAKING
350°
35 mins.
20 mins.

Preheat oven to 350°. Bake the large loaf in the moderate oven for about 35 minutes. The small ones will be done in about 20 minutes. When tapping the bottom crust yields a hard and hollow sound, the bread is done.

FINAL STEP

Remove bread from the oven and place on a metal rack to cool. Frost the large loaf with a drizzle of confectioners' icing. Circle with red candied cherries and slivers of green candied cherries. For the smaller ones, drizzle the tops with confectioners' icing and cap each with a perfect walnut half.

GREEK TRINITY EASTER BREAD

[ONE LARGE CLOVERLEAF LOAF]

A triad of small loaves, together on a baking sheet, forms a cloverleaf that becomes a traditional Greek Easter bread. Representing the Trinity, the three joined loaves are sliced individually and a slice of each is served to each member of the family.

The recipe makes a large bread that should be used in the home rather than carried somewhere or even frozen simply because it is so large —about 13 or 14 inches across. It is often hard to find that much space in the freezer. The loaves can be pulled or cut apart and rejoined, but it may be better to divide the dough to make two not-so-impressively large breads.

It is a rich, solid bread, colorful on the inside with split maraschino cherries and bits of lemon peel.

INGREDIENTS

3 packages dry yeast
½ cup warm water (105°–115°)
½ cup milk, scalded
½ cup (1 stick) butter, room temperature
½ cup sugar
½ teaspoon salt
3 eggs, room temperature
½ cup currants or raisins
Grated rind of two lemons
5½ to 6 cups all-purpose or bread flour, approximately
1 ten-oz. jar maraschino cherries, cut in half and drained
Icing: 1 cup confectioners' sugar, 1 or 2 tablespoons warm milk and ½ teaspoon vanilla or lemon juice

BAKING SHEET

One baking sheet, greased or Teflon

PREPARATION
20 mins.

In a large mixing bowl dissolve the yeast in water. Stir and set aside.

In a saucepan scald the milk, remove from heat

and add butter, sugar and salt. Allow the mixture to cool to lukewarm. Pour the cooled milk mixture into the large bowl and stir with the yeast. Add the eggs, currants or raisins, lemon rind and 3 cups of flour. Beat with a wooden spoon until smooth—about 80 strong strokes. Add the cherries and stir them into the batter. Add 2½ or 3 cups of flour, ½ cup at a time, until the dough becomes a rough mass and cleans the sides of the bowl.

KNEADING
10 mins.

Turn the dough out onto a floured work surface to begin the kneading process. When the mass has absorbed sufficient flour to lose its stickiness, either continue to knead by hand for 10 minutes or knead with the dough hook for 5 minutes. The loaf will be soft and elastic. If the dough hook tears the cherries, continue by hand.

FIRST RISING
1 hour

Return the dough to the mixing bowl, cover with plastic wrap and put in a warm (80°–85°), draft-free place until doubled in volume. You can test if it has risen by poking a finger in it; the dent will remain.

SHAPING
15 mins.

Remove the plastic wrap, punch down the dough with a soft blow of the fist—and let rest for 10 minutes. For one loaf, divide the dough into 3 equal parts. Round each into a smooth ball and arrange like a cloverleaf on the baking sheet. If for two smaller loaves, first divide dough into two parts. Fashion each into a 3-part cloverleaf as described for the larger loaf.

SECOND RISING
45 mins.

Cover with wax paper or foil and return to the warm place until the separate balls of dough have joined and are about doubled in bulk.

BAKING
375°
45 mins.

Preheat oven to 375°. Bake in the oven until the crust has taken on a lovely light brown color. When a wooden toothpick or metal skewer inserted in the center of one loaf comes out clean and dry, it is done. It is too unwieldy to turn over to tap the crust for doneness.

FINAL STEP

Remove bread from the oven and carefully place bread on a wire cooling rack. When cool, frost with confectioners' sugar icing and decorate with candied fruits and chopped nuts.

If the loaf is to be carried as a gift, cut a piece of cardboard to support it.

The loaf is good warm and uniced, and delicious

toasted. It will freeze for months. It is better to frost when it comes out of the deep freeze.

ELECTION DAY BREAD

[ONE LARGE TUBE LOAF]

While it is unlikely that many votes were ever bought by a gift of this loaf, as a New England legend would have you believe, I have found it an excellent coffee bread to serve to a jovial election eve crowd in front of the television set, and to poll watchers in the neighbor's garage. It is studded with nuts and bits of fruit, and has a lovely smell of cinnamon and nutmeg. It may be frosted with confectioners' icing or served plain as it comes from the oven (though cooled).

INGREDIENTS

2 packages dry yeast
1½ cups warm water (105°–115°)
2 teaspoons sugar
4½ cups all-purpose flour
1 teaspoon salt
1¼ teaspoons cinnamon
¼ teaspoon *each* clove and mace
½ teaspoon nutmeg
¾ cup (1½ sticks) butter or shortening, room temperature
1 cup sugar
2 eggs, room temperature
1½ cups raisins
¾ cup chopped nuts
½ cup chopped citron
1 tablespoon of flour, to dredge
Icing: Confectioners' sugar frosting which includes 1 cup confectioners' sugar, 1½ tablespoons orange juice, ½ teaspoon of vanilla and a pinch of salt

BAKING PAN

One 10-inch tube pan, greased or Teflon.

PREPARATION
10 mins.

This is a *batter* bread to be prepared in two stages so don't be carried away by election trends and add so much flour that it must be kneaded.

In a bowl dissolve the yeast in warm water. Measure in 2 teaspoons of sugar and 1½ cups of flour. Beat well with a wooden spoon, about 150 strong strokes.

FIRST RISING
30 mins.

Cover the bowl with plastic wrap, set in a warm place. The batter will rise high in the bowl and be quite stringy when stirred down.

On a length of wax paper sift together the remaining 3 cups of flour with the salt, cinnamon, clove, mace, and nutmeg.

In a small bowl cream the butter (or shortening) and the sugar. About 25 minutes after the batter has been put to rise, add the eggs to the creamed butter. Beat well. At 30 minutes, remove the plastic wrap and stir down the batter. Spoon in the creamed mixture and blend together. Add the flour-salt-spice mixture a spoonful at a time, beating after each addition. The mixture must be smooth.

Dredge the raisins, nuts and citron in a tablespoon of flour, and stir them into the mixture.

FORMING
5 mins.

Pour batter into the pan. Level it off with the spoon, which if dipped in cold water will slip easily over the sticky batter.

SECOND RISING
1½ hours

Cover the pan with wax paper and put in the warm place (80°–85°) until the batter has risen to twice its original height.

BAKING
375°
1¼–1½ hours

Preheat oven to 375°. This is a thick batter and will take considerable time in the moderate oven to bake. When a metal skewer or a wooden toothpick inserted in the loaf comes out with no batter clinging to it, the bread is done.

FINAL STEP

Remove bread from the oven. Let the bread cool in the pan for 10 minutes before turning it onto a metal rack to cool. Spread with confectioners' frosting while the bread is still warm.

ENGLISH CHRISTMAS BREAD

[TWO ROUND PLUMP LOAVES]

English tradition holds that if this loaf is baked Christmas Eve, the bread will never mold. If a slice of the bread is allowed to remain on the table after the Christmas Eve dinner, the home will never be without bread in the coming year. It rises up in lovely brown loaves.

INGREDIENTS

5½ cups all-purpose flour, approximately
2 packages dry yeast
1½ cups water
½ teaspoon nutmeg
1 teaspoon *each* allspice and caraway
½ cup (1 stick) butter
½ cup sugar
2 teaspoons salt
2 eggs, room temperature
½ cup dried currants
⅓ cup raisins, light or dark
⅓ cup finely cut-up citron or candied fruit peel
Confectioners' icing: 1 cup confectioners' sugar, 1 tablespoon warm water or milk, and ½ teaspoon vanilla extract
Decorations: 6 candied red cherries, halved
½ cup slivered almonds

BAKING SHEET

One 11 x 17 baking sheet, greased or Teflon.

PREPARATION
15 mins.

The first part of this recipe is for the mixer. In the mixing bowl place two cups of the flour and the yeast. Blend in the mixer briefly. In a saucepan, pour the water, nutmeg, allspice, caraway, butter, sugar, and salt. Heat until warm. The butter needs only to soften—not melt. Stir constantly. Pour this into the flour-yeast mixture. Add the eggs. Beat ½ minute at low speed, scraping the bowl several times. Beat 3 more minutes at high speed.

Unless the machine is heavy-duty, stop the mixer at this point and take up a wooden spoon. Add currants, raisins and citron. Gradually add more flour (about 3 cups) to form a soft dough.

KNEADING
6 mins.

Turn the dough out on a floured counter top or board; knead until smooth and elastic. Place in a greased bowl, turning to assure that the whole ball is coated lightly to keep it from crusting. Cover tightly with plastic wrap.

FIRST RISING
1 hour

Place the bowl in a warm spot until the dough has doubled. You can test if it has risen by poking a finger in it; the dent will remain.

SHAPING
5 mins.

Punch down the dough, kneading briefly to work out the air bubbles. Divide the dough in two pieces. Shape each into a ball and place on opposite corners of the baking sheet.

SECOND RISING
1 hour

Cover with wax paper and leave in a warm place (80°–85°).

BAKING
350°
45 mins.

Preheat oven to 350°. Bake in the oven. When the loaves are well browned and tapping the bottom crust yields a hard and hollow sound, they are done.

FINAL STEP

Remove bread from the oven and place on a wire rack. Let cool completely before frosting with confectioners' icing—1 cup confectioners' sugar, 1 tablespoon warm water or milk, and ½ teaspoon vanilla extract. Let the icing run down the sides and drip off. In the center form a wreath of red cherries. Sprinkle slivered nuts over it all.

JULEKAGE

[ONE LARGE OR TWO SMALL LOAVES]

The delicate and gingery taste of cardamom is the principal accent of Danish Christmas fruit loaf. While it is in the oven it will fill the house with a festive fragrance. Makes delicious toast.

INGREDIENTS

2 packages dry yeast
1 pinch sugar
½ cup warm water (105°–115°)
3 to 4 cups all-purpose flour, approximately
¼ cup sugar
¼ cup non-fat dry milk
1½ teaspoons salt
½ teaspoon vanilla
½ teaspoon grated lemon peel
2 eggs, room temperature and lightly beaten
½ teaspoon ground cardamom
½ cup (1 stick) butter, room temperature
1 cup mixed candied fruit, chopped medium fine

BAKING PANS

One large (9 x 5) baking pan or two small (7½ x 3½) pans, greased or Teflon. If glass pans are used, reduce oven heat 25°.

PREPARATION
20 mins.

In a small bowl sprinkle yeast and sugar over the water. Stir with a fork and let stand while the dry ingredients are being mixed.

Pour 2 cups of flour into a large bowl and add sugar, milk and salt. Stir. Form a well in the dry ingredients. Pour in yeast, vanilla, grated lemon peel, eggs and cardamom. Blend well. Add butter. Beat the mixture thoroughly—50 strokes.

Dice the candied fruit into small bits and blend into the batter. Stir in the balance of the flour, a half cup at a time, first with the spoon and then by hand. The dough will be oily because of the butter content and will easily clean the sides of the bowl.

KNEADING
8 mins.

Turn out on a floured board or counter top and knead until the dough is shiny and elastic.

FIRST RISING
1 hour

Place the dough back in the mixing bowl; cover tightly with plastic wrap. Move to a warm place (80°–85°) until the dough has risen to about twice its original size. You can test if it has risen by poking a finger in it; the dent will remain.

SHAPING
10 mins.

Punch down dough and knead for 30 seconds to press out bubbles. If for two loaves, divide with a sharp knife. Shape the dough into a ball, and let rest under a towel for 3 to 4 minutes. Form loaf by pressing the dough into a flat oval, roughly the length of the baking pan. Fold the oval in half, pinch the seam tightly to seal, tuck under the ends, and place in the pan, seam down. Repeat with the second loaf.

SECOND RISING
45 mins.

Cover the pans with wax paper and return to the warm place until the dough has doubled in bulk.

BAKING
350°
45 mins.

Preheat oven to 350°. Bake the loaves in the center of the oven until the crust is golden. To test, turn one loaf out of its pan and tap the bottom crust with a forefinger. A hard hollow sound means the bread is baked. If not, return to the oven for an additional 10 minutes. If the tops of the loaves appear to be browning too quickly, cover with a piece of foil or brown sack paper. Midway in the bake period and again near the end of it shift the pans so the loaves are exposed equally to temperature variations in the oven.

FINAL STEP — Remove bread from the oven, turn from the loaf pan (or pans) and cool on wire racks. Julekage will keep exceptionally well for up to three weeks if it is wrapped tightly in aluminum foil.

KULICH

[TWO LOAVES]

The traditional Easter bread of old Russia, Kulich was such a delicate creation that bakers put pillows around the pan of dough so that it would not fall. Walking with heavy boots through the kitchen was forbidden until the loaves were safely out of the oven. These precautions are unnecessary today.

The initials "XV"—meaning Christ Is Risen—are shaped on the top of the loaf with tiny strips of dough or sprinkled on the frosting with colored sprinkles. I do one of each. The decorated top is cut off and replaced each time the loaf is sliced. To some, the frosted top resembles the snow-covered domes of old Russian churches.

INGREDIENTS

2½ to 3 cups all-purpose flour, approximately
¼ cup sugar
1 teaspoon salt
1 teaspoon grated lemon peel
1 package dry yeast
½ cup milk
¼ cup water
2 tablespoons butter, room temperature
1 egg, room temperature
¼ cup *each* chopped blanched almonds and raisins
Icing: 1 cup confectioners' sugar, 1 tablespoon milk and ½ teaspoon vanilla
Colored sprinkles

BAKING TINS — Two greased 1-pound coffee cans, or other cans of about the same volume.

PREPARATION
20 mins.

In a large mixing bowl combine ¾ cup of flour, sugar, salt, lemon peel and yeast.

In a saucepan, over low heat, pour the milk and water. Add the butter which needs only to soften. Pour the liquid into dry ingredients and beat 100 strokes with a large wooden spoon—or 2 minutes at medium speed of electric mixer. Scrape bowl. Add egg and ½ cup or more of flour to make a thick batter. Beat at high speed for 2 minutes—or 150 strong strokes with the spoon.

With the wooden spoon and fingers, work in additional flour to make a soft dough that cleans the sides of the bowl.

KNEADING
10 mins.

Turn out on a lightly floured work surface and knead with a strong push-turn-fold action until the dough is smooth, elastic and feels alive under the hands. (The dough hook will do this in about 6 minutes.)

FIRST RISING
1 hour

Place in a greased bowl, turning to coat the entire ball. Cover the bowl with plastic wrap and put in a warm place (80°–85°) until dough has risen to double its size.

SHAPING
15 mins.

Punch down the dough and turn it onto the work surface again. Press the dough flat, sprinkle with almonds and raisins—work them into the dough. Divide the dough into two large pieces, with a small piece about the size of a golf ball set aside to make the initials.

With the hands, shape each large piece into a ball and, with the smooth side up, press into the greased coffee cans. Be certain, however, that the dough fills only *half* the tin. If necessary, reduce the amount of dough and bake the excess in another pan.

To create the letters "XV" in dough, roll out the small reserved piece into a pencil-thin rope about 24 inches long. Cut into 6 pieces. Cross two strands to form the "X"—and bend the other to make the "V."

SECOND RISING
45 mins.

Cover the cans with wax paper and let dough rise in a warm place until it has almost reached the top of the tins—about 45 *watchful* minutes. Don't let it rise above.

BAKING
350°
35 mins.

Preheat the oven to 350°. Place in a moderate oven for 35 minutes or until light brown, and a wooden toothpick or metal skewer inserted in the center of the loaf comes out clean and dry. The loaf will have pulled away from the sides of the can.

FINAL STEP

Remove bread from the oven. Let cool in the tins for about 10 minutes before turning loaves out onto a metal cooling rack. When the loaves have cooled, you may wish to decorate the one without the dough initials.

Frost with confectioners' icing and allow it to drip down the sides. Form the XV with colored sprinkles.

The decorated top is sliced off and is either used to cover the loaf while it is being consumed or is presented to an honored guest at the Easter feast.

SWISS CHRISTMAS BREAD

[TWO LOAVES]

It begins the night before with the mixture of fruit and nuts under brandy, filling the kitchen with the intriguing aroma of a very special kind of loaf in the making. A slice will show a swirl of brandied fruit in dough that has taken on some of the russet of the liquor.

INGREDIENTS

½ cup *each* sliced dried pears, raisins, chopped blanched almonds and mixed chopped red and green candied cherries
¼ cup chopped citron
1 teaspoon grated lemon peel
½ teaspoon *each* ground clove, cinnamon and nutmeg
½ cup brandy
1 package dry yeast
¼ cup warm water (105°–115°)
¾ cup milk
¼ cup (1 stick) butter, room temperature
¼ cup sugar
1 teaspoon salt
4 cups all-purpose flour, approximately
1 egg, room temperature and beaten
2 tablespoons flour—to dust moist fruit
Confectioners' icing: 1 cup confectioners' sugar, 2 tablespoons milk, and ⅛ teaspoon vanilla
8 whole almonds and ¼ cup slivered almonds
4 red candied cherries, halved

BAKING PANS

Two medium (8½ x 4½ loaf pans, greased or Teflon, metal or glass. If the latter, decrease oven heat 25°.

PREPARATION
20 mins.

The night before—
In a bowl combine the pears, raisins, almonds and red and green cherries. Add the citron, lemon peel,

the ground cloves, cinnamon and nutmeg. Stir in the brandy. Several times during the evening, move the fruit so that it has an opportunity to absorb all of the brandy it can. Cover tightly with plastic wrap.

25 mins.

The next day—
Dissolve yeast in the warm water, adding a pinch of sugar to hasten the fermentation process. Stir the mixture briskly with a fork or metal whip.

In a saucepan heat milk, and add butter, sugar and salt. In a large bowl make a well in 4 cups of flour and pour in warm milk mixture, also pour in any brandy not soaked up by the fruit. This also serves to cool the milk somewhat so it will not harm the yeast to be added. With a wooden spoon pull in some of the flour from the sides, and add the yeast. Stir. Each time cut in more of the flour. Beat one egg lightly and add to the bowl. When thoroughly mixed, work by hand for 3 or 4 minutes. The dough will be soft but not sticky. (If it's sticky, use a bit more flour.)

KNEADING
8 mins.

Turn out on a floured board or counter top and knead until the dough is smooth and elastic.

FIRST RISING
1 hour

Place the dough in a greased bowl, cover with plastic wrap and let rise in a warm place (80°–85°) until double.

SHAPING
20 mins.

First, the brandied fruit. Spread the fruit on a paper towel and pat it dry. Dust the fruit with 2 or 3 tablespoons flour so that no excess liquid is carried into the dough.

Work the fruit into the dough. Press the dough flat and spread about half of the fruit on top of it. Fold in the fruit, knead gently—and add the rest of the fruit in a similar manner. The moist fruit may leave brown streaks through the dough but I find this attractive when the bread is sliced.

Divide into two pieces and pat into oblong shapes. Place in the pans.

SECOND RISING
1½ hours

Cover loosely with wax paper or tea towel and place in a warm spot until double in bulk.

BAKING
400°
10 mins.

Preheat oven to 400°. Brush the loaves with melted butter and place in the hot oven. After 10 minutes reduce heat and bake the loaves for 50 minutes longer.

350°
50 mins.

Midway in the baking period (30 minutes) switch the tins and turn them around so that they get the oven heat evenly.

FINAL STEP

Remove bread from the oven. Turn the two loaves out on a wire rack to cool. Frost with confectioners' icing flavored with almond extract. Almonds and red cherries on the icing add a festive note.

PORTUGUESE SWEET BREAD

[SIX SMALL LOAVES]

A cross of dough baked over a colored egg identifies this small individual loaf of Portuguese Sweet Bread. The golden breads are about six inches in diameter and each has a nested egg—to the delight of a small child (or of a hostess in need of an unusual table decoration). The bread is unusually fine textured and equally good made into rolls.

INGREDIENTS

6 colored eggs, uncooked or cooked. Use Easter egg dye
2 packages of dry yeast
¼ cup warm water (105°–115°)
1 cup milk, heated
1 cup sugar
¼ cup (1 stick) butter
1 teaspoon salt
3 eggs, room temperature and well beaten
6 to 7 cups all-purpose flour, approximately

BAKING SHEET

One baking sheet, greased or Teflon.

PREPARATION

Traditionally, in Portugal the eggs are not colored, but in America, eggs at Easter call for a rainbow selection of colors and tints. They can be either cooked or uncooked. Baking the loaf also bakes the eggs.

20 mins.

In a small bowl or cup dissolve yeast in water and beat with a fork or metal whisk to speed the action.

In a large bowl pour the milk over sugar, butter and salt. Stir until butter melts and milk has cooled to lukewarm. Beat in eggs and yeast mixture. Gradually beat in 2 cups of flour—blending well with 100 strong strokes of a wooden spoon. Add 3 or 4 more cups, a portion at a time, until the dough becomes a rough mass and cleans the sides of the bowl.

If the dough feels slack or wet, add ½ cup more flour.

KNEADING
12 mins.

Flour the work surface. Turn the soft dough onto it and knead until it is smooth and elastic. Small air-filled blisters will appear under the surface of the dough.

FIRST RISING
2 hours

Return the dough to the bowl. Pat the dough with butter or shortening and place a length of plastic wrap tightly over the bowl. Put in a warm place where there will be no drafts until it has more than doubled in volume.

SHAPING
40 mins.

Punch down the dough and turn out onto the work surface. Divide the dough into 6 pieces for individual loaves. Fashion each into a ball. Pinch off a quarter of each and set aside. Press the dough into a flat round piece (about ½-inch thick) and make an indentation in the center for 1 egg. Carefully press each egg into its own nest.

Roll out the small piece of dough into a long 12-inch rope. Cut in two pieces and form an "X" over the egg. Pinch ends to the underside of the loaf but do not fasten the strands where they cross over the egg. Fold a strip of foil into a 1-inch-high collar that will force the dough into a thicker loaf than if it were permitted to rise and spread without restraint. Make the collar larger than the dough, or about 7 inches in diameter. Set it around the small loaf, allowing 1 inch between the 6 collars on the baking sheet. Fasten the collar securely closed with a pin or paper clip. These collars should be removed after 20 minutes in the oven so the sides will brown.

Plain rolls can be made with this dough by fashioning smooth balls of dough, about 1 inch in diameter, and putting them about ¼ inch apart in a lightly greased 9-inch square pan. This dough will fill two pans.

SECOND RISING
45 mins.

Cover with wax paper and return to the warm place until about doubled in volume.

BAKING
350°
30 mins.

Preheat oven to 350°. Place in a moderate oven and bake until the loaves are golden brown. Remove the foil collars after 20 minutes so the sides will brown. Test for doneness by sticking a wooden toothpick into one of the loaves. If it comes out clean and dry the loaves are baked.

FINAL STEP — Remove bread from the oven. Place the loaves on a metal rack to cool. These can be frozen successfully but I find that on occasion the color will peel slightly. This seldom bothers a young child, however.

NISU

[TWO BRAIDED LOAVES]

Nisu, of Finnish origin, is a fine-textured white bread that has the delicate flavor and aroma of cardamom, hinting of festive occasions and the holidays. The dough is braided and brushed with a glaze of egg yolk and milk just before it goes into the oven.

INGREDIENTS

5 to 6 cups all-purpose flour, approximately
1 package dry yeast
¾ cup non-fat dry milk
2 teaspoons salt
3 tablespoons sugar
1½ cups hot tap water (120°–130°)
3 tablespoons butter, room temperature
1 egg, room temperature
2 teaspoons ground cardamom
Glaze: 1 egg yolk
1 tablespoon milk

BAKING PANS — Two medium (8½ x 4½) baking pans, greased or Teflon. If glass, reduce oven heat 25°.

PREPARATION
15 mins.

In a large mixer bowl measure 3 cups flour and stir in yeast, milk, salt, sugar and water. Add butter, egg and cardamom. Beat in the electric mixer at medium-high speed for 2 minutes, scraping down the sides several times.

Stop the machine. Stir in the balance of the flour, a half cup at a time, first with the spoon and then by hand. The dough will be a rough, shaggy mass that will clean the sides of the bowl. If the dough continues moist and sticky, add small sprinkles of additional flour.

KNEADING
8 mins.

Turn the dough onto a lightly floured work surface—counter top or bread board—and knead with the rhythmic 1-2-3 motion of push-turn-fold. The dough will become smooth and elastic, and bubbles will form under the surface of the dough. Break the kneading rhythm occasionally by throwing the dough down hard against the work surface. Knead for about 8 minutes (6 minutes under the dough hook).

FIRST RISING
45 mins.

Place the dough in the mixing bowl and pat with buttered or greased fingers to keep the surface from crusting. Cover the bowl tightly with plastic wrap and move to a warm place (80°–85°) until the dough has risen to about twice its original size. Judge this by the distance it creeps up the sides of the bowl. You can test if it has risen by poking a finger in it. If the dent remains, the dough is ready to be braided.

SHAPING
20 mins.

The dough is to be made into two braided loaves. Divide the dough evenly into two pieces. Cut each piece into three equal portions. Place a cloth or wax paper over them and let them relax for 5 minutes.

Roll each piece under the palms into a length about 12 inches long. If the dough resists rolling and pulls back, roll each partially—moving on to the next while the others relax. Come back to the first and finish.

Lay the 3 strands side by side. Begin the braid in the middle and move to the end. Turn the dough around and finish. Repeat with the other loaf. Tuck the braid under to fit the pan and place it in the baking pan.

SECOND RISING
45 mins.

Place the pans in the warm place, cover with wax paper and leave until the center of the dough has risen to 1 inch above the level of the edge of the pan. Meanwhile, preheat the oven to 350°.

BAKING
350°
30–35 mins.

Brush the loaves with egg yolk mixed with milk. Don't let the mixture run against the pan or it may stick. Place in the oven. When the loaves are brown and tapping the bottom crust yields a hard hollow sound, they are done. If not, return to the oven for an additional 10 minutes. Midway in the bake period, shift the pans so the loaves are exposed equally to temperature variations in the oven. If the tops appear to be browning too quickly cover them with brown paper or a piece of foil.

FINAL STEP

Remove bread from the oven, turn from the pans, and place on the metal rack to cool before slicing.

ITALIAN EASTER BREAD

[ONE CIRCULAR LOAF]

The Easter Rabbit loves this loaf—5 colored eggs nested in the braid of a nut-rich dough. The colored eggs are uncooked which dictates care in tucking them into place in the twist.

It is baked at Easter by both the Swiss and Italians, and frosted with a sugar icing and decorated with colored sprinkles. Working the fruit and nuts into the dough after the first rise is a sticky business but once by that it is easy going and fun to make. Young children are great helpers but watch those raw eggs.

INGREDIENTS

5 uncooked eggs, to color
2½ to 3½ cups all-purpose flour, approximately
¼ cup sugar
1 teaspoon salt
1 package dry yeast
⅔ cup milk
2 tablespoons shortening
2 eggs, room temperature
½ cup chopped mixed candied fruit
¼ cup chopped blanched almonds
½ teaspoon anise seed
Icing: 1 cup confectioners' sugar, 1 tablespoon milk, ⅛ teaspoon vanilla, and colored sprinkles

BAKING SHEET

One baking sheet, greased or Teflon.

PREPARATION
15 mins.

In a large mixing bowl, mix thoroughly 1 cup of flour, sugar, salt and yeast.

In a saucepan combine milk and shortening and place over low heat until the liquid is warm and the shortening is soft or melted. Pour the milk into the bowl. Beat for 2 minutes at medium speed in an electric mixer—or 125 strokes with a wooden spoon. Add eggs and ½ cup of flour or enough to make a thick batter. Beat at high speed for 2 minutes—or with the wooden spoon.

With the spoon stir in enough additional flour to make a rough ball of dough that cleans the sides of the bowl.

KNEADING
10 mins.

Turn out on a floured work surface—counter top or bread board—and work in additional flour, if necessary, to overcome any stickiness. If the mixer has a dough hook, return the dough to the bowl and put under the hook for 6 minutes. Otherwise, knead by hand on the work surface until the dough is smooth and elastic—and feels alive under the hands. Small bubbles will appear under the surface of the dough.

FIRST RISING
1 hour

Place the dough in the mixing bowl, pat lightly with oil or butter, cover tightly with plastic wrap and put in a warm place (80°–85°) until doubled in bulk. Meanwhile, combine the fruit, nuts and anise seed.

SHAPING
30 mins.

Punch down the dough and return it to the lightly floured work surface. Knead in the fruit-nut-seed mixture. This will be a sticky job but keep the syrupy fruit powdered with flour until the pieces are worked into the dough.

Divide the dough in half. Roll each piece into a 24-inch rope. Work the rope carefully under the hands because the strength of the dough has been weakened somewhat by the fruit and nuts. The rope will roll better if the flour on the work surface is first wiped off so the dough will not slip under the pressure of the hands.

Loosely twist the ropes together and form a ring on the baking sheet. Pinch the ends together. Brush the dough with melted shortening. Push aside the twist to make a nesting place for each egg. The egg is raw so handle tenderly; nevertheless, push it down into the dough as far as possible.

SECOND RISING
1 hour

Cover the bread with a length of wax paper and return to the warm place until double in bulk.

BAKING
350°
35 mins.

Preheat oven to 350°. Place in the oven. A wooden toothpick inserted in a twist will come out clean and dry when properly baked.

FINAL STEP

Remove bread from the oven and place on a cooling rack. When the bread is cool, carefully drizzle confectioners' sugar frosting on the twist—between the eggs—and decorate with colored sprinkles. If it is to be frozen, decorate when ready to serve.

GUGELHUPF

[ONE ROUND RING]

A Christmas breakfast favorite in Austria, this handsome, crusted ring is imbedded with a score of whole almonds and dusted with powdered sugar. On the inside: rum-soaked raisins. A favorite Viennese dessert, Gugelhupf (pronounced google-hupf) is toasted and served with butter and jam. Coffee and tea make a fine accompaniment. The light, delicious bread is usually baked in a fancy mold (Bundt or Turk's Head) or an angel food cake pan. It is on the sweet side with a subtle rum and almond accent.

INGREDIENTS

½ cup golden raisins
¼ cup dark rum
1 package dry yeast
¾ cup warm water (105°–115°)
½ cup sugar
¼ (1 stick) cup butter
2 eggs, room temperature
2 tablespoons non-fat dry milk
¼ teaspoon salt
2½ cups all-purpose flour
1½ teaspoons grated lemon peel
1 tablespoon melted butter to coat pan
¼ cup finely ground almonds
18 to 20 whole blanched almonds
Confectioners' sugar, to dust

BAKING PAN

One mold or tube cake pan, buttered.

PREPARATION
45 mins.

Place raisins in a small bowl and soak them in the rum.

20 mins.

In a small bowl, sprinkle yeast over water. Stir and set aside.

With an electric mixer cream the sugar and butter until it is fluffy and light. Break in the eggs, one at a time, while beating the mixture. Add yeast, milk, salt and flour. Beat at a medium speed with mixer for 2 minutes, or with a wooden spoon. The batter-like dough will be smooth and can be poured or spooned. It will rise without kneading since the beating is sufficient to form the gluten. Drain the raisins and add them to the mixture. Add the lemon peel. Blend the mixture well.

FIRST RISING
2 hours

Scrape down the sides of the bowl. Cover tightly with plastic wrap. Put the bowl in a warm place until dough has more than doubled in volume.

SHAPING
15 mins.

Meanwhile, choose a heavy 1½-quart tube mold or a 10-inch angel food cake pan and with a pastry brush generously butter the sides. Shake the pan or mold to coat the lower two-thirds of the sides with the finely ground almonds. Arrange the whole almonds in an attractive pattern on the bottom of the pan.

Stir down the dough and with 2 large spoons dip the batter into the mold or pan—without disturbing the almonds.

SECOND RISING
1 hour

Cover with a length of plastic wrap and let rise until doubled in size in a warm, draft-free place.

BAKING
350°
25–30 mins.

Preheat oven to 350°. Place in the oven until a metal skewer inserted in the ring comes out clean and dry. Watch the bread carefully so it does not burn. Cover with foil or brown paper if it begins to brown too rapidly. It will bake a light golden brown.

FINAL STEP

Remove bread from the oven. Turn it out on a cake rack to cool. Just before serving, dust lightly with confectioners' sugar.

ANISE KUCHEN

[TWO ROUND LOAVES]

This German festive bread looks like a large four-leaf clover tied with gay colored ribbons. A thoughtful gift for the holidays, the golden brown loaf, speckled with bits of orange and lemon peel, has a spicy anise flavor. Especially good toasted, it keeps well frozen.

INGREDIENTS

1 package dry yeast
1½ cups warm water (105°–115°)
1 cup (2 sticks) butter or margarine, room temperature
½ cup sugar
Grated peel of 1 lemon
Grated peel of 1 orange
1 teaspoon salt
½ teaspoon *each* mace and nutmeg
3 tablespoons anise, crushed or ground
3 eggs, room temperature
½ cup instant non-fat dry milk
7 cups all-purpose flour, approximately
1 tablespoon salad oil, to brush

BAKING SHEET AND PAPER

One large baking sheet, greased or Teflon. Four 30-inch strips of 1½-inch-wide heavy brown paper to duplicate ribbons to be tied around the loaves after baking.

PREPARATION
20 mins.

In a medium-size bowl briskly beat yeast into water with a fork or metal whisk.

In a large bowl cream butter and gradually add sugar, blending until the butter is soft and fluffy. Mix in lemon and orange peel, salt, mace, nutmeg and ground anise seed. Add eggs, beating well after each addition. Stir in yeast and add milk.

Beat in the flour, a cup at a time, until the dough is soft and not sticky. Work it with the hands when it gets too stiff to beat with a wooden spoon. When the dough has cleared the bowl and is not absorbing additional flour, turn out on a lightly floured board or counter top.

KNEADING
18 mins.

Cover the dough and let it rest 10 minutes before starting the kneading. The dough should be kneaded for about 8 minutes, or until it is smooth and elastic.

FIRST RISING
50 mins.

Place the dough back in the large bowl (which has been washed and greased) and set in a warm place (80°–85°) until it has doubled in bulk.

SHAPING

Punch down the dough, turn it onto work surface again, knead briefly to push out the gassy bubbles and cut into two pieces with a knife. Shape into two rectangular loaves—about 8 by 5 inches. Place on the baking sheet, leaving space between the loaves for expansion. Grease the tops lightly with salad oil applied with a brush or the fingers. Tie each loaf with two brown paper strips—one lengthwise and one around the middle. Pin, clip, or staple the paper ribbons together but do so loosely so that the dough can expand without pinching off a quarter. The paper will leave depressions for colored ribbons to be tied later. Repeat: tie loosely—enough so that a finger can slip under the paper.

SECOND RISING
40 mins.

Cover with wax paper or foil resting on water glasses (so it doesn't touch the dough) and put in a warm place until almost doubled in bulk.

BAKING
350°
45 mins.

Preheat oven to 350°. Bake in the oven. When the loaves are golden brown and tapping the bottom crust yields a hard hollow sound, they are done. Turn the sheet or the loaves at midpoint in baking so they will have even exposure.

FINAL STEP Remove bread from the oven. When the loaves have cooled, remove the paper strips and replace with bright ribbons 1½ inches wide. A fine gift, and particularly good when toasted.

FINNISH EASTER BREAD

[TWO LARGE LOAVES]

The pungent flavors of lemon, orange and cardamom identify this rich Finnish festive loaf as *Pääsiäisleipä*—a cylindrical bread that is traditionally baked in milking pails to celebrate the arrival of new calves and the springtime abundance of dairy foods.

The whole loaf is cut into quarter wedges—and each wedge is then cut into triangular slices. It is a delicious bread spread with only butter or with soft cheeses such as cream cheese, Brie or Camembert. Excellent, too, with thin slices of Swiss, Edam or Gouda. In brief, good with all cheeses.

It is made with white and rye flours and prime dairy products—the best cream, the best eggs and the best butter.

INGREDIENTS

2 packages dry yeast
½ cup warm water (105°–115°)
1½ cups light cream or undiluted evaporated milk, room temperature
2 cups all-purpose flour
5 egg yolks
1 cup sugar
1 cup (2 sticks) butter, soft or melted and cooled
1½ teaspoons salt
2 teaspoons *each* ground cardamom and grated lemon peel
2 tablespoons grated orange peel
1 cup golden raisins
1 cup chopped blanched almonds
1 cup milk, room temperature
2 cups rye flour
4 to 4½ cups all-purpose flour, approximately

BAKING PAILS Traditionally, the loaf is baked in a pail—a gallon (4-quart) pail, ungalvanized. Two 2-quart sand pails or two 2-pound coffee cans or the equivalent in volume in other combinations of pails or cans may be used. It may be well to have a stand-by coffee can in the event there is too much dough at the last moment.

PREPARATION
10 mins.
45 mins.

In a large bowl combine yeast in the water. Stir in cream and the all-purpose flour. Blend with a large wooden spoon until the mixture is smooth. Cover with plastic wrap and let the sponge rise in a warm place (80°–85°) until it has doubled in size.

15 mins.

Remove the plastic wrap, stir down and add egg yolks, sugar, butter, salt, cardamom, lemon peel, orange peel, raisins, and almonds. Beat well until thoroughly combined. Stir in the milk and rye flour until blended; stir in the remaining white flour—½ cup at a time—to make a firm dough. Work the flour into the dough with the fingers when it gets too difficult to use the spoon. The dough will clean the sides of the bowl and form a rough mass.

KNEADING
8 mins.

Sprinkle a small amount of flour on the work surface and turn the dough onto it. Knead with a strong push-turn-fold motion until the dough is smooth and elastic.

FIRST RISING
45 mins.

Return dough to the bowl (which has been cleaned and greased), cover with plastic wrap and return to the warm place until it has doubled in bulk.

SHAPING
15 mins.

Punch the dough down, and work into a smooth ball. To make one large loaf, place the dough in the 4-quart pail, with the rounded top up. It should come to no more than the mid-point on the side of the pail. If there is an excess, take from the bottom and bake in a small can or pan. The dough can be divided for the two 2-quart pails or 2-pound coffee cans. Again, the dough should come only halfway up the side of the can. If too much, form a small ball for a smaller can.

SECOND RISING
40 mins.

Cover the cans loosely with wax paper and return to the warm place until the dough *almost* reaches the top of the can. If it goes too high, the expansion in the oven may force the heavy mushrooming crown so high that it leans and breaks off.

Preheat the oven to 350°, and arrange the shelves so that the tall cans will go on the lowest one to provide sufficient headroom for the loaf or loaves.

BAKING
350°
1¼ hours

Place the loaf or loaves in the oven. The large gallon-size loaf will take about 75 minutes while the smaller 2-quart loaves, about 60 minutes. Before removing from the oven, test for doneness with a long straw, wooden skewer or metal skewer. If the bread is baked the straw will come clean and dry from the center of the loaf. It will be golden brown and loose in the pail.

FINAL STEP

Remove bread from the oven and immediately brush the top with butter. Allow the loaf to rest in the pan for about 15 minutes before turning it onto a metal cooling rack.

CHRISTOPSOMO

[TWO ROUND LOAVES]

This Greek Christmas bread is decorated across the top with an early form of the Christian cross. It is a round loaf, rich with egg and scented with anise. Serve it warm, spread with sweet or regular butter. Later, serve toasted with honey. Initials, birth dates and ages can also be fashioned to celebrate other occasions.

INGREDIENTS

2 packages dry yeast
1 cup warm water (105°–115°)
¼ cup dry non-fat milk
1 cup (2 sticks) butter, room temperature
4 eggs, room temperature and slightly beaten
¾ cup sugar
2 teaspoons crushed anise seed
1 teaspoon salt
7 cups all-purpose flour, approximately
1 egg white, slightly beaten
9 candied cherries or walnut halves

BAKING SHEET

Baking sheet, greased or Teflon.

PREPARATION
20 mins.

With a fork or metal whip, blend yeast with water in a large bowl, and let stand for about 5 minutes.

Combine the yeast mixture, milk, 2 cups of flour, butter, eggs, sugar, anise seed, and salt. Blend thoroughly with a large wooden spoon. Gradually beat in the balance of the flour.

KNEADING
10 mins.

Turn dough onto a lightly floured board or counter top and knead until dough is smooth and elastic. If the dough is slack (too moist), add more flour.

FIRST RISING
1½ hours

Place in a large bowl (the one in which you mixed the dough). The bowl does not have to be greased since there is ample fat in the dough to keep it from encrusting. Tightly cover with plastic wrap and let rise in a warm place (80°–85°) until almost doubled in size.

SHAPING
20 mins.

Punch dough down and knead it briefly to work out the bubbles. Cut the dough into two pieces. Return one piece to the bowl while you make the first loaf. Pinch or cut off two small pieces, each about 2 inches in diameter, and set aside. Knead the large piece into a smooth ball on unfloured board, and place on one corner of the baking sheet. Flatten into an 8-inch round loaf, about 2 inches thick.

Shape the small balls into 12-inch-long strands by rolling and stretching each under the palms on the unfloured board. Cut a 4-inch-long slash into each end of the two ropes. Cross ropes at the center of the round loaf. Do *not* press down. Curl the slashed end sections to form 1½-inch circles. Place a walnut or candied cherry in each curl and in the center of the cross. Carefully brush the loaf with beaten egg white, taking special care to brush where the cross joins the loaf. Repeat with second piece.

SECOND RISING
1 hour

Cover the loaves with wax paper resting on water tumblers so the paper will not touch the dough. Let rise until almost doubled in size.

BAKING
350°
45 mins.

Preheat oven to 350°. Bake in the oven until a wooden toothpick inserted in center of loaf comes out clean.

FINAL STEP

Remove bread from the oven. Serve hot, or let cool on wire rack. Cut in wedges or slices. Wrap in foil to reheat in a 350° oven for about half an hour.

CHOREKI–GRECIAN SWEET BRAID

[TWO LARGE OR FOUR SMALL BRAIDS]

Choreki is a Grecian sweet bread, braided, that is festive any time of year. It is plump and the crust is shiny and sprinkled with chopped almonds and sesame seeds. The texture is excellent, thanks to three eggs (which give it tenderness) and it has richness that demands one more slice. A faint suggestion of anise but not overwhelmingly so. The recipe is for two large 16-inch loaves—or four smaller ones (10-inch), just right for one meal for a family of four, or for gift-giving.

INGREDIENTS

5½ cups all-purpose flour, approximately
2 packages dry yeast
1 cup hot tap water (120°–130°)
⅓ cup non-fat dry milk
1 teaspoon ground anise seed
½ cup shortening, part butter
½ cup sugar
1 teaspoon salt
3 eggs, room temperature
Topping: 1 tablespoon milk mixed with 1 egg
2 tablespoons *each* of chopped almonds and sesame seeds
2 tablespoons sugar to be sprinkled over topping

BAKING SHEETS

Two small or one large baking sheet, greased or Teflon.

PREPARATION
15 mins.

In large mixer bowl measure 2 cups flour. Add yeast—stir together.

Into a saucepan measure water, milk, anise seed, shortening, sugar and salt. Stir well and pour slowly into dry ingredients. Beat 25 strokes, and add eggs. In electric mixer, beat briefly at slow speed so the ingredients are not thrown out of the bowl, and increase speed to high for 3 minutes.

Stop mixer and take up the wooden spoon to work in additional flour, 1 cup at a time, until dough is roughly shaped and cleans the bowl.

KNEADING
8 mins.

Turn dough out onto a floured work surface—counter top or bread board. Knead until smooth—about 8 minutes by hand (5 minutes with a dough hook).

FIRST RISING
1 hour

Return to the bowl which has been wiped clean or washed, and butter dough so that a crust will not form during the rising period. Cover with plastic wrap and put in a warm place (80°–85°) free from drafts until the dough has risen to about double its bulk. You can test if it has risen by poking a finger in it; the dent will remain.

SHAPING
25 mins.

Punch down dough and turn out on the floured surface. Cover with a cloth and let rest for 10 minutes. Divide dough into two parts. To shape one loaf, divide the large piece into three smaller but equal pieces. Under the palms roll each piece into a long rope-like strip, about 16 inches in length. Place the lengths side by side on the work surface. Start in the middle and braid toward each end. Pinch each end so the braids will not break loose when they rise. Repeat with second piece. Place on baking sheet.

SECOND RISING
1 hour

Cover the two braids with a length of wax paper and return to the warm place.

BAKING
350°
45 mins.

Preheat oven to 350°. Before the loaf goes into the oven beat the milk into the egg and brush it over the braids. Sprinkle with almonds and sesame seeds—and the sugar.

Bake in the oven until well browned and a wooden toothpick or metal skewer inserted in the center of the loaves comes out clean and dry.

FINAL STEP

Remove bread from the oven and place on wire racks to cool. It is delicious warm from the oven.

ANISE LOAF

[ONE LARGE OR TWO SMALL TWIST LOAVES]

Sesame seeds are sprinkled liberally on the crust but the inside of the loaf belongs to anise, not pronounced enough to be licorice but light and delicate. Dark bits of anise seed, pulverized in the blender or crushed under a heavy spoon, dot the dough.

It can become an Easter loaf, if you desire, by simply nesting a tinted but uncooked egg among the braids. Makes marvelous toast. Freezes well for another day.

INGREDIENTS

1 cup milk
2 tablespoons butter
3 tablespoons sugar
½ teaspoon salt
1 package dry yeast
3 cups all-purpose flour, approximately
1 egg, well beaten, and at room temperature
2 tablespoons anise seeds, crushed
Glaze: Beaten egg white or yolk sprinkled with
2 tablespoons sesame seeds

BAKING SHEET

One baking sheet, greased or Teflon.

PREPARATION
25 mins.

In a saucepan heat milk, butter, sugar and salt until the liquid is warm and the butter is soft or melted. Cool to lukewarm and pour into a large mixing bowl. Sprinkle in the yeast and stir to blend well. Add 1 cup of flour and beat vigorously with a spoon. Break the egg into the batter, and add the crushed anise seeds. Beat by hand or with the electric mixer for 3 minutes, at high speed. Scrape down the sides of the bowl one or two times during the beating.

Stop the mixer. Gradually add 1 to 2 cups of flour and beat in with the spoon until it becomes too difficult. Work in flour by hand until it has formed a rough mass that cleans the sides of the bowl.

KNEADING
8 mins.

Turn the dough onto a lightly floured work surface—counter top or bread board—and knead the dough until it is smooth and elastic.

FIRST RISING
50 mins.

Place in a greased bowl, cover tightly with plastic wrap and put in a warm, draft-free place until the dough is light and doubled in bulk.

SHAPING
20 mins.

Punch the dough down and turn it out on the floured work surface again. For two loaves, divide the dough in half. Each half is divided into three equal pieces. Roll each piece under the palms until it is about 12 inches long. Place the three side by side on the baking sheet and braid.

Repeat with the second loaf. Brush the top of each with beaten egg white or yolk, mixed with a tablespoon of water, and sprinkle with sesame seeds.

SECOND RISING
45 mins.

Cover with wax paper and return to the warm place until the loaves have doubled in size.

BAKING
350°
35 mins.

Preheat oven to 350°. Place the pans in the oven. When the loaves are golden brown and tapping the bottom crust yields a hard and hollow sound, they are done. A soft thud means underdone—return to the oven for an additional 10 minutes.

FINAL STEP

Remove bread from the oven and place on a metal cooling rack.

CHALLAH

[TWO BRAIDED LOAVES]

Challah (pronounced hal-la) is a lovely yellow egg-rich and light textured white bread steeped in history. While the word "challah" has come to mean this loaf of braided bread, the preparation of the dough for baking in the Jewish kitchen is "the act of Challah" in which the woman takes a small part of the dough to burn in the oven as an offering. She thereby reenacts her origin at the Creation when she sprang from man's rib. The remaining dough may then be baked as she chooses, usually in the braided form.

The Hebrew law of Challah requires that the quantity of flour to be kneaded into dough be no less than the weight of 43 and one-fifth eggs, or 2½ quarts or 3½ pounds. The portion to be separated as the Challah offering is to be no less than the size of an olive.

INGREDIENTS

1 package dry yeast
5 cups all-purpose flour, approximately
2 tablespoons sugar
1½ teaspoons salt
⅓ cup butter or margarine, room temperature
1 cup hot tap water (120°–130°)
1 pinch saffron
3 eggs and 1 egg white, room temperature
Glaze: 1 yolk (from egg above)
2 tablespoons sugar
1 teaspoon cold water
½ teaspoon poppy seeds, to sprinkle

BAKING SHEET

Large baking sheet, greased or Teflon.

PREPARATION
15 mins.

In a large bowl mix yeast, 2 cups flour, sugar, salt and butter or margarine. Gradually add water to dry ingredients and beat at medium speed of electric mixer for 2 minutes. Scrape bowl occasionally. Add saffron, 3 eggs and 1 egg white (reserving the yolk). The batter will be thick. Beat for 2 minutes at high speed. Put aside the electric beater and continue mixing in flour with a wooden spoon. Add about 3 additional cups of flour, one at a time, until the rough mass is no longer sticky. If it is moist, add small amounts of flour until the dough cleans the side of the bowl.

KNEADING
8 mins.

Turn the dough out onto a floured surface and knead until the dough is smooth and elastic. (Six minutes with a dough hook.)

FIRST RISING
1 hour

Return dough to the mixing bowl which has been washed or wiped clean and greased. Turn the dough so that it is oiled on all sides.

Cover the bowl tightly with a length of plastic wrap and place it in a warm draft-free place until dough has doubled in bulk.

SHAPING
25 mins.

Punch the dough down and knead out the bubbles. Divide the dough in half.

To braid, divide each half into three equal pieces. With the hands roll each piece into a 12-inch length. Lay rolls parallel to each other. Start the braid in the middle and work to one end. Pinch the ends securely together. Turn around and complete the other end. Repeat with second piece.

Place the two braids on baking sheet.

Beat together remaining egg yolk, sugar and cold water. Carefully brush braids with the mixture. Sprinkle with poppy seeds.

SECOND RISING
1 hour

Don't cover the braids for the second rise. They will double in bulk.

BAKING
400°
30 mins.

Preheat oven to 400°. Bake in the oven until the braids test done when a wooden toothpick inserted in the center comes out clean and dry. The loaves will be a shiny golden brown.

FINAL STEP

Remove bread from the oven. Carefully remove from baking sheet and cool on wire racks. A long braided piece fresh from the oven is fragile and should be handled with care (and a spatula) until it cools and has stiffened a bit.

PANETTONE

[ONE OR TWO TALL LOAVES]

A tall rich loaf from Lombardy that embraces piñon nuts, citron, white and dark raisins and anise. Cut into wedges to serve. Italians serve this special loaf, which originated in Milan, not only at Christmas but at Easter, weddings, christenings, and other special occasions. Coffee and wine accompany it beautifully.

INGREDIENTS

3 packages dry yeast
½ cup warm water (105°–115°)
1 pinch of sugar
6 egg yolks, room temperature
1 teaspoon vanilla extract
½ teaspoon grated lemon peel
½ teaspoon salt
¼ cup sugar
1 tablespoon ground anise
2 to 3 cups all-purpose flour
½ cup (1 stick) butter, room temperature
⅓ cup diced candied citron
¼ cup white raisins, rinsed and drained
¼ cup dark raisins, rinsed and drained
2 tablespoons piñon (pine) nuts
2 tablespoons melted butter to brush loaf

BAKING PANS

There are several possibilities. One is to pat the dough into a round loaf, cut a cross on the top of the ball, and bake. It is traditional, however, to bake it in a tall receptacle so that it stands majestic, waiting to be cut into long wedges. Two 1-pound cans or one 2-pound can will create a tall loaf with a blossoming top. A can with color and printing will brown the loaf faster and better than an unadorned shiny metal one. If the loaf is done but too light in color, leave it out of the can and return it to the oven for another 6 to 8 minutes.

PREPARATION
25 mins.

In a small bowl or cup sprinkle yeast over water and whip with a metal whisk or fork to hasten the action. Add a pinch of sugar. Set aside for a few minutes.

Pour the yeast mixture into a large bowl. With a large wooden spoon stir in egg yolks, vanilla, lemon peel, salt, sugar and anise. Blend in 2 cups of flour, a half cup at a time, and beat 100 strokes until the dough pulls away from the sides in strands. Cut the butter into 8 or 10 pieces, and mix 2 or 3 pieces at a time into the dough.

The citron, raisins (white and dark) and the piñon nuts can be added now or *after* the first rise. I prefer to do it here because the fruit and nuts are much easier to introduce into the thin mixture; it is more difficult to get the dough to accept the fruit after kneading. The concern is possible discoloration of the dough by raisins which I find negligible. If the raisins are added *after* the first rise, pat them dry on paper towels and dust them with 1 tablespoon of flour so additional moisture is not introduced into the dough.

Add about 1 cup more flour, a little at a time, mixing it now with your hands. The dough should be firm and no longer sticky. It will be somewhat slick, however, because of the butter.

KNEADING
10 mins.

Turn the dough onto a bread board or counter top, lightly floured, and knead until it is smooth and shiny. The skin will seem lightly blistered.

FIRST RISING
1 hour

Put the dough back in the bowl and pat all over with buttered or greased fingers to keep the surface from crusting. Cover the bowl tightly with plastic wrap and move to a warm place (80°–85°) until the dough has risen to about twice its original size (judged as it creeps up the sides of the bowl). You can test if it has risen by poking a finger in it; the dent will remain.

SHAPING
10 mins.

Pat into a ball and place on a greased or Teflon baking sheet, if that is your choice, or grease the 1 large or 2 small cans according to the suggestions above. The cans will be about half filled with dough.

SECOND RISING
1 hour

Cover lightly with wax paper and return to the warm place until the dough has doubled in bulk—near but not over the top of the rim of the can. Preheat oven to 400°. Remove middle shelf; otherwise the tall loaf will push its way into the top of the oven.

BAKING
400°
10 mins.
350°
30–40 mins.

Brush the top of the dough with melted butter. Bake the loaf or loaves on the bottom shelf in a hot oven for 10 minutes. Reduce heat to 350° and bake for an additional 30 to 40 minutes longer. Midway during the baking, butter again and rotate tins so they are exposed to a different part of the oven. The loaves will be crisp and brown when they are done. Pierce with a metal skewer; if it comes clean the loaf is done. If the loaf tests done but the sides are not brown enough to suit you, return to the oven (without the tin) for another 5 or 10 minutes. Watch the loaf closely so that it doesn't overbrown.

FINAL STEP Remove bread from the oven. Handle the tall loaf or loaves with special care while they are hot; they are somewhat fragile. Place on wire rack until they are cool. Panettone stays fresh for a long while, if it is well wrapped in plastic wrap or foil. Cut and served in wedges, it is an excellent companion with coffee or wine.

RUSSIAN EASTER BREAD–KULICH

[TWO LOAVES]

Of the two recipes for Kulich in the book, this is the more elaborate—a half dozen egg yolks, almost a pound of butter, and saffron soaked in brandy. As a final touch and to give it an unusual texture, 3 stiffly beaten egg whites are worked into the dough when the kneading is almost finished. The kneading for this loaf will consume almost one hour if it is to achieve the smoothness and elasticity that Kulich should have.

The crown of the loaf is decorated with a rose laid on white or pink confectioners' sugar frosting. The loaf is cut horizontally and the top slice is always saved to use as a lid.

INGREDIENTS
2 packages dry yeast
¼ cup warm water (105°–115°)
1 cup warm milk (105°–115°)
1 teaspoon salt
2 cups all-purpose flour
½ teaspoon saffron
2 tablespoons brandy
6 egg yolks, room temperature
1½ cups sugar
1½ cups (3 sticks) butter, melted and cooled to 130°
6½ cups all-purpose flour, approximately
1 cup candied fruit
1 cup ground blanched almonds
1 cup raisins

1 teaspoon vanilla
1 teaspoon ground cardamom
3 egg whites
Icing: 1 cup confectioners' sugar
    1 tablespoon milk
    ½ teaspoon vanilla
1 small artificial rose

BAKING TINS

Two greased 2-pound coffee cans. Cut wax paper circles to place on the bottom of the cans to facilitate removing the loaves when baked.

PREPARATION
1¼ hours

In a small bowl dissolve yeast in ¼ cup warm water. Stir briefly with a fork or whisk.

In a large bowl measure the milk, salt, flour and the yeast solution. Blend with 25 strokes of a wooden spoon, cover the batter with plastic wrap and put in a warm place (80°–85°) for 1 hour or until it is light and bubbly.

Meanwhile, dry the saffron in a 250° oven for about 10 minutes, powder under a spoon and stir it into the brandy. Set aside.

In a bowl beat the egg yolks with the sugar—and pour into the risen batter. Stir it well and add the cooled butter, a little at a time, and the flour. The flour is stirred in, first with a spoon and then by hand, until the dough is a shaggy, rough mass that cleans the sides of the bowl.

In another bowl combine the candied fruit, almonds and raisins. Sprinkle in the saffron-brandy infusion, vanilla and cardamom. Stir it well and set aside.

KNEADING
1 hour

Turn the dough out onto a work surface liberally covered with flour. Begin the lengthy kneading process to make the dough smooth and elastic. Allow 45 minutes to 1 hour to achieve this. After kneading for fifteen minutes, flatten the dough into a large oval and spread the fruit mixture over it. Fold it into the dough. If the addition of the fruit mixture moistens the dough to the point of stickiness, add ¼ cup more flour and work it in. Continue kneading.

Next, beat 3 egg whites until they are stiff and work them into the dough by hand. The addition of whites will turn the dough into a sticky blob; but turn and work it with a metal spatula or metal scraper until the whites are completely incorporated. Sprinkle with a bit more flour to cut stickiness.

SHAPING
20 mins.

Grease the coffee cans or other tall, cylindrical baking tins. Cut wax paper circles to fit the bottom of the tins, and grease them before placing in the bottom of the tins. The baked loaves will easily slip out of the tins if this procedure is followed.

Fill each tin only halfway with dough. Moisten the fingers and pat the tops smooth.

RISING
1½ hours

Cover the tins with wax paper. Put in a warm place until the dough doubles in bulk—or comes just to the edge of the tins—but no higher!

BAKING
350°
1 hour

Preheat oven to 350°. Arrange the oven shelves so that tall tins are placed on the bottom one. Bake in the oven until a metal skewer inserted in the center of a loaf comes out clean and dry. If moist particles cling to the probe, return the loaf to the oven for an additional 10 minutes. Then test again.

FINAL STEP

Remove bread from the oven. Allow the loaves to stand about 10 minutes before turning out of the tins, onto a cooling rack. If a loaf sticks to the sides of the tin, circle around the loaf with a long thin knife blade to loosen.

When cool, ice with confectioners' frosting, pink or white, and decorate with a small paper or plastic rose. To serve, cut horizontal slices, beginning at the top. The decorated top slice is saved as a lid for the loaf.

HUNGARIAN CHRISTMAS BREAD

[TWO LONG LOAVES]

Mâkos és Diós Kalács is the impressive name of this festive bread distinguished by a black swirl of poppy seeds and raisins wrapped in a rich light dough.

INGREDIENTS

1 package dry yeast
⅔ cup warm water (105°–115°)
1 pinch sugar
1 cup (2 sticks) butter, room temperature
¼ cup sugar

½ teaspoon salt
2 tablespoons grated lemon peel
¼ cup non-fat dry milk
3½ cups all-purpose flour, approximately
1 cup ground poppy seeds
1 cup sugar
½ cup raisins
½ cup milk
Glaze: 1 egg beaten, mixed with 1 teaspoon water

BAKING SHEET — One 11 x 17 baking sheet, greased or Teflon.

PREPARATION
15 mins.

In a small bowl or cup dissolve 1 package yeast in the water. Stir in a pinch of sugar to hasten the yeast action. Let stand for a few minutes.

In a medium bowl combine butter, sugar, salt, 1 tablespoon lemon peel and milk. Add alternately 2½ cups of flour and the yeast mixture. Blend with a large wooden spoon—100 strokes. When the dough has formed a soft ball turn it out on a floured board or counter top.

KNEADING
10 mins.

Knead until the dough is smooth and not sticky. Add a little more flour (perhaps ½ cup or more) if necessary.

FIRST RISING
1 hour

Turn the dough into a bowl, cover tightly with plastic wrap and place in a warm spot (80°–85°) until it has doubled in bulk.

SHAPING
20 mins.

While the dough is rising, prepare the poppy seed filling. Combine ground poppy seeds, sugar, raisins, milk and remainder of lemon peel and cook in a double boiler over water until the mixture is of spreading consistency. Stir constantly. It will thicken in about 10 minutes. Remove from the heat and cool to room temperature.

20 mins.

Punch the dough down, divide in half, and roll each piece into a long rectangle about ¼-inch thick. Spread the flat pieces with the cooled poppy seed filling. Roll like a jelly roll. Pinch the seams together so that the filling does not bubble out when it heats and the dough begins to expand. Place the rolls on the baking sheet. Brush with the beaten egg glaze.

SECOND RISING
30 mins.

Cover the rolls with wax paper laid across water glasses so the paper does not touch the moist dough. Let rise. Brush again with the glaze.

BAKING
325°
50 mins.

Preheat oven to 325°. Bake the rolls in the oven. If the tops brown too rapidly in the latter part of the baking, cover with a piece of brown paper.

FINAL STEP

Remove bread from the oven and place on wire racks and cool. This keeps well frozen.

HOSKA

[TWO BRAIDED LOAVES]

This Czechoslovakian loaf has three tiers of braids—each braid successively smaller. It is a spectacular holiday bread that is glazed and decorated with whole almonds that bake to a beautiful deep brown. It is light, tender and a bit sweet.

INGREDIENTS

2 packages dry yeast
1¼ cups warm water (105°–115°)
¼ cup non-fat dry milk
5½ cups all-purpose flour, approximately
2 teaspoons salt
¾ cup sugar
2 eggs, room temperature
½ cup (1 stick) butter, room temperature
¼ cup chopped citron
¼ cup raisins, white or dark
¼ cup chopped almonds
1 tablespoon melted butter to brush braids
Glaze: 1 egg mixed with 1 tablespoon water
Decoration: ½ cup whole blanched almonds

BAKING SHEET

Baking sheet, greased or Teflon.

PREPARATION
12 mins.

In a small bowl or cup sprinkle the yeast over the water. Stir briskly to hasten the yeast action.

Into a large bowl measure milk, 3 cups of flour, salt and sugar, and form a well. Pour the yeast mixture into the well, and gradually pull the flour into the liquid with a large wooden spoon. Add eggs. Stir briefly. Add butter which must be soft (or melted). Beat 100 times until the mixture is smooth. Stir in additional flour (about 2½ cups), first with the spoon and then by hand. The dough will be soft but not sticky.

KNEADING
10 mins.

Turn out on a lightly floured board or counter top—and knead until it is smooth and elastic. The dough is so rich with butter that it will quickly lose its stickiness. If the dough seems moist ("slack," bakers call it), work in ¼ cup more flour.

FIRST RISING
1 hour

Place in a bowl and cover tightly with plastic. There is no need to grease the bowl because of the fat in the dough. Allow to double in bulk.

SHAPING
40 mins.

Punch down the dough and turn it out on a floured work surface. Flatten it out and sprinkle about half the fruit-nut mixture on top. Begin to work it into the dough. Flatten the dough again, and spread the remainder of the mixture on top. Continue working the dough with your fingers until the fruit and nuts are distributed throughout the dough. Working fruit in now, rather than earlier, makes it unlikely the fruit will discolor the dough as it might have during a lengthy kneading.

Braiding dough is fascinating once you get the hang of it. If the braid doesn't look right the first time, unbraid and start over.

Divide the dough into two pieces. Put one piece back in the bowl; this will become the second loaf later.

Divide the first piece into two equal parts. One of these divide into three equal pieces. Roll each under the palms of the hands—pulling and patting—until they are about 14-inches long. Children's putty requires the same technique. Place the three strands, which now look like small ropes, on the baking sheet, and form into a braid. Pat it into shape and brush the top with melted butter. Divide two-thirds of the second piece into three equal pieces. Form a second and smaller braid about 12-inches long. Place this on top of the first braid. If you fear it might slip, anchor it fore and aft with wooden picks. Butter the top in preparation for the third and final braid.

With the remaining small piece of dough make a third braid about 10-inches long. This is placed (in triumph) on top of the second braid. Again pin it down if it looks wobbly. (My first loaf so overwhelmed me that I pierced it through, from top to bottom, in two different places, with bamboo skewers usually reserved for the barbecue.)

Form the second loaf in the same manner with the dough reserved in the bowl.

SECOND RISING
1 hour

Cover carefully with wax paper and place in the warm place until the loaves have doubled. If the braids shift, gently push them back into position.

For the glaze, beat the egg into the tablespoon of water. Brush the braided loaves with the egg mixture, and then place on each loaf about 18 or 20 whole almonds—at random.

BAKING
375°
45 mins.

Preheat oven to 375°. Bake in the oven. When tapping the bottom crust yields a hard hollow sound, they are done. (Or insert a metal skewer or wooden toothpick into the centers. They are done if the pick comes out clean.)

FINAL STEP

Remove bread from the oven and cool on wire racks.

DRESDEN CHRISTMAS FRUIT BREAD

[TWO LONG LOAVES]

A stollen-type Yule bread, shaped in a long rectangle rather than as a crescent, it begins with rum poured over dried and candied fruit and left to soak for at least an hour—or, better still, overnight. Exchanged throughout Germany as a holiday gift, the loaf will keep through the festive season wrapped in foil.

INGREDIENTS

1 cup mixed candied citrus peel
¼ cup candied angelica, if available
½ cup dried currants
½ cup seedless raisins
½ cup candied cherries, halved
½ cup rum, light or dark
¼ cup warm water (105°–115°)
2 packages dry yeast
1 pinch of sugar
2 tablespoons flour (to dredge fruit)
1 cup milk
¾ cup sugar

1 tablespoon salt
½ teaspoon almond extract
½ teaspoon grated lemon peel
6 cups of all-purpose flour, approximately
2 eggs, room temperature
¾ cup (1½ sticks) butter, room temperature and cut into bits
1 cup blanched and slivered almonds
4 tablespoons melted butter
¼ cup confectioners' sugar to brush dough

BAKING SHEET

One 11 x 17 baking sheet, greased or Teflon.

PREPARATION
45 mins.

An hour or more before baking (or even the night before) combine in a small bowl the citrus peel, angelica, currants, raisins and cherries—and pour the rum over them. Stir the mixture to moisten all the pieces, and set aside.

Pour the water into a small bowl and sprinkle yeast on top. Add a pinch of sugar to help start the yeast action. Stir with a fork or small metal whip to completely dissolve the yeast.

Drain the fruit, reserving the rum, and pat the fruit dry with paper towels. Place the fruit in a paper sack with 2 tablespoons of flour and shake vigorously to coat the pieces. Set aside.

In a medium saucepan, combine milk, ½ cup of the sugar and salt; heat to lukewarm, stirring constantly, until sugar is dissolved. Off the heat, stir in reserved rum, almond extract, lemon peel and yeast mixture.

In a large bowl pour 3 cups of flour and with a wooden spoon slowly stir in the yeast mixture. Beat the eggs until frothy. Stir them into the bowl, followed by small pieces of the softened butter which can either be room temperature or melted. Beat 100 times. Add more flour, about 2 cups. When the dough can be gathered into a soft ball, turn it out on the counter top or a bread board sprinkled generously with flour.

KNEADING
12 mins.

Knead the dough, adding flour if it is sticky. When the kneading is finished, gently work the fruit and almonds into the dough. Don't work it unnecessarily long, for some of the fruit, especially the raisins, may discolor the dough.

FIRST RISING
2 hours

Place the dough in a bowl and cover tightly with plastic wrap. Put the bowl in a warm spot (80°–85°) in the kitchen until the dough doubles.

SHAPING
25 mins.

Turn out the dough, punch it down and knead it for a few seconds to press out the bubbles.

Divide into two pieces, and put one back in the bowl until you are ready to shape the second loaf. With a rolling pin work the dough into a rectangle about 12 inches long, 8 inches wide, and about ½ inch thick. Brush the dough with warmed butter and sprinkle with 2 tablespoons of sugar. Fold one long side just over the center of the strip. Fold the other long edge over the seam—overlapping by about 1 inch. Press both of the outside edges firmly but lightly to prevent the top from lifting up during proofing and baking. The ends of the loaf should be tapered slightly by patting them. Also push the sides together to mound the loaf in the center. The finished loaf will be about 13 inches long and about 3½ to 4 inches wide. Repeat with second piece.

SECOND RISING
1 hour

Place the loaves on an 11 x 17 baking sheet. Brush them with melted butter. Cover with wax paper (resting on glass tumblers to keep the paper off the dough) and set in a warm place until doubled in bulk.

BAKING
375°
50 mins.

Preheat oven to 375°. Bake in the oven until golden brown and crusty. Midway through the baking period, turn the loaves halfway around so that they are equally exposed to any temperature variations in the oven.

FINAL STEP

Remove bread from the oven. Transfer to wire racks. Either serve warm from the oven, or let it mature 3 days before reheating and serving. Just before serving, coat heavily with confectioners' sugar sprinkled from a sifter or small sieve.

BOHEMIAN CHRISTMAS BREAD

[TWO MEDIUM BRAIDED LOAVES]

The Christmas season calls for at least one braided bread and this two-tiered loaf is a good one for the table and to make for friends. Iced and decorated with pecans and red and green cherries, it is a holiday spectacle. Makes superb toast.

INGREDIENTS

2 packages dry yeast
¼ cup warm water (105°–115°)
Pinch of sugar
1 cup milk, heated
½ cup sugar
1 tablespoon salt
⅛ teaspoon mace
1 lemon rind grated
¼ cup (½ stick) butter, room temperature
2 eggs or 4 egg yolks, room temperature
5 to 6 cups all-purpose flour, approximately
½ cup raisins
½ cup cut-up almonds
Confectioners' icing: 1 cup confectioners' sugar, 1 tablespoon warm water or milk and ¼ teaspoon almond extract
¼ cup whole pecans
8 red and green candied cherries, halved

BAKING SHEET

One 11 x 17 baking sheet, greased or Teflon.

PREPARATION
20 mins.

In a small bowl or cup blend yeast into the water. Add sugar to speed the process. Beat with a fork or metal whip to dissolve the yeast granules. Let stand 3 to 5 minutes.

Pour the milk into a large bowl with sugar, salt, mace, lemon rind and butter. If milk is pasteurized there is no need to *scald* it. Cool to lukewarm. Add eggs, half the flour (2½ cups) and the yeast mixture to the bowl. Beat until smooth—about 100 strokes. Blend in the raisins and almonds. Gradually stir in more flour (about 3 cups) to form a soft, elastic dough.

KNEADING
7 mins.

Turn dough out onto lightly floured work surface—counter top or bread board. Knead by hand until the dough is smooth and elastic. (If a dough hook is used, it will take only about 4 minutes.) Place in a greased bowl and turn to coat all of the dough. Cover with plastic wrap.

FIRST RISING
1½ hours

Place the covered bowl in a warm spot (80°–85°) until the dough has doubled in bulk.

SHAPING 30 mins.	Punch down the dough and turn out on the floured board or counter top. Divide the dough into two pieces, and place one in the bowl to reserve for the second loaf. Divide the piece of dough into 4 equal parts. Let them rest for 10 minutes. Shape 3 of the 4 pieces into smooth, rope-like strips, about 14-inches long. Place them side by side on the baking sheet. Beginning in the middle, braid toward each end. Make a tight rather than a loose braid. Pinch ends together and tuck under. Divide the fourth piece into 3 equal parts. Shape into strips about 10-inches long in the same manner. Make another braid, and place it down the center of the larger braid. If the small braid is difficult to place, with a knife or razor make a ½-inch cut along the top of the large braid and lay the smaller one in the depression. If necessary use wooden toothpicks to hold in place. Repeat with second piece.
SECOND RISING 1 hour	Cover with wax paper. Place in a warm place (80°–85°) and let rise until double in bulk.
BAKING 400° 10 mins. 350° 40 mins.	Preheat oven to 400°. Place in the hot oven for 10 minutes, turn temperature down to 350° for an additional 40 minutes, or until bread tests done when tapped on bottom crust. A hard hollow sound means the bread is baked.
FINAL STEP	Remove bread from the oven and place on wire rack to cool. Remove wooden toothpicks. Ice, if desired, with confectioners' frosting. Decorate with candied cherries and pecans.

REBECCA'S CHALLAH

[TWO BRAIDED LOAVES]

It takes patience to wait out the three risings that this fine challah requires but the braided golden brown loaves are worth it. The home baker should plan to rise early to have the bread ready for the evening meal.

This recipe calls for an unusual way to start the yeast. It is mixed with sugar, flour and water in a tall water glass. When the yeast reaches the lip of the glass, it has "proofed" (shown proof it is alive) and is ready to be stirred into the waiting flour, eggs and shortening.

The role of challah in the Jewish home is described in the recipe for Challah, page 344. During Rosh Hashanah and Yom Kippur, challah is baked in the shape of a ladder symbolizing the hope that prayers of thanksgiving will mount to heaven. On Rosh Hashanah, it is customary to dip a slice of challah in honey to symbolize the sweetness of the New Year.

INGREDIENTS

2 packages dry yeast
8 teaspoons plus ½ cup of sugar
8 cups all-purpose flour, approximately
2¼ cups warm water (105°–115°)
½ cup vegetable oil
2 tablespoons salt, preferably kosher
3 eggs
1 tablespoon poppy seeds to sprinkle on tops

BAKING SHEET

One baking sheet, greased or Teflon.

PREPARATION
25 mins.

The yeast, 2 teaspoons sugar and 2 tablespoons all-purpose flour are placed in a tall water glass. Stir in ¾ cup warm water. Set aside until the liquid reaches the lip of the glass.

In a big bowl, measure 4 cups of flour. Add 1½ cups warm water (105°–115°), ½ cup vegetable oil, ½ cup sugar, salt and 2 eggs, and mix them together thoroughly. When yeast reaches the lip of the glass (about 15 minutes), add it to the batter. Mix, and gradually add 3 more cups of flour. The dough will be a rough, shaggy mass that will clean the sides of the bowl. If the dough continues to stick to the hands, add several sprinkles of flour.

KNEADING
8 mins.

Turn the dough onto a lightly floured work surface—counter top or bread board—and knead with the rhythmic 1-2-3 motion of push-turn-fold. The dough will become smooth and elastic, and bubbles will rise under the surface of the dough. Sprinkle with flour if the dough should continue moist or sticky.

FIRST RISING
1½–2 hours

Place dough in mixing bowl and pat with buttered or greased fingers to keep the surface from crusting. Cover the bowl tightly with plastic wrap and move to a warm place (80°–85°) until the dough has risen to about twice its original size. You can test if it has risen by poking a finger in it; the dent will remain.

SECOND RISING
1½ hours

Knock down dough. If it is sticky, add ½ cup flour, kneading to produce a soft dough. The kneading can be done right in the bowl, if you wish. Knead for only 2 minutes. Oil the top of the dough and replace the plastic wrap. Let rise until doubled.

SHAPING
18 mins.

Punch down. Knead to press out the bubbles. Divide the dough into 2 equal pieces—and divide each of these into 3 small parts. Place under wax paper or a towel and let rest on the counter top for 5 minutes to relax the dough. Roll each piece under the palms into a 10-inch roll. Place 3 rolls side by side and braid from the center. Repeat with remaining pieces. Set on baking sheet.

THIRD RISING
1 hour

Cover braids with wax paper. Set them in the warm place to double in bulk.

BAKING
350°
45–55 mins.

Preheat oven to 350°. Combine the remaining egg and 6 teaspoons of sugar and brush each loaf. Sprinkle with poppy seeds, if you wish. Bake in the oven until the loaves are a lovely golden yellow. The loaves, while hot, are too fragile to turn over to test for doneness by tapping the bottom crust. Instead, use a metal skewer or wooden toothpick. Insert it between the braids near the center of a loaf. If it comes out clean and dry, the loaf is done.

FINAL STEP

Remove bread from the oven. Use a spatula under the loaves to lift them off the baking sheet and onto the metal rack to cool. They are easier to handle when cool.

PANETTONE DI NATALE

[ONE LARGE LOAF]

Two sheets of dough, one heavy with fruit and nuts, the other, plain, rolled together and baked into a circular loaf in a tube pan, become Italian Christmas Fruit Bread. This is richer than most other panettone recipes but that is as it should be—it's for the holidays.

INGREDIENTS

1 package dry yeast
½ cup lukewarm water (105°–115°)
½ cup all-purpose flour
¾ cup (1½ sticks) butter, room temperature
½ cup sugar
3 eggs, room temperature
3 egg yolks, room temperature
1 teaspoon vanilla
1 teaspoon salt
4 cups all-purpose flour, approximately
⅓ cup raisins, rinsed and patted dry
½ cup *each* shredded candied lemon peel, citron and chopped blanched almonds
1 tablespoon sugar
2 dozen whole blanched almonds

BAKING PAN

Tube pan, buttered or Teflon.

PREPARATION
20 mins.

In a small bowl dissolve yeast in water. Stir briskly with a fork or metal whisk. Blend in ½ cup flour and let the sponge stand until it is bubbly—about 5 minutes.

In a large bowl cream together butter and sugar and follow this with eggs and egg yolks. Beat thoroughly until well mixed. Add yeast, vanilla, salt and about 4 cups of flour—one cup at a time. Stir with a wooden spoon until it becomes too difficult to turn—then work in by hand. When it is soft, but not sticky, turn from the bowl onto a floured board or counter top.

KNEADING
6 mins.

Knead the dough and divide the ball in two equal parts. One half is put aside to rest while the other half receives the raisins, candied peel, citron and chopped nuts. Work the fruit and nuts in well.

FIRST RISING
50 mins.

Keep the two halves separate. Place them in greased bowls, cover tightly with plastic wrap and move to a warm place (80°–85°) to rise until doubled in bulk. You can test if they have risen by poking a finger in them; the dents will remain.

SHAPING
30 mins.

Punch down the two doughs, turn them onto the floured surface, and knead again for 3 minutes. Butter pan, sprinkle it with sugar, and stud the bottom with whole blanched almonds.

Roll the plain dough into a triangle. (The long side —about 24 inches—will encircle the tube, with the ends overlapping.) Roll out the fruit dough the same size. Lay it on top of the plain. Beginning at the base of the triangle, roll up the two doughs, and fit them into the prepared pan. Try an experimental circle before dropping the dough into the pan to be certain the ends overlap, and, together, are about the same thickness as the center of the roll.

SECOND RISING
1 hour

Cover the pan with wax paper and place in a warm spot to rise until dough has doubled in bulk.

BAKING
400°
10 mins.
350°
50 mins.

Preheat oven to 400°. Bake in a hot oven for 10 minutes, reduce the oven temperature to moderate (350°) and continue to bake for another 50 minutes, or until the loaf tests done. Insert a metal skewer or wooden toothpick into the center of the loaf. If it comes out clean and dry, the loaf is done. If moist particles cling to the probe, return the loaf to the oven for an additional 10 minutes. Test again.

FINAL STEP

Remove bread from the oven and turn from the pan and place on a cooling rack. Slice in wedges.

PORTUGUESE HONEY BREAD

[THREE SMALL LOAVES]

Imagine the spiced richness in a loaf that includes sugar, honey *and* molasses as well as butter, sweet sherry and 4 spices. It comes out of the oven a solid brown brick that is aged at room temperature for 5 days before slicing thin to serve with tea or eggnog or holiday punch. Unlike fruit cake, it contains only a small quantity of fruit and nuts. Fine for gifts.

INGREDIENTS

1 cup (2 sticks) butter, room temperature
¾ cup molasses
1½ cups sugar
⅓ cup honey
¼ cup instant potatoes
¼ cup sweet sherry
⅓ cup chopped candied fruit
1 tablespoon diced candied citron
½ cup broken walnuts
¾ teaspoon ground cloves

2 teaspoons anise seed, ground
2 tablespoons cinnamon
¼ teaspoon black pepper
½ teaspoon baking soda
6½ cups all-purpose flour

BAKING PANS

Three small (7½ x 3½) baking tins, metal or Teflon, buttered, lined with wax paper and buttered again.

PREPARATION
20 mins.

This is a large recipe so use a large bowl in which to cream the butter, molasses, sugar and honey with a wooden spoon until fluffy. Blend in potatoes, sherry, candied fruit, citron, walnuts, cloves, anise, cinnamon, pepper and baking soda. Add 3 cups of flour. Mix well, and then begin to work the mixture with the hands. Add the balance of the flour—3 cups. It is now a heavy, crumbly mixture that does not have either the elasticity of yeast dough nor the creaminess of the usual batter. Preheat oven to 250°.

SHAPING
10 mins.

Divide the mixture among the three pans. Press the dough into the corners and pat the tops smooth. The fingerprints that are left will come out when the loaves rise in the oven. (A kitchen scale is convenient in dividing the dough equally.) The dough will come to about ½ inch from top of the pan.

BAKING
250°
3 hours

Bake in the oven. The loaves will rise an inch or so, and longitudinal cracks will appear in the tops.

FINAL STEP

Remove bread from the oven. Cool in pans on wire rack for 10 minutes. With care, turn the loaves from the pans. Gently peel off the paper and discard. The loaves are fragile when warm and could be broken. The bread may be sliced when warm but after the loaves have cooled they are to be aged at room temperature for at least 5 days, wrapped tightly in foil. The loaves will keep sealed or resealed for months, and can be frozen after maturing. Slice thinly.

SAFFRON CHRISTMAS WREATH

[ONE 14-INCH CIRCULAR LOAF]

Wreath-shaped, this bread gets its creamy yellow color and unusual flavor and aroma from a tablespoon of freshly ground saffron. Place a 3-inch ball of dough in the center hole to bake, and it becomes a Christmas star wreathed for the holidays.

INGREDIENTS

1 tablespoon of saffron
1 package dry yeast
¼ cup warm water (105°–115°)
1 cup milk or half-and-half
½ cup butter, room temperature
1 egg, room temperature
¼ cup sugar
1 teaspoon salt
4 cups all-purpose flour, approximately
1 cup raisins
Glaze: 1 egg beaten with 1 tablespoon milk
½ cup slivered almonds
3 tablespoons granulated sugar
3 red glacéed cherries, halved

BAKING SHEET

One baking sheet, greased or Teflon.

PREPARATION
20 mins.

In a slow oven (250°) dry 1 tablespoon saffron for about 20 minutes until it can be pounded to a powder in a mortar, or by a large spoon pressing the saffron against the bottom of a small bowl.

Dissolve the yeast in water and set aside.

15 mins.

In a saucepan heat 1 cup milk, adding butter and cool to lukewarm. Stir in the ground saffron. Pour the milk and yeast in a large bowl and stir in the beaten egg, sugar, salt and 2 cups of flour. Mix well—about 100 strokes. Add the raisins, and continue to stir vigorously until the dough is thick and glossy. (More flour will be added later.)

FIRST RISING
1 hour

Cover the bowl with plastic wrap and let the sponge rise in a warm place (80°–85°) until it has doubled in bulk.

KNEADING
8 mins.

The kneading *follows* the rising in this recipe. Add more flour—about 2 cups—to make a firm dough, turn out onto a floured board or counter top and knead until it is smooth and elastic.

SHAPING
25 mins.

Roll and press the dough into a long 27-inch roll. Cut off a 3-inch piece and reserve for the center. Fashion a large ring on the oiled or Teflon baking sheet, joining the ends by pinching them firmly together. Cut the ring with scissors at ½-inch intervals—about two-thirds of the way through the dough—and alternately turn the slices to the left and to the right.

Pat the ring into shape. The center should be about 6 inches across. Roll the 3-inch piece into a ball, place it in the center of the wreath. Flatten it slightly but be certain there is a clear space between it and the larger ring. Remember, both will expand during the rising process.

Brush the wreath and the center piece with lightly beaten egg mixed with milk, sprinkle with slivered blanched almonds and granulated sugar. Place 6 red glacéed cherries at intervals around the wreath.

SECOND RISING
1 hour

Cover carefully with wax paper and place in a warm spot (80°–85°) until doubled in bulk.

BAKING
375°
45 mins.

Preheat oven to 375°. Place baking sheet in the oven and bake until loaf tests done when a wooden toothpick inserted in the wreath comes out clean.

FINAL STEP

Remove bread from the oven. Let the wreath cool on the baking sheet for about 15 minutes before attempting to move it to the wire rack for further cooling. Slip it off the baking sheet gently so it does not break. When it is cool, place it on a circular piece of cardboard if it is to be carried.

CARDAMOM EASTER BREAD

[ONE BRAID]

A tinted egg peeking through the braids of this rich cardamom-flavored loaf makes this bread perfect for Easter. Be certain the egg is colored with regular Easter egg dye rather than chance it with ordinary food coloring that may run off the egg and discolor the loaf. It is also important that the egg be tucked deep under the braids so it will not be pushed out when the dough rises.

It makes a handsome loaf for Easter morning, especially if it is served to children. The egg, of course, is removed before that part of the bread is sliced.

INGREDIENTS

1 uncooked egg in shell, tinted red
1 package dry yeast
¼ cup warm water (105°–115°)
⅓ cup sugar
¼ cup (½ stick) butter, room temperature
½ teaspoon salt
½ cup milk, hot
2 teaspoons ground cardamom
3½ cups all-purpose flour, approximately
1 egg, room temperature
Glaze: ¼ cup milk
Sprinkle of sugar

BAKING SHEET

One baking sheet, greased or Teflon.

PREPARATION
20 mins.

Color the egg and set aside.

In a small bowl or cup dissolve yeast in water. Whip with a metal whisk or fork to hasten the action.

In a large mixing bowl put sugar, butter and salt—and over it pour the milk. Stir until butter is soft and milk has cooled to lukewarm. Add cardamom. Blend in 1 cup of flour with 25 strong strokes with a wooden spoon. Stir in the egg (not the colored one) and yeast. Add remaining flour, a half cup at a time, first with the spoon and then by hand, until a rough ball is formed and the dough pulls away from the sides of the bowl.

KNEADING
8 mins.

Turn the ball of dough onto a floured work surface—a counter top or bread board—and knead with a rhythmic push-turn-fold motion. (If a dough hook on the mixer is used, knead for 6 minutes.) The dough will be well kneaded when it is smooth, elastic and no longer sticky.

FIRST RISING
1¼ hours

Place the ball of dough in a greased bowl, cover tightly with plastic wrap and put in a warm draft-free place (80°–85°) until it has doubled in bulk.

SECOND RISING
1 hour

Turn back the plastic wrap, punch down the dough, replace the cover and let rise until almost doubled again.

SHAPING
30 mins.

Turn the dough out on a lightly floured work surface, knead for 60 seconds or until the bubbles have been forced out of the risen dough—and divide the dough into three equal parts. Cover them with a towel or wax paper and let them rest for about 10 minutes.

Roll each part under the heel of the hands to form a strand about 16-inches long, with slightly tapered ends. Line them up parallel on the greased baking sheet, and braid them loosely without stretching. Begin in the middle and work toward either end. Pinch the strands together at the ends. Carefully fashion a nest for the tinted egg under the strands in the middle of the loaf.

THIRD RISING
45 mins.

Cover the braid with wax paper and return to the warm place until it has almost doubled in size.

BAKING
375°
40 mins.

Preheat oven to 375°. Brush the loaf with milk and sprinkle with sugar. Place in the oven. When the loaf is golden brown and tapping the bottom crust yields a hard hollow sound, the bread is baked. If not, return to the oven for an additional 10 minutes. Midway in the bake period, shift the loaf—turn it halfway around—so it is exposed equally to temperature variations in the oven.

FINAL STEP

Remove bread from the oven. A braided bread while still hot from the oven is fragile so handle it carefully when removing to a metal cooling rack. It can be sliced while still warm—or served cold, or toasted.

SIXTEEN

Cheese Breads

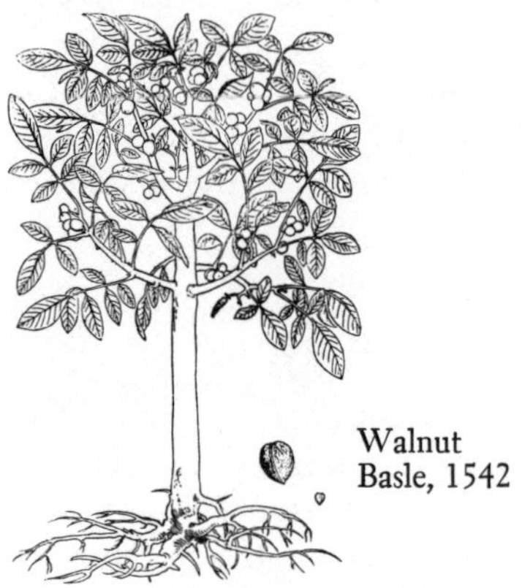

Walnut
Basle, 1542

Cheese and bread began a happy relationship about 9,000 years ago, give or take a millennium, when both were discovered by man. It is certain that he was soon putting them together and enjoying the nourishing good taste of the two in combination, each in its unique way enhancing the flavor of the other.

Cheese *in* bread is a late-arriving creation of the union. Cheese may be added to the mixture as just another ingredient so that it becomes indistinguishable except for the subtle richness and aroma it gives the loaf. It may be encased in a blanket of dough so that it retains its form. It may be sprinkled on the top to melt into the crust and add color and appeal.

And to all bread, cheese gives its taste.

Many of the recipes here call for sharp Cheddar cheese of good quality. The Russian loaf is made with a medium-soft cheese, a Munster, one of the best melting cheeses. All are natural cheeses, with one exception; a process cheese is called for in the Twisted Cheese Loaf. Cheese shaved or grated for bread sticks or the tops of loaves should be one of the Cheddars, a Swiss, or any similar dry cheese.

There are two things to remember about cheese in bread. It will soften the loaf and make for a closer grain. The loaf should be baked longer to avoid a slight sogginess caused by melted cheese.

Cheese is a great food, and it is a high compliment to bread to use cheese in its preparation.

CHEESE CASSEROLE BREAD

[TWO LOAVES]

There is no kneading to this cheese bread—four minutes beating with a wooden spoon or an electric mixer. The batter can be divided among a number of different pans. I usually put half in a 1-quart casserole and divide the remaining dough between two 6-inch fluted brioche tins. Other combinations are possible—remember to fill dough halfway in whatever pan or casserole you choose.

Slice or cut into wedges. Excellent toasted and keeps well frozen.

INGREDIENTS

4 to 5 cups bread or all-purpose flour
3 tablespoons sugar
1 tablespoon salt
2 packages dry yeast
2 cups hot tap water (120°–130°)
⅓ cup non-fat dry milk
2 tablespoons shortening, room temperature
1½ cups grated Cheddar cheese
1 egg, room temperature and beaten

BAKING PANS

Two 1-quart casseroles, greased, or any combination suggested above.

PREPARATION
15 mins.

In a large bowl, combine 2 cups flour, sugar, salt and yeast.

In a saucepan combine water, milk and shortening. Gradually add it to the dry ingredients and beat 150 strokes with a wooden spoon or 2 minutes at medium speed in the electric mixer. Scrape the bowl occasionally. Add cheese, egg and enough flour (about ½ cup) to make a thick batter but not so thick as to stop the mixer. Beat at high speed for 2 minutes or 150 additional strokes with the spoon.

With the spoon, stir in additional flour—about 2 cups—to make a stiff but manageable batter.

RISING
40 mins.

Cover the bowl with plastic wrap and put in a warm place (80°–85°) until batter is doubled in volume. Preheat oven to 375°.

FORMING
5 mins.

Stir down batter and beat vigorously for about 30 seconds. Turn into the prepared casseroles or tins.

BAKING
375°
45 mins.

Bake in the oven. The loaves will be done when a wooden toothpick inserted in the center of a loaf comes out clean and dry.

FINAL STEP

Remove bread from the oven and turn from casseroles or tins and cool on wire racks.

CHEESE SHORTBREAD

[A DOZEN PIE-SHAPED SERVINGS]

While it looks deceptively like an ordinary pie crust, this cheese creation is something else again. Rich (and short). A delicate wedge of goodness, it is fragile in the making, fragile in the cutting—but a joy to eat even in crumbs and pieces. With coffee or tea.

INGREDIENTS

1 cup grated Swiss cheese, room temperature
7 tablespoons butter or margarine, room temperature
¼ teaspoon salt
1½ cups all-purpose flour

BAKING PAN

One 9-inch layer cake pan or flan ring, lightly buttered.

PREPARATION
10 mins.

In a medium bowl combine cheese with butter, salt and flour. Work the mixture with your hands until it is a smooth ball. Too sticky, add a bit more flour. Too stiff, a teaspoon of cold water.

SHAPING
15 mins.

With a rolling pin, roll out the dough between two lengths of wax paper until it is slightly larger than the bottom of the pan or ring. Peel back the paper with care, quickly invert the dough over the pan and let it drop in. Press the dough snugly into the bottom. Neatly trim around the circle of dough because you will shortly be giving it a new edge. Fashion the scraps into a long, thin roll—long enough to go around the inside of the pan. Press the new edge onto the pastry, and flute it as you would pie crust.

With a knife or pastry wheel cut the shortbread 6 times across to make a dozen servings. If a flan ring was used, remove it and spread the wedges ½ inch apart. Separations or no, the demarcations will remain and make it easier to cut after it comes from the oven.

BAKING
400°
14 mins.

Preheat oven to 400°. Bake in the oven until it browns only faintly. Don't overbake. It can burn quite easily. Remove from the oven.

FINAL STEP

When it has cooled, cut down the lines again and remove from the baking pan.

CHEDDAR CHEESE BREAD

[TWO LOAVES]

There is more than one cup of cheese in each of the two 1½-pound loaves of this recipe. Toasted, it is outstanding but be careful that it doesn't burn. Watch it carefully, too, in the oven after 15 minutes; cover it with foil or brown paper if it gets too dark (and close to burning). It is the abundance of cheese that does it.

Thanks to the butterfat in the cheese, it is a soft and pliable dough, easy to work and not sticky at all.

A toasted slice is a good base for a creamed dish—chipped beef, chicken a la king, creamed mushrooms, or the like.

INGREDIENTS

1 package dry yeast
¼ cup warm water (105°–115°)
1¾ cups milk, heated
¼ cup sugar
2 teaspoons salt
2 tablespoons butter
3 cups sharp Cheddar cheese, shredded
5½ cups all-purpose or bread flour, approximately

BAKING PANS

Two medium (8½ x 4½) loaf pans, greased or Teflon. If glass, reduce oven heat 25°.

PREPARATION
25 mins.

In a small bowl sprinkle yeast over the water and stir to dissolve. Set aside while preparing the milk-cheese mixture.

Heat milk to scalding in a saucepan and stir in sugar, salt, butter and 2 cups of cheese. Stir until the butter and cheese are melted. Set aside to cool to lukewarm.

In a mixing bowl combine 2½ cups of flour, cheese mixture, yeast and the other cup of cheese. With an electric mixer beat for 2 minutes at medium speed—or 150 strong strokes with a wooden spoon. Either way, the batter must be smooth.

Add the additional flour, a cup at a time, stirring in with the wooden spoon and then by hand, until the dough is rough-formed and leaves the sides of the bowl. If it is wet or slack, add an additional half cup of flour.

KNEADING
10 mins.

Turn out on a floured surface—bread board or counter top—and knead with a strong push-turn-fold motion until it is smooth and elastic.

FIRST RISING
1½ hours

Return to the mixing bowl, pat the dough with shortening on all surfaces, and cover the bowl tightly with plastic wrap. Place in a warm spot (80°–85°) until dough has doubled in bulk.

SHAPING
15 mins.

Turn back plastic wrap, punch down dough and turn out on the floured surface. Divide in half. Round into balls, cover with wax paper and let rest for 10 minutes. Flatten the balls with the fist, fold in half, pinch the seams tightly together, turn the seams under, and plump into loaves to fit into the baking pans.

SECOND RISING
1 hour

Cover the pans with wax paper and return to the warm place until the dough has doubled in volume. It will rise about 1 inch above the edge of the pans.

BAKING
375°
40 mins.

Preheat oven to 375°. Bake in the oven until the loaves test done with a wooden toothpick or metal skewer. If done, the pin, inserted in the middle of the loaf, will come out clean and dry. This loaf browns easily so watch it closely after the first 15 minutes. If necessary, cover with foil or brown paper to keep it from getting too brown and perhaps burning.

FINAL STEP

Remove bread from the oven. Turn the loaves from the pans onto metal cooling racks.

CHEESE CARAWAY BATTER BREAD

[ONE LOAF]

This loaf is like other batter or no-knead breads—best served when fresh baked. It has a dark crust and a light interior speckled with caraway seeds. Its positive cheese and spicy flavor makes fine toast for a barbecue, a soup dinner or to serve with salad.

INGREDIENTS

1 package dry yeast
1 cup warm water (105°–115°)
1 cup grated Cheddar cheese (4 oz.)
1 teaspoon caraway seeds (crushed in blender)
2 tablespoons shortening, room temperature
2 tablespoons sugar
2 teaspoons salt
2½ cups all-purpose flour

BAKING PAN

One large (9 x 5) loaf pan, greased or Teflon. If glass, reduce oven heat 25°.

PREPARATION
20 mins.

In a large bowl sprinkle the yeast on the water, and stir briskly with a fork or whisk to hasten the fermentation action.

When yeast mixture has started to bubble—in about 5 minutes—add cheese, caraway seeds (broken up in the blender, or in a bowl, under a heavy spoon), shortening, sugar, salt and 1½ cups of flour. Beat this mixture with an electric mixer for about two minutes, scraping down the sides of the bowl once or twice. Or do 100 vigorous strokes with a large wooden spoon. The beating is substituting for kneading to form the necessary gluten in a yeast bread.

The mixture will be too heavy for a light electric mixer so put it aside and stir in the remaining flour with the spoon, a little at a time. Work the dough with the spoon until it is smooth.

FIRST RISING
45 mins.

Cover the bowl tightly with plastic wrap and let dough rise in a warm place (80°–85°) until it has doubled in bulk.

FORMING
10 mins.

Stir down batter with about 25 strokes and pour into a large loaf pan. Spread evenly with a rubber spatula, and pat top of loaf with a floured hand to smooth the surface. The pan will be less than half filled.

SECOND RISING
45 mins.

Cover with wax paper and return to the warm place until it has doubled in bulk. It will rise not quite to the lip of the pan.

BAKING
375°
45 mins.

Preheat oven to 375°. Bake in the oven. When tapping the bottom crust yields a hard hollow sound, the loaf is done.

FINAL STEP — Remove bread from the oven and turn from pan to a wire rack. Let it cool before slicing. It can be frozen and reheated with good results.

BUTTERMILK CHEESE BREAD

[ONE LARGE LOAF]

Buttermilk is the liquid in this quickly made loaf flavored with sharp Cheddar cheese. The texture is not as fine as other white breads but I like its coarseness, nevertheless.

The time saved in making this loaf is fairly substantial—about one third—since the electric mixer takes over the chore of mixing the dough, and only a 5-minute kneading is called for, plus only one rising of the dough. It is a very alive dough and will rise handsomely above the edge of the tins. The different flavor and texture result from the use of two leavening agents, yeast and baking powder, a combination that was used extensively at one time in the Western states.

INGREDIENTS

2 packages dry yeast
¾ cup warm water (105°–115°)
1¼ cups of buttermilk, room temperature
4½ to 5 cups all-purpose flour, approximately
2 tablespoons sugar
2 teaspoons *each* baking powder and salt
1 cup shredded sharp Cheddar cheese

BAKING PANS — One large (9 x 5) loaf pan, greased or Teflon, or a combination of 1 medium and 1 small pan. If glass, reduce oven heat 25°.

PREPARATION
15 mins.

In a mixing bowl dissolve yeast in water. Stir briefly with a whisk to help get the action started. Set aside for 5 minutes. Add buttermilk, 2½ cups of flour, sugar, baking powder and salt. Blend for ½ minute at low speed in an electric mixer. Scrape down sides of the bowl and increase speed to medium for 2 minutes.

Stop the machine and with a wooden spoon stir in cheese and remaining flour until the dough forms a rough mass and cleans the sides of the bowl.

KNEADING
5 mins.

Turn the dough onto a floured work surface, and knead. Add a half cup additional flour if the dough is slack or wet and sticky.

SHAPING
10 mins.

For one large loaf, roll dough into a rectangle 2 inches wider than the width of the pan. Roll from the short side into a tight roll, like a jelly roll—pressing each end to seal. Tuck ends under and place seam down in the buttered loaf pan. Brush lightly with melted butter. For two loaves, divide the dough and shape each as above.

RISING
1 hour

Cover with wax paper and put in a warm place (80°–85°) until doubled in bulk. The top of the dough will have risen about 1 inch above the edge of the pan. You can test if it has risen by poking a finger in it; the dent will remain.

BAKING
425°
35 mins.

Preheat oven to 425°. Place the pan (or pans) on a shelf in a low position in the oven so the bread will not brown too quickly. Loaves will be done when deep brown and pulled away from the sides of the pan. When tapping the bottom crust yields a hard hollow sound, the bread is done. If not, return to the oven—without the pan, if you wish a deep brown all-over crust—for an additional 10 minutes. However, if the tops of the loaves appear to be browning too quickly, cover with a piece of foil or brown sack paper.

FINAL STEP

Remove bread from the oven. Turn from pans and place the loaves on wire racks to cool. Brush with melted butter for a lovely rich glow.

WALNUT CHEDDAR LOAF

[ONE LOAF]

A quick bread that relies for its good and unusual taste on mustard, cayenne, Worcestershire sauce and a sharp Cheddar cheese, this loaf is right for a brunch or luncheon or to carry along on a picnic. Double the recipe for one medium and two small loaves—extras for gifts to the hostess. The loaf will have a broken ridge down the crust which will be light brown with orange cheese flecks and bits of brown nuts peeking through.

The loaf is equally good warm or cold. It can be reheated if wrapped in foil. The slices are almost too small for the conventional toaster but it is delicious toasted in the old-fashioned machine that drops its sides.

INGREDIENTS

2½ cups all-purpose flour
2 tablespoons sugar
2 teaspoons baking powder
1¼ teaspoons salt
½ teaspoon *each* dry mustard and baking soda
Dash of cayenne pepper
¼ cup shortening
1 cup grated sharp Cheddar cheese
½ teaspoon Worcestershire sauce
1 egg, room temperature
1 cup buttermilk, room temperature
1 cup chopped walnuts

BAKING PAN

One medium (8½ x 4½) loaf tin, greased or Teflon. If a glass pan, reduce oven heat 25°.

PREPARATION
20 mins.

Preheat oven to 350°.

In a large bowl mix flour, sugar, baking powder, salt, dry mustard, baking soda and cayenne. Use pastry blender and fingers. Work in the shortening. It will resemble coarse bran. Stir in the grated cheese.

In a small bowl combine Worcestershire sauce, egg and buttermilk. Stir this into the flour mixture until it is moistened—but no longer. Mix in the nuts.

FORMING
5 mins.

Turn the batter into the pan. Smooth top with a spatula.

BAKING
350°
55 mins.

Place in the oven. The loaf is done when a wooden toothpick inserted in the center comes out dry and clean.

FINAL STEP

Remove bread from the oven. Turn the loaf out of the pan immediately and carefully place it on a metal rack to cool before slicing.

CHEESE CARROT BREAD

[TWO LOAVES]

The cheese and bits of carrot give this light crusted bread a golden color usually associated with eggs, of which there are none in this recipe. The carrot slivers complement the cheese which toasting brings out in flavor and aroma. It is good for sandwiches.

INGREDIENTS

1 package dry yeast
1¾ cups warm water (105°–115°)
1 pinch sugar
2 tablespoons sugar
⅓ cup non-fat dry milk
2½ cups sharp Cheddar cheese, grated
¼ cup raw carrot, grated
3 tablespoons shortening (vegetable oil)
2 teaspoons salt
5 to 6 cups all-purpose flour, approximately

BAKING PANS

Two medium (8½ x 4½) loaf pans, greased or Teflon. If glass, reduce oven heat 25°.

PREPARATION
20 mins.

In a large mixing bowl sprinkle yeast over water. Stir to dissolve and add a pinch of sugar to hasten the fermentation. Let rest for 3 or 4 minutes.

Add 2 tablespoons sugar, milk, cheese, carrot, shortening and salt. Stir with a wooden spoon or electric mixer (low) for 30 seconds to mix well.

Add 3 cups flour and beat at medium speed for 3 minutes or 100 strokes with the wooden spoon. Add 2 cups or more flour, mixing with the spoon and then by hand until the dough pulls away from the sides of the bowl.

KNEADING
8 mins.

Turn dough out onto a floured surface—counter top or board. In the early stages it will be sticky but this will become less so as small portions of flour are added and the moisture is absorbed. Knead until the ball is smooth and satiny.

FIRST RISING
50 mins.

Return the dough to the bowl (which has been washed and greased), cover tightly with plastic wrap to retain moisture and heat, and place in a warm spot until doubled in bulk. You can test if it has risen by poking a finger in it; the dent will remain.

SHAPING
10 mins.

Remove wrap, punch dough down with the fist and fingers, turn out on the floured surface and cut into two equal pieces with a sharp knife. Shape into two loaves and put into loaf pans.

SECOND RISING
45 mins.

Cover with wax paper and return to the warm place until doubled in bulk.

BAKING
350°
45 mins.

Preheat oven to 350°. Bake in the oven until they are a golden brown. When tapping the bottom crust yields a hard hollow sound, they are done.

FINAL STEP

Remove bread from the oven. Turn out on wire cooling rack.

CHEESE STRAWS

[ABOUT THREE DOZEN]

Long thin twists of pastry dough, generously overlaid with dry cheese and sprinkled with caraway seeds, these are fine to serve with cocktails or at a buffet. They are easy to prepare, and are baked in a hot oven for no longer than 10 minutes. They need not all be the same precise length. Cut them from a roughly shaped rectangle—and if some are an inch or so shorter than the others, no matter.

INGREDIENTS

2 cups all-purpose flour
½ teaspoon salt
⅔ cup (1¼ sticks) butter, room temperature
¼ cup cold water
1 egg, well beaten
1½ cups finely grated Cheddar, Swiss or other dry cheese
1 tablespoon caraway seeds

BAKING SHEETS

One or more baking sheets, greased or Teflon, depending on the capacity of the oven.

PREPARATION
20 mins.

First, the pastry dough for the straws—

On a pastry or bread board sift the flour and make a well in the center. Sprinkle in the salt. Break or cut butter in small pieces into the well, and pour in the water. Work the ingredients in the well into a smooth paste, and gently pull in the flour to form the dough. A scraper or metal spatula will help turn and work the soft dough.

KNEADING
5 mins.

Knead dough lightly and wrap in wax paper.

REFRIGERATING
1 hour or more

Chill the wrapped dough in the refrigerator.

SHAPING
15 mins.

Roll the chilled pastry dough into a rectangle that is about ¼-inch thick. If you have a small oven, plan to bake the straws in two or more batches. Reserve the unneeded dough in the refrigerator until ready for the next batch. Preheat oven to 400°.

Brush the prepared dough with egg, and sprinkle heavily with the cheese shavings and caraway seeds.

With a sharp knife or pastry wheel cut strips about 6 to 8 inches long and ½-inch wide. Twist each strip 4 or 5 times and lay in rows on the baking sheet.

BAKING
400°
10 mins.

Bake in the oven watching carefully that the straws don't go beyond that time and scorch. They will be a delicate light brown, and the cheese will have melted and bubbled.

FINAL STEP

Remove from the oven. Spread the straws on a wire rack. Serve hot or cold. These keep very well stored in an airtight jar or can for several days.

Reheat in a slow (250°) oven.

CHEESE BREAD

[ONE LARGE LOAF]

Thyme and marjoram darken this loaf and give it good flavor but the red bits of pimiento give it color and an unforgettable taste. It reminds me always of a pimiento cheese spread my mother made for picnics on the shores of an Indiana lake more than fifty years ago. Both delicious. This one toasts, and, of course, is good picnic bread. The dough is soft and delicate and rolls into a loaf with no trouble.

INGREDIENTS

3¾ cups all-purpose flour, approximately
1 package dry yeast
3 tablespoons all-purpose flour
2 tablespoons butter or margarine
1 tablespoon sugar
1 teaspoon salt
½ teaspoon powdered marjoram
¼ teaspoon powdered thyme
1 cup milk (or 1 cup water and ¼ cup non-fat dry milk)
⅓ cup sharp Cheddar cheese, grated
¼ cup chopped pimiento
Melted butter or shortening to brush loaf

BAKING PAN

One large (9 x 5) loaf pan, greased or Teflon. If glass, reduce oven heat 25°.

PREPARATION
25 mins.

In a large mixing bowl blend 2 cups flour and yeast. Fashion a well in the flour in the center of the bowl.

In a medium saucepan, over medium heat, blend 3 tablespoons flour with butter. Add sugar, salt, marjoram and thyme. Stir in milk. Stir, cooking until smooth and thick. Remove from heat, and add the cheese and pimiento. Stir until the cheese has melted, and the mixture is warm (120°)—but not hot.

Pour the cheese mixture into the flour well; beat, slowly pulling the flour into the mass in the center of the bowl. Blend—about 50 strokes. Add the balance of the flour, in two portions, working until smooth after each addition. When the dough is too difficult to beat with the wooden spoon, work in the flour with the hands until it forms a rough mass and is not sticky.

KNEADING
6 mins.

Turn out on a floured board or counter top and knead until it rounds up in a ball, smooth and elastic. If the ball slumps, it is too soft. Add a bit more flour. Kneading will take about 6 minutes—4 minutes with an electric mixer equipped with a dough hook. Don't be rough with this dough because the pimiento pieces are fragile. Work the dough slowly but positively.

FIRST RISING
1 hour

Turn the dough back into the large bowl, pat the ball with a film of butter or shortening, and place in a warm spot (80°–85°) until it has almost doubled in bulk. Cover the bowl tightly with plastic wrap to keep the moisture in and to prevent a crust from forming.

SHAPING
5 mins.

Punch down and turn out onto the floured surface. Pat and shape into a loaf. Place in the large loaf pan.

SECOND RISING
50 mins.

Cover with wax paper and return to the warm place until the loaf has doubled in bulk—and is peeking over the edge of the pan.

BAKING
375°
45 mins.

Preheat oven to 375°. Brush the loaf with melted butter or shortening and place in the oven. When the loaf is golden brown and tapping the bottom crust yields a hard hollow sound, the bread is done. (A cake testing pin inserted in the center will come out clean if bread is done.) If not, return to the oven without the pan for 5 minutes.

FINAL STEP Remove bread from the oven. Turn out on a metal rack to cool. Brush with melted butter or shortening if you want a soft loaf (and cover with a tea towel). It will be more crisp, of course, with nothing brushed on.

TABASCO CHEESE BREAD

[ONE ROUND LOAF OR FOUR MINIATURE LOAVES]

A dash of Tabasco with the grated Cheddar cheese gives this loaf a nippy cheese flavor. Make this recipe in small or miniature loaves for children who will love it toasted. Baked in a larger pan, it is excellent for sandwiches. The loaf has a highly glazed crust and a slice streaked with yellow cheese.

INGREDIENTS
1 package dry yeast
¼ cup warm water (105°–115°)
1 pinch of sugar
1 cup milk heated to warm (105°–115°)
3 tablespoons butter or margarine, room temperature
1 tablespoon salt
3 to 4 cups all-purpose flour, approximately
1 cup grated sharp Cheddar cheese, room temperature
¼ teaspoon Tabasco sauce
Glaze: 1 egg yolk mixed with ¼ cup milk or cream

BAKING PANS One shallow round 8-inch cake pan or four miniature baking pans, greased or Teflon.

PREPARATION
25 mins.
In a small bowl or cup dissolve yeast in water, stirring briskly with a metal whisk or fork to hasten the action. Add sugar.

In a saucepan heat milk, butter and salt to lukewarm. Pour both the milk and yeast mixture into a large bowl, and add 2 cups of flour. Blend well with 25 strokes. Add the cheese and Tabasco. Blend in thoroughly. Add 1 cup of flour and begin to work the mixture by hand. Carefully add more flour, ¼ cup at a time, until the dough has lost its wetness and cleans the sides of the bowl.

KNEADING
7 mins.
Turn the dough onto a lightly floured surface—counter top or board. Have flour in a small sifter can or in the opened flour container so that small amounts of flour

can be sprinkled on the dough if it should become sticky in the early stages of kneading. Knead (4 minutes with a dough hook) until the dough is smooth and elastic. Then knead for another 1 minute for good measure.

FIRST RISING
1 hour

Place the dough in the large greased bowl, cover tightly with plastic wrap and put in a warm place (80°–85°) until it has doubled in bulk.

SHAPING
15 mins.

Punch the dough down in the bowl, knead briefly and turn out on the floured surface. With a large sharp knife cut the ball into as many pieces as you have decided to make into loaves. (See dough volume chart, page 23.)

For the round loaf, shape the dough into a ball. Press into the cake pan, filling out to the edges.

For a miniature loaf, press the ball into a flat oval, roughly the length of the pan. Fold the oval in half, pinch the seam tightly to seal, tuck under the ends, and place in the pan, seam down. Repeat with the other pieces.

SECOND RISING
50 mins.

Cover the pans loosely with wax paper and return them to the warm place until loaves have doubled in bulk, or just begin to peek above the edge of the pans.

BAKING
400°
10 mins.
350°
20–30 mins.

Preheat the oven to 400°. Glaze the loaves with the yolk and milk mixture. Place in the hot oven for 10 minutes, then reduce heat to 350° and bake the small loaves for an additional 20 minutes. Bake the large loaf for another 25 or 30 minutes. When tapping the bottom crust yields a hard hollow sound, they are done.

FINAL STEP

Remove bread from the oven. Turn from pans and leave on wire rack to cool.

PEPPER CHEESE LOAF

[TWO LOAVES]

At first it is the taste of the cheese, and then, the pepper, quite a lot of it, that the tongue is aware of. It is a fickle loaf. Eaten cold, the pepper dominates. Warm from the oven or toasted, the cheese flavor comes to the fore. Whichever, it is unusual and delicious. The cheese creates swirls and small fissures of yellow, while the pepper makes a pattern of black specks against the white dough.

Baked in coffee cans, the cylindrical loaf is cut into round slices for the table. A fine bread with a soup dinner, great for unusual sandwich slices on a buffet, and superb toasted, always.

INGREDIENTS
2½ to 3 cups all-purpose or bread flour, approximately
1 package dry yeast
2 tablespoons sugar
1 teaspoon salt
2 teaspoons black pepper, freshly ground
1 cup warm water (105°–115°)
1 tablespoon shortening
2 cups (6 ounces) sharp Cheddar cheese, coarsely grated

BAKING TINS
Two 1-pound coffee cans or 2 small (7½ x 3½) loaf pans, greased.

PREPARATION
15 mins.
In a mixer bowl blend 1 cup of flour, yeast, sugar, salt and ground pepper. (The cheese comes later, after the first rising.) Add water and shortening (I use vegetable oil in this recipe). Beat in the electric mixer at low speed for 30 seconds, scraping the bowl once or twice. Then, at high speed, beat 3 more minutes. Stop the mixer.

With a wooden spoon stir in additional flour, a half cup at a time, to form a soft dough that is elastic.

KNEADING
8 mins.
Turn out on a floured work surface—counter top or bread board—and knead with a strong push-turn-fold action. Add more flour if necessary to control the stickiness. (About 5 minutes with a dough hook.)

FIRST RISING
45 mins.
Place the ball of dough in a lightly greased bowl, cover tightly with plastic wrap and put in a warm place (80°–85°) until doubled in bulk. You can test if it has risen by poking a finger in it; the dent will remain.

SHAPING
10 mins.
Punch down the dough and work it briefly under the hands to press out the bubbles. Spread half of the cheese on the dough and fold in. Knead for 1 minute and sprinkle on the balance of the cheese. This is not an easy job because the dough does not want to accept the cheese. After a few minutes of tucking in loose pieces, however, it will, and all will be well.

With a sharp knife, divide the dough. Shape the

pieces into balls, and let them rest under a towel for 3 or 4 minutes. One ball should fill the prepared coffee can about halfway, no more. Press the dough into the container. Repeat with the second can. If for loaf pans, form by pressing a ball of dough into a flat oval, roughly the length of the baking tin. Fold the oval in half, pinch the seam tightly to seal, tuck under the ends, and place in the loaf pan, seam under. Repeat with the second ball of dough.

SECOND RISING
1 hour

Place the containers in the warm place, cover with wax paper and leave until the center of the dough has risen to the edge of the tin in the can or 1 inch above in the loaf pan.

BAKING
400°
35 mins.

Preheat oven to 400°. Place in the oven until the crust is a deep brown and the loaves test done. Turn out one loaf from its can or pan and tap the bottom crust with a forefinger. A hard hollow sound means the bread is baked. If not, return to the oven (without the pan, if you wish a browner crust) for an additional 10 minutes. If the loaves appear to be browning too quickly, cover with a piece of foil or brown sack paper.

FINAL STEP

Remove bread from the oven. Turn from containers and place on wire racks to cool. Serve either warm from the oven or reheated later. This bread freezes especially well, and will keep for six months or longer.

SWISS CHEESE POTATO BREAD

[ONE LARGE RING LOAF]

Diced Swiss cheese melts and spreads through this fine loaf to create a wonderfully soft and tender slice. It is basically a potato bread with cheese added. The loaf bakes a light brown with dark pieces of crusted cheese melted into the surface. It should be baked in an 8-inch tube pan, either an angel food tin or a Bundt pan. I like the hills and valleys of the latter.

INGREDIENTS

3 cups all-purpose flour, approximately
1 package dry yeast
1 teaspoon *each* sugar and salt
¼ cup instant potato

1½ cups hot tap water (120°–130°)
5 tablespoons butter or margarine, melted
2 eggs, room temperature
1 cup diced or grated Swiss cheese

BAKING PAN — One 8-inch tube pan, greased or Teflon. Angel food or Bundt pan will do fine.

PREPARATION
12 mins.

Measure 1½ cups of flour into a large mixing bowl, and stir in yeast, sugar, salt, potato and water. Beat in electric mixer for 30 seconds. Add the melted butter, two eggs and diced or grated Swiss cheese. Turn mixer to high for 2 minutes.

Stop mixer. Stir in the balance of the flour, a half cup at a time, first with the spoon and then by hand. The dough will be a rough, shaggy mass that will clean the sides of the bowl. If the dough continues slack and sticky, add a small amount of flour.

KNEADING
8 mins.

Turn the dough onto a lightly floured work surface—counter top or bread board—and knead with the rhythmic 1-2-3 motion of push-turn-fold. The dough will become smooth and elastic, and bubbles will rise under the surface of the dough. (Knead 6 minutes with a dough hook.)

FIRST RISING
1 hour

Place the dough in the mixing bowl and pat with buttered or greased fingers. Cover the bowl tightly with plastic wrap and move to a warm place (80°–85°) until the dough has risen to twice its original size.

SHAPING
10 mins.

Punch down the dough, turn it onto the work surface again, and let it rest for 2 minutes. Roll it under the palms to about 20 inches in length. Lay the length of dough in the prepared tube or Bundt pan. Overlap the ends slightly and pinch together.

SECOND RISING
45 mins.

Cover the pan with a length of wax paper and return to the warm place until dough has doubled its size.

BAKING
375°
45–55 mins.

Preheat oven to 375°. Bake in the oven until it tests done. A metal skewer inserted in the center of the loaf will come out clean and dry when it is done. Ten minutes before the bake period is ended, carefully turn the ring out of the pan onto a baking sheet. Return to the oven. This will give the loaf a lovely over-all brown that it would not otherwise have. But handle carefully. It is fragile when it is hot.

FINAL STEP

Remove bread from the oven. Slide the loaf off the baking sheet onto a metal rack to cool before slicing.

TWISTED CHEESE LOAF

[TWO LOAVES]

Cheese provides the lovely yellow color as well as its own distinctive flavor, but there is a piquancy in the taste that may confound you until you discover 12 ounces of beer among the ingredients. The two go together beautifully in bread, as they do together elsewhere. Toasted, it is superb.

There is a different way, too, of putting the twist in the loaf that makes it easy to do. Use only process cheese.

INGREDIENTS

1 can or bottle (12 ounces) beer or, if preferred, 1½ cups milk
½ cup warm water
2 tablespoons sugar
1 tablespoon salt
2 tablespoons butter or margarine
1 package (8 ounces) process Swiss or American cheese
5 cups all-purpose flour, approximately
2 packages dry yeast

BAKING PANS

Two medium (8½ x 4½) loaf pans, greased or Teflon. Reduce oven heat 25° if glass pans are used.

PREPARATION
30 mins.

In a large saucepan combine the beer, water, sugar, salt, butter and cheese. Heat until warm but the cheese need not completely melt. Lift off the heat and cool to very warm (120°–130°).

In a large mixer bowl measure in 2 cups of all-purpose flour and yeast. Add the warm mixture and beat at medium speed in the electric mixer for 3 minutes. Stir in the balance of the flour, a half cup at a time, first with the spoon and then by hand. The dough will be a rough, shaggy mass that will clean the sides of the bowl. If the dough continues slack, and moisture breaks through, add a small amount of additional flour.

KNEADING
6 mins.

Turn the dough onto a lightly floured work surface—counter top or bread board—and knead with the rhythmic 1-2-3 motion of push-turn-fold. The dough will become smooth and elastic, and bubbles will rise under the surface of the dough. Break the kneading rhythm occasionally by throwing the dough down hard against the counter top. (Knead 5 minutes with a dough hook.)

FIRST RISING
1 hour

Place the dough back in the bowl and pat with buttered or greased fingers to keep the surface from crusting. Cover the bowl tightly with plastic wrap and move to a warm place (80°–85°) until the dough has risen to about twice its original size (as judged by how high it creeps up the bowl).

SHAPING
15 mins.

Punch down the dough. Knead for 30 seconds to press out the bubbles. Divide the dough into two equal pieces. (Each will weigh about 1½ pounds.) Roll into a rectangle 12 inches by 5 inches. Cut each rectangle into 3 long strips, leaving them joined at one end by a ½-inch piece. Braid the strips. Tuck under the ends to make the dough about the same length as the bake pan. Place in the pan.

SECOND RISING
45 mins.

Place the pans in the warm place, cover with wax paper and leave until the center of the dough has risen ½ inch above the level of the edge of the pan.

BAKING
350°
40–45 mins.

Preheat oven to 350°. Bake in the oven until they are a golden brown. When tapping the bottom crust yields a hard hollow sound, they are done. If not, return to the oven for an additional 10 minutes. Midway in the bake period, and again near the end, shift the loaves so they are exposed equally to the temperature variations in the oven.

FINAL STEP

Remove bread from the oven. Turn from the pans and place on a metal rack to cool before slicing.

BOVRIL AND CHEESE LOAF

[ONE SMALL LOAF]

Bovril Toast was on the breakfast menu at Harrods, the famous department store in London, and it was delicious. Spread like thick jam, it was dark brown, salty and tasted of fine English beef which it was. I wrote the Bovril people to inquire if the beef extract might not also be used *in* bread rather than on it.

Miss D. W. Flowerdew, nutritionist, said yes, certainly, and sent this recipe tested in the Bovril experimental kitchen in London.

Bovril is available in a small 4-ounce glass bottle in the U.S. and Canada in large food markets and food specialty shops. Bovril is not inexpensive, be forewarned.

INGREDIENTS

1 package dry yeast
¼ cup warm water (105°–115°)
1 tablespoon Bovril
¼ cup warm water (105°–115°)
1½ to 2 cups all-purpose flour, approximately
1 teaspoon salt
2 teaspoons butter, room temperature
1½ cups grated sharp Cheddar cheese
To brush: 1 teaspoon milk

BAKING PAN

One small (7½ x 3½) loaf pan, greased or Teflon. If glass, reduce oven heat 25°.

PREPARATION
18 mins.

Sprinkle the yeast into the ¼ cup of water in a small bowl, and stir briskly to dissolve. Set aside.

Stir the Bovril into the ¼ cup of water to dissolve. Set aside.

Measure 1 cup flour into a mixing bowl and stir in salt. Drop butter into the flour and rub it into the mixture with the fingertips.

Pour both the yeast and Bovril mixture into the dry ingredients, and blend together. Stir in the Cheddar cheese. Add balance of the flour, a half cup at a time, first with the spoon and then by hand. Work it into a rough ball. If the dough is moist and sticky, sprinkle on a bit more flour.

FIRST RISING
1 hour

Kneading will come later. Now cover the bowl with plastic wrap and put in a warm place (80°–85°) until dough has doubled in size.

KNEADING
10 mins.

Turn back the plastic wrap, take out the dough and place it on a lightly floured work surface—counter top or bread board—and knead. It is such a small portion of dough that it will be difficult to maintain a rhythm in the kneading.

SECOND RISING
45 mins.

Return the dough to the bowl, replace the plastic wrap and put it in the warm place until the dough has doubled in volume.

SHAPING
10 mins.

Punch down the dough, turn it onto the work surface again, and knead for 30 seconds to press out the bubbles. Make the dough into a ball and let it rest under a towel for 4 minutes to relax it. Form the loaf by pressing the ball of dough into a flat oval, roughly the length of the prepared baking pan. Fold the oval in half, pinch the seam tightly to seal, tuck under the ends, and place in the pan, seam down.

THIRD RISING
40 mins.

Cover the dough with a piece of wax paper, and return it to the warm place until the dough has risen to the level of the edge of the pan.

BAKING
425°
30–40 mins.

Preheat oven to 425°. Brush the top of the loaf with milk, taking care that none of it runs to the sides of the pan where it may stick during the baking. Bake in the oven until the loaf tests done. When tapping the bottom crust yields a hard hollow sound, it is baked. Midway in the bake period and again near the end of it turn the loaf around in the oven.

FINAL STEP

Remove bread from the oven. Place the loaf on a wire rack to cool before serving. This makes delicious toast. It will keep for more than a week if wrapped tightly in foil or plastic, and can be frozen for several months.

A fine bread treat for a company brunch or a buffet.

KHACHAPURI—*GEORGIAN CHEESE BREAD*

[ONE LOAF]

The dough in this delightful loaf from the Russian Caucasus is rolled thin and baked around a filling of creamed Munster cheese. The dough is lifted up in folds around the cheese, and the folds are twisted into a small knot on top. It is baked to a lovely over-all brown.

Sliced thinly, the bread goes well at a brunch or a tea, as well as served with cocktails or with soup. In Georgia it is also made into small diamond-shaped tarts sold by street vendors.

INGREDIENTS

2 cups all-purpose flour, approximately
1 package dry yeast
1 teaspoon salt
2 teaspoons sugar
¼ cup non-fat dry milk
½ cup hot tap water (120°–130°)
4 tablespoons butter, room temperature
Filling: 1 pound Munster cheese
1 tablespoon butter
1 egg

BAKING PAN

One round 9-inch pan, greased or Teflon, with 1½- or 2-inch sides. You may wish to use a dark, well-used pan. A shiny new aluminum pan will not allow the loaf to become a deep rich brown.

PREPARATION
15 mins.

First, the dough.

In a mixing bowl measure 1 cup of flour and stir in the yeast, salt, sugar, milk, and the water. Add butter.

Beat in the electric mixer at medium-high speed for 3 minutes, or an equal length of time with a wooden spoon.

Stop mixer. Stir in the balance of the flour, a half cup at a time, first with the spoon and then by hand. The dough will be a rough, shaggy mass that will clean the sides of the bowl. If the dough is slack, and the moisture breaks through, add small sprinkles of flour.

KNEADING
8 mins.

Turn the dough onto a lightly floured work surface—counter top or bread board—and knead with the rhythmic 1-2-3 motion of push-turn-fold. The dough will become smooth and elastic, and bubbles will form under the surface of the dough. If it sticks to the hands or to the work surface, sprinkle on a little flour. Break the kneading rhythm occasionally by crashing the dough down hard against the counter top.

FIRST RISING
1 hour

Place the dough back in the clean mixing bowl and pat with buttered or greased fingers to keep the surface from crusting. Cover the bowl tightly with plastic wrap and move to a warm place (80°–85°) until the dough has risen to about twice its original size.

SECOND RISING
45 mins.

Turn back the plastic and punch down the dough with the fingers. Fold the sides of the dough over the center, and turn the ball over. Replace the plastic and return to the warm place.

THE FILLING
15 mins.

In the meantime, grate the cheese and combine it with the butter and egg in a large mixing bowl. Beat vigorously until it is smooth. Puré in a food mill or rub it through a fine sieve, with the back of a large spoon, over a bowl.

SHAPING
20 mins.

Punch down the dough, knead for 30 seconds to press out the bubbles. Let the dough rest on the lightly floured work surface for 4 or 5 minutes. Roll the dough into a large circle, about 22 inches in diameter. Stop for a moment or so halfway through the process to allow the dough to relax. This makes it much easier to work.

Slip the cake tin under the round of dough, taking care not to tear it. Carefully press the dough down into the pan, leaving the excess draped over the sides.

Spoon the filling onto the dough and mound about 3 inches high. Plan to make 6 or 8 drapes of dough into the center. Lift the edge up and over the filling. Continue around the pan until all the dough is folded into the center. Gather the ends of the dough that meet in the center and twist into a small knot.

RESTING
15 mins.

Set the loaf aside to rest for 15 minutes while the oven heats to 375°.

BAKING
375°
1 hour

Bake in the oven until the loaf is golden brown. It is difficult to test for doneness in the usual way because the hot cheese filling is misleading if pierced with a metal skewer. Rely on the color of the dough.

FINAL STEP

Remove bread from the oven. Let the loaf rest for 15 minutes before lifting it out of the pan with a broad spatula, and onto the rack to cool. It is fragile while hot so be careful with it.

When the loaf has cooled, slice and serve.

SEVENTEEN

Potato Breads

Potato Plant
Frankfort-am-Main, 1620

The potato—and the water it is boiled in—has long been a favorite of the American home baker because it produces a crisp crust and a moist slice, with a delightful home-baked flavor. Instant potato flakes or granules can be substituted; however, you do forgo the dividend of potato water that comes with doing the boiling yourself.

The potato grew wild in Peru and was taken to Europe by Spanish explorers in 1530. It reached England and Ireland in 1586. The first authenticated report of the potato in the U.S. was in Londonderry, N.H., in 1719. Because the stock came from Ireland, it was known thereafter as the Irish potato.

Experiment, too, with potato flour and potato starch. In a recipe that calls for 4 cups of white flour, substitute ½ cup of potato flour or starch for 1 cup of white flour. Increase the proportion over a number of bakings until you learn what makes the most desirable crispness and crunchiness of a loaf.

ROADSIDE POTATO BREAD

[THREE HUSKY LOAVES]

Farm kitchens for years have been filled with the lovely aroma of fresh baked potato bread which has the crusty goodness and special texture that only the addition of potato seems to give a loaf of white bread. There is an easier way than peeling, cooking and mashing potatoes because now it can be done with instant potato flakes. Milk substitutes for the starch-rich water in which the potatoes were boiled, giving the bread increased nutritional value and helping to brown the crusts.

This is a recipe from a Pennsylvania farm wife who sold her potato bread in a small roadside market. With 10 cups of flour, it makes a large batch of dough.

INGREDIENTS

10 cups all-purpose or bread flour, approximately
2 packages dry yeast
1 cup non-fat dry milk
⅓ cup sugar
1 tablespoon salt
⅓ cup instant potato flakes
3 cups hot tap water (120°–130°)
⅓ cup lard or butter, room temperature
Cornmeal, to dust pans

BAKING PANS

Three medium (8½ x 4½) loaf pans, greased or Teflon. If glass, reduce oven heat 25°.

PREPARATION
15 mins.

Put 4 cups of flour in a large mixing bowl and stir in the dry ingredients—yeast, milk, sugar, salt, and potato flakes. Pour in water and beat 2 minutes by hand with a wooden spoon or with an electric mixer at medium speed. Add the lard, beat until it has been thoroughly worked into the batter. Add additional flour, a cup at a time, working first with a spoon and then with the fingers until the dough is moist, roughly formed but not sticky. You will sense when it is accepting no more flour.

KNEADING
8 mins.

Turn the dough out on a lightly floured surface—counter top or bread board. Cover and let rest for about 15 minutes. Knead until the dough is soft, smooth and is elastic and alive under your hands.

FIRST RISING
1½ hours

Return to a greased bowl, turning the dough to oil it all over. Cover with plastic wrap and put it in a warm place (80°–85°) until it has doubled in bulk.

SECOND RISING
45 mins.

Turn back the plastic wrap and with the fingers and fist punch down the dough; cover again. Let rise until doubled.

SHAPING
10 mins.

Turn out onto the floured work surface and divide into 3 equal parts. Round into balls, cover with a cloth or wax paper and let them rest for 10 minutes. Meanwhile, prepare the pans. Sprinkle bottoms and sides of pans with cornmeal to give the crust an interesting look. Shape dough into loaves and place in pans.

THIRD RISING
1 hour

Cover the pans with wax paper and return to the warm place. Let rise until doubled.

BAKING
375°
50 mins.

Preheat oven to 375°. Place in the oven until the loaves are a rich brown. When tapping the bottom crust yields a hard hollow sound, they are done.

FINAL STEP

Remove bread from the oven. Turn from pans and place on metal racks to cool. This bread freezes well, and makes delicious toast.

POTATO BRAID

[TWO BIG HUSKY BRAIDED LOAVES]

This old-fashioned farm recipe has been used by fine home bakers for almost as long as the potato has been in North America. The potato, both the flesh and the water in which it is boiled, gives this bread an unusually good texture. Potato water has long been considered ideal for making yeast dough. It is a joy to work—plump and alive under the hands. It can be made with instant mashed potatoes (with good results) but that's a different loaf entirely. This is the way it has been done for many generations—and the bread is unexcelled.

INGREDIENTS

3 or 4 medium potatoes, peeled and boiled (reserve water)
2 packages dry yeast
½ cup warm water (105°–115°)
1½ cups potato (through a sieve)
½ cup shortening, room temperature
1 cup potato water, hot (120°–125°)
2 tablespoons sugar
2 teaspoons salt
¼ cup non-fat dry milk
5½ cups all-purpose or bread flour, approximately
Glaze: 1 egg white and 1 tablespoon water
Sprinkle of sesame seeds

BAKING SHEET OR PANS — One baking sheet or two large (9 x 5) loaf pans, greased or Teflon, metal or glass. If the latter, reduce oven heat 25°.

PREPARATION 30 mins. — Peel and boil 3 or 4 medium-size potatoes until they are done. Pour off the water and reserve.

20 mins. — In a small bowl or cup scatter the yeast over water and stir briskly with a wire whisk to hasten its action. Set aside.

In a large bowl mash 1½ cups of potato, forcing it through a sieve. (Keep the balance of the potato and water in the refrigerator for the next bread baking.) Add shortening to the hot potato, and with a wooden spoon stir until it is melted. Add the potato water, sugar, salt and milk. Blend with 50 strokes.

Pour in the yeast mixture, stir and add 2 cups of flour. Beat until smooth and the dough forms strands from the sides of the bowl. Gradually stir in the remaining flour, working it in with the hands when the dough gets too difficult to stir with a utensil.

The dough should be elastic but firm since it must hold its shape unsupported on a baking sheet (if that's your selection).

KNEADING 8 mins. — Turn out the dough on a lightly floured board or counter top. Potato bread dough is springy and easy to knead. Knead, adding more flour if the dough should stick to the board or the fingers. (About 6 minutes with a dough hook.)

FIRST RISING 45 mins. — Put the dough in a greased bowl, cover tightly with plastic wrap and put in a warm place (80°–85°) until double in bulk.

SHAPING 25 mins. — Braided potato loaves are a delight to make since the dough is so easy to work. They can either be panned or hearth-baked on a sheet.

For two large pans, make the braids about 10-inches long. If for a baking sheet, about 14 inches.

Punch down the dough, turn it onto work surface again, and divide into two pieces. Set one piece aside for the second loaf. Now divide the one piece into three. Let them relax for 2 or 3 minutes before rolling them back and forth under the palms to stretch them out. Lay them side by side, and braid from the middle to each end. Repeat with the second loaf.

For a loaf pan, tuck under the ends and fit into the pans.

For the baking sheet, pinch ends tightly together.

SECOND RISING
45 mins.

Cover the loaves carefully with wax paper (hold aloft with water tumblers) so the expanding dough won't touch it. Place in a warm place until double in bulk.

BAKING
400°
10 mins.
350°
35 mins.

Preheat oven to 400°. Brush the loaves with the egg white glaze and sprinkle liberally with sesame seeds. Bake in the hot oven for 10 minutes—reduce heat to 350° and bake for an additional 35 minutes. When tapping the bottom crust yields a hard hollow sound, they are done. If not, return to the oven for an additional 10 minutes. If the loaves appear to be browning too quickly, cover with a piece of foil or brown sack paper.

Midway in the bake period shift the loaves—turn halfway around—so that they are exposed equally to the eccentricities of the oven.

FINAL STEP

Remove from oven and place on wire racks to cool. This bread freezes well and is superb toasted. These are big loaves.

POTATO BREAD

[TWO LOAVES]

There is a wonderful fragrance about this bread that reaches into every nook of the house. In this recipe there is no substitute for potato water—the liquid in which potatoes are boiled. Instant potato flakes could be used as the chief ingredient but they do not produce the important by-product, the starch-rich water. Two potatoes are all that is needed, and boiling them will produce the necessary 1½ cups of liquid.

It makes a lovely white loaf that is delicious warm from the oven, and toasted. It freezes well, wrapped tightly in plastic wrap or foil.

INGREDIENTS

Two small- to medium-size potatoes, peeled and boiled (reserve water)
1 package dry yeast
¼ cup warm water (105°–115°)
1½ cups potato water, heated to 120°
¼ cup (½ stick) butter, room temperature

1 tablespoon salt
2 tablespoons sugar
¾ cup boiled potatoes, riced or mashed (see above)
6 cups all-purpose or bread flour, approximately

BAKING PANS Two medium (8½ x 4½) loaf pans, greased or Teflon. If glass, reduce oven heat by 25°.

PREPARATION
30 mins.

Beforehand, boil potatoes in water sufficient to make 1½ cups liquid for the recipe. Add nothing to the potatoes in the cooking process. Rice or mash them. Set both potatoes and liquid aside.

15 mins.

In a small bowl dissolve the yeast in water. Stir briskly with a whisk or fork.

Heat the potato water (120°) and pour over the butter, salt and sugar in a large bowl. Stir until butter has melted; add mashed potato and yeast. Gradually, a cup at a time, add flour to the mixture. Stir in with a large wooden spoon and when the dough begins to form, work with the hands. It will be a rough mass that will clean the sides of the bowl.

KNEADING
8 mins.

Turn the dough onto a floured work surface—counter top or bread board—and begin to knead with a strong push-turn-fold motion of the hands. If the dough is slack or moist (and sticky) add small amounts of flour. When properly kneaded, the dough will be smooth, elastic and feel alive under the hands.

FIRST RISING
1½ hours

Return the dough to the bowl, pat it with buttered fingers so that it will not crust, and cover with plastic wrap. Put in a warm place (80°–85°) until the dough has more than doubled in bulk.

SHAPING
20 mins.

Turn back the plastic wrap, punch down the dough and turn it out again on the floured work surface. Knead for 30 seconds to work out the bubbles. With a knife cut the dough in two pieces. Let them rest under a towel for 10 minutes before shaping into loaves. Flatten each piece into an oval, fold in half, pinch the seam tightly closed, pat into shape and drop into the pan—seam under.

SECOND RISING
35 mins.

Cover the loaves with wax paper or foil and let them rise in a warm place until doubled in volume.

BAKING
400°
15 mins.
350°
25 mins.

Preheat oven to 400°. Bake in a hot oven for 15 minutes, reduce heat to 350°. Continue baking until the loaves are a golden crusty brown, and leave the sides of the pans—about 40 minutes total time. When tapping the bottom crust yields a hard hollow sound, they are baked.

FINAL STEP

Remove from the oven. Turn the loaves onto a metal rack to cool before serving.

POTATO STARTER WHITE BREAD

[THREE MEDIUM LOAVES AND A DOZEN DINNER ROLLS]

This loaf is a country kind of bread, with a raw potato starter and lard for shortening.

There is more time spent in preparing this loaf than for most breads because the starter has to be made (page 284) and, before it can be used, it must double in volume so there is enough for the recipe as well as to replenish the starter jar. It has a delicious flavor, however, that makes the extra time seem worth it—especially when toasted.

INGREDIENTS

2 cups Raw Potato Starter (see page 284)
1½ cups *each* water and all-purpose flour
2½ cups warm water (105°–115°)
1 cup non-fat dry milk
4 tablespoons sugar
½ teaspoon ginger
1 package dry yeast
7½ cups all-purpose flour, approximately
4 tablespoons lard or other shortening, room temperature
3 teaspoons salt

BAKING PANS AND SHEET

Three medium (8½ x 4½) baking pans, greased or Teflon, and one baking sheet (for rolls), greased or Teflon. If glass pans are used reduce oven heat 25°.

PREPARATION
Overnight

The night before, pour the starter into a bowl and add 1½ cups *each* water and flour. Mix well. Cover tightly with plastic wrap and place in a warm spot overnight.

20 mins.

On bake day, turn back the plastic covering, stir well and pour 2 cups of the starter into a large bowl. Set aside. Return the remaining starter to the jar and place in the refrigerator for future starter breads.

To the starter add warm water, milk, sugar, ginger, yeast and 3 cups of flour. Stir thoroughly and let stand 3 minutes. Add the lard, salt and 3 cups additional flour, ½ cup at a time, stirring first with the spoon and then working by hand. The dough will be a soft, ragged mass that cleans the sides of the bowl.

KNEADING
8 mins.

Spread flour on the work surface and turn out the dough. Knead with a strong push-turn motion until it is smooth and elastic. If moisture should break through, sprinkle flour on the dough and on the hands. Soon it will lose its stickiness and feel alive and somewhat rubbery under the palms.

FIRST RISING
1 hour

Return the dough to the bowl, pat with shortening so the air does not form a crust, and cover tightly with plastic wrap. Set in a warm place (80°–85°) until it has doubled in bulk.

SHAPING
12 mins.

Punch down the dough and turn it out onto the work surface again. Knead 30 seconds to press out the bubbles; divide dough into four equal pieces. Shape three into loaves by flattening each into an oval as wide as the length of the pan. Fold in half, seal the seam tightly, and pat into shape. Place in the pan with the seam and ends tucked under.

For a delightful variation to accompany a salad or soup, roll one of the three pieces into a rectangle, brush with soft butter, sprinkle with pepper and celery seed, roll up tightly and seal. Fashion the fourth piece into a dozen dinner rolls if you wish.

SECOND RISING
45 mins.

Cover the dough with wax paper and return to the warm place until doubled in bulk or has reached the edge of the pans.

BAKING
375°
45 mins.

Preheat oven to 375°. Bake in the oven until the loaves are deep brown and loose in their pans. The rolls will be baked in about 25 minutes.

FINAL STEP

Remove bread from the oven. Turn the loaves onto a wire rack to cool before serving. This makes marvelous toast.

SISTER JENNIE'S POTATO BREAD

[TWO LOAVES]

One cup of potato passed through a sieve or food mill gives this loaf of Shaker bread a positive potato flavor. It rises high and grandly above the edge of a large bread pan. The moisture in the potato supplies most of the liquid except for a quarter cup of water used to dissolve the yeast.

A member of a Shaker community in Ohio, Sister Jennie said to allow eight hours for this loaf to rise, but I find that it can be done in considerably less time.

She also advised—

"Bread rises more quickly in the daytime when the kitchen fires are kept going than at night when only the embers smolder on the hearth; therefore 4 hours in the daytime is equal to 12 hours of rising at night."

Finally:

"Bread is the one food one can eat thrice daily and not tire of."

INGREDIENTS

1 cup mashed potato (unseasoned)
1 package dry yeast
¼ cup warm water (105°–115°)
2 eggs, beaten
½ cup sugar
¼ teaspoon salt
4 cups bread flour, approximately
½ cup (1 stick) butter, room temperature

BAKING PANS

Two large (9 x 5) baking pans, greased or Teflon. If glass, reduce oven heat 25°.

PREPARATION (FIRST STEP) 15 mins.

Beforehand, mash potatoes and put them through a sieve or food mill. Set aside.

Dissolve yeast in warm water in a small bowl or cup. Stir briskly with a fork or whisk to hasten the action.

In a large bowl combine the potato, eggs, ¼ cup sugar, salt, yeast and 2 cups flour. Stir until a rough ball has formed. Don't knead at this stage.

FIRST RISING 2 hours

Cover the bowl with plastic wrap and put in a warm place (80°–85°) until dough doubles in volume. Meanwhile, cream the butter and the remaining ¼ cup of sugar. Set aside.

PREPARATION (SECOND STEP) 10 mins.

Remove the plastic wrap and beat down the batter. Stir in the creamed butter and sugar. Add the balance of the flour, a half cup at a time, first with the spoon and then by hand. The dough will be a rough, shaggy mass that will clean the sides of the bowl. If the dough continues moist and sticky, sprinkle on small amounts of flour.

KNEADING
8 mins.

Turn the dough onto a lightly floured work surface—counter top or bread board—and knead with the rhythmic 1-2-3 motion of push-turn-fold. The dough will become smooth and elastic, and bubbles will rise under the surface of the dough. (Knead 6 minutes under the dough hook.)

SECOND RISING
1½ hours

Place the dough back in the mixing bowl and pat with buttered or greased fingers. Cover the bowl with plastic wrap and leave in the warm place until the dough has risen to about twice its original volume. You can test if it has risen by poking a finger in it; the dent will remain.

SHAPING
10 mins.

Punch down dough, turn it out onto the work surface again, and knead for 30 seconds to press out the bubbles. With a sharp knife, divide the dough into two pieces. Shape into balls. Let rest under a towel for 3 to 4 minutes. Form a loaf by pressing the ball into a flat oval, roughly the length of the bread pan. Fold the oval in half, pinch the seam tightly to seal, tuck under the ends, and place in the pan, seam down. Repeat with the second loaf.

THIRD RISING
40 mins.

Place the loaves in the warm place, cover with wax paper and let them rise to double their volume.

BAKING
375°
40 mins.

Preheat the oven to 375°. Bake in the oven until golden brown and test done. Turn one loaf out of its pan and tap the bottom crust with a forefinger. A hard hollow sound means the bread is baked. If not, return to the oven for an additional 10 minutes. If the tops of the loaves appear to be browning too quickly, cover with a piece of foil or brown sack paper. Midway in the bake period, and again near the end of it, shift the pans so the loaves are exposed equally to temperature variations in the oven.

FINAL STEP

Remove bread from the oven. Turn from the pans and place on a metal rack to cool before slicing. This loaf will keep well for several days, wrapped in plastic or foil. It also will keep for 4 or 5 months in the freezer. It makes fine toast.

EIGHTEEN

Vegetable Breads

Pumpkin
Basle, 1542

A vegetable is only a vegetable in most kitchens and seldom is it considered an ingredient for bread. A shame. Some lend a most interesting texture and taste to a loaf.

There are four vegetables in these eight recipes—hardly a major challenge to a green thumb—but they make delicious breads. Carrot, onion, pumpkin, and tomato are the four although smaller portions of these and others are among ingredients elsewhere in the book.

CARROT BREAD

[TWO LOAVES]

An intrigued young friend calls this "rabbit bread." It is not. It is a wonderfully moist and delicate loaf that uses two cups of finely shredded carrots in a dough already quite yellow with 4 eggs. I usually bake carrot bread in two 1-pound coffee cans and serve it either sliced in wedges or in rounds. This loaf will keep for several weeks and freezes particularly well.

INGREDIENTS
2 cups raw carrot, finely shredded
4 eggs, room temperature
2 cups sugar
1¼ cups salad oil

3 cups all-purpose flour
2 teaspoons baking powder
1½ teaspoons baking soda
¼ teaspoon salt
2 teaspoons cinnamon

BAKING PANS

Two medium (8½ x 4½) loaf pans, greased or Teflon, or two 1-pound coffee cans. Be certain to place a circle of wax paper on the bottom of the cans to make it easier to remove the cylindrical loaves. Also, line the loaf pans with wax paper for easier removal. If glass pans are used, reduce oven heat 25°.

PREPARATION
10 mins.

Beforehand, shred raw carrots to make 2 cups and set aside. In a large bowl beat the eggs, and add the sugar gradually, beating until thick. Add oil gradually, and continue beating until thoroughly combined. Stir in flour, baking powder, baking soda, salt, and cinnamon, and blend until the mixture is smooth. Stir in the carrots.

FORMING
3 mins.

Pour the batter into pans.

BAKING
350°
1 hour

Let batter stand in the pans while the oven heats to 350°. Place tall cans on a lower shelf or the crowns of the loaves may push into the top of the oven. Bake loaves until they test done when a metal skewer inserted in the center of a loaf comes out clean and dry. If the batter is moist and clings to the probe, return the bread to the oven for an additional 10 minutes. Test again.

FINAL STEP

Remove bread from the oven. Let the loaves stand in the pans for 10 minutes before turning the bread onto a metal rack to cool. Patiently allow the loaf in the coffee can to work free by gently forcing it downward by a smooth thrust of the arms.

PUMPKIN WALNUT BREAD

[TWO LOAVES]

While it has been pumpkin pie that has won warm accolades for home bakers for generations, pumpkin in bread adds a new taste dimension to the vegetable's popularity that began at least 9,000 years ago in the Mexican highlands. There are also two cups of chopped walnuts divided between the two loaves, and these add color and a roughness to the texture that is pleasing.

Either fresh cooked or canned pumpkin can be used in this recipe. I suggest using a dark brown sugar to give the bread a richer look.

INGREDIENTS

1¾ cups cooked pumpkin, fresh or canned
1½ cups brown sugar, firmly packed
½ cup (1 stick) butter, room temperature
3 eggs, room temperature
5 cups all-purpose flour
2 tablespoons baking powder
1 teaspoon cinnamon
½ teaspoon *each* salt and nutmeg
2 cups walnuts, chopped

BAKING PANS

Two medium (8½ x 4½) loaf pans, greased or Teflon. If glass, reduce oven heat 25°.

PREPARATION
15 mins.

In a large bowl mix together pumpkin, brown sugar, butter and the eggs, lightly beaten. Blend. On a length of wax paper sift together flour, baking powder, cinnamon, salt and nutmeg.

Spoon or pour dry ingredients into the pumpkin mixture. Mix thoroughly. Stir in walnuts. Preheat oven to 350°.

FORMING
5 mins.

Pour into pans. Push the mixture into the corners with a spoon or spatula. Form the batter slightly higher along the sides than in the middle—to compensate for the rising crown during baking.

BAKING
350°
1 hour

Bake in the oven until a loaf tests done when a metal skewer inserted in the center comes out clean and dry. If moist particles cling to the probe, return the loaf to the oven for an additional 10 minutes. Test again.

FINAL STEP

Remove bread from the oven. Let the bread cool 10 minutes before turning it out of the pans. Warm quick bread is more fragile than a yeast loaf and should be handled with care. This loaf will develop a richer flavor if allowed to age a day or so before slicing. It will keep for at least two weeks wrapped in plastic or foil.

ONION TWIST BREAD

[TWO LOAVES]

In the kitchen, during the bake period, there can be no question that the chief ingredient of this loaf is onion.

The bread has the strength of aroma and taste to please the most discriminating onion fancier. While it is less strong after the loaf has cooled, it renews itself with vigor in the toaster.

The bread looks good as a twist—two pieces wrapped together and dropped into a baking pan. I use a French bread pan which is 1 inch longer and 1 inch narrower than a medium pan and gives the loaf an attractive elongated shape. The twists can also be laid directly on a baking sheet. However, be certain the ends are pinched together tightly.

Don't look for salt among the ingredients below. It is in the soup mix.

INGREDIENTS

4 to 4½ cups all-purpose flour
2 packages dry yeast
⅓ cup non-fat dry milk
1½ cups hot tap water (120°–130°)
2 tablespoons shortening, room temperature
2 tablespoons sugar
1 package onion soup mix (1⅜ oz.)
2 tablespoons grated Parmesan cheese
1 egg, room temperature

BAKING PANS OR SHEET

Two medium (8½ x 4½) baking pans, greased or Teflon, or one baking sheet, greased or Teflon. If glass pans are used, reduce oven heat 25°.

PREPARATION
20 mins.

In a large mixer bowl combine 2 cups of flour and yeast. In a saucepan measure milk, water, shortening, sugar, soup mix and cheese. Stir over low heat until warm (120°). Pour this into the dry mixture, add the egg and beat at low speed in the electric mixer for 30 seconds. Scrape down bowl.

Turn mixer to high for 3 minutes. Stop the mixer, and with a wooden spoon gradually stir in more flour to form a soft dough that will clean the sides of the bowl.

KNEADING
8 mins.

Sprinkle the work surface with flour and turn the dough onto it. Knead until the dough is smooth and elastic (5 minutes with a dough hook).

RESTING
20 mins.

Cover the dough with the inverted bowl and let rest on the counter top.

SHAPING
15 mins.

To make two twist loaves, divide the dough into 4 parts. Shape each piece into a smooth 12-inch roll. Twist 2 pieces together and press ends to seal. Tuck under the sealed ends, place loaf in prepared tin. Loaves can also be baked on a baking sheet. Place them 2 inches apart.

RISING
45 mins.

Cover with wax paper or foil until doubled in size. Dough will rise to about ½ inch above the edge of the pan.

BAKING
375°
40 mins.

Preheat oven to 375°. Bake in the oven until the crusts have browned. The loaves will draw away from the sides of the pans. When tapping the bottom crust yields a hard hollow sound, the bread is done.

FINAL STEP

Remove bread from the oven. Turn out on metal cooling racks. Brush with butter for a nice soft finish.

NON

[EIGHT PIECES]

Rolled as thin as the thickness of the freshly chopped onion in the dough will allow, Non is a delicious unleavened flat bread from the steppes of Central Asia. There it is served at breakfast with a type of sour yogurt or with a sharp cheese, or at a luncheon with fruit and tea. The recipe can easily be doubled or trebled for a large buffet or barbecue where it will find an enthusiastic reception.

INGREDIENTS

3 tablespoons butter, room temperature
1 cup onions, finely chopped
½ cup warm water (105°–115°)
1 teaspoon salt
1½ to 2 cups all-purpose flour, approximately

BAKING PAN

One heavy 10-to-12-inch pan or griddle to place over high heat.

PREPARATION
15 mins.

Melt 1 tablespoon of butter in a heavy skillet set over high heat, add onions, reduce the heat to low, and cook 3 to 5 minutes, or until the onions are soft but not brown. Place them in a small bowl and cool to room temperature.

Melt remaining butter in the skillet and pour into a large mixing bowl. Add water, onions, salt and 1½ cups of all-purpose flour, a half cup at a time. Work the dough into a ball. If it sticks to the fingers, add 1 or 2 teaspoons additional flour.

KNEADING
1–2 mins.

Turn out on a lightly floured work surface and knead only until the dough is slightly firm. Dust with flour if it sticks to the work surface or fingers.

SHAPING
15 mins.

Divide the dough into 8 pieces and shape each into a ball. Cluster them on the floured work surface and let them rest 3 minutes. Roll each ball into an 8-inch round. If the dough resists, move on to another round and return to the first one later. In the meantime it will have relaxed, and it will flatten and stretch with much less effort. Set the rounds aside as you complete them.

BAKING
3–4 mins. for each

Use either an ungreased pan, a metal griddle, or a soapstone griddle (such as I use). Place it over a high heat. When a drop of water vaporizes the moment it hits the hot surface, place 1 round in the center. Brown for 3 or 4 minutes on each side. Don't be concerned if the rounds brown unevenly.

FINAL STEP

Remove from the heat. Place the bread on a rack to dry, and bake and dry the remaining rounds in the same fashion.

Serve the bread in a basket or other porous container.

If the bread should become limp in a day or so, place the rounds in a single layer on a baking sheet and bake in a 250° oven for 5 to 10 minutes or until they are again crisp.

SERENDIPITY BREAD

[ONE ROUND LOAF]

Originally this was to have been a batter bread but during a football game on television I overshot the quantity of flour and came up with an absolutely delicious kneaded loaf. The rosemary and dill are particularly strong in a toasted slice.

If you want it as a batter bread there is no problem. Stop with 2 cups of flour.

INGREDIENTS

3 cups all-purpose flour, approximately
1 package dry yeast
¼ cup non-fat dry milk
1½ tablespoons sugar
1 teaspoon salt
1 cup hot tap water (120°–130°)
2 teaspoons shortening, room temperature
1 tablespoon instant minced onion
½ teaspoon *each* dried dill weed and rosemary
Topping: Swish of melted butter and a sprinkle of salt

BAKING PAN

One 8- or 9-inch cake or pie pan, greased or Teflon. If glass, reduce oven heat 25°.

PREPARATION
15 mins.

In a mixing bowl measure 1 cup of flour and add the yeast, milk, sugar and salt. Stir to mix.

In a saucepan pour the water over the shortening, and stir in onion, dill weed and rosemary. Pour the liquid into the flour and beat at slow speed 30 seconds; increase to medium high for 3 minutes. Turn off the mixer, gradually add additional flour, first with a spoon and then by hand, until a soft mass has formed and pulled away from the sides of the bowl.

KNEADING
8 mins.

Sprinkle flour on the work surface and turn out the dough to knead. With a strong push-turn-fold action knead the dough—adding a small portion of flour if it is wet and sticky—until it is smooth and elastic under the hands.

FIRST RISING
1½ hours

Return the dough to the mixing bowl, pat the dough with greased or buttered fingers and cover tightly with a length of plastic wrap. The dough will double in volume. You can test if it has risen by poking a finger in it; the dent will remain.

SHAPING
10 mins.

Remove the plastic wrap, punch down the dough. Drop it on the floured work surface. Work it by hand for a moment or two to force out the air bubbles. Form into a round ball, flatten slightly, and place in the pan.

SECOND RISING
45 mins.

Cover the pan with wax paper and return to the warm place until dough doubles in bulk.

BAKING
400°
15 mins.
350°
35 mins.

Preheat oven to 400°. Bake in a hot oven for 15 minutes. Reduce heat to 350° for an additional 35 minutes or until the loaf is golden brown. A wooden toothpick inserted in the loaf will come out clean and dry when done.

FINAL STEP

Remove bread from the oven and place on a metal rack to cool. Brush with melted butter and sprinkle lightly with salt (coarse preferably).

TOMATO CARAWAY BREAD

[FOUR SLENDER LOAVES]

Two cups plus of tomato juice in dough to make 4 long loaves is sufficient to color them a salmon pink and to give a definite but not overpowering taste of tomato. The caraway seeds sprinkled on beaten egg brushed on the crust may be substituted by either poppy or sesame seeds with equally good results. The dark seeds (caraway or poppy) contrast nicely with the pinkish brown crust.

INGREDIENTS

6 to 6½ cups all-purpose flour, approximately
1 package dry yeast
2¼ cups tomato juice
2 tablespoons butter or margarine, room temperature
2 teaspoons salt
2 tablespoons sugar
Glaze: 1 egg, slightly beaten, and 1 tablespoon caraway or other seeds

BAKING SHEET

Baking sheet or sheets, greased or Teflon. Four loaves may require more than the one sheet.

PREPARATION
20 mins.

In a large mixing bowl measure 2 cups of flour, and the yeast. Stir.

Pour the tomato juice in a saucepan, add the butter, salt and sugar—and warm over a low heat to melt or soften the butter. Liquid should be warmed to 110° to 120°. Pour the tomato blend in the flour and beat 50 strokes with a wooden spoon or 30 seconds at low speed in an electric mixer. Add 1 cup flour and beat

150 strong strokes with the spoon or 3 minutes at high speed with the mixer.

Stop the beater, and continue to add flour, beating with the spoon until stiff and then work in the flour by hand. The dough will be a soft mass that cleans the sides of the bowl.

KNEADING
8 mins.

Turn the dough onto a work surface, lightly dusted with flour, and begin the kneading process—push-turn-fold. Add small sprinkles of flour if the moisture should break through.

FIRST RISING
1 hour

Place the dough back into the bowl, pat it with greased fingers, and cover tightly with a length of plastic wrap. Put in a warm place (80°–85°) until dough has doubled in bulk. You can test if it has risen by poking a finger in it; the dent will remain.

SHAPING
15 mins.

Turn dough out onto work surface again. These are long thin loaves shaped by first dividing the dough in four parts. Roll each into a rectangle—as long as the length of the bake sheet. Roll into a tight roll, making certain the seam and ends are pinched together. If this seam is not a secure one, the roll may unwind as the bread expands in the oven. After the seam has been sealed, roll the length of dough back and forth under the palms to smooth it, and to lengthen it if necessary. Place on the bake sheet. Repeat with the other pieces.

SECOND RISING
45 mins.

Cover with wax paper and return to the warm place until the loaves have doubled in size.

BAKING
375°
30 mins.

Preheat oven to 375°. Brush the loaves with the beaten egg and sprinkle with caraway seeds. Place in the oven. When lightly browned and tapping the bottom crust yields a hard hollow sound, they are done.

FINAL STEP

Remove bread from the oven. Place on a metal rack to cool before serving, or freezing.

CARROT-COCONUT BREAD

[ONE LARGE OR TWO SMALL LOAVES]

At one point in the preparation of this curious loaf it will look like a carrot salad liberally mixed with shredded coconut. Even when the flour is blended in, and the batter has been spooned into the pans, it does not look like bread. The flour will all but disappear and it seems unlikely that it will soon become a dark brown brick of delicious goodness—a taste reminiscent of fruit cake and macaroons. And the carrots, for some strange reason, don't taste like carrots at all.

It should age for 3 or 4 days in the refrigerator before serving. This recipe will make 2 small loaves, an ideal size for gift giving.

INGREDIENTS

3 eggs, room temperature
½ cup oil
1 teaspoon vanilla
2 cups *each* finely shredded carrots and packaged grated coconut
1 cup *each* raisins and chopped walnuts
2 cups all-purpose flour
½ teaspoon salt
1 teaspoon *each* baking soda, baking powder, and cinnamon
1 cup sugar

BAKING PANS

One large (9 x 5) loaf pan, greased or Teflon, or two small (7½ x 3½) pans, metal or glass. If glass, reduce oven heat 25°. Line pan or pans with buttered wax paper.

PREPARATION
15 mins.

In a large bowl break the eggs and beat until light in color. Stir in oil and vanilla. Blend in the carrots, coconut, raisins and nuts. In another bowl sift or blend together the flour, salt, baking soda, baking powder, cinnamon and sugar. Sift or spoon these dry ingredients into the carrot-coconut mixture. Stir only until it is well blended. The flour will all but disappear as it is absorbed by the wet ingredients. No matter.

FORMING
3 mins.

Spoon the mixture into the prepared tin or tins. Let stand while the oven heats to 350°.

BAKING
350°
1 hour

Bake in the oven until the loaf is a dark golden brown and tests done when a wooden toothpick inserted in the center of a loaf comes out clean and dry.

FINAL STEP

Remove bread from the oven. Let the loaves cool completely on the wire rack before wrapping tightly in plastic wrap or foil to put in the refrigerator to mature for 2 or 3 days before serving.

ONION LOVER'S BREAD

[ONE LARGE OR TWO SMALL BRAIDS]

This is a braided loaf, in which each braid is filled with a mixture of onions, butter, garlic salt, Parmesan cheese, poppy seeds and paprika. Its antecedents can be traced to pizza but it took imagination and daring to wrap six such ingredients in a lovely bread dough, braid them into a twist, and bake. The result (and you *must* love onion) is uncommonly good. It is a bread that will be remembered.

INGREDIENTS

1 package dry yeast
4 cups all-purpose flour, approximately
1¼ cups hot tap water (120°–130°)
¼ cup sugar
1½ teaspoons salt
⅓ cup non-fat dry milk
½ cup (1 stick) butter, softened
1 egg, room temperature
Filling: ¼ cup butter, melted
1 cup finely chopped onion or ¼ cup instant onions
1 tablespoon *each* grated Parmesan cheese and poppy seeds
1 teaspoon *each* garlic salt and paprika

BAKING SHEET

One baking sheet, greased or Teflon. The braid can also be baked in a tin.

PREPARATION
20 mins.

The dough is prepared first, and while it is rising the filling is made.

In a large mixer bowl, stir yeast into 2 cups of flour. In a saucepan add water to the sugar, salt, dry milk and butter. When the butter is quite soft, but not necessarily melted, add the egg and pour all the liquid into the flour-yeast. Blend at a low speed until moistened. Increase speed to medium and beat for 2 minutes. The beating can be done with a wooden spoon, if preferred.

Stop the mixer and stir in by hand 1½ or 2 additional cups of flour to form a soft dough that cleans the sides of the bowl. Unlike most other yeast dough this one will be allowed to rise *before* kneading.

FIRST RISING
1 hour

Cover the bowl tightly with plastic wrap and let rise in a warm place (80°–85°) until dough is light and doubled in volume.

THE FILLING

Melt the butter in a medium saucepan. Remove from heat and stir in the other ingredients—the onion, cheese, poppy seeds, garlic salt, and paprika. Mix thoroughly and set aside until ready to form the braids.

KNEADING AND SHAPING
8 mins.

Knock down the dough and turn out on a floured work surface. The dough may be slightly sticky because it is quite soft. However, toss or throw the dough down hard against the work surface until it becomes elastic and is no longer sticky. Keep the fingers dusted with flour and scrape the sticky dough from the counter top with a metal spatula or knife blade.

25 mins.

Let the dough relax for about 5 minutes and then roll it into a 12 x 18-inch rectangle. For one loaf, cut into three 4-inch-wide strips, or, for two loaves, six 9 x 4-inch strips. If the strips pull back and shrink when they are cut from the larger piece, let them rest for 2 or 3 minutes and roll to size.

Carefully spread the filling on the pieces, leaving a ½-inch margin around the edge. This permits a good seal that will hold and not open when the braids begin to expand in the oven.

Roll each piece from the long side. Stop the roll one inch from the edge. *Lift the edge up to the roll and pinch together*. Don't take the roll to the edge for this will push the filling onto the clear margin and make it difficult to get a firm seal.

Lift the rolls onto the baking sheet and braid 3 rolls together, pinching the ends together tightly.

SECOND RISING
45 mins.

Cover with a length of wax paper and place the baking sheet in a warm place until the braids have doubled in bulk.

BAKING
350°
35 mins.

Preheat oven to 350°. Bake in the oven. When the loaves are golden brown and tapping the bottom crust yields a hard hollow sound, they are done.

FINAL STEP

Remove bread from the oven. Place on a metal rack to cool somewhat before serving. The bread is especially good served warm from the oven, however.

NINETEEN

Spice Breads

Saffron
Lyons, 1579

Breads made with spices and herbs fill the house with provocative aromas and gladden the tongue with piquant tastes.

A spice is a part of a plant grown in the tropics, be it root, seed, leaf, or bark. Pepper. An herb is a leaf of a plant grown in the temperate zone. Mint.

While spices and herbs are used frequently in recipes throughout the book, they do not dominate or take charge of the flavor as they do in this chapter. There are three exceptions, strongly spiced, found elsewhere: Jalapeño (Corn), and Pepper Cheese Loaf and Tabasco Cheese Bread (Cheese).

Spices and herbs are perishable. Use them shortly after purchase while the flavors are at their best. Keep tightly closed and store in a cool place.

HERB AND CELERY BREAD

[ONE LARGE OR TWO SMALL LOAVES]

Ground sage, nutmeg and celery seed give this yeast bread a spiciness that is a particular delight when toasted. It can be baked on a flat sheet or in a pie pan, a casserole, or large brioche tins.

It is an easy loaf to make.

INGREDIENTS

3 to 3½ cups all-purpose or bread flour, approximately
1 package dry yeast
1½ teaspoons salt
¼ cup non-fat dry milk
2 tablespoons sugar
2 tablespoons shortening, room temperature
½ teaspoon nutmeg
1 teaspoon ground sage
2 teaspoons celery seed
1 cup hot tap water (120°–130°)
1 egg, room temperature

BAKING SHEET, PAN, TINS OR CASSEROLE

One baking sheet or 9-inch pie pan, greased or Teflon. Option: Two 6-inch brioche tins or one 2-quart casserole.

PREPARATION
15 mins.

In a large bowl measure 1½ cups of flour and add yeast, salt, dry milk, sugar, shortening, nutmeg, sage, and celery seed. Mix thoroughly—150 strong strokes. When the water is poured in, add egg and stir. Gradually add flour—¼ cup at a time—until the dough is formed into a rough shaggy mass. If the moisture persists in breaking through, add ¼ cup of flour and work it into the dough.

KNEADING
8 mins.

Knead on a lightly floured work surface until smooth. In the early stages keep flour dusted on the fingers and on the work surface. The dough will grow responsive and alive under the hands.

FIRST RISING
1 hour

Return the dough to the bowl, pat with buttered fingers, cover the bowl with plastic wrap and put in a warm place (80°–85°) until the dough has doubled.

SHAPING
8 mins.

Punch down the dough and turn onto the floured work surface again. Knead for 30 seconds to press out the bubbles. For one large loaf, shape into a ball, place on a baking sheet, or in a 9-inch pie plate or 2-quart casserole. For two loaves, divide the dough with a sharp knife and fashion each piece into a ball. Put in large 6-inch brioche tins.

SECOND RISING
50 mins.

Move the loaf or loaves to the warm place and cover with a length of wax paper. Let rise until double in bulk.

BAKING
400°
30–35 mins.

Preheat oven to 400°. Place in the oven. When tapping the bottom crust yields a hard hollow sound, they are done. If the crust is soft, return the loaf to the oven for an additional 10 minutes.

FINAL STEP

Remove bread from the oven. Place on wire racks to cool. Brush with melted butter or milk.

PAIN d'EPICES

[ONE LARGE OR TWO SMALL LOAVES]

This version of a famous French spice bread is a compact loaf that anchors its reputation on anise, cinnamon, honey, almonds, citron, orange peel and 3 tablespoons of rum. Slice when it is cool and spread with butter and honey. It is even better the second or third day.

INGREDIENTS

1¼ cups hot tap water (120°–130°)
1 cup sugar
¾ cup honey
2½ teaspoons baking soda
1 pinch salt
3 tablespoons rum
1 teaspoon *each* ground anise seed and cinnamon
4 cups all-purpose flour
3 tablespoons chopped blanched almonds
2 tablespoons chopped citron
½ teaspoon grated orange peel

BAKING PANS

One large loaf pan (9 x 5), greased or Teflon, or two small (7½ x 3½) pans. Metal or glass. If the latter, reduce oven heat 25°.

PREPARATION
15 mins.

In a small mixing bowl pour water and add sugar, honey, baking soda and a pinch of salt. Stir until it is dissolved. Mix in the rum, anise seed and cinnamon.

Measure flour into a large mixing bowl and pour in the liquid—stirring slowly but thoroughly to make a smooth batter. Drop in the almonds, citron and orange peel. Stir several times to mix throughout the batter. Preheat oven to 450°. Butter the tins and line with wax paper. Butter again.

FORMING
3 mins.

Pour the batter into the tin or tins. With a rubber scraper or spoon form a shallow depression down the center of the loaf, with the batter slightly higher along the sides. This will compensate for the rise of the center during baking.

BAKING
450°
10 mins.
350°
50–60 mins.

Place the bread in a very hot oven for 10 minutes; reduce the heat to moderate for an additional 50 or 60 minutes. The loaf will test done when a wooden toothpick inserted in the center comes out clean and dry.

FINAL STEP

Remove bread from the oven. Turn the tins on their sides and carefully pull out the loaves by tugging gently on the wax paper. Let the loaves cool (preferably overnight) before slicing thinly.

FINNISH CARDAMOM LOAF

[TWO ROUND LOAVES OR TWO BRAIDS]

A white loaf of Finnish origin, it is delicately flavored with cardamom, the aromatic seeds of an East Indian herb, a member of the ginger family. This loaf is uncommonly good for breakfast or brunch, especially warm from the oven or toasted. It can become a colorful festive loaf by braiding the dough and baking in loaf pans. Give it a drizzle frosting with confectioners' sugar icing.

INGREDIENTS

2 packages dry yeast
6 to 7 cups all-purpose or bread flour, approximately
2 cups warm water (105°–115°)
1½ teaspoons cardamom
⅓ cup sugar
2 teaspoons salt
¼ cup shortening
1 egg, room temperature
Icing: 1 cup confectioners' sugar
2 tablespoons water or milk
½ teaspoon vanilla or lemon juice

BAKING PANS

Two 9-inch layer pans, greased or Teflon (for round loaves), or two medium (8½ x 4½) loaf pans, greased or Teflon, for braids. If glass, reduce oven heat 25°.

PREPARATION
15 mins.

In a large mixing bowl stir yeast into 3 cups of flour. Measure the water, cardamom, sugar, salt and shortening into the flour and stir to blend it well. Add the egg.

Beat with a wooden spoon 100 strong strokes, or 3 minutes fast speed in the electric mixer. Stop beater, and take up the spoon. Continuc to work in the additional flour, a portion at a time, with the spoon and then the fingers.

KNEADING
8 mins.

When the dough is soft but not sticky, turn from the bowl onto a lightly floured work surface—a counter top or bread board. (Knead 8 minutes; 4 with the dough hook.)

FIRST RISING
1 hour

Place the dough in a buttered bowl, turn it over so that it is buttered on all sides. Cover the bowl tightly with plastic wrap and put in a warm place (80°–85°) until dough has doubled in bulk. You can test if it has risen by poking a finger in it; the dent will remain.

SHAPING
10 mins.

Punch down the dough to press out the bubbles. Let it rest on the counter, with the piece of plastic wrap over it, for about 10 minutes.

15 mins.

For ordinary loaves, cut the dough into two pieces, gently shape with the hands into flat round loaves to fit into the 9-inch round pans.

For braids, divide dough for one loaf into three equal parts. With the palms of the hands, roll each piece into a smooth rope about 12 inches long. Place them close together and then braid from the center to the ends. Pinch the braids together, tuck under the ends and drop into the greased medium loaf pans.

SECOND RISING
45 mins.

Cover the pans with buttered wax paper (to keep the dough from sticking) and put in a warm place until dough has doubled in bulk. The braided loaves will rise an inch or so above the edge of the pan.

BAKING
400°
45 mins.

Preheat oven to 400°. Bake in the oven. When loaves are well browned and tapping the bottom crust yields a hard hollow sound, they are done. If not, return to the oven (without pans if you wish) for an additional 10 minutes.

FINAL STEP

Remove bread from the oven. Place on racks and brush the round loaves with melted butter. After the braided loaves have cooled, frost with confectioners' sugar icing. Blend the confectioners' sugar with water or milk and vanilla or lemon juice.

SAVORY BREAD

[TWO LOAVES]

This has a fragrance of onion and garlic that is fascinating in a bread. These two, plus thyme, caraway, pepper and hot Tabasco, will give a delightful perfume to the kitchen in the early stages of preparation and carry on until after the loaves are taken from the oven. The seasonings are carried in a buttered layer in the loaf which bakes to a fat plumpness. Excellent with soups, barbecue meals and spaghetti.

Use all fresh garlic and onion—no powdered or dried products!

INGREDIENTS

5 cups all-purpose flour, approximately
1 tablespoon sugar
1 tablespoon salt
1 package dry yeast
1¼ cups milk
⅓ cup (⅝+ stick) butter, room temperature
2 eggs, room temperature
½ cup (1 stick) butter, room temperature
2 garlic cloves, mashed
1 teaspoon minced onion
1 teaspoon thyme
½ teaspoon *each* caraway seed and fresh ground black pepper
¼ teaspoon Tabasco
Glaze: 1 egg yolk and 2 tablespoons cream or milk, to brush

BAKING PANS

Two medium loaf pans (8½ x 4½), greased or Teflon, glass or metal. If glass, reduce baking temperature 25°.

PREPARATION
20 mins.

In a large mixing bowl combine 2 cups flour, sugar, salt and the yeast.

In a saucepan heat the milk with ⅓ cup butter until the milk is warm. The butter need not melt.

Lightly beat the eggs and add to the flour mixture, and then pour in milk and butter mixture. Beat with an electric mixer at a low speed until the flour is moist; increase speed to medium and beat for 3 minutes.

If you are beating it with a wooden spoon, do so for about 100 strong strokes or until the batter begins to string away from the sides of the bowl. Beat by hand and blend in the additional 3 cups or more of flour with the fingers. Work the dough into a mass that is no longer sticky.

KNEADING
6 mins.

Turn the dough out on a floured work surface and knead. (Four minutes with the dough hook on a Kitchen Aid mixer.) The dough will be warm and alive under your hands.

FIRST RISING
1 hour

Return the dough to the bowl and pat the dough with buttered fingertips to cover the surface entirely. Put in a warm (80°–85°) draft-free place until the dough has doubled in bulk.

While the dough is rising, prepare the seasoned butter. In a small bowl, cream the butter and add garlic cloves which have been crushed under the flat surface of a kitchen knife with a blow of the fist. Add minced or grated onion, thyme, caraway seed, black pepper and Tabasco.

SHAPING
15 mins.

Punch down the dough and remove from the bowl. Divide into two pieces. Roll each piece into a rectangle about 8 by 14 inches. With a spatula spread half the seasoned butter over the dough, leaving a 1-inch margin. Roll up the rectangle and pinch the seam tightly closed. Tuck in the ends and drop into the pan. Repeat with the second loaf.

SECOND RISING
1½ hours

Cover the loaves with wax paper and return to the warm place. Let them rise until the dough reaches the top of the pan.

BAKING
350°
45 mins.

Preheat oven to 350°. Brush the loaves with egg yolk mixed with cream or milk. Place the pans in the oven. The crusts will be bright brown when done. Test by inserting a wooden toothpick in the center of the loaf. If it comes out clean and dry the loaf is done.

FINAL STEP

Remove bread from the oven. When you turn the loaves out of their pans do so over paper towels because some of the butter may have run out of the seams and collected in the bottom of the tins.

Place the loaves on metal racks to cool before serving. This loaf toasts and freezes well. It should not be served with delicately flavored dishes. It is a rugged bread that demands and gets attention.

DILLY CASSEROLE BREAD

[ONE LOAF]

Dilly Casserole Bread is one of everyone's favorite home baked loaves. At the drop of a pan, a home baker will give you a pet dilly recipe—all harking back to the winning entry in a national baking contest several years ago. The major ingredient of all is cottage cheese but some will use dill weed instead of dill seeds while others recommend butter instead of margarine. Whatever the refinements, it is a fine bread that is easy to make, and has a delightful aroma while being baked, toasted and eaten.

INGREDIENTS

1 package dry yeast
¼ cup warm water (105°–115°)
1 cup cottage cheese, room temperature
2 tablespoons sugar
1 tablespoon instant onion bits
2 teaspoons dill seeds (or dill weed)
1 teaspoon salt
¼ teaspoon baking soda
1 egg, room temperature
2¼ to 2½ cups all-purpose flour, approximately
Glaze: ½ teaspoon melted butter to brush top, and sprinkle of salt

CASSEROLE

One 1½ quart (approximately 7 inches diameter, 4 inches deep) casserole, greased.

PREPARATION
20 mins.

Sprinkle yeast over water in a large mixing bowl. Stir briskly with a fork or metal whisk to hasten the action.

In a saucepan heat cottage cheese until warm to the touch (110°–120°). Pour cottage cheese into yeast mixture in the bowl and add the sugar, onion bits, dill seeds (or dill weed), salt, baking soda and egg. Add flour, a half cup at a time, to make a stiff batter, beating well after each addition.

FIRST RISING
1 hour

Cover with plastic wrap and let rise in a warm place (80°–85°).

FORMING
5 mins.

Remove the plastic wrap and stir down with 20 strong strokes. Turn into casserole.

SECOND RISING
45 mins.

Cover with a piece of wax paper and return to the warm place until the batter doubles in volume. Keep the wax paper away from the expanding batter or it may collapse when the paper is pulled away.

BAKING
350°
40–50 mins.

Preheat the oven to 350°. Bake in the oven until the loaf is deep brown and crusty. A wooden toothpick or metal skewer inserted in the center of the loaf will come out clean and dry when the bread is done. If moist particles cling to the probe, return the loaf to the oven for an additional 10 minutes. Cover with foil or brown paper the last 15 minutes to prevent excessive browning.

FINAL STEP

Remove bread from the oven. Immediately brush with butter and sprinkle lightly with salt. Allow the bread to cool for 10 minutes before removing it from the casserole and placing on the metal rack to cool.

ORANGE CINNAMON SWIRL BREAD

[TWO LOAVES]

This loaf gets its sugar and spice flavor from sugar and spice. The sugar and cinnamon are spooned onto the flattened-out dough and then, like a jelly roll, rolled up. Orange juice and grated orange peel are in the dough and give it tartness. Good warm, and fine toasted.

INGREDIENTS

1 package dry yeast
¼ cup warm water (105°–115°)
1 cup milk, scalded (or 1 cup hot tap water and ⅓ cup non-fat dry milk)
½ cup sugar
¼ cup shortening
1½ teaspoons salt
1 tablespoon grated orange peel
¾ cup orange juice
6½ to 7 cups all-purpose flour, approximately
1 egg, room temperature, slightly beaten
½ cup sugar
1 tablespoon cinnamon
2 teaspoons water
Frosting: 1 cup confectioners' sugar
1 teaspoon grated orange peel
4 teaspoons orange juice

BAKING PANS

Two medium (8½ x 4½) loaf pans, greased or Teflon, metal or glass. If the latter, reduce oven heat 25°.

PREPARATION
15 mins.

In a small bowl or cup dissolve yeast in water. Beat briefly with a spoon or whisk to help the process. Set aside.

In a bowl pour the milk, sugar, shortening, salt, orange peel and orange juice—and cool to lukewarm. With a wooden spoon stir in 2 cups of flour, and beat until smooth—about 100 strong strokes. Pour in the yeast mixture and 1 slightly beaten egg. Beat well. Add the remaining flour, a cup at a time, mixing first with the wooden spoon and then with the fingers, until the dough has lost its stickiness and has pulled away from the sides of the bowl.

KNEADING
10 mins.

Turn out on a lightly floured work surface—counter top or bread board—and knead. (Five minutes with a dough hook.) Add a bit more flour (¼ of a cup) if the moisture works through the surface of the dough and it sticks to the fingers or counter top.

FIRST RISING
1 hour

Place in a greased bowl, turning dough to be certain it is filmed with the oil on all sides. Cover the bowl tightly with plastic wrap and place in a warm spot (80°–85°), free from drafts, until the dough has doubled in bulk.

SHAPING
10 mins.

Fold back the plastic wrap and punch down the dough. Turn it out on the floured work surface; divide into two pieces. Cover with a cloth or a piece of wax paper and let the two pieces rest.

Combine the sugar and cinnamon.

15 mins.

Roll each piece into a rectangle about 15 x 7 inches. Each will be about ½-inch thick. Spread each rectangle with half the sugar-spice mixture. Sprinkle carefully with a teaspoon of water and smooth with a spoon or spatula. Roll from the narrow side. Seal the edges securely by pinching tightly along the seam. Tuck in the ends and place seam down in tins.

SECOND RISING
45 mins.

Cover the pans with wax paper and return them to the warm place until the dough has doubled in bulk.

BAKING
375°
325°
40 mins.

Preheat oven to 375°. Bake for 10 minutes at 375°, reduce heat to 325° and bake for 30 minutes, or until the loaves test done. A wooden toothpick inserted in the center of a loaf will come out clean and dry if the loaf is done. Also, if tapping the bottom crust yields a hard hollow sound, it is done.

FINAL STEP

Remove bread from the oven. Turn out on a metal rack to cool. When the loaves have cooled, frost with icing made from confectioners' sugar, orange peel and orange juice.

SIX HERBS BREAD

[TWO OR SIX LOAVES]

This light and airy loaf is the delight of the baker and the herbalist who loves the aroma and taste of herbs. The recipe is a vehicle for any of six herbs—dill, savory, basil, oregano, thyme, or marjoram. Your choice of herbs is added after the first rise.

Choose your two favorite herbs—divide the dough, and work one herb into one piece of dough, the second herb into the other.

No kitchen ever smelled better than one in which herb bread was baking or being toasted.

INGREDIENTS

1 package dry yeast
6 to 6½ cups all-purpose flour
2 tablespoons sugar
2 teaspoons salt
¾ cup non-fat dry milk
2¼ cups hot tap water (120°–130°)
2 tablespoons shortening, room temperature
Choice of these herbs:
- 1 tablespoon dill
- 1 tablespoon savory
- 1½ teaspoons basil
- 1½ teaspoons oregano
- 1½ teaspoons thyme
- 2¼ teaspoons marjoram

BAKING PANS

Two medium (8½ x 4½) loaf pans, greased or Teflon, or six small (5½ x 3¼) pans. If glass pans are used, reduce oven heat 25°.

PREPARATION
15 mins.

Blend yeast and 2 cups of flour in a large mixing bowl. Add sugar, salt, milk and 2¼ cups of water. Beat with a wooden spoon 125 strong strokes, or 3 minutes at medium speed with electric mixer. Add shortening. Continue beating until the soft batter forms strings from the sides of the bowl—about 2 minutes. Gradually add the additional flour, a cup at a time, first with the spoon and then by hand, until the dough has formed a rough mass and can be worked.

KNEADING
8 mins.

Turn the dough onto a floured work surface—counter top or bread board—and if the dough feels slack or moist or wet beneath its skin, add ½ cup additional flour. Keep a coating of flour on the dough as you begin to knead. Add more flour to the work surface if the dough sticks to the counter or the fingers.

Kneading is finished when the dough is smooth and satiny, and feels alive under the fingers (6 minutes with dough hook).

FIRST RISING
1 hour

Place in a greased bowl, turning to film all sides, cover bowl with plastic wrap and put in a warm place (80°–85°), free from drafts, until the dough has doubled in bulk.

SHAPING
15 mins.

Select and measure two herbs. Set aside. Turn dough out onto the work surface again. Knead the dough briefly to work out air bubbles. Cut the dough in half; set aside one piece. Flatten dough under the palms and sprinkle on the first herb. Fold over dough, knead for 2 minutes or until the spice is mixed throughout the piece. Form this into one medium loaf or three small loaves. Shape and place into the appropriate pan or pans.

Repeat with the other herb and dough.

SECOND RISING
45 mins.

Cover the pans with wax paper and put in the warm place until dough has doubled in size or has expanded about 1 inch above the edge of the pans.

BAKING
375°
45 mins.

Preheat oven to 375°. Bake in the oven. A wooden toothpick inserted in the center of the loaf will come out dry and clean if the loaf is baked.

FINAL STEP

Remove bread from the oven. Turn from pans immediately and place on metal racks to cool.

SWEDISH CARDAMOM BRAID

[TWO PLUMP LOAVES]

There is something undeniably hand-crafted in the appearance of a braided loaf, and this handsome plump bread, delicately seasoned with cardamom and dotted throughout with raisins, achieves the look with only a few twists. It is a rich bread—three sticks of butter in less than four pounds of dough. It keeps well, toasts beautifully (but must be watched), freezes well, and, overall, is a wholly satisfying baking experience.

INGREDIENTS

2 packages dry yeast
½ cup warm water (105°–115°)
½ cup milk scalded
½ cup sugar
1 teaspoon salt
1½ cups (3 sticks) butter, room temperature
2 eggs, room temperature
6 cups all-purpose flour, approximately
2 teaspoons ground cardamom
¾ cup seedless raisins
Glaze: 1 egg white, slightly beaten
2 tablespoons sugar

BAKING SHEET

Large baking sheet, greased or Teflon.

PREPARATION
15 mins.

In a small bowl or cup sprinkle yeast over water. Beat briskly with whisk or fork until the granules are dissolved.

In a mixing bowl pour milk over sugar, salt, and butter. Stir to soften butter. When the liquid has cooled to lukewarm add yeast mixture, eggs, 3 cups of flour, cardamom, and raisins. With wooden spoon or electric mixer beat until smooth—about 3 minutes. Stir in additional flour, a cup at a time, first with the spoon and then by hand. The dough will form a rough mass and clean the sides of the bowl. It will not be sticky because of the large amount of shortening. The dough should be firm but not stiff.

KNEADING
8 mins.

Turn the dough out onto a lightly floured work surface, counter top or bread board. With a strong push-turn-fold action, knead until it is smooth and elastic (about 5 minutes with the dough hook).

FIRST RISING
1 hour

Return the dough to the bowl (which does not need to be greased because of the high butter content of the dough). Cover the bowl with plastic wrap and put the bowl in a warm place (80°–85°) until dough has doubled in volume.

SHAPING 20 mins.	Punch down, turn out on a floured surface. Knead briefly to work out the air bubbles. Divide the dough into two pieces. Reserve one. Cut the other into 3 equal parts—and roll each under the palms into a fat roll about 12 inches long. Braid these loosely, with no more than 5 or 6 twists. Pinch the ends closed. Place the braid on the baking sheet. Repeat with the reserve dough.
SECOND RISING 50 mins.	Cover with wax paper and return to the warm place until doubled in bulk.
BAKING 350° 45 mins.	Preheat oven to 350°. Before baking, brush with the slightly beaten egg white mixed with sugar. Bake in the oven until the loaves test done. The crust will be a rich brown, and a wooden toothpick inserted in the center of the loaf will come out clean and dry.
FINAL STEP	Remove bread from the oven. Use a metal spatula to lift the braid off the baking sheet because the hot loaf is somewhat fragile and might break or bend. Cool on a metal rack before serving.

SAFFRON WREATH

[ONE LARGE OR TWO SMALL WREATHS]

Saffron—a full tablespoon of it—gives this handsome bread deep color and fine taste. It is a rich loaf with cream, milk, butter, egg and sugar. The wreath is formed, brushed with egg, and sprinkled with sugar and slivered almonds. Serve warm from the oven at a special breakfast, brunch or tea.

INGREDIENTS

1 tablespoon saffron
1 package dry yeast
¼ cup warm water (105°–115°)
½ cup *each* milk and cream
½ cup (1 stick) butter, room temperature
1 egg, room temperature
¼ cup sugar
1 teaspoon salt
4 cups all-purpose flour, approximately
1 cup raisins or ⅓ cup *each* candied lemon peel, citron and nut meats
Topping: Slightly beaten egg, sprinkle of sugar and 2 tablespoons slivered almonds

BAKING SHEETS

One large baking sheet, greased or Teflon, or 2 medium sheets for smaller loaves.

PREPARATION
30 mins.

Beforehand, dry a tablespoon of saffron in a slow oven (250°) for about 20 minutes. Pound it in a mortar or powder in a bowl under a heavy kitchen spoon.

20 mins.

In a small bowl or cup dissolve yeast in water. Beat briskly with a fork or whisk to hasten the fermentation. Set aside.

Warm the milk, cream and butter in a small saucepan over low heat until butter is quite soft or melted. Add powdered saffron to the milk.

In a large bowl beat the egg, sugar, salt and the yeast. Pour in the milk-saffron mixture and blend well. Gradually, a half cup at a time, stir in enough flour to make a *thin batter*. Add the raisins or the optional fruit and nuts. Beat about 100 strokes until the batter is thick and glossy.

FIRST RISING
1 hour

Cover the batter with plastic wrap and put it in a warm place (80°–85°) to rise to double in bulk.

KNEADING
8 mins.

Stir down the dough and add more flour to form a soft mass. Turn onto a floured work surface and knead vigorously until the dough is elastic and no longer sticks to the fingers. If the dough is moist or slack, dust small amounts of flour on the dough and hands.

SHAPING
30 mins.

Allow the dough to rest 10 minutes. This lets the dough relax and makes it easier to work.

For a large wreath use all of the dough. Divide the dough for two smaller wreaths. To fashion a wreath, roll the dough under the palms into a cylinder about 20- or 24-inches long. Bend this into a circle, pinch the ends together tightly to close the circle, and lay on a baking sheet. Flatten the dough to about an inch in thickness with the palms of the hands. With sharp scissors cut the ring three-quarters through from the outside, at ½-inch intervals. Turn these pieces alternately to the right and left to form the wreath pattern. Repeat with the second wreath.

Brush with beaten egg, sprinkle with sugar (regular or decorator's) and slivered almonds.

SECOND RISING
1 hour

Cover with wax paper and return to the warm place to double in size.

BAKING
375°
45 mins.

Preheat oven to 375°. Bake in the hot oven until the wreath is delicately browned.

FINAL STEP

Remove the wreath from the oven with care and place on a wire rack to cool. If the wreath is to be moved about, cut a cardboard to give it support underneath. This loaf is excellent warm or cold. It freezes well despite its rather cumbersome shape.

CINNAMON SWIRL LOAF

[TWO LOAVES]

The cinnamon swirl loaf is always a delight to cut because it reveals a pretty brown sugar-and-spice layer jelly-rolled in the white bread.

One note of caution: make certain the dough is rolled tight and then secured by pinching the seam before placing it in the loaf pan. I have had it pull during the first rise so that the seam broke loose. If it does this, carefully turn out the offending loaf—pinch the seam closed, and again put the seam on the bottom of the tin. If the loaf should deflate with this handling, leave it for 30 minutes and it will rise again.

INGREDIENTS

4½ to 5½ cups all-purpose flour, approximately
¼ cup sugar
1 teaspoon salt
1 package dry yeast
1¼ cups of milk
¼ cup (½ stick) margarine or vegetable shortening, room temperature
2 eggs, room temperature
⅓ cup sugar
1½ teaspoons cinnamon
1 tablespoon melted butter

BAKING PANS

Two medium (8½ x 4½) loaf pans, greased or Teflon, glass or metal. If glass, reduce oven heat 25°.

PREPARATION
15 mins.

In a large mixing bowl measure 2 cups flour, sugar, salt and yeast.

In a saucepan combine milk and shortening. Heat

over a low heat until the liquid is warm. The shortening does not have to melt. Gradually add to the dry ingredients and beat with a wooden spoon 100 strong strokes—or 2 minutes at medium speed with an electric mixer. Add eggs and enough flour to make a thick batter. Beat for 3 minutes at high speed or with a spoon. Stop beater. With the spoon, finish working in the additional flour, a half cup at a time. The dough will be roughly formed but no longer sticky.

KNEADING
10 mins.

Turn the dough onto a lightly floured work surface—counter top or bread board—and knead with the 1-2-3 motion of push-turn-fold. The dough will become smooth and elastic, and bubbles will rise under the surface of the dough. Sprinkle more flour on the ball of dough if it is slack or moist, or continues to stick to the hands or work surface. (Knead 6 minutes with a dough hook.)

FIRST RISING
1 hour

Place the dough back in the mixing bowl and pat with buttered or greased fingers to keep the surface from crusting. Cover the bowl tightly with plastic wrap and move to a warm place (80°–85°) until the dough has risen to about twice its original size (judged as it expands up the sides of the bowl). You can test if it has risen by poking a finger in it; the dent will remain.

SHAPING
20 mins.

Meanwhile, combine the sugar and cinnamon.

Punch down dough, turn it onto work surface again, and knead for 1 minute to press out bubbles. Divide dough into two pieces. Roll each piece into a 12 by 8-inch rectangle. Brush lightly with butter, keeping it away from the edge of the dough where the seam will be formed. Sprinkle with half the cinnamon-sugar mixture. Roll tightly from the short side, as with a jelly roll. Seal edges firmly or they may come unsealed as I have warned. Seal ends of loaf and fold underneath. Place the loaf with the seam down in the pan. Repeat with the remaining dough.

SECOND RISING
1 hour

Cover the loaves with wax paper and return to the warm place until dough rises about 1 inch above the edge of the pan.

BAKING
350°
40 mins.

Preheat oven to 350°. Bake in the oven until the light brown loaves test done when a toothpick inserted in the center of a loaf comes out clean and dry. When tapping the bottom crust yields a hard hollow sound, they are done.

FINAL STEP

Remove bread from the oven. This bread is delicious toasted, and fills the kitchen and the house with a wonderful sugar-and-spice aroma. Freezes well, too.

TWENTY

Fruit and Nut Breads

Orange Tree
Lyons, 1579

Fruits and nuts are admirable companions. They are teamed in half of these thirty-three recipes, and stand alone in the others. For instance, Apricot Layered Bread is apricot alone, but Apricot Nut Bread is the fruit plus chopped pecans. Avocado Bread is made with pecans, while Lemon Bread is the fruit alone.

There are thirteen kinds of fruit and four kinds of nuts among the ingredients in this chapter.

GLAZED RAISIN LOAF

[ONE LARGE OR TWO SMALL LOAVES]

Buttermilk and eggs are combined in this recipe to make a moist, finely textured slice studded with dark raisins. Lemon or orange juice is mixed into the confectioners' icing. I have found this to be an all-around satisfactory loaf, especially for the new baker.

INGREDIENTS

1 package yeast
¼ cup warm water (105°–115°)
1 cup seedless raisins
¼ cup (½ stick) butter or other shortening
¼ cup sugar
1½ teaspoons salt

½ cup buttermilk, room temperature
4 cups all-purpose flour, approximately
2 eggs, room temperature, slightly beaten
Glaze: 1 cup sifted confectioners' sugar
1½ tablespoons orange or lemon juice

BAKING PANS

One large (9 x 5) loaf pan, greased or Teflon, or one medium (8½ x 4½) and one small (7½ x 3½) pan. (See dough volume chart, page 23.) If glass pans are used, reduce oven heat 25°.

PREPARATION
15 mins.

In a small bowl or cup dissolve the yeast in water.

In a large bowl combine raisins, butter, sugar, salt and buttermilk. Measure in 1½ cups of flour—beat well, 75 strokes. Pour in the yeast and the beaten eggs. Blend thoroughly.

Gradually add the remaining flour, ½ cup at a time, first with the spoon and then by hand, until the mass of dough is soft and has dropped away from the sides of the bowl. If the dough continues moist and sticky, dust flour on the hands and dough.

KNEADING
10 mins.

Turn out on a lightly floured work surface and knead vigorously (6 minutes with a dough hook). The dough will be smooth and elastic.

FIRST RISING
1½ hours

Place the dough back into the bowl, pat it with buttered fingers, cover the bowl with plastic wrap and put in a warm place (80°–85°) until dough has doubled in size.

SHAPING
20 mins.

Turn back the plastic wrap, punch down the dough, turn it onto the work surface again, and let it rest for 10 minutes. Divide the dough into as many pieces as you want loaves and form each by rolling into a flat rectangle—as wide as the length of the pan. Roll up dough, sealing well at each turn. Press down on the ends of the loaf to seal, and tuck under as you place it in the pan.

SECOND RISING
50 mins.

Cover with wax paper and allow the dough to double in bulk. You can test if it has risen by poking a finger in it; the dent will remain.

BAKING
375°
30 mins.

Preheat oven to 375°. Bake in the oven until the loaves are well browned and loose in their pans. Turn one loaf out of its pan and tap the bottom crust with a forefinger. A hard hollow sound means the bread is done. If not, return to the oven for 10 minutes.

FINAL STEP

Remove bread from the oven. Place the hot loaves on a wire rack to cool before drizzling with confectioners' frosting—1 cup sifted confectioners' sugar and 1½ tablespoons orange or lemon juice.

If the bread is to be frozen don't ice until it comes out of the freezer.

RAISIN CASSEROLE BREAD

[TWO LOAVES]

This casserole bread is easy to make and produces a raisin loaf that tastes only of raisins—no other flavor gets in the way. The batter is sticky, however, and when it is prepared and poured into the casserole, dip fingertips and the spoons into cold water to prevent a sticky mess when smoothing it out.

The bread will rise impressively in the oven.

INGREDIENTS

4 cups all-purpose flour
2 packages dry yeast
½ cup sugar
1 teaspoon salt
½ cup non-fat dry milk
1½ cups hot tap water (120°–130°)
¼ cup (½ stick) margarine, room temperature
1 egg, room temperature
1 cup seedless raisins

BAKING CASSEROLES

Two 1-quart casseroles, greased.

PREPARATION
15 mins.

Measure 2 cups of flour, yeast, sugar, salt and milk into a large mixing bowl. Stir.

In a saucepan combine water and margarine. When the margarine is quite soft, pour the liquid into the flour bowl. Beat slowly in the electric mixer until the flour is absorbed and then turn to medium high speed for 2 minutes. Scrape the bowl occasionally while adding the egg and 1 cup additional flour.

The batter may be too thick for the beaters so stop

the machine and stir in 1 more cup of flour with a large wooden spoon. The mixture will now be quite stiff but workable with a spoon. Remember this is batter—not a dough to be kneaded.

RISING
1 hour

Clean the sides of the bowl with the spoon and cover it with a length of plastic wrap. Place in a warm (80°–85°) draft-free spot until the batter has doubled in size.

FORMING
10 mins.

Turn back the plastic wrap, stir down the batter. Drop in the raisins and beat for 30 seconds. Spoon or pour into the casseroles. Wet the fingertips and utensils to push the dough into the corners and smooth down the top of the loaves.

BAKING
350°
45 mins.

Let the batter stand while the oven heats to 350°. Bake in the oven until the bread is loose in the pans, and is well browned and crusted.

FINAL STEP

Remove bread from the oven. Turn from the casseroles and let cool on metal racks before serving or freezing.

LEMON BREAD

[ONE LOAF]

A fine home baker (Mrs. Lena Lynch) in the small southern Indiana farm community of Hindostan created this lemon loaf, glazed during baking with a thick sugary lemon mixture. The result is a crispy, candied crust and a moist yellow slice. For the lemon rind, I use a vegetable peeler and then slice or chop the strips of skin.

INGREDIENTS

1 lemon, with rind grated (or peeled, as above)
6 tablespoons butter or margarine, room temperature
1 cup sugar
1 tablespoon lemon extract
2 eggs, room temperature
1½ cups all-purpose flour
¼ teaspoon salt
1½ teaspoons baking powder
½ cup milk
Topping: ½ cup sugar mixed with 3 tablespoons lemon juice

BAKING PAN — One large (9 x 5) loaf pan, greased or Teflon, glass or metal. If glass, reduce oven heat 25°.

PREPARATION
20 mins.

First, peel or grate the lemon rind, and then squeeze out 3 tablespoons of juice for topping. Reserve both.

In a large bowl, cream the butter with the sugar, add lemon extract and eggs, beating well after each egg has been dropped into the bowl. On a length of wax paper, sift together the flour, salt and baking powder. Stir ½ cup at a time into the butter and egg mixture, alternating with the milk and lemon rind. Stir the dough thoroughly but only until it is well blended.

FORMING
3 mins.

Turn into the loaf pan. With a rubber scraper push the batter into the corners and level the surface of the loaf.

BAKING
325°
45 mins.
10 mins.

Bake in the oven for about 45 minutes. In the meanwhile dissolve ½ cup sugar in 3 tablespoons of lemon juice. Remove the loaf from the oven and carefully spoon the lemon topping over the crust. Return it to the oven for 10 minutes. Insert a metal or wooden skewer into the center of the loaf at the end of the bake period. If it comes out clean and dry the loaf is done. If moist particles cling to the probe, return the loaf to the oven for an additional 10 minutes.

FINAL STEP — Remove bread from the oven. Let the loaf cool and the glaze harden for about 10 minutes before turning it out on a wire cooling rack.

PEANUT BATTER BREAD

[ONE LARGE OR TWO SMALL LOAVES]

The crunchy bite in this peanut batter bread is provided by a quarter cup *each* of chunky peanut butter and finely chopped peanuts. The peanuts give the loaf only a light brown color but a solid flavor of nuts. It has always seemed reasonable to expect this loaf of bread to appeal principally to children and I am surprised when the adults join me in enjoying it.

INGREDIENTS

1 package dry yeast
1¼ cups warm water (105°–115°)
¼ cup chunk style peanut butter
¼ cup brown sugar, firmly packed

2 teaspoons salt
¼ cup finely chopped salted peanuts
3 cups all-purpose flour

BAKING PANS — One large (9 x 5) loaf pan, greased or Teflon, or two small (7½ x 3½) pans. If glass, reduce oven heat 25°.

PREPARATION
15 mins. — In a mixing bowl sprinkle the yeast over the water and stir briskly with a fork or whisk to dissolve.

Measure in the peanut butter, sugar, salt, chopped peanuts and 1½ cups of flour. Beat at medium speed with the electric mixer for 2 minutes, scraping sides and bottom of bowl occasionally. Or use a wooden spoon—200 strong vigorous strokes by hand.

Stop the beater and add the rest of the flour, ½ cup at a time, stirring until the mass is smooth.

FIRST RISING
45 mins. — Cover the bowl tightly with plastic wrap and put in a warm place (80°–85°) until batter has doubled in bulk.

FORMING
5 mins. — Stir down the batter with a dozen strong strokes. Spread evenly in the large pan or two small ones. Dampen fingers and pat top of the loaves to smooth the surface.

SECOND RISING
40 mins. — Cover the pans with wax paper and return to the warm place until batter has doubled in volume.

BAKING
375°
45 mins. — Preheat the oven to 375°. Place in the oven until the loaves are lightly browned and loose in their pans. Cover with foil if the loaves start to brown too fast. When tapping the bottom crust yields a hard hollow sound, they are baked. If not, return to the oven—without the pan if you wish a deep brown over-all crust—for an additional 10 minutes. Midway in the bake period shift the pans so the loaves are exposed equally to temperature variations.

FINAL STEP — Remove bread from the oven. Cool on a wire rack before serving. Freezes well.

CHERRY PECAN BREAD

[ONE LARGE LOAF]

This quick bread—a light brown and shiny crust—is an especially handsome loaf. It displays a pink slice studded with red cherry pieces and pecan chunks. The maraschino flavor, however, is not pronounced despite a dozen cherries and the cherry juice. There is also orange juice.

INGREDIENTS
1 (4 oz.) bottle of maraschino cherries, to be chopped
1 egg, room temperature
1 cup sugar
2 tablespoons butter, melted
¼ cup *each* cherry juice, orange juice and water
2 cups all-purpose flour
3 teaspoons baking powder
¼ teaspoon baking soda
1 teaspoon salt
1 cup chopped pecans

BAKING PAN
One medium (8½ x 4½) baking pan, greased or Teflon. If glass, reduce oven heat 25°.

PREPARATION
20 mins.
Preheat oven to 350°.

Pour off the cherry juice and reserve. With a sharp knife, quarter the cherries. In a bowl beat the egg, add the cherries and stir in the sugar and melted butter. Pour in cherry and orange juices and water. On a length of wax paper, sift or stir together the flour, baking powder, baking soda, and salt. Add these to the liquid mixture, a spoonful at a time, and blend together thoroughly. Add the chopped nuts, and stir in.

FORMING
3 mins.
Pour the batter into the pan. Push into the corners and level with spoon or spatula.

BAKING
350°
1¼ hours
Place in the oven until the crust is well browned (and perhaps cracked open). When a wooden toothpick inserted in the loaf comes out clean and dry, the loaf is done.

FINAL STEP
Remove bread from the oven. Let rest in the pan 10 minutes before removing to a wire rack to cool. This loaf is better seasoned for a day or so before slicing. Wrap with foil or plastic wrap.

BLUEBERRY PECAN BREAD

[ONE LARGE OR TWO SMALL LOAVES]

This loaf has all of the credentials for goodness—blueberries (or huckleberries), pecans, orange juice, orange rind and butter. I use frozen blueberries picked in the summer by a family picker on a northern Indiana pick-it-yourself farm. Baked in this loaf, the blueberries form blue pools of moist fruit. Decorative and good.

INGREDIENTS	1 cup washed blueberries or huckleberries, patted dry 1¾ cups all-purpose flour ⅔ cup sugar 1½ teaspoons baking powder ½ teaspoon *each* baking soda and salt Juice and grated rind of 1 orange 2 tablespoons butter, room temperature ½ cup boiling water, approximately 1 cup chopped pecans ¼ cup flour
BAKING PAN	One large (9 x 5) pan, greased or Teflon, or two small (7½ x 3½) pans. If glass, reduce oven heat 25°. Line the pans with buttered wax paper to keep the loaves from sticking.
PREPARATION 10 mins.	While the blueberries (or huckleberries) are being washed and dried on paper toweling, preheat oven to 350°.
20 mins.	In a large bowl sift together flour, sugar, baking powder, baking soda and salt. In a measuring cup pour the juice and grated rind of 1 orange, and add butter. Add boiling water sufficient to make ¾ cup. Stir this liquid into the dry ingredients, blending well. In a separate bowl, combine the berries, chopped pecans and ¼ cup sifted flour. Add this to the batter, taking care not to mash the berries.
FORMING 3 mins.	Pour the batter into pans (or pan).
BAKING 350° 1 hour	Place the pans in the oven and bake until the bread tests done when a wooden toothpick inserted in the loaf comes out clean and dry.
FINAL STEP	Remove bread from the oven. Turn the pan on its side, carefully pull the loaf out by gently tugging on the wax paper lining. Cool on metal rack.

LEMON RICH TEA LOAF

[ONE LOAF]

Despite its genteel name, this bread is surprisingly robust in its outward appearance—a fat loaf with a deep brown crust. Inside, the egg-rich loaf is finely textured, and delicately flavored with lemon. It toasts beautifully.

INGREDIENTS

1 package dry yeast
¼ cup warm water (105°–115°)
⅓ cup milk, scalded
¼ cup sugar
¼ cup (½ stick) butter, room temperature
1 egg, room temperature
2 egg yolks, room temperature
½ teaspoon salt
1½ teaspoons grated lemon peel
¼ teaspoon lemon extract
3 cups all-purpose flour, approximately

BAKING PAN

One large (9 x 5) loaf pan, greased or Teflon. If glass, reduce oven heat 25°.

PREPARATION
20 mins.

In a small bowl sprinkle yeast over the water and stir briefly with a fork or whisk to speed the action. Set aside.

Pour milk into a large bowl and add sugar and butter. Stir to melt, and allow to cool to lukewarm. Beat the egg and yolks together. Stir the egg mixture and yeast into milk in the bowl. Add salt, peel and extract.

Stir in flour, a half cup at a time, to make a soft dough. Beat first with a wooden spoon and then work with the hands until the dough is smooth. All of this is done in the bowl. There is no other kneading. Because of the butter, it will not be sticky even though it is quite soft and somewhat moist.

FIRST RISING
1¼ hours

Leave dough in bowl, cover tightly with plastic wrap and let rise in a warm place (80°–85°) until doubled in bulk. You can test if it has risen by poking a finger in it; the dent will remain.

SHAPING
5 mins.

Turn dough out on floured surface and press out air bubbles by kneading briefly. Flatten the dough into an oval with the hands—fold in half, pinch the seam tightly closed, tuck under the ends, and place in the pans.

SECOND RISING
1 hour

Cover the tins with wax paper and return to the warm place. Let the dough rise until it has doubled in volume, perhaps an inch above the side of the pan.

BAKING
375°
10 mins.
350°
30 mins.

Preheat oven to 375°. Bake 10 minutes in the moderately hot oven, reduce heat to 350° for an additional 30 minutes or until done. A wooden toothpick inserted in the center of the loaf will come out clean and dry when the loaf is baked. Also, tapping the bottom crust will yield a hard hollow sound.

FINAL STEP

Remove bread from the oven. Turn out on a metal rack and allow the loaves to cool before slicing, or freezing.

SAFFRON-LEMON BREAD

[TWO SMALL LOAVES]

The color is yellow. It could not be otherwise with its mix of lemon, saffron and eggs. While saffron is a subtle spice, it adds considerable strength to the color of the bread. Spread slices with softened cream cheese or butter for sandwiches.

INGREDIENTS

⅛ teaspoon powdered saffron
½ cup shortening, room temperature
¾ cup sugar
2 teaspoons grated lemon peel
2 eggs, room temperature
⅔ cup water
2 tablespoons lemon juice
2 cups all-purpose flour
2 teaspoons baking powder
¼ teaspoon baking soda
½ teaspoon salt

BAKING PANS

Two small (7½ x 3½) baking pans, greased or Teflon. If glass, reduce oven heat 25°.

PREPARATION
20 mins.

Beforehand, place the saffron in a small baking dish or pan and heat in a 250° oven for 10 to 15 minutes until it is dry and can be powdered under a heavy spoon. Preheat the oven to 350°.

In a large bowl, cream shortening, sugar, saffron

and lemon peel. Beat in eggs, one at a time. Mix water and lemon juice together and stir it into the mixture.

On a length of wax paper, sift together flour, baking powder, baking soda and salt. Slowly add this to the wet ingredients and blend thoroughly with a large spoon.

FORMING
3 mins.

Pour or spoon the batter into the loaf pans and level with the spoon or a rubber spatula.

BAKING
350°
35 mins.

Place the pans in the moderate oven for about 35 minutes. A wooden toothpick or metal skewer, inserted in center of the loaf, will come out dry and clean if the loaves are done.

FINAL STEP

Remove bread from the oven. Allow the loaves to cool in the pans for 10 minutes before turning them onto the wire racks to finish cooling.

COCONUT BANANA BREAD

[ONE LOAF]

This loaf has the smell of coconut and the taste of banana, a tropical pair that have always done well together. The coconut flakes are toasted in the oven before they are mixed with the banana. Later, in the oven, as part of the dough, the flakes will bake a deep brown against the lighter brown crust. It is a moist loaf that is fine for tea sandwiches.

INGREDIENTS

1 cup flaked coconut, to toast
⅓ cup (⅝ stick) butter or margarine, room temperature
⅔ cup sugar
2 eggs, room temperature
3 tablespoons milk
1 teaspoon lemon juice
½ teaspoon almond extract
2 cups sifted all-purpose flour
1 teaspoon baking powder
½ teaspoon *each* baking soda and salt
1 cup mashed ripe bananas (about 2 medium bananas)

BAKING PAN

One large (9 x 5) loaf pan, greased or Teflon, glass or metal. If glass, reduce oven heat 25°.

PREPARATION
25 mins.

First, toast the coconut on a baking sheet in a moderate oven (350°) or under the broiler until lightly browned. Stir flakes occasionally and keep a watchful eye on them so they don't burn. Remove from the oven and set aside to cool. Leave oven on.

In a large mixing bowl cream together butter and sugar. Beat in the eggs, one at a time. Stir in milk, lemon juice, and almond extract. Sift flour again into the mixing bowl with the baking powder, baking soda, and salt. Blend thoroughly.

Cut banana into small pieces in a bowl and mash well with a fork. Work banana into the mixture, and gently fold in toasted coconut. (Reserve a large pinch of coconut to sprinkle on the top of the loaf.)

FORMING
5 mins.

Pour the mixture into a loaf pan, pushing the dough into the corners and leveling the top with a rubber scraper.

BAKING
350°
1 hour

Bake in the oven until a metal skewer or wooden toothpick inserted in the center comes out clean.

FINAL STEP

Remove bread from the oven. Let the loaf cool in the pan for about 10 minutes before carefully turning it out onto a wire rack. Allow it to cool completely before serving.

ORANGE-RAISIN-NUT BREAD

[TWO LOAVES]

This is an unusual yeast bread because it uses more than 2 cups of orange juice, rather than milk or water, for the liquid. A delicious raisin-nut loaf, the orange, nevertheless, dominates. The addition of the raisins before kneading will give the dough a brownish cast but I find this appealing. This happens when the raisins break up under the hands of a strong kneader or the pull of a dough hook. Add the raisins after the first rise if you want to preserve the whiteness of the loaf.

These loaves will not rise as high as loaves made with water or milk because of the acidity of the juice.

INGREDIENTS

6 to 6½ cups all-purpose flour
1 package dry yeast
2 tablespoons sugar
2¼ cups warm orange juice (120°)
2 tablespoons shortening
2 teaspoons salt
1 cup seedless raisins
½ cup chopped walnuts
1 tablespoon grated orange peel
Icing (if desired): 1 cup confectioners' sugar
1 tablespoon milk
⅛ teaspoon vanilla extract
Decorations: 2 tablespoons chopped walnuts
2 teaspoons grated orange peel

BAKING PANS

Two medium (8½ x 4½) loaf pans, greased or Teflon, glass or metal. If glass, reduce oven heat 25°.

PREPARATION
15 mins.

In a large mixing bowl combine 2½ cups of flour, yeast and sugar. Heat orange juice and shortening in a small saucepan until the liquid is warm—120°. Pour the juice in the flour and beat with a wooden spoon, 100 strong strokes, or for 3 minutes at high speed with an electric mixer. Add salt. Mix in raisins, nuts and grated peel.

Mix in additional flour, ½ cup at a time, first with the spoon and then by hand, until the dough pulls away from the sides of the bowl and forms a rough ball.

KNEADING
8 mins.

Sprinkle flour on the work surface and turn the dough onto it. Keep a coating of flour on the dough as you begin to knead. Knead with a strong push-turn motion with the heel of the hand (6 minutes with a dough hook). The kneading is finished when the dough no longer sticks and is smooth and satiny (recognizing that the raisins and nuts will be bumpy).

FIRST RISING
1 hour

Put the dough in a greased bowl, turning to coat all sides, cover tightly with plastic wrap and put in a warm (80°–85°) draft-free place until it has doubled in bulk. You can test if it has risen by poking a finger in it; the dent will remain.

SHAPING
10 mins.

Turn the dough out onto the work surface and cut in half. Knead briefly to work out the air bubbles. Form each half into a loaf and place in a pan.

SECOND RISING
50 mins.

Cover the pans with wax paper and return to the warm place until the dough has risen ½ inch above the edge of the pan.

BAKING
375°
45 mins.

Preheat oven to 375°. Place the loaves in the oven until they are nicely browned and pull away from the sides of the pans. When tapping the bottom crust yields a hard hollow sound, they are baked.

FINAL STEP

Remove from the oven, turn out of pans, and place on metal cooling racks. When cool, these loaves may be frosted with a mixture of confectioners' sugar, milk and vanilla extract. Sprinkle with chopped nuts and grated orange peel.

PEANUT BUTTER BREAD

[ONE LOAF]

For those crazy about peanuts and peanut butter, this is their loaf. Warm from the oven or toasted, the bread gives off an inviting aroma of roasted peanuts. This recipe came to me roundabout from the Kona Coast of the Big Island of Hawaii where roasting coffee, not peanuts, is their forte.

INGREDIENTS

1½ cups hot tap water (120°–130°)
¾ cup peanut butter
¾ cup non-fat dry milk
½ cup sugar
¼ teaspoon salt
1 egg, room temperature
2 cups all-purpose flour
4 teaspoons baking powder
¾ cup chopped salted peanuts

BAKING PAN

One medium (8½ x 4½) loaf pan, greased or Teflon. If glass, reduce oven heat 25°.

PREPARATION
12 mins.

In a large bowl slowly pour water over peanut butter while stirring. Add milk, sugar, salt, egg and flour. Measure in the baking powder and the peanuts. Beat together with 25 strong strokes. Put aside to rest while the pan is greased. Preheat oven to 325°.

FORMING
3 mins.

Spoon into the prepared pan and push into the corners with a spoon or spatula.

BAKING
325°
1 hour

Bake in the oven until the loaf tests done when pierced in the center with a metal skewer or wooden toothpick. If it comes out clean and dry, the loaf is done. If moist particles cling to the probe, return the loaf to the oven for an additional 10 minutes. Test again.

FINAL STEP

Remove bread from the oven. Let the bread cool 10 minutes before turning it out of the pan. It will develop a richer flavor if allowed to mature for at least a day at room temperature wrapped in foil or plastic.

WALNUT BREAD

[ONE LOAF]

This is a white bread that goes into the loaf pan as a batter, carrying with it a liberal portion of walnuts. Try it spread with cream cheese. Delicious.

INGREDIENTS

3 cups all-purpose flour
4 teaspoons baking powder
1 teaspoon salt
¾ cup sugar
1 cup chopped walnuts
1 egg, room temperature
1½ cups milk, room temperature
2 tablespoons melted butter

BAKING PAN

One medium (8½ x 4½) loaf pan, greased or Teflon. If glass, reduce oven heat 25°.

PREPARATION
20 mins.

Preheat oven to 350°. In a bowl sift or stir together flour, baking powder, salt and sugar. Stir in walnuts. In a small bowl beat the egg into the milk. Pour into dry ingredients and stir only until the flour is moistened. Add the butter and blend it into the mixture.

FORMING
3 mins.

Cut a piece of wax paper to fit the bottom of the greased pan, and pat into place with buttered fingers. Pour the batter into the pan and push it with a spoon or spatula into the corners and level the top.

BAKING
350°
1 hour

Bake in the oven. Test for doneness by inserting a wood or metal skewer in the center of the loaf. If it comes out clean and dry the loaf is done. If not, return it to the oven for an additional 10 minutes. Test again.

FINAL STEP

Remove bread from the oven. Carefully turn the hot loaf out of the pan, and place it on a wire rack to cool before serving.

APRICOT NUT BREAD

[TWO LOAVES]

This no-knead loaf gets its rough texture from rolled oats. While dried apricots and pecans are expensive, they are worth having in this dark, molasses-flavored bread. Let it develop its full flavor for a day or so before slicing.

INGREDIENTS

2 packages dry yeast
½ cup warm water (105°–115°)
1½ cups boiling water
1 cup rolled oats
¼ cup dark molasses
¼ cup sugar
½ teaspoon *each* nutmeg and ginger
1 tablespoon salt
4½ cups all-purpose flour
¾ cup finely cut dried apricots
¾ cup chopped pecans
2 tablespoons butter or margarine

BAKING PANS

Two large (9 x 5) loaf pans, greased or Teflon, or in other combinations according to the dough volume chart on page 23. If glass pans are used, reduce oven heat 25°.

PREPARATION
10 mins.

In a small bowl sprinkle the yeast on the water, and briskly stir with a whisk or fork to hasten the fermentation. Set aside for 3 minutes.

In a large bowl pour the boiling water over the rolled oats, molasses, sugar, nutmeg, ginger, and salt. Blend, and let it cool until it is lukewarm to the touch. The yeast mixture will be well risen; pour it into the oats mixture, and add half the flour. Blend with about 20 strokes. Add remaining flour, a half a cup at a time, with the fruit, nuts, and shortening. Blend. There is no kneading.

FIRST RISING
1 hour
Cover the bowl with plastic wrap and put in a warm place (80°–85°) until dough has doubled in bulk.

FORMING
5 mins.
Remove the plastic wrap, beat down the dough and pour into the pans.

SECOND RISING
45 mins.
Cover the pan lightly with wax paper and return to the warm place. The dough will reach the top of the pan—so elevate the paper on tumblers so it won't touch.

BAKING
375°
50 mins.
Preheat oven to 375°. Bake in the oven until the loaves test done when pricked with a metal skewer. They are done if the pin comes out clean. If not, leave them in the oven 5 minutes longer.

FINAL STEP
Carefully remove from loaf pans to wire cooling racks.

TROPICAL BREAD

[ONE LOAF]

A colorful loaf that displays the browns of nuts, bran and banana and the orange of apricot bits. The bran gives it rough texture; the apricots, chewiness. The banana *must* be ripe if it is to blend smoothly with the other ingredients. Makes a rich loaf that is best a day or so after baking.

INGREDIENTS
⅔ cup sugar
⅓ cup shortening, room temperature
2 eggs, room temperature
1 cup ripe banana, mashed
¼ cup buttermilk
1¼ cups all-purpose flour
1 teaspoon baking powder
½ teaspoon *each* salt and baking soda
1 cup 100% Bran cereal
¾ cup dried apricots, chopped into bits
½ cup chopped walnuts

BAKING PAN
One 9 x 5 loaf pan, greased, glass or metal. If glass, reduce oven heat 25°. Line the pan with buttered wax paper to prevent the loaf from sticking.

PREPARATION
12 mins.
Preheat oven to 350°. In a large bowl cream sugar and shortening, and add eggs. Beat thoroughly. In a separate small bowl, mash banana well—and combine with buttermilk. Over a piece of wax paper sift together the

flour, baking powder, salt, and baking soda; add alternately with banana mixture to the creamed mixture. Stir in the bran, apricots (cut into small bits) and the walnuts. Stir only until it is well blended.

FORMING
2 mins.

Pour into pan.

BAKING
350°
1 hour

Bake in the oven until it tests done when pierced with a metal skewer or a wooden toothpick—and it comes out clean. It will probably have an interesting crack running the length of the crust but that is the way this bread behaves.

FINAL STEP

Remove bread from the oven. Let the loaf cool in the pan for about 10 minutes, and then carefully remove to a wire rack. This bread—delicious any time—is even better the second and third days.

NUBBY PEANUT LOAF

[ONE LOAF]

This is the peanut-iest for kids and peanut-addicted adults. Chopped salted peanuts are liberally scattered throughout the dough. Serve it fresh from the oven with butter, or as sandwiches—or toasted for breakfast.

INGREDIENTS

½ cup salted peanuts, chopped
1½ cups whole wheat flour
1 package dry yeast
1 cup hot tap water (120°–130°)
⅓ cup non-fat dry milk
3 tablespoons sugar
1 teaspoon salt
2 tablespoons shortening
1 egg, room temperature
1½ to 2 cups all-purpose flour, approximately

BAKING PAN

One medium (8½ by 4½) baking pan, greased or Teflon. If glass, reduce oven heat 25°.

PREPARATION
20 mins.

Beforehand, chop the salted peanuts (skinned) into fine bits. In a mixing bowl measure whole wheat flour and over it sprinkle yeast. Stir together with either a spoon or an electric mixer at slow speed.

Add the water, milk, sugar, salt and shortening. Beat for 30 seconds at low speed, and add the egg and chopped peanuts. Stir in sufficient white flour to make a thick batter and beat at medium speed, or by hand, for 3 minutes. Stop the mixer and gradually add additional white flour, first by spoon and then by hand, until a rough mass has formed.

KNEADING
6 mins.

Turn the dough out on a lightly floured work surface—counter top or bread board—and with a push-turn-fold motion knead the bread until it is smooth and elastic. If the dough is sticky or moist, add additional flour, a small portion at a time.

FIRST RISING
1 hour

Place the dough in the bowl; cover tightly with plastic wrap and put in a warm (80°–85°), draft-free place until the dough has doubled in volume. You can test if it has risen by poking a finger in it; the dent will remain.

SHAPING
10 mins.

Punch down the dough and turn out on the floured work surface. Shape into a loaf by pressing it into a flat oval, folding it in half, pinching the seam together tightly, and placing it in the bread pan, seam down.

SECOND RISING
45 mins.

Cover the pan with a piece of wax paper and return it to the warm place until the center of the dough is slightly above the top of the pan.

BAKING
400°
40 mins.

Preheat oven to 400°. Place the loaf in the oven. If the crust is browning too rapidly in the last half of the baking period, cover the loaf with brown paper. When a wooden pick inserted in the loaf comes out clean and dry, the bread is baked.

FINAL STEP

Remove bread from the oven. Turn the loaf out of the pan onto a metal rack to cool before serving.

ORANGE NUT BREAD

[ONE LARGE OR TWO SMALL LOAVES]

A compact light brown brick of orange and nuts—a jagged tear down the center of the crust in which an orange and sugar mix is spooned while the loaf is still in the oven. Fresh or frozen orange juice and grated orange rind give a fine odor and flavor to this waxy bread.

INGREDIENTS	2½ cups all-purpose flour 3 tablespoons baking powder 1 teaspoon salt 1 cup sugar ⅓ cup non-fat dry milk ¼ cup shortening, room temperature ¼ cup fresh or frozen orange juice ¾ cup water 1 egg, room temperature 3 tablespoons grated orange rind 1 cup chopped walnuts
BAKING PANS	One large (9 x 5) or two small (7½ x 3½) loaf tins, greased or Teflon, glass or metal. If glass, reduce baking heat 25°.
PREPARATION 12 mins.	Sift into a large bowl: the flour, baking powder, salt, sugar and milk. With a pastry blender or fingers cut in the shortening. Pour in orange juice, water and add the egg. With a large wooden spoon mix only enough to dampen the dry ingredients. Add the grated rind and chopped walnuts and mix them in well—but don't overbeat. Preheat oven to 350°.
FORMING 5 mins.	Beforehand, butter the pan and line the sides and bottom with a length of wax paper. Butter the paper in place before pouring in the dough. It will be thick so spread the batter into the corners with a rubber scraper. Leave the sides slightly higher than the center—to allow for the loaf to expand and level off in the oven.
BAKING 350° 50 mins. 10 mins.	Bake in a moderate oven for about 50 minutes. Remove loaf from oven and carefully spoon a mixture of ½ cup sugar and 3 tablespoons of lemon juice over the crust. Return to the oven for 10 minutes, or until it tests done. A wooden toothpick or metal skewer will come out clean and dry when inserted in the middle of the loaf. If moist particles cling to the probe, return the loaf to the oven for 10 additional minutes.
FINAL STEP	Remove bread from the oven. With the loaf pan turned on its side, carefully coax out the hot bread by tugging gently on the wax paper. Let the loaf mature, or age, overnight before serving.

LEMON NUT BREAD

[ONE LOAF]

This is not a large loaf but it is big in goodness—rich, moist and delicately flavored with lemon and nuts. A thick mixture of lemon juice and sugar is laid on the crust with a spoon when the loaf comes from the oven. The crust is pricked 20 or 30 times with a metal skewer or a wooden toothpick and the syrup spooned on.

INGREDIENTS
½ cup of shortening
1 cup sugar
2 eggs, room temperature, lightly beaten
1¼ cups all-purpose flour
2 teaspoons baking powder
¼ teaspoon salt
½ cup milk, room temperature
½ cup finely chopped walnuts
Grated rind of 1 lemon
Glaze: ¾ cup sugar, juice of 1 lemon

BAKING PAN
One medium (8½ x 4½) loaf pan, greased or Teflon. If glass, reduce oven heat 25°.

PREPARATION
15 mins.
Preheat oven to 350°. In a large bowl cream together shortening and sugar. Slightly beat the eggs and add to the creamed sugar. On a length of wax paper sift together the flour, baking powder and salt, and spoon this into the mixture, alternately with the milk. Add walnuts and lemon rind. Blend thoroughly—but only enough to mix it well.

FORMING
3 mins.
To facilitate turning it out after it is baked, grease the pan, line the sides and bottom with wax paper—and grease again. Pour into the loaf pan.

BAKING
350°
1 hour
Bake in the oven until the loaf tests done when pierced in the center with a metal skewer. If it comes out clean and dry, the loaf is done. (Keep skewer handy for the crust-piercing procedure to follow.)

FINAL STEP
15 mins.
Remove bread from the oven. While the loaf is still hot and in the pan, prick the top with 20 or 30 holes, using a wooden toothpick or a metal skewer—and spoon on the mixture of ¾ cup sugar and the juice of 1 lemon. If there is a long break in the crust (and there

should be) be sure to coat this as well. Slowly the crust will absorb all of the lemon mixture. Allow the loaf to stand for 15 minutes, and then carefully turn it on its side and remove from the pan. Again, handle gingerly since quick breads can be fragile. Cool completely before serving at a gala breakfast, brunch, teatime or as a late afternoon special snack.

PRUNE AND BLACK WALNUT BREAD

[ONE LOAF]

The dark and woodsy flavor of black walnuts dominates this waxy, moist loaf found on dinner tables in southern Indiana and Kentucky. The most tedious part of the recipe is taking the seeds out of the prunes, unless you are a prune buff which I've never been—except for this delicious bread. (Of course, there are pitted prunes.)

INGREDIENTS

1 cup prunes, soaked and drained
1 egg, room temperature
1 cup sugar
2 tablespoons butter, melted
2 cups all-purpose flour
3 teaspoons baking powder
¼ teaspoon baking soda
1 teaspoon salt
½ cup prune juice
¼ cup orange juice
1 cup black walnut meats, rough cut

BAKING PAN

One medium (8½ x 4½) metal or glass loaf pan, greased or Teflon. If a glass pan is used, reduce oven heat 25°.

PREPARATION
20 mins.

Beforehand, soak the prunes for about 1 hour in a bowl in water to cover. Drain the prunes and cut them in small pieces, discarding seeds.

In a large bowl beat the egg, stir in sugar and prunes. Melt butter and add it to the prune mixture. Sift together flour, baking powder, baking soda and the salt and add it, a half cup at a time—alternating with prune and orange juices—to the mixture in the large bowl. When this has been blended in, drop in the chopped nut meats and stir them thoroughly into the dough. Preheat the oven to 350°.

FORMING
10 mins.

A warm loaf of quick bread is more fragile than a yeast bread and must be removed from the pan with care. Before pouring the batter into the pan, it is better to grease the pan, line it with wax paper, especially the bottom, and butter the paper in place. The loaf then can be easily removed from the pan.

Pour batter into the pan. Cut through the mixture once or twice with a knife or rubber spatula to be certain the loaf is level and the mixture fills the corners.

BAKING
350°
1 hour

Bake in the oven. The loaf will rise and probably crack down the center. Test for doneness with a metal skewer or wooden toothpick. Insert it in the center of the loaf; if it comes out clean the loaf is done.

FINAL STEP

Remove bread from the oven. Let the loaf cool in the pan for about 10 minutes and then carefully remove it to a metal cooling rack.

HONEY PINEAPPLE BREAD

[ONE LARGE OR TWO SMALL LOAVES]

While this honey-colored loaf has a full cup of honey among its ingredients, it is the unmistakably tropical aroma of pineapple—in its preparation as well as in the loaf—that sets it apart. Whole bran and walnuts are added to give it a pleasant and slightly rough texture. A good slice to go with coffee, or a glass of port.

INGREDIENTS

2 tablespoons salad oil
1 cup honey
1 egg, room temperature and slightly beaten
2 cups all-purpose flour
2 teaspoons baking powder
1 teaspoon salt
1 cup whole bran
1 cup pineapple juice
¾ cup chopped walnuts

BAKING PANS

One large (9 x 5) baking pan, greased or Teflon, or two small (7½ x 3½) loaf tins. If glass, reduce oven heat 25°.

PREPARATION
15 mins.

Preheat oven to 350°.

In a bowl measure in oil, honey and egg. This sticky mess does blend together so stir it well for about 60 seconds. Add flour, baking powder, salt, whole bran and pineapple juice. Stir just enough to absorb the dry ingredients. Fold in the nuts.

FORMING
5 mins.

Prepare the pans by greasing and covering the bottoms with wax paper to make it easier to remove the loaves when baked. Pour the batter into the pans. Just be certain the pans are about half filled with batter. Push into the corners and level tops with spoon or spatula.

BAKING
350°
1–1¼ hours

Place in the oven until the loaf or loaves are honey colored. The loaves will test done when a wooden toothpick inserted in the center of a loaf comes out clean and dry. No batter will be sticking to it.

FINAL STEP

Remove bread from the oven. Let cool in the pans for 10 minutes before removing to a wire rack. Peel the paper off the bottom of each loaf. Allow loaf to age at least a day for a richer and more flavorful bread.

ORANGE BREAD

[TWO LOAVES]

While most orange breads fall into the quick bread category, this handsome loaf—flavored with orange juice and orange peel—is yeast-raised. It has a crust that is deep brown and a slice that is light orange in color. When it comes from the oven, brush with milk for a soft glaze.

INGREDIENTS

1 package dry yeast
¼ cup warm water (105°–115°)
1¾ cups hot tap water (120°–130°)
¼ cup orange juice
¼ cup grated orange peel
½ cup sugar
1½ teaspoons salt
3 tablespoons shortening, room temperature
7½ cups all-purpose flour, approximately
1 egg, room temperature

BAKING PANS

Two medium (8½ x 4½) baking tins, greased or Teflon. If glass is used, reduce oven temperature 25°.

PREPARATION
20 mins.

In a small bowl dissolve the yeast in warm water. Stir briskly with a fork or whisk to hasten the action. Set aside.

In a large bowl combine hot tap water, orange juice, orange peel, sugar, salt and shortening. Add 2 cups of flour and mix well. Add egg and the yeast mixture. Beat 150 strong strokes with a wooden spoon until batter is smooth and begins to pull away from the sides of the bowl in strands. Gradually add more flour, ½ cup at a time, first with the spoon and then with the fingers, until a soft mass of dough is formed.

KNEADING
8 mins.

Turn the dough out onto a lightly floured work surface (counter top or bread board) and knead with a strong push-turn-fold motion until it is smooth and elastic. If the dough seems slack or unduly moist, add ¼ cup or so additional flour. (The kneading will take about 5 minutes with a dough hook.)

FIRST RISING
1½ hours

Place the dough in a greased bowl, turning once to coat all of the surfaces, and cover tightly with a length of plastic wrap. Put the bowl in a warm place (80°–85°), free of drafts, until the dough has doubled in volume. You can test if it has risen by poking a finger in it; the dent will remain.

SHAPING
10 mins.

Turn back the plastic wrap, punch down the dough with a blow of the fist, and let it rest for 10 minutes. Divide the dough in half. Form a ball with each piece, flatten it into an oval, fold in half, pinch the seam closed, and pat into a loaf that will fit into the pan. Repeat with the second piece.

SECOND RISING
1¼ hours

Cover pans with wax paper and return to the warm place until the dough rises about 1 inch above the pan.

BAKING
375°
45 mins.

Preheat oven to 375°. Place in the oven and bake until the crusts are a golden brown and the loaves are loose in their pans. When tapping on the bottom crust yields a hard hollow sound, they are done.

FINAL STEP

Remove bread from the oven. Turn from the pans, and place on a wire rack. I sometimes rub the crusts with the wrapping paper from a quarter pound of butter or brush with milk or cream for a lovely soft look.

RAISIN-ORANGE BREAD

[TWO LOAVES]

A fat, moist loaf replete with raisins, this bread is iced with a frosting of chopped walnuts beaten into a blend of confectioners' sugar, butter and orange juice. There are bits of orange peel in the yellow eggy dough which contrasts nicely with the dark raisins. In the oven it raises two or three inches above the pan to give the bread an open and airy texture.

Toasts beautifully, and freezes well if wrapped tightly in plastic wrap or foil.

INGREDIENTS

5 to 5½ cups all-purpose flour, approximately
2 packages dry yeast
1 cup milk } or 1¼ cups water and
¼ cup water } ½ cup non-fat dry milk
1 orange rind, grated
1 teaspoon ginger
½ cup *each* butter and sugar
1½ teaspoons salt
2 eggs, room temperature
1½ cups raisins
Glaze: 1 cup confectioners' sugar
2 teaspoons butter, room temperature
½ cup walnuts, finely chopped
2 to 4 tablespoons orange juice

BAKING PANS

Two medium (8½ x 4½) baking tins, greased or Teflon. If glass, reduce oven heat 25°.

PREPARATION
20 mins.

In a large mixer bowl, measure 2 cups of flour and sprinkle the yeast over it. Blend with a wooden spoon. In a saucepan, measure milk, water, orange rind, ginger, butter, sugar and salt. Put it over a low heat until it is warm (120°), stirring constantly. Pour this mixture into the flour and yeast, add eggs and beat with the electric mixer at low speed until the flour is moistened. Beat 3 minutes at high speed, or for the same length of time with a wooden spoon.

Stop the mixer, scrape down the bowl and stir in the raisins. Gradually add more flour to form a soft mass that cleans the sides of the bowl. Work the flour in by hand when the dough gets too stiff for the spoon.

KNEADING
6 mins.

Turn the soft dough out onto a lightly floured work surface—counter top or bread board, and knead with a strong push-turn-fold motion until the dough is smooth and elastic. If the dough is sticky or too moist (slack) add ½ cup flour and work it into the dough.

FIRST RISING
1¼ hours

Return the ball of dough to the bowl, pat with buttered fingers, and cover tightly with plastic wrap. Set the bowl in a warm place (80°–85°) until the dough has doubled in size. You can test if it has risen by poking a finger in it; the dent will remain.

SHAPING
20 mins.

Punch down the dough in the bowl, turn it out on a floured surface and knead briefly (1 minute) and let rest under a towel or piece of wax paper for about 15 minutes. Divide the dough into 2 parts, press each part into a flat oval, fold in half, pinch the seam tightly closed and pat into the shape of a loaf. Place in the pans and, with a sharp knife or razor blade, make 3 diagonal slashes ¼ inch deep across the top of each loaf.

SECOND RISING
1 hour

Cover the pans with wax paper and put in the warm place until dough has doubled in volume.

Meanwhile, prepare the topping: blend the confectioners' sugar with the butter, walnuts and orange juice to spreading consistency.

BAKING
375°
50 mins.

Preheat oven to 375°. Place the loaves in the hot oven until well browned. When tapping the bottom crust yields a hard hollow sound, they are done.

FINAL STEP

Remove bread from the oven. While the loaves are warm, spread the topping on the top crusts. However, allow the loaves to cool before serving.

GERMAN RAISIN BREAD

[A CHOICE OF LOAVES]

Whole almonds or pecans encrusted on the loaf—top and bottom—are a sign that this is a special bread. The sweet dough, tinted faintly with cinnamon, is finely textured and moist with potato. However, it is the big swirl of raisins, nuts, candied fruit and cinnamon inside that gives the loaf its character and exceptionally good taste. Whole nut meats are placed in the bottom of the baking pan before the loaf is set in, and then more nuts, dipped in egg, are placed on the top.

This recipe will make 3 medium loaves and 2 small ones—ideal for gifts. Warm to serve. Freeze sealed in foil or plastic.

INGREDIENTS

2 packages dry yeast
1 teaspoon sugar
½ cup lukewarm water (105°–115°)
8 cups all-purpose flour, approximately
1 tablespoon salt
2 tablespoons butter or margarine, room temperature
1 cup finely sieved cooked potato or ¼ cup instant potato mixed in 1 cup water
2 cups warm milk (105°–115°)
2 eggs, room temperature, and slightly beaten
1 cup sugar
¼ cup (½ stick) butter, melted
1 teaspoon cinnamon
The filling: 1½ cups of raisins
1½ cups coarsely chopped candied cherries
1 cup finely chopped nuts
½ cup chopped citron
½ cup sugar
1½ teaspoons cinnamon
4 tablespoons soft butter
24 whole almonds or pecans
1 beaten egg

BAKING PANS

Three medium (8½ x 4½) and two small (7½ x 3½) loaf pans, greased or Teflon, glass or metal. If glass, reduce oven heat 25°. Other choices of loaf sizes may be made by consulting the dough volume chart on page 23.

PREPARATION
Sponge
20 mins.

In a small bowl or measuring cup, dissolve yeast and sugar in water. Stir and set aside.

In a large mixing bowl stir 4 cups of flour and salt. Add butter or margarine and potato. Stir in milk and the yeast mixture. Mix thoroughly—100 strokes.

2 hours

Cover the bowl with plastic wrap and move to a warm place (80°–85°), free from drafts. Allow the sponge to rise until doubled in volume.

Dough
10 mins.

Turn back plastic wrap, stir sponge briefly. Add eggs, sugar, butter and cinnamon. Gradually add more flour

—about 3 or 4 cups, sufficient to form a soft mass that cleans the sides of the bowl. If it is moist and sticky, add ¼ cup or more flour.

8 mins.

Turn the dough onto a floured work surface and knead with a strong push-turn-fold action until the dough is smooth and elastic. Keep the work surface and fingers dusted with flour until the dough has lost all of its stickiness and becomes firm under the hands.

FIRST RISING
1 hour

Return the dough to the bowl, cover again and let rise until double in bulk.

Meanwhile, prepare the filling by mixing in a bowl the raisins, chopped candied cherries, chopped nuts, and citron. In a cup combine and have ready sugar and cinnamon. Melt butter in a small pan.

SHAPING
30 mins.

Turn the dough out onto the lightly floured work surface, counter top or bread board, and knead briefly to press out the bubbles. Divide the dough into however many loaves you have decided to bake. (See the dough volume chart, page 23.)

Roll each piece into a rectangle (9 x 12 for a medium loaf). Brush with butter and spread on the sugar and cinnamon mix. Leave a dry 1-inch margin around the edges so that a strong seam can be made. Divide the fruit-nut mixture among the pieces of dough. Smooth in place but keep it away from the margins.

Roll as you would a jelly roll, starting from a short side. Make the roll tight to avoid air spaces in the finished loaf. When the roll is almost to the end of the rectangle, *lift up* the edge of dough and pinch it to the roll. Don't take the roll all the way to the edge because this could push the filling into the cleared margin. Fold the ends to seal.

Scatter a few nuts on the bottom of the pans before placing the loaves.

SECOND RISING
1 hour

Cover the loaves with the wax paper and move them to the warm place until they have doubled in volume.

BAKING
350°
45 mins.

Preheat oven to 350°. Dip 12 or 15 nuts in beaten egg in a cup and lightly press in a pattern on top of each loaf. Bake in the oven until the loaves are nicely browned and loose in their pans. Turn one loaf out of its pan and tap the bottom crust with a forefinger. A hard hollow sound means the bread is done. If not, return loaf to the oven, without the pan if you wish a deeper over-all brown crust.

FINAL STEP

Remove bread from the oven. Turn the loaves out onto wire racks to cool. Brush each loaf generously with melted butter.

APPLE TEA BREAD

[ONE MEDIUM OR TWO SMALL LOAVES]

A tart Greening apple (smooth of skin and waxy) is considered the apple for apple pie, especially in New England, and it is prized, too, for apple bread. This loaf is delicious, however, made with any cooking apple—thanks to butter, brown sugar, sour cream, cinnamon, nutmeg, ginger, and walnuts. Slice thinly and serve for tea, breakfast or at a special brunch.

INGREDIENTS

1 cup tart cooking apples, finely chopped
½ cup (1 stick) butter, creamed
¾ cup brown sugar
2 eggs, room temperature
2 tablespoons sour cream or buttermilk, room temperature
2 cups all-purpose flour
2 teaspoons baking powder
1 teaspoon *each* baking soda and salt
¼ teaspoon *each* cinnamon, nutmeg and ginger
1 cup chopped English walnuts

BAKING PANS

One medium (8½ x 4½) loaf pan, or two small (7½ x 3½) pans, greased or Teflon, metal or glass. If the latter, reduce oven heat 25°. The loaves will come out of the pans with less trouble if they are greased and then lined with wax paper.

PREPARATION
20 mins.

Beforehand, finely chop apples to make 1 cup. Reserve.

In a medium bowl cream the butter, and beat in the brown sugar until light and fluffy. Add 2 eggs, beating each into the mixture. Stir in sour cream or buttermilk and the cup of chopped apples.

In a separate bowl sift or stir together the flour, baking powder, baking soda, salt, cinnamon, nutmeg, and ginger. Add chopped walnuts and toss them well.

Stir the dry ingredients into the apple batter, and mix thoroughly.

FORMING
2 mins.
Spoon the batter into the pans and level the tops.

RESTING
20 mins.
Put aside to rest. Preheat the oven to 350°.

BAKING
350°
45–60 mins.
Bake the large loaf in the moderate oven for about 1 hour, and the smaller loaves 45 minutes, or until a wooden toothpick or metal skewer inserted in the center of the loaf comes out clean and dry.

FINAL STEP
Remove bread from the oven. Let the bread cool 10 minutes before removing from the pans. Place on metal rack to finish cooling.

APRICOT LAYERED BREAD

[ONE LOAF]

This loaf has several touches that make it an unusual bread. There is a layer of purée of apricot sandwiched midway in the loaf which is topped with dribbles of hot butter and sprinkles of brown sugar before it is thrust into the oven. It is a moist loaf and the apricot may dribble when the loaf is cut warm but allow it to set and it will slice nicely. While it is a delicious loaf, it may be too sticky as finger food—so serve with a fork.

INGREDIENTS
1 cup dried apricots
Water to cover
½ cup sugar
2 cups all-purpose flour
2 teaspoons baking powder
½ teaspoon salt
¼ cup (½ stick) butter or margarine
1 cup milk
2 eggs, room temperature and beaten
Topping: 1 tablespoon *each* melted butter and brown sugar

BAKING PAN
One medium loaf pan (8½ x 4½), greased or Teflon. If a glass pan is used, reduce oven heat 25°.

PREPARATION
1¼ hours
First, the apricots. In a medium saucepan cover the apricots with cold water, bring water to a boil and sim-

mer, covered, until they are soft. This will take about 45 minutes. Remove the cover and cook over a low heat until nearly all of the water is cooked away. Put apricots through a food mill or press them through a fine sieve, add ½ cup sugar to the purée and beat with a fork until the sugar is worked into it. Set aside. Preheat oven to 375°.

15 mins. — Sift flour, baking powder and salt into a large bowl. With two knives (or the fingers), cut in the butter and then, with a wooden spoon, stir in milk combined with beaten eggs. Stir only enough to moisten the flour.

FORMING
10 mins. — Pour half the batter into the pan, smooth it out and with a spoon spread it with the apricot purée. Add the remaining batter. Sprinkle the batter with the melted butter and brown sugar.

BAKING
375°
40 mins. — Place in the oven and bake until a meter skewer or wooden toothpick inserted in the center of the loaf comes out dry and clean.

FINAL STEP — Remove bread from the oven. Carefully turn out the loaf onto a metal cooling rack.

VEL'S DATE BREAD

[TWO SMALL LOAVES]

The twenty members of the Hindostan Women's Booster Club in a small farming community in the rolling hills of southern Indiana put together a book of favorite recipes which they sold to underwrite the club's "service and work." This is one member's recipe for date bread that produces a rich brown waxy loaf packed with date and walnut bits.

INGREDIENTS

1½ cups boiling water
1½ cups chopped dates
1¼ cups sugar
1 egg, room temperature
2 teaspoons baking soda
½ teaspoon salt
1 teaspoon vanilla
1 tablespoon butter, melted
2½ cups all-purpose flour
1 cup walnuts, chopped

BAKING PANS — Two small (7½ x 3½) loaf pans, greased or Teflon. If glass, reduce oven heat 25°. Line the pans with buttered wax paper to keep the loaves from sticking.

PREPARATION
20 mins. — In a bowl pour the boiling water over the dates and let soak. Preheat the oven to 325°.

10 mins. — Stir into dates the sugar, egg, baking soda, salt, vanilla, and butter. In a separate bowl measure the flour and add chopped walnuts. Dredging in flour will keep the nuts from sinking in the batter. Add the flour-nut mixture to the wet ingredients, and mix thoroughly.

FORMING
5 mins. — Pour the mixture into the pans, push into the corners with a spoon and smooth the tops.

BAKING
325°
50 mins. — Bake in the oven until the loaves test done when a metal skewer inserted in the center comes out dry and clean. If moist particles cling to the probe, return the pans to the oven for an additional 10 minutes.

FINAL STEP — Remove bread from the oven. Allow to cool in the pans 10 minutes before turning the pans on their sides to pull out the loaves with a gentle tug on the paper lining. This loaf will keep nicely for a fortnight or more wrapped in plastic. Keeps frozen for several months.

AVOCADO BREAD

[ONE LOAF]

This is the loaf to serve on St. Patrick's Day. Not too surprisingly, it is green. Green bread can be beautiful and it can be good. The avocado taste is subtle but it is there nevertheless. There will be a slightly tan crust over the loaf but the interior is green. Try it sliced thin and spread with whipped cream cheese.

INGREDIENTS
1 egg, room temperature
½ cup mashed ripe avocado, room temperature
½ cup buttermilk or sour milk, room temperature
1 cup chopped pecans
2 cups all-purpose flour, sifted
¾ cup sugar
½ teaspoon *each* baking soda and baking powder
¼ teaspoon salt

BAKING PAN — One medium (8½ x 4½) loaf pan, Teflon or greased, glass or metal. If glass, reduce oven heat 25°. For ease of turning out the loaf, first butter the pan and then line the long sides and the bottom with one piece of wax paper. Butter it.

PREPARATION
20 mins.

In a medium bowl combine the slightly beaten egg, avocado, buttermilk or sour milk and pecans. Set this aside while proceeding with the dry ingredients.

In another medium bowl sift together sifted flour, sugar, baking soda, baking powder and salt. Pour in avocado, mixing it only until all of the flour is moistened. Don't overblend. Preheat oven to 350°.

FORMING

Pour the mixture into the pan, push into the corners with a spoon or spatula and smooth on top.

BAKING
350°
1 hour

Bake in the oven until it tests done when pierced with a metal skewer or wooden toothpick. If the probe comes out clean, the loaf is done. It will have a fine green valley down the middle, with light brown crust on either side.

FINAL STEP

Remove bread from the oven. Turn it out of the pan with care. Peel off the paper and allow the loaf to cool on a wire rack. It will be better flavored after it has matured into the second day.

ORANGE PEEL BREAD

[COMBINATION OF LOAF SIZES]

Fresh orange or tangerine peel and a cup of water go into an electric blender, and are then cooked down with sugar into a thin syrup that carries the orange taste into the loaf. The brown sugar gives the chewy loaf its deep color.

INGREDIENTS

¾ cup orange or tangerine peel
1 cup water
1 cup sugar
1 cup brown sugar, firmly packed
1 tablespoon butter or other shortening
1 egg, room temperature
1 cup finely chopped walnuts
3½ cups white flour
3 tablespoons baking powder
½ teaspoon salt
1 cup milk, room temperature

BAKING UTENSIL — One large (9 x 5) loaf pan, greased or Teflon, or three greased 1-pound coffee cans. For other size loaf pans see dough volume chart on page 23. A loaf can be turned out of a pan quicker and cleaner when the pan is first buttered, lined with wax paper and buttered again. If glass, reduce oven heat 25°.

PREPARATION
15 mins. — In the electric blender whirl peel and water at high speed until the peel is cut into fine pieces. (Or put just the peel through a food chopper with fine blade three times.) Combine 1 cup sugar with the peel mixture in a saucepan, and bring to a boil. Boil, stirring constantly, for about 15 minutes or until the liquid has been reduced to 1 cup. Set aside.

15 mins. — Combine the brown sugar and butter with a fork in a large bowl until the butter is in tiny coarse lumps. With a wooden spoon, stir in the egg, walnuts and the orange peel mixture until well blended, about 25 strokes. On a length of wax paper, sift the flour, baking powder and salt together, and add to the mixture ½ cup at a time. Alternately pour in milk. Mix only until it is just combined—no longer.

FORMING
3 mins. — Pour the dough in pan or pans you want from the volume chart or one 9 x 5 loaf pan or three 1-pound cans, and level with a rubber scraper.

BAKING
350°
45–60 mins. — Preheat oven to 350°. Bake in a moderate oven 45 minutes for the smaller loaves, and 1 hour for the large loaf. Pierce in the center of a loaf with a metal skewer or wooden toothpick. If it comes out clean and dry, the loaf is done. If moist particles cling to the probe, return the loaf to the oven for an additional 10 minutes.

FINAL STEP — Remove bread from the oven and carefully turn out on a wire rack to cool.

CAPE COD CRANBERRY BREAD

[ONE LARGE OR TWO SMALL LOAVES]

Cranberries, orange and nuts blend together exceptionally well in this loaf from a kitchen on the Massachusetts shore. The coarsely chopped cranberries are mixed with an orange that has been fed through the fine blade of a food chopper. The result is colorful (the red and orange bits) and piquant (the slight acid of the cranberries). The loaf is shiny brown and while it is not large it is an excellent holiday gift. After it has aged for a day, slice and serve with coffee, tea or a glass of port.

INGREDIENTS

1 orange, finely ground
1½ cups cranberries, coarsely chopped
1 cup sugar
1 egg, room temperature, beaten
2 cups all-purpose flour
1½ teaspoons baking powder
1 teaspoon salt
½ teaspoon baking soda
¼ cup shortening
½ cup chopped walnuts

BAKING PANS

One large loaf pan (9 x 5), buttered or Teflon, or two small pans (7½ x 3½). If glass, reduce oven heat 25°.

PREPARATION
30 mins.

Prepare the orange by cutting it into 8 sections and removing the seeds and the center membrane with the tines of a fork. Feed the flesh and rind through the finest blade of a food chopper. Spoon the ground orange into a measuring cup and add boiling water to make a full cup. Coarsely chop the cranberries.

In a medium bowl combine the cranberries, sugar, beaten egg and orange mixture. Put aside.

In a large bowl sift together flour, baking powder, salt and baking soda. With a pastry blender or two knives, cut in the shortening until the mixture is uniformly coarse. Pour in the cranberry mixture. Stir only until it is mixed and moist. Do not beat. Stir in the chopped nuts.

FORMING
5 mins.

Butter the pan or pans and line with wax paper cut to fit. Butter the paper in place and pour in the batter.

RESTING
20 mins.

Let the batter stand while the oven is heating to 350°.

BAKING
350°
50–60 mins.

Bake the bread in the oven about 1 hour. (The smaller loaves may take 10 minutes *less* time.) Test for doneness with a toothpick inserted in the center of the loaves. If it comes out clean and dry, the loaves are done.

FINAL STEP

Remove bread from the oven. Turn on the side and carefully pull the loaves out by pulling the wax paper. Use equal care in peeling the paper off the loaves. Let the bread cool on a metal rack before slicing. It will have greater flavor the following day.

BRAN DATE BREAD DELUXE

[ONE MEDIUM LOAF]

At first it is the bran that dominates this dark handsome loaf but then gradually the palate is aware of wheat and the richness of the walnuts and dates. This recipe is adapted from one in an early edition (1943) of *The Joy of Cooking* in which the authors said, in the best Michelin tradition, "this recipe is worthy of three stars." It remains so.

It is a heavy, moist brick that makes wonderful sandwiches with butter or cream cheese.

INGREDIENTS

2 cups chopped dates
2 cups boiling water
2 eggs, room temperature
¾ cup brown sugar
2 cups whole wheat flour
2 teaspoons baking powder
1 teaspoon baking soda
2 cups bran
1 teaspoon vanilla
1 cup chopped walnut meats

BAKING PAN

One medium (8½ x 4½) loaf pan, greased or Teflon, metal or glass. If glass, reduce oven heat 25°. The loaf will come out of the pan with ease if the long sides and bottom are lined with a length of wax paper after the pan is greased. Be certain to butter the paper.

PREPARATION
20 mins.

Chop the dates and place them in a bowl and pour 2 cups boiling water over them. Set aside.

In a large bowl beat the eggs until light and slowly add the brown sugar—beating constantly. When this is creamy gradually add 1 cup whole wheat flour, baking powder, and baking soda. Add one half the date mixture and the other 1 cup of whole wheat flour, the bran and vanilla. When this is blended, add the second portion of the date mixture and the chopped nut meats.

FORMING
10 mins.

Pour or spoon the mixture into the pan. Let it stand while the oven heats to 350°.

BAKING
350°
1 hour

Place the pan in the oven and bake until the loaf is a deep crusty brown and tests done when a wooden toothpick inserted in the center of the loaf comes out clean and dry.

FINAL STEP

Remove bread from the oven. Turn the pan on its side and pull the loaf out by tugging gently on the wax paper edges. Peel the paper from the loaf and leave it to cool on a metal rack. This loaf will be better if allowed to age overnight; then it will be delicious. It keeps well for several days wrapped in plastic, or can be frozen for months.

CRANBERRY NUT BREAD

[TWO SMALL OR ONE LARGE LOAF]

This bread is a treat not only during the weeks of Thanksgiving and Christmas—considered the cranberry season, certainly—but whenever this bright red berry is on the market. Cranberries (also called mossberries) give the loaf a slight tartness (acidulousness) and spot it with bits of bright color. Orange peel and orange juice heighten the flavor. I usually make two small 1-pound loaves; one for home and the other a gift.

INGREDIENTS

2 cups all-purpose flour
1 cup sugar
1½ teaspoons baking powder
½ teaspoon baking soda
1 teaspoon salt
¼ cup shortening
¾ cup orange juice
1 tablespoon grated orange rind
1 egg, room temperature and beaten
½ cup chopped nuts
1 cup cranberries, coarsely chopped

BAKING TINS

One large (9 x 5) or two small (7½ x 3½) loaf tins, greased or Teflon. If glass, reduce oven heat 25°.

PREPARATION
20 mins.

In a large bowl sift together flour, sugar, baking powder, baking soda, and salt. With a pastry blender or two knives cut in the shortening until the mixture resembles coarse cornmeal.

In a small bowl combine orange juice and grated rind with the beaten egg. Pour the liquid into the dry ingredients and mix just enough to dampen. Don't beat. Carefully fold in the nuts and cranberries.

FORMING
3 mins.

Whichever pan or pans you choose (see dough volume chart, page 23), butter well, line the long sides and bottom with one length of wax paper, butter paper in place—for easy removal of the loaf. The mixture will be stiff and must be pushed into the corners of the pan with a spoon or spatula. Form it slightly higher on the sides to compensate for the rising crown.

RESTING
20 mins.

While the oven preheats to 350°, allow the filled pan to rest.

BAKING
350°
1 hour

Bake in the oven until the loaf tests done when pierced in the center with a metal skewer or wooden toothpick. If it comes out clean and dry, the loaf is baked. If moist particles cling to the pin, return the loaf to the oven for an additional 10 minutes. Test again.

FINAL STEP

Remove bread from the oven. Carefully turn from the pan, peel the wax paper away and cool on a metal rack. An easy way to remove the loaf is to turn the pan on its side, tug gently at the leading edges of the wax paper to work the loaf loose. Allow the loaf to age overnight before slicing.

PORTUGUESE NUT AND FRUIT BREAD

[TWO ROUND LOAVES]

A delicate bread, flavored heavily with ground almonds, its good taste rests also on butter, raisins, fruit peel, and a garniture of candied fruits, whole almonds, pine nuts and coarse decorating sugar. It is finely textured, moist and delicious. Serve for breakfast, brunch or buffet. The bread rises up and around a small ovenproof cup or dish that protects the center hole during the baking.

INGREDIENTS

5 to 6 cups all-purpose flour, approximately
1 cup sugar
1 tablespoon salt

2 packages dry yeast
½ cup non-fat dry milk
1¼ cups hot tap water (120°–130°)
¼ pound (1 stick) butter, room temperature
3 eggs, room temperature
3 tablespoons *each* raisins, diced mixed candied peel and chopped almonds
1 egg, room temperature and lightly beaten
Topping: Whole almonds, candied fruit, pine nuts, and coarse decorating sugar

BAKING SHEETS

Two baking sheets, greased or Teflon. Two 2½-inch ovenproof baking dishes.

PREPARATION
20 mins.

In a large mixer bowl measure 2 cups of flour, sugar, salt, yeast and milk. Stir together.

In a saucepan pour the water over the butter, stir and pour into the dry ingredients. Beat 100 strokes with a wooden spoon or 3 minutes at medium speed in an electric mixer. Add the 3 eggs, one at a time, and continue beating until blended. Stop the mixer and gradually work in the remaining flour, ½ cup at a time, sufficient to make a soft mass that cleans the sides of the bowl. When the spoon can no longer stir the dough, use the fingers.

KNEADING
10–12 mins.

Turn the dough onto a floured work surface and knead with a strong push-turn-fold motion, for 10 or 12 minutes until the dough is smooth and elastic. (Knead with the dough hook for 8 minutes.)

5 mins.

Flatten the dough into a large oval, and pour the raisins, peel and almonds over it. Fold the edges in and begin to work the mixture into the dough.

FIRST RISING
1 hour

Return dough to the bowl, pat with buttered fingers, cover tightly with plastic wrap and put in a warm place (80°–85°) until doubled in volume.

SHAPING
20 mins.

Meanwhile, prepare the baking sheets and the 2½-inch heatproof baking dishes. Butter the dishes on the outside.

Punch down the dough, turn it onto the work surface again, divide in half, knead briefly to press out the bubbles, and then poke or tear a finger-hole in the center of the dough. Gently enlarge the hole until the center will slip over the small prepared dish. Pat into shape and place the dough and its center dish on a baking sheet. Repeat with second piece.

SECOND RISING
50 mins.

Cover with wax paper and return to the warm place until doubled in volume. You can test if it has risen by poking a finger in it; the dent will remain.

BAKING
350°
1 hour

Preheat oven to 350°. Brush the loaves with beaten egg and decorate with whole almonds, red and green bits of candied fruit and whole pine nuts. Press these gently into the dough. Sprinkle with coarse granulated or decorating sugar. Bake in the oven until golden brown and crusty. Test with a wooden toothpick pushed into the loaf—if it comes out clean and dry the loaves are baked. If the loaves are placed in the oven on two shelves, alternate the pans after 30 minutes of the bake period. Do this twice more during the baking, and, at the same time, turn the loaves on the baking sheets so they are exposed to all parts of the oven.

FINAL STEP

Remove bread from the oven and carefully place the loaves on metal racks to cool before serving. Don't tear the inner ring of dough when removing the dish. Cut around it on the underside with a sharp knife if it is reluctant to drop out. This bread will keep for days wrapped in foil or plastic. It also freezes well for several months.

SELKIRK BANNOCK

[THREE LOAVES]

In 1859, in the Scottish town of Selkirk, southeast of Edinburgh, a baker, Robbie Douglas, opened a shop in the Market Place to sell a bannock that was to bring fame to Robbie and to the community. He imported his raisins from Turkey and bought butter made from milk produced on selected neighboring pastures. His fame and recipe still live. It is a weighty, rounded loaf, flat on the bottom and curved on top, with about half of its weight in fruit. This is an adaptation of his original recipe that I found in Edinburgh.

INGREDIENTS

4 to 5 cups all-purpose flour, approximately
1 package dry yeast
2 teaspoons salt

1½ cups hot tap water (120°–130°)
1 cup (2 sticks) butter, room temperature
½ cup (4 oz.) lard, room temperature
1 cup sugar
2 pounds raisins, sultanas or dark

BAKING PANS
Three round 8- or 9-inch cake pans, greased or Teflon, with 1½-inch sides.

PREPARATION
15 mins.
Measure 1 cup of flour into a large mixing bowl and stir in the yeast, salt and water, and put aside for a moment. Cream together the butter, lard and sugar in a separate bowl. Thoroughly combine the two mixes.

Stir in the remaining flour, a half cup at a time, first with the spoon and then by hand as the dough becomes more firm. It will be buttery and oily, hence won't cling to the bowl. Add flour sufficient to make a dough that is firm but elastic.

KNEADING
6 mins.
Place the dough on a lightly floured work surface and knead for 2 minutes. Add the raisins. This is a large measure and it will take a few minutes before the dough will accept them but in the meantime you will be kneading the dough as you work them in. Knead for a total of 6 minutes or until all of the raisins are in, and it is an elastic, firm ball that will hold its own shape in the pan.

SHAPING
6 mins.
Divide the dough into 3 parts. Mold each piece into a large round bun, and place in the pan. It should not touch the sides of the pan but rise up in a gentle curve away from the sides.

RISING
30 mins.
Cover the pans with wax paper and place in a warm spot (80°–85°). If the paper sticks to the dough, rest it on water tumblers above the dough.

BAKING
350°
1¼ hours
Preheat the oven to 350°. Bake in the oven. When tapping the bottom crust yields a hard hollow sound, they are done. If the crust should brown too quickly, cover with a piece of foil or brown sack paper.

FINAL STEP
Remove bread from oven; carefully place the loaves on metal racks to cool.

The Selkirk bakery suggests—

"It is cut into thin slices and eaten with or without butter. It is rich but not over-rich, and the butter that it contains is very noticeable. It is very economical since little is required and it keeps well. Wrapped in a cloth and placed in a tin, it will keep moist and palatable for a month or longer."

Of course, it can be frozen and left for several months.

RAISIN-NUT BRAID

[TWO LOAVES]

Chopped walnuts and raisins are so thick in this rich dough that some will fall out when the long strands are braided. Push them back in anywhere. Others will have the appearance of wanting to come out but won't. They will be surrounded and held firmly in an elastic grip when the dough expands.

There is a rugged handsomeness about this loaf that could come only from under the hands of a home bread maker.

INGREDIENTS

1 package dry yeast
¼ cup warm water (105°–115°)
2 cups milk, warm (105°–115°)
½ cup *each* sugar and shortening, room temperature
2 teaspoons salt
6 to 7 cups all-purpose or bread flour, approximately
1 cup *each* seedless raisins and chopped walnuts
Topping: 1 cup confectioners' sugar, 1 tablespoon milk and ½ teaspoon vanilla. Several candied cherries, cut in half

BAKING SHEET

One baking sheet, greased or Teflon.

PREPARATION
15 mins.

In a small bowl or cup dissolve the yeast in the water. Stir briskly with a fork or metal whisk. Set aside.

In a large bowl pour the milk, sugar, shortening and salt. Stir in the yeast. Measure in 3 cups of flour—beat well, about 150 strong strokes. Stir in raisins and nuts. Gradually add remaining flour, ½ cup at a time, first with the spoon and then by hand, until a rough, soft mass has formed. It will pull away from the sides of the bowl until only a film of dough remains. A dough hook will absolutely clean the sides of the bowl; a hand operation will not. Scrape down the film or coating with the fingertips or the edge of the spoon or spatula.

KNEADING
6 mins.

Spread flour on the work surface—counter top or bread board—turn the dough onto this. If it is moist (slack) and sticky, work in a little more flour. Presently it will become elastic and no longer sticky.

FIRST RISING
1½ hours

Return the dough to the bowl, pat with butter or shortening on the fingertips, and cover tightly with plastic wrap. Put in a warm place (80°–85°) until the dough has doubled in bulk. You can test if it has risen by poking a finger in it; the dent will remain.

SHAPING
25 mins.

Remove the plastic wrap, punch down the dough and turn it onto the floured work surface again. Cut the dough in two equal pieces. Shape each into a ball, cover and let rest for 10 minutes.

The rest period is important. The gluten must relax, otherwise you are constantly trying to stretch it when it wants to pull back.

Divide each half into 3 pieces. Roll each into a strand 20 inches long. However, give the dough time to relax by rolling the first strand out to only 10 inches, and then do the second and third strands to get them started. Return to #1 (which has now relaxed) and complete the braid to its full 20 inches. Then go back to the other two. If some of the nuts and raisins spill out tuck them back into a crack or fold.

Lay the 3 strips side by side and braid by starting in the center, working to either end. Pinch the ends tightly together. Avoid stretching the strands. Repeat for the other half piece. Place both braids on the baking sheet.

SECOND RISING
1 hour

Cover the braids with a layer of wax paper and return to the warm place. The braids will double in volume.

BAKING
375°
20–25 mins.

Preheat oven to 375°. After the braids have risen, be certain they are still pinched tightly together at the ends. Place them in the oven until they are light brown. Test by piercing between the braids with a toothpick. If it comes out dry, and not damp with dough, the braid is done.

FINAL STEP

Remove bread from the oven. Handle the hot braids carefully as they may crack apart. Lift from the bake sheet with a spatula and place on a metal rack to cool. While slightly warm, spread crust with the confectioners' icing. Decorate with candied cherries.

If a large braid is to be given as a gift or to be carried away, it is wise to place a piece of cardboard, trimmed to size, under it.

TWENTY-ONE

Little Breads

Fennel
Lyons, 1579

These wonderful small breads range from Tennessee Beaten Biscuits to Baps from Edinburgh. This is a chapter in which I have assembled all of the one-bite or two-bite recipes from my kitchen. There is no reason for mixing Bath Buns with Croissants or Hot Cross Buns with Sopaipillas except none are very big and all are very good.

CAMPER'S BAKING POWDER BISCUITS

[A DOZEN OR SO]

These should not be reserved exclusively for the High Sierra or a canoe trip. They are too good. They can be served at home at any meal and to any company. Most of the ingredients—flour, baking powder, salt and non-fat dry milk—can be carried pre-mixed in packages and all that need be added is shortening and water. The warm fat from just-fried bacon is a good shortening.

INGREDIENTS

1 cup all-purpose flour
1 teaspoon baking powder
¼ teaspoon salt
2 tablespoons non-fat dry milk
3 tablespoons butter, margarine or bacon drippings
¼ cup cold water, approximately

BAKING SHEET OR FRY PAN — Lightly greased or Teflon pan or baking sheet for camp stove oven or reflector oven. These can also be baked in a fry pan over the campfire coals.

PREPARATION
8 mins. — Measure the flour into a bowl and stir in baking powder, salt and dry milk. Work the shortening into the flour mixture with the fingertips until it becomes tiny floured granules. Gradually dribble in the water to make a soft dough, using first a spoon and then the fingertips. If too much water is added and the dough becomes sticky, sprinkle on a little flour.

KNEADING
30 seconds — This isn't kneading in the usual sense. It really is more mixing.

SHAPING
5 mins. — Pat the dough into a rough rectangle about ¾ of an inch thick. With a sharp knife cut the dough into 2-inch squares. Cluster the fragments together and bake them, too.

BAKING
450°
10–12 mins. — Bake in the oven or in a reflector oven until a rich brown and raised about 1½ to 2 inches high.

They may also be cooked in a fry pan on the stove, and each must be turned several times to assure even through-and-through baking.

FINAL STEP — Remove from the oven and serve immediately. Stow one or two in a pocket for a snack later on the trail.

BUTTERMILK BISCUITS

[A DOZEN]

These never rise very high in my oven—perhaps no more than half an inch—but they are absolutely delicious golden discs. I use yellow cornmeal to give them the golden tone but it is the buttermilk and lard, combined with the meal, that makes it a fine breakfast biscuit.

INGREDIENTS

1 cup all-purpose flour
½ teaspoon salt
1 teaspoon sugar
¼ teaspoon *each* baking soda and baking powder
⅓ cup yellow cornmeal
⅓ cup lard, room temperature
⅓ cup buttermilk, approximately
2 tablespoons butter, melted to brush

BAKING SHEET	One baking sheet, greased or Teflon.
PREPARATION 10 mins.	Preheat oven to 450°. Sift the flour, salt, sugar, baking soda and baking powder into a mixing bowl. Add cornmeal, and stir to blend. Cut in the lard with a pastry blender or the fingertips until the mixture is like coarse meal. Slowly dribble in the buttermilk, sufficient to barely hold the dough together yet with enough body to roll or pat flat. The amount of buttermilk may vary according to the ability of the flour to absorb it.
SHAPING 5 mins.	On a lightly floured work surface roll or pat the dough to ⅓ of an inch thick, and cut with a 2-inch cutter. These biscuits are delicate so lift them with a broad spatula or putty knife and place them on the baking sheet about a half inch apart. Brush with the melted butter.
BAKING 450° 12–15 mins.	Bake in the oven.
FINAL STEP	Remove biscuits from the oven. Serve piping hot. These are unusually good served at room temperature, too.

BUTTERMILK BRAN MUFFINS

[ABOUT THREE DOZEN]

The women of Hindostan, in southern Indiana (population: about 20 families), make a delicious bran muffin, part All-Bran and part Bran Buds (both Kellogg's). The result is a light, moist and completely satisfying muffin, though not as dark or as heavy as some.

The batter can be kept in a bowl in the refrigerator, tightly sealed with plastic wrap, and used as desired over a period of one or two weeks.

INGREDIENTS	1 cup All-Bran 2 cups Bran Buds 1 cup hot tap water (120°–130°) ½ cup vegetable shortening, room temperature 1½ cups sugar 2 eggs, room temperature 2½ cups all-purpose flour

2½ teaspoons baking soda
1½ teaspoons salt
2 cups (1 pint) buttermilk, room temperature

MUFFIN PANS — Muffin pans, greased or Teflon, with 36 cups for the full recipe.

PREPARATION
12 mins.

Preheat the oven to 350°.

Measure All-Bran and Bran Buds into a bowl and pour water over them. Set aside for a few moments until needed.

In a large bowl cream the shortening, sugar and eggs. On a length of wax paper sift the flour, baking soda and salt. Add this to the sugar-egg mix, alternately with the buttermilk. Stir in the moist bran and blend them all together well.

FORMING
3 mins.

Spoon the batter into the prepared muffin cups—about half full.

BAKING
350°
15–18 mins.

Bake in the oven until the muffins have raised and test done when a wooden toothpick inserted in the center of a muffin comes out clean and dry. If particles cling to the probe, return to the oven for 3 or 4 minutes. Test again.

FINAL STEP — Remove muffins from the oven. Allow the muffins to remain in the pans for 10 minutes before removing them. Serve warm or at room temperature. Either way, they are excellent.

BREADSTICKS

[ANY NUMBER]

Start with any dough—white, whole wheat, rye—roll out under the palms, pencil-thin and 6 or 8 inches in length. Bake for 20 minutes in a hot oven. There are a dozen variations—sprinkled with cheese, salt, nut meats, or any of your favorite herbs and spices.

INGREDIENTS — Bread dough, fresh-made or left over and frozen from some other baking project.

BAKING SHEET — One baking sheet, greased or Teflon.

BAKING
425°
20 mins.

Place about ½ inch apart on the baking sheet, and bake until the breadsticks are crisp and brown.

FINAL STEP

Remove from the oven. Arrange on a metal rack to cool. They may be stored in an airtight can or wrapped in plastic or frozen.

BENNE SEED BISCUITS

[ABOUT TWO DOZEN]

In Southern cooking and baking recipes the wild sesame seed is called the benne seed. One of its traditional uses is in the benne seed biscuit. The dough is rolled wafer thin and baked no longer than 8 to 10 minutes. It has an uncommon flavor that will intrigue guests.

INGREDIENTS

2 cups all-purpose flour
½ cup margarine or butter, room temperature
1 teaspoon baking powder
½ teaspoon salt
½ cup milk
½ cup roasted benne or sesame seeds

BAKING SHEET

One baking sheet, greased or Teflon.

PREPARATION
10 mins.

Preheat oven to 350°. Measure flour into a mixing bowl and rub in the margarine or butter with the fingertips. Stir in the baking powder, salt and milk. Blend thoroughly with 30 or 40 strokes. Add the benne or sesame seeds and work them into the dough.

SHAPING
15 mins.

Lightly flour the work surface—counter top or bread board—and turn out the dough. Roll wafer thin (⅛ of an inch or the thickness of two sesame seeds placed side by side) and cut circles with a 2-inch cutter. Arrange the circles on the baking sheet.

BAKING
350°
8–10 mins.

Place the baking sheet in the oven.

FINAL STEP

Remove biscuits from the oven. Place the biscuits on a metal rack and sprinkle lightly with salt. Serve when warm, but they are equally good at room temperature.

CORN PONES

[TWELVE TO FIFTEEN]

Two of the South's basic crops—corn and peanuts—are natural companions in this unleavened bread. While corn pone can be almost any corn bread made without milk or eggs, this version has ground raw peanuts as the added ingredient.

It is not an elegant bread, certainly—rough in texture and form—nevertheless it has a nutty flavor that is unusual and good.

I freeze a half dozen of these and carry them with me when I bicycle through the rolling hills of southern Indiana. By the time I cycle to the top of the sixth or seventh hill they are thawed—and delicious.

INGREDIENTS

4 tablespoons ground unroasted peanuts
3 cups stone ground cornmeal
1 teaspoon salt
¼ cup cooking oil (corn preferred)
2 cups boiling hot water

BAKING SHEET

One baking sheet, greased or Teflon.

PREPARATION
10 mins.

Beforehand grind or chop finely the raw peanuts.

In a bowl measure peanuts, cornmeal, salt, cooking oil and water. Mix for 2 minutes, adding more water if necessary to form a dough that clings together and is not dry.

SHAPING
8 mins.

Preheat oven to 350°. When the mixture has cooled, use two tablespoons to shape the ½-inch-thick cakes on the baking sheet. Use a heaped tablespoonful for each cake, patting it into a round, flat shape—about 3 inches in diameter—with the spoons, or fingers.

BAKING
350°
40–50 mins.

Bake in the oven until crisp.

FINAL STEP

Remove bread from the oven. Serve warm with butter and honey. Or carry on a trip.

ITALIAN BREADSTICKS

[ABOUT FOUR DOZEN]

Breadsticks in my kitchen are irregular creations to say the least. My big hands simply cannot consistently roll out a slender length of dough the diameter of a lead pencil. So, I take great pride in breadsticks that may be short or long or thin or fat, and a bit bumpy here and there. Nevertheless, they are delicious and I have yet to see anyone scorn them for their lack of uniformity or beauty.

INGREDIENTS

1 package dry yeast
⅔ cup warm water (105°–115°)
2 tablespoons *each* salad oil and olive oil
1 teaspoon salt
1 tablespoon sugar
2¼ cups all-purpose flour, approximately
Glaze: 1 egg, beaten
3 tablespoons either poppy or sesame seeds—or half the breadsticks with one and half with the other

BAKING SHEET

One baking sheet, greased or Teflon.

PREPARATION
15 mins.

In a large bowl stir the yeast into the water and set aside for 3 minutes. Measure and pour in salad oil, olive oil, salt, sugar and 1 cup of flour. Beat 100 strokes or until it is smooth. Gradually add enough of the remaining flour to make a soft dough. If the dough is slack or wet, add ¼ cup more flour.

KNEADING
6 mins.

Turn the dough onto a floured work surface and knead until smooth and elastic. Break the kneading rhythm occasionally by throwing the dough down hard against the counter top.

FIRST RISING
1 hour

Place the dough in the bowl, cover tightly with plastic wrap and put in a warm place (80°–85°) until the dough has doubled in bulk.

SHAPING
20 mins.

Punch dough down. Divide in half and then cut each half into 24 equal pieces—48 in all. Roll each under the palms into a slender cylinder about the length and diameter of a pencil. Place side by side on the baking sheet, leaving ½ inch between them. Brush with the beaten egg and sprinkle with poppy or sesame seeds, or both.

SECOND RISING
30 mins.

Cover with wax paper and return to the warm place until almost doubled in size.

BAKING
325°
30 mins.

Bake in the oven until the sticks are a light golden brown. Very thin sticks take less time and should be removed from the oven earlier.

FINAL STEP

Remove sticks from the oven and place them on a wire rack to cool. Keep in an airtight jar for several days, or freeze wrapped in plastic wrap for longer periods.

WHEAT-GERM BISCUITS

[A DOZEN]

Since the very essence of the wheat taste rests in the germ, this biscuit has a special appeal for those who like the full flavor of the dark grains. Not only is it good eating, but it supplies a bonus of wheat nutrients to the family.

It can be made in a very short while—less than 35 minutes from measuring the flour to serving.

INGREDIENTS

1½ cups all-purpose flour
½ cup wheat germ
1 tablespoon baking powder
1 teaspoon salt
¼ cup shortening
¾ cup milk, room temperature

BAKING SHEET

One baking sheet, ungreased or Teflon.

PREPARATION
10 mins.

Preheat oven to 450°. Measure flour into a bowl and stir in wheat germ, baking powder and salt. Cut in shortening with a pastry blender, or the fingers, and work it until it looks like coarse meal. Pour in milk and stir until all of the ingredients are moistened, no more.

KNEADING
45 seconds

Turn the dough onto a lightly floured work surface and knead 15 or 20 times.

SHAPING
10 mins.

Roll the dough ½ inch thick. Cut with a 2-inch cutter. Place the rounds on baking sheet.

BAKING
450°
12–15 mins.

Bake in the oven until the biscuits are a lovely brown.

FINAL STEP

Remove biscuits from the oven and serve warm.

CRUSTY WATER ROLLS

[EIGHTEEN]

This is an attractive round roll, glazed with a mixture of egg yolk and water, and peppered on the bottom with cornmeal. Beaten egg whites are folded into the dough to add to the leavening of the yeast and to give the roll a special softness. These are fine as dinner rolls, and because they are not overly sweet, they can be served at a buffet broken open to be filled with small pieces of meat, such as teriyaki steak, or a sliver of ham or turkey.

INGREDIENTS

1 cup warm water (105°–115°)
1 tablespoon sugar
1½ teaspoons salt
1 package dry yeast
3½ to 4 cups all-purpose flour, approximately
2 tablespoons vegetable oil
2 egg whites
1 tablespoon cornmeal
Glaze: 1 egg yolk
1 tablespoon water

BAKING SHEET

One baking sheet, greased or Teflon.

PREPARATION
18 mins.

In a large bowl mix together water, sugar, salt and yeast. Stir until ingredients are dissolved. Add 1 cup flour and the oil. Beat with vigorous strokes into a smooth batter. Set aside.

Beat egg whites until they are stiff but not dry. Fold these into the batter. The dough may seem slow to accept the whites but it will within a minute or two. Stir in the balance of the flour, a half cup at a time, first with the spoon and then by hand.

KNEADING
8 mins.

Turn the dough onto a lightly floured work surface—counter top or bread board—and knead with a rhythmic 1-2-3 motion of push-turn-fold. The dough will become smooth and elastic, and bubbles will rise under the surface of the dough. Sprinkle more flour on the dough and work surface if it continues to be sticky. (Knead 6 minutes with the dough hook.)

FIRST RISING
1 hour

Place dough back in the mixing bowl and pat with buttered or greased fingers. Cover the bowl tightly with plastic wrap and move to a warm place (80°–85°) until the dough has risen to about twice its original size.

SECOND RISING
15 mins.

Turn back plastic wrap and punch down dough with the fingers. Turn the edges into the center and turn over in the bowl. Return plastic wrap and let bread rise.

SHAPING
20 mins.

Turn the dough onto the work surface, knead for 30 seconds to press out the bubbles and cut into 18 equal pieces. Shape each into a neat round ball, dip the bottom in cornmeal and place on the prepared baking sheet. Place them about 1½ inches apart.

THIRD RISING
50 mins.

Cover with wax paper and return to the warm place until the rolls have about doubled in size.

BAKING
400°
15–20 mins.

Preheat oven to 400°. Brush each with the egg yolk beaten with the 1 tablespoon water. Place in the oven until the rolls are a bright shiny brown.

FINAL STEP

Remove rolls from the oven. Place them on a metal rack to cool somewhat before serving. They are best, of course, served right from the oven but these do keep well for a week or more.

CORN STICKS

[BETWEEN FIFTEEN AND TWENTY]

Each grain of cornmeal is left distinct and separate in this recipe that can be used for corn sticks, muffins or gems. There is a roughness about the surface of the baked bread that I find particularly appealing.

INGREDIENTS

½ cup all-purpose flour
2½ teaspoons baking powder
1 teaspoon sugar
½ teaspoon salt
1½ cups cornmeal
1 egg, room temperature
¾ cup milk, room temperature
3 tablespoons butter, melted

BAKING PANS OR TINS

Fifteen to 20 corn stick molds or muffin tins, oiled.

PREPARATION
8 mins.

Preheat the oven to 425°. Sift or stir together flour, baking powder, sugar and salt in a bowl. Mix in cornmeal and blend thoroughly. In another bowl beat egg until it is light in color, and stir in milk and melted butter. Using as few strokes as possible, stir the egg mixture into the cornmeal. The batter will be lumpy.

FORMING
2 mins.

Pour batter into prepared corn stick molds or muffin tins.

BAKING
425°
20–25 mins.

Bake in the oven until they are crisp and hard on the surface.

FINAL STEP

Remove bread from the oven. Serve hot with sweet butter.

FENNEL AND SALT BREADSTICKS

[BETWEEN FIFTY AND SEVENTY]

These fennel breadsticks—sprinkled with fennel and coarse salt—have brown crisp crusts and tender speckled-white insides. They are rolled by hand which gives them a pleasant home-fashioned irregularity. I do half of them with coarse salt sprinkled on the crust and the balance with fennel. The beer is optional. Breadsticks accompany soups and salads well, and are fine to nudge into soft dips.

INGREDIENTS

1 package dry yeast
¾ cup *each* warm water (105°–115°), salad oil, and beer
1½ teaspoons salt
1 tablespoon fennel seed
4½ cups all-purpose flour, approximately
Glaze: 1 egg beaten with 1 tablespoon water
1 tablespoon *each* coarse salt and fennel seed to sprinkle on breadsticks

BAKING RACK AND SHEET

Wire racks placed on baking sheets.

PREPARATION
10 mins.

In a large bowl, briskly stir yeast into water. Let stand for 3 or 4 minutes. Add salad oil, beer (or another ¾ cup water), salt and fennel seed. With a large wooden spoon, beat in 3 cups of the flour—about 75 strokes.

KNEADING
6 mins.

Spread remaining flour on a bread board or counter top and turn out the soft dough into the center of it. Keeping the fingers and the edges of the dough coated with flour, fold the dough to the center, pushing down with the palms of the hands. Continue kneading until the dough is smooth and elastic.

RISING
50 mins.

Place the dough in a greased bowl, cover tightly with plastic wrap and put in a warm place (80°–85°) until doubled in bulk. Preheat oven to 325°.

SHAPING
15 mins.

If you have a kitchen or postal scale, use it to achieve some uniformity in the size of the breadsticks. Knead the dough for a ½ minute to push out the bubbles. Pinch off 1½-inch-diameter balls, weigh them until you can judge them to be equal without weighing. Roll the balls under the palms of the hands until each is a long slender pencil-shaped rope, about 18 inches. Snip in half. Roll each briefly again and place ropes on the wire racks, which will go into the oven. Space about ½ inch apart. Carefully brush the tops with the egg-water mixture. Sprinkle some with fennel seeds and others with coarse salt. While finishing one batch, keep remaining dough covered in bowl. Repeat the shaping for the next and subsequent batches.

BAKING
325°
25 mins.

Bake in the oven until they are evenly browned.

FINAL STEP

Remove breadsticks from the oven. Cool on wire racks and then place in sealed plastic bags. Store at room temperature for use within a week or so, or freeze.

CORNMEAL WAFERS

[SERVED IN SQUARES]

This recipe is embarrassingly simple for being as delicious as it is. An ideal companion to a soup or cut into small bits for hors d'oeuvres, this unusual bread is a crisp paper-thin blanket of cornmeal batter spread over a hot baking sheet and put in a hot oven for just a few minutes. It is strongly reminiscent of the taste and smell of hot fried mush on a cold winter's day in a warm kitchen. I have never tried freezing it because none has ever been left for the experiment.

INGREDIENTS
1½ cups boiling water
1 cup white or yellow cornmeal
Pinch of salt
¼ cup melted bacon drippings

BAKING SHEET
One baking sheet, greased or Teflon.

PREPARATION
6 mins.
In a mixing bowl pour boiling water on the cornmeal to make a light batter (that can be spread thinly over the baking sheet). Season with salt and add bacon drippings. Preheat the oven to 425°.

BAKING
425°
6 mins.
Preheat baking sheet in the oven, brush it with drippings and spread the mush over it *very thinly*. This recipe will spread over *three* 10 x 14 baking sheets, so spread it wafer-thin. Bake until the bread is lightly browned. The thicker the batter is on the sheet the longer it will take the wafer to bake, and to brown.

FINAL STEP
Remove the sheet from the oven, cut into squares, and serve hot.

OATMEAL MUFFINS

[ABOUT ONE DOZEN]

This begins by soaking a cup of oatmeal in a cup of buttermilk for a half hour or more, and ends later with a dozen lovely light brown muffins coming out of the oven. Oatmeal gives the muffins a softness and a distinctive texture. The brown sugar is added last and is not completely broken up in the batter so that small pools of brown sweetness are left for the guest to find.

INGREDIENTS
1 cup rolled oats
1 cup buttermilk
1 cup all-purpose flour
½ teaspoon *each* salt and baking soda
1½ teaspoons baking powder
½ cup melted shortening or salad oil
1 egg, room temperature and beaten
½ cup brown sugar, firmly packed

MUFFIN TINS
Muffin tins, greased or Teflon—about 12 medium cups.

PREPARATION
15 mins.
Preheat oven to 350°. In a large bowl combine rolled oats and buttermilk. Allow the oats to soak for 30 min-

utes or longer. (Sometimes I will let them go overnight.)

On a length of wax paper sift the flour, salt, baking soda and baking powder. Stir the shortening and beaten egg into the oatmeal mixture. Blend in dry ingredients and mix only long enough to moisten. Drop in brown sugar. Stir but don't beat. Ideally, the brown sugar should remain suspended in the batter in small pea-size chunks.

FORMING
3 mins.

Spoon batter into the muffin tins.

BAKING
350°
25 mins.

Bake in the oven until brown.

FINAL STEP

Remove bread from the oven. Turn from muffin tins and serve while they are hot.

DANISH OAT CAKES

[ABOUT A DOZEN]

It is called Havregrynskage and while it is a hard cake and not a bread, it is fun to make, good to eat and a conversation food. The oats are cooked in butter and sugar, drenched in corn syrup—and packed solid in muffin tins. They are chilled for several hours in the refrigerator before serving. The Danes serve them with a cold buttermilk soup which they sometimes pour over the cakes.

INGREDIENTS

½ cup (1 stick) butter
¼ cup sugar
2 cups instant oatmeal
¼ cup white corn syrup

BAKING TINS

A muffin tin with 9 or 12 cups.

PREPARATION
20 mins.

In a large heavy skillet, over moderate heat, melt the butter and stir in the sugar with a wooden spoon. Let them cook together for about 30 seconds. Add oatmeal and, stirring occasionally, cook for 10 minutes or until the oatmeal is a golden brown. Remove from heat and stir in the white corn syrup. It will be quite thick and sticky.

FORMING
5 mins.

Rinse the muffin tin with cold water and shake out any excess moisture. Pack the cups firmly with the oatmeal mixture.

REFRIGERATION
3 hours

Place the filled muffin pan in the refrigerator for at least 3 hours.

FINAL STEP

Loosen the cakes by running a knife around the edges and slipping them out of their cups.

MAPLE SUGAR BISCUITS (AND VARIATIONS)

[TWO DOZEN]

This fine basic dough offers limitless possibilities in creating biscuits, ranging from apple and lemon to herb and maple sugar. This recipe is the basic dough made into a biscuit sprinkled generously with shaved maple sugar.

A lemon biscuit can be made by pressing a half lump of sugar, dipped in lemon juice, into each after cutting into rounds. When they come out of the oven, sprinkle with grated lemon rind and serve.

Ad infinitum.

INGREDIENTS

2 cups all-purpose flour
1 teaspoon salt
2 teaspoons baking powder
4 to 6 tablespoons butter, room temperature
¾ cup milk, approximately

BAKING SHEET

One baking sheet, greased or Teflon.

PREPARATION
10 mins.

Preheat oven to 450°. Measure flour into a bowl and stir in salt and baking powder. Cut butter into the dry ingredients, using a pastry blender, two knives or the fingertips. Gradually stir in ¾ cup of milk to make a soft but not sticky dough.

KNEADING
30 seconds

Knead dough on a lightly floured work surface with floured fingers for 30 seconds, no longer.

FORMING
10 mins.

For the maple sugar variation, roll into a sheet ½ inch thick. (The lemon biscuit round should be ¾ inch thick.) Cut the floured dough with a biscuit cutter or knife into rounds. Place on the baking sheet. Brush them with melted butter and sprinkle generously with ½ cup of maple sugar shaved from a block.

BAKING
450°
12–15 mins.

Bake in the oven until the biscuits are a golden brown.

FINAL STEP

Serve warm to your guests.

MOTHER'S BISCUITS

[TWO DOZEN]

Baking powder biscuits were so beautifully done by my mother that for a long time I felt intimidated by the thought of doing a panful myself. Finally, I dared. I did it with this recipe from a delightful book, *Cross Creek Cookery*, by the author of *The Yearling*, Marjorie Kinnan Rawlings. The mother is hers. My mother's recipe was not committed to paper. But I am satisfied this biscuit is just as good as my mother's, so I have no qualms about putting it here as a loving tribute to all mothers and to the millions of biscuits they have baked for happy children.

INGREDIENTS

2 cups all-purpose flour
5 teaspoons baking powder
½ teaspoon salt
2 tablespoons butter
1 cup milk (scant), room temperature

BAKING SHEET

One baking sheet, greased and cornmeal-dusted or Teflon.

PREPARATION
10 mins.

Preheat the oven to 450°. Mix flour, baking powder and salt together in a bowl, and sift twice. Work in the butter with the fingertips until it resembles coarse grain. Pour in only enough milk to hold the dough together. The exact amount varies with the flour.

FORMING
6 mins.

While it is considered heresy to handle biscuit dough needlessly, Mrs. Rawlings' mother believed that to make a flaky, layered biscuit one had to roll out the dough, fold it over itself in four layers, roll out again to a thickness of ½ inch, and cut with a 2-inch cookie cutter. Place biscuits on the baking sheet.

BAKING
450°
12–14 mins.

Bake in the oven until a golden brown and raised to about 1½ to 2 inches.

FINAL STEP

Remove biscuits from the oven. Serve hot.

WHEAT-NUT ROLLS

[THREE DOZEN]

Cracked wheat (bulgur) soaked in cold water overnight gives these wheaty rolls an unusual texture and taste.

This is a large recipe and it will make about three dozen rolls. I usually make a dozen in the shape of butterhorns, another dozen as clover leaves in a muffin pan, and, finally, a dozen fan-tans. (See pages 519–520 for shapes of rolls.)

INGREDIENTS

½ cup quick cooking cracked wheat (bulgur)
1 cup cold water
½ teaspoon salt
1 package dry yeast
2 cups warm water (105°–115°)
¾ cup non-fat dry milk
½ cup sugar
¼ cup vegetable oil
1 tablespoon salt
1 egg, room temperature and slightly beaten
6 cups all-purpose flour, approximately

BAKING SHEET AND MUFFIN PANS

Select baking sheet and muffin pans after you decide what kind of shape you wish to make and how many.

PREPARATION
Overnight

Overnight, soak the cracked wheat (bulgur) in cold water and salt.

20 mins.

On bake day, dissolve yeast in the water in a large bowl. Stir in the milk, sugar, oil, salt and egg. Add the soaked wheat mixture.

Measure in 3 cups flour and beat vigorously 75 strokes, or 2 minutes at medium speed in the electric mixer. Stop the mixer. Stir in the balance of the flour, a half cup at a time, first with the spoon and then by hand. The dough will be a rough, shaggy mass that will clean the sides of the bowl. If the dough continues slack, and is sticky, sprinkle on additional flour.

KNEADING
8 mins.

Turn the dough onto a lightly floured work surface—counter top or bread board—and knead with the rhythmic 1-2-3 motion of push-turn-fold. The dough will become smooth and elastic, and bubbles will rise under the surface of the dough. Sprinkle more flour on the dough if it is slack or moist. Occasionally change the kneading rhythm by raising the dough above the table and banging it down hard against the surface. (Knead 6 minutes with the dough hook.)

FIRST RISING
50 mins.

Place the dough in the mixing bowl and pat with buttered or greased fingers to keep the surface from crusting. Cover the bowl tightly with plastic wrap and move to a warm place (80°–85°) until the dough has risen to about twice its original size. You can test if it has risen by poking a finger in it; the dent will remain.

SHAPING
20 mins.

Remove plastic wrap, punch down dough and turn onto floured work surface. Make into rolls according to desired shapes on pages 519–520. Place in muffin tins or on baking sheet.

SECOND RISING
35 mins.

Cover the rolls carefully with wax paper, holding the paper off the dough by resting it on upturned water glasses, if necessary, and put in the warm place until rolls have doubled in volume.

BAKING
375°
20–25 mins.

Preheat oven to 375°. Bake in the oven until they are a light golden brown. Don't burn or scorch by leaving them in the oven too long.

FINAL STEP

Remove rolls from the oven. Serve the rolls warm. These freeze very well, however. Reheat before serving.

HOT CROSS BUNS

[ABOUT THREE DOZEN]

This recipe for one of the Easter season's legendary breads—hot cross buns—produces a speckled nut-brown dough loaded with cloves, nutmeg, currants and candied fruit. A white cross of confectioners' icing is the distinctive mark of this bread that is in every child's book of nursery rhymes and is supposed to have originated in pagan England. Even today, a hot cross bun baked on Good Friday is believed to have special curative powers.

INGREDIENTS

1 cup sugar
½ cup plus 2 tablespoons butter, melted
4 eggs, separated, and at room temperature
2¼ cups milk, lukewarm
1 package dry yeast
7 to 8 cups all-purpose or bread flour, approximately
1½ teaspoons salt
1 teaspoon nutmeg
¼ teaspoon powdered cloves
1 cup currants
½ cup chopped candied fruits
Glaze: 1 egg yolk
2 tablespoons of water
Icing: 1 cup confectioners' sugar
1 tablespoon milk
1 teaspoon lemon juice

BAKING SHEET

Baking sheet, greased or Teflon.

PREPARATION
30 mins.

The day before—
In a large bowl mix the sugar, ½ cup of melted butter, egg yolks, well beaten, and milk. Sprinkle yeast over the mixture in the bowl and stir in. Sift 4 cups of flour with the salt, nutmeg, cloves—beat into the batter.

3 hours

Beat egg whites until frothy but not quite stiff, and work into the batter. Sprinkle in currants and candied fruit. Add additional flour, a cup at a time, and work it into the dough, first with a spoon and then by hand, until it is a rough mass. Knead it in the bowl for 2 or 3 minutes. Don't make it a stiff dough but leave it soft and elastic. Cover the top of the bowl with plastic wrap and let stand in a warm place (80°–85°) while it rises, about 3 hours.

REFRIGERATION
Overnight

Punch down dough. Store the bowl in the refrigerator overnight.

On the following day—
Remove bowl from the refrigerator and allow it to stand for about 1 hour at room temperature.

KNEADING 10 mins.	Turn the dough out onto a floured work surface and knead until the dough is elastic and smooth.
SHAPING 20 mins.	Divide the dough into equal parts in successive steps—2-4-8-16-32 pieces, and shape into balls. Place the balls about 1 inch apart on the baking sheet.
RISING 1½ hours	Brush the balls with the remaining melted butter, cover with wax paper and place in the warm spot to rise until doubled.
BAKING 375° 25 mins.	Preheat oven to 375°. Turn back the wax paper. With a razor blade or scissors, cut a cross on the top of each bun. Brush with egg yolk and water. Place in the oven until nicely browned. If oven space is limited several batches may be baked.
FINAL STEP	Remove buns from the oven. Place on wire racks. When cool, form a cross on each bun with fairly firm confectioners' icing.

POPOVERS

[A DOZEN OR SO]

Popovers are unpredictable. Popovers are good to eat. There isn't very much to a popover. It is an ungainly-looking device for getting butter, jams, jellies and honey into the mouth.

The popover owes it all to steam levitation. It is done without yeast or chemicals of any kind. Only steam raises it high, and then drops it into a clumsy shape. Popovers are good to eat.

There should be at least one popover recipe in every home baker's repertoire. This is a good one.

INGREDIENTS	1 cup all-purpose flour (sift before measuring) ¼ teaspoon salt 1 tablespoon sugar 1 tablespoon butter, melted, or salad oil 1 cup milk, room temperature 2 large eggs
BAKING PANS AND CUPS	Greased muffin pans, heavy cast iron popover pans or ovenproof custard cups. Makes a dozen popovers in ⅓-cup-size pans, ten in ½-cup-size pans, and eight in 5- or 6-ounce glass cups.

PREPARATION
12 mins.

Preheat the oven to 400°. Mix flour in a bowl with salt and sugar. Add butter or oil, milk and eggs, and beat at medium-high speed in the electric mixer until very smooth. A hand beater can also be used. Beat for 3 minutes. Popover batter can also be made in a blender. Combine all of the ingredients and whirl at high speed 45 seconds. Stop the blender and scrape down the sides after the first 10 seconds.

FORMING
2 mins.

Fill the cups half full with batter.

BAKING
400°
40 mins.
or
375°
50–55 mins.

Bake in 400° oven for a dark brown shell with a moist interior. Bake in 375° oven for a light popover with a drier inside.

Keep door of the oven closed during the bake period to prevent a collapse under a draft of cold air.

FINAL STEP

Remove popovers from the oven. Turn from the pans and serve hot. Prick the popovers with a skewer if you like a dry interior. Leave them in the turned-off oven, door slightly ajar, for 8 to 10 minutes.

SOPAIPILLAS

[EIGHTEEN TO TWENTY-FOUR PUFFS]

Sopaipillas, fried in hot oil, come from the stove puffed like small balloons, and almost as light. The dough is rolled wafer-thin (⅛ inch), cut in 2-inch or 3-inch squares, and dropped into the pan of hot oil.

The sopaipillas are served hot from the kettle. Break off a corner of the puff, fill with honey and it becomes a fine accompaniment for highly seasoned Mexican-type dishes.

INGREDIENTS

1¾ cups all-purpose flour
2 teaspoons baking powder
1 teaspoon salt
2 tablespoons shortening, room temperature
⅔ cup cold water, approximately

COOKING KETTLE

One deep kettle, with 2 inches vegetable oil or fat. Also a slotted spoon.

PREPARATION
8 mins.

Preheat the oil or fat, 385° to 400° while the preparation continues. Sift flour, baking powder and salt into a mixing bowl. Cut shortening into the flour with a pastry blender or the fingers. It will look like coarse meal.

Add only enough water to make a stiff dough.

KNEADING
4 mins.

Turn onto a lightly floured work surface—counter top or bread board—and knead until smooth.

RESTING
10 mins.

Cover with a towel or a length of wax paper and let rest.

SHAPING
5 mins.

Roll dough into a rectangle, about 12 by 15 inches, and no more than ⅛ inch thick. With a pastry wheel or knife cut into 2- or 3-inch squares.

FRYING
1 to 2 mins.

When the oil is very hot drop 2 or 3 squares into it. Turn several times with a slotted spoon so each sopaipilla puffs and browns evenly. Remove and drain on paper towels.

FINAL STEP

Serve immediately with honey.

SOUR SKONS

[ONE LARGE SCONE TO SERVE EIGHT]

A cupful of oatmeal soaked in buttermilk for two days is the base for this delicious caraway-flavored scone (skon) from the Orkney Islands, to the north of the Scottish mainland. It is best done on a griddle.

The somewhat spare 2-sentence recipe that I copied down in Scotland began—"Soak up some oatmeal in buttermilk for a few days, then take it and beat it up with flour into which you have stirred a little baking soda, sugar to taste (don't over-sweeten), and a few caraway seeds." The second sentence said lay it on the griddle. End of recipe.

INGREDIENTS

1 cup oatmeal
1 cup buttermilk
1 teaspoon *each* sugar and baking soda
½ teaspoon *each* salt and caraway seeds
1¼ cups all-purpose flour

GRIDDLE OR BAKE SHEET

Heavy griddle or baking sheet, ungreased.

PREPARATION
2 or 3 days
10 mins.

Two or three days before, measure oatmeal into a small bowl and stir in buttermilk. Cover with plastic wrap and set aside to soak. Stir once each day.

On bake day, stir down the soaked oatmeal. In a separate bowl mix together sugar, baking soda, salt, caraway seeds and flour. Pour the wet mixture into the dry ingredients, and stir to blend thoroughly.

SHAPING
5 mins.

Pat the dough into a circular loaf, about 8 inches in diameter and ¾ of an inch thick. Allow it to rest while the griddle heats over a burner.

BAKING
Griddle
Hot
60 mins.

Test the griddle with a sprinkle of flour. If the flour turns deep brown within 10 seconds the griddle is ready for the scone. Lay the scone on the griddle and, with a knife, score the top into 8 pie-shaped pieces, cutting lightly into the dough, no more than ¼ of an inch deep.

Bake for 4 minutes and turn to bake 4 minutes on the other side. Reduce heat to medium and bake 45 to 55 minutes. During the bake period turn the scone every 10 minutes. Insert a wooden toothpick diagonally into the scone to test for doneness. If it comes out clean and dry the scone is done. If moist particles cling to the probe, leave on the griddle for an additional 10 minutes.

Oven
425°
30 mins.

The scone can be baked in the oven. Arrange scone on the baking sheet, score as above, and place in the oven until it tests done.

FINAL STEP

Lift the scone off the griddle with a spatula. Place on the metal rack to cool somewhat before serving. Break along the scored lines.

MRS. MACNAB'S SCONES

[SIXTEEN SMALL SCONES]

King Frederick of Prussia rode often from Balmoral Castle in Scotland, where he was a visitor, to the farm cottage of Mrs. Macnab near Ballater to eat her celebrated scones. While it is not possible to impart Mrs. Macnab's lightness of touch, her recipe in other hands does produce a delicious scone, white and soft on the inside, brown and crisp on the out.

The secret of success, according to Mrs. Macnab, was not working the dough with the hands except just once when kneading it.

INGREDIENTS	2 cups all-purpose flour, approximately 1 teaspoon *each* salt and baking soda 2 teaspoons cream of tartar 3 tablespoons butter, room temperature 1 egg, room temperature and lightly beaten ½ cup buttermilk, room temperature
BAKING SHEET	One baking sheet, greased or Teflon.
PREPARATION 10 mins.	Heat oven to 375°. In a mixing bowl measure flour, salt, baking soda and cream of tartar. Stir thoroughly. With the fingers rub the butter into the dry ingredients. Gradually stir beaten egg and buttermilk into the flour mixture. If it is too moist and sticks to the hands, add a sprinkle of flour.
KNEADING 2 mins. or less	Turn the dough onto a lightly floured work surface—counter top or bread board—and knead *as little as possible* to achieve a soft and pliable ball.
SHAPING 12 mins.	Divide the dough into 4 equal parts. Flatten each with the knuckles—not the rolling pin—into a round disc, about 6 inches in diameter and ½ inch thick. Prick a dozen times with the tines of a fork. With the moist edge of a kitchen knife cut into quarters. Lift each onto the baking sheet.
BAKING 375° 15 mins.	Bake in the oven until they are a lovely light tan. Don't scorch.
FINAL STEP	Remove scones from the oven. Serve while hot at breakfast, tea or brunch. I have frozen these but they are much better freshly prepared.

ENGLISH MUFFINS

[ABOUT TWO DOZEN]

An English muffin is a true English muffin only when it is torn apart to be toasted. Never cut with a knife! Even the best muffin, once sliced, can never regain the forever-lost taste sensation that comes with the toasting —in various degrees of golden brown—of the rough peaks and valleys in a torn-apart muffin. This recipe is for a good English muffin ready to be torn apart—not sliced.

These will not look like packaged English muffins, of precise size and shape. There will be irregular shapes among them, but so much the better.

INGREDIENTS

1 package dry yeast
¼ cup warm water (105°–115°)
1 cup hot tap water (120°–130°)
3 tablespoons butter, room temperature
2 tablespoons sugar
1 teaspoon salt
½ cup non-fat dry milk
5 to 5½ cups all-purpose flour, approximately
1 egg, room temperature
1 tablespoon cornmeal for sprinkling on work surface

BAKING GRIDDLE

Heavy metal or soapstone griddle.

PREPARATION
15 mins.

In a small bowl or cup dissolve yeast in the warm water. Stir with a fork or whisk to hasten the fermentation action. Set aside.

In a large mixing bowl measure hot water, butter, sugar, salt, milk, and 3 cups flour. Blend. Add yeast mixture. Beat at medium speed in mixer for 2 minutes, or 150 strokes with a wooden spoon. Beat in egg.

Turn off mixer and with a spoon stir in remaining flour, ¼ cup at a time, until the dough is a rough mass that cleans the sides of the bowl.

KNEADING
8 mins.

Turn the dough onto a floured work surface—counter top or bread board—and knead with a strong push-turn-fold motion until the dough is smooth, elastic and feels alive under the hands. (This dough kneads well under a dough hook—about 6 minutes.)

FIRST RISING
1 hour

Pat the ball of dough with lightly greased fingertips and return to the mixing bowl. Cover with plastic wrap and set in a warm place (80°–85°) until the dough has risen to twice its original size.

SHAPING
10 mins.

Turn back the plastic wrap, punch down the dough, knead for 30 seconds and set aside to rest for 10 minutes.

Sprinkle the work surface with cornmeal, and turn the dough onto it. Roll out the dough until it is ¼ inch thick. If it resists the rolling pin and pulls back, let it rest at intervals for 1 or 2 minutes. Cut into 3-inch rounds.

SECOND RISING
45 mins.

Sprinkle the surface again with cornmeal and put the rounds together under a towel and let rise on the counter top or bread board until they are doubled in size to about ½ inch thick.

BAKING
16 mins.

Heat a heavy griddle to hot. Bake the muffins for 2 minutes on each side. Reduce heat and bake 6 additional minutes on each side or a total of 16 minutes. Don't scorch.

FINAL STEP

Remove muffins from the griddle. Cool on metal rack before toasting. Pull apart with the tines of a fork or the fingers to toast. These freeze well and keep for months in the deep freeze.

BEATEN BISCUITS

[ABOUT THREE DOZEN]

There are three ways to make beaten biscuits. One is to beat the dough with a rolling pin, a flatiron or the side of a cleaver. Some use an ordinary hammer. Do this "30 minutes for family, and 45 minutes for company." A second is to run the dough, over and over again, through metal or wooden rollers in a hand-operated machine that looks like the clothes wringer from an old-fashioned washing machine. It is known as a beaten-biscuit machine, a kneader or a brake. Most are antiques, highly prized by their owners. The dough can also be put through the coarse blade of a food or meat grinder with satisfactory-to-good results.

The biscuits are cut from dough about ½ inch thick. They will rise a little, and will be crisp, short (because of the lard), dry, somewhat hard, and delicious.

The true mark of a beaten biscuit buff is splitting the biscuit with the tines of a fork. Never a knife or fingers.

The traditional biscuit is 1½ to 2 inches in diameter and made with a special cutter that presses six prongs through the center of the biscuit as it cuts. These holes can also be made with the tines of a fork. In Virginia, it is customary to form the biscuit by squeezing the dough between the thumb and forefinger to make a ball the size of a small egg. Pinched off, it is patted flat and pricked with a fork.

This recipe, which comes from a fine home baker in Concord, Tennessee, Mrs. Don Whitehead, was tested by airmail. She airmailed biscuits to me to use as a bench mark for excellence; I airmailed mine to her for a critique. Our biscuits were never exactly alike because I beat mine with a rolling pin while she rolled hers in a hundred-year-old machine with nickel-plated rollers.

There is somewhere a recipe for making beaten biscuits with an electric mixer. This would be unthinkable to a beaten-biscuit purist, and I tell this only as a matter of record.

A beaten biscuit party can be a crashing success. Let the guests take turns beating on the dough for 45 minutes, and they will have a half hour to recharge their energies before *their* biscuits come out of the oven for dinner.

INGREDIENTS

7 cups sifted all-purpose flour
2 teaspoons *each* salt and baking powder
2 tablespoons sugar
1 cup (½ pound) lard, room temperature
1⅓ cups milk (half-and-half for an even richer dough)

BAKING SHEET

Baking sheet, *un*greased or Teflon.

PREPARATION
15 mins.

Sift flour into a large bowl and add salt, baking powder and sugar. Stir to mix. Cut lard into small pieces and drop into dry ingredients. With a pastry blender or hands, work lard into the flour.

Pour 1 cup milk into the bowl and work it into the mixture. Add the balance of the milk if it is needed to hold the dough together. Remember, it is to be a fairly stiff dough—be sparing of the liquid. Knead the dough with the hands for 2 or 3 minutes until you are certain it will cling together in one mass and not fragment with the first blow of a blunt instrument.

RESTING
½–1 hour

Cover dough and put aside to rest.

BEATING
30–45 mins.

Assuming no beaten biscuit machine is available, select a place on a counter top or table that is the height most comfortable for prolonged beating. Don't beat frantically. Use measured beats. When the dough has been beaten crosswise in one direction, shift the dough or your position so that you are beating across the previous pattern. When the dough is flattened, fold it 2 or 3 times, into a ball, and continue beating. The dough will become silky and elastic. Bubbles may form and pop when beaten.

Remember: there are two other methods open to you—between the rollers of the machine, or 4 or 5 times through a meat grinder (coarse blade).

SHAPING
15 mins.

Preheat oven to 400°. Roll the dough into a sheet ½ inch thick. Use a 1½- or 2-inch cutter. Pierce each round twice with the tines of a fork. Place on the baking sheet.

BAKING
400°
25–30 mins.

Bake in the oven until the biscuits begin to brown—but only lightly.

FINAL STEP

Remove biscuits from the oven. Serve warm. These keep for several days in a tightly closed plastic bag. Wrap in foil to reheat. They freeze nicely for up to 6 months.

BATH BUNS

[TWO DOZEN LARGE BUNS]

The savory Bath Bun was first made in the English city of Bath, west of London on the river Avon. The rich valley has the only mineral springs in Great Britain and the Roman colonists were inspired to build a spa there—hence the name.

The delicately browned, sparkling, glazed sweet buns were first served in the fine homes along Bath's wide terraced streets.

Mace, the ground outer covering of the nutmeg and somewhat stronger, is the seldom-recognized flavoring. Finally, there are three different glazes put on the buns to give them their fine rich color.

INGREDIENTS

3 eggs, beaten
5 to 6 cups all-purpose flour, approximately
1 package dry yeast
½ cup sugar
1 teaspoon salt
½ teaspoon mace
⅓ cup non-fat dry milk
1½ cups hot tap water (120°–130°)
¼ cup (½ stick) butter or margarine, room temperature
1 cup raisins or currants
Glazes: 1 egg yolk
1 tablespoon lemon juice
3 tablespoons sugar
1 tablespoon milk

BAKING SHEET

One or more baking sheets, greased or Teflon, depending on the size of the oven.

PREPARATION
15 mins.

Beat 3 eggs together in a small bowl and set aside.

In a mixing bowl measure 2 cups of flour and stir in the yeast, sugar, salt, mace, milk and water. Add eggs and beat in the electric mixer at slow speed for 30 seconds to blend. Add butter or margarine and beat at medium-high speed for 3 minutes, or for an equal length of time with a wooden spoon.

Stop the mixer. Stir in the balance of the flour, a half cup at a time, first with the spoon and then by hand. The dough will be a rough, shaggy mass that will clean the sides of the bowl. If dough continues moist and sticky, add several sprinkles of flour.

KNEADING
8 mins.

Turn the dough onto a lightly floured work surface—counter top or bread board—and knead with the rhythmic 1-2-3 motion of push-turn-fold. The dough will become smooth and elastic, and bubbles will rise under the surface of the dough. If the dough is sticky, sprinkle on additional flour. Break the kneading rhythm by occasionally throwing the dough hard against the counter top. (Knead 6 minutes under the dough hook.)

FIRST RISING
2 hours

Place the dough in the clean mixing bowl and pat with buttered or greased fingertips to keep the surface from crusting. Cover the bowl tightly with plastic wrap and move to a warm place (80°–85°) until the dough has risen to about twice its original size. You can test if it has risen by poking a finger in it; the dent will remain.

SHAPING
15 mins.

The Bath Bun is about 4 inches in diameter. Begin by punching down the dough and working in the currants or raisins. Form in a ball, cut into 24 equal size pieces—about the size of a large egg. One will weigh about 2 ounces. Work the pieces into balls, and flatten on top. Place them on the bake sheet, leaving 1½ inches between the rolls.

Brush each with the beaten egg yolk. Next, with a spoon, lightly coat the top of each with the lemon juice mixed with sugar.

SECOND RISING
45 mins.

Place the baking sheet in the warm place, cover carefully with a length of wax paper. The buns will double in bulk.

BAKING
350°
25 mins.

Preheat oven to 350°. Before putting the rolls in the oven brush each with milk for a rich glaze.

Bake in the oven until the buns test done. Tap one on the bottom crust. A hard hollow sound means the bun is baked.

FINAL STEP

Remove from the oven. Place on a metal rack to cool before serving. These keep well for several days wrapped in plastic or foil.

BAPS

[EIGHT ROLLS]

The bap—the traditional breakfast roll of Scotland—is a puffed-up bun with a deep impression right in the middle of it where the baker's thumb has been pressed to keep the bun from blistering. The bap is brushed with milk twice before it goes into the oven to give it a rich glaze. Break the warm bap apart, spread with butter and jam. Delicious.

The grandfather of a British Prime Minister was known as "sma' Baps" by the young boys of Edinburgh because the baps sold in his bakery reputedly were smaller than those baked by his fellow tradesmen. I got the recipe in Edinburgh but they are not "sma' Baps."

INGREDIENTS

2 cups all-purpose flour, approximately
1 package dry yeast
¼ cup non-fat dry milk
½ teaspoon salt
1 teaspoon sugar
2 tablespoons lard, room temperature
¾ cup hot tap water (120°–130°)
To brush: ¼ cup fresh or evaporated milk

BAKING SHEET

One baking sheet, greased or Teflon.

PREPARATION
15 mins.

Sift flour into a bowl and stir in the yeast, milk, salt and sugar. With the fingers, rub the lard into the dry ingredients. Gradually pour in water, stir with a spoon and work with the fingers until a soft ball of dough is formed. Sprinkle on more flour if the dough is sticky, or a bit more water if it is too dry to hold together and knead.

In this recipe the dough rises once *before* it is kneaded.

FIRST RISING 30 mins.	Cover the bowl with plastic wrap and put in a warm place (80°–85°) until dough has doubled in size.
KNEADING 4 mins.	Turn dough out onto a lightly floured work surface—counter top or bread board—and knead until soft and elastic.
SHAPING 15 mins.	Divide the dough into 8 equal pieces. Let rest for 5 minutes before forming the baps. Make an oval of each piece—about 3 inches long, 2 inches wide and ½ inch thick. Place on the baking sheet and brush with milk.
SECOND RISING 15 mins.	Cover the baps with wax paper, holding the paper off the buns with a water glass, and set in a warm place.
BAKING 400° 15–20 mins.	Preheat the oven to 400°. Brush the baps with milk for a second time. Moisten a thumb and press it all the way down into the center of each bap. Bake in the oven until a lovely golden brown.
FINAL STEP	Remove from the oven. Serve warm.

WHOLE WHEAT ROLLS

[TWO DOZEN]

This recipe produces an unusual dinner roll. It is made with equal amounts of whole wheat and all-purpose flour and flavored with molasses. I make mine into tiny cloverleaf rolls in which each third is bite size. Exceptionally good.

INGREDIENTS	2¼ cups all-purpose flour, approximately 2 packages dry yeast ⅓ cup non-fat dry milk 1 tablespoon salt 2 tablespoons sugar 3 tablespoons molasses ¼ cup shortening, room temperature 1½ cups hot tap water (120°–130°) 2¼ cups whole wheat flour
BAKING SHEET AND MUFFIN TINS	One baking sheet, greased or Teflon. One dozen muffin cups, greased or Teflon.

PREPARATION
15 mins.

Measure flour into a large mixing bowl and stir in yeast, milk, salt, sugar, molasses, shortening and water. Beat at medium speed in electric mixer for 2 minutes, or with a wooden spoon for an equivalent length of time.

Stop mixer. Stir in whole wheat flour, a half cup at a time, first with the spoon and then by hand. The dough will be a rough, shaggy mass that will clean the sides of the bowl. If the dough continues moist and sticky, sprinkle with small amounts of all-purpose flour.

KNEADING
8 mins.

Turn the dough onto a lightly floured work surface—counter top or bread board—and knead with the rhythmic 1-2-3 motion of push-turn-fold. The dough will become smooth and elastic, and bubbles will rise under the surface. Break the kneading rhythm by occasionally throwing the dough hard against the work surface. (Knead 6 minutes under a dough hook.)

FIRST RISING
50 mins.

Place the dough in the mixing bowl and pat with buttered or greased fingers. Cover the bowl with plastic wrap and move to a warm place (80°–85°) until the dough has risen to twice its original volume. You can test if it has risen by poking a finger in it; the dent will remain.

SHAPING
15 mins.

Remove the plastic wrap and knock down the dough with the fingertips. Turn out onto the floured work surface and knead for 30 seconds to press out the bubbles. Let the dough rest for 5 minutes and then pinch off dough for whichever roll you choose (see pp. 519–520). Form round or oblong and place them on the baking sheet, or in muffin tins. I like to make tiny cloverleafs in muffin cups that are only 1¾ inches in diameter. Each of the three small balls of dough is no larger than a cherry.

SECOND RISING
35 mins.

Place the pans in the warm place, cover with wax paper and leave until rolls have doubled in volume.

BAKING
400°
15 mins.

Preheat oven to 400°. Bake in the oven until they are a dark brown. Lift one out of its cup and tap the bottom crust. It should be firm and hard.

FINAL STEP

Remove from the oven and serve warm.

BUTTERY ROWIES

[EIGHTEEN ROLLS]

Buttery Rowies, also called Aberdeen Butter Rolls, are flaky rectangles that have a fried taste and texture even though they are baked in the oven. The mixture of butter and lard is slathered on a thin rectangle of dough which is then folded over, rolled, folded, rolled, folded—a total of three times, much as is done with flaky pastry or croissants. They are best served warm from the oven.

INGREDIENTS

3 cups all-purpose flour, approximately
1 package dry yeast
1 tablespoon sugar
1 teaspoon salt
1½ cups hot tap water (120°–130°)
¾ cup (1½ sticks) butter, room temperature
¾ cup lard, room temperature

BAKING SHEET

One baking sheet. Be certain the sheet has a lip all the way around or fashion one with foil so the melted butter and lard do not run into the oven.

PREPARATION
15 mins.

Measure 1½ cups flour into a large mixing bowl and stir in yeast, sugar, salt and water. Beat in electric mixer at medium-high speed for 2 minutes.

Stop mixer. Stir in the balance of the flour, a half cup at a time, first with the spoon and then by hand. The dough will be a rough, shaggy mass that will clean the sides of the bowl. If the dough continues slack and moist, and is sticky, add a small amount additional flour.

KNEADING
8 mins.

Turn the dough onto a lightly floured work surface—counter top or bread board—and knead with the rhythmic 1-2-3 motion of push-turn-fold. The dough will become smooth and elastic, and bubbles will rise under the surface of the dough. Sprinkle on a little flour if the work surface or the fingers are sticky. Break the kneading rhythm occasionally by throwing the dough hard against the counter top. (Knead 6 minutes under the dough hook.)

RISING
1 hour

Place the dough in the mixing bowl and pat with buttered or greased fingers to keep the surface from crusting. Cover the bowl tightly with plastic wrap and move to a warm place (80°–85°) until the dough has risen to about twice its original size—as judged by how it creeps up the sides of the bowl. You can test if it has risen by poking a finger in it; the dent will remain.

REFRIGERATION
30 mins.

When it has risen, knock it down, turn it out onto work surface again, and knead for 30 seconds to press out the bubbles. Place in a clean bowl, cover with plastic wrap and put in the refrigerator to chill.

In the meantime, cream together the butter and lard. Divide into 3 equal parts on a length of wax paper and set aside.

SHAPING
10 mins.

Roll the dough on a lightly floured work surface to a rectangle 3 times as long as it is wide—12 by 4 inches, for example. The first butter-lard portion is to be spread on this.

Turn 1
20 mins.

Spread it over the dough but leave a 1-inch margin around the edge with no butter on it. Fold the dough in three, as you would a business letter. Wrap in wax paper and return to the refrigerator to chill the dough.

Turn 2
20 mins.

Roll out, spread on the second portion of the butter and lard, fold in three. Refrigerate to chill.

Turn 3
20 mins.

Roll out, spread on the third portion of the butter and lard, fold in three. Refrigerate to chill. Preheat oven to 400°.

15 mins.

Roll out until the dough is a rectangle 3 times as long as it is wide. It should be about ¼-inch thick. With a pastry wheel or wet knife blade cut into rectangles, about 1½ by 4½ inches. Place on a baking sheet that has a full lip, and leave a space of 1½ inches between.

BAKING
400°
20–25 mins.

Place rolls in the oven until raised, flaky and light brown.

FINAL STEP

Remove from the oven. These can be served to guests warm while the baker calls an old Scottish street cry—
"Bawbee Baps and Buttery Rowies!"

BRIOCHE

Brioche, in all of its forms, deserves a special place in a book on bread for it is one of the most sophisticated products to come out of the home oven. The brioche stands by itself with its own special kind of butter-rich flavor and fine texture.

The word "brioche" comes from two old French words—*bris* (break) and *hacher* (stir). The reference is to the butter that is "broken" from its hard form and stirred into the dough.

While brioches are most often made in a fluted tin—a cocky topknot on a ball of dough (Brioche à Tête)—there is Brioche au Fromage, Brioche en Couronne (crown brioche), and brioche this and brioche that. A delightful version one seldom sees in the U.S. but beloved by all French school children is Brioche Chocolat—a strip of chocolate baked in the folds of brioche dough.

Brioche dough can be used for the delicate cases that contain many sweet and savory dishes, rissoles, flans and other dishes and pastries.

Two brioche recipes are here. Easy Brioche has the look and form of the best. It lacks some of the subtle richness and fine texture inherent in the French Brioche.

FRENCH BRIOCHE

[BASIC DOUGH]

This recipe is the traditional brioche.

The dough is soft, easily stirred but sticky. To get it from this stage to where it will become elastic and pull away from the hands demands 10 minutes in a heavy-duty electric mixer, or 20 minutes by hand. The latter technique calls for lifting the sticky dough out of the bowl and crashing it back against the bottom. The next step, common to all brioche recipes, is to chill the rich dough for several hours so that it can be shaped into a variety of forms. Without the chilling, it would be impossible to work.

INGREDIENTS

2 packages dry yeast
1 cup warm water (105°–115°)
¼ cup non-fat dry milk
1 tablespoon sugar
2 teaspoons salt
4½ cups all-purpose flour
1 cup (2 sticks) butter, room temperature
5 eggs, room temperature
Glaze: 1 egg yolk
1 tablespoon milk
If you choose to bake Brioche au Fromage, dice 2 cups

(½ pound) Swiss cheese to knead into the basic dough after the first rising. Brioche Chocolat will take 1 square of chocolate (1 oz.) for each piece to be made. Break the square and lay the two pieces end to end.

BAKING TINS, SHEET AND PANS

Select the proper number of brioche or muffin tins and grease them well. For a crown brioche, a greased or Teflon baking sheet. Brioche loaves: two large (9 x 5) baking pans, greased or Teflon, or four small (5 x 2½) pans. If glass, reduce oven heat 25°.

PREPARATION
15 mins.

Sprinkle yeast over the water in a large bowl. Stir to hasten the yeast's action. Add the milk, sugar, salt and 2 cups flour. Beat in the electric mixer 2 minutes at medium-high speed, or for an equal length of time with a large wooden spoon. Add the butter and continue beating 1 minute.

Stop the mixer. Add eggs, one at a time, and remaining flour, a half cup at a time, beating thoroughly with each addition.

The dough will be soft and sticky, and it must be beaten until it is shiny, elastic and pulls from the hands.

20 mins.

Grab the dough in one hand, steadying the bowl with the other, and pull a large handful of it out of the bowl, about 14 inches aloft, and throw it back—with considerable force! Continue pulling out and slapping back the dough for about 18 to 20 minutes. Don't despair. It is sticky. It is a mess but it will slowly begin to stretch and pull away as you work it.

—or—

10 mins.

A heavy-duty mixer, at medium speed, can do this in about 10 minutes.

RISING
2–3 hours

Cover the bowl with plastic wrap and put it in a warm place (80°–85°) until dough has doubled in volume.

REFRIGERATION
4 hours or overnight

Stir down the dough. Place the covered bowl in the refrigerator. The rich dough must be thoroughly chilled before it can be formed.

SHAPING

PETITES BRIOCHES
25 mins.

[18 to 20 pieces]

Bring the dough out of the refrigerator and divide into portions that will half fill a muffin cup or fluted brioche tin, approximately ¼ cup each. Place all but 4 or 5 of these pieces on a floured baking pan, cover with wax paper and return them to the refrigerator to keep cold while shaping a few at a time.

Pinch about one-fifth off each individual piece of dough (for its topknot) and set aside. Shape the large piece into a ball and place it in the tin. Moisten a thumb or finger and press deep into the center of the brioche. Form the small ball of dough into a pear-shaped piece and fit it carefully into the finger depression. With a knife point, tuck the topknot securely into place. Repeat with the balance of the refrigerated dough.

Cover the shaped brioches with wax paper resting on water tumblers to keep the paper from coming in contact with the sticky dough. Move the tins to a warm place (80°–85°).

BRIOCHE À TÊTE
10 mins.

[one or two loaves]
This makes one or two loaves with topknot. Remove the dough from the refrigerator, pinch off one-fifth of the entire piece (for the topknot) and shape as you would a petite brioche. Use a large 9-inch fluted brioche mold or a 2-quart round baking pan. This recipe will also make two medium-size brioches by using two smaller 7-inch molds. Cover with wax paper and move to the warm place.

BRIOCHE EN COURONNE
15 mins.

[one crown or ring]
Shape the chilled dough into a round flat cake, about 2 inches thick. Place on baking sheet. Form a ring by piercing the dough in the center, pulling the dough apart with the hands pulling against each other. Work the rough edges into the dough as the hands move around the ring. Make the center hole about 5 inches in diameter. With a razor blade lightly slash the top of the ring at 2-inch intervals.

Cover with wax paper resting on a water tumbler placed in the hole. Put in a warm place to rise.

BRIOCHE LOAVES
10 mins.

[two large or four small loaves]
Shape the chilled dough into two loaves and place them in two large (9 x 5) baking pans or 4 small (5 x 2½) pans. Cover with wax paper and move to a warm place.

BRIOCHE AU FROMAGE
5 mins.

Knead 2 cups (½ pound) diced Swiss cheese into the basic recipe after it has risen and before it is refrigerated. Shape in any of the forms desired.

BRIOCHE CHOCOLAT
18 mins.

[eight pieces]
Divide the chilled dough into 8 pieces. Press each into a rectangle 4 x 8 inches. This will be folded over the chocolate to form a 4 x 4 inch square. Place the piece of chocolate in the center of one half of the rectangle and fold the other half over it. Press the edges tightly to seal. The chocolate can also be rolled in the rectangle of dough to form a roll rather than the flat bun-like piece. Place on the baking sheet, cover with wax paper and move to the warm place. (The French baker makes 8 diagonal cuts with a razor blade across the brioche.)

SECOND RISING
2 hours

When the brioche forms have been covered with wax paper, put them in the warm place until doubled in bulk.

BAKING
400°
Varies

Preheat oven to 400°. Carefully brush the tops with egg yolk and milk glaze.

Bake the Petites Brioches about 20 minutes, or until nicely browned and a metal or wooden skewer comes out clean and dry when inserted.

The large Brioche à Tête is baked 20 minutes in the hot oven, the heat is reduced to 350° and it is baked for an additional 40 minutes, or a total of 1 hour. Test the brioche for doneness.

Brioche en Couronne is baked in the hot oven for 40 minutes, or until the ring is well browned and a metal or wooden skewer comes out clean and dry when inserted.

Brioche loaves are baked at 400° for 15 minutes, the heat is reduced to 350° for an additional 25 minutes. Test for doneness.

Brioche Chocolat pieces are baked in the hot oven for 25 minutes, or until they test done. Rather than pierce to test (the melted chocolate in the center will defeat this), tap one on the bottom crust. If it is crisp and sounds hard it is done.

FINAL STEP

Remove brioches from the oven. Place on a metal rack to cool.

Cool them thoroughly before freezing in an airtight plastic bag or foil.

EASY BRIOCHE

This is the easier brioche to make because it is stirred rather than beaten to form the rich satiny dough necessary for a good brioche.

INGREDIENTS

½ cup (1 stick) butter, room temperature
⅓ cup sugar
1 teaspoon salt
¾ cup hot tap water (120°–130°)
¼ cup non-fat dry milk
1 package dry yeast
3 eggs, room temperature
1 egg yolk
3½ cups all-purpose flour
Glaze: 1 egg white
1 tablespoon sugar

BAKING TINS

Two dozen muffin cups (2¾″), greased or Teflon, or fluted brioche tins for Petites Brioches. Other forms are suggested in the recipe for French Brioche.

PREPARATION
20 mins.

Cream butter, sugar and salt in a large bowl. Pour in the water and stir in milk, yeast, eggs, egg yolk and 1½ cups of flour. Beat in an electric mixer at medium-high speed for 2 minutes.

Stop the mixer and continue with a spoon if the mixer is laboring or overheating. Stir or beat in the balance of the flour—2 cups—and beat vigorously for 2 minutes.

FIRST RISING
2 hours

Cover the bowl with plastic wrap and put in a warm place (80°–85°) until dough has risen to more than twice its original size.

REFRIGERATION
4 hours or overnight

Turn back plastic wrap and stir down the dough. Beat for 2 minutes with strong strokes. Replace plastic and place in the refrigerator.

SHAPING

Punch down, and form into any of the brioches described in detail for French Brioche (see page 510):

Petites Brioches	Brioche en Couronne
Brioche à Tête	Brioche Chocolat
Brioche Loaves	Brioche au Fromage

SECOND RISING
2 hours

Follow French Brioche.

BAKING
400°
Varies

Follow French Brioche.

FINAL STEP

Remove brioches from the oven. Cool on a metal rack and serve.

CROISSANTS

[MAKES EIGHTEEN]

The croissant, to me, has always been the *ne plus ultra* of baking. There is nothing finer for breakfast than a croissant, with its layers and layers of brown flaky goodness.

For a long time I dared not try making them because they seemed so fragile. Watching a 14-year-old apprentice in a small French provincial bakery make fifty of them in no time at all resolved it for me. I would try them the moment I got home. I did, and with great success. Not as perfectly formed as the French lad made them, but as delicious. His excellent advice to me: keep the butter and dough cold and you won't get into trouble.

Croissants are easy to freeze for a later day. Take them out of the oven 5 to 10 minutes early, when they are not quite done, and brown them later when they are to be served.

INGREDIENTS

2¾ cups all-purpose flour
1 package dry yeast
¼ cup non-fat dry milk
1 tablespoon sugar
½ teaspoon salt
1 cup hot tap water (120°–130°)
1 cup (2 sticks) butter, refrigerated

BAKING SHEET

One baking sheet, *un*greased or Teflon.

PREPARATION
18 mins.

In a large mixer bowl measure 1 cup flour and stir in the yeast, milk, sugar, salt and water. Blend with 50 strokes of a large wooden spoon. Stir in balance of the flour, a half cup at a time, first with the spoon and then by hand. Scrape loose the bits of flour and dough particles in the bowl with the fingertips and spatula. Carefully add the last of the flour because the dough must be workable but not stiff. Work in only enough flour to make a ball of dough that can be lifted out of the bowl and placed on the work surface.

KNEADING 4 mins.	Knead only enough to feel the dough become slightly elastic and draw back when it is pushed.
FIRST RISING 1½ hours	Place dough in the mixing bowl and pat with buttered or greased fingers. Cover the bowl with plastic wrap and move to a warm place (80°–85°) until the dough has risen to *three* times its original size. Before you set the dough aside, visualize how high up the sides of the bowl the dough must come to treble its volume.
SECOND RISING 1 hour	Turn back the plastic cover. Punch down the dough and knead for 30 seconds. Replace the cover and return the bowl to the warm place to double in size.
12 mins.	Meanwhile, prepare the butter by filling a bowl with cold water. Place sticks of butter in the water and work them between the fingers into one piece. Two or three cubes of ice in the water may help to prevent the butter from getting oily and sticking to the fingers. On a length of wax paper, fashion a 5 x 5 inch square of butter. It will be about ⅜ of an inch thick. Fold the wax paper around the butter square, place on a dish and put in the refrigerator.
30 mins.	Punch down the dough, knead for 30 seconds to press out the bubbles and place in a bowl. Cover with plastic wrap and put in the refrigerator.
SHAPING	At any time in the process when butter oozes from the dough and becomes sticky under the roller or hands, return it to the refrigerator to harden. Place the chilled dough on a lightly floured work surface and roll into a rectangle 8 by 12 inches. With the tip of a knife lightly score the rectangle into thirds, across the narrow part. Unwrap the butter and place it in the upper two-thirds of the rolled-out dough. Be certain there is an inch-wide border of unbuttered dough around the upper 3 edges. This will allow the dough to seal together when it is folded which it would not do if buttered.
Turn 1 3 mins.	Fold the lower (and unbuttered) third over the center third. Bring the upper third down on top of the center. This means there is now a sandwich of dough-butter-dough-butter-dough.
6 mins. Turn 2	Lightly flour the work surface and the dough. Turn the dough 90 degrees so the unsealed ends are at 12 and 6

o'clock before you. Without turning the dough in the process, roll it into a rectangle 6 by 12 inches. Don't roll over the ends for this might force the butter out of the dough. Start 1 inch from one end and stop 1 inch from the other.

Fold again in thirds.

REFRIGERATION
1 hour

Wrap the folded dough in wax paper and place in the refrigerator to chill. Don't leave it too long, however, because it will start to rise and separate the layers.

Turn 3
10 mins.

Unwrap the dough and lightly tap with a rolling pin to expel the bubbles, if any. Cover and let rest for 5 minutes, again to relax the dough. Lightly flour the work surface and dough, roll again into a 6 by 12 inch rectangle. If the butter is too cold to roll, tap with the rolling pin for a moment or two to soften it slightly. Fold the rectangle again.

Turn 4
6 mins.

Again roll the dough into a 6 by 12 inch rectangle. Fold into thirds again. This is the final turn, and there are now 55 layers of dough in the rectangle.

REFRIGERATION
1½ hours or
overnight

Wrap and chill in the refrigerator before forming, or leave overnight in the coldest part of the refrigerator covered with a pie tin and weighted down with 3 or 4 pounds of handy and heavy foodstuffs.

SHAPING
25 mins.

On a lightly floured work surface roll the dough into a rectangle no more than ⅛ inch thick—about the height of the small letters in this sentence. Mark and cut the dough into a series of 5-inch squares. Cut each square into a triangle.

Before rolling the croissant, flour the work surface. Gently and lightly roll the triangle with the rolling pin to the ⅛-inch thickness it was before being cut out of the square. You may have noticed that it drew in slightly when cut.

With the fingers, roll each triangle from the long 7½-inch edge toward the apex. Stretch the dough ever so slightly as you begin to roll and then hold the tip under a finger while you roll towards it—again, keeping the dough under some tension. Pinch the tip to the middle section of the roll. Shape each into a crescent but tighter than a half circle. The point is toward you and tipped down to touch the baking sheet. Repeat for each and place on the ungreased baking sheet about 1½ inches apart.

RISING
1 hour

Cover the croissants with wax paper and let rise in a warm place (80°–85°) until double in size.

BAKING
375°
25 mins.

Preheat oven to 375°. Bake on the middle rack of the hot oven until the croissants are a golden brown. Parisians like theirs a deeper brown so bake for an additional 5 minutes. If you want to freeze them take from the oven when they are raised and well-formed but only beginning to brown.

FINAL STEP

Remove bread from the oven. Cool on a rack but serve while warm, if possible. For freezing, cool on a rack and package airtight. They are fragile so handle them carefully. Place them in some remote part of the freezer where they won't get damaged. Thaw to bake and return to a 375° oven 12 to 15 minutes until rolls are the desired brown.

DINNER ROLLS

[A BASIC DOUGH (TWO TO THREE DOZEN PIECES)]

While any yeast dough (except batter) can be made into dinner rolls, there is one that I think is more elegant and delicious than all the rest. It bakes into a lovely light golden roll that won for my mother several blue ribbons at the Indiana State Fair. No matter what special dish she placed before her guests, it was her rolls that drew the most flattering remarks from men—and requests for the recipe from wives.

This is Lenora's recipe for what she called, simply, her "yeast rolls." Here it is made into most of the dinner roll shapes—Parker House, Bowknots, Rosettes, Butterhorns, Crescent, Cloverleaf, Fan-tans and Pan Rolls.

INGREDIENTS

½ cup potato, mashed or prepared "instant"
1 package dry yeast
¼ cup warm water (105°–115°)
1 egg, room temperature
¼ cup sugar
½ cup milk, room temperature
⅓ cup (⅝ of a stick) butter or margarine
½ teaspoon salt

3 to 3½ cups all-purpose flour, approximately
To brush: 4 tablespoons (½ stick) butter or margarine

BAKING SHEET, MUFFIN PANS AND/OR CAKE PAN

Baking sheet or sheets for Parker House, Bowknots, Rosettes, Butterhorns and Crescent rolls. Cloverleaves and Fan-tans are placed in muffin tins, while Pan Rolls are set in 8- or 9-inch cake pans. Select the proper ones and grease (if not Teflon).

PREPARATION
15 mins.

First, prepare the potato, whether from fresh potato or dehydrated "instant."

In a small bowl sprinkle yeast over water, stir together with a fork and set aside.

In a large bowl, blend egg and sugar. Add potato, milk, butter and salt. Mix together, add yeast and 2 cups flour. Beat 1 minute or 100 strokes. Gradually stir in additional flour, ½ cup at a time, first with wooden spoon and by hand as the dough becomes firm. Work the flour into the moist ball until it cleans the sides of the bowl and has lost much of its stickiness. It is an easy dough to work because of its high butterfat content.

KNEADING
8 mins.

Turn the soft dough onto a floured work surface and knead with a strong push-turn-fold motion until it becomes smooth and velvety under the hands. Keep the hands and work surface dusted with flour.

FIRST RISING
1¼ hours

Return the dough to the bowl, stretch a length of plastic wrap across the top and place in a warm spot (80°–85°) until dough has risen to double its volume.

SHAPING

The dough (4 cups of which weigh about 2 pounds) can be made into one shape of dinner roll or divided among the various shapes, as desired.

PARKER HOUSE
20 mins.

[28 to 32 pieces]
Dust the work surface with flour. Divide the dough in half. Roll the first piece into a circle, ⅜ inch thick. Cut with a 2½- or 3-inch biscuit cutter. If you have a French-type rolling pin no more than 1½ inches in diameter, place it in the center of the small rounds of dough. Carefully roll toward each end to create a valley in the center of the round. The center will be about ⅛ inch thick while the ends will be thicker. Or you may press the rounded handle of a knife into the dough to achieve much the same result. Keep the roll-

ing pin or knife handle dusted with flour as you work.

Carefully brush each round to within ¼ inch of the edges with melted butter. This will allow the baked roll to open as a pocket.

Fold over the round of dough so the cut edges just meet. Pinch with fingers to seal and press the folded edge (the hinge) securely. Place each about ½ inch apart on a baking sheet as completed. Repeat with the remainder of the dough, if desired.

BOWKNOTS AND ROSETTES
20 mins.

[24 pieces]
Dust the work surface with flour. Divide the dough in half. Roll one piece into a 12-inch rope. Divide into 12 pieces. Roll each into a slender 8-inch rope. For a Bowknot, tie each into a knot. For a Rosette, bring one end up and through the center of the knot, bringing the other end over the side and under. Place on a baking sheet 1 inch apart; press end to the sheet to keep them from untying.

BUTTERHORNS AND CRESCENTS
20 mins.

[16 pieces]
Dust the work surface with flour. Divide the dough into two pieces. Roll each into an 8-inch circle. Let the dough relax 3 minutes before cutting into eight wedges with a pastry wheel or knife. Roll up wedge, toward the point, pulling and stretching the dough slightly as you roll. For Butterhorns, place each on baking sheet, with points underneath. For Crescents, roll wedge in the same manner but curve each into a crescent as it is placed on the baking sheet.

CLOVERLEAF
15 mins.

[12 pieces]
Dust the work surface with flour. Divide the dough into two pieces. With palms, roll each into a 16-inch rope. If the rope draws back, allow it to relax for 3 minutes before proceeding. Cut each length into 18 pieces. Shape each into a small ball; place three in each muffin cup.

FAN-TANS
20 mins.

[24 pieces]
Dust the work surface with flour. Divide the dough into two pieces. Roll each into an 8 x 16 inch rectangle—twice as long as it is wide. If the dough pulls back, let it relax for three minutes. Brush with butter. With a pastry wheel or knife, cut the dough across the narrow width into five 1½-inch strips. Stack the five strips

and cut stack into 12 pieces. Place each in a 2½-inch muffin cup, with the cut side of the dough up.

PAN ROLLS
15 mins.

[24 pieces]
Dust the work surface with flour. Divide the dough into two pieces and, with the hands, roll dough into a 12-inch rope. Cut into 12 pieces. Shape each into a ball; tuck under the cut edges to draw the surface of the dough tight. Arrange in the pan.

SECOND RISING
30 mins.

Brush the tops with melted butter, cover with wax paper and place in warm place until rolls have doubled in size.

BAKING
400°
12–16 mins.

Preheat oven to 400°. Place rolls in the oven and bake until a golden brown.

FINAL STEP

Remove from oven and place on rack to cool. Immediately brush with melted butter.

TWENTY-TWO

Special Breads

Rice
Lyons, 1579

In a book of more than 300 bread recipes there are a few that demand special attention, and fit in no conventional category. This chapter is a collection of these recipes.

German Honigkuchen and Rice Bread have little in common except they are so different that they deserve each other. The same goes for Bacon Batter Bread, Lardy Loaf, Tea Brack, and a true French aristocrat, Gannat, to mention but six of fourteen.

PULLED BREAD

This is something done *to* bread, not a new bread in itself. Shaggy chunks torn from a loaf, trimmed of its crusts, are buttered and baked for 30 minutes in a slow oven. Result: golden crisps of *pulled* bread. They should be done fresh for a party or dinner, but they will keep in the refrigerator to be reheated. They are the ultimate crouton.

INGREDIENTS	1 (or part) loaf white bread, crusts removed 3 tablespoons butter, melted
BAKING SHEET	One baking sheet, metal or Teflon.
PREPARATION 20 mins.	Preheat oven to 300°. With one or two forks tear out chunks of bread about 1 inch wide and 2 inches long. Brush these jagged chunks on all sides with melted butter and arrange on the baking sheet.

BAKING
300°
30 mins.

Place the baking sheet in the middle shelf of the oven until the chunks are crisp and golden brown.

FINAL STEP

Remove bread from the oven. Serve immediately. They can be held for a day or two in the refrigerator but reheat before serving.

BACON BATTER BREAD

[TWO LOAVES]

Big, husky loaves, brown-flecked with pieces of bacon, this bread has the cold-winter-morning taste of crisp fried bacon. It is unusual to season a bread with coriander which is reserved for soups, salads, puddings and cheeses, but in this loaf it complements the bacon and underscores the whole wheat. It is a batter, and will rise without kneading. It will probably be too thick to pour, and too wet to lift with the hands. I have found that two spoons is the easiest way to transfer the batter from the bowl to the pans.

INGREDIENTS

¼ lb. uncooked bacon or enough to make ⅓ cup crumbled fried bacon
2 tablespoons bacon drippings (from the above)
1 cup whole wheat flour
4 cups all-purpose or bread flour
2 packages dry yeast
2 teaspoons salt
¼ teaspoon ground coriander
½ cup non-fat dry milk
2 cups hot tap water (120°–130°)
¼ cup brown sugar, firmly packed
1 egg, room temperature

BAKING PANS

Two medium (8½ x 4½) loaf pans, greased or Teflon. If glass, reduce oven heat 25°.

PREPARATION
15 mins.

Cook bacon to make ⅓ cup of crumbled bacon, and reserve it and 2 tablespoons of the drippings.

In a mixer bowl measure the whole wheat flour, 3 cups of all-purpose or bread flour, yeast, salt, ground coriander, milk, drippings and water. Blend at low speed in the electric mixer for 30 seconds, or for the same length of time with a large wooden spoon. Add brown sugar, egg and bacon. Stir. Increase mixer speed to high for 3 minutes—or 200 strokes with the spoon.

Stop the mixer and add the remaining flour. Blend it well.

FIRST RISING
50 mins.

Scrape down the sides of the bowl, cover it tightly with plastic wrap and put in a warm (80°–85°) place until the batter has doubled in volume.

FORMING
5 mins.

Turn back the plastic covering and stir down the batter. Lift it with spoons into the pans. Push into the corners of the pans with a spoon, and smooth the tops.

SECOND RISING
30 mins.

Cover pans with the plastic or wax paper and return the pans to the warm place. The batter will rise to the edge of the pans.

BAKING
375°
40 mins.

Preheat oven to 375°. Place the pans in the oven and bake until the loaves are a deep brown. The loaf is done when a metal skewer or wooden toothpick inserted in the center comes out clean and dry. If moist particles cling to the probe, return the loaf to the oven for an additional 10 minutes. Test again.

FINAL STEP

Remove bread from the oven. Carefully turn the hot loaves out onto a metal rack to cool before serving or freezing.

CRACKLING BREAD

[ONE LOAF]

Butchering time on the farm in winter means rendering lard, and a delicious by-product—cracklings. These are pieces of fat that have been cooked in a large vat and squeezed dry in a lard press. The hot lard runs into a tub and some of the cracklings are saved for crackling bread.

This is a rich loaf, essentially a corn bread that is flavored strongly with ground cracklings. The slice is an attractive golden yellow, with pieces of crackling much in evidence.

Cracklings may be found packaged in specialty food stores or, more often, at a supermarket, slaughterhouse or frozen-food plant. Then, too, some farmers still butcher and have cracklings but their number is diminishing rapidly.

INGREDIENTS

¼ cup all-purpose flour
1½ cups cornmeal, white or yellow
½ teaspoon baking soda
¼ teaspoon salt
1 cup *each* sour milk or buttermilk, and cracklings
1 egg, room temperature

BAKING PAN

One medium (8½ x 4½) baking pan, greased or Teflon, metal or glass. If the latter, reduce oven heat by 25°.

PREPARATION
15 mins.

In a bowl combine flour, cornmeal, baking soda, salt, sour milk or buttermilk. Stir in the cracklings and the egg. Blend thoroughly.

FORMING
3 mins.

Pour batter into the baking pan and with a rubber spatula smooth the surface.

BAKING
400°
30 mins.

Preheat oven to 400°. Bake in the oven until the bread is well browned. Pierce the center of loaf with a metal skewer. If it comes out clean and dry, the loaf is done.

FINAL STEP

Remove bread from the oven. Crackling bread is best when eaten warm. It can be frozen successfully but should be reheated in a 300° oven for 15 minutes before serving.

CAMPER'S FRYING PAN BREAD

[SERVES TWO HUNGRY MEN]

Frying pan bread, a type of bannock, is not meant to be served at a gourmet's table but at 10,000 feet high in the Sierra Nevada, alongside Evolution Lake, or on the Colorado River, the night before going through Upset Rapids. It has a heavy crust and a taste of old-fashioned shortcake without the strawberries.

Mix the dry ingredients in a plastic bag before you leave home—flour, baking soda and salt. Open the bag at camp, pour in a little Colorado or other river water, work it between the fingers and drop the dough into the skillet.

The party will remember you forever—not for upsetting the supply boat in the rapids—but for the hot bread.

INGREDIENTS

1 cup all-purpose or bread flour
1 teaspoon baking powder
¼ teaspoon salt
½ cup water, approximately (add cautiously)
Options: 1 tablespoon sugar (for crisper crust)
1 fresh or powdered egg (thickness and richness)
Milk instead of water
⅓ tablespoon shortening (keeping quality)

FRYING PAN

The camp fry pan.

PREPARATION
10 mins.

While the ingredients are being assembled and mixed, heat the frying pan and grease it.

If pre-assembled at home, remove about 2 tablespoons from the plastic bag to hold in reserve. Stir in only enough water, about ½ cup, to make a firm dough. Work this with the fingertips to blend thoroughly. If it is too wet, carefully add the reserve dry ingredients.

SHAPING
5 mins.

Form dough into a round cake, about 1 inch thick. It will not have a soggy center (and it will be crustier) if you poke a finger through the middle of the cake, and shape a hole 2 inches in diameter. The loaf will be about 8 inches across.

BAKING
15–30 mins.

Lay the bannock in the warm oiled skillet. When a bottom crust has formed, shake it loose so that it does not get stuck. When the dough has hardened, flip it over with the help of a spatula. Brown the two sides evenly by turning the bannock occasionally. If a lively fire is going, prop the pan at an angle so the heat will reach the bannock from the top.

The bread is done when tapping the crust yields a hard, hollow sound. If you discover that it is not done when you break off a piece, put bannock and the piece back in the skillet for a few more minutes. The bread can also be tested with a wooden splinter inserted in the dough—if it comes out clean and dry, the bannock is done.

FINAL STEP

Serve immediately—although it is delicious pulled from a jacket pocket and eaten on the trail or in a boat.

GLUTEN BREAD

[ONE LOAF]

While gluten bread is a dietetic loaf, a toasted slice has a crisp bite and a pleasant nutlike flavor. The flour is expensive (almost eight times as much as all-purpose flour) so it will probably be reserved for special diets.

To make gluten flour, white flour goes through a washing process that takes away most of the starch and leaves the gluten, which is then processed into a light brown flour. Gluten, of course, is the wonderful substance found chiefly in wheat flour, which forms an elastic network in yeast dough to trap gas bubbles and expand the dough.

INGREDIENTS

2½ to 3 cups gluten flour, approximately
1 package dry yeast
1½ teaspoons sugar
1½ teaspoons salt
⅓ cup non-fat dry milk
1½ cups warm water (105°–115°)
1 tablespoon vegetable oil

BAKING PAN

One medium (8½ x 4½) pan, greased or Teflon. If glass, reduce oven heat 25°.

PREPARATION
12 mins.

In a large bowl pour 1½ cups flour, yeast, sugar, salt and milk. Stir together. Add water and vegetable oil. Beat with a wooden spoon 1 minute or 100 strokes. Unlike other yeast doughs, gluten dough will immediately pull together in a ball and quickly clean the sides of the bowl. Gradually add flour, a tablespoon at a time, until the dough loses its wetness and can be worked without sticking to the hands.

KNEADING
8 mins.

Turn onto a board or counter top lightly dusted with gluten flour. Knead with a strong push-turn-fold motion. While the dough will be fairly stiff, it will become smooth and elastic under the hands.

FIRST RISING
1¼ hours

Place the dough in a greased bowl, cover with plastic wrap and put in a warm place (80°–85°) until dough has doubled in bulk.

SHAPING
10 mins.

Punch down the dough in the bowl. Turn it out on the work surface and knead for 30 seconds to work out the bubbles. Press the ball of dough into a flat oval, about the length of the baking pan. Fold the oval in half, pinch the seam tightly to seal, tuck the ends, and place in the pan, seam down.

SECOND RISING
1 hour

Place the pan in the warm place, cover with wax paper and leave until the center of the dough has risen to the edge of the pan.

BAKING
400°
25 mins.
350°
20 mins.

Place in the hot oven 25 minutes, reduce heat to 350° for an additional 20 minutes. Halfway through the bake period turn the pan. Loaf is done when it makes a hollow sound when thumped on the bottom.

FINAL STEP

Take from oven and place on cooling rack. If this is to be the bread supplement for only one person in the household, you may wish to slice just enough bread for three days, wrap and store; freeze the balance.

PAIN PERDU—LOST BREAD

Pain Perdu begins with a humble slice of stale bread (or lost bread) but emerges a proud dish dipped in seasoned milk and frothy eggs and dropped into a skillet of hot butter. Its name and recipe comes from the French Cajuns who settled two centuries ago in Louisiana. It can be served at breakfast with coffee or tea, and bacon on the side. Served with honey, jelly and powdered sugar, it is a light dessert for a special luncheon. At dinner it is an ideal side dish with hamburgers.

Pain Perdu made with slices of Buckwheat Bread (page 235) is a marvelous brunch surprise. Warm growing-up memories of my grandmother Condon and her buckwheat cakes!

INGREDIENTS

2 large eggs, separated
1 pinch salt
1 pinch cream of tartar
½ cup cold sweet milk
¼ teaspoon *each* vanilla (or brandy) and nutmeg
½ cup (1 stick) butter
2 tablespoons vegetable oil
6 to 8 slices of stale bread

EQUIPMENT

One large heavy skillet.

PREPARATION
20 mins.

Separate the eggs, and in a deep mixing bowl beat egg whites with salt and cream of tartar until they peak. Pour in the yolks and continue beating. Add milk, vanilla (or brandy) and nutmeg. When the ingredients have been blended set aside.

6 mins. per slice — In a large heavy skillet measure the butter and vegetable oil, and place over a hot burner. Dip each bread slice into the egg-milk mixture—to coat both sides—and drop into the skillet. The bread will brown rapidly—not more than 3 minutes to a side. Turn with a spatula to brown the other side. Remove and drain on paper toweling.

FINAL STEP — There are a number of toppings—maple syrup or sugar lightly sprinkled on the top or jelly or sugar and cinnamon or honey.

RICE BREAD

[ONE PLUMP LOAF]

A baking procedure is reversed for this unusual loaf. A piece of foil is laid over the batter-filled pan *before* it goes into the oven, and removed at mid-point in the baking process rather than being put on late to protect the bread from overbrowning.

A fine vehicle for spreads, it has a good texture but because of its compactness it should always be toasted or served warm from the oven. It loses its attractive qualities when it is cold.

INGREDIENTS

3 cups rice flour
¼ cup sugar
1 teaspoon salt
6 teaspoons baking powder
⅓ cup non-fat dry milk
2 cups water
1 egg, room temperature
⅓ cup melted butter or other shortening
To brush: 1 teaspoon melted butter

BAKING PAN — One medium (8½ x 4½) loaf pan, greased or Teflon. If glass, reduce heat in oven 25°.

PREPARATION
15 mins. — Preheat oven to 375°. Measure flour into a mixing bowl and add sugar, salt and baking powder. In another bowl, dissolve milk in water, and add the egg and butter or shortening. Gradually add the liquid ingredients to the dry mixture, stirring gently but do not overmix.

FORMING
10 mins.

Pour batter in the loaf pan, brush top with melted butter and let it rest for 5 minutes.

BAKING
375°
30 mins.
350°
45 mins.

Before placing the loaf pan in the oven, cover it loosely with a strip of aluminum foil which has been pierced two or three places to allow the moisture to escape. Place the pan in the oven. Bake for 30 minutes; remove foil cover; reduce temperature to 350°, and continue baking for about 45 minutes more. A wooden toothpick or metal skewer inserted in the center of the loaf will come out clean and dry when done. If moist particles cling to the probe, return the loaf to the oven for an additional 10 minutes.

FINAL STEP

Remove bread from the oven. This is a moist bread and fragile when hot, so carefully remove from pan and place it on wire rack to cool. This bread should always be served warm.

Slice the quantity needed for each meal and warm in toaster or oven to serve. Store in a plastic bag.

SAUSAGE BREAD

[TWO ROUND LOAVES]

One pound of small link sausages—cut into 1-inch lengths—is liberally scattered in these two loaves. A round flat bread, it is made with rich ingredients that include rather large portions of sugar, eggs and milk. The sausage pieces are added after the bread has been kneaded and it takes patience to get the dough to accept them. But it will.

It is a fine breakfast bread, and good to serve with soups.

INGREDIENTS

1 pound sausage links
2 packages dry yeast
¼ cup warm water (105°–115°)
1 cup sugar
1 cup hot milk
¼ cup (½ stick) butter, room temperature
1 teaspoon salt
3 eggs, room temperature
5 cups all-purpose flour, approximately

BAKING PANS

Two 8-inch pie pans, greased or Teflon.

PREPARATION
25 mins.

Cut sausages into 1-inch lengths, place in a small saucepan, cover with water, and parboil over low heat for about 10 minutes. Drain, and sauté in a skillet until cooked.

In a small bowl or cup sprinkle yeast over water. Stir briskly with a whisk or fork to dissolve.

In a large mixing bowl combine sugar, milk, butter and salt. Stir the mixture until butter has melted and the mixture has cooled to lukewarm. Beat in eggs and the yeast mixture. Stir in 2 cups flour and beat 3 minutes at fast speed with electric mixer or 150 strokes with a wooden spoon.

Stop the mixer. Stir in the balance of the flour, a half cup at a time, first with the spoon and then by hand. The dough will be a rough, shaggy mass but it will clean the sides of the bowl.

KNEADING
10 mins.

Turn the dough out onto a lightly floured work surface —counter top or bread board—and knead until the dough is smooth and small blisters appear under the surface. Add more flour to the board if the dough seems moist or slack. (Knead 6 minutes with a dough hook on an electric mixer.)

FIRST RISING
1½ hours

Place the dough back in the mixing bowl and pat all over with buttered or greased fingers to keep the surface from crusting. Cover the bowl tightly with plastic wrap and move to a warm place (80°–85°) until the dough has risen to about twice its original size (judged as it creeps up the sides of the bowl). You can test if it has risen by poking a finger in it; the dent will remain.

SHAPING
20 mins.

Punch the dough down and turn it out of the bowl. Knead it briefly, and flatten it down. Spread half the sausage pieces on the dough and fold them into the mass. Knead for 1 or 2 minutes. Flatten the dough again —and spread the balance of the sausage bits on the dough. Continue to knead the dough until the sausage bits are uniformly scattered throughout the bread.

Divide the dough into two pieces and shape both into flat round loaves. Press them into the bottoms of pie tins. They will fill the bottom of the pans and come halfway up the sides.

SECOND RISING
1 hour

Cover the tins with wax paper and return the loaves to the warm place until the dough has doubled again in bulk.

BAKING
375°
40 mins.

Preheat the oven to 375°. Bake the loaves in the oven until they are a rich brown color. When tapping the bottom crust yields a hard hollow sound, they are baked. Don't rush the loaves, however, because the dough near the sausage pieces will not bake as fast as the other.

FINAL STEP

Remove bread from the oven. Turn out of pans and place on metal racks to cool thoroughly before slicing.

IRISH WHISKEY LOAF

[ONE LOAF]

Since this Irish whiskey loaf occupies the high ground between bread on the one hand, and cake on the other, it is included here. Not only does it have a fine robust name but it has a fine taste as well.

INGREDIENTS

The peel of one lemon or orange
3 tablespoons of Irish whiskey
1¼ cups dark raisins or sultanas
¾ cup (1½ sticks) of butter, room temperature
¾ cup sugar
3 eggs, room temperature
2½ cups sifted all-purpose flour
1 pinch salt
¾ teaspoon baking powder

BAKING PAN

One lined and buttered 7-inch cake pan, regular or Teflon.

PREPARATION
5 hours

Four or five hours before: Peel the rind of a lemon or orange and soak in the Irish whiskey. Two hours later, lift out and discard the rind, and put the raisins in the flavored whiskey for another two or three hours.

15 mins.

Preheat the oven to 350°. Cream butter and sugar together. Add eggs one at a time, with a teaspoon of flour, and beat well at each stage. Sift the flour, salt, and baking powder together and fold into the egg-butter mixture. Lastly, fold in the whiskey and raisins.

FORMING
3 mins.

Pour batter into the pan.

BAKING
350°
45 mins.

Place in the oven. Halfway through the baking period reduce the heat to about 300°. You can test if it is baked by piercing loaf with a metal skewer or wooden

300°
45 mins.

toothpick. If it comes out clean and dry the loaf is baked.

FINAL STEP

Remove bread from the oven. Place on a wire rack to cool. Slice and eat while fresh. Serve this to a great aunt with a glass of port.

HONIGKUCHEN

[THIRTY OR SO PIECES]

Honigkuchen—German honey cake—is not a bread but it was put into the book because it is made with a kind of dough, is baked in an oven—and is delicious. Three good reasons for its being here.

A sweet which meant festivity and joy to the Germans of old, Honigkuchen calls for a full cup of honey, one of the earliest sweeteners used in Germany.

The dough is spread thin (about ½ inch) in a jelly-roll pan. When it comes from the oven, almonds are pushed into the hot cake and, if desired, an almond glaze is brushed on. Cut into rectangles or fancy shapes, Honigkuchen is aged 3 or 4 days before eating and it can be stored for 3 or 4 months in a tightly covered can or jar.

INGREDIENTS

To Prepare Pan: 1 tablespoon butter, room temperature
2 tablespoons all-purpose flour

Topping: 1 cup blanched almonds, whole or slivered

Dough: 5 cups all-purpose or bread flour
1½ teaspoons baking powder
¼ cup almonds, pulverized in blender or in mortar
3 tablespoons chopped candied citron
1 tablespoon cocoa, unsweetened
1 teaspoon *each* cloves and cinnamon
2 teaspoons ground cardamom
1 teaspoon finely grated lemon peel
½ teaspoon almond extract
1 cup honey
1 cup sugar
½ cup cold water

Almond Glaze: 1 cup confectioners' sugar
½ teaspoon almond extract
1 teaspoon lemon juice
2 tablespoons cold water

BAKING PAN

One 11 x 17-inch jelly-roll pan. Coat the bottom and sides with butter and sprinkle on the flour. Tip from side to side to spread the flour evenly. Turn the pan over, tap the bottom to remove excess flour. Set aside.

PREPARATION
25 mins.

Preheat oven to 350° and toast the almonds on a second baking sheet (not the one prepared with butter and flour). Stir frequently until they are lightly browned, about 10 minutes. Don't let them burn. Take them out but leave oven on.

In a large bowl, measure flour and stir in baking powder, ¼ cup pluverized almonds, citron, cocoa, cloves, cinnamon, cardamom, lemon peel and almond extract.

Bring the honey, sugar and water to a boil in a large saucepan over a moderate heat, stirring only to help dissolve the sugar. Reduce heat and simmer, uncovered, for 6 minutes. Pour the honey mixture over the flour mixture and beat together with a wooden spoon until a smooth batter is formed.

FORMING

Spoon the dough onto the prepared jelly-roll pan and, with the fingers, pat and spread it as evenly as possible over the pan. Dampen the fingers with water to work the warm, sticky mixture.

BAKING
350°
18 mins.

Bake on the middle shelf of the oven until the top is firm to the touch.

FINAL STEP

Remove the pan from the oven. Lightly score lines on the cake with a pastry wheel (and a yardstick), but don't cut. Press almonds into each piece, singly or in a pattern.

If glazing the cake, brush the top with the sugar-almond-lemon-water mixture. If an almond pops loose, secure it with a brush of glaze on its underside.

With the pastry wheel or knife, follow the scored lines and cut the sheet into pieces.

Lift to cool on a rack before storing for several days before serving. Keep in a tightly covered jar for several months.

TEA BRACK

[ONE LOAF]

So few things in the U.S. cater to the tea drinker's fancy (as opposed to coffee-this-and-coffee-that) that tea brack, with the cold beverage as one of its chief ingredients, gives a double reward. Thinly sliced, the moist, dark loaf is also delicious served *with* tea. I think so well of this loaf that I once flew to Paris with it under my arm as a house gift.

INGREDIENTS	1 cup white raisins ¾ cup dried currants ¼ cup chopped candied peel 1½ cups brown sugar 1½ cups cold tea (orange pekoe is fine) ¼ cup rum or brandy is optional (but good) 2 cups all-purpose or bread flour 1½ teaspoons baking powder ½ teaspoon *each* cinnamon, nutmeg and salt 1 egg, room temperature, well beaten
BAKING PAN	One medium (8½ x 4½) loaf pan, greased or Teflon. If glass, reduce oven heat 25°. To facilitate turning out the loaf after it has baked, butter or grease the pan, line the long sides and bottom with a length of wax paper, and butter again. Leave the ends of the paper sticking out about ½ inch so the loaf can be pulled from the pan.
PREPARATION Overnight	The night before: in a bowl combine raisins, currants, chopped mixed candied peel, brown sugar and cold tea. Add a dollop of brandy or rum (¼ cup) to give it a secret goodness. Cover with plastic wrap so that no moisture escapes.
15 mins.	The next day: preheat oven to 325°. In another bowl mix together, with fingers or a spoon, remaining dry ingredients—flour, baking powder, cinnamon, nutmeg and salt. Pour dry ingredients into tea-fruit mixture, stir well and add the egg which has been well beaten. The mixture will be thin.
FORMING 3 mins.	Pour or spoon the batter into the pan.
BAKING 325° 1½ hours	Bake the loaf slowly in the oven until a metal skewer or wooden toothpick comes out dry when pierced into the loaf.

FINAL STEP — Remove from the oven. Place on a wire rack for about five minutes before removing from the pan. Let it cool completely before it is cut. Serve with butter or cream cheese.

TREACLE BREAD

[ONE ROUND LOAF]

Molasses—treacle in Ireland—gives this loaf its lovely dark color. Its flavor is equally rich and dark, and, according to one Irish baker, "especially good for the little ones." Blackstrap molasses (without sulfur dioxide), found in many food specialty shops, will impart an even darker look and flavor.

INGREDIENTS

- 4 cups all-purpose or bread flour
- 1½ tablespoons sugar
- 1 teaspoon *each* baking soda and cream of tartar
- ½ teaspoon salt
- 1 pinch ginger
- ½ cup raisins or currants or both
- 1 to 1¼ cups milk
- 2 tablespoons treacle (molasses)
- 1 tablespoon milk—to brush on top

BAKING SHEET — One baking sheet, greased or Teflon. Flour or cornmeal also may be dusted on the greased sheet to facilitate removing the loaf.

PREPARATION
15 mins. — Preheat the oven to 400°. In a bowl sift together flour, sugar, baking soda, cream of tartar, salt and ginger. If the sifter is a bother, do this with the fingers or a fork, stirring and tossing the ingredients around until they are thoroughly mixed. Mix in the raisins or currants, or a combination of the two. In a saucepan heat the milk with the treacle (molasses) until the mixture is warm and blended. Make a well in the center of the dry ingredients and add enough of the warm milk mixture to make a light elastic dough. Work dough as little as possible to combine the ingredients.

KNEADING
2–3 mins. — Working with the dough (still in the bowl to save an extra cleanup of the counter top), knead.

SHAPING
5 mins.

Put the dough on a baking sheet and pat it into a round loaf about 1½-inches high. With a razor blade or sharp knife cut a cross ½-inch deep across the top, and brush the surface with milk.

BAKING
400°
40 mins.

Bake the loaf in the oven until it sounds hard and hollow when tapped on the bottom crust.

FINAL STEP

Remove bread from the oven. Place on wire rack to cool immediately when it comes from the oven. If the appetities are hearty and dining informal, break the loaf into quarters—otherwise slice.

LARDY LOAF

[TWO SMALL ROUND LOAVES]

The rich color and solid compactness of a Lardy Loaf in the window of a small bake shop in Balcombe, England, caught my eye one morning bicycling through the tiny village in Sussex, south of London. Brian Bristow, the baker, gave me his recipe which came originally from a baker in Gloucestershire. Packed with sugar and raisins, it is a rich loaf that is quite flaky and "short" because of the lard. It has a taste strongly reminiscent of my grandmother Condon's doughnuts. Slice it thinly and serve with tea. Children will love it anytime, of course, and rejoice in the moist pockets of sugar.

INGREDIENTS

1 package dry yeast
½ cup warm water (105°–115°)
1¾ cups all-purpose flour, approximately
1 teaspoon salt
1 cup raisins (dark or white or a mix)
¾ cup lard, room temperature
¾ cup sugar

BAKING PANS

Two round tins, about 6 inches in diameter and 2 inches deep. I use fluted brioche tins—6 inches across at the top, 4 inches at the bottom.

PREPARATION
5 mins.

In a bowl dissolve yeast in warm water. Stir it briskly to hasten the action. Stir in 1 cup of flour and the salt, and then add additional flour, a teaspoon at a time, to make a dough that is soft, pliable and does not stick to the fingers.

KNEADING
15 mins.

Knead this small ball of dough for about 5 minutes before adding the raisins. Work them into the dough carefully. Set aside to rest while creaming the lard and sugar in a small bowl. Divide the lard-sugar mix in half; drop one portion in the bowl with the dough. Reserve the other portion. With a wooden spoon and fingers, blend the mixture into the dough. It will be a stringy mess for a moment but add small sprinkles of flour to help control the stickiness. When it is a cohesive mass, and not stringy and sticky, knead for an additional 3 minutes.

FIRST RISING
1 hour

Cover bowl tightly with plastic wrap and put in a warm place (80°–85°).

SHAPING

Lift off the plastic wrap, punch down the dough and turn out on a floured work surface. Divide the dough in two pieces. Form each into a ball and let rest for 3 minutes. Roll each ball into a circle of dough about 10 inches in diameter (about ⅛ inch thick). Divide the reserved lard-sugar and place half of it in the center of the rolled-out dough. Carefully lift the edges, overlap them over the lard-sugar. Pinch the seams together. Turn the loaf over and place it in pan, the overlapping edges under. Repeat with the second loaf.

SECOND RISING
45 mins.

Cover with wax paper and put both pans in the warm place until the dough has doubled in bulk—the center rising slightly above the edge of a 2-inch pan.

BAKING
325°
1 hour

Preheat the oven to 325°. Place pans on the middle shelf of the oven and bake until the loaves are a deep rich brown.

FINAL STEP

Remove bread from the oven. Carefully place the hot loaves on a metal rack to cool. The loaves are especially good when served warm. However, they can be frozen—and reheated in the oven before slicing.

GANNAT

[TWO ROUND LOAVES]

A handsome loaf made with butter, brandy, a dozen eggs and diced Swiss cheese, Gannat is yellow, moist and delicious. Despite its list of expensive ingredients, Gannat is an easy bread to make. This recipe will make two lovely brown loaves, 9 inches in diameter and standing about 4 inches high.

Gannat, named for a small city in France where it is a regional favorite, is an unusual gift. Not an everyday kind of bread, list the chief ingredients on the card bearing the name of the bread so the recipient can have the joy of knowing what he is getting.

INGREDIENTS

1 package dry yeast
¼ cup warm water (105°–115°)
4 cups all-purpose flour, approximately
1 cup (2 sticks) butter, room temperature
5 tablespoons brandy
6 eggs } beaten together
6 egg yolks }
½ teaspoon salt
1 cup diced Swiss cheese
Glaze: 1 egg, beaten
1 tablespoon milk

BAKING PANS

Two 9-inch round cake pans, greased or Teflon, with sides 1½ to 2 inches high.

PREPARATION
25 mins.

In a small cup or bowl dissolve yeast in water. Set aside for 5 minutes until it begins to foam and bubble.

Sift 1 cup of flour into a large bowl and push it aside to form a hole in the center. Pour the yeast liquid in the hole and pull in the flour to form a firm dough. It may be necessary to add a little more warm water if the flour is unusually absorbent.

Lift out the dough while you fill the bowl with warm water (90°–100°). Place the dough in the water. It will sink but in 8 to 10 minutes it will rise to the surface. (Don't leave it in the water once it has risen or it will break apart. Be ready to lift it out when it surfaces.)

In a second bowl place 4 cups of flour, and add the butter, brandy, eggs and egg yolks (beaten together), and salt. Mix to a soft dough, and stir in the diced Swiss cheese.

KNEADING
5 mins.

When the ball of dough rises to the surface of the water, lift out and gently knead it into the egg dough. If it is sticky, add additional flour until firm enough to knead.

FIRST RISING 1 hour	Place the dough in the mixing bowl. Cover the bowl tightly with plastic wrap and move to a warm place (80°–85°) until the dough has risen to twice its original volume.
SHAPING 5 mins.	Punch down the dough, knead for 30 seconds to press out the bubbles. Divide the dough in half. Form each piece into a ball and place in the pans. Push the ball down and into the angles of the pan.
SECOND RISING 45 mins.	Cover with wax paper and return to the warm place until it has doubled in volume.
BAKING 425° 40–45 mins.	Preheat oven to 425°. Brush the bread with mixture of egg and milk. Bake in the oven until it is a golden brown. Pierce the center of the loaf with a metal skewer. If it comes out clean and dry, the loaf is done. If moist particles cling to the probe, return the loaf to the oven for an additional 10 minutes.
FINAL STEP	Remove bread from the oven. Turn from cake pan and cool on a metal rack before serving, or wrapping as a gift. It keeps well in the deep freeze. Each will weigh about 2 pounds, a substantial loaf.

TWENTY-THREE

An Outdoor Oven

From "The Queene-Like Closet"
London, 1670

Long after I had accumulated all the gear needed to bake any kind of loaf, I decided to build an outdoor oven modeled after those used to make the big crusty farmhouse loaves found in many parts of the world. Made of a mixture of mud and cement daubed over a shell of bricks and held together with reinforcing rods and lengths of chicken wire, the oven had only one compartment. A roaring fire was built in this, and kept going for two or three hours. The deep bed of coals was raked out, the floor quickly swept and mopped, and the loaves laid directly on the bricks.

The first time I built a fire in it, the 600-degree heat sent long cracks through the adobe mud. It didn't matter, fortunately, for these would open when the oven was hot, and close when it grew cold. I found I could judge the baking temperature by the width of the cracks.

I did, however, bend a piece of galvanized metal over the top of the oven which I left in place during Indiana's cold winter. I was afraid the severe freeze and thaw of February and March might work some of the adobe loose if I didn't protect it from moisture seeping into the cracks. The metal shield has worked fine, serving the same purpose as the broad lean-to roofs that Quebec farmers build over their outdoor ovens to protect them from the Canadian winter.

My oven was built along lines suggested in an article in *Sunset* magazine (August 1971) on the Pueblo adobe oven.

The oven produced fine big loaves, heavily crusted, and deep brown. The hot floor gave the loaves a quick boost that they could not get in an ordinary kitchen oven. Often the oven was too hot for bread but just right to begin a standing rib roast (500°). An hour later the bread would follow (350°). Only a thick wooden door on the oven gave a degree of control over the oven heat. Opened: it cooled down rapidly. Closed: the temperature would move up, then hold on a plateau for a long time before gradually falling off.

One convenient thing about using homemade adobe is that a hammer or sledge will break it apart if ever you should tire of it in the yard. If it were of solid concrete, it would take dynamite and a jack hammer to remove it.

Build one. Not only is it a great conversation piece, it also bakes fine bread.

(If you would like directions for building an adobe oven, write to the author in care of Simon and Schuster.)

Suppliers

From "The Kitchen Companion"
Philadelphia, 1844

Before going afield for supplies, especially the flours, check at home. There is a growing trend in supermarkets across the country to give the home baker a much wider selection of flours. Part of the baking renaissance.

The complete list of flours of many of the big millers, such as Robin Hood, Gooch and Ceresota (unbleached white), is available to grocers in 5- and 10-pound packages. These will cost you considerably less than the 1- and 2-pound specialty packs by the smaller mills. Ask your grocer.

Don't overlook the possibility of buying a 100-pound bag direct from a mill in your area. Share it with others who bake if that's too much flour to handle. The savings will be great.

If the search is unsuccessful, there are, of course, several specialty mills that distribute nationally through gourmet and health food shops, department store food sections and some supermarket chains.

National

Byrd Mill Co.
P.O. Box 5167
Richmond, Va. 23220

—Can be found almost anywhere. You may wish to write for a mail order catalogue. All basic flours and mixes but at premium prices.

Elam's Flours
Elam Mills
Broadview, Ill. 60153

—Its striped yellow and red box is a familiar sight in many stores. Includes all basic flours.

El Molino Mills
3060 West Valley Boulevard
Alhambra, California 91803
—In health food stores primarily. Write for mail order catalogue. Fine selection of all flours as well as bread mixes.

Regional

Mail orders know no geographic limits, of course, but the pocketbook does when it comes to postal rates. Here is an assortment of suppliers. Hopefully one will be near you.

The East

The Vermont Country Store
Weston, Vermont 05161
—All basic grains, stone-ground. Catalogue 25¢ includes great variety country store items. Quality products.

Lekvar by the Barrel
H. Roth & Son
First Avenue at 82nd Street
New York, N.Y. 10028
—Some flours but outstanding selection of spices, baking pans, molds, accessories.

The Great Valley Mills
Quakertown
Bucks County, Penna. 18951
—Stone-ground flours since 1710. Wide selection. Also molasses, spices.

Midwest

Sioux Millers
R. R. 1
Whiting, Iowa 51063
—Complete inventory of whole grain flours, cereals, and natural unrefined foods. Stone-ground. Quality.

Hatch's IGA International Food Store
1711 North College Avenue
Bloomington, Indiana 47401
—The store can supply almost every flour and ingredient in this book. Write for prices.

Brownville Mills
Brownville, Nebraska 68321
—Processors and distributors of natural foods including all basic flours, stone-ground. Write for price list.

Southwest
Arrowhead Mills, Inc.
Box 866
Hereford, Texas 79045
—This Deaf Smith County mill has a complete line of basic flours, all from organically grown grains. Also a complete line of natural food staples. Write for impressive price list.

West
See El Molino Mills above.

Dietetic
The American Dietetic Association
620 North Michigan Avenue
Chicago, Ill. 60611
—$1.00 for recipe booklet containing wheat, milk, egg-free and gluten-free recipes.

Superintendent of Documents
Government Printing Office
Washington, D.C. 20402
—10¢ Home and Garden Bulletin #147—Baking for People with Food Allergies.

Quaker Oats Co.
Merchandise Mart Plaza
Chicago, Ill. 60654
—Wheat, milk and egg-free recipes from Mary Alden.

Special Pans
Little Old Bread Man
500 Independence Ave. S. E.
Washington, D.C. 20003
—A French-type pan of aluminum, designed by a Washington, D.C., home baker. Write for prices.

Index